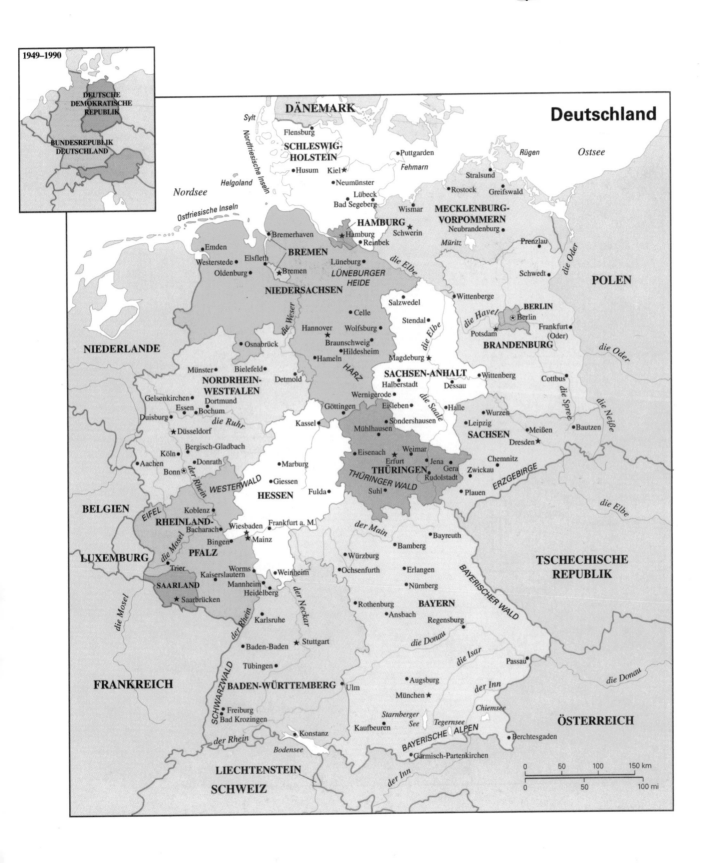

Deutschland

1949–1990

DEUTSCHE
DEMOKRATISCHE
REPUBLIK

BUNDESREPUBLIK
DEUTSCHLAND

DÄNEMARK

Sylt

Nordfriesische Inseln

Flensburg

SCHLESWIG-
HOLSTEIN

Puttgarden

Fehmarn

Rügen

Ostsee

Husum • Kiel ★

Helgoland

Nordsee

Neumünster •

Stralsund

Lübeck
Bad Segeberg

Wismar

Rostock •
Greifswald

Ostfriesische Inseln

HAMBURG

Schwerin

MECKLENBURG-
VORPOMMERN

Neubrandenburg

Bremerhaven •

Hamburg ★
Reinbek •

Müritz

Prenzlau •

Emden •

BREMEN

Lüneburg •

die Elbe

Schwedt •

POLEN

Westerstede •
Oldenburg •

Elsfleth •
★ Bremen

LÜNEBURGER
HEIDE

Salzwedel •

Wittenberge •

die Havel

BERLIN
★ Berlin

die Oder

NIEDERSACHSEN

Celle •

Stendal •

Potsdam ★

Frankfurt
(Oder)

NIEDERLANDE

Hannover •
★

Wolfsburg •

die Elbe

BRANDENBURG

die Oder

Osnabrück •

Braunschweig •
Hameln • Hildesheim

Magdeburg ★

Münster •
Bielefeld •

HARZ

SACHSEN-ANHALT

Wittenberg •

Cottbus •

die Spree

Detmold •

Halberstadt •

Dessau •

die Neiße

NORDRHEIN-
WESTFALEN

Wernigerode •

Eisleben •

die Saale

Halle •

Wurzen •

Bautzen •

Gelsenkirchen •
Dortmund •
Essen • Bochum •

Göttingen •

Sondershausen •

Leipzig •
Meißen •

SACHSEN

Duisburg •
★ Düsseldorf

die Ruhr

Kassel •

Mühlhausen •

Weimar •

Dresden ★

Bergisch-Gladbach •

Eisenach •

Erfurt •

Jena •

Chemnitz •

Köln •
Aachen •
Bonn •

Donrath •

Marburg •

THÜRINGEN

Gera •
Rudolstadt •

Zwickau •

ERZGEBIRGE

der Rhein

WESTERWALD

Giessen •

THÜRINGER WALD

Plauen •

die Elbe

BELGIEN

EIFEL

HESSEN

Fulda •

Suhl •

Koblenz •

RHEINLAND-

Bacharach •

Wiesbaden •
Frankfurt a. M.

der Main

Bayreuth •

TSCHECHISCHE
REPUBLIK

LUXEMBURG

die Mosel

Bingen •
★ Mainz

Bamberg •

PFALZ

Würzburg •

Erlangen •

Trier •

Worms •
Kaiserslautern •
Mannheim •

Weinheim •

Ochsenfurth •

Nürnberg •

BAYERISCHER WALD

SAARLAND

★ Saarbrücken

Heidelberg •

der Neckar

Rothenburg •

BAYERN

Ansbach •

Regensburg •

FRANKREICH

Karlsruhe •

der Rhein

die Donau

Passau •

SCHWARZWALD

Baden-Baden •
★ Stuttgart

der Inn

die Donau

Tübingen •

die Isar

BADEN-WÜRTTEMBERG

Ulm

Augsburg •

ÖSTERREICH

Freiburg •
Bad Krozingen •

München ★

Starnberger
See

Chiemsee

Tegernsee

Konstanz •

Kaufbeuren •

BAYERISCHE ALPEN

Berchtesgaden •

Bodensee

der Inn

Garmisch-Partenkirchen •

LIECHTENSTEIN

der Inn

SCHWEIZ

| 0 | 50 | 100 | 150 km |

| 0 | 50 | 100 mi |

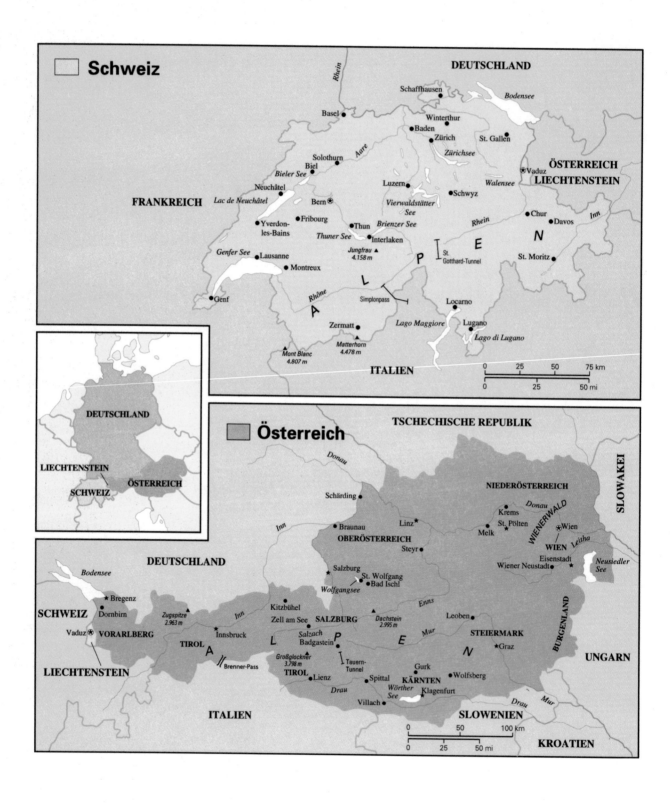

VORSPRUNG

THIRD EDITION

A Communicative Introduction to German Language and Culture

Thomas A. Lovik
Michigan State University

J. Douglas Guy
Northern Essex Community College

Monika Chavez
University of Wisconsin, Madison

HEINLE
CENGAGE Learning·

Australia • Brazil • Japan • Korea • Mexico • Singapore • Spain • United Kingdom • United States

***Vorsprung: A Communicative Introduction to German Language and Culture*, Third Edition**
Thomas A. Lovik, J. Douglas Guy, Monika Chavez

VP, Editorial Director: PJ Boardman

Publisher: Beth Kramer

Acquiring Sponsoring Editor: Judith Bach

Editorial Assistant: Gregory Madan

Senior Media Editor: Morgen Gallo

Executive Brand Manager: Ben Rivera

Market Development Manager: Courtney Wolstoncroft

Senior Content Project Manager: Aileen Mason

Senior Art Director: Linda Jurras

Manufacturing Planner: Betsy Donaghey

Rights Acquisition Specialist: Jessica Elias

Production Service: PreMediaGlobal

Text and Cover Designer: Roycroft Design

Cover image: © Hundertwasser Archive, Vienna; © Erich Lessing / Art Resource, NY 738 Grass for those who cry, 1975

Compositor: PreMediaGlobal

For product information and technology assistance, contact us at
Cengage Learning Customer & Sales Support, 1-800-354-9706

For permission to use material from this text or product, submit all requests online at **www.cengage.com/permissions**. Further permissions questions can be emailed to **permissionrequest@cengage.com**.

Library of Congress Control Number: 2012951235

Student Edition:
ISBN-13: 978-1-133-60735-9
ISBN-10: 1-133-60735-7

Loose-leaf Edition:
ISBN-13: 978-1-133-93760-9
ISBN-10: 1-133-93760-8

Heinle
20 Channel Center Street
Boston, MA 02210
USA

Cengage Learning is a leading provider of customized learning solutions with office locations around the globe, including Singapore, the United Kingdom, Australia, Mexico, Brazil and Japan. Locate your local office at **international.cengage.com/region**

Cengage Learning products are represented in Canada by Nelson Education, Ltd.

For your course and learning solutions, visit **www.cengage.com.**

Purchase any of our products at your local college store or at our preferred online store **www.cengagebrain.com**.

Instructors: Please visit **login.cengage.com** and log in to access instructor-specific resources.

Printed in the United States of America
1 2 3 4 5 6 7 16 15 14 13 12

Contents

Preface   xv

To the Student   xxiii

1 KAPITEL EINS
Fangen Sie bitte an. 1

ANLAUF I Annas Albtraum............2

Strukturen:
I. Understanding commands and requests.....8
   The imperative.........................8
   A. Formation of the formal imperative......8
   B. The word *bitte*......................9

Wissenswerte Vokabeln:
Aktivitäten im Klassenzimmer 9

Sprache im Alltag:
Breaking into a conversation with **Entschuldigung, Verzeihung, Pardon**......................7

ANLAUF II Annas Traum...............10

Strukturen:
II. Describing yourself and others...........18
    A. The verb **sein;** subject pronouns.......18
    B. The pronoun *you* 19
III. Asking for someone's name 20
     The verb **heißen** 20
IV. Asking for information and clarification....25
    Question formation 25
    A. Information questions................25
    B. Yes/no questions 26
V. Identifying people and classroom objects...27
   A. Noun gender and number...........27
   B. The nominative case: definite
      articles **der, das, die**...............28
   C. The nominative case: indefinite articles
      and **kein** 29
   D. The nominative case 34
   E. Pronoun substitution................35

Wissenswerte Vokabeln:
Das Alphabet 21
Die Zahlen 22
Aussehen..............................23
Das Klassenzimmer, der Hörsaal............27
Die Farben 29
Länder und Nationalitäten 31

Brennpunkt Kultur:
Greetings and farewells 11
Titles of address 16
Where German is spoken 32

Sprache im Alltag:
Abbreviated forms of **ein**................30

2 KAPITEL ZWEI
Familie und Freunde 39

ANLAUF
Anna Adler stellt sich vor . . . 40

ABSPRUNG
Anna schreibt eine E-Mail . . 58

ZIEL
Eine E-Mail schreiben 74

Strukturen:
I. Indicating possession or ownership 48
   The verb **haben** 48
II. Expressing what you like and don't like 52
   The expression **gern haben** . . 52
III. Describing actions 53
   Present tense of regular verbs . . 53
   A. Conjugation of regular verbs in the present tense 53
   B. Present tense equivalents in English and German 53
IV. Talking about what you like and don't like to do 54
   Verbs + the adverb **gern** 54
   A. Present tense of verbs with **gern**. 54
   B. Position of **gern** and **nicht** gern 55
V. Talking about what you have and don't have 56
   The accusative case. 56
   A. Definite and indefinite articles. 56
   B. Masculine *N*-nouns 57

Strukturen:
VI. Referring to people and things. 64
   Accusative pronouns 64
VII. Creating variety and shifting emphasis 65
   Position of subject and verb . . 65
VIII. Describing daily activities. . . 71
   Regular present tense verbs: verbs with separable prefixes and two-verb constructions . 71
IX. Expressing negation 73
   Position of **nicht** 73

Zielaktivitäten 74
Wortschatz. 77

Wissenswerte Vokabeln:
Annas Familie. 40
Die Familie und die Verwandten. . 46
Studienfächer 51

Wissenswerte Vokabeln:
Die Monate 62
Die Wochentage 66
Zeitausdrücke. 67
Die Uhrzeit. 68
Onkel Hannes' Alltag 72

Brennpunkt Kultur:
German immigration to North America 47
Types of universities in Germany . . 76
Sprache im Alltag:
Abbreviated **ich**-forms of verbs . . . 48
Expressions with the verb **haben**. . 50

3 KAPITEL DREI
Was gibt es in Heidelberg und Mannheim zu tun? 79

ANLAUF
Was halten wir von Anna?
Was hält sie von uns? 80

ABSPRUNG
Heidelberg und
Mannheim 100

ZIEL
Ein Gedicht über meine
Stadt . . 114

Strukturen:
  I. Describing activities 86
    Present tense of stem-vowel
    changing verbs 86
  II. Expressing relationships or
    ownership 90
    Nominative of possessive
    adjectives 90
  III. Expressing additional and
    contrastive information and
    justification 92
    Coordinating conjunctions . . 92
  IV. Stating personal preferences . . 93
    The adverb **lieber** 93
  V. Expressing what you would like
    to do 94
    The modal verb **möchte** 94

Strukturen:
  VI. Expressing possibilities 109
    The modal verb **können** . . 109
  VII. Talking about people and things
    that you know 112
    The verb **kennen** 112
  VIII. Expressing relationships or
    ownership 112
    Accusative of possessive
    adjectives 112
  IX. Talking about more
    than one item 113
    Noun plurals 113

Zielaktivitäten 114
Wortschatz 117

Wissenswerte Vokabeln:
Lebensmittel 96

Wissenswerte Vokabeln:
Freizeitaktivitäten 108
Die Landeskunde Deutschlands . 110

Deutsch im Beruf 1: 119

Brennpunkt Kultur:
Mealtimes in German-speaking
countries 95
The metric system 97
Sprache im Alltag:
Assumptions with **bestimmt, sicher,
wahrscheinlich,** and **wohl** 81
Es gibt ... Was gibt es?
Was gibt's 90
Specifying amounts 98
Bitte schön 98

Brennpunkt Kultur:
Heidelberg und Mannheim 106
Sprache im Alltag:
Nur „Bahnhof" verstehen 83

4 KAPITEL VIER
Unterwegs 121

ANLAUF
Mutters Ratschläge 122

ABSPRUNG
Die Radfahrprüfung – ein
Führerschein für Kinder . . 140

ZIEL
Fahrradunfälle 158

Strukturen:
I. Telling friends or relatives to
   do something 131
   The informal imperative . . . 131
   A. The **du**-imperative 131
   B. The **ihr**-imperative 133
   C. Inclusive suggestions:
      the **wir**-imperative 133
II. Expressing ability, fondness, and
    expected obligation 135
    Modal verbs (I) 135
    A. Expressing ability:
       können 135
    B. Expressing fondness and desire:
       mögen and **möchte** 137
    C. Expressing expected obligation:
       sollen 138

Strukturen:
III. Expressing permission, prohibition,
     necessity, and strong desire . . 146
     Modal verbs (II) 146
     A. Expressing permission:
        dürfen 146
     B. Expressing necessity:
        müssen 147
     C. Expressing strong desire:
        wollen 148
     D. Modal verb summary . . . 148
IV. Expressing spatial movement, the
    recipient of something,
    opposition, and omission . . . 155
    Prepositions with the
    accusative 155

Zielaktivitäten **158**
Wortschatz **161**

Wissenswerte Vokabeln:
Das Gepäck 128

Wissenswerte Vokabeln:
Eigenschaften 153

Brennpunkt Kultur:
Studienmöglichkeiten für
Deutschlernende 123
Sprache im Alltag:
Assumptions with **wohl** and
wahrscheinlich 126

Brennpunkt Kultur:
Rad fahren 145
Mit der Bahn fahren 150
Mit dem Auto fahren 157

Brennpunkt Kultur:
Frankfurt am Main 159

5 KAPITEL FÜNF
Freundschaften 163

ANLAUF	ABSPRUNG	ZIEL
Die Geschichte von Tante Uschi und Onkel Hannes 164	Erstes Date: Worauf man beim ersten Date achten soll . . .184	Freunde geben Freunden Ratschläge. 198

Strukturen:

I. Talking about past events . . 170
   The conversational past. . . . 170
   A. The auxiliaries **habetn**
      and **sein**. 170
   B. Past participles. 172
   C. Prefixes of past
      participles 176
   D. Past participles of **sein**
      and **haben** 179

Strukturen:

II. Expressing complex ideas
    with a subordinating
    conjunction 192
    A. The subordinating
       conjunction **dass** 192
    B. The subordinating
       conjunction **ob** 192
III. Expressing a condition 193
    Subordinate clauses
    with **wenn** 193
IV. Giving reasons 194
    Subordinate clauses
    with **weil** 194
 V. Expanding on an
    opinion or idea. 195
    Infinitive clauses with **zu** . . . 195
VI. Positioning information in
    a German sentence. 196
    A. Subject-verb inversion . . 196
    B. Two-part placement of
       German verbs 196
    C. Verb forms at the end of
       a subordinate clause. . . . 196

Zielaktivitäten **198**
Wortschatz. **201**

Wissenswerte Vokabeln:

Das Wetter 180
Die Jahreszeiten 182

Wissenswerte Vokabeln:

Freundschaft und Liebe 190

Brennpunkt Kultur:
Hansestadt Hamburg 177
Sprache im Alltag:
Article with first names. 165
Ganz. 181

Brennpunkt Kultur:
Bekannte oder Freunde? 189
Sprache im Alltag:
Expressing fondness or love. 191

6 KAPITEL SECHS
Willkommen in Tübingen 203

ANLAUF
Anna zieht ins
Wohnheim ein. 204

ABSPRUNG
Kleine Zimmer, kleine
Miete – Leben im
Studentenwohnheim 220

ZIEL
In dieser Stadt 236

Strukturen:
  I. Expressing the beneficiary or
    recipient of an action 212
    The dative case 212
    A. The dative case: personal
      pronouns. 212
    B. The dative case: definite and
      indefinite articles, and
      possessive adjectives. 214
  II. Indicating location 215

Strukturen:
  III. Expressing temporal and spatial
     relationships. 226
     Dative prepositions. 226
  IV. Expressing attitudes and
     conditions such as gratitude,
     pleasure, ownership, and need
     for assistance 230
     Dative verbs and
     expressions. 230
     A. Dative verbs. 230
     B. Adjectives with the
       dative case 231
     C. Idiomatic expressions with
       the dative case 231
  V. Specifying what you are talking
     about 233
     Der-words 233

Zielaktivitäten **236**
Wortschatz **239**

Wissenswerte Vokabeln:
Das Studentenzimmer und
die Möbel 204
Ein Einfamilienhaus, die
Stockwerke 216

Wissenswerte Vokabeln:
Körperteile 232

Brennpunkt Kultur:
Wo Studenten wohnen 211
Sprache im Alltag:
Expressions with animals. 205
Emphasizing one's opinion 228

Brennpunkt Kultur:
Tübingen. 225

Literarisches Deutsch:
Zwei Liebesgedichte . . 241

7 KAPITEL SIEBEN
Man kann alles in der Stadt finden 243

ANLAUF
Barbara muss ein Konto
eröffnen 244

ABSPRUNG
Freiburgs Trainer Robin Dutt:
„Bei uns lebt Multikulti" . .266

ZIEL
Mein Leben als
Film 282

Strukturen:
I. Expressing location and
   destination 250
   Two-case prepositions: **wo?** versus
   wohin? 250
   A. Two-case prepositions 250
   B. More about **an**, **auf**,
      and **in** 253
II. Giving directions 261
   Prepositional phrases; **hin**
   and **her** 261
   A. Prepositional phrases indicating
      location 261
   B. The prefixes **hin**
      and **her** 262
   C. Verbs commonly used with
      two-case prepositions 262

Strukturen:
III. Talking about when events
    happen 274
    Time expressions in the dative
    and accusative case 274
    A. Time expressions in the
       dative case 274
    B. Time expressions in the
       accusative case 274
IV. Talking about means of
    transportation 276
    The preposition **mit** with the
    dative case 276
V. Expressing time, manner,
   and place 278
   Word order for time, manner,
   and place 278
VI. Expressing the purpose for
    an action 280
    The subordinating conjunction
    damit 280

Zielaktivitäten **282**
Wortschatz **285**

Wissenswerte Vokabeln:
Wo gehst du gern hin? 254
Wo macht man das in der
Stadt? 256

Wissenswerte Vokabeln:
Wie kommt man dahin? 277

Brennpunkt Kultur:
Studentenermäßigungen 245
Einkaufen. 253
Stuttgart. 260
Sprache im Alltag:
Names of cities with **an/am** 255

Brennpunkt Kultur:
Fußball und Profi-Sport in
Mitteleuropa 265
Sprache im Alltag:
Expressing regularity 275

Brennpunkt Kultur:
München 284

8 KAPITEL ACHT
An der Uni studieren 287

ANLAUF
Ein Gruppenreferat 288

ABSPRUNG
Die beste Uni für mich . . .306

ZIEL
Ausreden im
Deutschkurs 328

Strukturen:

I. Talking about activities we do for
ourselves 296
Reflexive verbs with accusative
reflexive pronouns 296
A. Reflexive and non-reflexive
usage of verbs 296
B. Verbs that always require a
reflexive pronoun 297
C. Word order in sentences with
reflexive pronouns 297
II. Talking about daily hygiene
routines 300
Reflexive verbs with dative
reflexive pronouns 300

Strukturen:

III. Talking about future events . . .318
A. The present tense with
a time expression 318
B. The future tense: **werden +**
infinitive 319
IV. Expressing probability 321
The verb **werden + wohl** 321
V. Specifying additional information
about actions 322
A. Using verbs with prepositional
objects 322
B. Using **da-** and
wo-compounds 324

Zielaktivitäten **328**
Wortschatz **331**

Wissenswerte Vokabeln:
Die tägliche Routine 298
Im Badezimmer 299
Krank sein 303

Sprache im Alltag:
Interjections, Rejoinders
and Particles 291
Brennpunkt Kultur:
Universitätskurse 295

Brennpunkt Kultur:
Das deutsche
Universitätssystem 314
Wie Studierende ihr Studium
finanzieren 317
Das deutsche Schulsystem 327
Sprache im Alltag:
Studieren vs. lernen 306

9 KAPITEL NEUN
Ein Praktikum in Wien 333

ANLAUF
Karl hat ein Vorstellungsgespräch bei der Wiener Staatsoper . . .334

Strukturen:
I. Providing additional information about topics 340
Nominative, accusative, and dative case relative pronouns 340
A. Nominative case relative pronouns. 340
B. Accusative case relative pronouns. 343
C. Dative case relative pronouns. 344
D. Relative pronouns after prepositions 344
II. Proposing activities, making suggestions 347
Present tense subjunctive with **würde, hätte, wäre**. 347
A. The present subjunctive of **werden** 347
B. The present subjunctive of **haben** and **sein**. 348

Wissenswerte Vokabeln:
Berufe 342

Brennpunkt Kultur:
Berufswahl und Berufsausbildung in deutschsprachigen Ländern. 346
Sprache im Alltag:
Wishing someone luck 338

ABSPRUNG
Wiener Musikleben und Musiker-Gedenkstätten . . .350

Strukturen:
III. Describing people and things (I) 358
Endings on adjectives after **ein**-words, **der**-words, or neither 358
A. Endings on adjectives after **ein**-words: nominative case 358
B. Endings on adjectives after **ein**-words: accusative and dative case 361
IV. Describing people and things (II) 362
Endings on adjectives after definite articles 362
A. Adjectives preceded by a definite article: nominative, accusative, and dative case endings 362
B. Endings on unpreceded adjectives 364
V. Comparing people and things. 367
Comparative and superlative forms of adjectives and adverbs 367
A. Comparative forms 367
B. Superlative forms. 369

Wissenswerte Vokabeln:
Eigenschaften von guten Bewerbern. 360
Österreichs Leute und Länder . .366

Brennpunkt Kultur:
Wien. 353
Österreich 365

ZIEL
Vorbereitung auf ein Jobinterview. 372

Zielaktivitäten 372
Wortschatz 375

Deutsch im Beruf 2: 377

10 KAPITEL ZEHN
Feste, Feiertage und Ferien 379

ANLAUF
Aschenputtel: Ein Märchen nach den Brüdern Grimm 380

Strukturen:
I. Narrating past events 388
The narrative past 388
A. Narrative past: regular (weak) verbs 388
B. Narrative past: irregular (strong) verbs 391
C. Narrative past: **sein, haben,** and the modal verbs 393
D. Narrative past: mixed verbs 394

ABSPRUNG
Braunwald autofrei: Ein Wintermärchen ... hoch über dem Alltag 396

Strukturen:
II. Talking about consecutive events in the past 406
The past perfect 406
A. Using the conjunction **nachdem** with the past perfect 406
B. Word order in sentences beginning with a subordinate clause 406
III. Talking about concurrent events in the past 407
Using the conjunction **als** . . .407
IV. Saying when events occur . . .408
Using **wenn** vs. **wann** vs. **ob** . .408
V. Expressing ownership 409
The genitive case 409
A. Masculine and neuter nouns 410
B. Feminine and plural nouns 410
C. Masculine **N**-nouns 410
D. Adjective endings 410
E. Proper names 411
F. The dative preposition **von** 411
G. Genitive prepositions . . . 411

ZIEL
Ein Schweizer Märchen 416

Zielaktivitäten 416
Wortschatz 419

Wissenswerte Vokabeln:
Märchen 380

Wissenswerte Vokabeln:
Die Schweiz – geografische Daten 404

Brennpunkt Kultur:
Die Brüder Grimm und ihre Kinder- und Hausmärchen 381
Karneval, Fasching, Fastnacht 390

Brennpunkt Kultur:
Die Schweiz 403
Fest- und Feiertage 405
Sprache im Alltag:
Urlaub oder Ferien? 396
Diminutives 402
Replacing the genitive in spoken German 412

11 KAPITEL ELF
Geschichte und Geografie Deutschlands 421

ANLAUF
Was würdest du dann
vorschlagen? 422

ABSPRUNG
Die Geschichte Berlins . . .442

ZIEL
Meine persönliche
Zeittafel 456

Strukturen:
I. Speculating about activities,
making suggestions 430
The subjunctive mood 430
A. The present subjunctive of
können and the other
modal verbs 431
B. Making polite requests and
suggestions 432
C. Making role-reversal statements
with **an deiner (Ihrer, etc.)
Stelle** ... and the present
subjunctive 435
D. The past-time
subjunctive 436
E. The double-infinitive
construction 436
II. Talking about unreal
situations 437
A. Expressing unreal conditions:
Wenn-clauses 437
B. Present Tense Subjunctive II
forms of regular, irregular, and
mixed verbs 438

Strukturen:
III. Talking about actions as a
process 450
The passive voice 450
A. The passive voice:
present tense 450
B. The passive voice:
narrative and
conversational past 451
C. The impersonal passive . . 453

Zielaktivitäten 456
Wortschatz 459

Wissenswerte Vokabeln:
Sehenswürdigkeiten in Berlin . . . 423

Brennpunkt Kultur:
Deutschland: von der Monarchie
zur Demokratie (I) 434
Deutschland: von der Monarchie
zur Demokratie (II) 444
Sprache im Alltag:
Confirming what someone said . . . 427

Brennpunkt Kultur:
Deutschland: von der Monarchie
zur Demokratie (III) 455

Brennpunkt Kultur:
Freistaat Sachsen: Leipzig
und Dresden 458

12 KAPITEL ZWÖLF
Ende gut, alles gut! 461

ANLAUF	ABSPRUNG	ZIEL
Oh, Stefan, wenn du nur wüsstest! 462	Warum Deutsch lernen? 470	Lernerbiografien . . . 480
		Zielaktivitäten **480**
		Wortschatz **483**
Brennpunkt Kultur: Der Einfluss der englischen und deutschen Sprachen aufeinander 468	**Brennpunkt Kultur:** Amerikaner und amerikanische Kultur im deutschsprachigen Mitteleuropa 475	**Literarisches Deutsch 2:** Zwei Gedichte 485
Sprache im Alltag: **Etwas** and **nichts** 466	Deutsche und österreichische Einflüsse auf Amerikas Kultur . . . 479	

Reference

Appendix   487

Grammar Summaries and Tables   488

Principal Parts of Irregular (Strong) and Mixed Verbs   494

German-English Vocabulary   497

English-German Vocabulary   525

Index   545

Vorsprung is a complete first-year program designed for beginning students of German. It offers a communicative introduction to the German language and culture and provides beginning German students with the necessary skills for successful communication in today's rapidly changing world by exposing them to a wealth of written and spoken authentic textual materials. The first two parts (Anlauf and Absprung) are organized around a spoken and written text, respectively. *Vorsprung* combines a focus on spoken and written texts with interactive, in-class activities that foster accuracy in the language and give students ample opportunity to practice realistic German in authentic contexts.

Chapter Organization

The Student Text is divided into twelve chapters, each focusing on a different aspect of German culture. Each chapter is divided into three main parts. (Chapter 1 deviates slightly from this format). The first two parts (**Anlauf** and **Absprung**) are organized around a written or spoken text. The third part (**Ziel**) is devoted to culminating and integrative tasks and activities. Extensive pre- and post-listening or reading work is provided. In addition, important structural and lexical aspects of German are systematically explored in the first two parts of each chapter (except Chapter 12, which practices material from all the other chapters). The storyline begun in the **Anlauf** part is continued with a listening text (**Endspurt**) on the *Vorsprung* Student Companion Website (cengagebrain.com).

Chapter opener Each chapter begins with a photo focusing on the cultural themes of the chapter. A statement of the chapter's communicative, structural, lexical, and cultural goals is included to provide students with an overview of what they can expect to learn in the chapter.

Anlauf (**Warm-up**) The first main section of each chapter (**Anlauf**) features the **Anlauftext**, an audio text in dialogue form, much like a graphic novel, which can also be found recorded on the in-text audio program. The **Anlauf** section presents new grammatical structures and important vocabulary in context, as well as the cultural theme of the chapter. Chapter 1 has two **Anlauf** sections.

Vorschau (**Preview activities**) The **Anlauf** section begins with the **Vorschau** activities, pre-listening activities that function as advance organizers. There is a variety of activities used for pre-listening. The **Thematische Fragen** (*Thematic questions*) help students activate prior knowledge of themes, vocabulary, and structures before listening to the **Anlauftext**. The **Wortdetektiv** or **Satzdetektiv** activities (*Word- or sentence-detective activities*) help students focus on synonyms and build their active vocabulary base. Other predictive activities help students establish context before listening to the text. The **Vorschau** section further promotes awareness of the culture of German-speaking countries and highlights cross-cultural contrasts.

Anlauftext The **Anlauftext** is recorded on the in-text audio program and is represented visually by a storyboard in the textbook. To aid comprehension, students can listen to the **Anlauftext** while following the visual cues of the storyboard in their texts. The storyboards are a unique feature of *Vorsprung*. In the **Anlauftext**, students meet Anna Adler, an American studying for a year in Germany, along with Anna's German relatives, the Günthers, and her new friends at the university in Tübingen. All these frame the story line and unify the contents of Chapters 1–12.

Rückblick (**Post-viewing**) The activities in the **Rückblick** section guide students from initial comprehension of the text to personalization of the topics in the text. The **Stimmt das?** (*True or false?*) activity, the first activity in the section, provides a quick check of the content to determine how much of the text students understood. The **Kurz gefragt** (*Short-answer questions*) activity guides students to produce more complete statements about the text. The **Textdetektiv** activity guides students as they explore the Anlauftext for grammatical and lexical structures to learn "how German works." Further activities encourage students to use the **Anlauftext** as a jumping-off point for giving more personal reactions to the text. An **Ergänzen Sie** (*Fill-in*) activity in the Student Activities Manual asks students to focus on new vocabulary in the context of the text.

Strukturen und Vokabeln **(Structures and vocabulary)** These sections (in chapters 1–11) appear after the **Rückblick** in the **Anlauf** and **Absprung** sections. Each is organized around a selection of important language functions, such as describing yourself, asking for information, or expressing likes and dislikes. Each language function is identified with a roman numeral.

The grammar structures needed to perform each language function are clearly and concisely explained in English. Numerous easy-to-interpret charts, tables and examples aid comprehension. In addition, the vocabulary needed to fulfill the language function is presented in sections called **Wissenswerte Vokabeln** (*Vocabulary worth knowing*). Groups of thematically related words and phrases are presented in a richly illustrated format, eliminating the need for translation. This contextual approach to vocabulary presentation coincides with the functional and thematic approach of the book. A wide variety of productive and receptive activities are interspersed throughout the **Strukturen und Vokabeln** sections to aid in language development.

Absprung **(Take-off)** The second main section of each chapter revolves around the **Absprungtext,** an authentic written text produced originally for native speakers of German. (Note that there is no **Absprung** section in Chapter 1.) The **Absprung** section parallels the format of the **Anlauf** section by beginning with pre-reading activities in a **Vorschau** section. Many of the same activity types are used here to activate prior knowledge and to prepare students for reading and understanding the text. The **Absprungtext** itself is reproduced in as authentic a format as possible. Text types offered in this section include advertisements, brochures, newspaper and magazine articles, online activities, interviews, letters, time lines, internet blog entries and articles, and fairy tales. All text types relate directly to the chapter theme and to the continuing story presented in the **Anlauf** sections, and were selected for their high frequency of occurrence and usefulness to students.

The **Absprungtext** is followed by post-reading activities featured in a **Rückblick** section, which is very similar to the **Rückblick** section that follows the **Anlauftext**.

The **Absprung** section ends with another **Strukturen und Vokabeln** section, which parallels the **Strukturen und Vokabeln** section at the end of the **Anlauf**. Additional high-frequency language functions and the grammar and vocabulary to perform them are also presented and practiced. Readings from the **Absprungtext** can also be found on the in-text audio program.

Ziel **(Target)** As its name implies, the **Ziel** section is the culminating point of the chapter (there is no **Ziel** section in Chapter 1). The **Zielaktivitäten** guide students in activities that recycle and review structures and vocabulary learned in the chapter in task-based progression. By completing these culminating activities, students will demonstrate their success in reaching the learning goals listed in the chapter opener.

Wortschatz (**Vocabulary list**) Each chapter ends with a **Wortschatz** section that lists all the active words and expressions taught in the chapter. The vocabulary has been categorized by semantic fields, which facilitates acquisition of new vocabulary by encouraging students to associate words and word families.

Other Features of the Chapter

Brennpunkt Kultur (**Focus on culture**) These cultural notes appear throughout the chapter, as appropriate. Each note provides background information and insightful commentaries in English on themes encountered in the chapter. They are rich in descriptive detail and include additional thematic German vocabulary. Each Brennpunkt Kultur note is followed by a thought-provoking cross-cultural activity called Kulturkreuzung, which encourages higher-level thinking about the cultural information and students' cultural assumptions. Starting in Chapter 4 this activity asks students to reflect on their own culture and the target culture using German. The *Vorsprung* Website provides Web addresses for additional information about the cultural notes.

Kulturnotiz (**Culture note**) Interspersed throughout the chapters are short cultural notes in the margin that alert students to interesting or useful cultural knowledge related to the task or topic at hand.

Sprache im Alltag (**Everyday language usage**) These short descriptions of variations in spoken German highlight useful vocabulary and expressions.

Freie Kommunikation (**Free communication**) These featured activities appear at regular intervals in the chapter, especially as the culminating activities for the **Strukturen und Vokabeln** sections. Students are guided through role-play situations in which they practice the communicative functions that have been introduced.

Schreibecke (**Writing activities**) These special activities accompany the **Freie Kommunikation** activities throughout the chapter. They provide students with authentic tasks and the opportunity to practice their written skills in short, manageable writing assignments.

Activity icons With the exception of the Kulturkreuzung, all activities are numbered consecutively throughout the chapter. Each activity is preceded by one of three icons:

RECEPTIVE

PRODUCTIVE

INTERACTIVE

AUDIO

WEB

Receptive activities require students to recognize printed utterances. Productive activities require them to produce their own utterances. Interactive activities are productive activities that involve two or more students working together.

Enrichment Sections

Vorsprung, Third Edition contains four two-page special enrichment sections. **Deutsch im Beruf** (*Career German*) appears after Chapters 3 and 9. The first of these sections highlights practical vocabulary and information about using German in the tourist industry right here at home. The second offers information about finding a job in which a knowledge of German is an asset. **Literarisches Deutsch** (*Literary German*) appears after Chapters 6 and 12. These two sections offer the opportunity to read lyric poetry by well-known authors from the nineteenth and twentieth centuries and by one anonymous poet from the Middle

Ages. Warm-up and comprehension activities ensure a successful first experience with the beauty of the German language as it is used in German literature.

Supplementary Materials for Students

Student Activities Manual (SAM) The **Student Activities Manual** is a three-part volume combining the **Schriftliche Übungen** (*Written exercises*), **Hörübungen** (*Listening exercises*), and **Video** activities for the *Vorsprung* program. All are coordinated with the *Vorsprung* text.

The **Schriftliche Übungen** provide practice on structures, vocabulary, reading comprehension, culture, and writing skills, all designed to expand upon the work in the Student Text. The **Hörübungen** are designed to be used in conjunction with the SAM Audio Program. The activities focus on developing aural comprehension of spoken German. The audio texts reflect the themes, structures, and vocabulary encountered in the Student Text. The **Video** activities have students work with the *Vorsprung Video DVD*.

Accompanying SAM Audio and Video files can be accessed through the Premium Website.

Companion Website This open access website offers basic assets like the Text Audio Program and the **Endspurttexte.** The Text Audio Program complements the twelve chapters of *Vorsprung.* Each chapter includes recordings of the **Anlauftext,** the **Absprungtext** (when appropriate), and any applicable dialogues from the textbook chapters.

A new feature to the Companion Website is an extension of the Student Text called **Endspurt.** The **Endspurt** continues the storyline of the **Anlauftext. Vorschau** activities, much like those in the **Anlauf** section of the Student Text, prepare students to listen to and understand the **Endspurttext.** The **Endspurttexte** themselves incorporate the structures and vocabulary of the chapter in a free-flowing dialogue spoken at normal speed by native speakers of German. While listening to the **Endspurttexte** online, students can simultaneously view art-based cues that help their listening comprehension. After listening to the **Endspurttext,** students do follow-up activities in the **Rückblick** section that foster both comprehension and expansion skills. Further practice of vocabulary and structures from the **Endspurt** feature can be found in the SAM.

Premium Website The Premium Website for **Vorsprung** includes the SAM Audio Program, Video Program, audio flashcards, tutorial quizzes, and a variety of activities and resources to help you practice German, review for quizzes and exams, and explore German-language websites.

Authors

Thomas A. Lovik (University of Minnesota, M.A.; University of California, Berkeley, Ph.D.) began learning German as a second language as a junior in high school. He currently teaches German language, linguistics, and culture courses at Michigan State University. He also trains graduate teaching assistants and future teachers of German. His summers are usually spent directing a study abroad program in Mayen, Germany, a small town in the Eifel region. Professor Lovik also has close ties to the cities of Freiburg, Heidelberg, Mannheim, and Tübingen.

J. Douglas Guy (Indiana University, B.A.; Middlebury College, M.A.) is adjunct professor of German at Northern Essex Community College, Haverhill, MA. He has made significant contributions to the development of instructional text and media for German and Russian programs as an editor and ghostwriter, and has been a presenter at state and national conferences. He regularly sponsors exchange programs at the secondary level. He has also worked as a court interpreter, translator, and freelance photographer.

Monika Lagler Chavez was born in Austria and studied German and History at the University of Vienna. She has an M.A. in German Studies from the University of New Mexico-Albuquerque and a Ph.D. in German Applied Linguistics from the University of Texas at Austin. She is Professor of German and Second Language Acquisition at the University of Wisconsin-Madison, where she directs the first- and second-year programs in German language. Her research interests include learner and teacher variables and classroom language use.

Acknowledgments

The original conviction that prompted the creation of the first edition of *Vorsprung*—that learning German can be enjoyable and that understanding the German language and culture can be a valuable tool in today's changing world— continues to prove itself true. The authors' efforts in writing *Vorsprung* have been bolstered by the many people who have provided support, encouragement, assistance, good humor, and vast amounts of patience. They are especially grateful to their colleagues in the profession who have the good sense to adopt *Vorsprung* for their students.

The authors are deeply indebted to the many people at Heinle, Cengage Learning, who believed in their project and nurtured it along the way:

> Judith Bach for her support and leadership of the Third Edition, and Jessica Elias for permissions clearance of texts, art and realia.

The authors also wish to express their sincere thanks to the many talented people who contributed so much to this Third Edition:

> Paul Listen for his richly informed background and careful reading, correction and development of the manuscript for the Third Edition of the textbook and Student Activities Manual.

> Developmental editors Cynthia Hall Kouré and Peggy Potter for their enthusiastic, inspired work on the first and second editions of the textbook.

> Barbara Lasoff for her superb contributions to the first edition manuscript of the book and the recording program.

> Timothy C. Jones for the lively, colorful storyboards and line art that gives *Vorsprung* its unique visual humor and edge.

> Stacy Drew at PreMediaGlobal for her yeoman's work on all aspects of the production of the textbook, Instructor's Annotated Edition, the Student Activities Manual and other ancillaries.

> Stacy Drew, Jena Gray, Jamie Jankowski, Paul Listen and Aileen Mason for their careful selection and preparation of new photography, realia and art, and especially for layout and design of the pages for the Third Edition.

> Elizabeth Glew for her many resourceful contributions to the first edition of the Student Activities Manual.

> Mary Gell for her creative work on the new test bank for the Third Edition, and Charlotte Antibus for setting the foundation in the first edition.

Doug Milles for the recordings of core texts, listening activities for the Student Activity Manual and the listening tests that accompany **Vorsprung.**

Margret Rettich for the generous permission to re-use her illustrations for the Aschenputtel fairy tale.

For their assistance in the acquisition of original recordings and other materials for the Third Edition and for their native speaker insights, the authors would like to thank the following people:

Gabrielle Beck (Hamburg), Karen Clausen (Hamburg), Max Coqui (Neu-Biberg), Anje Naomi Decke (Berlin), Kristi Decke (Berlin), Jörg Frey (Goethe-Institut Boston), Gerda Grimm (Hoisdorf), Katja Günther (Frankfurt/Main), Karin Heidenreich (Fürth), Hans Ilmberger (Ahrensburg), Carol Jedicke (Berlin), Françoise Knaack (Keltern), Robert Meckler (Fürth), Folke-Christine Möller-Sahling (Goethe-Institut Boston), Christine Müller (Luzern), Silvia Solf (Stuttgart) and Florian Will (Berlin), and numerous tourist offices throughout Austria, Germany and Switzerland.

At Michigan State University: Minna Eschelbach, Monika Gardt (Heidelberg), Senta Goertler, Robert Gretch, David Kim, Angelika Kraemer, Eva Lacour, Elizabeth Mittman, Steve Naumann, George Peters, Carl Prestel (Tübingen), Nathan Pumplin, Theresa Schenker (Jena), Thomas Spranz-Fogasy (Mannheim), Matthias Steffan (Mannheim), Karin Wurst, and Thomas Achternkamp, Olaf Böhlke, and Volker Langeheine for their creative improvisation work on the Zieltexte.

At University of Wisconsin, Madison: The graduate students and faculty at the University of Wisconsin-Madison for ideas that in tangible and intangible ways helped to shape **Vorsprung.**

The authors also thank their students at Michigan State University, Northern Essex Community College, Beverly High School, Newburyport High School and the University of Wisconsin, Madison for their involvement and feedback during class testing of materials for the Third Edition. Special thanks to the teaching assistants, students and faculty at the University of Wisconsin, Madison and Michigan State University who have taught with **Vorsprung** and whose feedback and contributions have been incorporated into the new edition.

For their valuable appraisal and feedback on manuscript the authors would like to thank the following reviewers:

Carlee Arnett, *University of California - Davis*

Robert Bledsoe, *Augusta State University*

Beate Brunow, *Wofford College*

Anne Culberson, *Furman University*

Robert Dewell, *Loyola New Orleans*

Karin Duncker, *Hoffmann, North Central College*

Laura Eidt, *University of Dallas*

Jennifer Ham, *University of Wisconsin-Green Bay*

Melissa Hoban, *Blinn College*

Robert Kelz, *The University of Memphis*

Antje Krueger, *Goucher College*

Michael Latham, *Roosevelt University*

Felecia Lucht, *Wayne State University*

Andrea Menz, *Carson-Newman College*

Barbara Merten-Brugger, *University of Wisconsin, Milwaukee*

Helen Morris-Keitel, *Bucknell University*

Mike Putnam, *Penn State University*

Hartmut Rastalsky, *University of Michigan*

Jon Sherman, *Northern Michigan University*

Regina Smith, *Grand Valley State University*

Jane Sokolosky, *Brown University*

Bruce Spencer, *University of Iowa*

Christopher Stevens, *University of California, Los Angeles*

Erika Strube, *Gloucester County College*

Magdalena Tarnawska, *University of California - Los Angeles*

Ilona Vandergriff, *San Francisco State University*

Anja Wagner, *Pennsylvania State University - Altoona*

Melitta Wagner Heaston, *University of Northern Colorado*

Lastly the author team sincerely and gratefully thanks their families for support of the project and their endless patience during the months and months of e-mail, research, writing, revision and other always urgent work on the Third Edition of **Vorsprung**.

My wife Mary and our kids Julianna and Will, who have grown up with Anna Adler and studied in Tübingen themselves.

TAL

Katherine Guy, a great foreign language professional in her own right, and our sons Jonathan and Nicolas.

JDG

My parents, Franz and Helga Lagler, and my brother, Franz Lagler, for helping collect materials; Gabe Chavez for accompanying me on trips for materials collections; my sisters-in-law Mari, Tita and Mona Chavez for forwarding numerous packages during my stay in New Mexico; my parents-in-law, Gabe and Josie Chavez, for housing and feeding me during various drafts; and many old friends in Austria and elsewhere for inspiration regarding characters' names and scenarios.

MLC

Vorsprung, Third Edition, offers students a communicative introduction to the German language and culture that fosters active use of the German language. The *Vorsprung* materials are designed to provide ample opportunity for you to practice realistic German in authentic contexts. While the program emphasizes all four language skills—listening, speaking, reading, and writing—it places a special emphasis on the development of good listening skills as a foundation for the other skills.

Did you know . . . ?

- that when children learn their own language, they develop their listening skills first?

- that you spend about 40% of your time each day listening in your own language?

- that listening skills do not erode as quickly as speaking skills?

- that good listening skills can prove valuable in the development of speaking and writing skills?

What does this mean for learning German?

- While doing listening activities, concentrate initially on comprehension without being too anxious about speaking. You will be asked to speak and write more German gradually, as your listening skills develop.

- Listen carefully to your instructor. He or she—along with the audio and video recordings—will be your primary models for good German.

- Listen carefully to other students in the class. You can learn a lot from them. Pay close attention to the words they use, their pronunciation, and their partner's comprehension and reaction to what they say.

- Listen carefully to what you are saying. This may seem difficult at first, but as time progresses it will become easier.

What else is important when learning German?

- **Learn to focus** on what you do understand and rely on your own intuition to guess at the meanings of words. Don't become discouraged by what you don't understand.

- **Have realistic expectations.** Real fluency in another language can take years of study and may seem slow at first; during the first few weeks you may only be able to produce a word or two. However, by the end of Chapter 6, you can fully expect to be speaking in sentences about your family, your possessions, and your likes and dislikes. After two years of study you will find yourself quite comfortable conversing in German.

- **Be realistic** in your expectations of your pronunciation of German. Nobody expects you to have perfect pronunciation right away. With practice and time, your pronunciation will improve. Remember, communication is the goal of *Vorsprung*.

- **Challenge yourself.** Try to express yourself in novel ways and go beyond using language that you have rehearsed extensively.

- **Develop good study skills.** Set aside enough time each day to listen to the recordings or read the texts several times until you are comfortable with them. Let the accompanying activities guide you through different levels of comprehension. Ask your instructor for help when things are unclear.

- **Assume responsibility** for your own learning. Prepare before you come to class. For example, you are expected to read the grammar explanations on your own. Class time should be used for learning experiences you cannot get on your own, especially for communication and interaction with other students, as well as listening to authentic spoken German. Make an effort to use German whenever you can and to learn to say everyday phrases in German. Try to acquire vocabulary that is relevant to your own communicative needs.

- **Study the models in *Vorsprung*** and be sure that you understand the structures and vocabulary used in them.

- **Know your learning style.** Develop an approach to working with the information provided in *Vorsprung* that suits your particular learning style or needs. Try to assess how you learn best; for example, through visualizing concepts or associating them with each other, through listening to recordings or hearing yourself formulate statements aloud, or perhaps through writing things down and underlining them. Do whatever you find helpful for learning German.

- **Develop a vocabulary strategy.** When learning new vocabulary, practice writing new words on note cards or identifying objects in your environment with stick-on tags. You may also find it helpful to record new vocabulary and play it back to yourself. Try to organize words into small, manageable groups categorized thematically, by gender, by ranking, or by some other system. Continually test your knowledge of these new words. Avoid memorizing lists of words. Learn to associate new words with the visual or linguistic context provided in *Vorsprung*.

- **Learn to use a dictionary,** but don't let your dictionary become a substitute for effective reading strategies. This can undermine your own ability to associate meaning with new words and may inhibit your acquisition of German.

- **Keep an open mind** to new information. Much of what you learn about the German language and culture may seem different and strange at first. Maintaining an openness to new things is an important tool in learning about another language and culture.

- **Expect to make lots of errors** as you learn German. However, you will also be expected to learn from your mistakes and to make fewer and fewer errors as you progress. When you do make mistakes in class, listen carefully to what your instructor says. It should be your model for fashioning your own speech. The authors and your instructor want to congratulate you for deciding to learn German. You have made a very exciting and valuable educational choice.

Viel Spaß!

Zucchi Uwe/Picture Alliance/Photoshot   *Die Studenten sind in Hörsaal 20.*

Fangen Sie bitte an.

In this chapter you will learn to introduce yourself, ask for and spell names, identify common classroom objects, and identify and describe classmates.

Kommunikative Funktionen

> Understanding and giving commands
> Making polite requests with **bitte**
> Describing yourself and others
> Asking for someone's name
> Asking for information and clarification
> Identifying people, nationalities, colors, and classroom objects

Strukturen

> The formal imperative
> The word **bitte**
> Subject pronouns
> The verb **sein**
> The three forms of the pronoun *you*
> The verb **heißen**
> Question formation (including **wie bitte?**)
> Noun gender and number
> The nominative case: definite and indefinite articles
> Negation with **nicht** and **kein**
> Subject of a sentence
> Predicate nominative
> Pronoun substitution

Vokabeln

> The alphabet
> The numbers 0 to 1000
> Adjectives for personal description
> Classroom objects
> Colors
> Country names and nationalities

Kulturelles

> Greetings and farewells
> Titles of address
> Where German is spoken

This previewing section helps you establish the context of the text and understand important text vocabulary.

The symbol for productive activities is ⮌ and the one for receptive activities is ⮎. Interactive activities have the pair or group icon ♙♙. Receptive activities require that students recognize a printed utterance. Productive activities require that students produce their own sentences in German. Interactive activities usually involve two or more students talking.

Previewing activities

Most German verbs in the infinitive (the equivalent of English *to + verb*, e.g., *to have*) end in **-en**. German nouns are always capitalized.

Annas Albtraum°

In **Anlauf I** you are going to meet Anna Adler, an American student from Fort Wayne, Indiana, who is planning to study in Tübingen, Germany, for a year. Although excited about her year in Tübingen, Anna is also nervous and exhausted and falls asleep. In her dream, Anna works through her fears about being in a class in Germany and not being able to say what she wants.

Vorschau°

  Deutschtest (*German test.*) Find out how much German you already know. Match the following German words with their English equivalents in the right-hand column.

Deutsch	Englisch
1. sprechen	a. to come
2. der Pass	b. German
3. kommen	c. to speak
4. Deutsch	d. the passport
5. Kanada	e. America
6. Deutschland	f. Germany
7. heißen	g. Canada
8. Amerika	h. to be called
9. haben	i. from (*a country*)
10. Willkommen!	j. car
11. aus	k. to have
12. Auto	l. Welcome!
13. fragen	m. to say
14. Mann	n. woman
15. Frau	o. to ask
16. sagen	p. man

2 Thematische Fragen (*Topical questions.*) Discuss the following questions with your instructor or in pairs.

1. What feelings might you have if you were going to study abroad for a year in a German-speaking country? What things might excite or concern you?
2. What apprehensions could a beginner have about the language learning process? Where might those apprehensions come from?
3. How did you feel about coming to your first German class?

> **Thematische Fragen.** These questions are intended as a warm-up exercise before you read the German text. They activate ideas about the topic and prepare you for the reading. Starting in **Kapitel 4** these questions will be in German.

3 Machen Sie bitte mit (*Please join in.*) Listen as your instructor models the commands below and then asks you to carry them out.

Stehen Sie auf.   Setzen Sie sich.   Drehen Sie sich um.

Gehen Sie an die Tafel.   Schreiben Sie.

4 Wortdetektiv (*Word detective.*) Which words convey approximately the same meaning? Match the German word to its logical English equivalent.

> **Wortdetektiv.** Intuition can be useful when it comes to deciphering new German words. You don't need to understand every word to get the gist of a text. Look for words that may be similar to English. Also remember that German nouns begin with capital letters and that verb infinitives end with **-en** or **-n**.

Deutsch	Englisch
1. *grau*	a. Excuse me!
2. *Entschuldigung!*	b. to ask
3. *fragen*	c. the dream
4. *der Traum*	d. nothing
5. *nichts*	e. gray

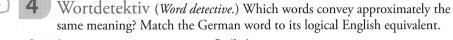

Deutsch	Englisch
6. *Gott sei Dank!*	f. to seek, to look for
7. *der Hörsaal*	g. quickly
8. *verstehen*	h. the lecture hall
9. *schnell*	i. Thank God!
10. *suchen*	j. to understand

Now listen to the recording. Study the pictures first, then listen to the text. You should not be reading along the first time you hear the text.

Anna hat einen Albtraum ...

Da ist die Universität in Deutschland: groß, grau, unpersönlich.

Anna sucht Hörsaal 20.

Anna fragt eine Studentin:

Entschuldigung! Bin ich hier richtig? Wo bin ich? Ist das hier Hörsaal 20?

Die Studentin sagt nichts.

Anna findet Hörsaal 20 und macht die Tür auf.

Aber die Tür knallt zu. Alle drehen sich um.

Rückblick°

Rückblick. This section guides you from understanding parts of the text to producing language based on the text.

Stimmt das? Do this exercise after reading the **Anlauftext** once to determine how much you understood.

5 Stimmt das? (*Is that correct?*) How much of the text can you remember without looking back at it? Look over the following statements and mark the true statements as **Ja, das stimmt.** Mark the false statements as **Nein, das stimmt nicht.** Then, listen as your instructor reads the statements aloud and models their pronunciation. If the statement is true, say **Ja, das stimmt.** If the statement is not true, say **Nein, das stimmt nicht.**

	Ja, das stimmt.	Nein, das stimmt nicht.
1. Anna hat einen Albtraum.	○	○
2. Die Universität ist groß, grau und unpersönlich.	○	○
3. Anna fragt eine Studentin: „Bin ich hier richtig?"	○	○
4. Die Studentin sagt: „Ja."	○	○
5. Anna findet den Hörsaal und macht die Tür auf.	○	○
6. Die Studenten sagen: „Hallo, Anna! Willkommen in Tübingen!"	○	○
7. Der Professor fragt: „Was suchen Sie?"	○	○
8. Anna ist nervös und sagt nichts.	○	○
9. Der Professor fragt Anna: „Wie heißen Sie? Wie heißen Sie?"	○	○
10. Annas Mutter sagt: „Anna! Anna! Anna! Wach auf!"	○	○

6 Ergänzen Sie (*Complete these sentences.*) Complete these questions and statements with words from **Anlauftext I.** Look back at the text as often as you like to read the sentences and see the words in context.

1. Anna hat einen _____.
2. Da ist die _____ in Tübingen: _____, grau und _____.
3. Anna sucht _____ 20.
4. Anna fragt eine _____: „Entschuldigung! Bin ich hier richtig?"
5. Die Studentin sagt _____.
6. Der Professor sagt: „ _____ Sie sich! Aber schnell!"
7. Der Professor fragt: „Wie _____ Sie?"
8. Der Professor fragt: „ _____ Sie das nicht? Wie heißen Sie?"
9. Der Professor sagt: „ _____ Sie an die Tafel!"
10. Annas Mutter sagt: „Anna! Anna! Anna! _____!"

7 Kurz gefragt (*Brief questions.*) Now try using what you have already learned to answer some simple German questions about Anna's dream. The two question words that recur frequently are **wer** [*who*] and **was** [*what*]. Be as complete in your answers as you can, but just a word or two may be enough.

1. Was sucht Anna?
2. Wer sagt: „Bin ich hier richtig?"
3. Was sagt die Studentin?
4. Wer sagt: „Setzen Sie sich!"?
5. Was fragt der Professor?
6. Was sagt Anna?
7. Wer sagt: „Anna! Anna! Anna! Wach auf!"?

© dean bertoncelj/Shutterstock.com

Bin ich hier richtig?

Sprache im Alltag: Breaking into a conversation with **Entschuldigung, Verzeihung, Pardon**

German speakers use one of several expressions to interrupt or engage a speaker politely in a conversation: **Entschuldigung! Verzeihung! Pardon!** All three mean essentially *Excuse me!* Whereas **Entschuldigung** frequently gets shortened to something like **Schuldigung, Verzeihung** and **Pardon** only occur in the full form. Since **Pardon** is French, it tends to be used more in regions where French is more commonly heard, e.g., in the west, or among speakers who are comfortable with the pronunciation of the word. **Verzeihung** tends to be the least commonly used form.

Pardon is pronounced like the French. The accent is on the last syllable and it is nasalized.

Strukturen

I Understanding commands and requests

The imperative

A. Formation of the formal imperative

The infinitive (**der Infinitiv**), the basic form of all German verbs, consists of a stem plus the ending **-n** or **-en**. The infinitive is the form listed in dictionaries and in the glossary at the end of this book.

Stem	+	Ending		Infinitive
geh	+	en	=	gehen to go
wander	+	n	=	wandern to hike

A formal command uses the infinitive form of the verb (**das Verb**). The formal imperative (**der Imperativ**) is usually formed by placing an infinitive-like verb at the beginning of the sentence followed by the pronoun **Sie** [*you*].

>**Schreiben Sie.**   *Write.*
>**Gehen Sie** an die Tafel.   *Go to the blackboard.*

The formal imperative for the verb **sein** [*to be*] is **seien.**

>**Seien Sie** still.   *Be quiet.*

In German, commands are sometimes written with an exclamation point (**!**). Speakers usually lower their pitch at the end of a command. The word **nicht** [*not*] is used to make a command negative. You will learn more about the position of **nicht** in **Kapitel 2**.

>**Schreiben Sie nicht!**   *Don't write!*

Seien Sie bitte still!

Strukturen und Vokabeln. This section guides you through many important features of German grammar necessary for communication. Annotations tell you which structures you are expected to produce and which ones you are only expected to recognize.

See the **Arbeitsbuch** (Student Activities Manual) for additional practice with structures and vocabulary.

© Andresr/Shutterstock

Wissenswerte Vokabeln: Aktivitäten im Klassenzimmer°

im ...: in the classroom

Understanding your instructor's requests

Stehen Sie still.

Laufen Sie.

Lachen Sie.

Machen Sie das Buch auf.

Machen Sie das Buch zu.

Lesen Sie das Buch.

B. The word *bitte*

The word **bitte** [*please*] softens commands and makes them into requests. **Bitte** can appear at the beginning, in the middle, or at the end of a request.

> **Bitte**, gehen Sie an die Tafel.
>
> Gehen Sie **bitte** an die Tafel.
>
> Gehen Sie an die Tafel, **bitte.**

---

8 **Bitte, stehen Sie auf** Listen as your instructor gives the following requests. You should only carry out requests given with **bitte**.

BEISPIEL   (Bitte) stehen Sie auf.

1. (Bitte) sagen Sie „Guten Tag".
2. (Bitte) setzen Sie sich (bitte).
3. (Bitte) gehen Sie (bitte) an die Tafel.
4. (Bitte) machen Sie die Tür auf.

Traum: dream

Annas Traum°

Now that she's awake, Anna realizes her fears were just a bad dream and that things in Tübingen will probably be a lot better. Her own experience learning German has actually been very good. In her daydream here, she knows that she will be able to say a lot in German, and she imagines how it will be to study in Germany and use the German language.

Vorschau

9 **Annas Albtraum** Your instructor will read each question about Anna's nightmare from **Anlauftext I**. Answer with a word or two in German.

1. Wer hat einen Albtraum – Anna oder der Professor?
2. Wo ist die Universität im Albtraum?
3. Ist die Universität persönlich° oder unpersönlich? groß oder klein?
4. Was macht Anna auf?
5. Was fragt der Professor? Was sagt Anna?
6. Was sagt Annas Mutter?

intimate

10 Thematische Fragen Discuss the following questions with your instructor or in pairs.

1. What fears were causing Anna anxiety in her nightmare?
2. Now that she is awake, what kind of positive daydream images might she have concerning:
   a. studying German in the future?
   b. the professors and instructors she might have?
   c. the students in her classes?
   d. her own skill in understanding and speaking German?

11 Wortdetektiv Which words convey approximately the same meaning? Match the German word to its logical English equivalent.

Deutsch	Englisch
1. freundlich	a. to answer
2. richtig	b. right
3. antworten	c. to come in
4. hereinkommen	d. in front
5. vorne	e. friendly
6. Platz nehmen	f. to take a seat
7. hineingehen	g. to greet
8. begrüßen	h. from where?
9. schön	i. to walk in, go in
10. woher?	j. to speak
11. sprechen	k. beautiful

Wortdetektiv. Use your intuition to guide your choices. Look for similar patterns in the words, e.g., **freundlich** looks like *friendly*. Also remember what you already know about capitalization of German nouns and endings on infinitives.

Brennpunkt Kultur

Greetings and farewells

Greetings such as **Guten Morgen!** and **Guten Tag!** are used to initiate conversations and to acknowledge other people, even if just in passing. In the German-speaking countries, people shake hands more often than in North America when they greet each other. Greetings differ according to geographic areas, time of day, and the social relationship of the people.

Guten Tag!

German has no single equivalent for the English greeting *hello!* Instead, German speakers use three different expressions depending on the time of day:

Until about 11 A.M.:	From about 11 A.M. until sundown:	After sundown:
Guten Morgen! *Good morning!*	**Guten Tag!** *Good day!*	**Guten Abend!** *Good evening!*

Speakers frequently shorten these greetings to **Morgen!, Tag!, 'n Abend!** From approximately 11 A.M. through lunch time, co-workers sometimes greet each other in passing with **Mahlzeit!** [*Have a nice meal!*].

In addition to these general greetings, many others are regionally unique. Austrians and Bavarians say **Servus!** with their friends and **Grüß Gott!** generally, instead of **Guten Tag!** The Swiss, particularly those in the region of Zurich (**Zürich**), greet everybody with **Grüezi!** Caution: Certain regional greetings sound out of place if used in a different part of the country, e.g., the southern **Grüß Gott** used in northern Germany.

Because of the growing influence of English throughout German-speaking countries, it is now quite common to hear **Hallo!** used as a friendly, neutral greeting by younger and middle-aged speakers.

To say good-bye, speakers use several different expressions. **Auf Wiedersehen** (or, just **Wiedersehen!**) is the generic expression for *good-bye*. **Tschüss** is more informal, although variations of it are heard by most speakers throughout Germany, Switzerland, and Austria.

Auf Wiedersehen! *Good-bye!*	**Tschüss!** *Bye!*	**Gute Nacht!** *Good night!*

Kulturkreuzung (*Cultural Intersection*)

Germans tend to greet people in situations where Americans and Canadians typically do not. How do you greet others in English? How does this contrast with German? Does the time of day play a role in your greeting? Do you typically shake hands? Do your greetings distinguish between people to show different degrees of formality? Do you say hello and goodbye differently to fellow students than to your professors?

Now listen to the recording. Study the pictures first, then listen to the text. You should not be reading along the first time you hear the text.

Anna sucht den Hörsaal und fragt eine Professorin:

Ich suche Hörsaal 20. Bin ich hier richtig?

Da ist die Universität in Tübingen: romantisch, historisch, schön.

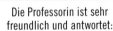

Die Professorin ist sehr freundlich und antwortet:

Ja, Sie sind hier richtig. Hörsaal 20 ist gleich da vorne.

Anna macht die Tür auf und geht hinein.

Der Professor begrüßt Anna.

Guten Morgen! Kommen Sie 'rein und nehmen Sie Platz. Setzen Sie sich, hier vorne.

© Cengage Learning 2014

Kulturnotiz. The room number is 020. A placeholder 0 is used in university buildings for ground floor room numbers.

Kulturnotiz. Annas Traum. Anna has some trouble understanding the professor because he speaks with an accent typical of the dialect in the Tübingen area. This dialect is called Swabian (**Schwäbisch**).

Rückblick

12 **Stimmt das?** How much of the text can you remember without looking back at it? Look over the following statements and mark the true statements as **Ja, das stimmt.** Mark the false statements as **Nein, das stimmt nicht.** Then, listen as your instructor reads the statements aloud and models their pronunciation. If the statement is true, say **Ja, das stimmt.** If the statement is not true, say **Nein, das stimmt nicht.**

	Ja, das stimmt.	Nein, das stimmt nicht.
1. Die Universität Tübingen ist historisch.	⊘	○
2. Anna ist nervös°. Sie sagt nichts°.	○	⊘
3. Anna fragt eine Professorin: „Bin ich hier richtig?"	⊘	○
4. Die Professorin antwortet: „Nein, Sie sind hier nicht richtig."	○	⊘
5. Der Professor heißt Professor Fachmann.	○	⊘
6. Er fragt Anna: „Wie heißen Sie?"	⊘	○
7. Anna versteht nicht und sagt: „Entschuldigung."	⊘	○
8. Der Professor fragt: „Wie heißen Sie? Wie ist Ihr Name?"	⊘	○
9. Anna antwortet: „Ich heiße Anna Adler."	⊘	○
10. Anna sagt, sie kommt aus den USA.	⊘	○
11. Der Professor sagt: „Sie sprechen gut Japanisch!"	○	⊘

nervous/nothing

13 **Ergänzen Sie** Complete these questions and statements with words from **Anlauftext II.** Look back at the text as often as you like to read the sentences and see the words in context.

1. Da ist die Universität in Tübingen: romantisch, historisch und _____.
2. Anna fragt eine _____: „Bin ich hier _____?"
3. Anna macht die _____ auf.
4. Der Professor fragt: „Wie heißen _____?"
5. Anna versteht nicht und sagt: „Wie bitte? _____."
6. Dann antwortet Anna: „Ich _____ Anna Adler."
7. Der Professor fragt: „_____ kommen Sie, Frau Adler?"
8. Anna antwortet: „Ich komme _____ Fort Wayne."
9. Der Professor sagt: „Ach, sind Sie _____?"
10. Der Professor sagt: „Sie _____ sehr gut Deutsch."
11. Anna sagt: „_____ schön!"

14 **Kurz gefragt** Now use what you have already learned to answer some simple German questions about Anna's daydream. Be as complete as you can, but just a word or two may be enough.

1. Wie ist die Universität in Tübingen?
2. Wie ist die Professorin?
3. Wie heißt der Professor?
4. Was fragt der Professor?
5. Was fragt und sagt Anna, wenn sie nichts versteht?
6. Woher kommt Anna?
7. Wie spricht Anna Deutsch?
8. Wie begrüßen die Studenten die Amerikanerin aus Fort Wayne?

15 Textdetektiv: **Anlauftext.** Use **Anlauftext II** to recognize important aspects of German structure and usage.

1. Look at these two examples from the text. Which letter appears at the end of the verb to designate what Anna – the subject – is doing?

   *Anna **sucht** den Hörsaal.*   *Anna **macht** die Tür auf.*

   a. –en   b. –e   c. –t *(c. circled)*

2. Look at these examples from the text. Which letter appears at the end of the verb to designate what Anna says she is doing?

   *Ich **heiße** Anna Adler.*   *Ich **komme** aus Fort Wayne.*

   a. –en   b. –e *(b. circled)*   c. –t

3. Look at these examples from the text. Which letter or letters appear at the end of the verb to designate that you are talking directly to another person?

   ***Kommen** Sie 'rein.*   *Wie **heißen** Sie?*

   a. –en *(a. circled)*   b. –e   c. –t

4. Indicate whether each of the following examples is a question (Q), a command (C), or a statement (S).

	Q	C	S
a. Sie sind hier richtig.	○	○	◉
b. Nehmen Sie Platz.	○	◉	○
c. Sind Sie Amerikanerin?	◉	○	○
d. Woher kommen Sie denn?	◉	○	○
e. Sie sprechen sehr gut Deutsch.	○	○	◉
f. Kommen Sie rein.	○	◉	○

5. Look at your answers in #4. Which two types of expressions have the verb at the beginning of the expression? Where is the verb in the third type of expression?

6. The professor addresses Anna as *Frau Adler* and introduces himself as *Professor Freund*. What does this imply about the relationship between German students and their professors? They are _____.

   a. very informal.   b. troubled   c. formal but polite *(c. circled)*

7. When does one use the following phrases appropriately when in a conversation? Match the related answers.

Occasion	Appropriate phrase
1. to say hello c Groß Gott (Bavaria)	a. Ach!
2. to thank someone e	b. Sehr angenehm!
3. to ask someone to repeat what they said d	c. Guten Tag!
4. to welcome someone f	d. Wie bitte?
5. to express one's pleasure at meeting someone b	e. Danke schön!
6. to express relief (for example, to have finally understood something) a	f. Willkommen!

Das bin ich. *Be careful to say only what you know how to say. Try to strike a balance between what you have already learned to say, and what you would like to express in the new language.*

 16 Das bin ich Tell a partner three things about yourself using Anna's statements about herself as your model.

BEISPIEL

Ich bin | *Amerikaner(in).*
| *Student(in).*
| *freundlich. / romantisch.*
| *groß. / schön.*

1. Ich bin ...
2. Ich heiße ...
3. Ich komme aus ...
4. Ich spreche ...

Brennpunkt Kultur 🌐 Web Search / Web Link

Titles of address

When addressing people they don't know well or people with whom they are not on intimate terms, German-speaking adults use a title before the person's last name. When talking to adults, it is better to err on the side of formality at first and use the title.

Herr (*for men*): **Herr Müller** — Mr. Müller
Frau (*for women*): **Frau Seifert** — Mrs. or Ms. Seifert
Fräulein (*for young girls*): **Fräulein Schmidt** — Miss Schmidt
Guten Morgen, Herr Müller. — Good morning, Mr. Müller.

Guten Tag, Herr Professor Winkler!

Fräulein, when used with a last name, should not be used for adult women. It is outdated and carries negative connotations. In restaurants, **Frau Ober** is beginning to replace **Fräulein,** traditionally used to call the waitress. To call a waiter, use **Herr Ober!**

In formal writing and speech and when talking about another person, German speakers also like to include the professional title of the person they are speaking with: **Guten Tag, Herr Professor Winkler.**

Kulturkreuzung

Do you use first names when you greet your friends? Do you use first names when greeting your professors? How do they greet you? Do you use titles when greeting older people?

16 VORSPRUNG

17 Guten Morgen (*Good morning.*) Practice the following dialogues with a partner until you feel confident enough to perform one from memory for the class.

1. PROFESSOR KÜHLMANN: Guten Tag, meine Damen° und Herren°.
        STUDENTEN: Tag, Professor Kühlmann.

ladies / gentlemen

2.   MUTTER: Morgen, Ulla. Kaffee?
            ULLA: Morgen, Mama. Ja, bitte.

3. HERR LANGE (*in München*): Grüß Gott.
        FRAU HILLGRUBER: Grüß Gott, Herr Lange.

18 Grüß Gott Select an appropriate greeting based on the time of day, the region, and the person you are to greet. You may need to consult the maps of Germany, Switzerland, and Austria in the front of your textbook. More than one answer may be possible.

Stuttgart *Guten Morgen*

Berlin *Guten tag*

Salzburg *Grüß Gott / Servus*

Innsbruck *Guten Gute nacht*

Zürich *Gruezi*

See the **Arbeitsbuch** (Student Activities Manual) for additional practice with structures and vocabulary.

The verb _sein._ Sein is an infinitive. It is the most irregular verb in German. You should memorize these forms.

The formal subject pronoun for *you* is **Sie**, always spelled with a capital **S**. The forms for *she* and *they* are spelled **sie** (lowercase **s**), but naturally at the beginning of a sentence, they have a capital **S**. In those cases, the verb form and context will help you avoid confusion with the formal **Sie** [*you*].

Strukturen

 Describing yourself and others

A. The verb *sein;* subject pronouns

A simple way to describe yourself or another person is to use a form of the verb **sein** [*to be*].

> **Ich bin** Amerikanerin.   *__I am__ (an) American.*
> **Sie sind** freundlich.   *__You are__ friendly.*

In the examples above, the words **ich** and **Sie** are called subject pronouns. They refer to individual people or things (singular pronouns) or groups of people or things (plural pronouns). Here are the present-tense forms of **sein.**

sein: *to be*		
Person	**Singular**	**Plural**
1st	ich **bin** *I am*	wir **sind** *we are*
2nd, informal	du **bist** *you are*	ihr **seid** *you are*
2nd, formal	Sie **sind** *you are*	Sie **sind** *you are*
3rd	er/sie/es **ist** *he/she/it is*	sie **sind** *they are*

← 19 Kurze Gespräche (*Short conversations.*) Fill in the blanks with the correct form of the verb **sein.** With a partner, practice reading the dialogues.

1. *Im Deutschunterricht°*

In German class

DOKTOR LANGE: Guten Abend. Ich _____ Bernd Lange. Wer _____ Sie?

HERR ADJEMIAN: Guten Tag, Doktor Lange. Ich _____ Herr Adjemian.

DOKTOR LANGE: _____ Sie Frau Fuji?

FRAU SATO: Nein, ich _____ Frau Sato. Die Frau da, das _____ Frau Fuji.

2. *An der Universität°*

At the university

INGRID: _____ der Hörsaal da vorne?

KARL: Ja, da _____ er.

INGRID: Und der Professor?

KARL: Er _____ auch schon da.

3. *Vor dem Hörsaal°*

In front of the lecture hall

ANNA: Pardon, _____ ihr Studenten hier?

KARL UND ULI: Ja, wir _____ beide Studenten.

ANNA: _____ hier Hörsaal 20?

KARL UND ULI: Ja, gleich da vorne.

B. *The pronoun* you

The German language has three different words for *you*. **Du** is used when speaking to a friend, a family member, a child, a pet, or when praying to God. Students, longtime colleagues, workers, and soldiers of equal rank typically also use **du** with each other.

> Bist **du** Studentin?   *Are you a student?*

The pronoun **ihr** is the plural form of **du**. Students, for example, use **ihr** when addressing more than one friend. It is used much like "*you guys*" or "*y'all*" in English.

> **Ihr** seid hier richtig.   *You (guys) are in the right place.*

Sie is used with one or more adults when the speaker wants to show respect for them or does not know them well. When students are in about the eleventh grade, teachers begin to address them with **Sie**.

> Wie heißen **Sie**?   *What is your name?* or *What are your names?*

You will use the **Sie**-form exclusively in the early chapters. Using **du** instead of **Sie** may be considered offensive by an unfamiliar person. If you are unsure which form to use, it is always safest to use **Sie** until the person to whom you are talking suggests that you use **du**.

Sie oder du?

© Cengage Learning 2014

> It is considered inappropriate and disrespectful to address a stranger with **du**. Some people feel insulted when not addressed properly.

> The pronoun **du** is also used by friends as an attention-getter; i.e., *hey:* **Du, Thomas, bist du nervös?**

→ 20 *Du, ihr* oder *Sie?* Decide whether Anna should use **du, ihr,** or **Sie** with the following people.

	du	ihr	Sie
1. the professor she asks for directions	○	○	○
2. the student she sits next to	○	○	○
3. her dog	○	○	○
4. Professor Freund	○	○	○
5. her mother	○	○	○
6. some friends in a pub	○	○	○

Strukturen

III Asking for someone's name

The verb *heißen*

The letter **ß** (called **Esszett**) is used instead of **ss** after long vowels or diphthongs. The Swiss do not use **ß**, only **ss**.

Besides the verb **sein,** German speakers also use the verb **heißen** (*to be called*) to introduce themselves.

　　Ich **heiße** Barbara Müller.　　*My name is Barbara Müller.*

These are the present-tense forms of **heißen.**

heißen: *to be called*		
Person	**Singular**	**Plural**
1st	ich **heiße**	wir **heißen**
2nd, informal	du **heißt**	ihr **heißt**
2nd, formal	Sie **heißen**	Sie **heißen**
3rd	er/sie/es **heißt**	sie **heißen**

Ich heiße Barbara.

Wie heißen Sie? German speakers often give their family name, followed by their entire name when responding to the question **Wie heißen Sie?** or **Wer sind Sie?**

👥 21 Wie heißen Sie? You are at a formal reception. Go around and ask five students what their names are using the verb **heißen.** Remember the names of the students you meet so you can introduce them to others. Below are some phrases to help you.

BEISPIEL　S1: *Guten Tag. Ich heiße Thomas Conrad. Wie heißen Sie?*

　　　　　　　S2: *Ich heiße Clausen, Karen Clausen.*

　　　　　　　S1: *Guten Tag, Frau Clausen. Sehr angenehm.*

　　　　　　　S2: *Sehr angenehm, Herr Conrad.*

　　　　S1 (*to S3*): *Das ist Karen Clausen.*

Guten Morgen. • Guten Tag. • Guten Abend. • Servus. • Grüezi. •
Grüß Gott. • Hallo. • Wie heißen Sie? • Wer sind Sie? • Ich bin …

Wissenswerte Vokabeln: das Alphabet

Spelling names

a	ah	**j**	jot	**s**	ess	**ß**	ess-tsett	**T**	großes „t"
b	beh	**k**	kah	**t**	teh	**ä**	ah-Umlaut	**t**	kleines „t"
c	tseh	**l**	ell	**u**	uh	**ö**	oh-Umlaut	**tt**	Doppel „t"
d	deh	**m**	emm	**v**	fau	**ü**	uh-Umlaut		
e	eh	**n**	enn	**w**	weh				
f	eff	**o**	oh	**x**	iks				
g	geh	**p**	peh	**y**	üppsilon				
h	hah	**q**	kuh	**z**	tsett				
i	ih	**r**	err						

BEISPIEL   Wie schreiben Sie „Professor"?
P-r-o-f-e-s-s-o-r oder P-r-o-f-e-Doppel „s"-o-r.
Wie schreiben Sie „Professorin"?
P-r-o-f-e-s-s-o-r-i-n oder P-r-o-f-e-Doppel „s"-o-r-i-n.

22 Das Alphabet Listen as your instructor models the sounds of the alphabet. Then repeat the sounds as instructed. Practice spelling the names of students in your class as well.

23 Wie bitte? (*Excuse me?*) You are working as a telemarketer in Vienna. Your job is to confirm the spelling of the names of people identified as winners of a trip to the United States. Choose a name from the telephone directory and call that person to confirm the spelling of his/her name. Take turns. Follow the model below.

Am Telefon

BEISPIEL   S1: *Guten Morgen. Hier ist Herr (Frau) _____. Wie heißen Sie bitte?*
S2: *Beck, Hans Beck.*
S1: *Wie bitte? Wie schreiben Sie das?*
S2: *B - e - c - k.*
S1: *Danke. Auf Wiederhören°.*

Beck, Hans, 22, Magdeburgerstr. 63	**233 94 37**
Bleisch, Ute, 16, Effingerg. 15, Stg. 2	**456 45 32**
Meißner, Günter, 13, Volkg. 7, Stg. 15	**812 69 54**
Schumm, Harry, 5, Marg. Gürtel 126, Stg. 2	**45 41 47**
Wurmisch, Hedwig, 16, Speckbacherg. 8	**647 04 31**

Was ist die Adresse?

Abbreviations are often used in telephone directories. Can you find the following address indications in the list shown here? **Effingergasse:** *Effinger Lane;* **Magdeburgerstraße:** *Magdeburger Street;* **Margareten Gürtel:** *Margareten Loop;* **Stiege:** *stairway, floor.*

Kulturnotiz. It is common in Germany, Austria, and Switzerland for speakers to answer the phone by giving their last name. Some speakers are increasingly using *Hallo* when answering phones.

Die Zahlen

Asking for personal information

0 = null	10 = zehn	20 = zwanzig	30 = dreißig
1 = eins	11 = elf	21 = einundzwanzig	40 = vierzig
2 = zwei	12 = zwölf	22 = zweiundzwanzig	50 = fünfzig
3 = drei	13 = dreizehn	23 = dreiundzwanzig	60 = sechzig
4 = vier	14 = vierzehn	24 = vierundzwanzig	70 = siebzig
5 = fünf	15 = fünfzehn	25 = fünfundzwanzig	80 = achtzig
6 = sechs	16 = sechzehn	26 = sechsundzwanzig	90 = neunzig
7 = sieben	17 = siebzehn	27 = siebenundzwanzig	100 = (ein)hundert
8 = acht	18 = achtzehn	28 = achtundzwanzig	101 = (ein)hunderteins
9 = neun	19 = neunzehn	29 = neunundzwanzig	1 000 = (ein)tausend

BEISPIEL Wie alt sind Sie? *Ich bin … Jahre alt.*

24 Autogrammspiel (*Autograph game.*) Walk around and find a classmate for each age listed below. When you find someone who matches the age description, have that person sign his/her name.

or

BEISPIEL S1: *Sind Sie achtzehn Jahre alt?*
S2: *Nein, ich bin … (oder°)*
Ja, ich bin achtzehn. Christina

1. 18 Jahre alt _____
2. 19 Jahre alt _____
3. 20 Jahre alt _____
4. 21 Jahre alt _____
5. über 25 Jahre alt _____

Wie alt sind sie?

Aussehen

Describing physical characteristics

Ich habe … • Er hat … • Sie hat …

braune Augen

grüne Augen

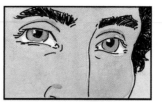
blaue Augen

die Brille: *glasses.* **Er hat eine Brille.**

lange Haare

kurze Haare

glatte Haare

krause Haare

wellige Haare

die Glatze: *bald head.* **Der Professor hat eine Glatze.**

blonde Haare

schwarze Haare

braune Haare

rote Haare

graue Haare

The word **hässlich** [*ugly*] is used to describe things. It is extremely rude to describe people as **hässlich** or ugly. Use the word **unattraktiv**.

schlank/mollig

groß/klein

alt/jung

hübsch/unattraktiv

Attraktiv is a synonym for **hübsch** and is used mostly for women. Men are referred to as **gut aussehend** [*good looking*].

BEISPIEL   Wie sehen Sie aus?° *Ich bin (schlank). Ich habe (schwarze Haare).*

What do you look like?

Illustrations © Cengage Learning 2014

→ **25** Wer ist das? (*Who is that?*) Match the descriptions below with the appropriate person in each photo.

1. Er ist 65 Jahre alt und hat kurze, graue Haare.
2. Er ist 5 Jahre alt, klein und hat dunkelblonde Haare.
3. Er ist 35 Jahre alt, schlank und hat kurze, braune Haare.
4. Sie ist 63 hat lange, glatte, blonde Haare.
5. Sie ist 32 Jahre alt, schlank und hat lange, glatte, dunkelbraune Haare.
6. Sie ist 6 Jahre alt, klein und hat hellbraune Haare.

Herr und Frau Winter

Herr und Frau Zwicker und die Kinder: Regina und Max

26 Anna ist jung (*Anna is young.*) Describe the characters you have encountered so far, using words from **Wissenswerte Vokabeln.** Try to use at least three descriptive words for each picture.

Anna Adler

die Professorin

Annas Mutter

Professor Freund

BEISPIEL Das ist Anna. Sie hat (*blonde Haare und blaue Augen*). Sie ist (*jung*) und sie ist (*schlank*).

27 Wie sehen sie aus? (*What do they look like?*) As a class, generate a list of famous personalities that you all know. Describe one of these people to a partner and see if your partner can guess whom you are talking about.

BEISPIEL S1: *Er ist … Er hat …*
Sie ist … Sie hat …

Strukturen

IV Asking for information and clarification

Question formation

There are two types of questions in English and German: information questions and yes/no questions.

A. Information questions

Information questions (**Ergänzungsfragen**) require an answer that provides specific information. They begin with one of the following question words.

wann?	when?	**Wann** ist das?	**When** is that?
warum?	why?	**Warum** sagt Anna nichts?	**Why** doesn't Anna say anything?
was?	what?	**Was** sucht Anna?	**What** is Anna looking for?
wer?	who?	**Wer** sagt das?	**Who** says that?
wie?	how?	**Wie** heißen Sie?	**What** is your name?
wo?	where?	**Wo** ist das Buch?	**Where** is the book?
woher?	from where?	**Woher** kommen Sie?	**Where** are you **from**?
wohin?	to where?	**Wohin** gehen Sie?	**Where** are you going (**to**)?

> Be careful not to confuse the meanings of **wer** *who* and **wo** *where*.

Information questions are formed with one of the question words, followed by the verb, then the subject. The speaker lowers his/her pitch at the end of an information question.

Wo bin ich?	*Where am I?*

Unlike English, German does not require a helping verb (e.g., *do/does*) to form questions.

Was sprechen Sie?	*What **do** you speak?*
Woher kommen Sie?	*Where **do** you come from?*

German does not always use the same question word as English does in similar expressions, and question words with prepositions are not usually separated in German as they are in English.

Wie heißen Sie?	***What** is your name?*
Wie ist Ihr Name?	***What** is your name?*
Woher kommen Sie?	***Where** are you **from**?*
	***Where** do you come **from**?*

The question *Wie bitte?*

Wie bitte? is commonly used to ask someone to repeat for clarification, much as we use *What?* or *Excuse me?* or *I beg your pardon?* in English.

WILLI: Guten Tag. Ich heiße Willi.
JULIANNA: Wie bitte?
WILLI: Willi. Mein Name ist Willi.

B. Yes/no questions

Yes/no questions (**Ja/Nein-Fragen**) give information which the person answering is expected to negate or confirm. They always begin with the verb and the pitch rises at the end of the question.

Sind Sie Amerikaner?	*Are you (an) American?*
Verstehen Sie Deutsch?	*Do you understand German?*

Note again that German does not require any helping verbs (e.g., *do/does*) to form questions.

---

†† 28 Drei Interviews Ask three different students the following questions.

BEISPIEL S1: *Wie heißen Sie?*
S2: *Tom.*

		1	*2*	*3*
1. Wie heißen Sie?		_____	_____	_____
2. Woher kommen Sie?	(aus …)	_____	_____	_____
3. Wo wohnen° Sie?	(in …)	_____	_____	_____
4. Wie alt sind Sie?		_____	_____	_____ (… Jahre alt)
5. Wie sehen Sie aus?	(Ich bin/habe …)	_____	_____	_____

live

Ich habe …   Ich komme …   Ich bin …

© keeweegirl/shutterstock.com

Strukturen

V Identifying people and classroom objects

A. Noun gender and number

All German nouns are capitalized, and every noun is categorized into one of three genders (**das Genus**): masculine, neuter, or feminine. Nouns often are accompanied by a definite article (**der bestimmte Artikel**) meaning *the*. The form this definite article takes (**der, das,** or **die**) depends on whether the noun is masculine, neuter, or feminine.

>   Masculine: **der** Professor, **der** Hörsaal
>   Neuter: **das** Buch, **das** Auto
>   Feminine: **die** Professorin, **die** Mutter, **die** Tafel

In German non-living things as well as living things are classified either as masculine (e.g., **der Hörsaal**), neuter (e.g., **das Zimmer**), or feminine (e.g., **die Tür, die Universität**). Some words for people are even categorized as neuter, e.g., **das Kind** (*the child*), **das Mädchen** (*the girl*). In the plural, the definite article for all nouns is **die**, regardless of their gender.

It is important to memorize the definite article (**der, das,** or **die**) that accompanies each new noun you learn.

Wissenswerte Vokabeln: das Klassenzimmer, der Hörsaal

Naming and identifying classroom objects

>   **BEISPIEL**   Was ist das? *Das ist die Uhr.*

You will learn about the formation of plural nouns in **Kapitel 3.**

der Tisch: the table

You may have noticed your instructor saying **auf den Stuhl** instead of **der Stuhl**. The difference will be explained in a later chapter.

29 Das Klassenzimmer Listen as your instructor models the commands below and then asks you to carry them out.

Zeigen Sie auf das Arbeitsbuch (das Buch, das Fenster).
Zeigen Sie auf die Lampe (die Landkarte, die Leinwand, die Steckdose, die Tafel, die Tür, die Uhr).
Zeigen Sie auf den Fernseher (den Beamer, den Papierkorb, den Schreibtisch, den Bleistift, den Stuhl, den DVD-Spieler).

30 Sie sind der Professor/die Professorin Ask your partner to identify as many classroom objects as possible.

BEISPIEL   S1: *Ist das die Kreide?*
            S2: *Ja, das ist die Kreide.* (oder)
                Nein, das ist der Stuhl. (oder)
                Ich weiß es nicht.°

I don't know.

B. The nominative case: definite articles *der, das, die*

Nouns can have different grammatical functions in sentences, and German uses a specific *case* to highlight each function. You have already seen that the definite article identifies the gender and number of a noun. The definite article also identifies the grammatical function (or case) of a noun in a sentence. You will learn about the grammatical functions of nouns later in this chapter.

For now, you should know that the nominative case is used for nouns serving as the subject of a verb, that is, the person or thing performing the action, and that the definite articles **der, das,** and **die** are used for nominative-case nouns.

der, das, die: *the*			
Case	**Masculine**	**Neuter**	**Feminine**	**Plural (all genders)**
Nominative	der	das	die	die

31 Ist das der Stuhl? (*Is that the chair?*) Fill in the blanks with **der, das,** or **die.**

1. Wo ist _der_ Schreibtisch?
2. Ist das _der_ Stuhl?
3. Wo ist _die_ Uhr?
4. Wo ist _der_ Papierkorb?
5. Ist das _der_ Fernseher?
6. Wie heißt _das_ Buch?
7. Ist _die_ Steckdose kaputt?
8. Ist _das_ Fenster auf°?
9. Wo ist _der_ Laptop?
10. Ist das _die_ Leinwand?

open

Ist das Fenster auf?

Wissenswerte Vokabeln: die Farben

Identifying objects by color

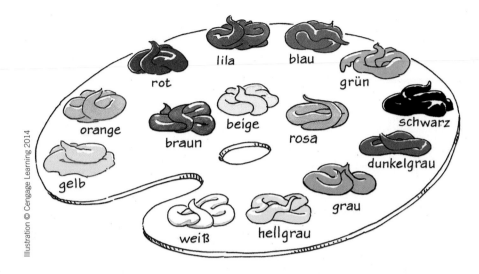

lila • blau • grün • rot • orange • beige • rosa • schwarz • braun • dunkelgrau • gelb • grau • weiß • hellgrau

32 Welche Farbe hat …? Work with a partner to describe the color of the classroom objects you now know.

die Tafel • die Tür • der Schreibtisch • die Wand • das Buch • die Leinwand • das Arbeitsbuch • der Papierkorb • der Stuhl • die Uhr • der Laptop/Computer

BEISPIEL   S1: *Welche Farbe hat der Stuhl?*
S2: *Der Stuhl ist schwarz.*
S1: *Richtig.* (oder)
Nein, der Stuhl ist braun.

33 Annas Klassenzimmer Complete the following description of Anna's classroom by providing **der, das,** or **die.**

Das Klassenzimmer ist relativ schön. *Der* Schreibtisch ist hellbraun. *Der* Papierkorb ist orange. *Die* Landkarte zeigt° Europa. *Die* Tafel ist nicht schwarz. Sie ist grün. *Die* Uhr ist kaputt. *Die* Professorin heißt Ziegler. Sie sagt: „Guten Morgen. Nehmen Sie bitte Platz." *Der* Stuhl von Frau Professor Ziegler steht vorne. *Die* Studenten° sprechen sehr viel Deutsch miteinander°. *Der* Fernseher ist an, aber *der* DVD-Spieler ist kaputt.

shows

students
with each other

C. The nominative case: indefinite articles and *kein*

1. The indefinite article: *ein*

The indefinite article (**der unbestimmte Artikel**) identifies the typical rather than the particular.

   Ein Klassenzimmer hat eine Tafel   *A classroom has a blackboard.*

   Eine Tafel ist grün oder schwarz.   *A blackboard is green or black.*

The indefinite articles in German are **ein** for masculine nouns, **ein** for neuter nouns, and **eine** for feminine nouns. All three correspond to *a* and *an* in English.

> **Kulturnotiz.** German classrooms frequently have a moveable green slate board that is cleaned with a wet sponge instead of an eraser.

Illustration © Cengage Learning 2014

As with the definite article, the indefinite article signals the gender (masculine, neuter, or feminine) and the grammatical function (or the case, e.g., nominative) of the noun in the sentence. Because **ein** literally means *one*, it cannot be used to refer to more than one item.

The following chart lists the nominative-case indefinite articles.

	Masculine	Neuter	Feminine	Plural
Nominative	ein	ein	eine	—

34 **Das Klassenzimmer** Professor Freund is talking about classroom objects with his German class. Fill in the following blanks with **ein** or **eine**.

PROFESSOR: Hier sind _eine_ Landkarte, _eine_ Leinwand und _ein_ Schreibtisch. Was ist das?

STUDENT: Das ist _eine_ Uhr.

PROFESSOR: Und was ist das?

STUDENT: Das ist _ein_ Stuhl.

PROFESSOR: Ist das _ein_ Fenster?

STUDENT: Nein, das ist _ein_ Fernseher, und das ist _ein_ Laptop.

2. Negating the indefinite article: *kein*

German has two ways of expressing negation. In **Anlauftexte I** and **II** you have already seen that speakers negate verbs with **nicht** [*not*].

Anna versteht **nicht**.   *Anna does **not** understand.*

To negate a non-specific noun, German speakers use a form of the word **kein** [*not a/an, no, or not any*].

Ist das ein Stuhl?   *Is that a chair?*
Nein, das ist **kein** Stuhl.   *No, that is **not a** chair. (It is a table.)*
  (Das ist ein Tisch.)

Ist Anna Kanadierin?   *Is Anna (a) Canadian?*
Nein, sie ist **keine** Kanadierin. *No, she is not (a) Canadian. (She is [an] American.)*
  (Sie ist Amerikanerin.)

The following chart lists the nominative-case forms of **kein.**

	Masculine	Neuter	Feminine	Plural
Nominative	kein	kein	keine	keine

††† **35** Ein Marsmensch° im Klassenzimmer Find a partner and pretend one of you is a Martian who cannot get his/her "Earth classroom" vocabulary right. The "Martian" asks whether various classroom objects are called by certain names. The "Earthling" confirms what the Martian says or contradicts with the correct information.

Martian

BEISPIEL   S1 (MARTIAN): *Ist das eine Tür?*
            S2 (EARTHLING): *Ja, das ist eine Tür.* (oder)
                            Nein, das ist keine Tür. Das ist eine Tafel.

Ist das eine Tür?

Illustration © Cengage Learning 2014

Wissenswerte Vokabeln: Länder und Nationalitäten°

Asking for personal information

countries and nationalities

	die Nationalität	
das Land	*Maskulin*	*Feminin*
die USA/Amerika	der Amerikaner	die Amerikanerin
England	der Engländer	die Engländerin
Japan	der Japaner	die Japanerin
Kanada	der Kanadier	die Kanadierin
Mexiko	der Mexikaner	die Mexikanerin
Österreich	der Österreicher	die Österreicherin
die Schweiz	der Schweizer	die Schweizerin
Italien	der Italiener	die Italienerin
Spanien	der Spanier	die Spanierin
Exceptions:		
Deutschland	der Deutsche	die Deutsche
	ein Deutscher	eine Deutsche
Frankreich	der Franzose	die Französin

⟳ **36** Anna ist Amerikanerin Make statements about the nationalities of the following people.

BEISPIEL   Jennifer: aus den USA *Jennifer ist Amerikanerin.*

1. Theo: aus der Schweiz
2. Michelle: aus Frankreich
3. Margaret: aus England
4. Franz: aus Österreich
5. Robert: aus den USA

6. María: aus Mexiko *mexikanerin*
7. Jill: aus Kanada *kanaderin*
8. Klaus: aus Deutschland *Deutsche*
9. Giuliana: aus Italien *Italienerin*
10. Juan Carlos: aus Spanien *Spanier*

Brennpunkt Kultur

 Web Search
Web Link

Where German is spoken

German is the native language (**die Muttersprache**) of an estimated 125 million people in Germany, Austria, Switzerland, and Liechtenstein. German is also an official language in Belgium, Italy (South Tyrol), Luxembourg, and Poland and is recognized as a minority language in the Czech Republic, Denmark, Hungary, and Romania. This makes it the most widely spoken language (24%) in the European Union. German is also spoken unofficially by substantial minorities in France (Alsace-Lorraine), Russia, Estonia, Latvia, Lithuania, Croatia, Serbia, Slovakia, Ukraine, and the former African colony of Namibia. It is also still spoken by immigrant populations throughout North and South America, especially in the United States, Brazil, Argentina, Canada, and Mexico. For many former foreign workers who have returned to their native countries, e.g., Turkey, Greece, Italy, Spain, and the former Yugoslavia, German is a second language.

Caro/Alamy

Because of Germany's strong economic position and leadership in the European Union, interest in learning German has increased dramatically in Eastern Europe since 1990.

Kulturkreuzung

Recent census data revealed that German is the third or fourth most widely spoken language other than English in many American states, and in many Canadian provinces as well. Is German spoken anywhere in your community or your state? Are there any German-language newspapers in your community? Do you have access to German-language media?

 37 Deutschland Look at the map of Germany in the front of your textbook and match the cities on the left with their locations on the right.

1. Heidelberg ist
2. Berlin ist
3. München ist
4. Erfurt, Weimar und Jena sind
5. Hannover und Göttingen sind
6. Bonn, Köln und Düsseldorf sind
7. Rostock und Stralsund sind
8. Frankfurt, Kassel und Gießen sind
9. Dresden und Leipzig sind
10. Bremerhaven ist

a. am Rhein in Nordrhein-Westfalen
b. an der Nordsee.
c. an der Ostsee in Mecklenburg-Vorpommern.
d. in Baden-Württemberg.
e. in Bayern.
f. in Hessen.
g. in Niedersachsen.
h. in Sachsen.
i. in Thüringen.
j. nicht weit° von Polen.

nicht weit: *not far*

38 Nein, sie ist keine Deutsche Your partner has incorrect information about the nationalities of the people listed in **Aktivität 36.** Respond to the questions with the correct information. Be sure to use **kein/keine** in your response.

BEISPIEL   Robert / Deutscher (aus den USA)

> S1: *Ist Robert Deutscher?*
> S2: *Nein, er ist kein Deutscher. Er ist Amerikaner.*

1. Franz / Deutscher (aus Österreich)
2. Theo / Amerikaner (aus der Schweiz)
3. Klaus / Kanadier (aus Deutschland)
4. Jill / Mexikanerin (aus Kanada)
5. Margaret / Österreicherin (aus England)
6. Juan Carlos / Italiener (aus Spanien)

39 Auf einer Party (*At a party.*) Use the following cues to ask students about their nationalities.

BEISPIEL   USA / Schweiz

> S1: *Sind Sie Amerikaner(in)?*
> S2: *Ja, ich bin Amerikaner(in). Und Sie?*
> S1: *Ich bin Schweizer(in).*

1. USA / Schweiz
2. Österreich / Japan
3. Kanada / Österreich
4. Deutschland / Italien
5. die Schweiz / Frankreich
6. Japan / Deutschland
7. Mexiko / Schweiz
8. England / Österreich
9. Spanien / England

40 Wer ist das? Here are some famous personalities. Using the questions below to guide you, ask each other as many questions as you can about each person.

Wer ist das? • Wie heißt er/sie? • Woher kommt er/sie? • Ist das … ? •
Ist er/sie Amerikaner/Amerikanerin? • Kommt er/sie aus Österreich?

BEISPIEL   S1: *Wer ist das?*
            S2: *Das ist Dirk Nowitzki.*
            S1: *Kommt er aus Amerika?*
            S2: *Nein. Er kommt aus Deutschland.*

Dirk Nowitzki

Diane Kruger

D. The nominative case

1. Subject of a sentence

In German the subject of a sentence (**das Subjekt**) is in the nominative case. The subject is the person or thing that performs the action described by the verb. It answers the question **wer?** (*who?*) regarding people, and the question **was?** (*what?*) regarding inanimate objects.

subject
Wer macht die Tür auf?   *Who is opening the door?*

subject
Der Professor macht die Tür auf.   *The professor is opening the door.*

subject
Was ist schwarz oder grün?   *What is black or green?*

subject
Eine Tafel ist schwarz oder grün.   *A blackboard is black or green.*

In an English sentence the subject is often the first word or phrase. In a German sentence the subject is frequently not the first word or phrase. Nevertheless, the subject always determines the ending of the verb.

        subject   *subject*
Da vorne ist **Hörsaal 20.**   ***Lecture Hall 20** is up ahead.*

Reading Strategy. Learn to identify the subject by how it fits grammatically with the verb.

Here is a summary chart of the nominative-case definite articles, indefinite articles, and forms of **kein.**

	Masculine	Neuter	Feminine	Plural
Definite article	der	das	die	die
Indefinite article	ein	ein	eine	—
kein	kein	kein	keine	keine

2. Predicate nominative

The predicate nominative (**das Prädikatsnomen**) restates the subject of the sentence and follows the verbs **sein** (*to be*), **heißen** (*to be called*), and a few others.

Sie ist **die Studentin aus Bonn.**   *She is **the (female) student from Bonn.***
Vorsprung ist **ein Deutschbuch.**   *Vorsprung is **a German textbook.***
Anna ist **Amerikanerin.**   *Anna is **(an) American.***
Der Professor heißt **Freund.**   *The professor's name is **Freund.***

In the sentences above, **Sie,** *Vorsprung,* **Anna,** and **Der Professor** are all subjects, and **die Studentin, ein Deutschbuch, Amerikanerin,** and **Freund** are all predicate nouns.

In German, the indefinite article is not used when stating a person's nationality, profession, or religion.

Er ist Amerikaner.   *He is (an) American.*
Sie ist Professorin.   *She is a professor.*
Klaus ist Katholik.   *Klaus is a Catholic.*

41 Deutsche Prominente° Match the prominent Germans on the left with their professions on the right.

celebrities

BEISPIEL S1: *Wer ist Franka Potente?*
S2: *Sie ist Filmschauspielerin.*

1. Franka Potente
2. Roger Federer
3. Heidi Klum
4. Michael Ohoven
5. Angela Merkel
6. Michael Schumacher
7. Dirk Nowitzki

a. die Bundeskanzlerin
b. Basketballspieler
c. Formel-1-Autorennfahrer
d. Model
e. Filmproduzent
f. Tennisspieler
g. Filmschauspielerin

E. Pronoun substitution

The pronouns **er, es,** and **sie** are used to replace the nouns in a sentence. By referring back to nouns, pronouns unify sentences into a tight narrative, thereby avoiding repetition and adding variety to sentences.

Der Tisch ist groß. **Er** ist braun.	***The table*** *is big.* ***It*** *is brown.*
Wo ist **das Buch?** Hier ist **es.**	*Where is **the book**? Here **it** is.*
Das ist **die Tafel. Sie** ist schwarz.	*That is **the board**. **It** is black.*
Wo sind **die Studenten?** Hier sind **sie.**	*Where are **the students**? Here **they** are.*

42 Wo ist der Tisch? – Hier ist er Ask your partner questions about the location of various people and objects using the question word **wo?** (*where?*). Use the appropriate personal pronoun (**er, es,** or **sie**) in your response.

BEISPIEL S1: *Wo ist der Tisch?*   S2: *Hier/Da° ist er.*

There

das Fenster? • die Tafel? • der Professor? • die Professorin? • das Buch? • der Stuhl? • die Wand? • der Fernseher? • das Arbeitsbuch? • der Schreibtisch?

43 Freie Kommunikation: **Jeopardy.** Form questions in German which accompany these statements from two categories: **Prominente Deutsche, Schweizer oder Österreicher** and **Prominente Amerikaner/Amerikanerinnen.** The monetary value of each item is listed.

Prominente Deutsche, Schweizer oder Österreicher

$ 10   1. Er/Sie ist der/die deutsche Bundeskanzler(in).
$ 20   2. Er kommt aus Österreich. Er spielt Hans Landa in *Inglourious Basterds.*
$ 30   3. Sie ist sehr attraktiv, hat blonde Haare und ist Model aus Deutschland.
$ 40   4. Er ist Tennis-Profi und Wimbledon-Meister aus der Schweiz.

Prominente Amerikaner/Amerikanerinnen

$ 10   1. Er ist der Präsident der USA.
$ 20   2. Er ist Ex-Präsident, Demokrat, Autor und Philanthrop.
$ 30   3. Sie ist Amerikanerin mexikanischer Abstammung° und Model.
$ 40   4. Sie ist Afro-Amerikanerin und Rock-Soul-Sängerin°. Sie ist über 70 Jahre alt und wohnt in der Schweiz.

of Mexican background
rock and soul singer

⬅ 44 Schreibecke: **Lesen Sie den *Stern*.** Fill in the subscription information for *Stern* with your name and information under **Angaben des Werbers** and include a friend's subscription under **Angaben des neuen *Stern*-Abonnenten**.

BEHALTEN SIE DEN ÜBERBLICK.

Ja, wir möchten alle *stern*-Vorteile!

Angaben des neuen *stern*-Abonnenten

Name, Vorname

Straße/Hausnummer

Postleitzahl   Wohnort

Telefonnummer   Geburtsdatum   *19*

E-Mail

Schicken Sie mir 1 Jahr lang wöchentlich den *stern* samt TV-Magazin zum Einzelpreis von zzt. € 2,30 statt € 2,50 inkl. Mehrwertsteuer und Versand. Falls ich nicht 6 Wochen vor Ablauf des vereinbarten Bezugszeitraumes kündige, verlängert sich mein Abonnement um jeweils 1 weiteres Jahr. Ich war in den letzten 6 Monaten nicht Bezieher des *stern*.

Ich bin damit einverstanden, dass Sie mir auch per Telefon oder E-Mail interessante Angebote unterbreiten (ggf. streichen).

Ich zahle bequem und bargeldlos per Bankeinzug (1/4-jährlich, zzt. € 29,90).

Bankleitzahl   Kontonummer

Geldinstitut

X

Datum   Unterschrift des neuen Lesers

Angaben des Werbers

Name, Vorname

Straße/Hausnummer

Postleitzahl   Wohnort

Telefonnummer   Geburtsdatum   *19*

E-Mail

Der neue *stern*-Abonnent und der Prämienempfänger dürfen nicht identisch sein. Die Zusendung meiner Prämie erfolgt nach Zahlungseingang (Zuzahlungsprämien werden per Nachnahme geliefert). Dieses Prämienangebot gilt nur innerhalb Deutschlands und solange der Vorrat reicht. Auslandspreise auf Anfrage.

Ich werbe den neuen Abonnenten. Als Prämie wähle ich:

☐ Best Choice: € 70,– Gutschein
Ohne Zuzahlung

☐ Prophete Mountainbike
Zuzahlung € 109,–

Ausschneiden und abschicken:
stern Kunden-Service · 20080 Hamburg

Bestell-Nr.: **241 947 W**

Stern/Gruner & Jahr

Abonnent: subscriber; Postleitzahl: postal code; Wohnort: city or town; Geburtsdatum: date of birth

WORTSCHATZ

Tutorial Quiz
Audio Flashcards

This vocabulary list represents words from **Kapitel 1** that you may want to use. The words have been categorized according to the thematic topics in this chapter. The **Ausdrücke** and **Andere Wörter** sections will provide a list of useful expressions and words found in the chapter.

Gruß- und Abschiedsformeln *Greetings and Farewells*

Guten Morgen! / Morgen! *Good morning.*

Hallo! *Hello*

Mahlzeit! *Have a good meal.* **(at lunchtime)**

Guten Tag! / Tag! *Good afternoon; Good day.*

Guten Abend! / 'n Abend! *Good evening.*

Gute Nacht! *Good night.*

Auf Wiedersehen! *Good-bye.*

Tschüss! *'Bye.*

Personen *People*

die Frau; Frau … *woman; Mrs. . . .*

das Fräulein; Fräulein … *young girl; Miss . . .* (for young girls only)

der Herr; Herr … *gentleman; Mr. . . .*

die Person *person*

der Professor / die Professorin[1] *(male/female) professor*

der Student / die Studentin *(male/female) student*

Länder *Countries*

das Land *country*

Deutschland *Germany*

England *England*

Frankreich *France*

Italien *Italy*

Japan *Japan*

Kanada *Canada*

Mexiko *Mexico*

Österreich *Austria*

die Schweiz *Switzerland*

Spanien *Spain*

die USA / Amerika *United States / America*

Nationalitäten *Nationalities*

die Nationalität *nationality*

der Amerikaner / die Amerikanerin *(male/female) American*

der Deutsche (ein Deutscher) / die Deutsche (eine Deutsche) *(male/female) German*

der Engländer / die Engländerin *(male/female) English person*

der Franzose / die Französin *(male/female) French person*

der Italiener / die Italienerin *(male/female) Italian person*

der Japaner / die Japanerin *(male/female) Japanese person*

der Kanadier / die Kanadierin *(male/female) Canadian*

der Mexikaner / die Mexikanerin *(male/female) Mexican*

der Österreicher / die Österreicherin *(male/female) Austrian*

der Schweizer / die Schweizerin *(male/female) Swiss person*

der Spanier / die Spanierin *(male/female) Spanish person*

Das Aussehen *Appearance*

das Aussehen *appearance*

die Augen *(pl.) eyes*

braune (grüne, blaue) Augen *brown (green, blue) eyes*

die Brille *(sg.) glasses*

die Haare *(pl.) hair*

blonde (schwarze, braune, rote, graue) Haare *blond (black, brown, red, gray) hair*

glatte (krause, wellige, lockige) Haare *straight (tightly curled, wavy, curly) hair*

lange (kurze) Haare *long (short) hair*

Farben *Colors*

die Farbe *color*

beige *beige*

blau *blue*

braun *brown*

gelb *yellow*

grau *gray*

grün *green*

lila *purple; violet*

orange *orange*

rosa *pink*

rot *red*

schwarz *black*

weiß *white*

dunkel *dark*

dunkelgrau *dark gray*

hell *light*

hellgrau *light gray*

Im Klassenzimmer; im Hörsaal *In the classroom; in the lecture hall*

der Hörsaal *lecture hall*

das Klassenzimmer *classroom*

die Universität *university*

das Arbeitsbuch *workbook*

---

[1]The feminine form of many professions and nationalities is formed by adding the suffix **-in** to the masculine form. Starting in **Kapitel 2,** noun plurals will also be included.

der **Beamer** *computer projector*
der **Bleistift** *pencil*
das **Buch** *book, textbook*
der **Computer** *computer*
der **DVD-Spieler** *DVD-player*
das **Fenster** *window*
der **Fernseher** *television set*
die **Kreide** *chalk*
der **Kuli** *ballpoint pen*
die **Lampe** *lamp*
die **Landkarte** *map*
die **Leinwand** *projection screen*
der **Papierkorb** *waste basket*
der **Schreibtisch** *desk*
die **Steckdose** *electrical outlet*
der **Stuhl** *chair*
die **Tafel** *board; chalkboard*
der **Tisch** *table*
die **Tür** *door*
die **Uhr** *clock*
die **Wand** *wall*

Fragewörter *Question words*

wann? *when?*
warum? *why?*
was? *what?*
wer? *who?*
wie? *how?*
wo? *where?*
woher? *from where?*
wohin? *to where?*

Verben *Verbs*

auf•machen *to open*
auf•stehen: Stehen Sie auf! *Stand up.*
heißen *to be called, named*
lachen: Lachen Sie! *Laugh.*
sein *to be*
sich setzen: Setzen Sie sich! *Sit down.*
stehen: Stehen Sie still! *Stand still.*
zeigen: Zeigen Sie …! *Point to . . .*

Adjektive *Adjectives*

alt *old*
attraktiv *attractive* (for females)
freundlich *friendly*

groß *big; tall*
gut *good*
gut aussehend *good-looking* (for males)
hübsch *pretty* (for females)
jung *young*
klein *little*
kurz *short*
lang *long*
mollig *chubby*, *heavy*
schlank *slender, thin*
schön *beautiful*
unattraktiv *unattractive*

Pronomen *Pronouns*

ich *I*
du *you* (singular, informal)
Sie *you* (singular, formal)
er *he; it*
es *it (he, she)*
sie *she; it*
wir *we*
ihr *you* (plural, informal)
Sie *you* (plural, formal)
sie *they*

Artikel *Articles*

der, das, die (die, *pl.*) *the*
ein, eine *a, an*

Ausdrücke *Expressions*

bitte *please*
danke *thank you*
Das ist … *That is . . .*
Er/Sie hat … *He/She has . . .*
Er/Sie kommt aus … *He/She comes from . . .*
Ich habe … *I have . . .*
Ich komme aus … *I come from . . .*
Ich spreche … *I speak . . .*
Ich weiß nicht. *I don't know.*
Ist das …? *Is that . . . ?*
Kommt er/sie aus …? *Does he/she come from . . . ?*
Sind Sie … Jahre alt? *Are you . . . years old?*
Und Sie? *And you?*

Welche Farbe hat …? *What color is . . . ?*
Wer ist das? *Who is that?*
Wer sind Sie? *Who are you?*
Wie bitte? *What?; Excuse me?; Pardon?*
Wie heißen Sie? *What's your name?*
Wie sehen Sie aus? *What do you look like?*
Woher kommt er/sie? *Where does he/she come from?*

Zahlen *Numbers*

die Zahl *number*
null, eins, zwei, drei, vier, fünf, sechs, sieben, acht, neun
zehn, elf, zwölf, dreizehn, vierzehn, fünfzehn, sechzehn, siebzehn, achtzehn, neunzehn
zwanzig, einundzwanzig, zweiundzwanzig
dreißig, vierzig, fünfzig, sechzig, siebzig, achtzig, neunzig
(ein)hundert, (ein)hunderteins
(ein)tausend

Andere Wörter *Other Words*

da *there*
ja *yes*
hier *here*
kein, keine (keine, *pl.*) *no, not one, not any*
nein *no*
nichts *nothing*
richtig *correct*
und *and*

Meine eigenen Wörter *My own words*

_____
_____
_____
_____
_____

Westend61/Jupiter Images

Im Sommer sitzt die Familie im Garten bei Kaffee und Kuchen.

Familie und Freunde

In this chapter you will learn how to talk about your family, your possessions, the subjects you study, the activities you like or routinely do, and when certain events occur.

Kommunikative Funktionen

> Indicating possession or ownership

> Expressing what you like and don't like

> Describing actions

> Talking about what you like and don't like to do

> Talking about what you have and don't have

> Creating variety and shifting emphasis

> Describing daily activities

> Expressing negation

> Expressing birthdates

Strukturen

> The verb **haben**

> Verbs (including **haben**) + the adverb **gern**

> Present tense of regular verbs

> The accusative case

> Accusative case pronouns

> Position of subject and verb

> Separable-prefix verbs and two-verb constructions

> Position of **nicht**

Vokabeln

> Die Familie und die Verwandten

> Studienfächer

> Die Monate

> Die Wochentage

> Zeitausdrücke

> Die Uhrzeit

> Der Alltag

Kulturelles

> German immigration to North America

> Types of universities in Germany

stellt ... : introduces herself

Anna Adler stellt sich vor°

Anna introduces herself and describes some of her favorite activities. She also introduces her immediate family. She talks about college, her German skills, and her anxieties and hopes as she looks ahead to a year studying abroad.

Vorschau

 1 Thematische Fragen Discuss the following questions with your instructor or in pairs.

1. What do you already know about Anna Adler? Where does she come from? Where is she going to study? How does she feel about it?
2. If you were going to contact family friends or relatives who lived in a foreign country and whom you had never met before, what would you tell them about yourself? What would you ask?

Wissenswerte Vokabeln: Annas Familie

Identifying family relationships

> **Annas Familie:** Note the absence of an apostrophe between the noun and the possessive **s.**

> **Wissenswerte Vokabeln:** This feature contains vocabulary that you are expected to learn and use.

© Cengage Learning 2014

Annas Eltern heißen Bob und Hannelore Adler.
Hannelore Adler ist die Mutter von Anna und Jeff.
Bob Adler ist der Vater von Anna und Jeff.
Hannelore und Bob haben zwei Kinder, Anna und Jeff.
Der Sohn heißt Jeff. Er ist der Junge in der Familie.
Die Tochter heißt Anna. Sie ist das Mädchen in der Familie. Anna ist Jeffs Schwester.
Jeff ist Annas Bruder.
Bob und Hannelore sind verheiratet. Sie sind Mann und Frau. Anna ist nicht verheiratet. Sie ist ledig.

BEISPIEL Sind Sie verheiratet? *Nein, ich bin ledig.*

2 Wer ist wer in der Familie Adler? (*Who's who in the Adler family?*)
Complete these sentences with the correct term for each relationship.

1. Anna Adler ist die _Tochter_ von Bob und Hannelore Adler.
2. Bob und Hannelore haben zwei _Kinder_: Anna und Jeff.
3. Jeff ist der _Sohn_ von Bob und Hannelore. Er ist der _Junge_ in der Familie.
4. Bob und Hannelore sind die _Eltern_ von Anna und Jeff.
5. Annas und Jeffs _Vater_ heißt Bob Adler.
6. Annas und Jeffs _Mutter_ heißt Hannelore Adler.
7. Jeff ist Annas _Bruder_. Er ist der _Junge_ in der Familie.
8. Anna ist Jeffs _Schwester_. Sie ist das _Mädchen_ in der Familie.
9. Bob und Hannelore Adler sind verheiratet. Sie sind Mann und _____
10. Jeff und Anna sind nicht verheiratet. Sie sind _____.

3 Wortdetektiv Which words convey approximately the same meaning?
Match the German word to its logical English equivalent.

Deutsch	Englisch
1. sportlich	a. to think; to mean
2. fliegen	b. athletic
3. aus	c. smart, clever
4. klug	d. to fly
5. meinen	e. from
6. hören	f. history
7. zu Hause	g. to hear, listen
8. die Geschichte	h. I would like to
9. ich möchte	i. I watch TV
10. ich sehe fern	j. at home
11. zwei Semester verbringen	k. to make better, improve
12. jetzt	l. to spend two semesters
13. Angst haben	m. to learn; to study (*for an exam, class*)
14. verbessern	n. to be afraid
15. lernen	o. now
16. die Musik	p. for example
17. spielen	q. I'm looking forward to
18. ich bin gespannt auf	r. a little bit (of)
19. ein bisschen	s. to play
20. zum Beispiel	t. music

Zum Beispiel is often abbreviated as **z. B.**

Track 1-4

Now listen to the recording.

Kulturnotiz. At German universities, the **Wintersemester** typically begins in early October and lasts until late March, with a break for **Weihnachten** and **Neujahr**. The **Sommersemester** begins in early April and ends in late June or early July.

Rückblick

4 **Stimmt das?** How much of the text can you remember without looking back at it? Look over the statements and mark the true statements as **Ja, das stimmt.** Mark the false statements as **Nein, das stimmt nicht.** Then, listen as your instructor reads the following statements and models their pronunciation.

	Ja, das stimmt.	Nein, das stimmt nicht.
1. Anna Adler ist Deutsche.	○	○
2. Anna kommt aus Fort Wayne, Indiana.	○	○
3. Sie spielt gern Basketball.	○	○
4. Sie hört gern Musik, Mozart zum Beispiel.	○	○
5. Annas Vater Bob ist 48 Jahre alt.	○	○
6. Annas Mutter Hannelore kommt aus Los Angeles.	○	○
7. Annas Bruder Jeff ist 16 und meint, er ist klug.	○	○
8. Anna möchte unbedingt ihr Deutsch verbessern.	○	○
9. Anna verbringt ein Semester in Zürich.	○	○
10. Anna hat ein bisschen Angst.	○	○

5 **Ergänzen Sie** Complete these statements with words from the **Anlauftext.** Look back at the text as often as you like to read the sentences and see the words in context.

1. Ist Anna Deutsche? Nein, sie ist _____.
2. Anna kommt _____ den USA.
3. Anna fliegt im August _____ Deutschland.
4. Anna sagt: „Ich spiele _____ Softball."
5. Anna sagt: „Ich _____ gern Musik, _____ _____ Mozart."
6. Annas Vater, Bob Adler, ist 48 _____ alt.
7. Annas Bruder _____ Jeff.
8. Anna ist Studentin. Sie studiert _____ und _____.
9. Anna sagt: „Ich spreche ein _____ Deutsch von zu Hause."
10. Anna sagt: „Dieses Jahr _____ ich zwei Semester an der _____ in Tübingen."
11. Anna sagt: „Ich habe ein bisschen _____."
12. Anna sagt: „Ich möchte so viel sehen und auch so viel _____."

Kulturnotiz. Akt. 6, Kurz gefragt: Germans may hold dual citizenship, carry two passports, and reside and work anywhere in the European Union.

6 **Kurz gefragt** Answer the questions with just a word or two. Review the question words before you begin.

was? = *what?*   **wo?** = *where?*
wann? = *when?*   **woher?** = *where . . . from?*
wie? = *how?*   **wohin?** = *where . . . to?*

1. Woher kommt Anna?
2. Wann fliegt Anna?
3. Wohin fliegt Anna?
4. Was macht Anna gern? Was sind Annas Hobbys?
5. Wie alt ist Annas Vater?
6. Woher kommt Annas Mutter?
7. Was ist Annas Mutter: Deutsche oder Amerikanerin?
8. Ist Annas Bruder sportlich?
9. Was studiert Anna?
10. Wo verbringt Anna dieses Jahr zwei Semester?

7 Jetzt sind Sie dran You are introducing yourself to a German class in Germany. Complete the statements below, then read them to your partner.

1. Ich heiße ___.
2. Ich komme aus ___.
3. Ich bin __ Jahre alt.
4. Meine Mutter heißt ___.
5. Sie ist ___ Jahre alt.
6. Sie kommt aus ___.
7. Mein Vater heißt ___.
8. Er ist ___ Jahre alt.
9. Er kommt aus ___.
10. Ich bin Student(in).

© CandyBox Images/shutterstock.com

Additional vocabulary:
ist gestorben = *has died*

8 Textdetektiv: **Anlauftext.** Look at the **Anlauftext** to answer the following questions about how German works.

1. Anna describes where she is from, where she is going, and what she will be doing. Prepositions such as *aus*, *nach*, *in*, and *an* play an important role in the descriptions. Find the German equivalents for the following expressions in the *Anlauftext*.
   a. from Germany _____
   b. from Fort Wayne _____
   c. from the U.S. _____
   d. to Germany _____
   e. in Tübingen _____
   f. at the university _____

2. *Annas Vater Bob ist Amerikaner. Annas Mutter Hannelore ist jetzt Amerikanerin.* Based on a comparison of the two words for "American" in these German sentences, we conclude that the noun ending with-*in* indicates:
   a. a plural (more than one)
   b. a woman
   c. an American

3. Anna explains: *Ich habe auch einen Bruder.* Underline in each of the following sentences the word that resembles *einen*.
   a. Ich habe keine Schwester.
   b. Meine Mutter ist 46 Jahre alt.
   c. Ich möchte unbedingt mein Deutsch verbessern.

   Which of those three German words means "no"? Which two mean "my"? The gender of the noun *Mutter* is feminine. Which letter on the preceding word shows that *Mutter* is feminine?

4. The opposite of *so viel* (so very much) is …
   a. unbedingt
   b. ein bisschen
   c. sehr

See the **Arbeitsbuch** (Student Activities Manual) for additional practice with structures and vocabulary.

Relationships created by re-marriage of a parent (e.g., stepfather, stepsister) are indicated by the prefix **Stief-: Stiefvater, Stiefmutter, Stiefkind, Stieftochter, Stiefschwester, Stiefsohn, Stiefbruder.** Relationships where siblings share only one biological parent are indicated by the prefix **Halb-: Halbbruder, Halbschwester.** Adoptive relationships are indicated by the prefix **Adoptiv-: Adoptivsohn, Adoptivtochter, Adoptiveltern.**

Someone who has left a spouse is **getrennt** (*separated*) or **geschieden** (*divorced*). Someone who has lost a spouse is **verwitwet** (*widowed*).

Wissenswerte Vokabeln: die Familie und die Verwandten

Identifying family relationships

der Mann, die Männer
die Frau, die Frauen
die Eltern (*pl.*)
die Mutter, die Mütter
der Vater, die Väter
das Kind, die Kinder
die Tochter, die Töchter
das Mädchen, die Mädchen
der Sohn, die Söhne
die Schwester, die Schwestern

der Bruder, die Brüder
der Junge, die Jungen
die Geschwister (*pl.*)
die Großeltern (*pl.*)
die Großmutter, die Großmütter
die Oma, die Omas
der Großvater, die Großväter
der Opa, die Opas

das Enkelkind, die Enkelkinder
die Enkelin, die Enkelinnen
der Enkel, die Enkel
die Tante, die Tanten
der Onkel, die Onkel
die Nichte, die Nichten
der Neffe, die Neffen
der Cousin, die Cousins
die Cousine, die Cousinen

BEISPIEL   S1: *Haben Sie Geschwister?*

S2: Ja, ich habe eine Schwester und einen Bruder.

Brennpunkt Kultur

 Web Search
Web Link

German immigration to North America

Anna, like approximately 23% of all Americans, has a German background. Germany's first immigrants to the new world came from the Lower Rhine city of Krefeld and settled in Philadelphia in 1683, establishing a German-speaking community called Germantown. New German, Swiss, and Austrian immigrants brought their German language and customs with them as they moved to places as diverse as southern Ontario, New York, Wisconsin, Indiana, California, Missouri, and Texas. With over 57 million Americans claiming German heritage, Germans are the largest single ethnic group in the U.S. Since 1983, German-Americans celebrate their ethnic heritage every year on October 6, German-American Day.

Many German-Americans take great pride in the continued use of the German language. In some smaller towns and rural areas, you can still hear German as their language of choice. The Amish, for example, worship in High German, but in daily conversation they use the German dialect their ancestors brought with them over 200 years ago. Cities such as New York, Chicago, and Los Angeles used to have large German-speaking communities, which have, with time, blended into the larger society. But you can still find German restaurants, bakeries, bookstores, German-speaking churches or newspapers in German, and sometimes even radio stations with a German-language program.

Bettmann/CORBIS

George Herman (Babe) Ruth ist ein berühmter Deutsch-Amerikaner.

Kulturkreuzung

Many immigrants from Germany, Austria, and Switzerland to the U.S. and Canada named their new homes after the cities they left behind. How many German city names can you identify in your state or province?

←⃝ **9** Die Familie Complete the following sentences using the information provided in the family tree.

BEISPIEL Anna ist die *Schwester* von Jeff.

1. Katja ist die_____ von Georg.
2. Annas _____ heißt Hannelore.
3. Katja ist Annas _____, und Georg ist Annas _____.
4. Onkel Hannes und _____ Ursula sind Katjas und Georgs _____.
5. Friedrich Kunz ist Katjas _____.
6. Bob und Hannelore Adler sind verheiratet: sie sind _____ und Frau.
7. Georg ist Katjas _____. Er ist der _____ in der Familie.
8. Bob Adler ist Katjas und Georgs _____.
9. Anna Adler ist Bobs und Hannelores _____. Sie ist das _____ in der Familie.
10. Anna und Jeff sind die zwei _____ von Hannelore und Bob Adler.
11. Werner Kunz, Ursula und Johannes Günther haben eine _____ in den USA, Anna.
12. Jeff ist Werners, Ursulas und Johannes' _____.

Strukturen

 Indicating possession or ownership

The verb **haben**

The verb **haben** (*to have*) expresses possession or ownership.

Ich **habe** auch einen Bruder.	*I also have a brother.*
Ich **habe** keine Schwester.	*I don't have a sister.*

Haben has the following present tense forms.

haben: *to have*		
Person	**Singular**	**Plural**
1st	ich hab**e**	wir hab**en**
2nd, informal	du ha**st**	ihr hab**t**
2nd, formal	Sie hab**en**	Sie hab**en**
3rd	er/sie/es ha**t**	sie hab**en**

 10 Wer hat was? (*Who has what?*) Put together meaningful sentences by matching the subjects from the left column with the correct forms of **haben** in the right column.

1. Ich …	a. haben eine intelligente Tochter.
2. Du …	b. habe keine Schwester.
3. Anna …	c. habt ein schönes Auto.
4. Herr Günther, Sie …	d. hat etwas Angst.
5. Ihr …	e. hast keine Verwandten in Deutschland.

Ich habe einen Bruder.

Peter Kneffel/EPA/Newscom

Sprache im Alltag: Abbreviated **ich**-forms of verbs

In conversational German, speakers often drop the standard **-e** ending of the **ich**-form. These short forms are common in conversation, but they are considered non-standard in writing. When a colloquial conversation is written, the deleted **-e** is sometimes indicated by the use of an apostrophe.

Ich **hab'** eine Frau und zwei Söhne.	Ich **hab'** keine Töchter.
Ich **hör'** gern Musik.	Und ich **spiel'** gern Softball.
Ich **hab'** Probleme mit …	

Courtesy of Manfred von Papen.

11 Ich habe Probleme mit … Complete each sentence with the correct form of **haben.**

BEISPIEL Der Patient *hat* Probleme mit der Religion.

1. Der Psychiater fragt: „ _____ Sie Probleme?"
2. Der Patient _____ viele° Probleme.
3. Der Patient sagt: „Ich _____ Probleme mit meiner Identität."
4. Die Studenten sagen: „Wir _____ Probleme mit Professor Bauer."
5. _____ der Psychiater Geldprobleme?
6. Anna fragt Georg: „_____ du Geldprobleme?"
7. Georg sagt: „Nein, _____ ich keine Geldprobleme. Ich arbeite° im Sommer."
8. Anna fragt Katja und Georg: „_____ ihr Geldprobleme?"
9. Katja und Georg sagen: „Im Moment _____ wir keine Probleme."

Sprache im Alltag: Expressions with the verb **haben**

German uses the verb **haben** with specific nouns denoting a state of being to express a physical or emotional condition.

Angst haben	*to be afraid*
Ich sehe einen Horrorfilm. Ich **habe Angst.**	
Hunger haben	*to be hungry*
Ich möchte etwas essen°. Ich **habe Hunger.**	
Durst haben	*to be thirsty*
Ich möchte etwas trinken°. Ich **habe Durst.**	
Zeit haben	*to have time*
Ich kann warten°. Ich habe **Zeit.**	

To negate such expressions, use **kein:** Ich habe **keinen** Hunger. / Ich habe **keinen** Durst. / Ich habe **keine** Zeit. / Ich habe **keine** Angst.

12 Interview First, fill in the information about you and your family in the column with the head **ich.** Then, ask your partner these questions and note his/her answers in the right column.

BEISPIEL   S1: *Haben Sie Geschwister?* | S1: *Haben Sie Geschwister?*
S2: *Ja, ich habe zwei Brüder* | S2: *Nein, ich habe keine Geschwister.*
und eine Schwester.

S1: *Wie heißen sie? (Wie heißt er/sie?)*
S2: *Sie heißen Hans, Franz und Constanze. (Er heißt Jörg. / Sie heißt Martina.)*

	ich	*mein Partner/meine Partnerin*
1. Haben Sie Eltern?	_____	_____
2. Wie heißen sie?	_____	_____
3. Wie alt sind sie?	_____	_____
4. Haben Sie Brüder?	_____	_____
5. Wenn° ja, wie heißen sie?	_____	_____
6. Wie alt sind sie?	_____	_____
7. Haben Sie Schwestern?	_____	_____
8. Wenn ja, wie heißen sie?	_____	_____
9. Wie alt sind sie?	_____	_____
10. Sind Sie verheiratet?	_____	_____
11. Wenn ja, wie heißt Ihr Mann / Ihre Frau?	_____	_____

Ich habe zwei Schwestern.

Wissenswerte Vokabeln: Studienfächer°

Identifying academic subjects

academic subjects

Biologie • Chemie • Medizin • Mathematik (Mathe) • Philosophie • Physik • Psychologie • Soziologie

Sprachen: Arabisch • Chinesisch • Deutsch • Englisch • Französisch • Russisch • Spanisch

W. Vok.: All sciences are feminine nouns. All languages are neuter.

BEISPIEL	Was studieren Sie?	*Ich studiere Betriebswirtschaft.*
	Welche Sprache lernen Sie?	*Ich lerne Deutsch.*
	Was haben Sie als Hauptfach?	*Ich habe Philosophie als Hauptfach.*
	Was haben Sie als Nebenfach?	*Ich habe Englisch als Nebenfach.*

If your field of study is not listed here, ask your instructor for its German name.

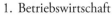

1. Betriebswirtschaft	5. Internationale Beziehungen	8. Kunst
2. Geschichte	6. Pädagogik	9. Ingenieurwesen
3. Informatik	7. Volkswirtschaft	10. Musik
4. Politikwissenschaft		

Illustrations © Cengage Learning 2014

Strukturen

 Expressing what you like and don't like

The expression **gern haben**

When talking about what they like, German speakers use the verb **haben** with the adverb **gern. Gern** usually appears at the end of the sentence or clause.

Ich **habe** meinen Deutschkurs **gern.**	*I like my German class.*
Meine Schwester **hat** Mozarts Musik **gern.**	*My sister likes Mozart's music.*
Haben Sie Mathe auch **gern?**	*Do you like math too?*

When talking about what they dislike, German speakers use the verb **haben** with **nicht gern,** which appears at the end of the sentence or clause.

Wir **haben** Musik **nicht gern.**	*We don't like music.*
Was? Ihr **habt** Musik **nicht gern?**	*What? You (guys/all) don't like music?*

Quantifiers such as **sehr** (*a lot*), **nicht so** (*not so*), and **nicht sehr** (*not much*) can be added to specify how much one likes or dislikes something.

Ich **habe** Biologie und Mathe **sehr gern.**	*I like biology and math a lot.*
Geschichte **haben** wir **nicht so gern.**	*We don't like history so much.*

 13 Interview: Studienfächer Ask another student the following questions.

1. Was haben Sie als Hauptfach?
2. Was haben Sie als Nebenfach?
3. Welche Kurse° haben Sie dieses Semester?
4. Welche Kurse haben Sie gern?
5. Welche Kurse haben Sie nicht so gern?

courses

Die Chemiestudenten machen ein Experiment.

14 Schreibecke: **Was wir gern haben.** In complete sentences describe which subjects you are studying this semester, which of these you like, and which ones you dislike. Based on the interviews in **Aktivität 13,** describe which students in the class share your schedule, likes, and dislikes.

To express the notion of *also,* insert **auch** after **haben.**

BEISPIEL   *Ich habe Deutsch, Mathe und Chemie. Jenny hat auch Deutsch. Ben und Katie haben auch Mathe. Ich habe Deutsch gern. Jenny hat ...*

Strukturen

 Describing actions

Present tense of regular verbs

A. Conjugation of regular verbs in the present tense

When talking about the activities that we or other people do, a subject pronoun is used along with a conjugated verb. Often a word or phrase follows the verb. Different subject pronouns require different endings on the verbs. Here are the present tense endings of the verb **spielen** (*to play*) as an example, followed by other important verbs.

spielen: *to play*		
Person	**Singular**	**Plural**
1st	ich spiel**e**	wir spiel**en**
2nd informal	du spiel**st**	ihr spiel**t**
2nd formal	Sie spiel**en**	Sie spiel**en**
3rd	er/sie/es spiel**t**	sie spiel**en**

> Notice there are three forms that are always identical to the regular infinitive: **wir** (*we*), **Sie** (*you*, formal), and **sie** (*they*). As you learned in **Kapitel 1,** the infinitive is the form listed in the dictionary and is composed of two parts: the stem (**spiel-**) and the ending (**-en**). The endings are attached to the verb stem.

Infinitive	gehen	heißen	kommen	meinen	studieren	verstehen
	to go	*to be named*	*to come*	*to think to mean*	*to study*	*to understand*
ich	geh**e**	heiß**e**	komm**e**	mein**e**	studier**e**	versteh**e**
du	geh**st**	heiß**t**	komm**st**	mein**st**	studier**st**	versteh**st**
Sie	geh**en**	heiß**en**	komm**en**	mein**en**	studier**en**	versteh**en**
er/sie/es	geh**t**	heiß**t**	komm**t**	mein**t**	studier**t**	versteh**t**
wir	geh**en**	heiß**en**	komm**en**	mein**en**	studier**en**	versteh**en**
ihr	geh**t**	heiß**t**	komm**t**	mein**t**	studier**t**	versteh**t**
Sie	geh**en**	heiß**en**	komm**en**	mein**en**	studier**en**	versteh**en**
sie	geh**en**	heiß**en**	komm**en**	mein**en**	studier**en**	versteh**en**

> **du heißt:** Note that the typical **-st** ending for **du** is reduced to **-t** when it follows **ss, ß, s,** or **z.**

Some other verbs you have already seen and used include **arbeiten** *to work;* **bleiben** *to stay, remain;* **finden** *to find, to think something is;* **fliegen** *to fly;* **fragen** *to ask;* **hören** *to hear, to listen to;* **lernen** *to learn, to study (for an exam, class);* **machen** *to do, to make;* **schreiben** *to write;* **trinken** *to drink;* **verbringen** *to spend (time);* and **wohnen** *to reside, live.*

B. Present tense equivalents in English and German

English has three possible meanings for one present tense German form.

Er **spielt** Mozart.
$\begin{cases} \text{He } \textbf{\textit{plays}} \text{ Mozart.} \\ \text{He } \textbf{\textit{does play}} \text{ Mozart.} \\ \text{He } \textbf{\textit{is playing}} \text{ Mozart.} \end{cases}$

> Note that, in general, for verbs like **arbeiten** and **finden,** which have a **-t** or **-d** at the end of the stem, an **e** is inserted between the stem and the endings **-st** and **-t: du arbeitest, er/sie/es arbeitet, ihr arbeitet; du findest, er/sie/es findet, ihr findet.**

The English use of *do* or *does* emphasizes the action expressed in the infinitive: *Yes, he does play Mozart.* There is no equivalent in standard German for this use of *do* or *does.* Instead, standard present tense is used, often in conjunction with **doch: Er spielt doch Mozart.**

You learned in **Kapitel 1** that to form a yes/no question, you reverse the position of the conjugated verb and the subject. Unlike English, German never uses helping verbs to form present-tense questions.

Spielt er auch Bach?
{ ***Does** he **play** Bach, too?*
***Is** he **playing** Bach, too?*

Studierst du Chemie?
{ ***Are** you **studying** chemistry?*
***Do** you **study** chemistry?*

---

15 Annas Familie Read Anna's statements. Then in groups or pairs, talk about Anna's family.

BEISPIEL Anna: Ich heiße Anna.
Annas Eltern (Hannelore und Bob Adler) • Annas Bruder (Jeff)

S1: *Annas Eltern heißen Hannelore und Bob Adler.*
S2: *Annas Bruder heißt Jeff.*

1. Anna: Ich heiße Anna.
   Annas Eltern (Hannelore und Bob Adler) • Annas Bruder (Jeff) • Annas Großeltern (Friedrich und Elfriede Kunz) • Annas Cousine (Katja) • Annas Cousin (Georg) • du (Engelbert)
2. Anna: Ich komme aus Fort Wayne.
   Katja und Georg (Weinheim) • Annas Großeltern (Bad Krozingen) • wir (den USA)
3. Anna: Ich spiele Softball.
   Jeff (Basketball) • Katja (Feldhockey) • Georg und Katja (Tennis) • Annas Mutter (Golf)
4. Anna: Ich höre gern Rockmusik.
   Katja (Oldies) • Annas Großeltern (klassische Musik) • Annas Eltern (Country) • Tante Uschi (Schlager°) • Jeff (Rapmusik) • wir (Indie-Rock)
5. Anna: Ich verstehe Deutsch.
   Katja (Englisch) • Georg (nur° Fußball) • Annas Großeltern (kein Englisch)

Strukturen

IV Talking about what you like and don't like to do

Verbs + the adverb *gern*

A. Present tense of verbs with *gern*

To talk about activities they like to do, German speakers use a verb that expresses the activity and add the adverb **gern** to the sentence.

Jeff **spielt gern** Basketball. *Jeff likes to play basketball.*
Sind Sie **gern** in Deutschland? *Do you like being in Germany?*

To talk about activities they dislike, German speakers add **nicht gern.**

Ich **fliege nicht gern.** *I **don't like to fly.***
Hören Sie Rapmusik **nicht gern?** *Don't you **like to listen** to rap music?*

easy listening hits

only

B. Position of *gern* and *nicht gern*

Depending on the context of the sentence and the intention of the speaker, **gern** and **nicht gern** occur in different places. In statements, **gern** and **nicht gern** can be placed after the conjugated verb or at the end of the sentence. Placement after the conjugated verb is more common. In yes/no questions, **gern** and **nicht gern** are also placed after the subject or at the end of the sentence.

Statement	Question
Jeff **spielt gern** Basketball.	**Spielt** Jeff **gern** Basketball?
Jeff **spielt** Basketball **gern**.	**Spielt** Jeff Basketball **gern**?
Jeff **spielt nicht gern** Softball.	**Spielt** Jeff **nicht gern** Softball?
Jeff **spielt** Softball **nicht gern**.	**Spielt** Jeff Softball **nicht gern**?

Jeff spielt gern Basketball.

Jeff spielt nicht gern Softball.

© Cengage Learning 2014

---

 16 Autogrammspiel Find a classmate who likes to do each activity, and have that person write his/her name next to the question.

BEISPIEL   S1: *Spielen Sie gern Tennis?*
S2: *Nein, ich spiele nicht gern Tennis.* (oder) *Ja, ich spiele gern Tennis.*

1. Spielen Sie gern Tennis?
2. Sprechen Sie gern Deutsch?
3. Trinken Sie gern Bier?
4. Gehen Sie gern einkaufen°?
5. Hören Sie gern Rockmusik?
6. Fliegen Sie gern?
7. Sehen Sie gern fern?
8. Gehen Sie gern wandern?

shopping

17 Was meinen Sie? Choose the phrases that apply to you, then tell a partner in complete sentences about yourself.

BEISPIEL   *Ich höre gern klassische Musik.*

1. gern klassische Musik hören
2. aus den USA kommen
3. gern einkaufen gehen
4. Deutsch interessant finden
5. die Semesterferien° in Florida verbringen
6. dieses Jahr nach Deutschland fliegen
7. eine Schwester haben
8. gern Tennis spielen

semester break

18 Schreibecke: **Meine Familie.** Use Katja's description of her own family as a model to write about your family.

My

> Meine° Familie wohnt in Weinheim.
> Mein Vater heißt Johannes Günther. Er ist 45 Jahre alt. Er ist nicht sehr alt. Er kommt aus Paderborn. Er spielt gern Tischtennis.
> Meine Mutter heißt Ursula Günther. Sie ist 48 Jahre alt. Sie ist sehr klug. Sie kommt aus Bad Kreuzingen. Sie spielt nicht gern Tischtennis.
> Mein Bruder heißt Georg. Er ist 16 Jahre alt. Er kommt aus Weinheim. Er meint, er ist sehr klug. Er hört gern Rockmusik. Er lernt nicht gern Englisch.
> Herzliche Grüße
> Katja

Strukturen

 Talking about what you have and don't have

The accusative case
A. Definite and indefinite articles

The subject of a sentence performs the action described by the verb and is in the nominative case (**der Nominativ**). It answers the questions **wer?** (*who?*) and **was?** (*what?*). The accusative case (**der Akkusativ**) is used to designate the direct object (**das direkte Objekt**). The direct object is the target or product of the action expressed by the verb and answers the questions **wen?** (*whom?*) and **was?** (*what?*).

Was hat Anna?	*What is Anna having?*
Anna hat **einen Traum.**	*Anna is having a dream.*
Was sucht Anna?	*What is Anna looking for?*
Anna sucht **den Hörsaal.**	*Anna is looking for the lecture hall.*
Wen fragt Anna?	*Whom does Anna ask?*
Anna fragt **eine Studentin.**	*Anna asks a (female) student.*
Was schreibt Anna?	*What is Anna writing?*
Anna schreibt **eine E-Mail.**	*Anna is writing an e-mail.*

You can identify the accusative case by looking at the ending on the article. The ending denotes both the gender (masculine, feminine, neuter) and the number (singular or plural) of the noun, as well as its function (direct object as opposed to subject, etc.). The following chart shows all the forms of the definite and indefinite articles, plus **kein** in the nominative and accusative case.

Case	Singular			Plural
	Masculine	**Neuter**	**Feminine**	**All Genders**
Nominative	**der** Mann	**das** Kind	**die** Frau	**die** Kinder
	ein Mann	**ein** Kind	**eine** Frau	—
	kein Mann	**kein** Kind	**keine** Frau	**keine** Kinder
Accusative	**den** Mann	**das** Kind	**die** Frau	**die** Kinder
	einen Mann	**ein** Kind	**eine** Frau	—
	keinen Mann	**kein** Kind	**keine** Frau	**keine** Kinder

Note that only the singular masculine forms are different in the nominative (**der, ein, kein**) and in the accusative (**den, einen, keinen**). Singular feminine and neuter forms as well as plural forms are identical in the nominative and in the accusative. Please also note that **kein** has the same endings as **ein**.

Ich habe einen Porsche, einen Audi, einen BMW, einen Mercedes und einen Trabi zu Hause.

B. Masculine *N*-nouns

A small group of masculine nouns adds an **-n** or **-en** ending to the noun itself to signal the change in function from subject to direct object. Pay special attention to these nouns, which include **der Herr (→ den Herrn), der Student (→ den Studenten), der Neffe (→ den Neffen)** and **der Junge (→ den Jungen).** In vocabulary sections, the extra accusative case ending will be noted in brackets. The second **-en** ending listed is the plural ending: **der Student, [-en], -en.**

Ich kenne **den Herrn.**	*I know the (gentle)man.*
Werner hat **einen Neffen** in Indiana.	*Werner has a nephew in Indiana.*

N-nouns are discussed mainly for recognition.

19 Ich habe ... zu Hause (*I have . . . at home*) Ask what your partner has at home. Report your findings to the class. As you listen to what other students say, write down their names next to what they have.

BEISPIEL S1: *Haben Sie einen Hund zu Hause?*
 S2: *Ja, ich habe einen Hund.*

Personen/Tiere°/Objekte	Mein Partner / Meine Partnerin	Andere Leute°
1. einen Hund	_____	_____
2. Geschwister	_____	_____
3. einen Bruder	_____	_____
4. zwei (drei, vier) Brüder	_____	_____
5. eine Schwester	_____	_____
6. zwei (drei, vier) Schwestern	_____	_____
7. ein Kind	_____	_____
8. einen Opa	_____	_____
9. einen Laptop	_____	_____
10. ein Deutschbuch	_____	_____

animals / other people

20 Meine Familie Work with a partner and take turns asking each other questions. Follow the model.

BEISPIEL Schwester in Mexiko

 S1: *Haben Sie eine Schwester in Mexiko?*
 S2: *Nein, ich habe keine Schwester in Mexiko. Ich habe eine Schwester in Kanada, in Edmonton. (oder) Ich habe überhaupt keine Schwester.*

1. Onkel in Österreich
2. Großvater in Kanada
3. Großmutter in Russland
4. Tante in China
5. Kinder in England
6. Cousin in Kalifornien
7. Sohn in Japan
8. Tochter in Australien
9. Nichte in Brasilien
10. Oma in Liechtenstein

German speakers use the word **überhaupt** to emphasize **kein. Ich habe überhaupt keine Verwandten in Deutschland.**

Ich habe überhaupt keine Hunde zu Hause.

© Cengage Learning 2014

Both **die E-Mail** and **das Mail** are used by Germans to mean *e-mail*.

The short version of **Ursula,** generally used by family and friends, is **Uschi.**

Anna schreibt eine E-Mail

In preparation for her year in Germany, Anna Adler decides to contact her relatives in Germany. Her mother's sister, Ursula, lives with her family in Weinheim. Anna hopes to spend some time with them before her German course in Tübingen begins. With help from her mother, Anna writes Tante Uschi an e-mail about her travel plans, her academic schedule in Germany, and her request to come for a visit. She asks Tante Uschi to write back.

Vorschau

← 21 Thematische Fragen Discuss the following questions with your instructor or in pairs.

1. If you were writing a letter or e-mail to relatives who lived in a foreign country and whom you'd never met, telling them that you wanted to come for a visit, what travel information would you include?
2. Suppose you wanted to visit these relatives before starting a study-abroad program in the country they live in. What would you tell them about yourself? What questions would you ask them?
3. Why might you prefer writing instead of calling someone abroad? Why would speaking a foreign language on the phone be more difficult than speaking it face to face with someone?

→ 22 Mein Tagtraum (*My daydream*) Imagine that you are going to Germany. How do you see yourself?

1. das Alter
   a. Ich bin fünfzehn Jahre alt.
   b. Ich bin zwanzig Jahre alt.
   c. Ich bin fünfzig Jahre alt.
2. der Beruf°/die Ausbildung°
   a. Ich bin Schüler(in)°.
   b. Ich bin Student(in).
   c. Ich habe einen Beruf.
3. die Personen
   a. Ich fliege allein.
   b. Ich fliege mit Freunden.
   c. Ich fliege mit meiner° Familie.

4. in Deutschland
   a. Ich gehe einkaufen.
   b. Ich studiere an der Universität.
   c. Ich besuche° meine Verwandten.
5. die Zeit
   a. Ich bleibe eine Woche.
   b. Ich bleibe einen Monat.
   c. Ich bleibe ein Jahr.
6. die Sprache°
   a. Ich spreche perfekt Deutsch.
   b. Ich spreche ein bisschen Deutsch.
   c. Ich spreche perfekt Englisch.

am visiting

occupation / education
elementary or high-school student

language

my

23 Wortdetektiv Which words convey approximately the same meaning? Draw a line from the German word to its logical English equivalent.

Deutsch	*Englisch*
1. um 8.15 Uhr	a. finally
2. ankommen	b. to send
3. schicken	c. at 8:15 A.M.
4. endlich	d. to arrive
5. zurück	e. back

6. kennenlernen	f. to call up
7. ganz allein	g. immediately
8. gleich	h. expensive
9. teuer	i. to get to know
10. anrufen	j. all alone

11. die Zeit	k. to visit
12. eine Bitte	l. to hope
13. die Leute	m. people
14. besuchen	n. a request
15. hoffen	o. time

E-Mail

viviamo/Shutterstock.com

24 Scanning Scanning is a reading technique used to identify specific information, without reading every word of the text. It also helps the reader to locate the features that are typical of a certain text type.

1. When composing a letter or an e-mail the writer generally observes certain conventions. Scan Anna's e-mail for these customary elements.
   a. a subject line
   b. a date
   c. an opening greeting
   d. a closing

2. Look over Anna's e-mail for answers to these questions.
   a. When is she arriving in Germany, and where?
   b. When does her German course begin?
   c. When does the actual fall semester begin?
   d. How does she express her wish to come for a visit? How does she repeat it?

Now read the text.

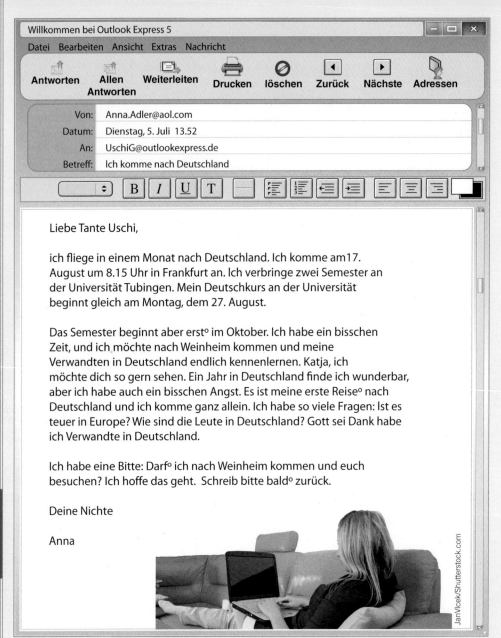

Willkommen bei Outlook Express 5

Datei   Bearbeiten   Ansicht   Extras   Nachricht

Antworten   Allen Antworten   Weiterleiten   Drucken   löschen   Zurück   Nächste   Adressen

Von: Anna.Adler@aol.com
Datum: Dienstag, 5. Juli 13.52
An: UschiG@outlookexpress.de
Betreff: Ich komme nach Deutschland

B   *I*   <u>U</u>   T

Liebe Tante Uschi,

ich fliege in einem Monat nach Deutschland. Ich komme am17.
August um 8.15 Uhr in Frankfurt an. Ich verbringe zwei Semester an
der Universität Tubingen. Mein Deutschkurs an der Universität
beginnt gleich am Montag, dem 27. August.

Das Semester beginnt aber erst° im Oktober. Ich habe ein bisschen
Zeit, und ich möchte nach Weinheim kommen und meine
Verwandten in Deutschland endlich kennenlernen. Katja, ich
möchte dich so gern sehen. Ein Jahr in Deutschland finde ich wunderbar,
aber ich habe auch ein bisschen Angst. Es ist meine erste Reise° nach
Deutschland und ich komme ganz allein. Ich habe so viele Fragen: Ist es
teuer in Europe? Wie sind die Leute in Deutschland? Gott sei Dank habe
ich Verwandte in Deutschland.

Ich habe eine Bitte: Darf° ich nach Weinheim kommen und euch
besuchen? Ich hoffe das geht. Schreib bitte bald° zurück.

Deine Nichte

Anna

not until

***erste ...** : first trip*

may
soon

> Family members close letters with **dein/deine: dein Thomas** (*your Thomas*), **deine Anna** (*your Anna*).

JanVlcek/Shutterstock.com

Rückblick

25 **Stimmt das?** How much of the text do you remember without looking back at it?

	Ja, das stimmt.	Nein, das stimmt nicht.
1. Anna fliegt im Juli nach Deutschland.	○	○
2. Anna kommt am 17. August in Frankfurt an.	○	○
3. Annas Deutschkurs beginnt am 27. August.	○	○
4. Anna möchte direkt nach Tübingen fahren.	○	○
5. Anna findet ein Jahr in Deutschland wunderbar.	○	○
6. Anna kommt ganz allein.	○	○
7. Anna hat keine Angst; sie spricht perfekt Deutsch.	○	○
8. Anna hat Verwandte in Deutschland.	○	○
9. Anna möchte Tante Uschis Familie endlich kennenlernen.	○	○
10. Tante Uschi soll° nicht zurückschreiben.	○	○

should

26 **Ergänzen Sie** Complete these questions and statements with words from the **Absprungtext.** Look back at the text as often as you like to read the sentences and see the words in context.

1. Ich _____ in einem Monat nach Deutschland.
2. Ich _____ am 17. August um 8 Uhr 15 in Frankfurt an.
3. Ich verbringe zwei _____ an der Universität in Tübingen.
4. Mein Deutschkurs _____ gleich am Montag, den 27. August.
5. Ich möchte nach Weinheim kommen und meine _____ in Deutschland endlich kennenlernen.
6. Ein Jahr in Deutschland ist wunderbar, aber ich habe auch ein bisschen _____.
7. Ich habe so viele _____.
8. Ist es _____ in Europa?
9. Wie sind die _____ in Deutschland?
10. Gott sei _____ habe ich Verwandte in Deutschland!
11. Ich habe eine _____: Darf ich nach Weinheim kommen und euch _____?

27 **Kurz gefragt** Answer these questions with just a word or two.

BEISPIEL S1: *Wann kommt Anna nach Deutschland?*
S2: *In einem Monat.* (oder)
Im August.

1. Wo kommt sie an?
2. Wo studiert sie?
3. Was studiert sie?
4. Wann beginnt das Semester?
5. Hat sie Angst?
6. Wo wohnen Annas Verwandte in Deutschland?
7. Wie findet Anna ein Jahr in Deutschland?
8. Wen möchte Anna in Weinheim besuchen?

28 Textdetektiv: **Absprungtext.** Look at the **Absprungtext** to answer the following questions about how German works.

1. The German word for 'Dear', when addressing a female relative in a letter is:
   a. Liebe   b. Deine   c. Ich

2. When closing an informal letter, females sign off with:
   b. Liebe   b. Deine   c. Auf Wiedersehen

3. Which preposition from the right column precedes each expression?
   (One preposition is used twice.)

Example from the text	Preposition
1. a date: ____ 17. August	a. am
2. a day of the week: ____ Montag	b. in
3. a geographic destination/where to: ____ Weinheim	c. nach
4. time of the day: ____ 8.15 Uhr	d. um
5. a geographic location/where: ____ Frankfurt: ____ Deutschland	

Wissenswerte Vokabeln: die Monate

Talking about birthdays

der Monat, -e

der Januar	... im Januar	am ersten Januar
der Februar	... im Februar	am zweiten Februar
der März	... im März	am dritten März
der April	... im April	am vierten April
der Mai	... im Mai	am fünften Mai
der Juni	... im Juni	am sechsten Juni
der Juli	... im Juli	am siebten Juli
der August	... im August	am achten August
der September	... im September	am neunten September
der Oktober	... im Oktober	am zehnten Oktober
der November	... im November	am elften November
der Dezember	... im Dezember	am zwölften Dezember

am dreizehnten ...
am vierzehnten ...
am fünfzehnten ...
am sechzehnten ...
am siebzehnten ...
am achtzehnten ...
am neunzehnten ...
am zwanzigsten ...
am einundzwanzigsten ...
am zweiundzwanzigsten ...
am dreiundzwanzigsten ...
...
am dreißigsten ...
am einunddreißigsten ...

SEPTEMBER

21

DVARG/Shutterstock.com

Ich habe am einundzwanzigsten September Geburtstag.

When writing German, use a period following a number to indicate an ordinal number: **1.** (*1st*). Form the spoken forms of ordinal numbers for 2, 4–6, and 8–19 by adding the ending **-ten** to the number: **zweiten.** For numbers above 19, add **-sten: zwanzigsten.** Ordinal numbers that have special individual forms are: **ersten** (*first*), **dritten** (*third*), and **siebten** (*seventh*).

BEISPIEL   S1: *Wann haben Sie Geburtstag?*
S2: *Im Januar.*

S1: *Wann haben Sie im Januar Geburtstag?*
S2: *Ich habe am fünfundzwanzigsten Januar Geburtstag.*

Kati hat am einunddreißigsten Mai Geburtstag.

29 **Wann haben Sie Geburtstag?** With a partner, state the date on which the following birthdays happen.

BEISPIEL   S1: *Wann haben Sie Geburtstag?*
S2: *Ich habe am dritten September Geburtstag.*

	Ich	Mein Partner/Meine Partnerin
1. Wann haben Sie Geburtstag?	_____	_____
2. Wann hat Ihre Mutter Geburtstag?	_____	_____
3. Wann hat Ihr Vater Geburtstag?	_____	_____
4. Wann hat Ihre Schwester Geburtstag?	_____	_____
5. Wann hat Ihr Bruder Geburtstag?	_____	_____
6. Wann hat Ihr Freund/Ihre Freundin Geburtstag?	_____	_____

Wann haben Sie Geburtstag?
Ihr and **Ihre** are the formal equivalents of *your.* You will learn more about this form in **Kapitel 3.**

To answer questions 2–6, use the subjects **Mein Vater (Bruder, Freund)** and **Meine Mutter (Schwester, Freundin)** to create full sentences. **Meine Mutter hat am zweiten April Geburtstag.**

Strukturen

 Referring to people and things

Accusative pronouns

In **Kapitel 1** you learned that pronouns must reflect the gender and number of the nouns they represent.

> Hier ist **ein Tisch. Er** ist neu.
> **Meine Mutter** heißt Helga. **Sie** spricht am Telefon.
> Das ist **mein Deutschbuch**. **Es** hat sehr schöne Fotos.

In each of the examples above, the highlighted pronoun in the second sentence is the subject of that sentence. The subject is always in the nominative case. Now look at the pronouns below in the examples. These pronouns are direct objects and are therefore in the accusative case. They are called **Akkusativpronomen.** A direct object answers the question **wen?** (*whom?*) or **was?** (*what?*).

Katja, ich möchte **dich** sehen.	*Katja, I would like to see **you**.*
Darf ich **euch** besuchen?	*May I visit **you guys**?*
Wo ist mein Vater? Ich sehe **ihn** nicht.	*Where is my father? I don't see **him**.*
Das ist meine Schwester. Möchtest du **sie** kennenlernen?	*That is my sister. Would you like to meet **her**?*
Hier ist mein Deutschbuch. Möchtest du **es** lesen?	*Here is my German book. Would you like to read **it**?*

Here are the nominative and accusative forms of the personal pronouns.

	Singular						Plural			
	1st	**2nd**		**3rd**			**1st**	**2nd**		**3rd**
Nominative	ich	du	Sie	er	es	sie	wir	ihr	Sie	sie
Accusative	**mich**	**dich**	**Sie**	**ihn**	**es**	**sie**	**uns**	**euch**	**Sie**	**sie**
	me	*you*	*you*	*him*	*it*	*her*	*us*	*you*	*you*	*them*

 30 Kombinieren Sie Select a logical response from the column on the right for each statement or question in the left column.

1. Ich liebe° dich, Annette!
2. Wie finden Sie Professor Bauer?
3. Kommt ihr heute vorbei?
4. Anna hat heute Shorts an.
5. Wer hat mein Deutschbuch?
6. Wo ist Frau Günther?

a. Ich weiß nicht°. Ich sehe sie nicht.
b. Katja trägt° sie auch.
c. Ich habe dich auch sehr gern, Hannes.
d. Claudia hat es jetzt.
e. Ich finde ihn sehr interessant.
f. Ja, wir besuchen euch heute.

*love / **weiß nicht**: don't know*
is wearing

31 Kurze Dialoge Supply the appropriate accusative pronouns (**mich, dich, euch, Sie,** or **uns**) in the dialogues below.

1. PROFESSOR: Sprechen Sie Deutsch? Verstehen Sie ____?
   STUDENTEN: Ja, wir verstehen ____, Herr Professor.
2. ENKEL: Opa? Opa? Hier bin ich.
   OPA: Ich höre ____, Kleiner°.   *little one*
3. OPA KUNZ: Wann besucht ____ Anna?
   OMA KUNZ: Sie kommt im August.
4. ANNA: Oma und Opa, ich möchte ____ besuchen. Geht das?
   OPA UND OMA KUNZ: Natürlich, geht das. Komm nach Bad Krozingen.

32 Interview With a partner, create short dialogues about what you like to do. Use pronouns in your answers to the questions.

BEISPIEL S1: *Lernen Sie gern Deutsch?*
            S2: *Ja, ich lerne **es** gern.* (oder) *Nein, ich lerne **es** nicht gern.*

1. Verstehen Sie das Buch?   4. Möchten Sie Tübingen sehen?
2. Möchten Sie Anna kennenlernen?   5. Möchten Sie die Familie besuchen?
3. Möchten Sie Georg kennenlernen?   6. Hören Sie gern Techno-Musik?

Strukturen

VII Creating variety and shifting emphasis

See the **Arbeitsbuch** (Student Activities Manual) for additional practice with structures and vocabulary

Position of subject and verb

In declarative sentences, the subject is generally the first element of the sentence, followed by the conjugated verb and the predicate (e.g., objects, prepositional phrases).

subject
Ich heiße Anna Adler.   *My name is Anna Adler.*

It is also common to begin a German sentence with something other than the subject. The first position can be occupied by a single word, a phrase, or an entire clause. Whenever an element other than the subject begins a sentence, the subject follows the verb as the third element of the sentence.

The purpose of placing an element other than the subject in first position is to emphasize that element.

	1	2 (Verb)	3 (Subject)	
Time phrase:	Dieses Jahr	verbringe	**ich**	zwei Semester in Deutschland.
Direct object:	Ein Jahr in Deutschland	finde	**ich**	wunderbar.
Expression:	Gott sei Dank	habe	**ich**	Verwandte in Deutschland.

Regardless of the position of the subject, the conjugated verb is always the second element of a sentence.

Please note that words like **ja** or **nein** and the conjunctions **und, aber, oder** (*and, but, or*) do not affect the word order: Ja, ich heiße Anna und ich bin Amerikanerin.

→ **33** Annas Pläne Combine the following sentence parts so they accurately reflect Anna's plans.

1. In Fort Wayne ...
2. In Frankfurt ...
3. Eine E-Mail ...
4. Erst im Oktober ...
5. In Weinheim ...
6. Zwei Semester ...
7. Ein Jahr in Deutschland ...
8. Ein bisschen Angst ...
9. In einem Monat ...
10. Den Opa und die Oma ...

a. habe ich schon.
b. finde ich wunderbar.
c. besuche ich meine Verwandten.
d. verbringe ich an der Universität in Deutschland.
e. sehe ich später°, im November oder Dezember.
f. fliege ich nach Deutschland.
g. schreibe ich an Tante Uschi.
h. beginnt das Semester in Tübingen.
i. komme ich an.
j. bin ich zu Hause°.

later

at home

Wissenswerte Vokabeln: die Wochentage

Talking about weekly schedules

Kulturnotiz: Most German calendars start the week with Monday instead of Sunday.

The word **Wochentag** is a compound made from **die Woche** (*week*) and **der Tag** (*day*). The gender of a compound is the gender of the last word.

der Wochentag, -e

der Sonntag	... am Sonntag
der Montag	... am Montag
der Dienstag	... am Dienstag
der Mittwoch	... am Mittwoch
der Donnerstag	... am Donnerstag
der Freitag	... am Freitag
der Samstag (*in Süddeutschland*)	... am Samstag
der Sonnabend (*in Norddeutschland*)	... am Sonnabend
das Wochenende	... am Wochenende

BEISPIEL

Was ist heute?	*Heute ist Montag.*
Was haben wir heute?	*Heute haben wir Mittwoch.*
Wann spielt Anna Softball?	*Am Donnerstag.*
Wie viele Tage hat die Woche?	*Sieben.*

→ **34** Jetzt sind Sie dran (*Now it's your turn*) Restate these sentences by positioning the underlined words in the first position and making all the necessary changes to word order.

1. Wir verbringen <u>ein Semester</u> an der Universität in Göttingen.
2. Wir haben <u>so viele Fragen</u>!
3. Wir fliegen <u>in drei Tagen</u> nach Frankfurt.
4. Wir verbringen das Wochenende <u>in Frankfurt</u>.
5. Wir fahren <u>dann</u> nach Göttingen weiter°.
6. Wir kommen <u>am Montag</u> in Göttingen an.
7. Der Deutschkurs an der Universität beginnt <u>gleich am Dienstag</u>.
8. Wir spielen <u>erst am Samstag</u> ein bisschen Fußball.

fahren weiter nach: *travel on to*

← **35** Was macht Katja heute? (*What's Katja doing today?*) Answer these questions about Katja's activities this week. Start your answer with the day of the week.

Was macht Katja heute?
When one takes brief notes in German and does not make complete sentences, the infinitive appears at the end.

tanzen ... : go dancing

Montag	Freitag
eine Postkarte schreiben	tanzen gehen°
Dienstag	**Samstag**
Tennis spielen	einen Spanischkurs haben
Mittwoch	**Sonntag**
mit Jutta Kaffee trinken	zu Hause bleiben
Donnerstag	**Notizen**
einen Pullover kaufen°	

buy

BEISPIEL Was macht Katja am Mittwoch? *Am Mittwoch trinkt sie ...*

1. Was macht Katja am Mittwoch?
2. Wann bleibt Katja zu Hause?
3. Wann geht Katja tanzen
4. Spielt Katja Tennis oder Fußball? Wann?
5. Was macht Katja am Montag?
6. Wann geht Katja einkaufen°? Was kauft Katja?
7. Hat Katja Samstag frei?

shopping

Zeitausdrücke°

time expressions

Expressing repeated activities

montags
dienstags
mittwochs
donnerstags
freitags
samstags, sonnabends
sonntags

BEISPIEL Wann lernen Sie? *Ich lerne montags und mittwochs.*

To express that an activity repeatedly or habitually takes place on a certain day, German speakers use the adverbial forms of the days of the week. They are written lower case (not capitalized) with an **-s** at the end.

👥 36 Wann machen Sie das? Your partner will ask you about activities you do. Answer with **am** plus the particular day of the week if you will engage in the activity this week. Use the name of the day only plus an added **-s** if you do the activity regularly.

BEISPIEL   S1: *Wann haben Sie Deutsch?*
S2: *Ich habe montags, mittwochs und freitags Deutsch.*

homework

1. Deutsch haben
2. einkaufen gehen
3. im Restaurant essen
4. Musik hören
5. Hausaufgaben° machen
6. zu Hause bleiben
7. tanzen gehen
8. Bier trinken

Die Uhrzeit

Telling time

Es ist sieben Uhr morgens.

Es ist Viertel nach eins.

Es ist Viertel vor zwei.

Es ist halb sechs.

Es ist fünf Minuten vor sechs.

Es ist fünf Minuten nach sechs.

Es ist zehn Uhr abends.
Es ist zweiundzwanzig Uhr.

Es ist Mittag.

Es ist Mitternacht.

Illustrations © Cengage Learning 2014

BEISPIEL   Wie viel Uhr ist es? *Es ist ...*

Fractions of hours may only be used for the 12-hour clock. **Viertel** (*quarter hour*) may be used to denote a quarter of an hour before or after a full hour. **Halb** means *half* and when used for telling time indicates that one half of the next full hour has passed. Thus, **halb zwei** means *one thirty*. Amounts of time which cannot be measured in halves or quarters are counted in minutes after (**nach**), or short of (**vor**) the full hour.

Expressing time periods

Wann kommt Anna in Frankfurt an?	Sie kommt **um** Viertel nach acht an.
	Sie kommt **um** acht Uhr fünfzehn an.
Wann haben Sie Deutsch?	Ich habe **von** acht (Uhr) **bis** acht Uhr fünfzig Deutsch.
Wann haben Sie Mathematik?	Ich habe **von** neun **bis** elf (Uhr) Mathematik.

A specific point in time is denoted by the use of **um,** followed by the time. An approximate point in time is expressed with **gegen**, followed by the time.

Anna kommt **gegen** acht Uhr an.   *Anna arrives about eight o'clock.*

↩ **37** Georgs Stundenplan Georg is a student in the 11th grade at the **Johannes Kepler Gymnasium** in Weinheim. Complete the sentences below, referring to his weekly schedule for help.

	Mo.	Di.	Mi.	Do.	Fr.
7.45	Mathe	—	Deutsch	—	Deutsch
8.35	Religion	Englisch	Mathe	—	Deutsch
9.25	Pause	Pause	Pause	Pause	Pause
9.45	Deutsch	Mathe	Englisch	Deutsch	Physik
10.30	Englisch	Physik	Geschichte	Sport	Sport
11.15	Geschichte	Erdkunde	—	Englisch	Erdkunde
12.00	Geschichte	Religion	Physik	Englisch	Mathe
12.55			Physik	Erdkunde	

BEISPIEL   Montags um ____ hat Georg Mathe.
Montags um Viertel vor acht hat Georg Mathe.

1. Mittwochs beginnt er um _____.
2. _____ hat er Physik um 10.30 Uhr.
3. Er geht freitags um _____ nach Hause°.
4. Religion hat er _____ und dienstags.
5. Er hat Erdkunde° freitags von _____ bis _____.
6. Montags hat er um _____ Religion.
7. Freitags hat er Mathe um _____.
8. Er hat montags bis freitags um _____ Pause.
9. Mittwochs hat er um _____ frei.

geht nach Hause: goes home

geography

Especially for official purposes, the 24-hour clock is used. When using the 12-hour clock, **morgens** (*in the morning*), and **abends** (*in the evening*) may be added for further clarification.

The beginning and end of an action is denoted by the use of **von** (starting point) and **bis** (end point).

Komm, schnell! Es ist schon halb sechs!

⬅ **38** Wann sendet er? (*When does it broadcast?*) Ask your partner about the radio stations shown.

Deutsche Radioprogramme in den U. S. A	**ILLINOIS & INDIANA**	**OHIO**
	WNWI 1080 AM Das Deutschlandecho mit Armin Homann Sam. & Son. 9:00 - 11:00 Uhr	**WCWA 1230 AM** Toledo DEUTSCHE RADIOSTUNDE TOLEDO Son. 9:00 – 10:00 Uhr Peter Petersen, Sprecher
FLORIDA **WIPO-FM 89** Titusville Son. von 16:30 -18:00 Uhr Die deutsch-polnische Stunde Frank & Ruth Mlodzianowski **WTIS-1110 AM** Tampa *Deutsche Funksendung* mit Susanne Nielsen Son. von 13:00-14:00 Uhr	**WKTA 1330 AM** Chicago **Der Funk am Morgen Seit 40 Jahren mit Alfred Richter** Samstag: 10:00-12:30 Uhr **Österreicher Rundfunk mit Manfred Gursch** Samstag: 12:30 - 15:00 Uhr	German-American Radio Shows with Dr. Joe Wendel **WCPN 90.3 FM** Cleveland jeden Sam. 20:00 – 21:00 Uhr **WCSB 89.3 FM** Cleveland jeden Son. 10:00 – 12:00 Uhr www.wcsb.org
	MISSOURI **WGNU 920 AM** St. Louis Die deutsche Schlagerparade Sprecher: Alfred Goerlich Jeden Son. von 14:30 - 16 Uhr	**WQRP 89.5 FM** Dayton jeden Sam. 10:00 – 13:00 Uhr **Melodies of Germany & Austria with Maritta**

BEISPIEL S1: *Wie heißt der Radiosender in Tampa?*
S2: *WTIS*

S1: *Wann sendet er auf Deutsch?*
S2: *Sonntags um 13 Uhr. (Sonntags von 13 bis 14 Uhr.)*

1. Titusville, Florida
2. Chicago
3. St. Louis
4. Toledo

Strukturen

VIII Describing daily activities

Regular present tense verbs: verbs with separable prefixes and two-verb constructions

Many German verbs that describe daily activities are composed of either a verb stem with a prefix or a two-verb construction.

- Prefixes that may be separated from the verb stem are always stressed and look like independent words, such as prepositions, e.g., **kommen** (*to arrive*), **aufstehen** (*to get up, stand up*), **umdrehen** (*to turn around*), **anfangen** (*to start*), **hören** (*to stop*), or adverbs, e.g., **sehen** (*to watch TV*), **kommen** (*to come back*)
- Two-verb constructions include **lernen** (*to get to know*), **gehen** (*to go shopping*), **gehen** (*to go to bed*), **gehen** (*to go for a walk*), and **gehen** (*to go hiking*).

Separable prefixes and the first verb in a two-verb construction are placed at the end of the main clause in a sentence.

In the infinitive form, verbs with prefixes are written as one word; verbs in two-verb constructions are always written separately except for **kennenlernen**. Despite this difference, they share similarities in word placement.

an•kommen	Ich **komme** im August **an**.	*I arrive in August.*
auf•stehen	**Stehen** Sie bitte **auf**.	*Get up, please.*
einkaufen gehen	Wir **gehen** um 8.00 Uhr **einkaufen**.	*We're going shopping at 8:00.*

Gern and **nicht gern** occur either right after the conjugated verb or right before the separable prefix or the infinitive

Ich **stehe (nicht) gern** samstags und sonntags auf. ⎫ *I (don't) like to get up on*
Ich stehe samstags und sonntags **(nicht) gern auf**. ⎭ *Saturdays and Sundays.*

Notice that the infinitive of **wandern** is formed with the stem (**wander-**) and the ending **-n**.

Separable-prefix verbs that occur in vocabulary lists in this book are marked with a bullet between the prefix and verb stem (e.g., **auf•stehen, zurück•kommen**). In standard German, these infinitives are written as one word (e.g., **aufstehen, zurückkommen**).

Prefixes that do not resemble independent prepositions or adverbs are not separable. Examples are **ver-** (**verbringen:** *to spend*) or **be-** (**besuchen:** *to visit*).

Ich stehe nicht gern auf.

Wissenswerte Vokabeln: Onkel Hannes' Alltag°

Talking about daily activities

1.
Um halb sieben **wacht** Hannes Günther **auf.**

2.
Um Viertel nach sieben **steht** Hannes **auf.**

3.
Um zehn vor neun **kommt** er im Büro **an.**

4.
Gegen zehn Uhr **ruft** er Tante Uschi **an.**

5.
Um halb sechs **hört** der Arbeitstag **auf.**

6.
Er **kommt** gegen sechs Uhr **zurück.**

7.
Um Viertel nach sechs **geht** Hannes mit Uschi **spazieren.**

8.
Um Viertel vor elf **gehen** sie **schlafen.**

Illustrations © Cengage Learning 2014

BEISPIEL   Wann stehen Sie auf?   *Ich stehe um … auf.*

39 Das Wochenende Ask your classmates whether they do the following activities on the weekend. Then determine the rank of these activities based on how many people in the class engage in them. Use the numbers 1 (most popular) to 6 (least popular).

BEISPIEL   *Stehen Sie vor sieben Uhr auf?*

	Person	Rang°
1. vor sieben Uhr aufstehen	____	____
2. einkaufen gehen	____	____
3. die Eltern anrufen	____	____
4. mit Freunden spazieren gehen	____	____
5. vor zehn Uhr abends zurückkommen	____	____
6. nach elf Uhr abends schlafen gehen	____	____
7. von sieben bis ein Uhr fernsehen	____	____

Kommen Sie vor zehn
Gehen Sie nach elf Uhr abends schlafen?
Sehen Sie von sieben bis ein Uhr fern?

Strukturen

IX Expressing negation

Position of **nicht**

The following rules governing the placement of **nicht** may be helpful to you.

1. In very basic sentences, **nicht** follows the verb but precedes a separable prefix.
   Sie kommt **nicht** an.

2. In yes/no questions, **nicht** remains at the end of the sentence, even though the verb occurs at the beginning of the question.
   Kommen Sie **nicht?**

3. In statements and questions with a direct object, **nicht** usually occurs at the end.
   Sie verstehen den Professor **nicht.**   Verstehen Sie den Professor **nicht?**

4. **Nicht** precedes most adverbs, adjectives, and prepositional phrases.

Er spielt **nicht gern** Tennis.	*He doesn't like to play tennis.*
Sie kommt **nicht aus Deutschland.**	*She isn't from Germany.*
Der Professor ist **nicht freundlich.**	*The professor is not friendly.*

When words like **Zeit** and **Kinder** are quantified with **viel** (*much, a lot of*) and **viele** (*many, a lot of*), however, the negation includes **nicht.**

Ich habe **nicht viel** Zeit.	*I don't have much time.*
Ich habe **nicht viele** Kinder.	*I don't have many children.*

> **Viel** is used to quantify things that cannot be counted: **viel Angst** (*much anxiety*). **Viele** is used to quantify things that can be counted: **viele Studenten** (*many students*). The opposite expressions are **wenig** (*little*) and **wenige** (*few*): **wenig Angst** (*little anxiety*), **wenige Studenten** (*few students*).

 40 Verstehen Sie den Professor? Answer in the negative, using **nicht.**

BEISPIEL   S1: *Verstehen Sie den Professor?*
              S2: *Nein, ich verstehe den Professor/ihn nicht.*

1. Verstehen Sie den Professor?
2. Sagen Sie gern „Guten Tag"?
3. Spielt er gern Fußball?
4. Haben Sie so viel Zeit?
5. Kommt Katja aus den USA?
6. Kommen Sie aus Deutschland?
7. Kommt Anna zurück?
8. Ist Anna sportlich?

> Remember to use a form of **kein** when you answer a question negatively about the availability or existence of someone or something: Hast du Zeit? – Nein, ich habe **keine** Zeit; Haben Sie Kinder? – Nein, ich habe **keine** Kinder.

41 *Nicht oder kein?* Decide whether to use **nicht** or a form of **kein** in your answers to these questions.

BEISPIEL   S1: *Haben Sie einen Bruder in Sankt Petersburg?*
              S2: *Nein, ich habe keinen Bruder in Sankt Petersburg.*

1. Haben Sie einen Bruder in Sankt Petersburg?
2. Sprechen Sie perfekt Deutsch?
3. Haben Sie einen Cousin in Weinheim?
4. Haben Sie Zeit?
5. Fliegen Sie heute nach Berlin?
6. Verstehen Sie Finnisch°?
7. Beginnen Sie die Hausaufgaben um sechs Uhr?
8. Stehen Sie sonntags um halb sieben auf?

das Finnisch: *the Finnish language*

film director

Eine E-Mail schreiben

Zielaktivitäten

42 Eine E-Mail an… Write an e-mail announcing your arrival in Germany to a famous German, expressing your desire to visit them in their hometown. Write to one of the people in the list below. You may wish to look up some information about this person on the Internet. You may also choose a different person.

Angela Merkel (Bundeskanzlerin) / Berlin
Heidi Klum (Fotomodell) / Bergisch Gladbach
Werner Herzog (Filmregisseur°) / München
Sido (Rapper) / Berlin
Mesut Özil (Fußballer) / Gelsenkirchen
Daniel Brühl (Filmstar) / Berlin und Barcelona
Moritz Bleibtreu (Filmstar) / Hamburg
Günter Grass (Schriftsteller) / Lübeck
Diane Kruger, (Filmstar) / Hildesheim
Clueso (Sänger) / Erfurt

Daniel Brühl

Heidi Klum

Build your message around the following components and phrases:

Component	Example phrases
greeting	Lieber _____! (for a man)/ Liebe _____! (for a woman)
who you are	Ich bin Student / Studentin an der Universität von _____.
your name	Ich heiße _____.
your family	Meine Eltern heißen _____. Mein Bruder heißt _____.
your hometown	Ich komme aus _____.
your German skills	Ich spreche ein bisschen/gutes/kein Deutsch.
a few adjectives that describe you	Ich bin _____.
the date, time, and place of of your arrival	Ich komme am _____ um _____ Uhr in _____ an.
where you wish to go and what you want to do there	Ich möchte nach _____ kommen und _____.
how familiar you are with Germany	Es ist meine erste/zweite/dritte/vierte Reise nach Deutschland.
a few questions you would like to ask about Germany	Ich habe so viele Fragen: ??
your daily habits, to make sure you are compatible	Ich stehe _____ auf.
your request	Ich habe eine Bitte: Darf ich _____?
closing	Ihr Fan Thomas / Monika

👥 43 Eine Konversation mit... Your famous person received your e-mail and is calling you to discuss your visit. He or she is asking you some questions about you, to see whether a visit will work for both of you. Take turns with another student in playing the roles of visitor and famous person. Finally, the famous person arrives at a decision and says:

Willkommen in _____ ! OR Tut mir leid, ich habe keine Zeit!

Here are a few possible questions to get you started:

Spielen Sie gern Fußball?
Hören Sie gern Musik?
Möchten Sie nach Berlin kommen?
Lernen Sie gern Deutsch?

44 Schreibecke: **Eine andere E-Mail schreiben** (*Writing another e-mail*). You are planning to attend a summer course in Switzerland in July. Write an e-mail to your pen pal Annette in Bern. Use Anna's e-mail earlier in the chapter for ideas.

45 Freie Kommunikation: **Das bin ich** (*That's me*). You are giving a speech to an Austrian class that wants to know what American students are like. Describe yourself in detail.

Brennpunkt Kultur

Web Search
Web Link

Types of universities in Germany

Until fairly recently, most German universities aspired to the ideal established by Wilhelm von Humboldt at Berlin University in 1810. Set up as an elite institution, meant for a small number of students who pursued research and study for the sake of learning alone, the university only granted advanced degrees to a limited number of students in a limited number of fields.

With increasing numbers of students since the 1960s and with changes in technology and science, this system has proved too inflexible. In response, many new types of universities were founded:

- **die technische Hochschule,** institutes of technology, for engineering and technology-driven fields with an emphasis on research;
- **die Fachhochschule,** special colleges with an emphasis on applied professions in the fields of business administration, design, engineering, health and human services, information sciences, and social work;
- creative and performing arts academies such as **die Kunsthochschule,** art academies, and **die Musikhochschule,** music conservatories, among others.

More recent reforms have shortened the time needed to earn a degree. Since 2010 all universities have been offering shorter degree programs that lead to Bachelor's or Master's degrees that are recognized across Europe and the U.S. Due to political and economic pressures and competition from universities abroad, a limited number of private universities have been founded and nine elite universities have been identified and funded to attract the best and brightest German and international students.

Philip Lange/Shutterstock.com

Humboldt-Universität zu Berlin, im Jahr 1810 gegründet

Kulturkreuzung

Think about the different courses of study available at your institution. Which ones are more theoretical in nature? Which ones are more applied or practical? Which courses of study aren't offered at your college? Why? What is different about the German system?

Die Familie und die Verwandten

der Bruder, ¨ *brother*
der Cousin, -s *(male) cousin*
die Cousine, -n *(female) cousin*
die Eltern *(pl.) parents*
der Enkel, - *grandson*
die Enkelin, -nen *granddaughter*
das Enkelkind, -er *grandchild*
die Familie, -n *family*
die Frau, -en *wife*
die Geschwister *(pl.) siblings; brothers and sisters*
die Großeltern *(pl.) grandparents*
die Großmutter, ¨ *grandmother*
der Großvater, ¨ *grandfather*
der Hund, -e *dog*
der Junge [-en], -en *boy*
die Katze, -n *cat*
das Kind, -er *child*
die Leute *(pl.), people*
das Mädchen, - *girl*
der Mann, ¨er *husband*
die Mutter, ¨ *mother*
der Neffe, [-n], -n *nephew*
die Nichte, -n *niece*
die Oma, -s *grandma*
der Onkel, - *uncle*
der Opa, -s *grandpa*
die Schwester, -n *sister*
der Sohn, ¨e *son*
die Tante, -n *aunt*
die Tochter, ¨ *daughter*
der Vater, ¨ *father*
die Verwandten *(pl.) family, relatives*

Die Universität und die Studienfächer

das Hauptfach, ¨er *major (area of study)*
   Was haben Sie als Hauptfach? *What's your major?*

der Kurs, -e *course*
das Nebenfach, ¨er *minor (area of study)*
das Semester, - *semester*
das Studienfach, ¨er *academic subject*
   Welche Fächer haben Sie? *What subjects are you taking?*
das Arabisch *Arabic*
die Betriebswirtschaft *business*
die Biologie *biology*
die Chemie *chemistry*
das Chinesisch *Chinese*
das Deutsch *German*
das Englisch *English*
das Französisch *French*
die Geschichte *history*
die Informatik *computer science*
das Ingenieurwesen *engineering*
Internationale Beziehungen *(pl.) international relations*
die Kunst *art*
die Mathematik (Mathe) *mathematics (math)*
die Medizin *medicine*
die Musik *music*
die Pädagogik *education (teaching)*
die Philosophie *philosophy*
die Physik *physics*
die Politikwissenschaft *political science*
die Psychologie *psychology*
das Russisch *Russian*
die Soziologie *sociology*
das Spanisch *Spanish*
die Volkswirtschaft *economics*

Die Monate

der Januar, der Februar, der März, der April, der Mai, der Juni, der Juli, der August, der September, der Oktober, der November, der Dezember

das Jahr, -e *year*
der Monat, -e *month*
Wann haben Sie Geburtstag? *When is your birthday?*
am ersten Januar *on the first of January*
im Januar *in January*

Die Wochentage

der Montag, der Dienstag, der Mittwoch, der Donnerstag, der Freitag, der Samstag *(Austria, Switzerland, southern Germany),* **der Sonnabend** *(northern Germany),* **der Sonntag**
der Arbeitstag, -e *work day*
der Tag, -e *day*
die Woche, -n *week*
das Wochenende, -n *weekend*
der Wochentag, -e *day of the week; weekday*
am Sonntag *on (this) Sunday*
am Wochenende *on the weekend*
heute *today*
   Was haben wir heute? *What day is it today?*
   Was ist heute? *What day is it today?*
sonntags *on Sundays (in general)*
die Uhr *clock; (clock) time*
die Zeit, -en *time*
Wie viel Uhr ist es? *What time is it?*
Es ist ... (Uhr). *It's . . . (o'clock).*
(fünf) Minuten nach (eins) *(five) minutes after (one)*
(fünf) Minuten vor (zwei) *(five) minutes to (two)*
halb (zwei) *half past (one) (i.e., halfway to two)*
der Mittag *noon*
die Mitternacht *midnight*
Viertel nach (eins) *quarter past (one)*
Viertel vor (zwei) *quarter to (two)*

abends *in the evening*
morgens *in the morning*
um (sechs) Uhr *at (six) o'clock*
gegen (sieben) Uhr *around (seven) o'clock*
von (neun Uhr) bis (zehn Uhr) *from (nine o'clock) until/to (ten o'clock)*

Aktivitäten des Alltags
an•fangen *to start*
an•kommen *to arrive*
an•rufen *to call up (on the phone)*
auf•hören *to stop*
auf•stehen *to get up, get out of bed; to stand up*
auf•wachen *to wake up*
beginnen *to begin*
besuchen *to visit*
bleiben *to stay, remain*
ein•kaufen *to shop*
fern•sehen *to watch TV*
finden *to find; to think that something is . . .*
fliegen *to fly*
fragen *to ask*
gehen *to go*
  nach Hause gehen *to go home*
  schlafen gehen *to go to bed*
  spazieren gehen *to go for a walk*
haben *to have*
  Angst haben *to be afraid, anxious*
  Durst haben *to be thirsty*
  frei haben *to have time off*
  gern haben *to like*
  Hunger haben *to be hungry*
  nicht gern haben *not to like*
hoffen *to hope*
hören *to hear; to listen to*
kaufen *to buy*
kennen•lernen *to get to know*
kommen *to come*
lernen *to learn; to study (for an exam, a class)*
machen *to do; to make*
  Hausaufgaben machen *to do homework*
meinen *to think; to mean*
schlafen *to sleep*

schreiben *to write*
sehen *to see*
spielen *to play*
studieren *to study*
tanzen *to dance*
trinken *to drink*
um•drehen *to turn around*
verbessern *to improve*
verbringen *to spend time*
verstehen *to understand*
wandern *to hike*
wohnen *to live*
zurück•kommen *to come back, return*

Ordnungszahlen
am ersten, zweiten, dritten, vierten, fünften, sechsten, siebten, achten, neunten, zehnten, elften, zwölften, dreizehnten, ..., zwanzigsten, einundzwanzigsten, ...

Kommunikation
die Bitte, -n *request*
die E-Mail *e-mail*
die Frage, -n *question*
die Leute *(pl.) people*
die Mail/E-Mail, das Mail *e-mail (the concept)*
die Postkarte, -n *postcard*
die Reise, -n *journey, trip*

Personalpronomen im Akkusativ
dich *you (sg. informal)*
es *it*
euch *you (pl. informal)*
ihn *him*
mich *me*
sie *her; them*
Sie *you (sg. & pl. formal)*
uns *us*

Adjektive
klug *smart*
ledig *single*
sportlich *athletic*
teuer *expensive*
toll *great*
verheiratet *married*
wunderbar *wonderful*

Ausdrücke
auf Deutsch *in German*
darf ich? *may I?*
ein bisschen *a little*
ich bin gespannt auf *I'm looking forward to*
ich möchte *I'd like*
nach Hause *(to) home*
nicht sehr *not very, not much*
nicht so *not so*
überhaupt kein *none at all*
zu Hause *at home*
zum Beispiel (z. B.) *for example*

Andere Wörter
aber *but*
allein *alone*
auch *also, too*
bald *soon*
dein Thomas / deine Anna *your Thomas/Anna (at the end of a letter)*
doch *yes (for emphasis)*
endlich *finally*
etwas *somewhat, a little*
für *for*
ganz allein *all alone*
gern *(after a verb) to like to do*
ich singe gern *I like to sing*
gleich *right away*
mit *with*
nur *only*
oder *or*
sehr *very*
viel *much, a lot*
viele *many, a lot*
von *of; from*
wen? *whom?*
wenig *little*
wenige *few*

Meine eigenen Wörter
_____
_____
_____
_____
_____

Studenten, Einwohner und Touristen finden Heidelbergs Altstadt romantisch und schön.

Was gibt es in Heidelberg und Mannheim zu tun?

In this chapter you will learn how to talk about the activities of others, what you like to do, and what you can do. You will begin using the informal form of *you* (du) with other students. You will also read about the German cities Heidelberg and Mannheim.

Kommunikative Funktionen
> Describing more actions and activities
> Expressing relationships or ownership
> Expressing additional and contrastive information and justifications
> Stating personal preferences
> Expressing what you would like to do
> Expressing possibilities
> Referring to people and things
> Talking about what you know as a fact and about people, places, and things
> Talking about more than one item

Strukturen
> Present tense of stem-vowel changing verbs
> Nominative and accusative of possessive adjectives
> Coordinating conjunctions
> The adverb **lieber**
> The modal verbs **möchte** and **können**
> The verbs **kennen** and **wissen**
> Noun plurals

Vokabeln
> Lebensmittel
> Freizeitaktivitäten
> Die Landeskunde Deutschlands

Kulturelles
> Mealtimes in German-speaking countries
> The metric system
> Heidelberg and Mannheim

Was halten wir von Anna? Was hält sie von uns?

The Günthers are talking about their American relative, Anna Adler, and make certain assumptions about her behavior and Americans in general, with whom they have had little direct contact. Anna, too, wonders about her German relatives. All this talk reveals some glaring stereotypes about Americans and Germans.

Vorschau

1 Thematische Fragen Discuss the following questions with your instructor or in pairs.

1. What are some of your assumptions about Germans and German culture?
2. Think about some German characters you have seen on TV or in a movie, e.g., on comedy shows, in war movies, in political thrillers. Brainstorm with classmates the titles of shows and the names of characters. How were the Germans portrayed? What stereotypes do these characterizations perpetuate?

2 Wortdetektiv Which words convey approximately the same meaning? Match the German word with its logical English equivalent. To guess the meaning of the German words, look for similarities with English (cognates), determine which English and German words belong to the same categories (nouns, verbs, adjectives), and use a process of elimination.

Deutsch	Englisch
1. das Gepäck	a. to eat
2. mit•bringen	b. perhaps
3. essen	c. to bring along
4. lächeln	d. luggage
5. vielleicht	e. something
6. etwas	f. to smile
7. das Schweinefleisch	g. always
8. tragen	h. train station
9. der Bahnhof	i. to wear
10. immer	j. pork
11. wahrscheinlich	k. there is
12. es gibt	l. probably

3 Verwandte Wörter entdecken°

1. A cognate is a word that has a similar form in two different languages, like the German **Haus** and the English *house*. Scan the statements in the **Anlauftext** (pages 82–83). Find six cognates in German.
2. Look at the statements and the drawings in the text and decide which daily habits or customs mentioned there lead to the creation of stereotypes about others.
3. Can you find another direct translation from English like **Kaugummi?**

discover

Sprache im Alltag: Assumptions with **bestimmt, sicher, wahrscheinlich,** and **wohl**

A person who makes an assumption generally expects the listener to confirm a suspicion or thought. In German, the words **bestimmt** (*undoubtedly, for sure*), **sicher** (*certainly, surely*), **wahrscheinlich** (*most likely, probably*), and **wohl** (*in all likelihood, no doubt, probably*) indicate that a statement is an assumption.

Anna spricht **sicher** nur Englisch.	*Anna certainly speaks only English.*
Sie trägt **bestimmt** immer Shorts und Turnschuhe.	*She always wears shorts and sneakers for sure.*
Es gibt **wahrscheinlich** keine gute Popmusik in Deutschland.	*There's probably no good pop music in Germany.*
Anna sieht **wohl** immer nur fern.	*Anna probably just watches TV all the time.*

---

 4 Bin ich typisch? Ask your classmates whether they are Americans. Every time a person indicates he/she is an American, confront him/her with one of the stereotypes listed below. Present these stereotypes in the form of assumptions, using **sicher, bestimmt,** and **wohl.** Your classmate says whether this stereotype applies to him/her.

BEISPIEL S1: *Sie kauen° wohl gern Kaugummi.*
S2: *Nein, ich kaue nicht gern Kaugummi. (oder)*
Ja, ich kaue gern Kaugummi.

chew

1. gern Kaugummi kauen
2. gern Rockmusik hören
3. nur Hamburger essen
4. immer Cola trinken
5. nur Englisch sprechen
6. gern Shorts und Turnschuhe tragen

Now listen to the recording. Try to identify the cultural stereotypes presented in the text.

Sprache im Alltag: **Nur „Bahnhof" verstehen**

The expression **nur Bahnhof verstehen** is a German idiom that literally means *to understand only train station*. It means *not to have a clue* or *to be unable to comprehend anything*.

Rückblick

Stimmt das? Do this exercise after reading the text once to determine how much you understood and how much you missed. Then reread the text until you feel confident that you understand it.

5 **Stimmt das?** How much of the text can you remember without looking back at it? Look over the statements and mark the true statements as **Ja, das stimmt**. Mark the false statements as **Nein, das stimmt nicht**. Then, listen as your instructor reads the following statements and models their pronunciation.

	Ja, das stimmt.	Nein, das stimmt nicht.
1. Tante Uschi meint, Anna isst nur Bratwurst.	○	○
2. Tante Uschi meint, Anna trinkt nur Bier.	○	○
3. Tante Uschi meint, Anna spricht viel Deutsch.	○	○
4. Tante Uschi meint, Anna lächelt immer, wie alle Amerikaner.	○	○
5. Katja meint, Anna versteht gut Deutsch.	○	○
6. Katja meint, Anna versteht nichts von Politik oder Fußball.	○	○
7. Onkel Hannes meint, Anna sieht immer fern.	○	○
8. Georg meint, Anna trägt immer Shorts und Turnschuhe.	○	○
9. Anna meint, die Günthers trinken nur Mineralwasser und essen vegetarisch.	○	○
10. Anna meint, die Günthers wandern jedes Wochenende.	○	○
11. Anna meint, es gibt gute Popmusik in Deutschland.	○	○

6 **Ergänzen Sie** Complete these sentences with words from the **Anlauftext**.

Tante Uschi

1. Anna _____ vielleicht nur Hamburger mit Ketchup und _____ nur Cola.
2. Anna _____ sicher nur Englisch.

Katja

3. Anna ist so freundlich und optimistisch. Sie _____ immer, wie alle Amerikaner.
4. Anna _____ nicht viel Deutsch, nur „Bahnhof".

Onkel Hannes

5. Anna _____ wohl immer nur _____.
6. Anna hat immer _____ im Mund.

Georg

7. Anna bringt viel _____ mit.
8. Anna _____ bestimmt immer Shorts und Turnschuhe.
9. Anna _____ wohl lange in Weinheim bei den Günthers.

Anna

10. Es _____ wahrscheinlich keine gute Popmusik in Deutschland.
11. Die Günthers _____ immer nur Schweinefleisch und trinken immer nur _____.

⊕ **7** Kurz gefragt Answer these questions. Try to create complete sentences.

Was, meinen die Günthers, ...

1. essen und trinken alle Amerikaner?
2. spricht Anna?
3. machen alle Amerikaner immer?
4. versteht Anna sicher nur?
5. bringt Anna mit?
6. hat Anna immer im Mund?
7. trägt Anna bestimmt?

Was, meint Anna, ...

8. essen und trinken die Günthers?
9. machen die Günthers jedes Wochenende?
10. gibt es wahrscheinlich nicht in Deutschland?

⊕ **8** Textdetektiv: **Anlauftext.** Use the *Anlauftext* to recognize important aspects of German structure and usage.

Kulturnotiz. Since most stores are closed on Sundays, people tend to take walks and spend time with friends and family.

1. The title of the *Anlauftext* is *Was halten wir von Anna? Was hält sie von uns?* Match the following people with the correct personal pronoun to identify who is being referred to in the title.

Personal pronoun	People referred to
a. wir	die Familie Günther
b. uns	Anna
c. sie	

2. The two verbs mentioned in the title, **halten** versus **hält**, have different endings. What other difference do you notice?
   a. They both have the same vowel.
   b. The *wir*-form of the verb has an *Umlaut* over the *a*, while the *sie*-form does not.
   c. The *wir*-form of the verb has no *Umlaut* over the *a*, while the *sie*-form does.

3. Look at the end-of-chapter *Wortschatz*. Which one of these verbs from the *Anlauftext* has no *Umlaut* in the infinitive but does have an *Umlaut* when it refers to an individual person (such as *sie [she]*)?
   a. sie trägt   b. sie lächelt   c. sie lacht

4. Match each *sie (they)* form with the corresponding *sie (she)* form and infinitive form.

sie (they)	sie (she)	Infinitive
a. gehen	trägt	trinken
b. trinken	spricht	essen
c. tragen	isst	tragen
d. sehen	sieht	gehen
e. lächeln	geht	lächeln
f. sprechen	trinkt	sehen
g. essen	lächelt	sprechen

5. Mark the following statements as true (T) or false (F) based on what you noticed in question 4. If an answer is false, what is correct?
   a. _____ The *sie (they)* form of a verb is identical to the infinitive of the verb.
   b. _____ The verbs *tragen, sprechen, essen*, and *sehen* have a different vowel in the *sie (they)* (or infinitive) form than in the *sie (she)* form.
   c. _____ The difference between the vowels is always the *Umlaut ä*.

Was isst du gern?

© Cengage Learning 2014

Strukturen

D Describing activities

Present tense of stem-vowel changing verbs

Many German verbs change their stem vowel (the main vowel of the verb) in the present tense **du-** and **er/sie/es**-forms. These verbs belong to a group of verbs called irregular verbs (**unregelmäßige Verben**) or strong verbs (**starke Verben**). Compare how the stem vowels change in the questions raised by the Günthers.

Anna fragt ...
Essen sie immer Schweinefleisch?
Do they always eat pork?

Sehen sie überhaupt fern?
Do they watch TV at all?

Familie Günther fragt ...
Isst sie vielleicht nur Hamburger?
Does she perhaps eat only hamburgers?

Sieht Anna wohl immer nur fern?
Does Anna just watch TV all the time?

With a few exceptions that will be noted later, the stem-changing verbs use the same present tense endings as the other regular verbs (**schwache Verben**) that have been introduced so far. Here are the present tense forms of the stem-changing verb **sehen** (*to see*). Note the **ie** in the **du** and **er/sie/es** forms: **du siehst, er/sie/es sieht.** Remember that the other forms of verbs like **sehen** do *not* change the stem vowel: **ich sehe, Sie sehen, wir sehen, ihr seht, sie sehen.**

Person	**sehen:** *to see*	
	Singular	**Plural**
1st	ich **sehe** (seh + **e**)	wir **sehen** (seh + **en**)
2nd, informal	du **siehst** (sieh + **st**)	ihr **seht** (seh + **t**)
2nd, formal	Sie **sehen** (seh + **en**)	Sie **sehen** (seh + **en**)
3rd	er/sie/es **sieht** (sieh + **t**)	sie **sehen** (seh + **en**)

Shown below are the four common vowel changes in the stems of such verbs. These verbs must be memorized.

> Other verbs in category 1 are **fallen** (*to fall*), **fangen** (*to catch*), **ein•laden** (*to invite*), **lassen** (*to let*), **schlafen** (*to sleep*), and **waschen** (*to wash*).

> Other verbs in category 4 are **fressen** (*to eat like an animal*) and **helfen** (*to help*).

1. **a > ä** **an•fangen** *to start* ich fange an, du fängst an, er/sie/es fängt an
   fahren *to drive* ich fahre, du fährst, er/sie/es fährt
   halten von *to think about* ich halte, du hältst, er/sie/es hält
   tragen *to wear; to carry* ich trage, du trägst, er/sie/es trägt

2. **au > äu** **laufen** *to run; to walk* ich laufe, du läufst, er/sie/es läuft

3. **e > ie** **sehen** *to see* ich sehe, du siehst, er/sie/es sieht
   lesen *to read* ich lese, du liest, er/sie/es liest

4. **e > i** **essen** *to eat* ich esse, du isst, er/sie/es isst
   geben *to give* ich gebe, du gibst, er/sie/es gibt
   nehmen *to take* ich nehme, du nimmst, er/sie/es nimmt
   sprechen *to speak* ich spreche, du sprichst, er/sie/es spricht
   vergessen *to forget* ich vergesse, du vergisst, er/sie/es vergisst
   werden *to become* ich werde, du wirst, er/sie/es wird

← **9** **Die Günthers** Choose a partner and one of the following two **Tabellen** about the Günthers. Your partner should refer to the other **Tabelle**. Note that **Tabelle B** is printed upside down. Ask each other what the Günthers like to do.

BEISPIEL S1: *Was macht Hannes gern in der Freizeit?*
S2: *Er läuft gern Ski.*
S1: *Was macht er gern im Sommer?*
S2: *Er fährt gern Wasserski°.*

Ski is always pronounced **Schi**.

to go waterskiing

the newspaper

fährt ... : likes to go bicycling

Tabelle A (S1):

	In der Freizeit	essen/trinken	im Sommer
Hannes	?	trinkt gern Weißwein	?
Anna	liest gern Zeitung°	?	trägt gern Shorts
Georg	fährt gern Rad°	?	fährt nach Italien
Katja	?	isst gern vegetarisch	?
Uschi	gibt Hannes einen Kuss	trinkt gern Eiskaffee	?
Bob	läuft 5 Meilen	?	?
Hannelore	?	?	wird schön braun

Tabelle B (S2): *(printed upside down)*

	In der Freizeit	essen/trinken	im Sommer
Hannelore	hört gern Musik	isst gern Wiener Schnitzel	?
Bob	?	isst Steak und Salat	sieht nicht viel fern
Uschi	?	?	fängt einen Spanischkurs an
Katja	spricht gern Französisch	?	fährt nach England
Georg	?	trinkt gern Cola	?
Anna	?	isst gern Hamburger	?
Hannes	läuft gern Ski	?	fährt gern Wasserski

10 Autogrammspiel Walk around and find a classmate for each activity listed below. When you find someone who does the activity, have that person sign his/her name.

BEISPIEL S1: *Trägst du gern Shorts?*
S2: *Nein, ich trage nicht gern Shorts.* (oder)
Ja, ich trage gern Shorts.
S1: *Unterschreib hier bitte.*

1. Trägst du gern Turnschuhe?
2. Liest du gern Zeitung?
3. Siehst du gern fern?
4. Sprichst du gern Deutsch?
5. Isst du gern Fleisch?
6. Trinkst du gern Bier?
7. Vergisst du oft die Hausaufgaben?
8. Wirst du dieses Jahr 21 Jahre alt?

11 Das Interview You are writing an article for the student newspaper. Interview a partner who plays an Austrian exchange student. Ask the following questions about his/her habits. Circle the response that matches your partner's answer, or have him/her supply one.

BEISPIEL S1: *Was isst du gern?*
S2: *Ich esse gern Hamburger.*

Fragen	*Antworten*			
1. Was isst du gern?	Hamburger	Bratwurst	Wiener Schnitzel	?
2. Was sprichst du gern?	Deutsch	Englisch	Spanisch	?
3. Was liest du gern?	Deutsch	Englisch	Französisch	?
4. Was trägst du gern?	Shorts	Turnschuhe	Lederhosen°	?
5. Was trinkst du gern?	Kaffee	Milch	Cola	?
6. Siehst du oft fern?	Ja, oft.	Nein, nicht oft.	Nein, überhaupt nicht.	?
7. Was machst du gern?	Auto fahren	Ski laufen	einkaufen gehen	?

leather pants

The verb **wissen**

Another verb that changes its stem vowel is **wissen** (*to know as a fact*).

wissen: *to know as a fact*		
Person	**Singular**	**Plural**
1st	ich **weiß**	wir **wissen**
2nd, informal	du **weißt**	ihr **wisst**
2nd, formal	Sie **wissen**	Sie **wissen**
3rd	er/sie/es **weiß**	sie **wissen**

The verb **wissen** changes its stem vowel to **ei** in the **ich, du,** and **er/sie/es** forms. The **ss** changes to **ß** in those forms as well. Furthermore, the **ich** and **er/sie/es** forms have no ending.

Ich **weiß** es.   *I know it.*

Wissen often refers to information that is expressed in a subordinate clause. The conjugated verb in the subordinate clause always occurs at the end.

Weißt du, dass Anna in Fort Wayne wohnt?	*Do you know that Anna lives in Fort Wayne?*
Ja, ich weiß, dass sie in Fort Wayne wohnt.	*Yes, I know that she lives in Fort Wayne.*

You will learn more about subordinate-clause word order in **Kapitel 5**.

12 **Weißt du das?** (*Do you know that?*) Answer the following questions with **Ja, das weiß ich**. or **Nein, das weiß ich nicht**. If you *do* know something, provide the requested information.

BEISPIEL   Weißt du, wie alt Anna ist?
Ja, das weiß ich. Sie/Anna ist zwanzig

1. Weißt du, wie alt Anna ist?
2. Weißt du, wann Anna nach Deutschland fliegt?
3. Weißt du, wo in Deutschland Annas Flugzeug landet?
4. Weißt du, wie Annas Verwandte in Deutschland heißen?
5. Weißt du, wo Annas Großeltern wohnen?
6. Weißt du, wer Georg ist?
7. Weißt du, wo Anna zwei Semester verbringt?
8. Weißt du, wann Annas Deutschkurs anfängt?

13 **(Stereo)typisch** The list below reflects stereotypical images of Americans and Germans. Determine to whom these stereotypes refer by creating ten complete sentences.

BEISPIEL   *Eine typische Amerikanerin lächelt immer.*

Ein typischer Amerikaner/Deutscher	spricht	eine Zigarette im Mund.	
	trinkt	jedes° Wochenende.	*every*
Eine typische Amerikanerin/Deutsche	isst	nur Englisch.	
	versteht	immer fern.	
	hat	immer Kaugummi im Mund.	
	trägt	etwas von Softball.	
	wandert	Cola mit viel Eis°.	*ice*
	sieht	Schokoladeneis°.	*chocolate ice cream*
	lächelt	etwas von Fußball.	
		Schweinefleisch.	
		Deutsch, Englisch und eine zweite Fremdsprache°.	*foreign language*
		nur Bier.	
		Turnschuhe und Shorts.	
		immer.	
		nichts von Politik.	
		Lederhosen / Dirndl.	
		einen Mercedes in der Garage.	

dicogm/Shutterstock.com

Strukturen

 Expressing relationships or ownership

Nominative of possessive adjectives

German speakers use possessive adjectives (**Possessivpronomen**) to express ownership or a relationship.

> Das ist **mein** Freund. Er heißt Jürgen.   *That's my friend. His name is Jürgen.*
> **Meine** Freundin läuft gern Ski.   *My girlfriend likes to ski.*

The ending of a possessive adjective denotes the case (e.g., nominative, accusative), gender (masculine, neuter, feminine), and number (singular or plural) of the noun that follows it. Here are the nominative forms for the possessive adjectives.

		Masculine ein/kein	Neuter ein/kein	Feminine eine/keine	Plural —/keine
		Possessive Adjectives (nominative forms)			
Singular	my	**mein** Vater	**mein** Kind	**meine** Mutter	**meine** Kinder
	your (informal)	**dein** Vater	**dein** Kind	**deine** Mutter	**deine** Kinder
	your (formal)	**Ihr** Vater	**Ihr** Kind	**Ihre** Mutter	**Ihre** Kinder
	his	**sein** Vater	**sein** Kind	**seine** Mutter	**seine** Kinder
	its	**sein** Vater	**sein** Kind	**seine** Mutter	**seine** Kinder
	her	**ihr** Vater	**ihr** Kind	**ihre** Mutter	**ihre** Kinder
Plural	our	**unser** Vater	**unser** Kind	**uns(e)re** Mutter	**uns(e)re** Kinder
	your (informal)	**euer** Vater	**euer** Kind	**eure** Mutter	**eure** Kinder
	your (formal)	**Ihr** Vater	**Ihr** Kind	**Ihre** Mutter	**Ihre** Kinder
	their	**ihr** Vater	**ihr** Kind	**ihre** Mutter	**ihre** Kinder

Possessive adjectives can be referred to as **ein-words** because they take the same endings for case, gender, and number as the forms of the indefinite article **ein**. This is true for all possessive adjectives (including **Ihr, ihr, unser, euer**), not just for those that are spelled with **-ein**. **Unser** frequently and **euer** always lose the internal **-e-** when an ending is added.

The **-er** on **unser** and **euer** is not an ending but part of the stem.

unser:	**unsere** Schwester
	unsre Schwester
euer:	**eure** Schwester

Note that possessive adjectives for masculine and neuter nouns are identical, as are the possessive adjectives for feminine nouns and plural nouns.

14 Meine Freunde Create interesting descriptions of your friends and relatives by combining the subjects in the left column with an appropriate verb from the middle and an item from the right column. Make up a few of your own, too.

der Freund = (male) friend; boyfriend. **die Freundin** = (female) friend; girlfriend.

Mein Freund	isst	kein Schweinefleisch.
Meine Freundin	trägt	immer fern.
Mein Vater	läuft	Spanisch, Deutsch und Englisch.
Meine Mutter	fährt	nicht.
Mein Bruder	sieht	sehr schnell°.
Meine Schwester	liest	gern Pizza.
Mein Deutschlehrer	spricht	keine Lederhosen.
Meine Deutschlehrerin	vergisst	gern Bücher.
Mein Opa		einen VW.
Meine Oma		viel.
		wenig.
		immer ihr/sein Passwort.

fast

Kulturnotiz: Lederhosen are not typical attire for most German men. They are mostly worn in Bavaria and parts of southern Germany and at traditional festivals.

Strukturen

 Expressing additional and contrastive information and justifications

Coordinating conjunctions

German speakers use coordinating conjunctions (**nebenordnende Konjunktionen**) to provide additional information (**und**), justification (**denn**), or contrast (**sondern, aber, oder**). There are five frequently used coordinating conjunctions.

aber	*but*
denn	*for, because*
oder	*or*
sondern	*but rather*
und	*and*

Coordinating conjunctions may conjoin words, phrases, or clauses. When used to conjoin clauses, a comma is inserted before the coordinating conjunction.

> Meine Mutter **und** ich spielen Tennis, **und** mein Vater spielt Golf.
>
> *My mother **and** I play tennis, **and** my father plays golf.*

Aber is commonly used in conversation to present an idea that contrasts what has been stated or implied so far.

> Anna ist gespannt auf das Jahr in Deutschland, **aber** ihre Mutter macht sich Sorgen.
>
> *Anna is excited about the year in Germany, **but** her mother is worried.*

Denn is used to provide an indisputable reason or justification.

> Ihr Freund kommt nicht, **denn** er fährt nach Hause.
>
> *Her friend isn't coming **because** he's going home.*

Oder is used to provide alternative information.

> Geht Hannes nach Hause, **oder** (geht er) zu Uschi?
>
> *Is Hannes going home, **or** (is he going) to Uschi's?*

Sondern introduces a clause, phrase, or noun that contradicts a preceding negative statement which usually contains **nicht.**

> Anna kommt **nicht** am Montag, **sondern** am Dienstag.
>
> *Anna is**n't** coming on Monday, **but (rather)** on Tuesday.*

Do not confuse the conjunction **denn** with the particle **denn** as used in questions like: **Woher kommen Sie denn?** The particle **denn** is used to show personal interest or to elicit further information after a misunderstanding. It does not join two clauses.

 15 **Warum machen sie das?** Match the statements in the left column with the appropriate justifications in the right column.

1. Mein Bruder isst oft Fleisch,
2. Unsere Tante isst gar kein Fleisch,
3. Meine Familie hört gern Musik,
4. Seine Schwester trägt heute Shorts und Sandalen,
5. Mein Bruder lächelt,
6. Unsere Großeltern sehen nie fern,
7. Euer Deutschlehrer trägt keine Lederhosen,
8. Ihre Mutter spricht Deutsch,

a. denn wir sind sehr musikalisch.
b. denn sie kommt aus Deutschland.
c. denn er kommt aus Norddeutschland.
d. denn es ist sehr warm.
e. denn er ist sehr glücklich°.
f. denn Fleisch ist zu teuer°.
g. denn sie haben keinen Fernseher.
h. denn er hat Fleisch gern.

happy
expensive

16 Sie ist Amerikanerin, aber ... Match the statements in the left column with the appropriate contrasting information in the right column.

1. Anna spricht Englisch,
2. Anna wohnt in Fort Wayne,
3. Herr Günther isst oft bei McDonalds,
4. Katja versteht Englisch,
5. Georg kommt aus Deutschland,
6. Frau Adler ist gut organisiert,
7. Es ist heute kalt,

a. aber Jeff trägt keinen Pullover.
b. aber sie vergisst oft ihre Brille.
c. aber sie spricht auch etwas Deutsch.
d. aber er trinkt nicht gern Bier.
e. aber sie hat Angst, Englisch zu sprechen.
f. aber sie hat Verwandte in Deutschland.
g. aber er bleibt schlank.

Strukturen

IV Stating personal preferences

The adverb **lieber**

You have already learned how to use **gern** to talk about activities that you like to do.

Ich spiele **gern** Tennis.   *I **like to** play tennis.*

To express a preference for one of two options, use **lieber** with a verb.

Spielst du **lieber** Tennis oder Fußball?   *Do you **prefer to** play tennis or soccer?*
Ich spiele **lieber** Fußball.   *I **prefer to** play soccer. (I **like to** play soccer **more**.)*

The expression **lieber ... als** (*rather than*) is used when stating a preference for one thing over another.

Ich spiele **lieber** Fußball **als** Tennis.   *I prefer to play soccer **rather than** tennis.*

                                  *(I **like** to play soccer **more than** tennis.)*

  17 Das mache ich lieber Ask each other about your personal preferences, using the appropriate verb. After you have finished, report back to the class.

BEISPIEL   *Lederhosen/Shorts tragen*
          S1: *Trägst du lieber Lederhosen, oder trägst du lieber Shorts?* (oder)
               Was trägst du lieber: Lederhosen oder Shorts?
          S2: *Ich trage lieber Shorts. Was trägst du lieber?*
          S1: *Ich trage auch lieber Shorts.*

          S1: *(Lori) sagt, sie trägt lieber Shorts.*
          S2: *(Raoul) sagt, er trägt lieber Shorts.*

1. Hamburger/Bratwurst essen
2. Englisch/Deutsch sprechen
3. Cola/Bier trinken
4. klassische Musik/Rockmusik hören
5. Softball/Fußball spielen
6. Birkenstock-Sandalen/Turnschuhe tragen
7. Mathematik machen/Literatur lesen
8. Auto/Fahrrad° fahren
9. einen Chemiekurs/Psychologiekurs machen
10. Das Frühstück/Mittagessen vergessen

bicycle

Strukturen

 Expressing what you would like to do

The modal verb **möchte**

German speakers use **möchte** to express what they or somebody else would like to have or would like to do. If it is used to express a preference for a certain action (what people would like to do), **möchte** acts as a modal verb. Modal verbs are helping verbs (**Hilfsverben**) that express under which conditions an action takes place. **Möchte** implies that the action is desired by the subject. The verb that expresses the desired action is used in the infinitive form. In simple declarative sentences with a modal verb, the infinitive occurs at the end of the sentence. You will be learning about other modal verbs in this chapter and **Kapitel 4**.

Ich **möchte** meine Verwandten in Deutschland **kennenlernen.**   *I would like to get to know my relatives in Germany.*

möchte: *would like (to)*				
Person	**Singular**		**Plural**	
1st	ich	**möchte**	wir	**möchten**
2nd, informal	du	**möchtest**	ihr	**möchtet**
2nd, formal	Sie	**möchten**	Sie	**möchten**
3rd	er/sie/es	**möchte**	sie	**möchten**

When **möchte** is used, the infinitive can be omitted if it is clear from the context what infinitive is implied. Infinitives that are commonly omitted are: **essen, trinken, fahren, gehen,** and **haben.**

Ich **möchte** bitte eine Cola (haben).   *I would like (to have) a cola, please.*
Er **möchte** nach Heidelberg (fahren).   *He would like to go to Heidelberg.*

---

 18 Was möchtest du lieber? Ask your partner questions about what he/she would prefer to do.

BEISPIEL   eine Cola / einen Kaffee trinken

S1: *Möchtest du lieber eine Cola oder einen Kaffee (trinken)?*
S2: *Ich möchte lieber einen Kaffee (trinken), und du?*
S1: *Ich möchte lieber eine Cola.*

1. eine Cola / einen Kaffee (trinken)
2. fernsehen / einen Film sehen
3. Turnschuhe / Sandalen tragen
4. Deutsch / Englisch sprechen
5. um sechs Uhr Morgen / um ein Uhr Mittag aufstehen
6. schwimmen / wandern (gehen)
7. ein großes Frühstück / ein großes Mittagessen (essen)
8. nach Heidelberg / nach München (fahren)
9. ins Museum / ins Restaurant (gehen)
10. ???

Mealtimes in German-speaking countries

Since eating customs are often the most distinctive aspects of a culture, they are frequently the means by which others form stereotypes. For example, in Germany, Austria, and Switzerland, it is common to hold the knife in the right hand and the fork in the left hand. Diners use the knife to push food onto the fork while resting their forearms on the edge of the table. In the United States, resting the forearms on the table may be considered rude mealtime behavior. In German-speaking central Europe, parents correct children who have their hands under the table.

In German-speaking countries, there are three to five distinct mealtimes. Breakfast (**das Frühstück**) usually consists of coffee or tea, some kind of fresh-baked bread (**das Brot**) or a crusty roll (**das Brötchen** in the north and **die Semmel** in southern areas). To accompany the bread there can be butter (**die Butter**), fruit jam (**die Marmelade**), honey (**der Honig**), cheese (**der Käse**), a unique German dairy spread called (**der) Quark,** or even cold cuts (**der Aufschnitt**). Some people round off their breakfast with a soft-boiled egg (**ein weich gekochtes Ei**), yogurt (**der/das Joghurt**), or breakfast cereal. Many Germans consider a nutritious breakfast the most important meal of the day and make it a sit-down family affair.

Mid-morning around 10:00 a.m., most people at work and school break for their "second breakfast" (**zweites Frühstück**), which may consist of a cup of yogurt, a piece of fruit, or a **belegtes Brötchen** with cold cuts or cheese.

Das Mittagessen is traditionally the main hot meal of the day. It often has three courses: (1) an appetizer (**die Vorspeise**), most often soup (**die Suppe**) or salad (**der Salat**); (2) the main course (**das Hauptgericht**) of meat or fish, potatoes or noodles or rice, and a vegetable; and (3) a dessert (**die Nachspeise / der Nachtisch**) of pudding, fruit, or ice cream, but not usually cake or pastry.

On special occasions or on weekends, many people enjoy coffee and cake (**Kaffee und Kuchen**) around mid-afternoon.

The last meal of the day, around 6 p.m., is called **das Abendbrot** or **das Abendessen.** It is essentially a reprise of breakfast: bread, butter, cold cuts, and cheese, along with tomatoes, salad, and cucumbers, or occasionally sausages and potato salad (**Würstchen mit Kartoffelsalat**) for variety. Tea, mineral water, beer, or wine completes the meal. In a growing number of working families, the main hot meal is now prepared in the evening.

Kulturkreuzung

Think about the differences between meals in German-speaking countries and in this country. What differences do you notice about breakfast? What kind of breakfast foods are unique to your area of the country, and to other areas of the country? Which breakfast seems healthier? What prevents people here from eating their big meal at noon? When is it probably healthier to eat the big meal of the day? When do people in this country take time out for coffee and pastries? How would guests here react if you served them cold cuts and tea for supper or for breakfast?

AISPIX by Image Source/Shutterstock.com

Was isst man zum Frühstück?

Wissenswerte Vokabeln: Lebensmittel

Talking about foods that we like

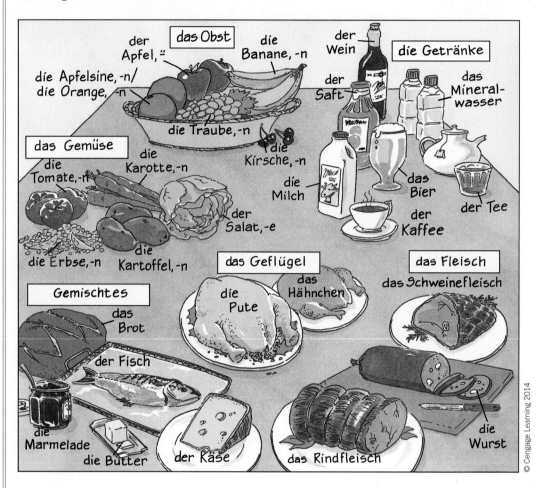

die **das Obst** die der der **die Getränke**
der **Apfel,** ¨ **Banane, -n** Wein
die Apfelsine, -n/ der das
die Orange, -n Saft **Mineral-**
wasser

das Gemüse die die
die **Karotte, -n** Kirsche, -n
Tomate, -n die das
der Milch Bier
Salat, -e der der Tee
die die Kaffee
die Erbse, -n Kartoffel, -n

das Geflügel **das Fleisch**
das das Schweinefleisch
Gemischtes die Hähnchen
das Pute
Brot

der Fisch

die die
Marmelade Wurst
die Butter der Käse das Rindfleisch

© Cengage Learning 2014

BEISPIEL Was isst du gern? *Ich esse gern Salat.*

© Cengage Learning 2014

19 Was isst und trinkst du lieber? Interview your partner about his/her preferences in food and drinks. After you have finished, report back to the class.

BEISPIEL Schweinefleisch/Rindfleisch
S1: *Was isst du lieber: Schweinefleisch oder Rindfleisch?*
S2: *Ich esse lieber Rindfleisch als Schweinefleisch.*

S1: (Karen) *isst lieber … als …*
S2: (Eric) *isst lieber … als …*

1. Schweinefleisch/Rindfleisch
2. Fisch/Fleisch
3. Gemüse/Obst
4. Wurst/Käse
5. Hähnchen/Fisch
6. Bier/Milch
7. Kaffee/Tee
8. Honig/Marmelade

The metric system

The metric system is used in Europe and much of the world outside the United States. Among other things, it is used when shopping, measuring body weight and height, and measuring distances between cities.

liquids
der Liter (l) = slightly more than a liquid
  quart
der Zentiliter (cl) = 0.01 liter

mass / weight
das Gramm (g) = about 35/1000 of
  an ounce
das Pfund (Pf) = 500 grams
das Kilo(gramm) (kg) = 1000 grams,
  2 metric pounds

length / height
der Meter (m) = slightly more than a yard

der Zentimeter (cm) = 0.01 meter

distance
der Kilometer (km) = 0.62 miles
  = 1000 meters

Gasoline is sold in liters, and some drinks are sold in centiliters. In a bar, wine may be ordered by a quarter/ an eighth liter (**ein Viertel / ein Achtel Weißwein, bitte**), and beer may be sold by the half liter (**ein Halbes**) or in a full liter (called **eine Maß** in Bavaria).

To specify a plural quantity, German speakers use the same form as the singular neuter form of the measurement: **500 Gramm Käse, zwei Pfund Äpfel.**

Wie weit ist es bis nach Köln?

Meats and breads are sold by the **Kilo.** Two pounds of hamburger may be ordered as **ein Kilo** or **1 000 Gramm Hackfleisch.** Germans (but not Austrians or Swiss) use pounds and might order **zwei Pfund Hackfleisch.** Amounts smaller than a pound are most frequently expressed in grams (**125 Gramm**) but can also be expressed in Germany as fractions of a pound (**ein halbes Pfund, ein Viertel Pfund**). In Austria, smaller food purchases are usually made in fractions of a **Kilo** or in **Deka** (multiples of 10), not in **Gramm** or **Pfund**. Body weight is expressed in kilos (**65,5 Kilo**) and height in meters and centimeters (**ein Meter siebzig Zentimeter**).

To say how far it is from one city to another, people use the expression **weit von** (*far from, away from*): **Heidelberg ist 20 Kilometer weit von Mannheim.**

Kulturkreuzung

While Canada and Great Britain converted to the metric system years ago, the United States still mostly uses the traditional English system of weights and measures. In what situations is the metric system used in the U.S.? Why has the country not converted completely to the metric system? What advantages does the metric system offer? What are the advantages of the English system? What obstacles discourage conversion to the metric system in the U.S.?

Sprache im Alltag: Specifying amounts

German speakers usually purchase small amounts of fresh cold cuts, cheese, meat, fruit, and vegetables each day for immediate consumption. Shoppers (**Kunden**) therefore often request very small amounts and salespeople (**Verkäufer**) ask for approval if the amount on the scale is a little above or below the desired weight.

KUNDE/KUNDIN: Geben Sie mir bitte 200 Gramm Leberwurst und 150 Gramm Gouda.
VERKÄUFER(IN): Darf° es etwas mehr° sein? (*oder*)
　　　　　　　Darf es etwas weniger° sein?

In addition to metric measurement, German speakers use several other expressions with non-count nouns. As with the metric system, German does not include a word for *of* with these expressions.

Die Studentin isst **ein Stück Käse**	The student is eating a piece of cheese.
Ich nehme **eine Scheibe Brot.**	I'll take a slice of bread.
Karl trinkt **eine Tasse Kaffee**	Karl is drinking a cup of coffee.
Lise möchte **ein Glas Wasser.**	Lise would like a glass of water.
Frau Lehlbach kauft **eine Flasche Olivenöl**.	Mrs. Lehlbach is buying a bottle of olive oil.

Masculine and neuter quantities like these (**das Glas, das Stück**) do not have separate plural forms.

Der Kellner bringt **zwei Glas Wein.**	The waiter is bringing two glasses of wine.
Barbara isst **drei Stück Käse.**	Barbara eats three pieces of cheese.

---

20 In der Bäckerei° Listen to the following dialogue, then practice it with a partner.

BÄCKER: Guten Tag. Bitte schön?
KUNDIN: Ich möchte ein Weißbrot und vier Brötchen.
BÄCKER: Sonst noch 'was?°
KUNDIN: Das war's.
BÄCKER: Das macht zwei Euro neunzig.
KUNDIN: Bitte schön.
BÄCKER: Danke. Und zehn Cent zurück.
KUNDIN: Auf Wiedersehen.
BÄCKER: Wiedersehen.

Sprache im Alltag: **Bitte schön**

The German expression **bitte schön** has several different meanings depending on the context in which it is used. German sales clerks use **Bitte schön?** (*May I help you?*) to initiate a sales dialogue. Customers use **Bitte schön** (*Here you go*) when laying their money on the counter to pay for the goods. When responding to **Danke schön,** all speakers in any situation use **Bitte schön** (*You're welcome.*)

Margin notes:

may / more
less

Germans are sticklers for the right beverage containers. Coffee may be drunk from a cup (**eine Tasse** or **ein Becher**), whereas hot tea is typically drunk from a glass (**ein Glas**) in a holder.

bakery

Track 1-7

Sonst ... : *(Would you like) anything else?*

Two common places to buy food are **das Lebensmittelgeschäft** (*grocery store*) and **der Supermarkt** (*supermarket*).

⊖ **21** Schreibecke: **Der Wocheneinkauf.** Make up a weekly food shopping list; write the amounts in **Gramm.** Use the items you have learned in the chapter and the following ad for ideas.

gute Lebensmittel

Rotkäppchen Riesling Sekt[1], tegut... Sekt brut[1] aus Trauben ökologischen Anbaus **oder Villa Maria Carla Rosé Frizzante IGT[1] oder Prosecco DOC[1]** aus Italien, aus Trauben ökologischen Anbaus, 1 l = 5,03 €, 0,75 l Flasche/ Bügelverschluss-Flasche

~~5,49~~   ~~5,99~~   **5,99**   **3.⁷⁷**
~~4,99~~

bis zu 37 % günstiger

Bio-Aktionstüte*
Inhalt:
1 Bio-Bauernbrot 1.000 g,
1 Bio-Baguette 250 g,
5 Bio-Rhönweck,
Tüte

herzberger bäckerei

3.⁹⁹
statt ~~5,73~~
30 % günstiger

Bio-Fleischwurst im Ring*
schmackhaft gewürzt

Bihophar Trachtenhonig oder Wabenecht Honig
verschiedene Sorten,
1 kg = 7,98 €, 500 g Glas

~~5,59~~   **3.⁹⁹**
bis zu 28 % günstiger

Spanischer Eisbergsalat
Klasse I, Stück

Bio

0.⁶⁶

Bio
100 g
0.⁸⁹
statt ~~1,29~~
31 % günstiger

Kombi-Angebot

Drei Berliner*
kaufen und
0,57 € sparen.

3 Stück nur
1.⁹⁸

Südafrikanische Bio-Weintrauben
hell, kernlos,
Sorte: „Prime Seedless",
Klasse II, 1 kg = 5,00 €,
500 g Schale

Bio

2.⁵⁰

frische Putenschnitzel*
eignet sich hervorragend für Fondue,
natur oder mariniert

100 g
0.⁹⁹
statt ~~1,22~~

Kombi-Angebot

Sechs Packungen
Happy Day Saft,
2 l kaufen und
4,94 € sparen.

10.–

Sorten frei wählbar.

From TEGUT grocery store flyer

Heidelberg und Mannheim

In anticipation of Anna's arrival, the Günthers, who live in Weinheim just north of Heidelberg, send her tourist brochures on Heidelberg and Mannheim. Heidelberg has many well-known attractions—a historic university, an old castle, and a scenic location on the Neckar River with vineyards nearby. Mannheim, Heidelberg's neighbor to the west on the Rhine, is known less for its tourist attractions and more for its industrial significance.

Vorschau

⮐ **22** Thematische Fragen Discuss the following questions with your instructor or in pairs.

1. What cities do you associate with Germany? Why?
2. What do you already know about Heidelberg? Where are you likely to get information about Heidelberg?
3. Heidelberg is considered one of Germany's most romantic cities. What makes a city romantic? What role does geography play in defining a romantic city? What sort of buildings and other tourist attractions might you find in Heidelberg that make it a "romantic city"?
4. What do you know about Mannheim?
5. Heidelberg, Mannheim, and Tübingen are all located in Germany's southwesternmost state, (**das Land**), Baden-Württemberg. There are a total of sixteen **Länder** in Germany. Which other ones have you heard of, and where are they?

Chris Howes/Wild Places Photography/Alamy

Mannheim: Kurfürstliches Residenzschloss.

23 Wortdetektiv Which words convey approximately the same meaning? Match the German word with its logical English equivalent.

Deutsch	Englisch
1. die Stadt (e.g., Berlin)	a. bicycle
2. das Fahrrad	b. bridge
3. segeln	c. to sail
4. die Brücke	d. castle, palace
5. das Schloss	e. city, town

6. der Einwohner	f. inhabitant, citizen
7. die Bibliothek	g. sightseeing attraction
8. die Sehenswürdigkeit	h. library
9. das Schwimmbad	i. to fish
10. angeln	j. swimming pool

11. die Jugendherberge	k. to ride horseback
12. reiten	l. church
13. die Kirche	m. bed & breakfast hotel
14. der Hauptbahnhof	n. main train station
15. die Pension	o. youth hostel

16. Altes Rathaus	p. water tower
17. der Wasserturm	q. plaza, square
18. die Trimm-dich-Pfade	r. student bar
19. der Platz	s. fitness trails
20. das Studentenlokal	t. old city hall

Heidelberg: das Große Fass.

Chris Howes/Wild Places Photography/Alamy

Die Universität Heidelberg

⟳ **24** Zum Text Tourist brochures often list facts and figures to provide a quick overview of a city and its attractions. The following ads contain information on Heidelberg and Mannheim. Scan the texts to find . . .

1. the phone number, fax number, and e-mail address for the two tourist information offices.
2. the number of hotel beds in Heidelberg and hotel rooms in Mannheim.
3. the year the university in Heidelberg was founded.
4. examples for how Heidelberg markets itself. (Scan the text for adjectives.)
5. the larger city: Is it Heidelberg or Mannheim?
6. how the information is presented, e.g., whole sentences? or just key words?

Now read the text.

Heidelberg

Universitätsstadt am Neckar, 150 000 Einwohner, davon 25 000 Studenten, 6 100 Betten (davon 3 340 in Hotels, 1 500 in Gasthöfen und Pensionen, Jugendherberge mit ca. 450 Betten, und 5 Campingplätze in der Umgebung.)

Freizeit: Freischwimmbad°, Hallenschwimmbad°, Reiten, Tennis, Angeln, Segeln, Großgolf, Minigolf, Fahrradverleih°, Neckarschifffahrt°, Zoo, Kinderparadies

Sehenswürdigkeiten: Heidelberger Schloss – das Große Fass – das Deutsche Apotheken-Museum, historische, romantische Altstadt am Neckar, älteste Universität Deutschlands (1386), Universitätsbibliothek, Alte Brücke, Heiliggeistkirche, Kurpfälzisches Museum, historische Studentenlokale, Bergbahn° zur Spitze des Königstuhls, dem Hausberg° von Heidelberg.

ⓘ Tourist- Information: Heidelberg Marketing GmbH
www.heidelberg-marketing.de
Telefon: 0049 (0) 6221 58 44 444
email: info@heidelberg-marketing.de www.facebook.com/Heidelberg
Fax: 0049 (0) 58 40 254

---

outdoor pool / indoor pool
bicycle rental / boat rides on the Neckar River

mountain railway / popular hilltop

Die älteste Universität Deutschlands means *Germany's oldest university.*

Mannheim

Stadt der Quadrate° an Rhein und Neckar im Herzen der ehemaligen° Kurpfalz, heute Metropolreregion Rhein-Neckar. Mannheim hat 325 000 Einwohner, 2 900 Zimmer mit 4800 Betten in Hotels, Gasthöfen und Pensionen, 99 Betten in der Jugendherberge. Kongresszentrum „Rosengarten", SAP Arena und Maimarkthalle/-gelände als Veranstaltungsstätten.

Freizeit: Campingplätze an Rhein und Neckar, beheizte Freischwimmbäder, Hallenbäder, Tennis, Squash, Angeln, Reiten, Segeln, Minigolf, Trimm-dich-Pfade

Sehenswürdigkeiten & Museen: Friedrichsplatz (eine der größten Jugendstilanlagen° Europas) mit Wasserturm (als Wahrzeichen°) und Wasserspielen°, Kurfürstliches Residenzschloss mit Schlosskirche (größtes Barockschloss° Deutschlands), Jesuitenkirche, Kunsthalle Mannheim, Planetarium, TECHNOSEUM – Landesmuseum für Technik und Arbeit, Nationaltheater, Kinder- und Jugendtheater im Kulturzentrum, Altes Rathaus und Untere Pfarrkirche St. Sebastian (Glockenspiel°) am Marktplatz, erste Popakademie Deutschlands, Rheinpromenade, sowie der Hafen°

ℹ Tourist-Information Mannheim
Willy-Brandt-Platz 3
68161 Mannheim
Telefon: (06 21) 10 293-8700

Telefax: (06 21) 293-8701
E-Mail: touristinformation@mannheim.de
www.tourist-mannheim.de

square blocks / former

Stadt der Quadrate means *city of squares* (like in a grid).

Art Nouveau / symbol / fountains

Baroque palace

chimes

harbor

Größtes Barockschloss means *the largest baroque* palace. It is similar to **die älteste Universität.** Both are superlative forms (*the most*).

Die Universität Mannheim ist in einem Barockschloss.

Rückblick

↵ **25** Stimmt das? How much of the text do you remember without looking back at it?

	Ja, das stimmt.	Nein, das stimmt nicht.
1. Heidelberg ist eine Industriestadt.	○	○
2. Mannheim liegt am° Rhein und am Neckar.	○	○
3. Mannheim hat 325 000 Einwohner.	○	○
4. In Heidelberg gibt es keinen Wassersport.	○	○
5. Für Kinder gibt es in Heidelberg den Zoo und das Kinderparadies.	○	○
6. Mannheim hat kein Schloss.	○	○
7. Heidelbergs Altstadt ist alt, kaputt und hässlich°.	○	○
8. Mannheim hat die älteste Universität Deutschlands.	○	○
9. Die Alte Brücke führt über° den Neckar.	○	○
10. Die Tourist-Information in Heidelberg findet man in historischen Studentenlokalen.	○	○

liegt ... : is situated on

ugly

führt ... : goes across

↵ **26** Was gibt's in Mannheim oder Heidelberg? Compare Mannheim's attractions to those of Heidelberg. Which of the following attractions and facilities do both cities offer and which are unique to Mannheim or Heidelberg?

Theater • Squash • Schloss • Segeln • Tennis • Kirche • Minigolf • Museum • Kunsthalle • Wasserspiele • Hallenschwimmbad • Reiten • Universität • Rathaus • Trimm-dich-Pfade • Popakademie • Studentenlokale • Neckar • das Große Fass • Hafen • Rhein • Campingplätze • Gasthöfe und Pensionen • Friedrichsplatz

Mannheim	*Heidelberg*	*Mannheim und Heidelberg*
_____	_____	_____
_____	_____	_____
_____	_____	_____
_____	_____	_____
_____	_____	_____

↵ **27** Wo findet man diese Leute? With a partner, determine where in Heidelberg or Mannheim you would most likely find these people during the day.

1. Tennisspieler	in der Bibliothek oder im Hörsaal
2. Pastoren	an der Universität
3. Schwimmer	im Schloss
4. deutsche Touristen	auf dem Tennisplatz
5. Professoren	in der Kirche
6. Studentinnen	im Schwimmbad
7. Heidelberger	im Museum
8. amerikanische Touristen	im Lokal

28 Ergänzen Sie Complete these statements with words from the **Absprungtext**.

1. Heidelberg ist eine _____ und hat 150 000 _____.
2. Es gibt in Heidelberg über 6 000 Betten in _____, in Gasthöfen und in _____.
3. Es gibt in Mannheim 120 Betten für junge Leute in der _____.
4. Das Heidelberger _____ ist das Symbol von Heidelberg.
5. Der _____ ist das Symbol von Mannheim.
6. Heidelberg hat eine historische, romantische _____ am Neckar.
7. Heidelbergs Altstadt ist historisch und _____.
8. Heidelbergs _____ ist die älteste in Deutschland (1386).
9. Heidelberger Studenten leihen Bücher für ihre Kurse aus der _____ aus°.   *leihen ... aus = ausleihen:*
   check out
10. Sonntags gehen Christen in die _____.
11. In Mannheim sieht man gute Dramen von Goethe und Schiller im _____.
12. Studenten gehen in historische _____ und trinken Wein und Bier.

29 Kurz gefragt Answer these questions with just a word or two, or a short phrase.

1. Welche Stadt hat mehr Einwohner: Heidelberg oder Mannheim?
2. Welche Freizeitaktivitäten in Heidelberg und Mannheim haben mit Wasser zu tun°?   *mit ... zu tun: to do with ...*
3. Welche Freizeitaktivitäten in Heidelberg haben mit Tieren° zu tun?   *animals*
4. Für welche Sportarten braucht° man einen Ball?   *needs*
5. Was sind zwei Sehenswürdigkeiten in der Nähe° vom Heidelberger Schloss?   *vicinity*
6. Wo ist die Heidelberger Altstadt? Und wie ist sie?
7. Wie kommt man über den Neckar? Man geht über ...
8. Wo hört und sieht man das Glockenspiel in Mannheim?

30 Textdetektiv: **Absprungtext.** Look at the *Absprungtext* to answer the following questions about these texts.

1. Just from their visual presentation, the intent behind these two texts is
   a. to promote Mannheim and Heidelberg as cities that have seen better days.
   b. to promote Mannheim and Heidelberg as brand new cities in Germany.
   c. to promote Mannheim and Heidelberg as historically rich and vibrant cities.

2. Apart from the heading that names the city, each text starts with
   a. a list of statistics about each city.
   b. the most important tourist attraction in each city.
   c. contact information.

3. These texts were written for an audience of
   a. students learning the German language.
   b. potential tourists.
   c. inhabitants of these two cities.

4. The authors of *Vorsprung* chose these texts because they (select all that apply)
   a. present cultural information that is relevant to the book's storylines.
   b. contain vocabulary that is easily guessable for speakers of English.
   c. might make students consider actually visiting.

Heidelberg and Mannheim

Heidelberg and Mannheim are a study in contrasts. Whereas Heidelberg was spared the devastation of aerial bombing in World War II, Mannheim was badly damaged. After the war Mannheim rebuilt its distinctive downtown square grid (**Quadrat**), which resembles many American cities. Heidelberg's romantic and bustling **Hauptstraße** meanders for over a mile from the **Bismarckplatz** past the **Theaterplatz** and the **Universitätsplatz**. Many small streets and walkways make up the **Altstadt**.

Heidelberg's reputation is built on its proud academic tradition. **The Heidelberger Schloss** is one of the most popular tourist attractions in Europe. The skull of *Homo heidelbergensis*, the earliest human remains in Europe, was discovered near Heidelberg in 1907 and is over 500,000 years old.

Mannheim's reputation is built on its past and current industrial innovations. In 1885, Carl Friedrich Benz invented the first automobile in Mannheim, which later evolved to become the first **Mercedes** automobile. Mannheim continues to be the home of mechanical and electrical engineering firms as well as car makers, but is also emerging as a popular music capital in Germany. Mannheim's sister city across the Rhein, Ludwigshafen, is home to BASF (Badische Anilin- und Soda-Fabrik), one of the largest chemical companies in the world.

St. Nick/Shutterstock.com

Das Heidelberger Schloss ist das Wahrzeichen von Heidelberg.

Kulturkreuzung

Can you identify two cities near each other like Heidelberg and Mannheim that represent a contrast between **Universitätsstadt** and **Industriestadt**?

31 Was möchtest du in Heidelberg sehen? Use the photos of Heidelberg below as a visual guide. Ask your partner what he/she would like to see in Heidelberg.

BEISPIEL   S1: *Möchtest du Heidelberg sehen?*
                S2: *Ja, ich möchte Heidelberg sehen, und du?*
                S1: *Ja, ich auch. (oder)*
                     Nein, ich nicht. (oder)
                     Nein, ich möchte Heidelberg nicht sehen.

BEISPIEL   S1: *Möchtest du das Schloss sehen?*
                S2: *Ja, ich möchte das Schloss sehen, und du?*
                S1: *Ja, ich auch. (oder)*
                     Nein, ich nicht. (oder)
                     Nein, ich möchte das Schloss nicht sehen.

Heidelberg
Der Neckar

Das Schloss
Das Große Fass im Schloss
Das Rathaus

Die Universität
Der Zoo
Die Studentenlokale
Die Heiliggeistkirche

Die Altstadt

Die Alte Brücke

All images courtesy of Tom Lovik.

Wissenswerte Vokabeln: Freizeitaktivitäten

Talking about what you can do and like to do

Fußball spielen

Klavier spielen

ins Kino gehen

tanzen

Ski laufen

reiten

kochen

lesen

Rad fahren

spazieren gehen

singen

angeln

segeln

Karten spielen

wandern

schwimmen

Illustrations © Cengage Learning 2014

BEISPIEL Was spielst du gern? *Ich spiele gern Tennis.*

32 Das Interview Find out as much as you can about your partner's leisure time activities. Write **ja** if you or your partner like to do the activity, and **nein,** if you do not.

BEISPIEL   S1: *Spielst du gern Karten?*
            S2: *Ja, und du?*

	Ich	*Mein Partner/Meine Partnerin*
Karten spielen	_____	_____
Fußball spielen	_____	_____
Klavier spielen	_____	_____
ins Kino gehen	_____	_____
reiten	_____	_____
kochen	_____	_____
lesen	_____	_____
Rad fahren	_____	_____
spazieren gehen	_____	_____
schwimmen	_____	_____
segeln	_____	_____

Similar to **Fußball spielen**, you can say **Baseball spielen, Basketball spielen, Golf spielen, Softball spielen, Tennis spielen,** and **Volleyball spielen.**

Similar to **Klavier spielen**, you can also say **Flöte** (*flute*) **spielen, Gitarre** (*guitar*) **spielen,** and **Geige** (*violin*) **spielen.**

Similar to **ins Kino gehen**, you can say **ins Konzert gehen, ins Museum, ins Restaurant, ins Café** and **ins Theater gehen.**

Strukturen

VI Expressing possibilities

The modal verb **können**

The modal verb **können** (*to be able to*) is used with an infinitive to express what a person can or cannot do or knows or doesn't know how to do.

    Ich **kann** Deutsch sprechen.   *I **can (know how to)** speak German.*

Like **möchte, können** may occur without an infinitive, when the implied infinitive is clear from the context. This happens particularly often in the context of languages.

    Angelika **kann** Deutsch (sprechen).   *Angelika **can** speak German.*

Like other modals, **können** has stem vowels that are different in the singular and in the plural. Also, the 1st and 3rd person singular forms have no endings.

You will learn more about these modal verbs in **Kapitel 4.**

können: *can; to be able to*		
Person	**Singular**	**Plural**
1st	ich k**a**nn	wir k**ö**nnen
2nd, informal	du k**a**nnst	ihr k**ö**nnt
2nd, formal	Sie k**ö**nnen	Sie k**ö**nnen
3rd	er/sie/es k**a**nn	sie k**ö**nnen

The pronoun **man** (*one*) is often used with **kann** to express what options are available.

    In Heidelberg **kann man** segeln.   ***You (one) can** sail in Heidelberg.*

Remember, when expressing what you know how to do, especially speaking languages, you can drop the infinitive.

👥 33 Kannst du das machen? Ask a partner how well he/she can do the following activities. Then check the appropriate columns.

BEISPIEL   S1: *Kannst du Tennis spielen?*
S2: *Ja, ich kann relativ gut Tennis spielen.*

Aktivität	sehr gut	relativ gut	nicht so gut	gar nicht
1. Tennis spielen	○	○	○	○
2. kochen	○	○	○	○
3. Ski laufen	○	○	○	○
4. schwimmen	○	○	○	○
5. Spanisch (sprechen)	○	○	○	○
6. Flöte spielen	○	○	○	○
7. tanzen	○	○	○	○
8. segeln	○	○	○	○

👥 34 Was kann man in deiner Stadt machen? Ask a partner the following questions about his/her hometown.

BEISPIEL   ins Kino gehen
S1: *Woher kommst du?*
S2: *Aus (Detroit).*
S1: *Kann man in (Detroit) ins Kino gehen?*
S2: *Ja.*

1. ins Kino gehen
2. am Fluss° Rad fahren
3. ins Konzert gehen
4. am Abend spazieren gehen
5. ins Theater gehen
6. Studentenlokale finden
7. ins Schloss gehen
8. ins Museum gehen
9. gute Hotels finden
10. alte Kirchen besichtigen°

am ... : at the river

to visit, tour

Wissenswerte Vokabeln: Die Landeskunde Deutschlands

Talking about geographic landmarks in Germany

↩ 35 Land und Leute kennenlernen Answer the following questions about Germany.

1. Welche drei Großstädte sind auch Bundesländer?
2. Welche drei Bundesländer haben die meisten° Einwohner?
3. Welche drei Bundesländer haben die wenigsten° Einwohner?
4. Welches Bundesland hat München als Hauptstadt?
5. Welche Bundesländer sind an der Ostsee?
6. Welche zwei Bundesländer sind direkt an der Nordsee?
7. Welche drei Bundesländer haben eine Grenze mit Frankreich?
8. Durch welche Bundesländer fließt° der Rhein?
9. Wie heißt die Hauptstadt von Rheinland-Pfalz?
10. In welchem Bundesland liegt Leipzig?

most
fewest

flows

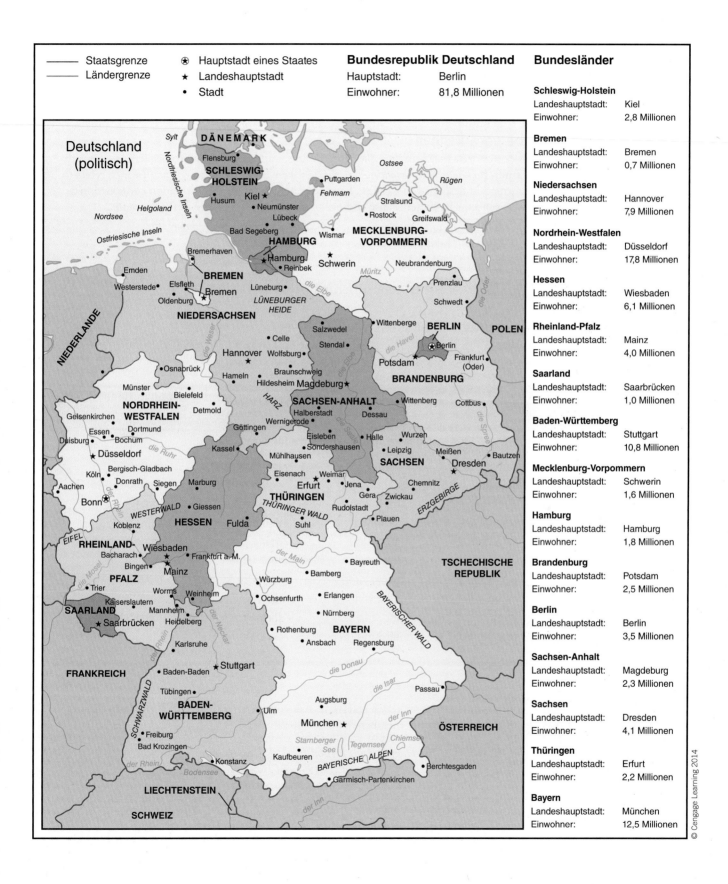

Deutschland (politisch)

——	Staatsgrenze
——	Ländergrenze
✪	Hauptstadt eines Staates
★	Landeshauptstadt
•	Stadt

Bundesrepublik Deutschland

Hauptstadt:	Berlin
Einwohner:	81,8 Millionen

Bundesländer

Schleswig-Holstein
Landeshauptstadt: Kiel
Einwohner: 2,8 Millionen

Bremen
Landeshauptstadt: Bremen
Einwohner: 0,7 Millionen

Niedersachsen
Landeshauptstadt: Hannover
Einwohner: 7,9 Millionen

Nordrhein-Westfalen
Landeshauptstadt: Düsseldorf
Einwohner: 17,8 Millionen

Hessen
Landeshauptstadt: Wiesbaden
Einwohner: 6,1 Millionen

Rheinland-Pfalz
Landeshauptstadt: Mainz
Einwohner: 4,0 Millionen

Saarland
Landeshauptstadt: Saarbrücken
Einwohner: 1,0 Millionen

Baden-Württemberg
Landeshauptstadt: Stuttgart
Einwohner: 10,8 Millionen

Mecklenburg-Vorpommern
Landeshauptstadt: Schwerin
Einwohner: 1,6 Millionen

Hamburg
Landeshauptstadt: Hamburg
Einwohner: 1,8 Millionen

Brandenburg
Landeshauptstadt: Potsdam
Einwohner: 2,5 Millionen

Berlin
Landeshauptstadt: Berlin
Einwohner: 3,5 Millionen

Sachsen-Anhalt
Landeshauptstadt: Magdeburg
Einwohner: 2,3 Millionen

Sachsen
Landeshauptstadt: Dresden
Einwohner: 4,1 Millionen

Thüringen
Landeshauptstadt: Erfurt
Einwohner: 2,2 Millionen

Bayern
Landeshauptstadt: München
Einwohner: 12,5 Millionen

Strukturen

VII Talking about people and things that you know

The verb kennen

To express that they know people, places, films, and books, German speakers use the verb **kennen** (*to know, to be acquainted with*). Unlike **wissen** (*to know as a fact*), which refers to information described in a clause, **kennen** generally refers to information contained in a direct object. The present tense endings of **kennen** are like those of regular verbs.

Kennst du unseren Nachbarn?	*Do you know our neighbor?*
Nein, ich **kenne** ihn nicht.	*No, I don't know him.*

When referring to cities by name, German speakers use the pronoun **es. Kennst du Mannheim? Ja, ich kenne *es* ziemlich gut. *Es* ist eine tolle Stadt.**

VIII Expressing relationships or ownership

Accusative of possessive adjectives

Earlier in this chapter, you learned about the possessive adjectives in the nominative case. Here are the accusative forms for the possessive adjectives.

		Masculine	Neuter	Feminine	Plural
		einen/keinen	ein/kein	eine/keine	—/keine
	Possessive Adjectives (accusative forms)				
Singular	my	**meinen** Vater	**mein** Kind	**meine** Mutter	**meine** Kinder
	your (informal)	**deinen** Vater	**dein** Kind	**deine** Mutter	**deine** Kinder
	your (formal)	**Ihren** Vater	**Ihr** Kind	**Ihre** Mutter	**Ihre** Kinder
	his	**seinen** Vater	**sein** Kind	**seine** Mutter	**seine** Kinder
	its	**seinen** Vater	**sein** Kind	**seine** Mutter	**seine** Kinder
	her	**ihren** Vater	**ihr** Kind	**ihre** Mutter	**ihre** Kinder
Plural	our	**uns(e)ren** Vater	**unser** Kind	**uns(e)re** Mutter	**uns(e)re** Kinder
	your (informal)	**euren** Vater	**euer** Kind	**eure** Mutter	**eure** Kinder
	your (formal)	**Ihren** Vater	**Ihr** Kind	**Ihre** Mutter	**Ihre** Kinder
	their	**ihren** Vater	**ihr** Kind	**ihre** Mutter	**ihre** Kinder

As in the nominative, the internal e is always dropped when adding an ending to **euer (eure, euren)** and optionally dropped when adding one to **unser (unsre, unsren).**

36 Freunde und Familie Ask your partner these questions about friends and family members.

BEISPIEL   S1: *Hier ist mein Freund Hans. Kennst du ihn?*
S2: *Ja, ich kenne deinen Freund Hans. (oder)*
Nein, ich kenne deinen Freund Hans nicht.

1. mein Freund Hans
2. meine Tochter Anna
3. Barbaras Bruder Karl
4. meine Freunde Volker und Katharina
5. Roberts Freundin Barbara
6. mein Partner Robert
7. meine Kinder Fabian und Helena
8. Katjas und Georgs Eltern

Strukturen

 Talking about more than one item

Noun plurals

In **Kapitel 1** you learned that every German noun is accompanied by **der, das,** or **die,** depending on the gender of the noun. There is only one definite article for the plural in both the nominative and the accusative cases: **die.** Here are the basic patterns for forming noun plurals.

You should memorize the gender and the plural form for each new noun as you learn it.

Plural marker	Singular	Plural
no ending	der Lehrer, das Fenster, der Onkel, das Mädchen	die Lehrer, die Fenster, die Onkel, die Mädchen
umlaut + no ending	der Vater, die Tochter, die Mutter	die Väter, die Töchter, die Mütter
-e ending	der Tag, der Freund, das Lokal	die Tage, die Freunde, die Lokale
umlaut + **-e** ending	der Gast, der Sohn, die Wurst	die Gäste, die Söhne, die Würste
-er ending	das Kind, das Bild	die Kinder, die Bilder
umlaut + **-er** ending	der Mann, das Schloss, das Buch	die Männer, die Schlösser, die Bücher
-n ending	der Neffe, die Tante, die Schwester	die Neffen, die Tanten, die Schwestern
-en ending	der Herr, der Professor, der Fotograf, der Automat, die Schönheit, die Möglichkeit, die Universität, die Zeitung	die Herren, die Professoren, die Fotografen, die Automaten, die Schönheiten, die Möglichkeiten, die Universitäten, die Zeitungen
-nen ending	die Studentin	die Studentinnen
change **-um** to **-en**	das Museum, das Studium	die Museen, die Studien
-s ending	der Chef, das Hotel	die Chefs, die Hotels

Good dictionaries list the plural changes of nouns. If two endings are listed, the second one is the plural ending. (The first ending denotes the genitive, a case that you will encounter in **Kapitel 10.**) The symbol - indicates no ending, ¨ indicates an umlaut, and **-e, -er, -n, -en, -s** indicate the ending. Feminine forms ending in **-in** may not show the plural form **-nen.**

The following simple rules may help you form certain plurals if you don't remember them. Examples of each case are included in the preceding chart.

- Neuter nouns with the suffix **-chen** add no plural ending.
- Feminine nouns ending in **-heit, -keit, -tät,** and **-ung** add **-en** in the plural.
- Nouns borrowed from English or French often (but not always) add **-s** in the plural.

Most nouns that add **-s** derive from a foreign language, mostly English. However, **der Computer**—like the words **Vater, Lehrer,** etc.—does not form the plural with **-s.**

 37 Wo ist der Plural? Circle all the features that indicate that the following words are plurals. If there are no features because a plural word looks the same as its singular form, underline the word.

Väter • Lehrer • Schwestern • Professoren • Studenten • Freunde • Hamburger • Türen • Kinder • Betten • Einwohner • Menschen • Straßen • Plätze • Fahrräder • Suppen • Colas • Familien

Ein Gedicht über meine Stadt
Zielaktivitäten

38 **Ein Gedicht** Read the following poem about the hometown of one of the
Vorsprung authors.

Danube

abbey

Melk, Österreich
Melk, Österreich
Melk an der Donau°
In Melk leben 6 000 Leute.
Melk gibt es seit mehr als tausend Jahren.
In Melk spricht man Deutsch – aber auch Englisch und ein bisschen
    Französisch oder Italienisch.
In Melk gibt es 380 Betten und 12 Restaurants.
In Melk können 380 Touristen schlafen.
Du kannst in Melk schlafen.
In Melk gibt es Sehenswürdigkeiten.
Melk hat ein Stift°, eine Altstadt, kein Hallenbad und keine Universität.
In Melk kann man Fahrrad fahren, mit dem Schiff auf der Donau fahren,
    spazieren gehen und auch Tennis spielen.
Melk ist schön, historisch und interessant
Möchtest du Melk sehen?
Sieh dir Melk an! Schlaf in Melk! Iss in Melk!
Melk an der Donau!
Mein Melk an der Donau – dein Melk an der Donau!

Ed Kashi/Corbis

Die Stadt Melk in Österreich ist über 1100 Jahre alt.

39 Ein Gedicht schreiben The structure of the poem is provided below. Use this structure to write a similar poem about your own hometown.

Melk, Österreich

Melk, Österreich	name of city and country or state
Melk an der Donau	full name, referencing a geographic landmark
In Melk leben 6 000 Leute.	population
Melk gibt es seit mehr als tausend Jahren.	age/history
In Melk spricht man Deutsch – aber auch Englisch und ein bisschen Französisch oder Italienisch.	languages spoken
In Melk gibt es 380 Betten und 12 Restaurants.	accommodations and restaurants
In Melk können 380 Touristen schlafen.	capacity for overnight guests
Du kannst in Melk schlafen.	make it personal
In Melk gibt es Sehenswürdigkeiten.	what there is
Melk hat ein Stift, eine Altstadt, kein Hallenbad und keine Universität.	the sights there (or not there)
In Melk kann man Fahrrad fahren, mit dem Schiff auf der Donau fahren, spazieren gehen und auch Tennis spielen.	activities that one can do
Melk ist schön, historisch und interessant	essential qualities
Möchtest du Melk sehen?	an inviting question
Sieh dir Melk an! Schlaf in Melk! Iss in Melk!	a series of imperatives
Melk an der Donau!	repeat first or second line
Mein Melk an der Donau – dein Melk an der Donau!	talk about it as yours and mine

 40 Schreibecke: **Meine Stadt: Information für Touristen.** Write a description of your home town or college/university town that you would like to send to some German friends. Include all the information that is relevant to tourists, e.g., about sports facilities, cultural events, historic sights, restaurants, and number of inhabitants.

41 Schreibecke: **Was kann man hier sehen?** You are anticipating a phone call from a young person from a Swiss village who is coming to your town for a one-year exchange. You will be speaking in German. Make some notes to yourself and write down at least five types of things in each category (**Unsere Stadt, Meine Universität**) that a person can see there. Think of all the things that might be different for your visitor.

BEISPIEL   *Hier kann man viele Parks sehen.*

Unsere Stadt		Meine Universität	
_____	_____	_____	_____
_____	_____	_____	_____
_____		_____	

42 Freie Kommunikation: **Rollenspiel: Ein Telefongespräch.** The Swiss exchange person calls you to get an understanding of life in your town. She/He is especially interested in getting a sense for the things she/he will see and need for a one-year exchange. Discuss the items you listed in the activity above. Here are some useful expressions:

Hallo
Hier ist ... ,
Ich möchte wissen ...
Was kann man dort sehen?
Gibt es viele ... ?
Vielen Dank für die Information.
Auf Wiederhören!

43 Freie Kommunikation: **Der neue Mitbewohner / Die neue Mitbewohnerin.** Your German roommate has just told you that one of his/her friends is coming to live with you. Since you feel your apartment is quite small and you know nothing about this person, ask your roommate questions about the new roommate's eating and drinking preferences, TV viewing habits, free-time activities, and any other personal traits. Discuss these issues in German.

Edvard March/Corbis

WORTSCHATZ

Tutorial Quiz
Audio Flashcards

Das Essen

das Frühstück *breakfast*

das Mittagessen *lunch*

das Abendbrot *light evening meal, supper*

das Abendessen *evening meal, supper*

die Vorspeise, -n *appetizer*

das Hauptgericht, -e *main course, entree*

die Nachspeise, -n *dessert*

der Nachtisch, -e *dessert*

der Apfel, ̈ *apple*

die Apfelsine, -n *orange*

der Aufschnitt *cold cuts*

die Banane, -n *banana*

das Bier, -e *beer*

die Bratwurst, ̈e *bratwurst*

das Brot, -e *bread*

das Brötchen, - *hard roll*

  ein belegtes Brötchen *roll spread with butter, jam, meat, etc.*

die Butter *butter*

die Cola, -s *cola*

das Ei, -er *egg*

  ein weich (hart) gekochtes Ei *soft-boiled (hard-boiled) egg*

das Eis *ice; ice cream*

die Erbse, -n *pea*

der Fisch *fish*

das Fleisch *meat*

das Geflügel *poultry, fowl*

das Gemüse *vegetable(s)*

das Getränk, -e *beverage, drink*

das Hackfleisch *ground beef*

das Hähnchen, - *chicken*

der Hamburger, - *hamburger*

der Honig *honey*

der/das Joghurt *yogurt*

der Kaffee *coffee*

die Karotte, -n *carrot*

die Kartoffel, -n *potato*

der Käse *cheese*

der Kaugummi, -s *chewing gum*

die Kirsche, -n *cherry*

der Kuchen, - *cake*

die Marmelade, -n *fruit jam, preserves*

die Milch *milk*

das Müesli *muesli (grain cereal)*

das Obst *fruit*

die Orange, -n *orange*

die Pute, -n *turkey*

der Quark *(a special German dairy spread)*

das Rindfleisch *beef*

der Saft, ̈e *juice*

der Salat, -e *lettuce; salad*

das Schweinefleisch *pork*

die Semmel, -n *hard roll (in southern Germany and Austria)*

die Suppe, -n *soup*

der Tee *tea*

die Tomate, -n *tomato*

die Traube, -n *grape*

das Wasser, ̈ *water*

  das Mineralwasser *mineral water*

der Wein, -e *wine*

die Wurst, ̈e *sausage*

Verben und Freizeitaktivitäten

die Freizeitaktivität, -en *leisure activity*

an·fangen *(er fängt an) to start, begin*

angeln *to fish*

besuchen *to visit*

essen *(er isst) to eat*

fahren *(er fährt) to travel*

Rad fahren *(er fährt Rad) to ride a bicycle (he's riding a bicycle)*

fern·sehen *(er sieht fern) to watch television*

geben *(er gibt) to give*

  Es gibt ... *There is/are . . .*

Was gibt es ... ? *What is (there) . . . ?*

Was gibt's? *What's up?*

ins Kino (Konzert, Theater) gehen *to go to the movies (concert, theater)*

halten *(er hält) to hold*

  halten von *to think of, have an opinion of*

Kaugummi kauen *to chew gum*

kennen *to know, be acquainted with (a person, a city)*

kochen *to cook*

können *to be able to, can*

lächeln *to smile*

laufen *(er läuft) to run*

  Ski laufen *to ski*

lesen *(er liest) to read*

mit·bringen *to bring along*

möchte *would like to*

nehmen *(er nimmt) to take*

reiten *to ride (horseback)*

schwimmen *to swim*

segeln *to sail*

sehen *(er sieht) to see*

singen *to sing*

spielen *to play*

  Fußball (Baseball, Basketball, Golf, Tennis, Volleyball) spielen *to play soccer (baseball, basketball, golf, tennis, volleyball)*

  Karten spielen *to play cards*

  Klavier (Flöte, Gitarre) spielen *to play piano (flute, guitar)*

sprechen *(er spricht) to speak*

tragen *(er trägt) to wear; to carry*

  Turnschuhe (Shorts) tragen *to wear athletic shoes (shorts)*

tun *to do*

  haben mit ... zu tun *to have to do with . . .*

vergessen *(er vergisst) to forget*

warten *to wait*
werden (er wird) *to become*
wissen (er weiß) *to know as a fact*

Die Stadt

der Bahnhof, -höfe *train station*
  der Hauptbahnhof, -höfe main/central train station
die Bibliothek, -en *library*
die Brücke, -n *bridge*
das Café, -s *café*
der Einwohner, - *inhabitant (male)*
die Einwohnerin, -nen *inhabitant (female)*
die Fußgängerzone, -n *pedestrian zone*
das Geschäft, -e *store*
  das Lebensmittelgeschäft (Musikgeschäft, Schuhgeschäft) *grocery store (music store, shoe store)*
die Hauptstraße, -n *main street*
die Kirche, -n *church*
die Kunsthalle, -n *art museum*
das Lokal, -e *pub, bar*
der Marktplatz, ̈e *market place*
das Museum, pl. Museen *museum*
der Platz, ̈e *plaza, square*
das Rathaus, ̈er *city hall*
das Restaurant, -s *restaurant*
  im Restaurant *in (at) a restaurant*
das Schwimmbad, ̈er *swimming pool*
  das Freibad *outdoor pool*
  das Hallenbad *indoor pool*
die Stadt, ̈e *city*
  die Altstadt *historic district*
der Supermarkt, ̈e *supermarket*
das Theater, - *theater*
der Turm, ̈e *tower*
  der Wasserturm *water tower*

Für den Touristen / Für die Touristin

das Bett, -en *bed*
der Campingplatz, ̈e *campground*
die Freizeit *free-time, leisure-time*
der Gasthof, ̈e *inn*
das Gepäck *luggage, baggage*
das Hotel, -s *hotel*
die Jugendherberge, -n *youth hostel*
die Pension, -en *guesthouse*
die Schifffahrt *boat ride*
das Schloss, ̈er *castle, palace*
die Sehenswürdigkeit, -en *sightseeing attraction*
das Zentrum, pl. Zentren *center*
  das Kongresszentrum, pl. Kongresszentren *convention center*
  das Kulturzentrum, pl. Kulturzentren *cultural center*
der Zoo, -s *zoo*

Im Geschäft und im Restaurant

der Becher *cup (ceramic, paper)*
die Flasche *bottle*
das Glas *glass*
das Gramm *gram*
das Kilo(gramm) *kilo(gram)*
der Kilometer *kilometer*
der Liter *liter*
der Meter *meter*
das Pfund *pound*
die Scheibe, -n *slice*
das Stück *piece*
die Tasse *cup*

Die Landeskunde Deutschlands

die Fläche, -n *land area*
der Fluss, ̈e *river*
die Landeskunde *geography*
die See, -n *sea*

die Nordsee *North Sea*
die Ostsee *Baltic Sea*

Possessivpronomen

dein *your (sg. informal)*
euer *your (pl. informal)*
ihr *her; their*
Ihr *your (sg. & pl. formal)*
mein *my*
sein *his; its*
unser *our*

Andere Ausdrücke

gar nicht *not at all*
in der Nähe (von) *in the vicinity (of)*

Andere Wörter

die Idee, -n *idea*
der Mensch, [-en], -en *person*
besser *better*
bestimmt *undoubtedly*
danach *afterward*
denn *because; then* (particle)
etwas *some(thing)*
immer *always*
langweilig *boring*
lieber *rather*
  lieber … als … *rather … than …*
man *one; you*
sicher *certainly, surely*
sondern *but, rather*
vielleicht *perhaps, maybe*
wahrscheinlich *most likely, probably*
wohl *in all likelihood, no doubt*
zuerst *first of all, firstly*
zuletzt *lastly*
zu viele *too many*

Meine eigenen Wörter

_____

_____

_____

_____

_____

_____

Many tourists who come to the United States and Canada are German speakers who love to visit, especially when prices for food, lodging, and transportation are a bargain by European standards. Major cities such as New York, Boston, Toronto, San Francisco, Atlanta, Chicago, Montreal, New Orleans, Orlando, Philadelphia, Vancouver, Washington, D.C., and Los Angeles are popular travel destinations. However, tourists from Germany, Austria, and Switzerland also flock to the sunny beaches of Florida and California, and to the wide-open spaces of Texas and the American Southwest.

Knowledge of German is often useful in the tourist industry for writing advertising copy, such as the ads you see here for San Francisco. It is also useful for interpreting for and assisting travelers whose command of English may be limited.

> The **Deutsch im Beruf** section will provide you with specific information about jobs in which you can use your language skills and will help develop language skills that are important on the job.
> In **Deutsch im Beruf 1,** you will read about employment opportunities in the tourist industry in the United States and as office support in German-speaking countries

1 **Wo sind die Touristen?** Have you heard anyone speak German where you live? The following is a list of places where you might encounter German-speaking tourists in the U.S. and Canada. Check the places where you have heard German spoken.

___ auf einem Oktoberfest   ___ am Flughafen (z. B. O'Hare in Chicago)
___ am Bahnhof   ___ im Hotel
___ auf der Straße   ___ im Restaurant
___ auf einem Campingplatz   ___ in einer Bank
___ am Strand°   ___ im Bus

beach

2 **Sehenswürdigkeit Nr. 1: Fisherman's Wharf** Tourist advertisements emphasize the positive and use colorful descriptive adjectives. Find the adjectives and nouns used in the text to describe Fisherman's Wharf.

1. Die _____ am Wasser.
2. Erleben Sie den _____ Fisherman's Wharf.
3. die _____ Attraktion in San Francisco
4. die _____ Aussicht auf die Bay
5. Restaurants mit vielen verschiedenen _____
6. Unterhaltung für die _____ Familie

Die Attraktion am Wasser.

Das beliebteste Ziel in San Francisco. Erleben Sie den historischen Fisherman´s Wharf, die klassische Attraktion in San Francisco. Schauen Sie in einem der kuriosen Stände im Freien hinein und probieren Sie ein Meeresfrüchte-Cocktail und lassen Sie sich vom verführerischen Aroma von frisch gebackenem Sauerteigbrot verführen, während Sie am Wharf entlang spazieren und die spektakuläre Aussicht auf die Bay genießen. Oder gehen Sie an Bord eines der historischen Schiffe am Wharf und erhaschen Sie einen Blick der berüchtigten Insel Alcatraz. Nur wenige Schritte von Ihrem Hotel finden Sie Restaurants mit vielen verschiedenen Spezialitäten, einzigartige Shops und Unterhaltung für die ganze Familie. Es ist immer etwas los am Wharf. www.visitfishermanswharf.com

Fisherman's WHARF SAN FRANCISCO

Reprinted by permission of San Francisco Chaperon.

3 **Sprechen Sie das deutlich aus** One important skill you should develop in order to use your German successfully on the job is clear pronunciation of the language. Practice the following German expressions for famous San Francisco attractions.

1. Die besten Stadtrundfahrten
2. Weingebiet
3. Sauerteigbrot
4. die Insel Alcatraz
5. Einzigartige Shops
6. Es ist immer etwas los am Wharf

4 **Kommen Sie bitte mit nach San Francisco!** Tourist ads often use verbs that describe activities tourists can do while visiting their destination. Find the verbs used in these ads and the one on the previous page to engage the reader and invite him or her to experience San Francisco actively.

booths full of oddities / outdoors experience

1. _____ Sie in einem der kuriosen Stände° im Freien° hinein.
2. _____ Sie° den historischen Fisherman's Wharf.
3. _____ Sie an Bord eines der historischen Schiffe.
4. _____ Sie Yosemite an einem Tag: _____ Sie mit dem Zug bis nach Merced ...
5. _____ Sie einen Aperitif und den Sonnenuntergang in unserer Bar.

Toranico/Shutterstock.com

Im Flughafen: Mit Flugticket und Gepäck kann sie endlich losfliegen!

Unterwegs

In this chapter you will learn how to make informal requests and express what you can, must, want to, should, and may do.

Kommunikative Funktionen

> Telling friends or relatives to do something

> Making inclusive suggestions

> Expressing ability, fondness, expected obligation, permission, prohibition, necessity, and strong desire

> Expressing spatial movement, the recipient of something, opposition, and omission

Strukturen

> The informal (**du-, ihr-**) imperative

> Inclusive suggestions (**wir-**imperative)

> Particles with the imperative

> Modal verbs (**können, mögen/möchte, sollen, dürfen, müssen, wollen**)

> Accusative prepositions

Vokabeln

> Das Gepäck

> Eigenschaften

Kulturelles

> Studienmöglichkeiten für Deutschlernende

> Rad fahren

> Mit der Bahn fahren

> Mit dem Auto fahren

> Frankfurt am Main

Mutters Ratschläge

Anna packt die Koffer für ihre Reise nach Deutschland. Sie ist gespannt auf das Jahr in Deutschland, aber ihre Mutter macht sich Sorgen wegen° Anna und der Reise. Sie gibt Anna Ratschläge, aber Anna will nichts davon hören. Anna hat andere Vorstellungen°. In Deutschland warten die Günthers auf° Annas Ankunft°. Tante Uschi hat auch ein paar Ratschläge für Katja und Georg.

macht ... wegen: *is worried about*

ideas / warten auf: *wait for*

arrival

> Beginning in **Kapitel 4,** most of the activity directions are given in German. Try to learn the meanings of the words used. They are used frequently.

answer / following

still

Kreuzen Sie... an: *check the appropriate category*

Vorschau

1 Thematische Fragen Beantworten° Sie die folgenden° Fragen auf Deutsch.

Anna ist noch° zu Hause in Indiana. Sie packt für zwei Semester in Tübingen. Was kommt mit nach Deutschland? Was bleibt zu Hause? Kreuzen Sie die passende Kategorie an° und bilden Sie dann Sätze.

BEISPIEL *Der warme Pullover kommt mit nach Deutschland.*
Der Hund bleibt zu Hause.

	Nach Deutschland	Bleibt zu Hause
1. der warme Pullover	○	○
2. die Kamera	○	○
3. die Kreditkarte	○	○
4. der Reisepass°	○	○
5. das Auto	○	○
6. der Fernseher	○	○
7. der Hund	○	○
8. die Familienfotos	○	○
9. das Adressbuch	○	○
10. der Laptop	○	○

passport

2 Für die Reise Was ist wichtig° für Sie, wenn Sie eine Reise machen? Kreuzen Sie an, was für Sie stimmt.

	Wichtig	Nicht wichtig
1. Verwandte oder Freunde besuchen	○	○
2. Shoppen gehen und Geld ausgeben	○	○
3. Andenken° kaufen	○	○
4. Sehenswürdigkeiten° (z. B. Schlösser) sehen	○	○
5. Ansichtskarten° schreiben	○	○
6. Alkohol trinken	○	○
7. Ihre Aktivitäten auf Facebook dokumentieren	○	○
8. Fotos machen	○	○
9. neue Leute kennenlernen	○	○
10. tanzen gehen	○	○

important

souvenirs
the sights
post cards

3 Wortdetektiv Welche Wörter und Ausdrücke° bedeuten° ungefähr° das Gleiche?

expressions / mean / approximately

Deutsch	Englisch
1. mit•nehmen	a. carefully
2. die Kleidung	b. clothing
3. ich muss	c. to take along
4. vorsichtig	d. I have to
5. sich Sorgen machen	e. to hitchhike
6. per Anhalter fahren	f. to worry
7. Andenken kaufen	g. suitcase
8. der Koffer	h. to buy souvenirs
9. Geld aus•geben	i. to help
10. ich soll	j. surrounding area
11. helfen	k. I should
12. die Umgebung	l. to spend money

Brennpunkt Kultur

Web Search
Web Link

Studienmöglichkeiten° für Deutschlernende *study options*

Courtesy of J. Douglas Guy.

Named for Germany's most famous classical author and playwright, Johann Wolfgang von Goethe (1749–1832), the **Goethe-Institut** promotes the German language and provides cultural events. The organization offers language classes at six sites in the U.S., three in Canada, and fourteen in Germany, representative of the 136 **Goethe-Institute** in 92 countries around the world. The institutes maintain lending libraries and organize cultural events such as film series, concerts, lectures, and traditional celebrations to enhance the understanding of German culture in the local community. Working on behalf of Austria, the **Austrian Cultural Institute** of New York City also organizes exhibits, film festivals, and lectures and facilitates student exchanges and dissemination of information about Austria. The **Swiss Institute** in New York, Switzerland's foremost cultural institute in the United States, promotes artistic dialogue between Switzerland and the U.S. through various cultural programs.

Many U.S. and Canadian colleges also offer study and internship programs abroad in Germany, Austria, or Switzerland. A year abroad enriches student appreciation for the German language and culture while raising that student's language skills to their highest level.

Kulturkreuzung

Wo in Deutschland, Österreich oder der Schweiz hat Ihre Universität Studienprogramme? Verbringt man ein oder zwei Semester im Ausland? Kennen Sie Studenten oder Studentinnen an Ihrer Universität aus Europa? Warum, meinen Sie, kommen diese Studenten an Ihre Universität?

Hören Sie gut zu. *(Listen carefully).*

Hannelore Adler hat viele Ratschläge für Anna, aber Anna interpretiert sie anders.

Frau Adler sagt: *Anna denkt:*

Trink nicht so viel Cola!

Dann muss ich wohl Bier trinken, aber das mag ich nicht.

Nimm genug warme Kleidung mit!

Darf ich zwei Koffer nach Deutschland mitnehmen?

Gib nicht zu viel Geld für Andenken aus!

Ich will aber Andenken kaufen.

Fahr nie per Anhalter!

Dann kann ich ein Fahrrad kaufen.

Tante Uschi hat auch viele Ratschläge für ihre Familie. Die Günthers haben auch Missverständnisse.

Und in mancher Hinsicht sind meine Schwester und ich verschieden°:   *different*

>Ich mag klassische Musik, aber sie nicht.
>Ich bin unsportlich, aber sie ist sehr sportlich.
>Ich bin relativ unsicher, aber sie ist sehr selbstsicher.
>Sie ist sehr locker und lustig, aber ich bin relativ steif und ernst.
>Sie ist sehr offen und gesellig, aber ich bin schüchtern.

51 Schreibecke: **Eine Onlineannonce.** Sie suchen einen Freund/eine Freundin online. Schreiben Sie, wie diese ideale Person sein soll. Schreiben Sie 8-10 Sätze. Was ist wichtig? Rauchen? Sportlich sein? Dann schreiben Sie 5 Sätze über Ihre eigene Person.

BEISPIEL *Ich suche einen Freund/eine Freundin. Er/Sie muss intelligent sein. Er/Sie sollte viel Kaffee trinken. Er/Sie sollte kein Bier trinken. Er/Sie sollte nur vegetarisch essen usw. Ich bin super schön und sehr selbstständig. Ich habe... Ich kann...*

Brennpunkt Kultur 🌐 Web Search / Web Link

Mit dem Auto fahren

The country that brought the world high-performance automobiles like Mercedes-Benz, Audi, Porsche, and BMW has a long-standing love of driving. German manufacturers like Opel and Volkswagen demonstrated high-quality engineering at an affordable price point, helping Germany acquire a world-wide reputation for quality cars and automotive products. Yet owning and driving a car in Germany is expensive. Fuel can cost as much as $9.00 (US) per gallon, and drivers are required to pay annual taxes and high insurance rates. Acquiring a driver's license **(der Führerschein)** is expensive by itself. Student drivers taking classes at a **Fahrschule** must be at least 17 years old and are required to take 25-45 hours of on-road instruction and another 11 hours of driving theory. This brings the investment to about €1000. After taking a first aid course, a vision test, a written test and a road test, applicants can earn their preliminary license (**die Prüfbescheinigung**). Once they reach the age of 18, they can upgrade to a full **Klasse B** or **BE** license. With this license, drivers are allowed to drive a passenger vehicle (**der Personenkraftwagen, der PKW**). Those wishing to drive a motorcycle, truck, or other motorized vehicle have to apply for different driver's licenses with different requirements.

Kulturkreuzung

Haben Sie ein Auto? Finden Sie Autofahren billig oder teuer? Warum? Können Sie ohne ein Auto leben?

Endspurt: Online Listening Text & Activities.

Fahrradunfälle

Zielaktivitäten

52 Der Fahrradunfall Lesen Sie den Text über den Fahrradunfall von Michael R. und dann schreiben Sie über einen fiktiven Fahrradunfall von Inge Stark.

occur

> ### Rund 75 % aller Fahrradunfälle passieren° zwischen Radfahrern und Autofahrern
>
> Ein sonniger Tag im Mai. Michael R., Fahrradfahrer aus Augsburg, hält an der Kreuzung: Die Ampel zeigt rot. Als es grün wird, will Michael R. losfahren. Doch links von ihm fährt eine große dunkle Limousine und will nach rechts abbiegen. Der Autofahrer sieht Michael nicht, biegt rechts ab und trifft ihn am Arm. Michael fällt vom Rad auf den Boden°. Der Autofahrer spricht am Handy, sieht ihn nicht und fährt einfach weiter. Michael steht auf, holt sein kaputtes Rad und schiebt° es nach Hause.

ground

pushes

Reprinted by permission of Allgemeiner Deutscher Fahrrad-Club.

53 Selber schreiben Inge Stark hat einen Fahrradunfall auf der Straße. Schreiben Sie über den Unfall. Benutzen Sie den Text in Aktivität 52 und die Ausdrücke in der folgenden Liste als Hilfe. Der erste Satz beginnt so:

BEISPIEL *Es ist ein ... Tag im September. Es ...*

> - ein sonniger/regnerischer/kalter Tag im September
> - 19 Uhr abends
> - dunkel
> - Inge Stark - sportliche Fahrradfahrerin aus Tübingen
> - an einer Ampel halten
> - viele Autos unterwegs / laut
> - ein alter Mann im Auto / nach rechts abbiegen
> - nicht so gut sehen können
> - Hunger haben
> - am Handy sprechen
> - nach Hause zum Abendessen fahren möchte
> - auf den Boden fallen
> - unvorsichtig
> - glücklich

Brennpunkt Kultur

Frankfurt am Main

Frankfurt am Main, located in the heart of Germany as its fifth-largest city on the banks of the Main River **(der Main)** in the state of Hesse **(Hessen),** is both the geographic crossroads of the country and its key economic center. The major gateway to Germany and the nation's most important transportation center, Frankfurt is home to Europe's busiest international airport, **der Frankfurter Flughafen,** the German international airline **Deutsche Lufthansa,** and the German Federal Railway, **die Deutsche Bahn.** Frankfurt is also the German "Wall Street": the home of the German federal bank **(die Bundesbank)**, the national stock exchange **(die Frankfurter Wertpapierbörse),** and many large corporations and publishing houses. Reflecting the city's important role in international finance, the Monetary Institute of the European Community **(das Europäische Währungsinstitut)** and the European Central Bank **(die Europäische Zentralbank)** are situated in Frankfurt. Frankfurt is also famous for its many trade fairs, among them **Messe Frankfurt**, the third largest in the world.

Courtesy of J. Douglas Guy.

MAINHATTAN pur
Frankfurt am Main
AVM Advanced Vision
Marketing u. Vertriebs GmbH

Der Römer in Frankfurt am Main: Diese junge Familie geht mit ihrem Kind durch Frankfurts Altstadt spazieren.

Frankfurt is a key center of German culture and history. Germany's most famous author, Johann Wolfgang von Goethe, was born there. In 1848, the city was the site of the first attempt to establish a united German nation through a representative assembly. Over 40% of Frankfurt's residents are of immigrant backgrounds, coming from one of 180 nationalities living in this multicultural city.

The people of Frankfurt enjoy a lively theater, opera, and music scene. They relax by visiting the numerous museums along the Main River **(das Museumsufer),** taking their children to the world-class **Frankfurter Zoo,** spending a day in the glass-enclosed **Palmengarten** (botanical garden), and sipping the popular local apple wine **(Stöffche** or **Äppelwoi (or Ebbelwoi))** in the cozy pubs of Sachsenhausen.

Kulturkreuzung

Welche Städte in den USA oder in Kanada kann man mit Frankfurt vergleichen°? *compare*
Wo ist die Börse in Kanada? In den USA? Wo ist der größte° Flughafen in den *largest*
USA? In Kanada? Wie heißt der/die bekannteste Schriftsteller(in)° von Kanada? *bekannteste ...: most*
Von den USA?   *famous writer*

ii 54 Freie Kommunikation: **Mutter/Vater und Tochter/Sohn.** Machen Sie dieses Rollenspiel mit einem Partner/einer Partnerin: Ihr Sohn/Ihre Tochter fährt bald nach Frankfurt. Welche Ratschläge haben Sie für ihn/sie? Wie reagiert Ihr Sohn/Ihre Tochter auf die Ratschläge?

BEISPIEL   S1 (MUTTER/VATER): *Sprich nicht mit Fremden!*
              S2 (SOHN/TOCHTER): *Was? Ich soll nicht mit Fremden sprechen? Wie*
                                 kann ich neue Leute kennenlernen?
              S1 (MUTTER/VATER): *Geh in die Uni und sprich nur mit den*
                                 Professoren und mit Studenten.

⬅ 55 Schreibecke: **Anna im Flugzeug.** Sie sind Anna im Flugzeug nach Frankfurt. Das Flugzeug landet in einer Stunde. Sie wissen, Sie sehen bald Ihre Verwandten und müssen dann Deutsch sprechen. Sie sind ein bisschen nervös. Was können Sie wohl sagen? Machen Sie sich zu den folgenden Fragen Notizen°.

1. Was sollen Sie in Deutschland machen? Was denken Sie? Was denken Ihre Eltern?
2. Was dürfen Sie in Deutschland nicht machen? Was denken Sie? Und Ihre Eltern?
3. Wie fühlen Sie sich jetzt?
4. Was wollen Sie machen, sobald° Sie in Weinheim sind?

notes

as soon as

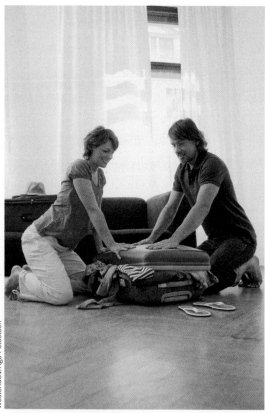

Westend61/Age Fotostock

Ich kann nicht alles mitnehmen. Was brauche ich wirklich für diese Reise?

WORTSCHATZ

Tutorial Quiz
Audio Flashcards

Die Reise

das Adressbuch, ¨er *address book*
das Andenken, - *souvenir*
die Bahn *railroad*
die Bordkarte, -n *boarding pass*
der Brief, -e *letter*
der Flug, ¨e *flight*
der Flughafen, ¨ *airport*
der Flugschein, -e *airline ticket*
das Flugzeug, -e *airplane*
das Geschenk, -e *gift*
der Hauptbahnhof, ¨e *main train station*
der Pass (Reisepass), ¨e *passport*
der Platz, ¨e *seat, place; space, room*
die Reise, -n *trip*
der Zug, ¨e *train*
mit der Bahn fahren *to travel by train*
per Anhalter fahren (er fährt per Anhalter) *to hitchhike*
unterwegs *underway*

Das Gepäck

das Handgepäck *carry-on luggage*
die Handtasche, -n *handbag, purse*
der Koffer, - *suitcase, trunk*
der Kulturbeutel, - *cosmetics / toiletries case*
der Rucksack, ¨e *backpack*
die Tasche, -n *bag*

Die Kleidung

der Anzug, ¨e *suit*
der Badeanzug, ¨e *(woman's) bathing suit*
die Badehose, -n *(man's) bathing suit*
die Bluse, -n *blouse*
der Handschuh, -e *glove*
das Hemd, -en *shirt*
das Hoodie, -s *hooded sweatshirt*
die Hose, -n *trousers, pants*

die Jacke, -n *jacket*
die Jeans (pl.) *jeans*
das Kleid, -er *dress*
die Kleidung, -en *clothing, clothes*
die Krawatte, -n *tie*
der Mantel, ¨ *overcoat*
der Pullover, - *pullover sweater*
der Rock, ¨e *skirt*
der/das Sakko, -s *sports jacket*
die Sandale, -n *sandal*
der Schal, -s *scarf*
der Schuh, -e *shoe*
die Socke, -n *sock*
der Stiefel, - *boot*
die Strumpfhose, -n *panty hose, stockings*
das T-Shirt, -s *tee-shirt*
die Unterhose, -n *underwear*
die Unterwäsche (pl.) *underwear*
der Wintermantel, ¨ *winter coat*

Die Toilettenartikel

das Deo, -s *deodorant*
die Haarbürste, -n *hair brush*
der Kamm, ¨e *comb*
der Lippenstift, -e *lipstick*
der Nagellack *nail polish*
der Spiegel, - *mirror*
die Zahnbürste, -n *toothbrush*
die Zahnpasta, -pasten *toothpaste*

Persönliche Gegenstände

die Bankkarte, -n *bank card, ATM card*
der Gegenstand, ¨e *object*
das Geld, -er *money*
das Handy, -s *cell phone*
der i-Pod, -s
die Kamera, -s *camera*
die Kreditkarte, -n *credit card*

der Laptop, -s *laptop computer*
das Portemonnaie, -s *wallet*
das Wörterbuch, ¨er *dictionary*

Die Eigenschaften

die Eigenschaft, -en *personal trait, quality, characteristic*
doof *goofy in an annoying way*
dumm *dumb*
einfallslos *uncreative*
ernst *serious*
faul *lazy*
fleißig *hardworking, industrious; busy*
gesellig *gregarious, sociable*
glücklich *happy*
heiter *funny, cheerful*
intelligent *intelligent*
interessant *interesting*
kreativ *creative*
laut *loud, noisy*
locker *relaxed, cool*
lustig *funny, jovial*
müde *tired*
musikalisch *musical*
nervös *nervous*
offen *open*
ruhig *quiet, peaceful, calm*
schüchtern *shy*
selbstsicher *self-assured*
sportlich *athletic*
steif *stiff, ill-at-ease*
sympathisch *likeable, pleasant, nice*
tot *dead*
unfreundlich *unfriendly*
unglücklich *unhappy*
unmusikalisch *unmusical*
unsicher *unsure, insecure*
unsportlich *unathletic*
unsympathisch *unlikeable, disagreeable*

Radfahren, Autos und Verkehr

der Ausweis, -e *identification card, permit*

der Radfahrausweis *bicycle permit*

das Auto, -s *automobile, car*

die Autobahn, -en *autobahn, freeway*

der (Auto)bus, -se *bus*

das Benzin *gasoline*

das Fahrrad, ¨-er *bicycle*

der Führerschein, -e *driver's license*

der Fußgänger, - *pedestrian*

die Kreuzung *the intersection*

das Moped, *-s moped*

die Prüfung, -en *test*

der Radfahrer, - / die Radfahrerin, -nen *cyclist, bicycle rider*

die Regel, -n *rule, regulation*

der Sicherheitshelm *safety helmet*

das Verbot, -e *ban, prohibition*

der Verkehr *traffic*

das Verkehrsschild, -er *traffic sign*

die Vorfahrt *right of way*

der Wagen, - *car*

der Weg, -e *path*

> **der Fußweg** *footpath*
>
> **der Radweg** *bicycle path*

gefährlich *dangerous*

geradeaus *straight ahead*

langsam *slow*

links *left*

rechts *right*

schnell *fast*

Akkusativpräpositionen

durch *through*

für *for*

gegen *against; around (a time)*

ohne *without*

um *around; at (a time)*

Modalverben

dürfen (er darf) *may; to be allowed to, permitted to*

> **ich darf nicht** *I must not*

können (er kann) *can; to be able to*

möchte (ich möchte, du möchtest, er/sie möchte, etc.) *would like to (immediate relevance)*

mögen (ich mag, du magst, er/sie mag, etc.) *to like (a thing, a person) (generally)*

müssen (er muss) *must; to have to, be required to*

> **ich muss nicht** *I don't need to*

sollen *to be supposed to; ought to*

wollen (er will) *to want to*

Andere Verben

ab•biegen *to turn*

ab•steigen *to get off (a bike)*

achten auf *pay attention to*

Angst haben *to be afraid*

an•halten *to stop*

auf•passen *to pay attention*

aus•geben (er gibt aus) *to spend (money)*

bedeuten *to mean, have the meaning of*

benutzen *to use*

beschreiben *to describe*

bezahlen *to pay*

brauchen *to need*

> **ich brauche nicht** *I don't have to*

denken *to think*

denken an ... *to think about . . .*

helfen (er hilft) *to help*

mit•nehmen (er nimmt mit) *to take (something) along*

packen *to pack*

schicken *to send*

schieben *to push*

Andere Wörter

ab und zu *now and then*

besonders *especially*

genug *enough*

gleich *similar, same*

leider *unfortunately*

mal *once*

neu *new*

nie *never*

niemand *nobody, no one*

noch *still; again*

oft *often*

spät (später) *late (later)*

> **spätestens** *at the latest*

zu spät *(too) late*

ungefähr *approximately*

vorsichtig *careful*

wichtig *important*

ziemlich *somewhat*

Andere Ausdrücke

das heißt (d. h.) *that is (to say)*

Hab keine Angst! Don't be afraid.

Mach dir keine Sorgen! *Don't worry.*

noch einmal *once again*

Meine eigenen Wörter

_____

_____

_____

_____

_____

Ein Spaziergang Hand in Hand kann echt romantisch sein.

FredFroese/iStockphoto.com

Freundschaften

In this chapter you will learn how to talk about events in the past, about personal relationships, the weather, and the seasons.

Kommunikative Funktionen
> Talking about past events
> Describing weather conditions and seasons
> Describing personal relationships
> Expressing what you know and don't know
> Expanding on an opinion or idea
> Giving reasons
> Positioning information in a German sentence

Strukturen
> The conversational past
> Subordinate clauses with **ob, dass, wenn,** and **weil**

> Expressions with **zu** + infinitive
> Word order: subject-verb inversion, two-part verbs, and verb position in subordinate clauses

Vokabeln
> Das Wetter
> Die Jahreszeiten
> Freundschaft und Liebe

Kulturelles
> Hansestadt Hamburg
> **Bekannte** oder **Freunde?**

Die Geschichte von Tante Uschi und Onkel Hannes

Onkel Hannes und Tante Uschi sitzen an einem Abend mit Anna zu Hause in Weinheim und sprechen über ihre Studienzeit in Hamburg. Hier erzählen° sie Anna, wie sie sich kennengelernt haben.

tell

Vorschau

1 Thematische Fragen: Meine Jobs Viele Studenten müssen arbeiten° und ihr Studium selbst° finanzieren. Kreuzen Sie die Jobs an, die Sie auch schon° gehabt haben. Bei welchen Jobs trifft° man interessante Leute°?

work
themselves
already / meets / people

	Meine Jobs	Jobs mit interessanten Leuten
1. in einer Kneipe als Kellner(in)° arbeiten	○	○
2. in der Bibliothek arbeiten	○	○
3. in einem Geschäft arbeiten	○	○
4. in einem Krankenhaus° arbeiten	○	○
5. Pizza ausfahren°	○	○
6. Nachhilfestunden geben°	○	○
7. im Restaurant kochen oder abwaschen	○	○
8. babysitten	○	○
9. Karten spielen und Geld gewinnen	○	○
10. Taxi fahren	○	○

waiter/waitress

hospital
deliver
***Nachhilfestunden … :** tutor*

2 Kennenlernen Sie finden jemanden attraktiv. Was machen Sie?

	Das mache ich.	Das mache ich nicht.
1. etwas fallen lassen°	○	○
2. viel Bier trinken	○	○
3. tolle° Kleider tragen	○	○
4. freundlich sein	○	○
5. die Person direkt ansprechen	○	○
6. wild tanzen	○	○
7. viel Geld ausgeben	○	○
8. etwas Intelligentes sagen°	○	○
9. Komplimente machen	○	○
10. anstarren° und warten	○	○

***fallen lassen:** drop*

cool

say

stare

3 Zeitdetektiv Hier sind Sätze im Präsens. Welche Sätze im Perfekt° bedeuten ungefähr das Gleiche?

conversational past

Präsens
1. Du hast eine Erkältung°.
2. Du tust mir leid°.
3. Er gibt nie Trinkgeld°.
4. Danach heiraten° wir.
5. Ich bin in Tante Uschi verliebt°.

6. Er küsst° mich.
7. Er sieht gut aus.
8. Ich gehe oft in die Kneipe.
9. Wir verbringen viel Zeit miteinander.
10. Ich lade sie ins Theater ein.

Perfekt
a. Er hat nie Trinkgeld gegeben.
b. Du hast eine Erkältung gehabt.
c. Ich war in Tante Uschi verliebt.
d. Du hast mir leidgetan.
e. Danach haben wir geheiratet.
f. Ich habe sie ins Theater eingeladen.
g. Ich bin oft in die Kneipe gegangen.
h. Er hat gut ausgesehen.
i. Er hat mich geküsst.
j. Wir haben viel Zeit miteinander verbracht.

cold
***Du ...:** I feel sorry for you*
tips
marry
in love

kisses

> The verb **sein** is frequently used in the simple past. This is explained later in this chapter.

 4 Gegensätze Finden Sie das Wort mit der umgekehrten° Bedeutung.

opposite

BEISPIEL Geld verdienen   *Geld ausgeben*

1. ganz schlimm
2. dort
3. zusammen
4. bald
5. arbeiten
6. erzählen

a. zuhören
b. später
c. spielen
d. hier
e. sehr gut
f. allein

> **Zeitdetektiv.** You will learn how to form the conversational past later in this chapter. For now, recognizing it is sufficient.

Sprache im Alltag: Article with first names

German speakers frequently use a definite article with first names to signal familiarity.

Die Uschi hat als Kellnerin gearbeitet.

Der Hannes war nervös.

Hamburger Wappen

Track 1-11

Hören Sie gut zu.

Onkel Hannes und Tante Uschi erzählen Anna, wie sie sich kennengelernt haben.

Uschi hat in Hamburg Pharmazie studiert und als Kellnerin in einer Studentenkneipe gearbeitet. Sie hat Geld fürs Studium verdient.

Ich bin oft in die Kneipe gegangen, weil mir die Uschi gut gefallen hat.

Ja, und er hat nie Trinkgeld gegeben. Wenigstens hat er gut ausgesehen ...

Und dann habe ich sie eines Tages ins Theater eingeladen, und nachher haben wir zusammen ein Bier getrunken. Wir haben leidenschaftlich diskutiert ...

Ja, aber nach dem zweiten Bier war ich etwas mutiger.

Leidenschaftlich diskutiert? Du warst so nervös, du hast keine drei Worte gesagt.

Und später haben wir einen romantischen Spaziergang an der Alster gemacht. Dort haben wir einander zum ersten Mal geküsst.

Romantisch, sagst du? Es hat die ganze Zeit geregnet, und du hast eine ganz schlimme Erkältung gehabt.

Aber du hast mich trotzdem geküsst!

Ich habe dich nur geküsst, weil du mir so leidgetan hast.

Note the meaning of the following words in the Anlauftext; **danach, nachher:** *after that, afterwards;* **trotzdem:** *nevertheless;* **und so weiter:** *and so on;* **weil:** *because;* **wenigstens:** *at least;* **zum ersten Mal:** *for the first time.*

© Cengage Learning 2014

Na, trotzdem ... Von da an haben wir viel Zeit miteinander verbracht. Wir haben oft zusammen gekocht und gegessen und sind auch abends ausgegangen.

Ja, wir haben tolle Nächte in St. Pauli durchgemacht. Getanzt, getrunken und so weiter ...

Und sonntags sind wir immer zum Fischmarkt gegangen ...

... und an der Elbe spazieren gegangen.

Er hat auch oft ein Liebesgedicht für mich geschrieben.

Ich liebe dich.

O je! Das habe ich ganz vergessen. Ich war bis über beide Ohren in die Uschi verliebt.

Deshalb haben wir uns auch verlobt.

Und bald danach haben wir geheiratet.

Rückblick

5 **Stimmt das?** Stimmen diese Aussagen zum Text? Wenn nicht, was stimmt?

	Ja, das stimmt.	Nein, das stimmt nicht.
1. Uschi hat in Heidelberg studiert.	○	○
2. Hannes hat Uschi sehr viel Trinkgeld gegeben.	○	○
3. Hannes und Uschi sind zusammen ins Kino gegangen.	○	○
4. Nachher haben Hannes und Uschi einen Spaziergang gemacht.	○	○
5. Hannes hat Uschi zum ersten Mal im Regen geküsst.	○	○
6. Uschi war krank° und sie hat Hannes leidgetan.	○	○
7. Uschi und Hannes haben viel Zeit zusammen verbracht.	○	○
8. Uschi hat ein Gedicht für Hannes geschrieben.	○	○
9. Hannes war in Uschi verliebt.	○	○
10. Uschi und Hannes haben geheiratet.	○	○

sick

··························

Complete the **Ergänzen Sie** activity in the Student Activities Manual before doing the next activity.

··························

sequence

6 **Gut organisiert** Wie ist die korrekte Reihenfolge°?

_____ haben in St. Pauli Musik gehört, getanzt, getrunken

_____ ist oft in die Kneipe gegangen

___1___ hat in der Kneipe gearbeitet

_____ haben einen romantischen Spaziergang an der Alster gemacht

_____ haben einander zum ersten Mal geküsst

_____ haben geheiratet

_____ hat Uschi ins Theater eingeladen

_____ haben viel Zeit zusammen verbracht

7 **Romantisch?** Welche Aktivitäten, die Uschi und Hannes zusammen gemacht haben, finden Sie romantisch? Welche langweilig? Kreuzen Sie **Romantisch** oder **Langweilig** an. Dann fragen Sie einen Partner/eine Partnerin.

BEISPIEL S1: *Findest du es romantisch oder langweilig, ins Theater zu gehen?*
S2: *Das finde ich romantisch (langweilig).*

	Romantisch		Langweilig	
	Ich	Partner(in)	Ich	Partner(in)
1. ins Theater zu gehen	○	○	○	○
2. zusammen ein Bier zu trinken	○	○	○	○
3. einen Spaziergang im Regen zu machen	○	○	○	○
4. eine Person zu küssen	○	○	○	○
5. ein Liebesgedicht zu schreiben	○	○	○	○
6. tanzen zu gehen	○	○	○	○
7. auf einen Fischmarkt zu gehen	○	○	○	○
8. zusammen zu kochen und zu essen	○	○	○	○

→ **8** Kurz gefragt Beantworten Sie diese Fragen auf Deutsch.

1. Was hat Tante Uschi in Hamburg gemacht?
2. Wie hat Onkel Hannes Tante Uschi kennengelernt?
3. Was war ihr erstes Date? Wer hat wen eingeladen?
4. Was haben sie nachher zusammen gemacht?
5. Wo haben sie einander zum ersten Mal geküsst? Wer hat wen geküsst?
6. Was haben sie von da an gemacht?
7. Was hat Onkel Hannes für Tante Uschi geschrieben?

→ **9** Textdetektiv: **Anlauftext.** Use the *Anlauftext* to recognize important aspects of German structure and usage.

Uschi …	hat in Hamburg Pharmazie studiert.
	hat als Kellnerin in einer Studentenkneipe gearbeitet.
Hannes …	ist oft in die Kneipe gegangen.
	hat nie Trinkgeld gegeben.
Uschi und Hannes …	haben oft zusammen gekocht.
	sind auch abends ausgegangen.

1. Look at the examples above. To express past activities, German speakers generally use . . .
   a. one verb.   b. two verbs.   c. three verbs.

2. One of the verbs is always . . .
   a. at the beginning of the sentence.   b. at the end of the sentence.

3. The first verb is always called a helping or auxiliary verb. It . . .
   a. is always a form of *haben*.   b. is always a form of *sein*.   c. can be either.

4. Which of the two verbs in the sentence has an ending that matches or agrees with the subject of the sentence?
   a. the first verb, the auxiliary verb   b. the second verb, the past participle

5. Look at the past participles in the examples above. What prefix do most have at the beginning? What two different types of endings do they have?

6. Match the past participles from the examples above with their infinitive forms.

Past Participle	Infinitive
a. gegangen	1. arbeiten
b. ausgegangen	2. studieren
c. studiert	3. ausgehen
d. gekocht	4. gehen
e. gegeben	5. kochen
f. gearbeitet	6. geben

7. Which of the two auxiliary verbs is more common?
   a. *sein*   b. *haben*

8. In the examples from the *Anlauftext*, the only verb that takes *sein* as its auxiliary verb of the past tense is . . .
   a. sehen.   b. gehen.   c. gefallen.   d. studieren.

Strukturen

 Talking about past events

The conversational past

When speaking or writing informally about past events, German speakers often use the conversational past, which is also sometimes called the present perfect tense (**das Perfekt**). The conversational past is formed with a present tense form of the auxiliary verb (**das Hilfsverb**), **haben** or **sein**, and the past participle of the verb (**das Partizip**). The past participle is frequently, although not always, identifiable by a **ge-** prefix and either a **-t** or **-en** ending. The past participle is always positioned as the last word in a sentence or clause.

| Onkel Hannes **ist** in die Kneipe **gegangen.** | *Uncle Hannes went to the pub.* |
| Onkel Hannes **hat** Tante Uschi **geküsst.** | *Uncle Hannes kissed Aunt Uschi.* |

The German conversational past (e.g., **sie hat geschrieben**) looks like the English present perfect *(she has written)*, but it does not have the same meaning. German present perfect is most commonly used for actions completed in the past. In contrast, the English present perfect often expresses uncompleted actions that continue into the present.

> *German conversational past*
> Ich **habe** einen Brief **geschrieben.**   *I **wrote** a letter.*
>
> *English present perfect*
> *I **have known** him for three years.*   Ich **kenne** ihn seit drei Jahren.

A few common verbs, such as **sein** and **haben,** seldom occur in their conversational past forms, even in informal language. Instead, they frequently appear in the simple past forms: e.g., **ich war** (*I was*) and **er hatte** (*he had*).

A. The auxiliaries *haben* and *sein*

As mentioned above, German speakers use the two auxiliaries **haben** and **sein** to form the conversational past. **Haben** is used with most verbs and is always used with a *transitive* verb (any verb that takes a direct object).

| Uschi **hat** Pharmazie studiert. | *Uschi studied pharmaceutics.* |
| Uschi und Hannes **haben** Bier getrunken. | *Uschi and Hannes drank beer.* |

Sein is used with verbs that express a change of location. Such verbs do not have a direct object and are called *intransitive* verbs.

Infinitive	Conversational past	
fahren	Ich bin gefahren.	*I drove; I went.*
fliegen	Ich bin geflogen.	*I flew.*
gehen	Ich bin gegangen.	*I walked; I went.*
kommen	Ich bin gekommen.	*I came.*
laufen	Ich bin gelaufen.	*I ran.*
reiten	Ich bin geritten.	*I rode horseback.*
schwimmen	Ich bin geschwommen.	*I swam.*
segeln	Ich bin gesegelt.	*I sailed.*

In general, the simple past is used more frequently (even in speaking) in northern regions, while the conversational past is used more frequently (even in writing) in southern regions.

You will learn more about the simple past in **Kapitel 10.**

When the verbs **fahren, fliegen, reiten, schwimmen,** and **segeln** are used with a direct object, they require haben: **Ich bin nach Hause gefahren vs. Ich habe dein Auto gefahren.**

The form of the past participle (**-en** or **-t** ending) in no way affects whether one uses **haben** or **sein** as the auxiliary.

Verbs that express a change of condition also require **sein**, as does the verb **bleiben**.

Infinitive	Conversational past	
auf•stehen	Ich bin früh aufgestanden.	*I got up early.*
auf•wachen	Ich bin aufgewacht.	*I woke up.*
bleiben	Wir sind zu Hause geblieben.	*We stayed home.*
sterben°	Sie ist gestorben.	*She died.*
werden	Sie ist böse geworden.	*She became angry.*

> *Note:* Verbs requiring **sein** appear in the vocabulary lists with the auxiliary verb **ist**.

to die

The auxiliary is conjugated to agree with the subject. The past participle is not conjugated.

Wir **sind** zum Fischmarkt **gegangen.**   *We went to the fish market.*
Anna **ist** mit Katja ins Kino **gegangen.**   *Anna went to the movies with Katja.*

The position of the subject has no influence on the position of the auxiliary or the past participle. Like all conjugated verbs, the auxiliary occurs in the second position in statements and in the first position in questions.

Statement
subject
<u>Hannes</u> **hat** Uschi **geküsst.**

subject
Bald danach **haben** <u>sie</u> **geheiratet.**

Question
subject
Hat <u>Hannes</u> Uschi **geküsst?**

subject
Haben <u>sie</u> bald danach **geheiratet?**

---

10   Was ist passiert°? Verbinden Sie einen Satz in der linken Spalte° mit einem Satz in der rechten Spalte.

happened / column

1. Die Kellnerin ist heute Morgen sehr müde.
2. Tante Uschi ist heute Apothekerin° in Weinheim.
3. Hannelore Adler hat eine E-Mail von Anna.
4. Anna kann nicht schlafen.
5. Barbara und Anna finden den Film sehr gut.
6. Tante Uschi liebt° Onkel Hannes.

a. Anna hat letzte Woche eine E-Mail geschrieben.
b. Onkel Hannes hat Tante Uschi geküsst.
c. Sie hat gestern Abend bis spät in der Kneipe gearbeitet.
d. Sie hat in Hamburg Pharmazie studiert.
e. Sie hat zu viel Kaffee getrunken.
f. Sie sind gestern° ins Kino gegangen.

pharmacist

loves / yesterday

Die Speicherstadt Hamburgs.

⏎ **11** Wo hast du studiert? Ergänzen Sie diese Sätze mit den passenden Formen von **haben** und **sein.**

1. KARL: Wo _____ deine Eltern studiert?
2. BEATE: Mein Vater _____ in Heilbronn zur Schule gegangen, aber er _____ in München Chemie studiert.
3. KARL: Aber du _____ doch hier zur Schule gegangen, nicht?
4. BEATE: Eigentlich° _____ ich in Amerika in den Kindergarten gegangen. Mein Vater _____ dort zwei Semester verbracht.
5. KARL: Wirklich?° Was _____ er dort gemacht?
6. BEATE: Er _____ seine Dissertation geschrieben. Wir _____ ein Jahr in Cambridge in Massachusetts gelebt. Dort _____ ich Englisch gelernt.

Actually

Really?

B. Past participles

All verbs can be classified as regular (weak—**schwach**), irregular (strong—**stark**), or mixed (combining characteristics of weak and strong verbs—**gemischt**). Whether a verb is regular, irregular, or mixed affects the form of the past participle, particularly its stem and its ending.

1. Regular (weak) verbs

Regular verbs (**regelmäßige Verben**), which include many verbs that have been recently incorporated into the German language, are sometimes referred to as weak verbs (**schwache Verben**).

- Most regular verbs form the past participle by keeping the present tense stem and adding the **ge-** prefix and the ending **-t.**

Other regular verbs include:

brauchen, hat gebraucht
fragen, hat gefragt
hören, hat gehört
kaufen, hat gekauft
kochen, hat gekocht
lachen, hat gelacht
lächeln, hat gelächelt
lernen, hat gelernt
machen, hat gemacht
meinen, hat gemeint
packen, hat gepackt
schicken, hat geschickt
setzen, hat gesetzt
tanzen, hat getanzt
wohnen, hat gewohnt
zeigen, hat gezeigt

Infinitive	Conversational past	
mailen	hat **ge** + mail + **t**	Sie hat uns gemailt.
spielen	hat **ge** + spiel + **t**	Die Kinder haben gespielt.
surfen	hat **ge** + surf + **t**	Ich habe gestern im Internet gesurft.
wandern	ist **ge** + wander + **t**	Anna ist viel gewandert.

- Regular verbs whose stem ends in **-t, -d, -gn, -chn,** or **-fn** require the ending **-et** to form the past participle.

Infinitive	Conversational past	
arbeiten	hat **ge** + arbeit + **et**	Ich habe gearbeitet.
flirten	hat **ge** + flirt + **et**	Uschi und Hannes haben geflirtet.
öffnen°	hat **ge** + öffn + **et**	Georg hat die Tür geöffnet.
regnen	hat **ge** + regn + **et**	Es hat so viel geregnet.
warten	hat **ge** + wart + **et**	Anna hat lange gewartet.

to open

- Most verbs ending in **-ieren** are regular, but they do not add the prefix **ge-.**

Infinitive	Conversational past	
fotografieren	hat fotografier + **t**	Wir haben viel fotografiert.
studieren	hat studier + **t**	Sie haben lange studiert.

12 Katjas Freund Roland Hier erzählt Katja, wie sie ihren Freund Roland kennengelernt hat. Schreiben Sie das richtige Partizip.

arbeiten • kaufen • lernen • machen • öffnen • regnen • spielen

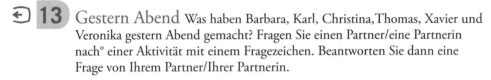

Ich habe Roland im Jugendklub kennengelernt. Er hat dort als Kellner _____. Es war im September. Das Wetter war miserabel. Es hat _____, und ich war total nass. Er hat mir die Tür _____, denn ich habe gerade (*just*) im Kaufhaus neue Kleidung _____ und ich hatte keine freie Hand. Er war ein richtiger Gentleman! Danach haben wir viel zusammen _____. Für die Schule haben wir beide (*both*) zusammen Mathe _____. Am Wochenende haben wir oft Tennis _____.

about

13 Gestern Abend Was haben Barbara, Karl, Christina, Thomas, Xavier und Veronika gestern Abend gemacht? Fragen Sie einen Partner/eine Partnerin nach° einer Aktivität mit einem Fragezeichen. Beantworten Sie dann eine Frage von Ihrem Partner/Ihrer Partnerin.

BEISPIEL S1: *Was hat Barbara gestern Abend gemacht?*
S2: *Sie hat Spaghetti gekocht.*
Und was hat Thomas gemacht?
S1: *Er hat telefoniert.*

Tabelle A (S1):

	Gespielt	Gemacht	Gelernt
Barbara	Billard gespielt	?	Mathe gelernt
Thomas	?	telefoniert	?
Karl	Karten gespielt	?	Physik gelernt
Christina	?	zu Hause gearbeitet	?
Xavier	Saxophon gespielt	?	?
Veronika	?	Xavier geküsst	?

Tabelle B (S2):

Veronika	X-Box gespielt	?	für ihr Examen gelernt
Xavier	?	viel fotografiert	Englisch gelernt
Christina	Gitarre gespielt	?	Deutsch gelernt
Karl	?	ein Buch gekauft	?
Thomas	Tischtennis gespielt	?	nichts gelernt
Barbara	?	Spaghetti gekocht	?
	Gespielt	**Gemacht**	**Gelernt**

Thomas hat telefoniert.

2. Irregular (strong) and mixed verbs

- Irregular verbs (**unregelmäßige Verben**), namely those verbs with a stem-vowel change in the present tense or one of the past tenses, are also called strong verbs (**starke Verben**). They generally include **ge-** and have the ending **-en** on the past participle.

Other irregular verbs include:

halten, hat gehalten
heißen, hat geheißen
helfen, hat geholfen
lesen, hat gelesen
schlafen, hat geschlafen
singen, hat gesungen
sprechen, hat gesprochen
tragen, hat getragen
tun, hat getan

Infinitive	Conversational past	
geben	hat **ge** + geb + **en**	Was hast du ihm gegeben?
lesen	hat **ge** + les + **en**	Ich habe das ganze Buch gelesen.

For many verbs, the vowel in the present tense stem changes in the past participle. For some verbs, one or more consonants change as well. There is no way to recognize which verbs change the stem vowel or consonant in the past participle. They must be memorized.

Infinitive	Conversational past	
gehen	ist ge + **gang** + en	Er ist mit mir ins Kino gegangen.
trinken	hat ge + tru**n**k + en	Wir haben doch kein Bier getrunken.

- Mixed verbs combine features of both regular and irregular verbs to form their past participles. Like regular verbs, they add a **-t** in the past participle and, like some irregular verbs, they change the stem in the past participle.

There are approximately 35 high-frequency irregular and mixed verbs. You will need to memorize their stem changes. Some English verbs can help you remember the German verb forms (e.g., *speak, spoken:* **sprechen, gesprochen**).

Infinitive	Conversational past	
bringen	hat ge + br**ach** + **t**	Was hast du mir gebracht?
denken	hat ge + d**ach** + **t**	Ich habe oft an dich gedacht.
kennen	hat ge + k**a**nn + **t**	Hast du sie gut gekannt?
wissen	hat ge + w**uss** + **t**	Ich habe das nicht gewusst.

The following list shows irregular and mixed verbs with their stem changes in the conversational past.

Note that some irregular verbs have a change in consonant spelling of the stem in the past participle: **essen, gegessen; nehmen, genommen; reiten, geritten; gehen, gegangen.**

	Infinitive	Conversational past	
No vowel change	**e**ssen	hat geg**e**ssen	Hast du gegessen?
	f**a**hren	ist gef**a**hren	Sie ist gefahren.
	l**au**fen	ist gel**au**fen	Ich bin nach Hause gelaufen.
	k**o**mmen	ist gek**o**mmen	Du bist spät gekommen.
ei > ie	schr**ei**ben	hat geschr**ie**ben	Anna hat einen Brief geschrieben.
ei > i	r**ei**ten	ist ger**i**tten	Er ist auf dem Land geritten.
e > a	g**e**hen	ist geg**a**ngen	Er ist nach Hause gegangen.
e > o	n**e**hmen	hat gen**o**mmen	Petra hat es genommen.
i > o	schw**i**mmen	ist geschw**o**mmen	Wir sind kurz geschwommen.
ie > o	sch**ie**ben	hat gesch**o**ben	Ich habe mein Rad geschoben.
i > u	f**i**nden	hat gef**u**nden	Herr Meyer hat sein Auto gefunden.

14 Autogrammspiel: Was hast du heute gemacht? Finden Sie für jede° Frage eine Person, die mit **Ja** antwortet. Bitten Sie diese Person um ihre Unterschrift.

each

BEISPIEL   S1: *Hast du heute Kaffee getrunken?*
S2: *Ja, ich habe heute Kaffee getrunken.*
S1: *Unterschreib hier bitte.*

1. Kaffee getrunken   _____
2. Hausaufgaben gemacht   _____
3. Pizza gegessen   _____
4. mit dem Bus zur Uni gefahren _____
5. eine E-Mail geschrieben   _____
6. Musik gehört   _____
7. eine Zeitung° gekauft   _____
8. Vokabeln gelernt   _____
9. gut geschlafen   _____
10. Deutsch gesprochen   _____
11. zu Hause gesungen   _____

newspaper

Kulturnotiz. People in German-speaking countries are twice as likely to read a newspaper every day compared to Americans. German newspapers also tend to have less advertising.

Ich habe heute Morgen eine Zeitung gekauft.

Bildagentur Hamburg/Alamy

15 Übertreibungen° Ein alter Freund beschreibt seine Kindheit°, aber er übertreibt auch gern. Sie müssen ihn oft an die Realität erinnern.

exaggerations / childhood

BEISPIEL   perfekt Deutsch sprechen/gar kein Deutsch spreche
S1 (DER FREUND): *Ich habe als Kind perfekt Deutsch gesprochen.*
S2 (SIE): *Nein, du hast als Kind gar kein Deutsch gesprochen.*

1. ein Auto kaufen/ein Fahrrad kaufen
2. viele Bücher lesen/Comichefte° lesen
3. jeden Morgen ein Bier trinken/jeden Morgen Orangensaft trinken
4. gesund° essen/ungesund essen
5. immer zur Schule laufen/immer zur Schule fahren
6. nie am Wochenende zu Hause bleiben/oft am Wochenende zu Hause bleiben
7. das Abendessen immer kochen/das Abendessen nie kochen
8. viele Briefe schreiben/viele E-Mails schreiben

comic books

healthy

C. Prefixes of past participles

1. Separable-prefix verbs

As you know, most verbs add **ge-** to form the past participle. A verb with a separable prefix (**trennbares Präfix**) inserts this **-ge-** between the prefix and the stem.

Hannes hat Uschi ins Theater ein**ge**laden.   *Hannes invited Uschi to the theater.*

The most common separable prefixes are: **ab-, an-, auf-, aus-, ein-, mit-, zu-, zurück-.** Here is a list of past participles of common verbs with separable prefixes. When spoken, the stress in the infinitive and in the past participle is always on the prefix: ***an**kommen, **an**gekommen.*

Infinitive	Conversational past	
ab•biegen	ist ab + **ge** + bogen	Ich bin rechts abgebogen.
an•kommen	ist an + **ge** + kommen	Magda ist schon angekommen.
auf•hören	hat auf + **ge** + hört	Der Professor hat gerade aufgehört.
aus•geben	hat aus + **ge** + geben	Hast du viel Geld ausgegeben?
ein•kaufen	hat ein + **ge** + kauft	Katja hat viel eingekauft.
fern•sehen	hat fern + **ge** + sehen	Wir haben ferngesehen.

Irregular and mixed verbs with separable prefixes undergo the same stem changes as the forms that have no separable prefix: **nehmen** (*to take*) → **hat genommen; an•nehmen** (*to assume*) → **hat angenommen.**

> Other separable-prefix verbs include:
>
> ab•steigen, ist abgestiegen
> an•fangen, hat angefangen
> an•halten, ist angehalten
> an•rufen, hat angerufen
> aus•gehen, ist ausgegangen
> ein•laden, hat eingeladen
> mit•bringen, hat mitgebracht
> mit•nehmen, hat mitgenommen
> weiter•fahren, ist weitergefahren
> zurück•kommen, ist zurückgekommen

shopping spree

was noch: what else

⤴ **16** Ein Einkaufsbummel° in Hamburg Es ist Abend. Onkel Hannes und Tante Uschi besuchen Hamburg. Katja ist zu Hause in Weinheim. Katja spricht am Telefon mit ihrer Mutter. Was sagt Katja? Was sagt Tante Uschi?

BEISPIEL
S1 (KATJA):   *Was hast du heute gemacht, Mama?*
S2 (TANTE USCHI): *Ich bin früh aufgestanden. Und was hast du gemacht, Katja?*
S1 (KATJA):   *Ich habe lange geschlafen. Und was hast du noch° gemacht, Mama?*

Tabelle A (S1, Katja):

Katja	Tante Uschi
lange geschlafen	?
Vati angerufen	?
Um 6 Uhr zurückgekommen	?
mit Claudia ferngesehen	?

Tabelle B (S2, Tante Uschi):

Tante Uschi	Katja
früh aufgestanden	?
an der Elbe spazieren gegangen	?
viele Sachen eingekauft	?
viel Geld ausgegeben	?

Yadid Levy/Anzenberger/Redux Pictures

Wir haben in Hamburg gut eingekauft.

Hansestadt Hamburg

Hamburg (**die Freie und Hansestadt Hamburg**), Germany's largest seaport and second largest city (1.8 million inhabitants), constitutes one of the 16 states (**Länder**) of the Federal Republic of Germany. Hamburg, as well as Berlin and Bremen, is a city-state with an independent status, which it owes to its history as a Hanseatic city.

The Hanseatic League (**die Hanse**) originated in the 13th century, when Hamburg and Lübeck agreed to reduce the trade barriers between them in order to foster trade in the North Sea and throughout the Baltic region. **Die Hanse** actively promoted trade, international contacts, and the accumulation of wealth, along with the relative independence that such economic wealth provided in a feudal society.

Eventually over 200 cities, including Bergen (Norway), Novgorod (Russia), London (England), Bruges (Belgium), and Gdansk (Poland) joined the league and profited from the trade network. Strategically located on the Elbe River (**die Elbe**) between the North Sea (**die Nordsee**) and the Baltic Sea (**die Ostsee**), Hamburg became a hub of Hanseatic trade and has proudly maintained its role as a center of international trade into the 21st century.

From its center along the banks of the Alster (**die Alster**), which is dammed and forms a large lake in the center of the city, Hamburg revels in its maritime history and its position as Germany's window on the world. Being a port city has fostered a cosmopolitan image and a tolerant tradition for which Hamburg is famous. The copper-roofed, neo-renaissance city hall (**das Rathaus**) serves as the seat of city-state government and dominates the skyline from the Alster. The **Jungfernstieg** is home to Hamburg's most exclusive shops and hotels. It passes over the canals (**Fleete**) that crisscross Hamburg and leads to the main shopping street, **Mönckebergstraße.**

The harbor section, **St. Pauli,** is home to the city's shipping and shipbuilding industries. The symbol (**das Wahrzeichen**) of Hamburg, **die Sankt Michaeliskirche (der Michel)**, the largest Baroque church in the city, is also located there. **St. Pauli** is also the location of northern Europe's largest entertainment and red light district, **die Reeperbahn.** St. Pauli's Fish Market (**der Fischmarkt**) is held every Sunday morning from six to ten o'clock. In 2008, part of the immense warehouse district on the waterfront (**die Speicherstadt**) was converted to **HafenCity,** which now provides upscale housing for 12,000 residents, sparkling new office space for 40,000, and a home for the city's newest concert hall, **die Elbphilharmonie**.

Santje/Shutterstock.com

Das Hamburger Rathaus dominiert das Stadtbild von der Alster her.

Hamburg is the birthplace of composers Johannes Brahms and Felix Mendelssohn, filmmaker Fatih Akin, fashion designer Karl Lagerfeld, and Chancellor Angela Merkel. In addition to being an important media, TV, and filmmaking center, Hamburg has over twenty theaters, the oldest opera house in Germany, three symphony orchestras, a ballet company, and numerous art museums and galleries. Hamburg is also home to one of Germany's largest urban universities (**die Universität Hamburg**). And not to be forgotten, Hamburg is the birthplace of the **Hamburger Steak,** chopped beef topped with a fried egg, which traveled to America, where it abandoned the egg but added a bun, mustard, and ketchup to become an American staple: the hamburger.

Kulturkreuzung

In der Geschichte Hamburgs spielt das Wasser eine große Rolle: die Elbe, die Alster, die Fleete, die Nähe° zur Nordsee und zur Ostsee. Ist Ihre Stadt an einem See° oder an einem Fluss, oder gibt es nur einen kleinen Bach° in der Nähe? Wie heißen diese Gewässer? Wie wichtig sind sie im wirtschaftlichen° Leben von der Stadt? Was kann man dort in der Freizeit machen? Was haben Sie dort schon gemacht°?

proximity / lake

brook

economic

***haben** ...: have done*

Katja hat ihren Vater angerufen.

Other inseparable-prefix verbs include:

**bedeuten, hat bedeutet
beginnen, hat begonnen
benutzen, hat benutzt
besuchen, hat besucht
bezahlen, hat bezahlt
verstehen, hat verstanden**

to lose

to spell

puzzle

wedding anniversary

For verbs ending in **-ieren**, stress is placed on **-iert**: stud*iert*.

wanted to

angry

👥 17 Interview Stellen Sie einem Partner/einer Partnerin die folgenden Fragen.

BEISPIEL S1: *Hast du heute gut geschlafen?*
S2: *Ich habe heute gut geschlafen.*

1. Hast du heute gut geschlafen?
2. Wann bist du aufgestanden?
3. Wann bist du heute zum Campus gekommen?
4. Wann bist du gestern zurückgekommen?
5. Hast du heute oder gestern eingekauft?
6. Wie viel Geld hast du gestern ausgegeben?

2. Inseparable prefix and *ieren* verbs

A verb with an inseparable prefix (**untrennbares Präfix**) does not add **ge-** in the past participle. When spoken, the stress is always on the stem of the past participle, not on the inseparable prefix: be*sucht*, ver*standen*.

Infinitive	Conversational past	
erzählen	hat erzähl + t	Mutti hat uns die Geschichte erzählt.
verbringen	hat verbrach + t	Sie hat ein Jahr in Afrika verbracht.
verdienen	hat verdien + t	Uschi hat viel Geld verdient.
vergessen	hat vergess + en	Monika hat Annas Geburtstag vergessen.
verlieren°	hat verlor + en	Sie hat ihr Handy verloren.

The most common inseparable prefixes are: **be-, ent-, er-, ge-, ver-,** and **zer-.**

Infinitive	Conversational past	
buchstabieren°	hat buchstabier + t	Fabian hat das Wort richtig buchstabiert.
diskutieren	hat diskutier + t	Sie haben Politik diskutiert.
studieren	hat studier + t	Wo hat Franz in den USA studiert?

⊸ 18 Das Happyend: Ein Rätsel° Onkel Hannes und Tante Uschi haben einander in Hamburg kennengelernt. Sie sind jetzt 25 Jahre verheiratet. Zum 25. Hochzeitstag° besuchen sie die Stadt wieder. Rekonstruieren Sie mit einem Partner/einer Partnerin die korrekte Reihenfolge der Geschichte von Uschi Kunz und Hannes Günther in Hamburg.

Vor 25 Jahren

_____ Hannes Günther und Uschi Kunz haben sich verliebt.
_____ Sie haben sich verlobt.
___1__ Uschi hat in Hamburg Pharmazie studiert.
_____ Uschi hat als Kellnerin wenig Geld verdient.
_____ Sie sind im Regen spazieren gegangen.
_____ Hannes hat Uschi ins Theater eingeladen.

Gestern

_____ Am Abend wollten° sie das Hamburger Ballett besuchen.
_____ Hannes hat die Karten im Hotel vergessen und Uschi war böse°.
_____ Sie haben das Ballett nicht verstanden.
_____ Hannes hat die Karten wiedergefunden und Uschi war wieder glücklich.
_____ Sie haben den Tag an der Alster verbracht.
_____ Sie haben in einer Kneipe etwas getrunken und über das Ballett diskutiert.

D. Past participles of *sein* and *haben*

The past participle of **sein** is **gewesen**. The past participle of **haben** is **gehabt**.

Tante Uschi **ist** in Hamburg Studentin **gewesen.**	*Aunt Uschi was a student in Hamburg.*
Du **hast** eine ganz schlimme Erkältung **gehabt.**	*You had a really bad cold.*

In spoken German, the simple past tense forms of **sein (ich war, du warst, er/sie/es war, wir waren, ihr wart, sie/Sie waren)** and **haben (ich hatte, du hattest, er/sie/es hatte, wir hatten, ihr hattet, sie/Sie hatten),** discussed in **Kapitel 10,** are frequently used instead of the conversational past to express the past tense.

Er **hat** Geburtstag **gehabt.** }	*He had a birthday.*
Er **hatte** Geburtstag.	
Sie **ist** krank **gewesen.** }	*She was sick.*
Sie **war** krank.	

---

19 Meine Kindheit Sprechen Sie zusammen über Ihre Kindheit. Benutzen Sie **sein** und **haben.**

BEISPIEL   S1: *Als Kind bin ich selten krank gewesen. Und du?*
S2: *Als Kind bin ich auch selten krank gewesen.*
Als Kind war ich auch selten krank.

1. oft/selten krank
2. sehr aktiv/sehr ruhig
3. oft im Kino/selten im Kino
4. sehr sportlich/nicht sehr sportlich
5. viele/wenige Erkältungen
6. viele/wenige Regeln
7. viele/wenige Spielsachen°
8. viele/ein paar° Spielkameraden°

toys
***ein paar:** a few / playmates*

20 Herrn Günthers Geschäftsreise° Ergänzen Sie diese Sätze mit der korrekten Partizipform.

Herr Günther ist letzte Woche auf Geschäftsreise in München _____ (sein). Dort hat er die letzten fünf Tage _____ (verbringen). Er ist gestern Abend aus München _____ (zurückkommen). Er ist um 21.15 Uhr am Bahnhof in Weinheim _____ (ankommen). In München hat er mit Kollegen an einem Projekt _____ (arbeiten). Das Projekt haben sie vor einem Jahr _____ (anfangen). Die Kollegen haben viel _____ (diskutieren). Aber zum Schluss° haben alle sehr gut an dem Projekt _____ (verdienen). Jetzt hat das Projekt _____ (aufhören). Alle sind nach Hause _____ (zurückfahren).
In München hat Herr Günther auch etwas Zeit für die Sehenswürdigkeiten _____ (haben). Am Samstag hat er das BMW-Museum _____ (besuchen). Dort hat er viele alte Autos und Flugzeuge _____ (sehen). Er ist sehr lange im Museum _____ (bleiben). Für seine Kinder hat er auch Andenken _____ (kaufen). Für Georg hat er ein Buch über den BMW Autokonzern _____ (finden). Für Katja hat er eine CD mit südamerikanischer Flötenmusik _____ (mitbringen). Seine Frau hat er auch nicht _____ (vergessen). Für sie hat er einen Schal _____ (kaufen). Er hat relativ viel Geld _____ (ausgeben).

business trip

***zum ... :** in the end*

Kulturnotiz. Bayerische Motoren Werke (BMW) was founded in the year 1917.

Wissenswerte Vokabeln: das Wetter

Describing weather conditions

humid / is; lit. lies

Alice/Shutterstock.com

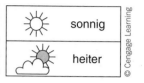

☼	sonnig
⛅	heiter

© Cengage Learning

Wie ist das Wetter heute?

Heute ist es | sonnig.
heiter.

Die Sonne scheint heute. Gestern hat die Sonne nicht geschienen.

Es wird heiß und schwül°. Die Temperatur liegt° bei vierunddreißig Grad Celsius.

Kathy Squires

Heute ist es | wolkig.
bedeckt.
windig.

Es gibt | viele Wolken.
Nebel heute.

Gestern hat es auch Nebel gegeben.

Es wird kühl. Die Temperatur | fällt.
sinkt.

Heute Morgen ist die Temperatur gesunken/gefallen.

⛅	wolkig
☁	bedeckt
≡	Nebel

© Cengage Learning

Guðjón Eyjólfur Ólafsson/Shutterstock.com

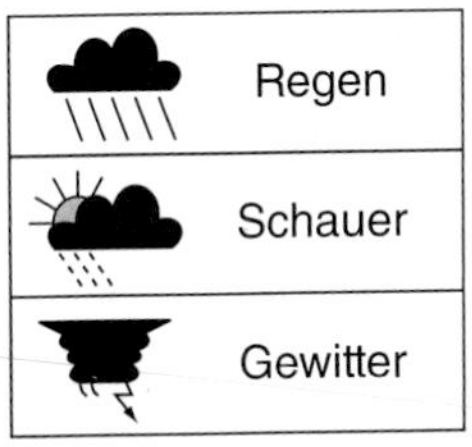

Regen
Schauer
Gewitter

© Cengage Learning 2014

Heute regnet es. Wir haben Regen. Gestern hat es den ganzen Tag geregnet.

Es gibt | Schauer.
Gewitter.

Das Wetter ist schlecht°. — *bad*

Es blitzt und donnert. In der Nacht hat es auch gedonnert und geblitzt.

Es ist | ganz nass°. — *wet*
nicht trocken°. — *dry*
wirklich mies°. — *rotten, lousy*

Es wird warm. Die Temperatur steigt°. — *is rising*

Heute schneit es. Wir haben Schnee. Am Wochenende hat es viel geschneit.

Es wird kalt. Die Temperatur liegt bei null Grad Celsius (um den Gefrierpunkt).

Morgen soll es sonnig aber kalt sein.

AP Photo/Markus Schreiber

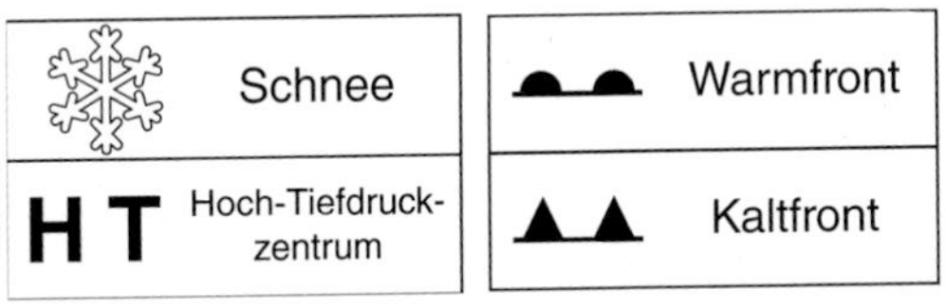

Schnee
H T
Hoch-Tiefdruck-zentrum
Warmfront
Kaltfront

© Cengage Learning 2014

Sprache im Alltag: **ganz**

The word **ganz** is used frequently in German. It can be used as an adjective (to mean *whole* or *all*) and as an adverb (to mean *really, quite,* or *very*).

Es hat den **ganzen** Tag geregnet.	*It rained **all** day.*
Das ist meine **ganze** Familie.	*This is my **whole** family.*
Ja, das finde ich **ganz** toll.	*Yes, I think that's **quite** good.*
Du hast eine **ganz** schlimme Erkältung gehabt.	*You had a **really** (**very**) bad cold.*

21 Wie ist das Wetter in Oslo? Das Wetter in Tübingen ist momentan nicht so gut. Anna sucht schönes Wetter! Sie liest die *Frankfurter Allgemeine Zeitung* und findet den Wetterbericht für Europa. Beantworten Sie die Fragen.

BEISPIEL S1: *Wie ist das Wetter in Oslo?*
S2: *In Oslo ist es bedeckt. Die Temperatur liegt bei drei Grad.*

1. Wien
2. Dublin
3. Bordeaux
4. Moskau
5. Rom
6. Istanbul
7. Athen
8. Madrid
9. München
10. Berlin
11. Nizza
12. Paris

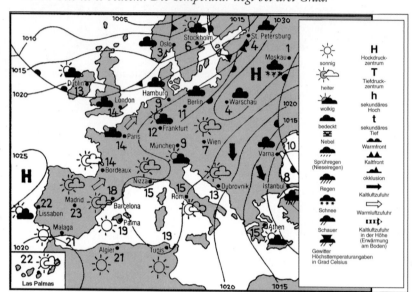

www.wetter.com

22 Das Wetter hier Beantworten Sie die Fragen.

1. Wie ist das Wetter heute?
2. Ist es heute bedeckt oder heiter?
3. Wie ist die Temperatur heute in Fahrenheit? In Celsius?
4. Haben wir heute Morgen Nebel gehabt?
5. Wie ist das Wetter gestern gewesen?
6. Wann hat es zuletzt geregnet?
7. Wann hat es zuletzt geschneit?
8. Wie soll das Wetter morgen (und übermorgen) sein?

Die Jahreszeiten

Talking about the seasons

der Frühling

der Sommer

der Herbst

der Winter

© Cengage Learning

BEISPIEL *Wie ist das Wetter im Winter?*

ii 23 Fragen zum Wetter Stellen Sie einem Partner/einer Partnerin diese Fragen über das Wetter.

1. Wie ist es im Sommer in Atlanta?
2. Wie ist das Wetter im Winter in Buffalo, New York?
3. Wie ist es im Frühling in Washington, D.C.?
4. Wie ist das Wetter im Herbst im Mittelwesten?
5. Zu welcher Jahreszeit regnet es hier am meisten?
6. Zu welcher Jahreszeit ist das Wetter hier sehr schlecht?
7. Wann haben wir das beste Wetter? Warum meinst du das?

> Vocabulary that might be important for your region: **der Sturm** (*storm*), **der Orkan** (*hurricane*), **der Tornado** (*tornado*), **der Wirbelsturm** (*whirlwind*).

ii 24 Rollenspiel: Gestern Abend Sie treffen° einen Freund/eine Freundin an der Uni. Der Freund/Die Freundin sieht sehr müde aus. Beginnen Sie die Konversation mit „Guten Tag". Stellen Sie dann die Frage: „Wie geht's?" Der Freund/Die Freundin erzählt, was er/sie gestern Abend gemacht hat. Hier sind einige Ideen. *meet*

nicht so gut geschlafen	bis spät gearbeitet
für eine Prüfung gelernt	Basketball gespielt
in die Kneipe gegangen	Hausaufgaben gemacht
eine Party besucht	die ganze Nacht mit Freunden telefoniert

ii 25 Rollenspiel: Letzten Sommer Sie treffen einen Freund/eine Freundin und sprechen über letzten Sommer. Beginnen Sie die Konversation mit: „Hallo." Hier sind einige Ideen.

im Sommer gemacht	zum Strand° gefahren
fast° immer geregnet	die Sonne hat geschienen
Wasserski gefahren	Baseball gespielt
eine Reise gemacht	mit Freunden ausgegangen
nichts Interessantes gemacht	viel gearbeitet und wenig verdient

beach
almost

ii 26 Ein Pechtag° Beschreiben Sie einen Tag, an dem nichts gut gegangen ist. Eine Person beginnt mit „Hallo, ___. Du siehst nicht so gut aus. Was ist los?°" Hier sind einige Ideen.

unlucky day
Was ...: *What's the matter?*

zu spät aufgestanden	kein Buch gehabt
Wasser nur kalt gewesen	Geld vergessen
das Handy verloren	krank geworden
keinen freien Parkplatz gefunden	usw.°

und so weiter

27 Schreibecke: **Einen Brief schreiben.** Sie sind heute nicht in den Deutschkurs gekommen. Schreiben Sie Ihrem Lehrer/Ihrer Lehrerin eine kurze E-Mail. Erklären° Sie, warum Sie nicht da waren. Was haben Sie gemacht?

Explain

zu lange schlafen • Auto kaputt • das Buch vergessen • Hausaufgaben nicht machen • krank sein

BEISPIEL *Lieber Herr ... (Liebe Frau ...),*

Erstes Date: Worauf man beim ersten Date achten soll

Anna hat in Weinheim die Liebesgeschichte von Tante Uschi und Onkel Hannes gehört. Sie möchte wissen, wie es mit dem Dating in Deutschland steht. Ist das alles wie zu Hause oder gibt es in Deutschland andere Regeln und andere Erwartungen? Anna sucht Informationen über das Dating in Deutschland und findet Ratschläge von der Mannheimer Psychologin Dr. Doris Wolf über das Online-Dating. Vielleicht ist Online-Dating nicht die beste Option…

Vorschau

➲ **28** Thematische Fragen I Wie kann man erkennen°, dass ein Date ein Date ist – und nicht ein ganz normales Treffen°? Markieren Sie.

	Ein Date	Ein ganz normales Treffen	Das tue ich nie!
1. Ich bin nervös.	○	○	○
2. Ich achte sehr auf die Zeit. Ich komme rechtzeitig an.	○	○	○
3. Ich plane vorher, was ich sagen möchte und wohin wir gehen sollen.	○	○	○
4. Ich muss/darf die Hälfte° bezahlen.	○	○	○
5. Ich trage besonders attraktive Kleidung.	○	○	○
6. Ich spreche über Probleme mit meinem Ex-Freund/mit meiner Ex-Freundin.	○	○	○
7. Ich stelle meinem Partner/meiner Partnerin viele Fragen.	○	○	○
8. Wir treffen uns in meiner Wohnung°.	○	○	○
9. Ich benehme mich° ganz wie mit meinen Freunden.	○	○	○
10. Wir reden (=sprechen) über Tabuthemen, wie zum Beispiel Sex, Religion oder Politik.	○	○	○
11. Ich rufe nachher an, denn ich möchte wissen, wie es war.	○	○	○
12. Ich schlage eine Zeit vor, wann wir uns wiedersehen sollen.	○	○	○

recognize
meeting

half

apartment
benehme …: *behave*

29 Thematische Fragen II Beantworten Sie die folgenden Fragen auf Deutsch.

1. Wie oft, glauben Sie, gehen Studenten an Ihrer Uni auf ein Date?
2. Mit wem gehen Sie auf Dates?
   a. mit niemandem
   b. nur mit Leuten, in die ich mich verliebt habe
   c. nur mit Leuten, die ich gern habe
   d. mit allen Leuten
   e. ???

3. Wer hat die besten Ideen für ein Date?
   a. Menschen im Internet
   b. meine Freunde
   c. meine Mutter
   d. ???

Treffen Sie sich auf neutralem Boden!

30 Phrasendetektiv Welche Phrasen bedeuten ungefähr das gleiche?

1. meine eigenen vier Wände
2. auf neutralem Boden
3. die Zeit begrenzen
4. deutlich machen
5. die Telefonnummer bekannt geben

a. klar machen, genau sagen
b. die Telefonnummer sagen
c. meine Wohnung
d. die Zeit einschränken/beschränken
e. auf neutralem Territorium

6. d. h.
7. auf keinen Fall
8. Vertrauen zum anderen (haben)
9. sich wie eine kleine graue Maus benehmen
10. ein Treffen ausmachen

f. keine individuelle Persönlichkeit haben
g. ein Date arrangieren
h. das heißt (zum Beispiel)
i. ganz bestimmt nicht
j. der anderen Person alles sagen können

11. offene Fragen
12. gutes Selbstvertrauen haben
13. man darf sich nicht wundern
14. auf jemanden gut wirken
15. die Anonymität aufgeben

k. keine Anonymität mehr wollen
l. man muss wissen, dass das passiert.
m. einen guten Effekt haben
n. sich selbst gern haben
o. eine Frage, die man nicht mit „Ja" oder „Nein" beantworten kann.

Lesen Sie jetzt den Text.

here: each other

Treffen Sie sich° auf neutralem Boden – in einer Kneipe, in einem Restaurant, in einem Park. Treffen Sie sich auf keinen Fall beim ersten Date in Ihren eigenen vier Wänden. Dies ist ein großes Risiko.

Begrenzen Sie von vornherein die Zeit für das erste Date. D. h., wenn Sie das erste Treffen ausmachen, dann machen Sie gleich deutlich, dass Sie nur 30 oder 60 Minuten Zeit haben.

other

Vor dem ersten Date keine Telefonnummern oder sonstige° Kontaktdaten (E-Mail-Adresse) bekannt geben. Geben Sie Ihre Anonymität erst auf, wenn Sie ein gewisses Vertrauen zum anderen gefasst haben – vielleicht beim zweiten Treffen?

caller ID

Schalten Sie die Rufnummer-Übertragung° Ihres Handy aus. So vermeiden Sie, dass der Angerufene Ihre mobile Telefonnummer erfährt.

yourself / pick up

Lassen Sie sich° nicht zu Hause abholen° und lassen Sie sich nach dem Date nicht nach Hause bringen. Lassen Sie sich nicht im Wagen des anderen ein Stück mitnehmen.

Interessieren ...: are you interested in / Wer ...: Whoever is interested in others

Interessieren Sie sich für° den anderen? Warum? Wer sich für andere interessiert°, ist interessant. Und wie macht man das? Ganz einfach durch offene Fragen. Das sind Fragen, auf die man nicht mit Ja oder Nein antworten kann. Offene Fragen beginnen immer mit Wie?, Warum?, Auf welche Weise?, Woher?

behave
sich wundern: *be surprised*
sich abwenden: *turn away*
sich fühlen: *feel*

Selbstvertrauen ist enorm wichtig. Mit einem guten Selbstvertrauen wirken Sie auf andere attraktiv und interessant. Wenn Sie sich wie eine kleine graue Maus benehmen°, dann dürfen Sie sich nicht wundern°, wenn andere in Ihnen auch die kleine graue Maus sehen und sich abwenden°.

failed / relationships

Reden Sie beim ersten Treffen nie darüber, wenn Sie sich einsam und unglücklich fühlen°. Auch gescheiterte° Beziehungen°, Probleme mit dem Ex oder der Ex sind Flirtkiller.

Absolut tabu sind auch Themen wie Politik, Geld, sexuelle Themen und – liebe Frauen, denkt daran – Kinderwunsch.

Dr. Doris Wolf – Diplom Psychologin, Psychotherapeutin

© PAL Verlag GmbH

Andersen Ross/Jupiter Images

Man kann neue Leute online kennenlernen und alte Freunde wiederfinden.

Rückblick

→ **31** Stimmt das? Stimmen diese Aussagen zum Text? Wenn nicht, was stimmt?

	Ja, das stimmt.	Nein, das stimmt nicht.
1. Das erste Date darf in der privaten Wohnung sein.	○	○
2. Das erste Date darf lang sein.	○	○
3. Man soll beim ersten Date die private Telefonnummer herausgeben.	○	○
4. Man soll dem Partner vom ersten Moment an vertrauen.	○	○
5. Eine Person ohne viel Selbstvertrauen ist wie eine kleine Maus.	○	○
6. Man darf keine offenen Fragen stellen.	○	○
7. Man soll Persönlichkeit zeigen.	○	○
8. Man kann auch über Sex, den/die Ex oder Politik sprechen.	○	○

> Complete the **Ergänzen Sie** activity in the Student Activities Manual before doing the next activity.

← **32** Kurz gefragt Beantworten Sie diese Fragen auf Deutsch.

1. Was ist für die Autorin das große Risiko beim ersten Date?
2. Warum soll man vor dem ersten Date nicht anrufen?
3. Wo soll man sich mit dem Partner beim ersten Date treffen? Und wo nicht?
4. Wie lang soll das erste Date maximal sein?
5. Welche Fragen soll man beim ersten Date stellen? Mit welchen Wörtern fangen diese Fragen an?
6. Wie zeigt man am besten Interesse an der anderen Person?
7. Welche Rolle spielt Selbstvertrauen beim ersten Date?
8. Welche Themen sind beim ersten Date tabu?
9. Wie finden Sie diese Datingtipps?

→ **33** Idiotisch, oder was? Die folgende Liste gibt mögliche Datingtipps. Wie finden Sie diese Tipps? Markieren Sie Ihre Meinung.

	Diesen Tipp finde ich ...		
Tipp	idiotisch	nützlich°	unterhaltsam°?
1. Triff dich° mit dem Partner in einer Kneipe!	○	○	○
2. Triff dich mit dem Partner in einem Park!	○	○	○
3. Gib dem Partner nicht deine Telefonnummer!	○	○	○
4. Stell dem Partner nur offene Fragen!	○	○	○
5. Nimm dir für das erste Date mindestens vier Stunden Zeit!	○	○	○
6. Zeig dem Partner viel Selbstvertrauen!	○	○	○
7. Sprich nicht über den/die Ex!	○	○	○
8. Sag nicht, dass du Kinder willst!	○	○	○

*useful / amusing
meet*

34 Textdetektiv: **Absprungtext.** Use the *Absprungtext* to recognize important aspects of German structure and usage.

1. Which imperative forms are used in the Absprungtext?
   a. formal ("Sie")   b. informal ("du")   c. inclusive ("wir")

2. The form of address implies that this text was written ...
   a. by friends for friends.
   b. by adults for other adults.
   c. by students for other students.

3. Who do you think is the target audience of this text? There may be more than one correct answer.
   a. teenagers
   b. college students
   c. single adults who may not have dated in a while
   d. young professionals just out of college

4. Which two of these verbs do not belong?
   sprechen • reden • geben • sagen • erzählen • nehmen
   What do the remaining verbs all express?
   a. oral communication   b. written communication   c. miscommunication

5. Look at this example sentence from the *Absprungtext*, especially the modal verb form:
   Diese Dinge <u>sollten</u> Sie beim ersten Date auf keinen Fall ansprechen.

   The modal verb *sollten*, in form and meaning, resembles the English modal verb:
   a. shall   b. should   c. must

6. Which of these three verb forms conveys the least urgency and, therefore, the greatest degree of politeness when giving directions to others?
   a. shall   b. should   c. must

zu ... : in pairs

35 Diskussion: Zusammen ausgehen In Europa geht man oft mit einer Gruppe aus. Bilden Sie eine Gruppe von drei Personen. Diskutieren Sie, welche Dinge man besser zu zweit° macht und welche man in der Gruppe machen kann. Welche Dinge machen Sie alle lieber zu zweit, welche lieber in der Gruppe?

BEISPIEL   S1: *Gehst du lieber zu zweit oder in einer Gruppe ins Kino?*
            S2: *Ich gehe lieber zu zweit ins Kino. Und du?*
            S3: *Ich gehe auch lieber zu zweit ins Kino. (oder)*
                Ich gehe lieber in einer Gruppe ins Kino.

Aktivität	Zu zweit	In der Gruppe
1. ins Kino gehen	○	○
2. in die Disko tanzen gehen	○	○
3. in ein Restaurant gehen	○	○
4. spazieren gehen	○	○
5. fernsehen	○	○
6. für eine Prüfung lernen	○	○
7. Sport treiben	○	○
8. in die Kneipe gehen	○	○
9. fürs Wochenende wegfahren	○	○

Brennpunkt Kultur

 Web Search
Web Link

Bekannte oder Freunde?

In North America it is common to call most of the people you know reasonably well your "friends." German speakers distinguish between two types of "friends." **Bekannte** (acquaintances) may be people you know quite well or those you have seen only once in your life: classmates, co-workers, members of a club, or people you know only superficially. Even when the first name is used, a **Bekanntschaft** (acquaintance relationship) of this type maintains a certain emotional distance as indicated by the continued use of **Sie** in conversation. While German speakers may have many **Bekannte,** they have only a few **Freunde.** A **Freund** or **Freundin** is an intimate friend or a person with whom one shares a very special, permanent bond that is rare and treasured. Young people may also call such a friend their **Kumpel.**

Esiline/Shutterstock.com

Charlotte ist meine beste Freundin.

In the relatively stable, less mobile cultures of central Europe, students often go through school with the same classmates, growing up together and evolving into a close circle of friends (**der Freundeskreis, eine Clique**). Whether they are of the same sex or opposite sex, such **Freunde** acquired in school often become close friends for life. When a **Bekanntschaft** among adults evolves into a **Freundschaft,** the new friends may acknowledge their special relationship with a ceremonial drink (**Brüderschaft trinken**). From this point on, they will use **du** with each other. Close friends of this type are usually referred to as **ein Freund von mir/eine Freundin von mir.** When German speakers refer to **mein Freund** or **meine Freundin,** they are talking about a person with whom they have a close relationship or even an intimate or romantic one.

Kulturkreuzung

Ist es im College leicht°, Freundschaften zu schließen°? Warum? Warum nicht? Machen Sie viel mit einer kleinen Clique oder sind Sie lieber mit ein oder zwei Personen zusammen? Haben Sie noch Kontakt zu Freunden aus der Schulzeit? Haben Sie lieber viele Bekannte oder nur ein paar gute Freunde? Mit wem sprechen Sie lieber über persönliche Dinge – mit Personen am College, mit Freunden von der Schule, mit Ihrer Familie? Wo findet man am besten Personen für ein Date?

*easy / **Freundschaften … :** to make friends*

Wissenswerte Vokabeln: Freundschaft und Liebe

Describing personal relationships

Sie sieht gut aus.
Er findet sie attraktiv.

Sie spricht ihn an.
Sie flirtet mit ihm.

Sie umarmt ihn.
Er küsst sie. Sie küsst ihn.
Sie schmusen.

Sie mögen einander. Sie haben einander gern. Er hat sie gern.
Sie hat ihn gern.

Sie verlieben sich ineinander. Es wird ernst. Er zieht ein. Sie leben zusammen.

Sie haben Krach miteinander.

Er hat Liebeskummer.

Sie versöhnen sich.

Sie verloben sich.

Sie lernen die Verwandten kennen.

Sie heiraten: sie werden Mann und Frau.

BEISPIEL   *Du hast einen neuen Freund/eine neue Freundin? Wie findest du ihn/sie?*

Illustrations © Cengage Learning 2014

Sprache im Alltag: Expressing fondness or love

German speakers use three expressions to describe fondness or love for a person. Expressions with **mögen** indicate fondness, while expressions with **lieb haben** indicate fondness verging on love. **Lieben** is used explicitly to indicate romantic love. Speakers tend to say "Ich hab' dich lieb" rather than "Ich liebe dich."

Ich mag dich.	*I like you.*
Ich hab' dich lieb.	*I am really fond of you.*
Ich liebe dich.	*I love you.*

36 **Ein Liebesgedicht** Schreiben Sie ein Liebesgedicht mit sechs Zeilen und lesen Sie dann das Gedicht der Klasse vor. Bilden Sie Sätze mit den folgenden Verben.

geheiratet	geschmust
ernst geworden	sich verlobt
gut ausgesehen	angesprochen
Liebeskummer gehabt	attraktiv gefunden
schön ausgesehen	sich verliebt
geküsst	angesehen

BEISPIEL *Er/Sie hat gut ausgesehen.*

37 **Aktivitäten mit Freunden** Kreuzen Sie an, wie oft Sie im letzten Jahr die folgenden Aktivitäten mit einem (Ihrem) Freund/mit einer (Ihrer) Freundin gemacht haben. Dann fragen Sie einen Partner/eine Partnerin.

BEISPIEL S1: *Wie oft bist du mit deinem Freund (deiner Freundin) Rad gefahren?*
S2: *Wir sind selten miteinander Rad gefahren. Und du?*
S1: *Wir sind oft miteinander Rad gefahren.*

	Nie 0 %	Selten 20 %	Oft 60 %	Sehr oft 80 %	Immer >100 %	
1. Rad gefahren	○	○	○	○	○	
2. ins Kino gegangen	○	○	○	○	○	
3. ins Restaurant gegangen	○	○	○	○	○	
4. zusammen ein Bier getrunken	○	○	○	○	○	
5. Hausaufgaben gemacht	○	○	○	○	○	
6. ein Buch gelesen	○	○	○	○	○	
7. ein Theaterstück° gesehen	○	○	○	○	○	*stage play*
8. Verwandte besucht	○	○	○	○	○	
9. über andere Leute gesprochen	○	○	○	○	○	
10. Pläne für die Zukunft° diskutiert	○	○	○	○	○	*future*

Strukturen

Ⅱ Expressing complex ideas with a subordinating conjunction

A. The subordinating conjunction *dass*

Frequently the factual knowledge expressed by speakers with the verbs **wissen, glauben,** or **denken** is in the form of an entire sentence or clause.

Ich **weiß, dass** es heute kalt ist.	*I know that it's cold today.*

A clause usually has a subject and a verb. When a clause stands by itself it is known as a sentence or main clause (der **Hauptsatz**). A dependent or subordinate clause (der **Nebensatz**) cannot stand alone; it depends upon a main clause and is introduced by a subordinating conjunction, e.g., **dass** (*that*) followed by the subject of the subordinate clause. A comma always separates a dependent clause from the main clause.

The conjugated verb of a subordinate clause comes at the end. Separable prefixes are reunited with the conjugated verb at the end of the clause. Auxiliary verbs follow past participles because they are conjugated.

Machen Sie gleich deutlich, **dass** Sie nur 30 oder 60 Minuten Zeit **haben.**	*Make it clear that you only have 30 or 60 minutes free.*
Weißt du, **dass** ich ein neues Auto **gekauft habe?**	*Do you know that I bought a new car?*
Er weiß nicht, **dass** ich ihn **sehen kann.**	*He doesn't know that I can see him.*

Dass may be omitted. In that case, the verb reverts to main clause position.

Du warst so nervös, **dass** du keine drei Worte gesagt **hast.**
Du warst so nervös, du **hast** keine drei Worte gesagt.

Speakers also often use a **dass**-clause to express that something is good **(gut)**, interesting **(interessant)**, important **(wichtig)**, etc., or that a person is disappointed **(enttäuscht)**, happy **(froh)**, sad **(traurig)**, etc. This is used with the structure **Es ist (gut, wichtig, interessant), dass …**

Es ist wichtig, **dass** wir Deutsch sprechen.	*It is important that we speak German.*
Es ist gut, **dass** das Wetter heute so schön ist.	*It is good that the weather is so nice today.*

B. The subordinating conjunction *ob*

To express that they do not know something, German speakers use a negated form of the verb **wissen** with the subordinating conjunction **ob** (*if, whether*), followed by a reference to the missing information. This is, in essence, an indirect yes/no question.

Ich **weiß nicht, ob** sie heute kommt.	*I don't know whether she is coming today.*

German speakers also use **ob** with the affirmative expressions **fragen, will wissen,** and **möchte wissen** to obtain more information.

Ich **frage, ob** sie kommt.	*I'll ask if she's coming.*
Sie **will wissen, ob** er sie wirklich geliebt hat.	*She wants to know whether he really loved her.*

Weißt du nicht, dass ich dich lieb habe?

Fabrice LEROUGE/Jupiter Images

38 Traumpartner(in) Welche Eigenschaften hat Ihr Traumpartner/Ihre Traumpartnerin? Wie wichtig sind diese Eigenschaften für Sie? Kreuzen Sie **Gar nicht wichtig, Wichtig** oder **Sehr wichtig** an. Fragen Sie dann einen Partner/eine Partnerin.

BEISPIEL   S1: *Ist es wichtig, dass dein Traumpartner sportlich ist?*
            S2: *Nein, es ist gar nicht wichtig. Ist es wichtig, dass deine Traumpartnerin viel Geld hat?*
            S1: *Nein, es ist nicht wichtig, dass sie viel Geld hat. Ist es wichtig, dass …?*

	Gar nicht wichtig	Wichtig	Sehr wichtig
1. Er/Sie hat viel Humor.	○	○	○
2. Er/Sie ist ehrlich°.	○	○	○
3. Er/Sie ist sportlich.	○	○	○
4. Er/Sie gibt viel Geld aus.	○	○	○
5. Er/Sie sieht gut aus.	○	○	○
6. Meine Eltern mögen ihn/sie.	○	○	○
7. Er/Sie mag die Natur.	○	○	○
8. Er/Sie liest viel.	○	○	○
9. Er/Sie trinkt keinen Alkohol.	○	○	○
10. Er/Sie spricht Deutsch und Englisch.	○	○	○
11. Er/Sie ist romantisch.	○	○	○
12. Meine Katze (Mein Hund) mag ihn/sie.	○	○	○

honest

39 Schreibecke: **Freund(in) oder Traumpartner(in)?** Gute Freunde sind nicht unbedingt Traumpartner. Beschreiben Sie in zehn Sätzen einen guten Freund/ eine gute Freundin mit dem Vokabular aus der Aktivität „Traumpartner(in)".

Strukturen

▌▌▌ Expressing a condition

Subordinate clauses with *wenn*

German speakers use the subordinating conjunction **wenn** (*when, whenever, as soon as, if*) to express when they do things and to express a condition. As in all subordinate clauses, the conjugated verb comes at the end of a **wenn**-clause.

Reden Sie nie darüber, **wenn** Sie sich einsam und unglücklich **fühlen.**   *Never talk about it **if** you are feeling lonely and unhappy.*

If a sentence begins with a **wenn**-clause, the main clause begins with the verb followed by the subject.

Wenn Sie das erste Treffen **ausmachen**, dann machen Sie gleich deutlich, **dass** Sie nur 30 oder 60 Minuten Zeit **haben.**   ***When** you agree on your first meeting, then make it immediately clear that you only have 30 to 60 minutes time.*

40 In welchen Situationen? Erzählen Sie, in welchen Situationen Sie etwas machen können. Verbinden Sie eine Aussage aus der linken Spalte mit einem Satz in der rechten Spalte und bilden Sie einen **wenn**-Satz.

BEISPIEL   Ich gebe die Anonymität auf. Ich habe Vertrauen zum anderen gefasst.
Ich gebe die Anonymität auf, wenn ich Vertrauen zum anderen gefasst habe.

1. Ich gehe im Winter Ski laufen.
2. Ich spreche so oft wie möglich Deutsch.
3. Ich spreche die Person direkt an.
4. Ich lade jemanden auf ein Date ein.
5. Ich gebe die Anonymität auf.
6. Ich arbeite im Sommer.
7. Ich lerne regelmäßig für meine Kurse.
8. Ich lasse mein Handy zu Hause.

a. Ich finde die Person attraktiv.
b. Ich möchte, dass mich niemand anruft.
c. Ich habe genug Selbstvertrauen.
d. Ich habe Vertrauen zum anderen gefasst.
e. Ich will in den Kursen gute Zensuren bekommen.
f. Ich will mein Deutsch verbessern.
g. Es hat genug geschneit.
h. Ich will Geld verdienen.

Strukturen

IV Giving reasons

Subordinate clauses with *weil*

To state a reason or a justification, German speakers use the subordinating conjunction **weil** (*because*). The verb in the subordinate clause occurs at the end of the clause.

More and more, many German speakers are now using main clause word order after **weil** and not putting the conjugated verb at the end.

Ich habe dich geküsst, **weil** du mir leidgetan hast.	*I kissed you because I felt sorry for you.*
Onkel Hannes hat ein Bier getrunken, **weil** er Durst hatte.	*Uncle Hannes drank a beer because he was thirsty.*

41 Warum machen sie das? Geben Sie einen Grund° für die folgenden Handlungen° an.

reason
actions

Other subordinating conjunctions are **bevor** (*before*), **nachdem** (*after*), and **obwohl** (*although*). They require placement of the verb at the end of the subordinate clause.

ordered

BEISPIEL   *Uschi und Hannes sind nach Hamburg gefahren, weil sie Hochzeitstag haben.*

1. Uschi und Hannes sind nach Hamburg gefahren,
2. Hannes ist zum Hotel zurückgegangen,
3. Uschi hat an der Alster einen Spaziergang gemacht,
4. Uschi hat eine Cola bestellt°,
5. Uschi ruft das Deutsche Schauspielhaus an,
6. Uschi und Hannes müssen um 17.00 Uhr zurück im Hotel sein,

a. er hat sein Geld im Hotelzimmer vergessen.
b. das Wetter heute ist so schön.
c. Katja ruft kurz nach 5 Uhr an.
d. sie haben Hochzeitstag.
e. sie hat Durst.
f. sie möchte für heute Abend Karten bestellen.

42 Warum lernst du Deutsch? Stellen Sie einem Partner/einer Partnerin die folgenden Fragen. Er/Sie gibt als Antwort einen Grund an.

BEISPIEL   S1: *Warum lernst du Deutsch?*
S2: *Ich lerne Deutsch, weil ...*

1. Warum lernst du Deutsch?
    a. Ich möchte Deutschland besuchen.
    b. Ich habe deutsche Verwandte.
    c. Ich möchte gut Deutsch sprechen.
    d. Ich möchte Deutschlehrer(in) werden.
    e. Ich muss es für Chemie (Musik, Geschichte usw.) lernen.
    f. …

2. Warum ist Deutsch wichtig?
    a. Meine Eltern (Großeltern) sprechen Deutsch.
    b. Über 90 Millionen Menschen sprechen Deutsch als Muttersprache.
    c. Mein Freund/Meine Freundin spricht Deutsch.
    d. Deutschland spielt eine führende Rolle in der Europäischen Union.

Strukturen

V **Expanding on an opinion or idea**

Infinitive clauses with *zu*

A variant of the subordinate clause is the **zu** clause. **Zu** is frequently used after an adjective or a noun with an infinitive to expand on an idea. While the verb still occurs at the end of the clause, it is not conjugated and occurs in the infinitive form after **zu.**

Es ist *einfach*, verliebt **zu sein.**	*It is easy to be in love.*
Es ist *uncool*, das **zu sagen.**	*It is uncool to say it.*
Anna hat *Zeit*, eine E-Mail **zu schreiben.**	*Anna has time to write an e-mail.*

Verbs with a separable prefix insert **zu** between the prefix and the stem in infinitive clauses.

Es ist einfach, ihn an**zu**rufen.	*It is easy to call him up.*

 43 Ist es cool? Kombinieren Sie zwei Satzteile und fragen Sie einen Partner/ eine Partnerin.

BEISPIEL   Ist es cool? Du lernst Deutsch.
S1: *Ist es cool, Deutsch zu lernen?*
S2: *O, ja! Es ist sehr cool, Deutsch zu lernen. Hast du Interesse, Japanisch zu lernen?*

1. Ist es cool?   Du kommst am Samstag mit.
2. Hast du Interesse?   Du liest das Buch.
3. Bist du neugierig°?   Du machst viel mit deinen Freunden.   *curious*
4. Seid ihr froh°?   Ihr fahrt im Sommer nach Italien.   *glücklich*
5. Ist es schwierig°?   Du besuchst Südamerika.   *difficult*
6. Ist es leicht?   Du lernst Deutsch/Arabisch.
7. Ist es gut?   Du hast wenige Freunde.
8. Hast du Zeit?   Du lernst Japanisch.

Strukturen

Positioning information in a German sentence

Features of German word order

You have learned three important features of German word order (**Wortstellung**).

A. Subject-verb inversion

In **Kapitel 2** you learned that in a main clause the conjugated verb always comes in the second position.

> Hannes **liebt** Uschi.   *Hannes loves Uschi.*

The subject may appear *after* the verb when the sentence begins with other elements.

direct object	*verb*	*subject*	
Das	hab'	<u>ich</u>	ganz vergessen.

adverb	*verb*	*subject*	
Sonntags	sind	<u>wir</u>	zum Fischmarkt gegangen.

On Sundays, we went to the fish market.

B. Two-part placement of German verbs

Some verb forms occur at the end of the main clause. In **Kapitel 4** you learned that in modal + infinitive constructions, the infinitive is placed at the end of a main clause.

> Fabian **muss** sein Fahrrad nach Hause **schieben.**   *Fabian has to push his bicycle home.*
> Sie **soll** laut **klingeln** und **weiterfahren.**   *She should ring her bell loudly and keep peddling.*

Remember that verbs with separable prefixes place the prefix at the end of the clause in the present tense.

> Herr Günther **ruft** Uschi um 10 Uhr **an.**   *Herr Günther calls up Uschi at 10:00.*

Earlier in this chapter you learned that the past participle is placed at the end of a main clause in the conversational past.

> Uschi **hat** in Hamburg Pharmazie **studiert** und als Kellnerin in einer Studentenkneipe **gearbeitet.**   *Uschi studied pharmaceutics in Hamburg and worked as a waitress in a student bar.*

C. Verb forms at the end of a subordinate clause

You learned earlier in this chapter that in German the conjugated verb is placed at the end of a subordinate clause.

> Franzi darf abbiegen, **wenn** kein Verkehr **kommt.**   *Franzi may turn if no traffic is coming.*
> Machen Sie gleich deutlich, **dass** Sie nur 30 oder 60 Minuten Zeit **haben.**   *Make it clear that you only have 30 or 60 minutes time.*

A subordinate clause may begin with a subordinating conjunction (e.g., **dass, ob, weil, wenn**) or with a question word (e.g., **wann, warum, was, wie,** or **wo).**

> ANNA: Weißt du, **wo** sie wohnt?   *Do you know where she lives?*
> KATJA: Nein. Ich weiß auch nicht, **wie** sie heißt.   *No. I don't know her name either.*

„Meint ihr, dass er der richtige für mich ist?"

The separable prefix appears joined with the verb at the end of a subordinate clause.

USCHI: Weißt du, wann Anna **ankommt?** *Do you know when Anna is arriving?*

KATJA: Nein, nur, dass sie vorher **anruft.** *No, only that she will call first.*

---

 44 Ob sie mich liebt? Karl und Inge sind Studenten an der Universität in Tübingen. Karl hat Inge kennengelernt und jetzt hat er Liebeskummer. Stellen Sie einem Partner/einer Partnerin Fragen.

BEISPIEL   S1: *Was weiß Karl über Inge?*
S2: *Er weiß, dass sie aus Ulm kommt. Und was weiß er nicht?*
S1: *Er weiß nicht, wie alt sie ist. Und was möchte er wissen?*
S2: *Er möchte wissen, ob sie gern italienisch isst.*

Karl weiß	*Karl weiß nicht*	*Karl möchte wissen*
1. Sie kommt aus Ulm.	Wie alt ist sie?	Isst sie gern italienisch?
2. Sie sieht gut aus.	Ist sie romantisch?	Geht sie gern spazieren?
3. Sie hat viel Humor.	Ist sie sportlich?	Tanzt sie gern?
4. Sie studiert Betriebswirtschaft.	Wohnt sie schon lange hier?	Mag sie die Natur?

Werner Dieterich/Alamy

Inge ist am Wochenende nach Ulm gefahren.

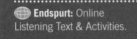
🌐 **Endspurt:** Online
Listening Text & Activities.

Freunde geben Freunden Ratschläge

Zielaktivitäten

 45 Ein katastrophales erstes Date Ihr Freund/Ihre Freundin war auf einem ersten Date. Er/sie hat ALLES falsch gemacht. Das Date war eine Katastrophe. Der Freund/Die Freundin erzählt zuerst, was passiert ist. Geben Sie dann Rat: Was soll Ihr Freund/Ihre Freundin jetzt machen?

Was ist passiert?

1. Sie wollen Ihrem Freund/Ihrer Freundin gern helfen, aber Sie müssen zuerst wissen, was passiert ist. Stellen Sie dem Freund/der Freundin einige Fragen. Was antwortet der Freund/die Freundin?

BEISPIEL   S1: *Wo war das Date?*
S2: *Das Date war in einer Kneipe.*

a. Wo war das Date?
in einer Kneipe / in meinem Studentenzimmer / in einem Hotel / im Kino / in einem Park / an der Uni / …

b. Wie lange war das Date?
drei Minuten / vier Stunden / den ganzen Tag / das ganze Wochenende / …

c. Was hast du getrunken?
Tee / Mineralwasser / vier große Flaschen Bier / drei Glas Whiskey / Kaffee / nichts / …

d. Worüber hast du gesprochen?
über meine dummen Professoren / über meinen Hund / über meinen Ex / über meine Ex / über Geld / über meine Religion / über den inkompetenten Kellner / über den Preis von Bier / über Politik / über …

e. Was hast du dem Date gegeben?
meine Telefonnummer / eine falsche Telefonnummer / meine Adresse / meine E-Mail-Adresse / einen falschen Namen / die Hand / einen dicken Kuss / die Restaurantrechnung° / …

f. Wie hast du gewirkt?°
extrem dumm / sehr naiv / ziemlich uninteressant / total verliebt / ganz betrunken / zu leidenschaftlich / sehr kalt / …

g. Was hat dein Date am Ende zu dir gesagt?
„Das war katastrophal." / „Wie romantisch!" / „Das war langweilig." / „Ich will dich vergessen." / „Ich möchte dich leidenschaftlich küssen." / „Ich will dich niemals wiedersehen." / „Darf ich dich wieder einladen?" / „Willst du mich heiraten?" / …

restaurant bill
Wie ...: *How did you come across?*

Die Geschichte erzählen

2. Erzählen Sie zuerst ein bisschen von Ihrem Freund/Ihrer Freundin. Geben Sie ein paar neue Details an. Sagen Sie, was *zuerst, später, dann, danach,* und *zuletzt / am Ende* passiert ist. Nicht vergessen: Nach Wörtern wie *zuerst, dann* usw. kommt gleich das konjugierte Verb an zweiter Stelle.

BEISPIEL *Meine Freundin Katie kommt aus Kalifornien. Sie ist achtzehn Jahre alt und studiert Biologie. Sie war auf einem Date. Das ist so passiert: Das Date war in einer Kneipe. Die Kneipe hat „The Smoking Gun" geheißen. Das Date hat aber nur drei Minuten gedauert. Katie hat nichts getrunken. Zuerst hat sie über ihren Ex gesprochen. Dann hat sie dem Date …*

Der Rat

3. Was soll Ihr Freund/Ihre Freundin jetzt nur machen? Geben Sie Ratschläge.

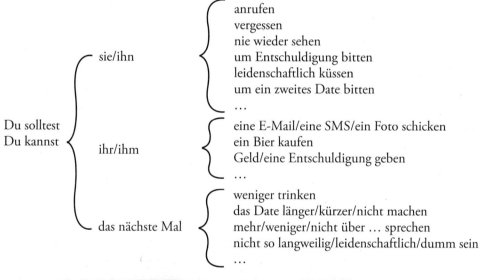

Du solltest
Du kannst

sie/ihn
- anrufen
- vergessen
- nie wieder sehen
- um Entschuldigung bitten
- leidenschaftlich küssen
- um ein zweites Date bitten
- …

ihr/ihm
- eine E-Mail/eine SMS/ein Foto schicken
- ein Bier kaufen
- Geld/eine Entschuldigung geben
- …

das nächste Mal
- weniger trinken
- das Date länger/kürzer/nicht machen
- mehr/weniger/nicht über … sprechen
- nicht so langweilig/leidenschaftlich/dumm sein
- …

Fuse/Jupiter Images

Hast du ihm deine Telefonnummer gegeben?

46 Schreibecke: **Eine Seifenoper° schreiben.** Schreiben Sie eine kurze Seifenoper (fünf bis acht Sätze). Benutzen Sie die Fragen unten und Wörter und Ausdrücke aus **Wissenswerte Vokabeln: Freundschaft und Liebe.** Viel Spaß!

1. Was ist der Titel der Seifenoper?
2. Wie heißen die Personen? Was sind die Eigenschaften jeder° Person?
3. Was ist vorher passiert°?
4. Was sind die momentanen Beziehungen°?

BEISPIEL   **Lieben und Leben:** *Die Personen heißen Beate, Torsten, Hanno und Sabine. Hanno findet viele Frauen attraktiv und sieht sehr gut aus. Beate ist hübsch und ziemlich lustig. Torsten [...] Vorher war Beate in Hanno verliebt, aber Hanno hat Sabine geküsst. [...] Beate ist jetzt böse auf Hanno. Sie geht mit Torsten aus und er ist in sie verliebt.*

47 Reisetagebuch Sie sind in Deutschland. Schreiben Sie in ein Reisetagebuch, was Sie schon gemacht, gesehen und gelernt haben. Schreiben Sie auch auf, was Sie noch lernen oder sehen wollen. Verwenden Sie Konjunktionen wie **dass, ob, weil** und **wenn** und die Fragewörter als Konjunktionen. Verwenden Sie auch die folgenden Konstruktionen: **Ich möchte/will wissen, ob ... ; Ich frage mich** (*wonder*), **ob ... ; In Deutschland ist es leicht, ... zu ....**

BEISPIEL   *Ich habe schon gesehen, wie freundlich die Leute sind. Ich habe schon viele nette° Leute kennengelernt. Ich möchte aber auch wissen, ob ...*

48 Wir sind verliebt! Sie studieren in Berlin und haben dort eine sehr nette Person kennengelernt. Sie verbringen schon viel Zeit miteinander, und Sie möchten bei dieser Person einziehen und mit ihr zusammenleben. Schreiben Sie einen Brief an Ihre Eltern. Informieren Sie Ihre Eltern über die Fragen:

> Wie und wo haben Sie sich kennengelernt?
> Was haben Sie zusammen gemacht?

Fragen Sie Ihre Eltern, ob sie dafür oder dagegen sind.

49 Freie Kommunikation: **Die Einladung.** Sie finden eine Person attraktiv und möchten sie in die Kneipe einladen. Die andere Person hat wenig Interesse. Sie sind aber sehr motiviert und geben nicht auf°. Wie überreden° Sie die Person, mit Ihnen auszugehen?

Möchtest du heute Abend auf eine Party gehen?

WORTSCHATZ

Tutorial Quiz
Audio Flashcards

In der Kneipe

der Kellner, - / die Kellnerin, -nen *waiter / waitress*

die Kneipe, -n *pub, bar*

das Trinkgeld, -er *tip, gratuity*

arbeiten (hat gearbeitet) *to work*

bestellen (hat bestellt) *to order*

verdienen (hat verdient) *to earn*

verkaufen (hat verkauft) *to sell*

Freundschaft, Liebe und Leute

der/die Bekannte, -n *acquaintance, casual friend*

die Beziehung, -en *relationship*

die Einladung, -en *invitation*

der/die Ex, - *former boyfriend/ girlfriend*

das Date, -s *date*

die Frau, -en *wife; woman*

der Freund, -e / die Freundin, -nen *friend*

die Freundschaft, -en *friendship*

der Junge, [-n], -n *boy, guy;* **die Jungs** *boys, guys (slang)*

der Kontakt *contact*

der Krach, ⸚e *argument, quarrel; noise*

Krach haben *to have a fight, quarrel*

der Kumpel, -s *buddy, pal*

die Leute *(pl.) people*

die Liebe, -n *love*

der Liebeskummer *lovesickness; heartbreak*

das Mädchen, - *girl*

der Mann, ⸚er *husband; man*

der Respekt *respect*

das Risiko, *pl.* **Risiken** *risk*

das Selbstvertrauen *confidence, self-respect*

der Streit *argument*

die Sympathie *likeability*

das Thema, *pl.* **Themen** *topic, theme*

das Treffen, - *meeting*

der/die Verlobte, -n *fiancé(e)*

das Vertrauen *trust*

ab•holen (hat abgeholt) *to pick up*

an•sprechen (spricht an, hat angesprochen) *to initiate a conversation (with someone)*

auf•geben (gibt auf, hat aufgegeben) *to give up*

aus•gehen (ist ausgegangen) *to go out*

aus•machen (hat ausgemacht) *to finalize, e.g., a date*

aus•schalten (hat ausgeschaltet) *to turn off*

aus•sehen (sieht aus, hat ausgesehen) *to look, appear*

begrenzen (hat begrenzt) *to limit*

bekannt geben (hat bekannt gegeben) *to reveal*

diskutieren (hat diskutiert) (über + acc.) *to discuss (a topic)*

ein•laden (lädt ein, hat eingeladen) *to invite; to ask out*

ein•ziehen (ist eingezogen) *to move in*

erfahren (erfährt, hat erfahren) *to find out; experience*

fertig•werden (wird, ist fertiggeworden) *to accept, come to grips with*

flirten (hat geflirtet) *to flirt*

heiraten (hat geheiratet) *to marry, get married*

küssen (hat geküsst) *to kiss*

lassen (lässt, hat gelassen) *to let, allow; to have someone do something*

leben (hat gelebt) *to live*

zusammen•leben (hat zusammengelebt) *to live together*

lieben (hat geliebt) *to love*

reden (hat geredet) (über + acc.) *to talk (about a topic)*

schmusen (hat geschmust) *to cuddle, make out*

treffen (trifft, hat getroffen) *to meet*

umarmen (hat umarmt) *to embrace, hug*

verliebt (in + acc.) sein *to be in love (with somebody)*

vermeiden (hat vermieden) *to avoid*

wirken (hat gewirkt) *to make an impression, appear to be*

attraktiv *attractive*

beide *both*

einander *each other*

einfach *simple; simply*

ernst *serious*

tabu *forbidden, taboo*

täglich *daily, every day*

wahr *authentic, real*

zusammen *together*

Ich habe dich lieb. *I am really fond of you. I love you.*

Ich liebe dich. *I love you.*

Ich mag dich. *I like you.*

Sie verlieben sich ineinander. *They fall in love with each other.*

Sie verloben sich. *They get engaged.*

Sie versöhnen sich. *They reconcile, make up.*

Vertrauen fassen zu (+ dat.) *to trust*

weit weg *far away*

zu zweit *as a couple; in twos*

zum ersten Mal *for the first time*

Das Gefühl

böse *angry*

deutlich *clear*

einsam *lonely*

enttäuscht *disappointed*

froh *happy*

gewiss *certain*

neutral *neutral*

offen *open*

stolz *proud*

traurig *sad*

unglücklich *unhappy*

Das Wetter

Wie ist das Wetter heute? *What's the weather like today?*

der Gefrierpunkt *freezing point*

das Gewitter *electrical storm, thunderstorm*

der Grad *degree*

der Nebel *fog*

der Regen *rain*

der Schauer, - *rain shower*

der Schnee *snow*

die Sonne, -n *sun*

der Sturm, ¨e *storm*

die Temperatur, -en *temperature*

das Wetter *weather*

die Wolke, -n *cloud*

blitzen: es blitzt (es hat geblitzt) *there is lightning*

donnern (es hat gedonnert) *to thunder*

fallen (fällt, ist gefallen) *to drop; to fall*

regnen (es hat geregnet) *to rain*

scheinen (hat geschienen) *to shine*

schneien (es hat geschneit) *to snow*

sinken (ist gesunken) *to sink; to drop*

steigen (ist gestiegen) *to rise; climb*

bedeckt *overcast*

heiß *hot*

heiter *clear, partly sunny*

kalt *cold*

kühl *cool*

mies *rotten, lousy*

nass *wet, damp*

schwül *humid*

sonnig *sunny*

trocken *dry*

warm *warm*

windig *windy*

wolkig *cloudy*

Die Temperatur liegt bei [zehn] Grad Celcius. *The temperature is [ten] degrees Celcius.*

Die Jahreszeiten

die Jahreszeit, -en *season*

der Frühling *spring*

der Herbst *autumn, fall*

der Sommer *summer*

der Winter *winter*

Zeitausdrücke

bald *soon*

bevor *before*

früher *earlier, in the past*

gestern *yesterday*

jetzt *now*

morgen *tomorrow*

erst *only, just;* **erst (seit)** *just since*

schon *already*

Andere Verben

an•fangen (fängt an, hat angefangen) *to start, begin*

beginnen (hat begonnen) *to begin*

bekommen (hat bekommen) *to get*

bringen (hat gebracht) *to bring*

erzählen (hat erzählt) *to tell, relate*

glauben (hat geglaubt) *to believe*

liegen (hat gelegen) *to lie*

los•fahren (fährt los, ist losgefahren) *to set off (on a trip)*

mailen (hat gemailt) *to e-mail*

öffnen (hat geöffnet) *to open*

passieren (ist passiert) *to happen*

sagen (hat gesagt) *to say*

sitzen (hat gesessen) *to sit*

sterben (stirbt, ist gestorben) *to die*

surfen (hat gesurft) *to surf*

verlieren (hat verloren) *to lose*

Andere Wörter

die Kontaktdaten (*pl.*) *contact information*

die Telefonnummer, -n *telephone number*

die Zeitung, -en *newspaper*

dass *that*

ob *whether, if*

trotzdem *nevertheless, in spite of that*

weil *because*

wenn *if, when, whenever*

zu *(+ inf.) to*

einfach *simple*

fertig *finished*

frei *free*

jede(r) *each*

leicht *easy; light*

richtig *right, proper; real*

schade *too bad, unfortunate*

schlecht *bad*

schlimm *bad, nasty*

schwierig *difficult, hard*

toll *fantastic, great*

eigentlich *actually*

fast *almost, practically*

ganz *really, very; whole*

   ganz nass *completely wet*

   ganz schlimm *really bad*

   die ganze Zeit *the whole time*

wenigstens *at least*

wirklich *really*

Andere Ausdrücke

auf keinen Fall *in no case, never ever*

auf neutralem Boden *on neutral ground*

ein paar *a few*

ich frage mich, ob … *I wonder if …*

und so weiter (usw.) *and so on, etcetera (etc.)*

von vornherein *right from the very start*

Was ist los? *What's the matter?*

Was noch? *What else?*

Meine eigenen Wörter

_____

_____

_____

_____

_____

Yoshihiro Takada/Jupiter Images

Tübingen ist eine tolle Universitätsstadt.

Willkommen in Tübingen

In this chapter you will learn to express giving or lending to others, talk about the location of things, make compliments, and talk about ailments.

Kommunikative Funktionen
> Expressing the beneficiary or recipient of an action
> Indicating location
> Expressing temporal and spatial relationships with dative prepositions
> Expressing gratitude, pleasure, ownership, and need for assistance
> Specifying what you are talking about

Strukturen
> The dative case
> Dative prepositions
> Dative verbs and expressions
> **Der**-words

Vokabeln
> Das Studentenzimmer
> Ein Einfamilienhaus
> Körperteile

Kulturelles
> Wo Studenten wohnen
> Tübingen

Anna zieht ins Wohnheim ein

Anna zieht in ein Tübinger Studentenwohnheim ein. Es heißt Waldhäuser-Ost. Barbara, eine Studentin im ersten Semester aus Dresden, hat das Zimmer neben Anna. Sie hilft Anna beim Einzug°.

hilft ... : helps Anna move in

Vorschau

Wissenswerte Vokabeln: das Studentenzimmer und die Möbel

Identifying objects

das Bild • die Gardinen, pl. • der Computer • der Drucker • das Bücherregal • die Stereoanlage • der Kleiderschrank • die Lampe • das Poster • der Spiegel • die Pflanze • das Radio • der Stuhl • der Schreibtisch • die Couch, das Sofa • der Sessel • das Waschbecken • der Wecker • die Kommode • der Fernseher • der Teppich • das Bett

Was ...: What kind of

BEISPIEL Was für° Möbel hast du im Zimmer? *Ich habe ...*

↩ **1** Hast du das im Zimmer? Fragen Sie einen Partner/eine Partnerin, was er/sie im Zimmer hat. Benutzen Sie die Akkusativformen: einen/keinen, ein/kein, eine/keine.

die Stereoanlage • das Wasserbett • das Telefon • der Mikrowellenherd • das Handy • die Kaffeemaschine • der Mini-Kühlschrank°

mini-refrigerator

BEISPIEL S1: *Hast du eine Stereoanlage im Zimmer?*
S2: *Ja, ich habe eine Stereoanlage. Und du?* (oder)
Nein, ich habe keine Stereoanlage.

2 Thematische Fragen Beantworten Sie diese Fragen auf Deutsch.

1. Was brauchen Studenten für die Universität? Machen Sie eine Liste.
2. Wohnen Sie mit anderen Studenten in einem Studentenwohnheim? Wie finden Sie das? Was können Sie da alles machen? Was ist verboten°?
3. Wohnen Sie zu Hause? Was können Sie da machen? Was ist verboten?

forbidden

3 Satzdetektiv Welche Sätze bedeuten ungefähr das Gleiche?

1. Anna zieht ins Wohnheim ein.
2. Ich bin selber erst vor einer Woche hier eingezogen.
3. Ich krieg' die Tür nicht auf.
4. Gib mir deinen Schlüssel. Ich schließ' dir die Tür auf.
5. Hier, guck mal, Anna!
6. Gefällt dir dein Zimmer denn nicht?

a. Von jetzt an wohnt Anna im Studentenwohnheim.
b. Ich kann die Tür nicht öffnen.
c. Ich wohne erst seit einer Woche im Wohnheim.
d. Schau mal, Anna!
e. Findest du dein Zimmer nicht schön?
f. Gib mir den Schlüssel. Ich mache die Tür auf.

7. Du hast einen Schrank für deine Klamotten.
8. Also, jetzt zeig' ich dir das Badezimmer, wenn es dir recht ist.
9. Du hast wirklich Schwein gehabt.
10. Du hast ein Privatbad bekommen: Klo, Dusche und Waschbecken.
11. Du, ich danke dir echt für die Hilfe!
12. Kannst du mir einen Stift leihen?

g. Das Badezimmer hast du für dich allein: Toilette, Dusche und Waschbecken.
h. Du hast einen Schrank für deine Kleidung.
i. Du hast wirklich Glück gehabt.
j. Ich zeige dir das Badezimmer, wenn das O.K. ist.
k. Kannst du mir einen Stift geben?
l. Vielen Dank für deine Hilfe.

Kulturnotiz. In German-speaking countries, floors are counted as follows: **das Erdgeschoss** *(first floor)*, **erster Stock** *(second floor)*, **zweiter Stock** *(third floor)*, etc.

Kulturnotiz. German door locks often include a deadbolt, which must be turned twice to lock the door.

Sprache im Alltag: Expressions with animals

German speakers like to use colorful expressions involving animals.

Schwein haben	*to be lucky*
Du **hast Schwein gehabt.**	
einen Bärenhunger haben	*to be hungry as a bear*
Er **hat einen Bärenhunger.**	
einen Vogel haben	*to be crazy*
Er **hat einen Vogel.**	
(einen) Kater haben	*to have a hangover*
Wir **haben** heute **einen Kater.**	
hundemüde sein	*to be dog-tired*
Ich **bin hundemüde.**	

Hören Sie gut zu.

> **Zum** + verb in the infinitive (**ein Bett zum Schlafen**)
> is the equivalent of *for* + *-ing* verb *(a bed for sleeping)*.

© Cengage Learning 2014

Heißt das, dass die Studenten hier in Deutschland nichts anderes machen als schlafen, aufstehen und lernen?

Na so ziemlich. Nur die Reihenfolge stimmt nicht so ganz. Also, wir stehen so gegen Mittag auf, dann schlafen wir in den Vorlesungen — na, und abends lernen wir, in den Studentenkneipen.

Also, jetzt zeig' ich dir dein Badezimmer, wenn es dir recht ist.

Mein Badezimmer? Ich habe ein eigenes Badezimmer?

Klein aber fein! Du hast wirklich Schwein gehabt! Meistens gibt es nur ein Gemeinschaftsbad oder einen Duschraum auf dem Gang, aber du hast ein Privatbad bekommen: Klo, Dusche und Waschbecken.

Vielleicht ist es doch eine Luxusbude.

Was soll ich dir noch schnell sagen? Also, eine Bar und Cola-Automaten gibt's unten im Keller, und die Telefonzellen, das Schwarze Brett und dein Postfach findest du im Erdgeschoss. Die Küche ist am Ende vom Korridor.

2. Stock
Annas Zimmer
Küche

1. Stock

Erdgeschoss
schwarzes Brett
Postfächer

Keller
Bar
Colaautomaten

Alles klar.

Du, ich muss zu einem Freund, aber ich komme später bei dir vorbei.

Danke, Barbara.

Gut. Kannst du mir einen Stift leihen? Ich schreibe dir die Zimmernummer von einem Freund aus Dresden auf. Er wohnt einen Stock tiefer.

Gut. Du, ich danke dir echt für die Hilfe!

Ja, bis gleich. Tschüss.

Rückblick

4 Stimmt das? Stimmen diese Aussagen zum Text? Wenn nicht, was stimmt?

Kulturnotiz. Because the legal drinking age in Germany for beer and wine is 16, it is quite common to find a student bar in residence halls.

Complete the **Ergänzen Sie** activity in the Student Activities Manual before doing the next activity.

	Ja, das stimmt.	Nein, das stimmt nicht.
1. Anna muss den Weg zu ihrem Zimmer alleine finden.	○	○
2. Barbara studiert schon lange in Tübingen.	○	○
3. Annas Zimmer ist gleich neben Barbaras Zimmer im zweiten Stock.	○	○
4. Anna kann die Tür nicht aufschließen. Barbara nimmt den Schlüssel und hilft.	○	○
5. Anna und Barbara finden, sie haben Luxusbuden im Studentenwohnheim.	○	○
6. Barbara meint es ironisch, wenn sie sagt, deutsche Studenten stehen erst gegen Mittag auf und schlafen in den Vorlesungen.	○	○
7. In diesem Wohnheim haben alle Zimmer ein Privatbad.	○	○
8. Es gibt eine Studentenkneipe im Erdgeschoss.	○	○
9. Die Studenten können am Ende vom Korridor selber kochen.	○	○
10. Anna leiht Barbara eine Zigarette.	○	○

5 Sie/Er weiß (nicht), dass … Welche Dinge weiß ein deutscher Student/eine deutsche Studentin wahrscheinlich nicht, wenn er/sie zuerst in ein amerikanisches Studentenwohnheim kommt? Welche Dinge weiß er/sie?

BEISPIEL   S1: *Weiß ein deutscher Student (eine deutsche Studentin), dass es eine Küche gibt?*
S2: *Nein, er (sie) weiß nicht, dass es eine Küche gibt.* (oder)
Ja, er (sie) weiß, dass es eine Küche gibt.

1. Es gibt eine Küche.
2. Man schläft in einem Bett.
3. *First floor* ist das Erdgeschoss.
4. Man kann Türen ohne Schlüssel abschließen.
5. Das Studentenwohnheim hat keine Bar.
6. Das Badezimmer hat ein Klo.
7. Die Studenten essen zusammen in der *cafeteria*.
8. Man darf nicht rauchen.

6 Textdetektiv: **Anlauftext.** Use the *Anlauftext* to recognize important aspects of German structure and usage.

1. Look at these examples from the *Anlauftext*. Each example has a boldface pronoun. Decide which pronoun the boldface pronoun looks more like: **mich** or **dich**.

	Looks more like *mich*	Looks more like *dich*
a. Das ist wirklich nett von **dir**.	○	○
b. dass du **mir** hilfst	○	○
c. Ich zeig **dir** dein Zimmer.	○	○
d. Gib **mir** deinen Schlüssel.	○	○

2. What do the meanings of verbs like **helfen, zeigen,** and **geben** suggest?
   a. that one person is providing something for another person
   b. that a person is acting alone
   c. that a person is taking something from another person

3. The pronoun forms **mir** and **dir** occur with verbs such as **helfen, zeigen,** or **geben**. In addition, as shown in example 1.a., they can also be prompted by …
   a. the adjective *nett*   b. the adverb *wirklich*   c. the preposition *von*

4. The question **Gefällt dir dein Zimmer?** is best translated as *Do you like your room?* However, unlike the English translation, *you* is not the subject of the German sentence. What is the literal translation of the German question?
   a. Does your room appeal to you?
   b. Can you accept your room?
   c. Where can your room be found?

5. The phrase **ein Schreibtisch zum Lernen** …
   a. uses a verb as a past participle
   b. uses a verb (infinitive) as an adjective
   c. uses a verb (infinitive) as a noun

6. The form **zum** is a contraction of
   a. the preposition *zu* and the article *das*
   b. the preposition *zu* and the article *dem*
   c. the preposition *zu* and the article *den*

7. The answer in 5 is accomplished by … (Mark all that apply.)
   a. capitalizing the verb
   b. giving the verb an article

⟵ **7** Unser Traumzimmer Sprechen Sie in einer Gruppe von drei Personen über Ihr Traumzimmer. Was haben Sie alles im Zimmer? Schreiben Sie eine Liste. Machen Sie dann eine Skizze° des Zimmers.

sketch

BEISPIEL   *In unserem Traumzimmer gibt es ein Wasserbett, eine …*
Das Zimmer ist … / Das Zimmer hat …

⟵ **8** Der Studentenalltag Was machen Sie als Student/Studentin jeden Tag? Kreuzen Sie zuerst an, was Sie jeden Tag machen. Notieren Sie dann die Reihenfolge (zuerst … , dann … , später …). Fragen Sie dann einen Partner/eine Partnerin.

BEISPIEL   S1: *Was machst du zuerst?*
S2: *Zuerst stehe ich auf.*
S1: *Und dann?*

Was?	Jeden Tag?	In welcher Reihenfolge?
1. frühstücken	◯	____
2. Kaffee trinken	◯	____
3. duschen°	◯	____
4. weggehen	◯	____
5. mit Freunden simsen°	◯	____
6. aufstehen	◯	____
7. den Wecker abstellen°	◯	____
8. Deutsch lernen	◯	____

to shower

to text

to turn off

†† 9 Freie Kommunikation: **Interview.** Stellen Sie einem Partner/einer Partnerin die folgenden Fragen.

1. Hast du eine Luxusbude? Wenn ja (nein), warum kann man das sagen?
2. Hat man hier im Wohnheim eine Küche auf dem Gang?
3. Gibt es eine Studentenbar im Studentenwohnheim? Kann man an der Uni überhaupt Bier kaufen oder trinken?
4. Kann man an der Uni Zigaretten kaufen?
5. Was hast du in deinem Zimmer?

†† 10 Rollenspiel: Neu im Wohnheim S1 ist neu im Wohnheim und sucht sein/ihr Zimmer. S2 wohnt schon im Wohnheim und hilft S1, das Zimmer zu finden. Was sagen Sie? Hier sind einige Ausdrücke.

Kannst du mir bitte helfen? • Das ist nett von dir. • Ich zeige dir … • Gib mir … • Hast du auch so ein … im Zimmer?

⇐ 11 Schreibecke: **Eine E-Mail an Katja.** Anna schreibt Katja Günther eine E-Mail. Sie will über ihren ersten Tag im Studentenwohnheim, über Barbara, ihr Zimmer und die Dinge im Keller und im Erdgeschoss schreiben. Aber Anna wird müde. Schreiben Sie Annas E-Mail fertig.

BEISPIEL   Liebe Katja,

heute bin ich im Studentenwohnheim Waldhäuser-Ost angekommen. Ich habe eine nette Studentin kennengelernt. Sie heißt Barbara Müller und kommt aus Dresden. Sie hat mir geholfen. Sie hat …

Zeichnung: Sepp Buchegger

…und wenn, liebe Eltern, mein Vermieter° mit dem Auto unterwegs ist, dann ist es sogar richtig gemütlich° hier.

landlord
cozy

Wo Studenten wohnen

Most universities in German-speaking countries are located in the center of town, and are rarely arranged in an insular, campus-like setting. Because the universities do not assume responsibility for housing all students, students must compete for a limited number of subsidized dorm rooms or find their own housing on the more expensive open market (**der Wohnungsmarkt**). The shortage of space in town near the classroom buildings has resulted in the construction of many residence halls (**Studentenwohnheime**), as well as many research buildings, on the outskirts of town. Most residence halls consist primarily of single rooms (**Einzelzimmer**), which contain a bed, a desk, a bookcase, and a small table and chair, some closet space or a freestanding wardrobe and a small sink. Older residence halls have communal toilets (**die Toiletten/die WCs**) and a shower room (**der Duschraum**). Each floor is also equipped with a communal kitchen (**die Gemeinschaftsküche**) where students can store food and cooking utensils, prepare and eat their own meals. A large cafeteria (**die Mensa**), located at or near the university, provides subsidized lunches and dinners for students and faculty, whether or not they live in one of the residence halls.

Caspar Benson/Getty Images

Hier ist der Schlüssel für die Wohnung.

According to 2009 data from Deutsches Studentenwerk, 12-13% of German students nationally live in residence halls, while 18% live with their parents. Fully 66% live in apartments. To assist domestic and international students with finding private housing in town, many universities offer a free housing service (**Zimmer- und Wohnungsvermittlung**). Only 1% of students nationwide rent rooms or apartments in private homes with a family (**zur Untermiete wohnen**), which often excludes cooking privileges and allows for little privacy. 5% of students nationwide live in residential cooperatives (**Wohngemeinschaften** or **WGs**), in which the housemates share costs and often the cooking, shopping, and cleaning responsibilities.

Kulturkreuzung

Wo wohnen Sie – privat oder im Studentenwohnheim? Muss man an Ihrer Universität im Studentenwohnheim wohnen? Welche Vorteile° bietet° das Studentenwohnheim: Einzelzimmer? Doppelzimmer? Gruppenzimmer? Was kostet ein Zimmer im Studentenwohnheim? Was kostet ein privates Zimmer? Wohnen viele Studenten zu Hause bei den Eltern?

advantages / offers

Strukturen

 Expressing the beneficiary or recipient of an action

The dative case

You have already learned that the nominative case is used for the subject of a sentence and the accusative case is used for the direct object. A third case, called the dative (**der Dativ**), is used for an indirect object, the beneficiary or recipient of an action, which is usually a person or an animal. The direct objects in these sentences are inanimate objects (**dein Zimmer, deinen Schlüssel, die Tür, einen Stift**) and appear in the accusative case.

Komm, ich zeig' **dir** dein Zimmer.	*Come on, I'll show your room to you.* *(Come on, I'll show you your room.)*
Gib' **mir** deinen Schlüssel.	*Give your key to me. (Give me your key.)*
Ich schließ' **dir** die Tür auf.	*I'll open the door for you.*

In English, indirect objects that follow direct objects usually include either *to* or *for* before the noun or pronoun (*for you, to me*). Notice that the German dative case, when used with people, does not need an accompanying preposition (**dir, mir**).

The dative answers the question **wem?** (*to whom? for whom?*).

Wem leiht Anna einen Stift?	*To whom is Anna lending a pen?*
Sie leiht **Barbara** einen Stift.	*She's lending a pen to Barbara.*
Sie leiht **ihr** einen Stift.	*She's lending her a pen.*

A. The dative case: personal pronouns

The indirect object in the dative case is often expressed as a personal pronoun. Here are the nominative, accusative, and dative forms of the personal pronouns.

	Singular						Plural			
	1st	**2nd**		**3rd**			**1st**	**2nd**		**3rd**
Nom.	ich	du	Sie	er	es	sie	wir	ihr	Sie	sie
Acc.	mich	dich	Sie	ihn	es	sie	uns	euch	Sie	sie
Dat.	**mir**	**dir**	**Ihnen**	**ihm**	**ihm**	**ihr**	**uns**	**euch**	**Ihnen**	**ihnen**
	(to/for) me	*(to/for) you*	*(to/for) you*	*(to/for) him*	*(to/for) it*	*(to/for) her*	*(to/for) us*	*(to/for) you*	*(to/for) you*	*(to/for) them*

Note that the dative forms **ihm** and **ihr** resemble their English counterparts *him* and *her*. However, the English forms *him* and *her* also correspond to the German accusative forms **ihn** and **sie**. **Ich kenne ihn/sie.** *I know him/her.*

When the direct object is a pronoun, it must come before the indirect object.

Kannst du mir deinen Stift leihen?	*Can you lend me your pen?*
Kannst du **ihn** mir leihen?	*Can you lend it to me?*

⤺ **12** Was leihen sie einander? Was leihen die folgenden Studenten/ Studentinnen einander? Unterhalten Sie sich mit einem Partner/einer Partnerin und benutzen Sie Personalpronomen in den Antworten.

BEISPIEL   S1: *Was leiht Rolf Barbara?*
S2: *Er leiht ihr seinen Computer.*

Tabelle A (S1):

	Rolf	Barbara	Carlos und Karla	Torsten	Anna
Rolf	—	?	seine Sporttasche	?	5 Euro
Barbara	Nichts	—	?	ihre Zeitung	?
Carlos und Karla	?	ihre Gitarre	—	ihr Radio	?
Torsten	sein Handy	?	?	—	sein Wörter-buch
Anna	?	ihre Haarbürste	ihr Shampoo	?	—

Tabelle B (S2):

	Rolf	Barbara	Carlos und Karla	Torsten	Anna
Rolf	—	seinen Computer	?	sein Auto	?
Barbara	?	—	ihre Karten	?	ihren Schlüssel
Carlos und Karla	20 Euro	?	—	?	ihr Fahrrad
Torsten	?	seinen Fernseher	seine CDs	—	?
Anna	ihr Auto	?	?	Geld	—

⤺ **13** Leihst du mir das? Leihen Sie Freunden oft etwas? Ein Partner/Eine Partnerin fragt, ob er/sie sich die folgenden Gegenstände von Ihnen leihen kann. Was antworten Sie?

BEISPIEL   S1: *Leihst du mir bitte dein Deutschbuch?*
S2: *Na klar! Ich leihe dir mein Deutschbuch.* (oder)
Nein. Mein Deutschbuch leihe ich dir nicht.

1. dein neues Auto
2. dein Fahrrad
3. deine Zahnbürste
4. deine Haarbürste
5. dein Shampoo
6. dein Handy
7. 100 Euro
8. 1 000 Dollar
9. deinen Pullover
10. deine Schuhe

↩ **14** Geburtstagsgeschenke Wem schenken° Sie die folgenden Gegenstände zum Geburtstag? Besprechen° Sie mit einem Partner/einer Partnerin, welche Leute welche Geschenke bekommen sollen. Besprechen Sie auch, warum.

give as a gift
discuss

BEISPIEL S1: *Wem schenkst du ein Auto zum Geburtstag?*
S2: *Ich schenke Mary ein Auto.*
S1: *Warum schenkst du ihr ein Auto?*
S2: *Weil ihr Auto kaputt ist.*

1. ein Auto
2. ein Flugticket nach Frankreich
3. Karten für ein Konzert
4. ein Fahrrad
5. einen Computer
6. Blumen°
7. einen Fernseher
8. ein Buch über Deutschland
9. einen Reisekoffer

a. Frankie ist ein großer Fan von HipHop.
b. Luise ist sehr sportlich.
c. Sabine ist Hobbygärtnerin.
d. Bastian ist ein Internet-Fan.
e. Holger sieht gern fern.
f. Elke fliegt nach Spanien.
g. Stefan studiert Deutsch.
h. James studiert Französisch.
i. Marys Auto ist kaputt.

flowers

> Remember that **ihr** is a possessive adjective (**ihr Auto:** *her car*) as well as a dative personal pronoun (**Ich gebe ihr das Auto:** *I give her the car*).

> **Geburtstagsgeschenke.** Remember that **weil** is a subordinating conjunction and requires the conjugated verb to be placed at the end of the clause.

B. The dative case: definite and indefinite articles and possessive adjectives

You can identify the dative case of a noun by looking at the ending on the article or possessive adjective. The following chart summarizes the dative forms of the definite and indefinite articles, **kein,** and the possessive adjectives. Note the similarity of the endings with the personal pronouns, e.g., **-m** for masculine and neuter forms and **-r** for feminine forms.

	Masculine	Neuter	Feminine	Plural
Nominative	der Vater	das Kind	die Mutter	die Freunde
Accusative	den Vater	das Kind	die Mutter	die Freunde
Dative	d**em** Vater	d**em** Kind	d**er** Mutter	d**en** Freund**en**
	ein**em** Vater	ein**em** Kind	ein**er** Mutter	kein**en** Freund**en**
	mein**em** Vater	mein**em** Kind	mein**er** Mutter	mein**en** Freund**en**
	dein**em** Vater	dein**em** Kind	dein**er** Mutter	dein**en** Freund**en**
	Ihr**em** Vater	Ihr**em** Kind	Ihr**er** Mutter	Ihr**en** Freund**en**
	sein**em** Vater	sein**em** Kind	sein**er** Mutter	sein**en** Freund**en**
	ihr**em** Vater	ihr**em** Kind	ihr**r** Mutter	ihr**en** Freund**en**
	unser**em** Vater	unser**em** Kind	unser**er** Mutter	unser**en** Freund**en**
	eur**em** Vater	eur**em** Kind	eur**er** Mutter	eur**en** Freund**en**

Nouns in the dative plural add the ending **-n** (**den Freunden, den Kindern**), unless

1. the regular plural is formed by adding **-s: die Autos → den Autos**
2. the plural already ends in **-n**: die Tanten → den Tanten

Just as they do in the nominative plural and in the accusative singular and plural, masculine N-nouns add **-n** or **-en** in the dative singular (e.g., **dem Herrn, dem Neffen, dem Studenten**) as well as in the dative plural (e.g. **den Herren, den Neffen, den Studenten**).

15 Wem gibt Stefan den Schlüssel? Was ist die logische Antwort? Fragen Sie einen Partner/eine Partnerin.

BEISPIEL   S1: *Wem gibt Stefan die Seminararbeit?*
S2: *Er gibt der Professorin die Seminararbeit.*

1. Stefan / die Seminararbeit geben
   a. seinen Eltern   b. der Professorin   c. einer Studentin

2. Barbara / ihre Haarbürste leihen
   a. der neuen Studentin   b. ihrer Katze   c. dem Professor

3. Anna / ein Kleid schenken
   a. ihrem Freund Karl   b. ihrer Freundin   c. ihrer Professorin

4. Karl / einen CD-Player kaufen
   a. seiner Professorin   b. seinem Bruder   c. seinem Hund

5. Barbara / einen Computer schenken
   a. ihrer Nachbarin   b. ihrer Katze   c. ihrem Vater

6. der Professor / die Prüfungen zurückgeben
   a. den Eltern   b. den Studenten   c. seiner Frau

7. Barbara / die Postkarte aus Italien schreiben
   a. der Bank in Tübingen   b. der Bundeskanzlerin   c. den Eltern in Dresden

Strukturen

Ⅱ Indicating location

Dative of location: *in der, im/in dem, in den*

The preposition **in** belongs to a group of prepositions called *two-case prepositions* (**die Wechselpräpositionen**) that can occur with either the accusative case or the dative case.

To indicate the location of a person, animal, object, or action, German speakers use **in** with a definite article in the dative case.

> Die Studenten essen **in der** Küche.   *The students eat in the kitchen.*
> Abends sind sie **in der** Kneipe.   *In the evening, they're in the bar.*

For the dative case of masculine and neuter nouns, a contracted form of **in dem** is frequently used: **im.**

> Eine Bar gibt's **im** Keller.   *There is a bar in the basement.*
> Was hast du **im** Zimmer?   *What do you have in the room?*

When referring to countries (**Deutschland**) or cities (**Tübingen**) as locations, German speakers use the preposition **in** without a definite article.

> **Tübingen**: Anna ist **in** Tübingen.   **Deutschland:** Tübingen ist **in** Deutschland.

However, names of certain countries always occur with a definite article, e.g., **die Schweiz** (*fem.*), **die Türkei** (*fem.*), or **die Vereinigten Staaten (die USA)** (*pl.*). When they are used in expressions indicating locations, the article must be changed to the dative case.

> **die Schweiz:** Bern ist eine Stadt **in der** Schweiz.
> **die Vereinigten Staaten (die USA):** Annas Familie lebt in den Vereinigten Staaten (in den USA).

The use of two-case prepositions with the accusative will be explained in **Kapitel 7.**

Wissenswerte Vokabeln: ein Einfamilienhaus, die Stockwerke

Describing the features of a house

Im zweiten Stock (m.)
1. das Kinderzimmer
2. die Treppe
3. der Hobbyraum

Im ersten Stock (m.)
4. das Gästezimmer
5. das Kinderzimmer
6. der Gang, der Flur
7. das Badezimmer
8. das Schlafzimmer
9. der Balkon

Im Erdgeschoss (n.)
10. die Garage
11. die Diele
12. der Eingang
13. die Rollläden
14. das Wohnzimmer
15. das Arbeitszimmer
16. die Küche
17. das Klo
18. die Waschküche

19. der Garten

Im Keller (m.)
20. der Abstellraum

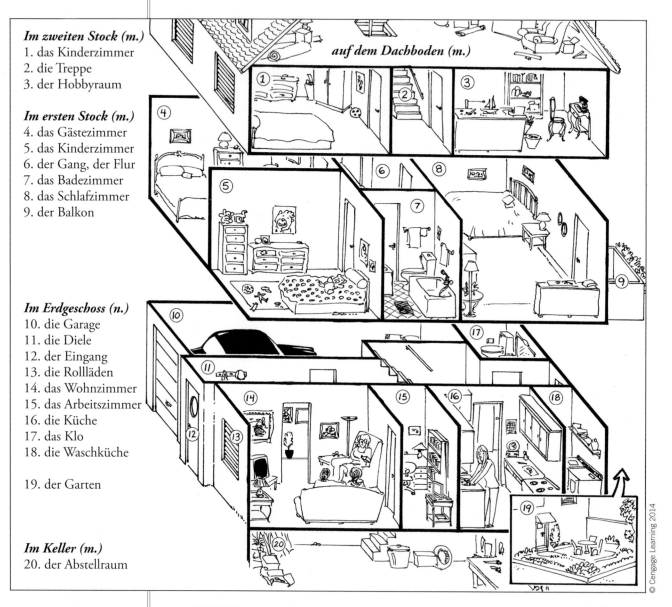

auf dem Dachboden (m.)

© Cengage Learning 2014

BEISPIEL Was ist im Keller?
Der Abstellraum ist im Keller.

Wo schläfst du?
Ich schlafe im Gästezimmer.

16 Wo machst du das? Kreuzen Sie das Zimmer an, in dem Sie diese Aktivitäten machen.

BEISPIEL   S1: *Wo schläfst du?*
                S2: *Ich schlafe im Schlafzimmer.*

	Im Schlafzimmer	Im Badezimmer	In der Küche	Im Wohnzimmer
1. schlafen	○	○	○	○
2. Kaffee trinken	○	○	○	○
3. baden	○	○	○	○
4. fernsehen	○	○	○	○
5. die Zeitung lesen	○	○	○	○
6. frühstücken	○	○	○	○
7. aufstehen	○	○	○	○
8. duschen	○	○	○	○
9. die Hausaufgaben machen	○	○	○	○
10. die Kleidung aufhängen°	○	○	○	○

hang up

17 Wo ist das Auto? Wo findet man normalerweise die folgenden Gegenstände?

BEISPIEL   S1: *Wo ist das Auto?*
                S2: *In der Garage.*

1. das Auto
2. der Fernseher
3. die Waschmaschine
4. die Kaffeemaschine
5. der Rasierapparat
6. das Doppelbett
7. die Stereoanlage
8. der Mikrowellenherd
9. die Rolle Toilettenpapier
10. die Couch
11. das Waschbecken
12. das Bücherregal
13. die Rosen, Tulpen und Tomaten
14. die Zahnbürsten
15. die alten Klamotten
16. das Kinderbett
17. das Handy

Uwe Landgraf/Shutterstock.com

18 Interview Stellen Sie einem Partner/einer Partnerin die folgenden Fragen.

1. Wohnst du in einem Haus, in einer Wohnung oder in einem Studentenwohnheim?
2. Wie viele Schlafzimmer hat dein Haus, deine Wohnung, dein Studentenwohnheim?
3. Wie viele Badezimmer hat dein Haus, deine Wohnung, dein Studentenwohnheim?
4. Hast du eine Küche?
5. Wo isst du normalerweise?
6. Was für Möbel hast du in deinem Zimmer?

ii 19 Entschuldigung, können Sie mir sagen,… Sie und ein Partner/ eine Partnerin sind Touristen und fragen einige Tübinger nach Sehenswürdigkeiten in Tübingen. Benutzen Sie den Stadtplan von Tübingen.

BEISPIEL   S1: *Entschuldigung, können Sie mir sagen, wo der Hölderlinturm ist?*
S2: *Der Hölderlinturm? Ja. In der Bursagasse 6.*
S1: *Danke schön.*

1. das Zimmertheater
2. die Blaue Brücke
3. der Club Voltaire
4. die Kunsthalle Tübingen
5. das Deutsch-Amerikanische Institut
6. das Stadtmuseum Kornhaus

Theater
1 Landestheater Württemberg-Hohenzollern, Eberhardtstr. 8 Theaterkasse Tel.: 9313149

2 Zimmertheater Bursagasse 16 Tel.: 92730

Kinos
3 Kino Arsenal Eine Institution. Programmkino. Anspruchsvolles° Programm, Kinokneipe Am Stadtgraben 33, Tel.: 51073

4 Kino Atelier Das Programmkino und Café Haag, der American Diner Am Haagtor, Tel.: 21225

5 Museum 1 + 2 Studio Museum Die Kino's mit Niveau° Am Stadtgraben 2, Tel.: 23661

6 Blaue Brücke 1 – 3 Friedrichstr., Tel.: 23661

7 Kino Löwen Kornhausstr., Tel.: 22410

Diskotheken
8 Zoo Diskothek, Kneipe, Konzerte. Schleifmühleweg 86. Tel: 40539

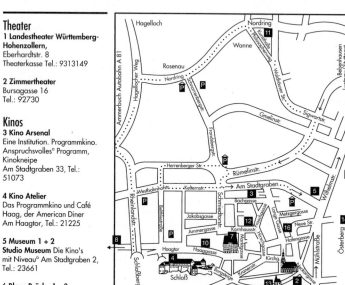

Veranstaltung/Konzert
9 Sudhaus Veranstaltungen, Konzerte, Kabarett. Hechinger Str. 203 Tel: 74696

10 Club Voltaire Kleinkunst, Konzerte. Haaggasse 26b, Tel.: 51524

Ausstellungen
11 Kunsthalle Tübingen, Philosophenweg 76

12 Stadtmuseum Kornhaus, Kornhausstr. 10

13 Hölderlinturm, Bursagasse 6

14 Institut Culturel Franco-Allemand, Doblerstr. 25

15 Deutsch-Amerikanisches Institut, Karlstr. 3

16 Galerie im Alten Schlachthaus, Metzgergasse 3

17 Auto- und Spielzeugmuseum Boxenstop Autos, Motorräder, Puppen°, (Blech) Eisenbahnen, Spielsachen° präsentiert in toller Atmosphäre Brunnenstr. 18, Tel.: 21996

anspruchsvolles:
sophisticated

mit … : with high standards

Puppen: dolls
Spielsachen: toys

cabaret

ii 20 Fragen über Tübingen Benutzen Sie den Stadtplan und beantworten Sie die Fragen über Tübingen.

BEISPIEL   S1: *Wo kann man ein anspruchsvolles Kinoprogramm finden?*
S2: *Im Kino Arsenal.*

1. Wo kann man Motorräder, Puppen und Spielsachen finden?
2. Wo kann man zwei Kinos mit Niveau finden?
3. Wo kann man Konzerte hören?
4. Wo kann man Kleinkunst° finden?
5. Wo kann man amerikanisches Essen finden?
6. Was möchten Sie in Tübingen sehen?

†† 21 Freie Kommunikation: **Rollenspiel: Ein Telefongespräch.** Sie haben eine neue Wohnung in Frankfurt. Sie rufen zu Hause an und sprechen mit Ihrer Mutter. Erzählen Sie ihr von der neuen Wohnung. Ihre Mutter ist sehr neugierig° und stellt viele Fragen.

curious

†† 22 Rollenspiel: In unserer Stadt Ein Student/Eine Studentin ist neu in Ihrer Stadt. Welche interessanten Dinge soll er/sie machen? Und wo?

⟵ 23 Schreibecke: **Mein Zimmer.** Beschreiben Sie Ihr Zimmer. Was haben Sie alles?

der Fernseher • die Kaffeemaschine • das Doppelbett • die Stereoanlage •
der Mikrowellenherd • die Couch • das Waschbecken • das Bücherregal •
der Computer • das Bild • das Poster • der Drucker • die Kommode •
die Pflanze • der Schreibtisch • der Sessel • die Kochplatte • die Lampe •
die Pinnwand • das Bett • die Klamotten • der Spiegel • der Taucheranzug

BEISPIEL *In meinem Zimmer habe ich einen Fernseher und einen Laptop.*

Courtesy of J. Douglas Guy.

In Kiel: Es ist etwas eng für Jan in seinem Zimmer im Wohnheim, aber der Balkon gefällt ihm sehr.

Kleine Zimmer, kleine Miete – Leben im Studentenwohnheim

Wo und wie man wohnt, ist ein großes Problem für viele Studenten in deutschen Universitätsstädten. Anna hat Schwein mit ihrem Zimmer im Studentenwohnheim, denn sie hat alles, was sie braucht. Im folgenden Artikel beschreibt die Autorin Anna Grabowski von der Deutschen Welle die Situation mit deutschen Wohnheimen.

Vorschau

24 Thematische Fragen Besprechen Sie die folgenden Fragen mit einem Partner/einer Partnerin auf Deutsch.

1. Wohnen Sie in einem Studentenheim, in einer Wohnung, in einem Haus, in einer WG oder bei den Eltern?
2. Was gibt es dort? Ist das in der Miete schon drin?

Gibt es … ?	Ja/Nein	Ist das in der Miete schon drin?
einen Internetanschluss	_____	_____
Elektrizität (=der Strom)	_____	_____
heißes Fließwasser	_____	_____
eine Heizung (für die kalten Tage)	_____	_____
eine Klimaanlage (für die heißen Tage)	_____	_____
ein Privatbad für Sie allein	_____	_____
ein Schlafzimmer für Sie allein	_____	_____
ein Fenster in Ihrem Zimmer	_____	_____
eine Küche für Sie allein	_____	_____
einen Gemeinschaftswäschetrockner°	_____	_____
eine Gemeinschaftswaschmaschine	_____	_____
einen Großfernseher	_____	_____
Farbe° an der Wand	_____	_____
einen Abstellraum	_____	_____
einen Parkplatz	_____	_____
einen Fitnessraum	_____	_____
ein Waschbecken	_____	_____
Kabelfernsehen	_____	_____

3. Wie viel Platz haben Sie für sich allein in Quadratmetern (m²)?
4. Auf einer Skala von 1–5 (5 ist am besten), wie viele Punkte geben Sie Ihrem Wohnplatz? Erklären Sie die Punkte.

communal clothes dryer

paint

10 square meters equal roughly 100 square feet.

🔁 **25** Phrasendetektiv Welche Phrasen bedeuten ungefähr das Gleiche?

1. praktisch und günstig
2. an Ort und Stelle sein
3. die Wände streichen
4. nirgendwo
5. unterkommen
6. durchschnittlich

   a. einen Platz zum Wohnen finden
   b. zum Beispiel (3+4+2+3) / 4 = 3
   c. praktisch und zu einem guten Preis
   d. da sein, existieren
   e. Farbe an die Wand machen
   f. nicht da und auch nicht dort

7. die Miete enthält Stromanschluss
8. öffentlich
9. man wählt eine Wohnform
10. das eigene Reich
11. Gemeinschaftsküche/-dusche
12. sich in der Miete niederschlagen

   g. wo man machen kann, was man will (wie ein König/eine Königin)
   h. man bestimmt, wo man wohnt
   i. einen Effekt auf den Preis für die Wohnung haben
   j. der Preis für Elektrizität ist in der Miete schon drin
   k. für alle, nicht privat
   l. alle kochen/duschen da

13. 17 Quadratmeter (m^2)
14. die Kochplatte
15. eng
16. höchstens
17. eine Wohnung teilen

   m. nicht breit oder weit genug
   n. 2–3 Personen wohnen in einer Wohnung zusammen
   o. ein heißer Ring, auf dem man kocht
   p. maximal
   q. fast 183 Quadratfuß

Courtesy of J. Douglas Guy.

In der Gemeinschaftsküche darf man jederzeit kochen und essen.

Fast so günstig wie im Elternhaus: Ein Zimmer im Studentenwohnheim

Praktisch und günstig, das sind die beiden Hauptargumente, wenn Studierende ins Wohnheim ziehen. Tisch und Bett stehen schon an Ort und Stelle, und Wände streichen muss man auch nicht.

Nirgendwo kommt man während des Studiums so günstig unter wie im Studentenwohnheim: Durchschnittlich kostet ein Wohnheimzimmer 182 Euro im Monat. In der Miete ist oft schon ein Internetanschluss enthalten. Zwölf Prozent der Studierenden in Deutschland wählen diese Wohnform. Bei Studenten, die für ein Auslandssemester nach Deutschland kommen, sind es sogar 40 Prozent. Neben den Wohnheimen, die mit öffentlichen Mitteln gefördert werden°, gibt es in fast allen Uni-Städten auch private Wohnheime.

Gemeinschaftsküche oder eigenes Reich

Wohnheim ist nicht gleich Wohnheim°: In manchen gibt es Gemeinschaftsduschen und nur eine Küche für viele, in anderen sogar eine Sauna und eine Bar im Keller – das schlägt sich dann aber auch in der Miete nieder°. Sophia aus Münster hat sich für die günstigere Variante entschieden: Ihr Appartement in einem Wohnheim des Studentenwerks Münster ist 17 Quadratmeter groß, hier schläft und lernt und arbeitet sie. Die beiden Kochplatten im Flur ihres Zimmers bleiben meist kalt, zum Kochen ist es ihr hier zu eng. Aber dafür liegt die Mensa der Uni gleich um die Ecke°.

Ganz schön praktisch

720 weitere Studierende leben in dem Wohnheim, Sophia kennt nur eine Handvoll von ihnen. Man trifft sich höchstens mal im Flur, ansonsten° ist die Atmosphäre anonym.

Kneipenabend und Brettspiele

In anderen Wohnheimen hingegen° gibt es regelmäßige Treffen in den Gemeinschaftsräumen oder auf der Wiese vorm Haus, Kneipenabende, Grillfeiern oder Spieletreffs. Ein gutes Angebot vor allem für Studierende, die neue Leute kennenlernen wollen. Und auch das gibt es: WG im Wohnheim. Vor allem neuere Wohnheime bieten auch Wohnungen an, die sich zwei oder drei Studierende teilen können. Küche und Bad werden dann gemeinsam genutzt°, und jeder hat sein eigenes Zimmer.

Marginal glosses:

die: ...: *that are supported by public funds*

Wohnheim ist ...: *Not all residence halls are the same*

schlägt sich nieder: *is reflected*

gleich ...: *right around the corner*

otherwise

on the other hand

werden genutzt: *are used*

Auremar/Shutterstock.com

In Gemeinschaftsräumen kann man zusammen lernen.

Rückblick

→ **26** Stimmt das? Stimmen diese Aussagen zum Text oder nicht? Wenn nicht, was stimmt?

	Ja, das stimmt.	Nein, das stimmt nicht.
1. Im Studentenwohnheim kann man günstig wohnen.	○	○
2. Die meisten deutschen Studenten wohnen nicht in einem Studentenheim.	○	○
3. Über 50 % der Studenten aus dem Ausland wohnen in Deutschland in einem Studentenwohnheim.	○	○
4. Alle Studentenwohnheime in Deutschland haben eine Bar im Keller.	○	○
5. Ein privates Bad hat jeder Bewohner im Studentenwohnheim.	○	○
6. Sophia kocht gern in ihrem Zimmer.	○	○
7. Sophia kennt nur wenige Studenten in ihrem Studentenwohnheim persönlich.	○	○
8. In manchen Studentenwohnheimen ist die Atmosphäre sehr persönlich.	○	○
9. In vielen neuen Studentenwohnheimen müssen sich nur 2–3 Leute ein Bad oder eine Küche teilen.	○	○

Complete the **Ergänzen Sie** activity in the Student Activities Manual before doing the next activity.

👥 **27** Kurz gefragt Beantworten Sie diese Fragen auf Deutsch.

1. Warum zum Beispiel nennt man das Leben in einem Studentenwohnheim „praktisch und günstig"?
2. Wie groß ist Sophias Appartement im Studentenwohnheim – in Quadratmetern und in Quadratfuß?
3. Wo isst Sophia meistens?
4. Was machen die Studenten in Studentenwohnheimen mit einer persönlichen Atmosphäre zusammen – zum Beispiel?
5. Was ist ein Vorteil von neueren Studentenwohnheimen?

← **28** Eine Umfrage° machen Fragen Sie andere Studenten im Kurs. Wie wichtig sind ihnen diese Dinge, wenn sie eine Wohnung wählen?

survey

BEISPIEL S1: *Wie wichtig ist dir ein schneller Internetanschluss?*
S2: *Er ist mir sehr wichtig.*

Make sure to conjugate the verb correctly. The example shows a singular subject. For a plural subject, use a plural verb. For example: **Wie wichtig sind dir Parkplätze für Autos?**

Wie wichtig ist/sind dir … ?	Extrem wichtig	Ziemlich wichtig	Nicht so wichtig	Total unwichtig
ein schneller Internetanschluss	○	○	○	○
ein großer Fernseher	○	○	○	○
ein privates Bad	○	○	○	○
ein eigenes Zimmer	○	○	○	○
ein großer Kühlschrank	○	○	○	○
Haustiere°	○	○	○	○
eine persönliche Atmosphäre	○	○	○	○
eine Heizung und Klimaanlage	○	○	○	○
Parkplätze für Autos	○	○	○	○

pets

29 Textdetektiv: **Absprungtext.** Use the *Absprungtext* to recognize important aspects of the structure and usage of the German language.

1. Underline all instances of the dative case in the examples below. Some examples have two dative phrases.
   a. Leben im Studentenwohnheim
   b. fast so günstig wie im Elternhaus
   c. Ein Wohnheimzimmer kostet 182 Euro im Monat.
   d. In der Miete ist ein Internetanschluss enthalten.
   e. Neben den öffentlichen Wohnheimen gibt es in fast allen Uni-Städten private Wohnheime.
   f. Zum Kochen ist es ihr (Sophia) zu eng.
   g. In manchen Wohnheimen gibt es eine Bar im Keller.
   h. Sophia kennt nur eine Handvoll von ihnen.
   i. Sophias Wohnung in einem Wohnheim
   j. Es gibt regelmäßige Treffen in den Gemeinschaftsräumen oder auf der Wiese.

2. The preposition **in** is used with the dative or the accusative case. Which of these phrases shows **in** with an accusative case? What is the verb used with the accusative?
   a. In der Miete ist oft schon ein Internetanschluss enthalten.
   b. Das sind die beiden Hauptargumente, wenn Studenten ins Studentenwohnheim ziehen.
   c. In manchen Wohnheimen gibt es Gemeinschaftsduschen.

3. The article you have just read mentions several advantages and disadvantages of various living situations using numbers. Adverbs and adjectives that quantify and contrast things are important features of such a text. Based on the context, guess what these adverbs and adjectives mean. Match each German word in boldface with its correct English equivalent.

German example	English equivalent of the adverb or adjective
1. **fast** so günstig wie im Elternhaus	a. at the most
2. **Durchschnittlich** kostet ein Wohnheim 182 Euro.	b. on average
	c. almost
3. bei Studenten aus dem Ausland sind es **sogar** 40 Prozent	d. even
4. Man trifft sich **höchstens** mal im Flur.	e. equal, identical
5. Wohnheim ist nicht **gleich** Wohnheim	

6. In **manchen** Wohnheimen gibt es Gemeinschaftsduschen.	f. other, different
7. In **anderen** Wohnheimen gibt es sogar eine Sauna.	g. as … as
8. Nirgendwo kommt man **so** günstig unter **wie** im Studentenwohnheim	h. on the other hand
9. In anderen Wohnheimen **hingegen** gibt es regelmäßige Treffen.	i. some, a few

Tübingen

Located approximately 40 kilometers south of the city of Stuttgart, Baden-Württemberg's urban capital and economic powerhouse, the old university city of Tübingen is distinguished by its historical town center (**die Altstadt**). Straddling the Neckar and Ammer rivers, Tübingen is known for its historic town hall (**das Rathaus**), a castle (**Schloss Hohentübingen**), and a myriad of half-timbered houses (**Fachwerkhäuser**) on narrow, winding streets. While the city boasts a population of just under 90,000, it owes its fame

Courtesy of J. Douglas Guy.

Stocherkahnfahren auf dem Neckar gehört zu den Studententraditionen in Tübingen.

to the 25,800 students at the **Eberhard-Karls-Universität,** who are continually drawn to this dynamic educational institution. Founded in 1477 with only 300 students, the university established a reputation for outstanding scholarship and teaching. It has attracted significant German intellectuals: the astronomer and mathematician Johannes Kepler; the philosopher G.W.F. Hegel; the Romantic author Ludwig Uhland; the 20th-century novelist Hermann Hesse; and the contemporary theologian Hans Küng. In the 18th century, the impassioned German poet Friedrich Hölderlin attended the university, but later descended into mental illness, spending the last 36 years of his life in a tower on the banks of the Neckar, now known as the **Hölderlinturm.** After the collapse of the Nazi government in 1945, the university at Tübingen was the first in Germany to reopen its doors. Since then the university has pursued international cooperation and collaborative projects, establishing academic partnerships with numerous American universities. The city of Tübingen has a partnership with the city of Ann Arbor, Michigan, in the U.S.

Courtesy of J. Douglas Guy.

In der Stadt Tübingen findet man viele enge Straßen.

Kulturkreuzung

Tübingen ist als Universitätsstadt sehr bekannt. Ist die Stadt, wo Sie jetzt studieren, auch als Universitätsstadt bekannt? Wie kann man Ihre Stadt sonst noch beschreiben? Die Eberhard-Karls-Universität ist über 535 Jahre alt. Wie alt ist Ihre Uni? Was studieren viele Leute an Ihrer Uni? Welche bekannten Leute haben an Ihrer Uni studiert?

Strukturen

 Expressing temporal and spatial relationships

Dative prepositions

There are eight prepositions that are always followed by the dative case (**die Dativ-präpositionen**). You already encountered some in earlier chapters. The translations of these prepositions are only approximate. Their meanings vary depending on the context.

> aus, außer, bei, mit, nach, seit, von, zu

1. Expressing origin: **aus** (*from, out of*)

   Khalid kommt **aus** Marokko. *Khalid is **from** Morocco.*

As with the preposition **in**, with dative prepositions be sure to alter the articles that accompany certain country names (e.g., **aus den USA/Vereinigten Staaten, aus der Türkei, aus der Schweiz.**

2. Expressing exclusion: **außer** (*except for*)

   Außer ihm sprechen alle Studenten Deutsch. ***Except for*** *him all the students speak German.*

When **außer** occurs in the same sentence with **auch** (*also*), it means *in addition to*

   Außer ihm sind **auch** Anna und Barbara hier. ***In addition to*** *him, Anna and Barbara are also here.*

3. Expressing location: **bei** (*at, near, with*)

   Das Studentenwohnheim ist **bei** der Autobahn. *The dorm is **near** the freeway.*

   Barbara hat in Moskau **bei** einer Frau gewohnt. *Barbara lived **with** a woman in Moscow.*

There are two translations of *to live with*: **leben/wohnen bei** and **zusammenleben/zusammenwohnen mit**. The preposition **bei** indicates a relationship of dependency, as in **Jeff lebt/wohnt bei seinen Eltern.** The preposition **mit** implies a relationship of shared responsibilities: **Franz lebt/wohnt mit seiner Freundin zusammen.**

Some common verbs used with **bei** are **arbeiten, essen,** and **vorbeikommen** (*to stop by*).

   Wir essen **bei** Stefanie. *We're eating **at** Stefanie's.*
   Werner arbeitet **bei** der Bank. *Werner works **at** the bank.*
   Karl kommt morgen **bei** uns vorbei. *Karl is stopping by (**at** our place) tomorrow.*

Note that German does not add a possessive **s** to the nouns or names describing a location: **bei Stefanie**.

4. Expressing accompaniment: **mit** (*with*)

   Besprechen Sie das **mit** einem Partner. *Discuss that **with** a partner.*

Expressing means: **mit** (*by*)

   Wir fahren **mit** der Bahn nach Rostock. *We're going **by** train to Rostock.*

5. Expressing time: **nach** (*after, past*)

   Es ist fünf **nach** drei. *It's five **after (past)** three.*
   Nach der Vorlesung gehen wir nach Hause. ***After*** *the lecture we'll go home.*

6. Expressing destination: **zu, nach** *(to)*

   People and institutions

Wir gehen **zu** Karl.	*We're going to Karl's (house).*
Anna geht **zur** (= **zu der**) Universität.	*Anna is going to the university.*

   German does not add **'s** to proper names when **zu** is used with a name: **zu Karl.**

   Cities, countries, and home

Ich bin dann **nach** Darmstadt gezogen.	*Then I moved **to** Darmstadt.*
Ich gehe **nach** Hause.	*I'm going home.*

Remember: The dative case—not **zu**—is used for the recipient of an action. **Gib' mir deinen Schlüssel.**

7. Expressing duration: **seit** *(since, for)*

The preposition **seit** is used with the present tense to express the present perfect (have *known, have been living*) in English.

Ich kenne Thomas **seit** dem Kindergarten.	*I have known Thomas **since** kindergarten.*
Ich lebe **seit** ein**em** Jahr in Heidelberg.	*I have been living in Heidelberg **(for)** a year.*
Ich lebe **seit** zwei Jahren in Deutschland.	*I've been living in Germany **(for)** two years.*

Unlike the other numbers, **ein** *(a)* takes endings when used with **seit: seit einem Jahr.**

Remember: The expression **zu Hause** means *at home.*

8. Expressing possession, association, or connection: **von** *(of, by, from)*

Der Bruder **von** Barbara wohnt noch zu Hause.	*Barbara's brother still lives at home.*
Das ist nett **von** dir.	*That's nice **of** you.*
Das Lied ist **von** Beethoven.	*The song is **by** Beethoven.*
Das Geschenk ist **von** Karl.	*The present is **from** Karl.*

Speakers often use **von** to indicate possession, e.g., **der Bruder von Barbara.** Standard German uses the possessive **s: Barbaras Bruder.**

   The prepositions **von, zu,** and **bei** frequently form contractions with the definite article.

von + dem = vom	am Ende **vom** Korridor	*at the end of the hall*
zu + dem = zum	ein Bett **zum** Schlafen	*a bed for sleeping*
zu + der = zur	Sie geht **zur** Universität.	*She's going to the university.*
bei + dem = beim	Karl war **beim** Arzt.	*Karl was at the doctor's.*

When used with an infinitive, **beim** means *while,* and **zum** means *for.*

beim Essen	*while eating*	**zum** Schlafen	*for sleeping*

Remember: The plural noun in the dative has the ending **-(e)n** or **-s**, e.g., **seit zwei Jahren.**

➜ **30** Oma und Opa Wählen Sie die richtige Dativpräposition.

1. Anna spricht (aus/seit/mit) ihren Großeltern.
2. OMA: Wir sind so froh, dass du (nach/zu/aus) uns gekommen bist, Anna.
3. OPA: Wir haben auch so gern die Briefe (aus/mit/von) dir und deiner Mutter gelesen. Es ist nur schade, dass sie nicht auch gekommen ist.
4. OMA: Ja, die Hannelore haben wir (seit/von/außer) fünf Jahren nicht mehr gesehen.
5. ANNA: Meiner Meinung nach wollte Mama im Dezember (zu/mit/bei) Papa (zu/aus/nach) Deutschland kommen, aber er muss Mitte Dezember für zwei Wochen nach Florida fahren.
6. OMA: Also, von mir aus kommen sie hoffentlich bald. Wie lange dauert° der Flug (außer/von/zu) Amerika?
7. ANNA: (Bei/Nach/Mit) dem Flugzeug dauert es sieben Stunden.

lasts

Sprache im Alltag: Emphasizing one's opinion

German speakers frequently use expressions with dative prepositions to express or emphasize an opinion. Which of the following expressions are used in the preceding activity?

meiner Meinung nach	*in my opinion*
mit anderen Worten	*in other words*
von mir aus	*as far as I am concerned*
(von) daher	*therefore*
aus diesem Grund	*therefore, that's the reason why*

31 Wie ich lebe Bilden Sie Sätze mit den folgenden Elementen.

1. Ich wohne
   a. bei meinen Eltern zu Hause.
   b. mit Freunden zusammen.
   c. allein.

2. Ich wohne … hier.
   a. seit wenigen Wochen
   b. seit vielen Monaten
   c. seit einigen Jahren

3. Ich arbeite
   a. bei (McDonald's).
   b. in der Mensa.
   c. zu Hause.

4. Ich esse oft
   a. mit meinem Mitbewohner.
   b. mit meiner Mitbewohnerin.
   c. allein.

5. Ich fahre … zur Uni.
   a. mit dem Rad
   b. mit dem Bus
   c. mit dem Auto

Ehrlich, ich bin mir da ganz sicher - die eine ist für Frauen mit Hosen und die andere für Frauen mit Rock.

Reprinted by permission of Erich Raauschenbach

32 Neue Leute kennenlernen Kreuzen Sie die beste Antwort an.

BEISPIEL S1: *Wann lernst du neue Leute kennen?*
S2: *Beim Essen.*

	Beim Lernen	Beim Schlafen	In der Freizeit	Beim Essen
1. neue Leute kennenlernen	○	○	○	○
2. vom Sommer träumen	○	○	○	○
3. Kollegen aus Kursen erkennen°	○	○	○	○
4. Kleingeld brauchen	○	○	○	○
5. ungeduldig° werden	○	○	○	○
6. über Physik und Deutsch lesen	○	○	○	○
7. mit Ausländern sprechen	○	○	○	○
8. einem Partner den Ball geben	○	○	○	○

see, recognize

impatient

33 Das ist nett von ihm Geben Sie eine passende Antwort auf die folgenden Bemerkungen°.

comments

BEISPIEL   Karl hilft Anna mit den Hausaufgaben.
Das ist nett von ihm.

Das ist | nett
| freundlich
| nicht nett
| unfair
| von …

1. Karl hilft Anna mit den Hausaufgaben.
2. Barbara hilft Anna beim Einzug.
3. Inge leiht sich immer das Fahrrad von° Barbara.
4. Wir leihen unseren Freunden gern Geld.
5. Karl gibt Carlos seine 20 Euro nicht zurück.
6. Zwei Studenten haben gestern den Test gesehen.
7. Ich habe meiner Freundin Blumen geschenkt.

leiht sich von: borrows from

34 Mein Tagesablauf Denken Sie an einen ganz normalen Tag. Schreiben Sie sechs Aktivitäten oder Termine° auf sechs Karten auf, z. B. (das) Aufstehen, die Vorlesung. Geben Sie dann einem Partner/einer Partnerin die gemischten Karten. Der Partner/Die Partnerin versucht, mit Fragen die richtige Reihenfolge der Aktivitäten und Termine festzustellen°. Benutzen Sie immer die Präposition **nach**.

appointments

determine

BEISPIEL   S1: *Was machst du nach der Vorlesung?*
S2: *Nach der Vorlesung esse ich.*
S1: *Was machst du nach …?*

35 Wie lange machst du das schon? Sie möchten Ihren Partner/Ihre Partnerin besser kennenlernen. Stellen Sie einander die folgenden Fragen.

BEISPIEL   S1: *Wie lange lernst du schon Deutsch?*
S2: *Ich lerne seit vier Monaten Deutsch.*

Was?
1. Deutsch lernen
2. (nicht/nicht mehr) rauchen°
3. Auto fahren
4. an dieser Uni studieren
5. selber kochen
6. im Studentenwohnheim wohnen

Wie lange?
seit ____ Jahren/Monaten/Wochen/Tagen
seit ____ Minuten/Stunden
noch nie

smoke

36 Interview Stellen Sie einem Partner/einer Partnerin die folgenden Fragen.

1. Bei wem wohnst du oder mit wem wohnst du zusammen?
2. Wie lange wohnst du schon in dieser Stadt?
3. Hast du einen Job? Wo arbeitest du?
4. Mit wem lernst du oft?
5. Wohin gehst du nach dem Unterricht°?
6. Wohin möchtest du fahren, wenn du Geld hast?
7. Aus welchem Land kommst du? Deine Eltern? Deine Großeltern?
8. Von wem bekommst du jedes Jahr ein Geschenk zum Geburtstag?

lecture, class

Strukturen

IV Expressing attitudes and conditions such as gratitude, pleasure, ownership, and need for assistance

Dative verbs and expressions

A. Dative verbs

There are five common verbs in German that always occur with the dative (**Dativverben**).

1. Expressing gratitude: **danken (hat gedankt)** *(to thank)*

    Ich danke dir für die Hilfe!   *Thanks for your help!*

2. Expressing pleasure: **gefallen (gefällt; hat gefallen)** *(to be appealing, pleasing)*

    Gefällt dir dein Zimmer denn nicht?   *Don't you like your room?*

3. Expressing like and dislike for food: **schmecken (hat geschmeckt)** *(to taste good)*

    Milch **schmeckt mir** nicht.   *Milk doesn't taste good to me.*

4. Expressing ownership: **gehören (hat gehört)** *(to belong to)*

    Der Bleistift **gehört ihr**.   *The pencil belongs to her.*

5. Expressing the need for assistance: **helfen (hilft; hat geholfen)** *(to help)*

    Kannst du **mir** bitte **helfen**?   *Can you help me, please?*
    Das ist wirklich nett von dir,   *It's really nice that you're helping me.*
       dass du **mir hilfst**.

German speakers often use **gefallen** or **schmecken** to make a compliment. The other person responds with a detail, or sometimes downplays the compliment.

> KARL: Dein Pullover gefällt mir echt°.
> BARBARA: Danke. Er ist aus Mexiko. *(oder)*   Danke. Aber er ist schon alt.

(margin note: really)

---

 37 Komplimente machen Machen Sie Komplimente. Verwenden Sie **gefallen** oder **schmecken**.

BEISPIEL   S1: *Dein Pullover gefällt mir echt gut.*
            S2: *Danke. Ich habe ihn erst vor ein*
               paar Tagen gekauft. (oder) *Ich*
               danke dir, aber er ist schon alt.
               (oder)   *Danke, mir auch.*

1. dein Pullover
2. deine Schuhe
3. dein Foto
4. deine Freunde
5. dein Poster
6. dein Zimmer
7. dieser Wein
8. diese Tomaten

(margin notes: iron; marriage)

Die Paar Probleme, Reprinted by permission of Cartoon Concept.

38 Ein Ratespiel Bilden Sie Gruppen von vier bis sechs Leuten. Eine Person ist der Gruppenleiter/die Gruppenleiterin. Jede Person in der Gruppe gibt dem Leiter/der Leiterin einen oder zwei Gegenstände. Dann zeigt der Leiter/die Leiterin der Gruppe jeden Gegenstand und fragt: „Wem gehört das?" Die anderen Leute in der Gruppe beschreiben den Besitzer/die Besitzerin°. Nennen Sie keine Namen!

Ein Ratespiel. The noun **der Student** adds **-en** in all cases but the nominative singular.

owner

BEISPIEL S1: *Wem gehört das Buch?*
S2: *Das gehört einem Studenten mit schwarzen Haaren.*
S3: *Gehört das Buch einem Studenten mit einer Brille?*
S1: *Ja.*
S4: *Ist es Jeremy?*
S1: *Ja.*

ein Student	mit	schwarzen (blonden, roten, braunen) Haaren
eine Studentin		blauen (braunen, grünen, grauen) Augen
		einer Brille

B. Adjectives with the dative case

Some adjectives appear in conjunction with the dative in order to indicate a temporary condition rather than a permanent quality. When used with the dative case, these adjectives always refer to people. They are **warm, heiß, kalt, schlecht,** and **langweilig.** It is important to use these adjectives correctly. Incorrect use with **heiß, kalt,** and **warm** may lead to unintended meanings.

Temporary condition		Permanent quality	
Mir ist langweilig.	*I am bored.*	Ich bin langweilig.	*I am a boring person.*
Ihr ist schlecht.	*She feels ill (nauseous).*	Sie ist schlecht.	*She is a bad person.*
Mir ist kalt.	*I'm (feeling) cold.*	Eis ist kalt.	*Ice is cold.*

 39 So fühle ich mich° jetzt Beschreiben Sie, wie Sie sich in dieser Situation fühlen.

fühle mich: feel

BEISPIEL Kannst du bitte das Fenster aufmachen? *Mir ist heiß.*

1. Kannst du bitte das Fenster zumachen?
2. Kannst du bitte die Heizung anmachen?
3. Ich möchte etwas Interessantes machen.
4. Ich kann jetzt nichts essen.

C. Idiomatic expressions with the dative case

Here are some common idiomatic expressions that require the dative case.

Wie geht es Ihnen/dir?	*How are you?*
Es/Das tut mir leid.	*I'm sorry.*
Der Arm tut mir weh.	*My arm hurts.*
Die frische Luft tut ihm gut.	*Fresh air is good for him.*
Das ist mir peinlich.	*That's embarrassing for me.*

Wissenswerte Vokabeln: Körperteile

Describing your body; talking about physical discomfort

BEISPIEL *Was tut dir weh?*
Mir tun die Füße (die Augen) weh. (oder)
Ich habe mir das Bein gebrochen.

die **Haut** = *skin;*
das **Herz** = *heart*

© Cengage Learning 2014

cause / effect

⊃ **40** Ursache° und Wirkung°: Mir tut der Arm weh Verbinden Sie eine Ursache mit einer Wirkung.

BEISPIEL Karl hat sich das Bein gebrochen.   *Ihm tut das Bein weh.*

1. Karl hat sich das Bein gebrochen.
2. Die Studenten haben heute sehr viel gelesen.
3. Frau Müller ist heute zum Zahnarzt° gegangen.
4. Ich habe Aspirin eingenommen.
5. Monika ist vom Fahrrad gefallen.
6. Stefan hat seine Wohnung eingerichtet und viele Möbel getragen.
7. Wir haben viel zu viel gegessen.
8. Anna und Barbara sind heute sehr weit gelaufen.
9. Die Musik im Konzert war zu laut.

a. Mir tut der Kopf nicht mehr weh.
b. Ihm tut das Bein weh.
c. Ihnen tun die Augen weh.
d. Ihr tun jetzt die Zähne nicht mehr weh.
e. Ihr tun die Knie noch weh.
f. Den Zuhörern tun die Ohren weh.
g. Ihm tun die Schultern und die Arme weh.
h. Ihnen tun die Füße weh.
i. Uns tut der Bauch weh.

dentist

41 Hast du Lust mitzumachen? Ihr Mitbewohner/Ihre Mitbewohnerin hat Pläne für den Abend. Sie haben aber gar keine Lust mitzumachen. Beantworten Sie die Fragen mit einer Ausrede° und sagen Sie, was Ihnen wehtut.   *excuse*

BEISPIEL   S1: *Ich gehe heute Abend essen. Hast du auch Lust zu essen?*
S2: *Nein, danke. Mir tut der Bauch weh.*

1. heute Abend essen gehen
2. mit Freunden Basketball spielen
3. einer Freundin beim Einziehen ins Studentenwohnheim helfen
4. um acht Uhr ins Hard-Rock-Konzert gehen
5. in einer Stunde eine Fahrradtour machen
6. Karten spielen
7. ein Bier trinken gehen

Strukturen

V Specifying what you are talking about

Der-words

Der-words have case endings similar to those of **der/das/die**. You have already encountered three common **der**-words in exercise direction lines in this text.

Singular		*Plural*	
dieser/dieses/diese	*this, that*	**diese**	*these, those*
jeder/jedes/jede	*each, every*	**alle**	*all (pl.)*
welcher/welches/welche	*which*	**welche**	*which (pl.)*

Wie fühlen Sie sich in **dieser** Situation?	*How do you feel in this situation?*
Welche Sätze bedeuten das Gleiche?	*Which sentences mean the same thing?*
Welche Studentin kommt aus den USA?	*Which student is from the US?*
Alle Studenten müssen eine Arbeit schreiben.	*All students have to write an exam.*
Ich kenne **diesen** Professor.	*I know that professor.*
Er steht **jeden** Tag um 6 Uhr auf.	*He gets up every day at 6:00.*
Kannst du **diesem** Studenten helfen?	*Can you help this student?*

> Time phrases with **dieser** and **jeder** employ the accusative case: **Anna ruft Stefan diesen Freitag/jeden Morgen an**.

Here are the nominative, accusative, and dative endings for **der**-words:

	Masculine	Neuter	Feminine	Plural
Nominative	dies**er** Mann	dies**es** Kind	dies**e** Frau	dies**e** Kinder
	jed**er** Mann	jed**es** Kind	jed**e** Frau	all**e** Kinder
	welch**er** Mann	welch**es** Kind	welch**e** Frau	welch**e** Kinder
Accusative	dies**en** Mann	dies**es** Kind	dies**e** Frau	dies**e** Kinder
	jed**en** Mann	jed**es** Kind	jed**e** Frau	all**e** Kinder
	welch**en** Mann	welch**es** Kind	welch**e** Frau	welch**e** Kinder
Dative	dies**em** Mann	dies**em** Kind	dies**er** Frau	dies**en** Kinder**n**
	jed**em** Mann	jed**em** Kind	jed**er** Frau	all**en** Kinder**n**
	welch**em** Mann	welch**em** Kind	welch**er** Frau	welch**en** Kinder**n**

42 Nimm diesen hier! Fragen Sie einen Freund/eine Freundin, ob er/sie Ihnen diese Gegenstände leihen kann.

BEISPIEL   einen Stift

> S1: *Kannst du mir einen Stift leihen?*
> S2: *Ja, nimm diesen Stift hier.*

1. einen Stift
2. ein Buch über Deutschland
3. ein Radio
4. ein Fahrrad
5. einen Laptop
6. eine Cola
7. einen 20-Euro-Schein
8. eine Lampe

decisions

43 Entscheidungen° am Bahnhof Barbara ist am Bahnhof. Sie hat aber noch keine konkreten Reisepläne. Karl hilft ihr. Suchen Sie sich einen Partner/ eine Partnerin und spielen Sie Barbara und Karl. Setzen Sie auch eine richtige Form von **welcher/welches/welche** in Barbaras Fragen ein.

BEISPIEL   S1 (BARBARA):   *Um welche Zeit soll ich nur abfahren: um vier Uhr oder um vier Uhr dreißig?*
                S2 (KARL):   *Fahr um vier Uhr ab.*

1. Um _____ Zeit soll ich nur abfahren: um vier Uhr oder um vier Uhr dreißig?
2. Mit _____ Zug soll ich nur fahren: mit einem Eilzug oder mit einem Lokalzug?
3. _____ Stadt soll ich nur besuchen: Bonn oder Hamburg?
4. _____ Buch soll ich im Zug lesen: mein Deutschbuch oder einen Roman?
5. _____ Musik soll ich für die Reise mitbringen: Jazz oder Rock?
6. _____ Freund oder _____ Freundin soll ich ein Souvenir kaufen: dir oder Anna?
7. Mit _____ Leuten soll ich im Abteil° sitzen: mit jungen oder mit alten?

Kulturnotiz. Der Lokalzug stops at every train station. **Der Eilzug** is a faster train with stops in larger towns and cities only. In addition, there are **Intercityzüge** and **Inter City Express (ICE)** trains, which stop only in very large cities. They are also more expensive than local trains.

compartment

exaggerations

44 Übertreibungen° Barbara beschreibt das deutsche Studentenleben. Sie übertreibt ein bisschen. Setzen Sie eine richtige Form von **jeder/jedes/jede** und **alle** ein. Benutzen Sie **alle** für Nominativ und Akkusativ Plural und **allen** für Dativ Plural.

1. _____ Tag müssen die Studenten um fünf Uhr morgens aufstehen.
2. Dann lernen _____ Studenten zwei bis drei Stunden.
3. Danach isst _____ Student und _____ Studentin nur ein Stück Brot mit Käse.
4. Dann gehen die Studenten zur Uni: sie gehen zu _____ Vorlesung.
5. Die Studenten stellen° viele Fragen und _____ Frage ist intelligent und wichtig.
6. _____ Professoren freuen sich° über die Fragen. Sie helfen _____ Studenten gern.
7. _____ Abend arbeiten die Studenten schwer.
8. Und _____ Wochenende lernen oder arbeiten sie auch. Sie haben keine Freizeit!

pose, ask
freuen sich: *are happy*

⬅ **45**

45 Die Küche In der Küche fehlen° viele Sachen. Der Hausmeister will wissen, was die Studenten in der Küche haben und was sie brauchen. Anna, Barbara, Karl und Inge schreiben eine Liste für den Hausmeister. Schreiben Sie an den Hausmeister für sie.

are missing

ein Herd • ein Fernseher • Töpfe • ein Faxgerät • ein Bett • ein Mikrowellenherd • Kochbücher • Fächer für Brot und Reis • ein Kühlschrank • eine Geschirrspülmaschine° • eine Kaffeemaschine • Tee und Kaffee • ein Spiegel° • ein Spülbecken° • ein Teppich • eine Brot- und Wurstschneidemaschine°

dishwasher / mirror
sink / bread and meat slicer

46 Freie Kommunikation: **Rollenspiel: In der Küche.** Sie sind mit einem Freund/einer Freundin in der Küche und möchten für eine Party eine Pizza machen. Ihr Freund/Ihre Freundin hilft Ihnen und gibt Ihnen, was Sie brauchen. Hier sind einige Ausdrücke.

der Teig

das Mehl

die Tomaten

der Käse

die Wurst

die Pilze *(pl.)*

die Oliven *(pl.)*

Salz und Pfeffer

das Öl

das Wasser

der Topf

der Löffel

das Messer

die Gabel

der Teller

der Herd

Kannst du mir helfen?	Ich helfe dir gern.
Wo ist/sind … ?	Leider haben wir das nicht.
Wem gehört/gehören … ?	Im Kühlschrank.
Gefällt/Gefallen dir … ?	Ich weiß es nicht.
Kannst du mir … geben?	Ich kann (den Käse) nicht finden.
Kannst du … finden?	Ja, klar.
schneiden°?	Leider, nein.
waschen?	

cut

In dieser Stadt
Zielaktivitäten

ad agency / (female) boss

↩ **47** Rundherum in dieser Stadt: eine Werbebroschüre Sie haben einen neuen Job bei einer Werbeagentur° und müssen Ihrer Chefin° den Text für eine Broschüre für eine kleine Fantasiestadt in Deutschland schreiben. Die Stadt heißt Neuheim am Main. In der Broschüre sollen Sie viele Informationen über Neuheim am Main geben. Geben Sie an, wo man gut essen und trinken kann (und was die Spezialitäten der Stadt sind), was für Musik man hören kann (und wo), wo man einen Spaziergang machen kann (und in welchen Jahreszeiten), was man mit Kindern tun kann (und wo) usw. Benutzen Sie diese Wörter: **die Schule, der Wald°, das Theater, der Zoo, der Club, das Stadtmuseum**. Beginnen Sie die Broschüre mit dem folgenden Satz.

forest

offers

BEISPIEL *Neuheim am Main bietet° dem Besucher viele Attraktionen und Sehenswürdigkeiten.*

playground

hiking path

inn

der See = *lake*
lawn for sunbathing

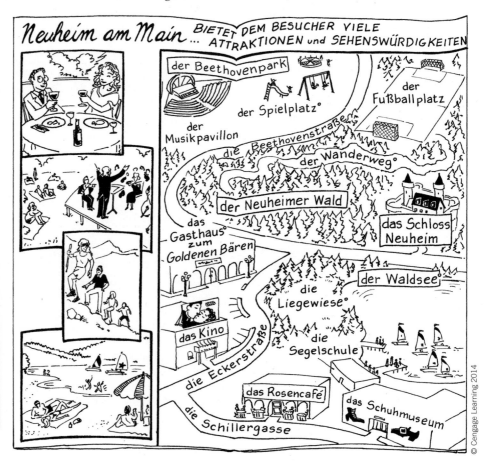

48 Einen Ausflug nach Neuheim Zwei Freunde planen einen Ausflug nach Neuheim. Eine Person (S1) will unbedingt nach Neuheim, die andere Person (S2) findet die Idee schlecht. Schreiben Sie einen Dialog. Schreiben Sie Argumente für und gegen verschiedene Aktivitäten in der Stadt. Verwenden Sie den Stadtplan. Kombinieren Sie Informationen aus den Spalten. Verwenden Sie auch typische *Redewendungen*. Ideen für einen *letzten Satz* finden Sie unten.

BEISPIEL

S1 [ILSE]: *Ich möchte nach Neuheim fahren und im Gasthaus zum Goldenen Bären Schnitzel essen.*

S2 [HEIDI]: *Ach nein! Vom Essen im Gasthaus Zum Goldenen Bären wird mir schlecht!*

S1 [ILSE]: *Also gut. Besuchen wir dann das Schuhmuseum.*

Aktivitäten in Neuheim

im Gasthaus Zum Goldenen Bären essen
das Schuhmuseum besuchen
einen Film im Kino sehen
im Neuheimer Wald wandern gehen
einen Kaffee im Rosencafé trinken

ein Stück Torte im Rosencafé essen
das Schloss Neuheim besuchen
auf dem Spielplatz Fußball spielen
segeln gehen
in der Sonne liegen

Reaktionen

	Negativ	Positiv
Vom Essen/Kino/Konzert/Kaffee/ Segeln/Wandern/Schuhmuseum/ Fußball ... Von der Musik, Sonne ... Von den Torten ...	... wird mir schlecht. ... wird mir langweilig. ... krieg' ich Kopfschmerzen. ... krieg' ich Bauchschmerzen. ... krieg' ich einen Muskelkater.	... werde ich fit und gesund. ... lerne ich was Neues. ... kann ich die Natur so richtig erleben. ... kann ich nicht genug kriegen. ... werde ich schön braun.
Das Essen/Kino/Konzert/Segeln/ Wandern/Schuhmuseum ... Den Kaffee ... Die Musik/Sonne ... Die Torten ...	... finde ich langweilig/ uninteressant. ... gefällt/gefallen mir überhaupt nicht. ... schmeckt/schmecken mir gar nicht.	... finde ich sehr interessant. ... gefällt/gefallen mir sehr. ... schmeckt/schmecken sehr gut.

Typische Redewendungen

Das stimmt (sicher/ganz bestimmt°)!/Das stimmt (sicher/ganz bestimmt) nicht!
Da hast du/habe ich (total) recht/unrecht.°
Dieses Argument ist vollkommen° (un)logisch.
Das ist doch ganz klar!
Das finde ich überhaupt nicht./Das finde ich schon.
Du hast ja keine Ahnung°, wie schön/schlimm/langweilig/spannend das ist!
Probieren wir es doch!°

certainly
Da hast du ...: *You are (totally) right/wrong.*
completely

keine ...: *no idea*
Let's give it a try!

Der letzte Satz

Also gut, machen wir das/fahren wir (nicht) nach Neuheim/bleiben wir zu Hause.

⮌ **49** Schreibecke: **Wie heißt mein Studentenwohnheim?** Beschreiben Sie Ihr Studentenwohnheim in zehn Sätzen, aber schreiben Sie nicht den Namen von dem Wohnheim auf! In welchem Stock wohnen Sie? Seit wann wohnen Sie dort? Was haben Sie alles? Welche Zimmernummer haben Sie? Was gefällt Ihnen gut/nicht gut? Dann geben Sie die Beschreibung einem Partner/einer Partnerin, und er/sie soll erraten°, in welchem Wohnheim Sie wohnen.

guess

50 Freie Kommunikation: **Rollenspiel: Beim Arzt°.** Patient(in): Sie sind ein Hypochonder. Sie gehen zum Arzt, denn Sie fühlen sich schon wieder° nicht sehr wohl. Beschreiben Sie dem Arzt Ihre Symptome. Arzt (Ärztin): Sie kennen diesen Patienten/diese Patientin sehr gut. Er/Sie ist ein Hypochonder. Sie wissen, dass die beste Lösung° ist, wenn Sie gut zuhören und viele Fragen über die Probleme stellen.

Doktor

again

solution

BEISPIEL

ARZT (ÄRZTIN):	*Wie fühlen Sie sich heute?*
PATIENT(IN):	*Mir tut der Bauch weh.* (oder)
PATIENT(IN):	*Können Sie mir helfen?*
ARZT (ÄRZTIN):	*Wo tut es Ihnen weh?*

Stocklite/Shutterstock.com

Beim Arzt

WORTSCHATZ

Tutorial Quiz
Audio Flashcards

Das Studentenleben, -

die Party, -s *party*

die Prüfung, -en *test, examination*

der/die Studierende, -n *student*

der Unterricht, -e *lesson, instruction, class*

die Vorlesung, -en *lecture, class*

Das Studentenzimmer, -

das Bett, -en *bed*

das Bild, -er *picture*

die Blume, -n *flower*

der Computer, - *computer*

die Couch or (Sw.) **der Couch, -s** or **-en** *couch*

der Drucker, - *printer*

die Gardine, -n *curtain*

der Internetanschluss, ⸚e *Internet connection*

die Klamotten *(pl.)* *things to wear, duds*

die Kommode, -n *chest of drawers*

die Möbel *(pl.)* *furniture*

die Pflanze, -n *green plant*

das Radio, -s *radio*

das Regal, -e *set of shelves*

    das Bücherregal *bookcase*

der Schrank, ⸚e *closet*

    der Kleiderschrank *wardrobe*

    der Kühlschrank *refrigerator*

der Schreibtisch, -e *desk*

der Sessel, - *armchair (North), chair (South)*

die Stereoanlage, -n *stereo set*

das Telefon, -e *telephone*

der Teppich, -e *rug, carpet*

das Waschbecken, - *(bathroom) sink*

der Wecker, - *alarm clock*

die Wohnung, -en *apartment*

Das Studentenwohnheim, -e

das Appartement, -s *apartment*

der Automat, [-en], -en *vending machine*

die Bar, -s *bar*

das Brett, -er *board*

    das Schwarze Brett *bulletin board*

die (Luxus)bude, -n *(luxury) student room (slang)*

der Duschraum, ⸚ *shower room*

das Einzelzimmer, - *single room*

das Fach, ⸚er *compartment, cupboard, container, shelf*

der Flur, -e *floor*

das Gemeinschaftsbad, ⸚er *shared/communal bathroom*

die Gemeinschaftsküche, -n *shared/communal kitchen*

die Kochplatte, -n *hotplate*

die Mensa, *pl.* **die Mensen** *university cafeteria*

die Miete, -n *rent*

das Postfach, ⸚er *mailbox*

der Schlüssel, - *key*

das Studentenwerk *student services*

das Studentenwohnheim, -e *residence hall*

das Studentenzimmer *student's room*

auf•kriegen (hat aufgekriegt) *to open (slang)*

auf•schließen (hat aufgeschlossen) *to unlock*

auf•schreiben (hat aufgeschrieben) *to write down*

ein•ziehen (ist eingezogen) *to move in*

leihen (hat geliehen) *to lend, loan*

Das Einfamilienhaus, ⸚er

das Bad, ⸚er *bath*

der Balkon, -s and -e *balcony*

der Boden, ⸚ *floor; ground*

der Dachboden, ⸚ *attic*

    auf dem Dachboden *in the attic*

die Diele, -n *entrance hall*

die Dusche, -n *shower*

der Eingang, ⸚e *entrance, front door*

das Erdgeschoss, -e *ground floor*

    im Erdgeschoss *on the first (ground) floor*

der Flur, -e *hallway, corridor*

der Gang, ⸚e *hallway, corridor*

der Garten, ⸚ *garden; yard*

das Haus, ⸚er *house*

    das Einfamilienhaus *single-family home*

der Keller, - *basement, cellar*

das Klo, -s (das Klosett) *toilet (colloq.)*

die Küche, -n *kitchen*

der Raum, ⸚e *room*

    der Abstellraum, ⸚e *storage room*

der Rollladen, ⸚ *roll-top shutter*

der Stock, *pl.* **die Stockwerke** *floor, story*

    im ersten (zweiten) Stock *on the second (third) floor*

die Toilette, -n *toilet*

die Treppe, -n *step; stairway*

die Waschküche, -n *laundry room*

das WC, -s *toilet*

das Zimmer, - *room*

    das Badezimmer, - *bathroom*

    das Schlafzimmer, - *bedroom*

    das Wohnzimmer, - *living room*

In der Küche

die Gabel, -n *fork*

der Herd, -e *stove*

der Löffel, - *spoon*

das Messer, - *knife*

der Pfeffer *pepper*
das Salz *salt*
der Teller, - *plate*
der Topf, ̈e *pot*
Guten Appetit! *Enjoy your meal.
  Bon appétit.*

Der Körperteil, -e
der Arm, -e *arm*
das Auge, -n *eye*
der Bauch, ̈e *stomach*
das Bein, -e *leg*
die Brust, ̈e *chest*
der Finger, - *finger*
der Fuß, ̈e *foot*
das Gesicht, -er *face*
das Haar, -e *hair*
der Hals, ̈e *throat*
die Hand, ̈e *hand*
die Haut *skin*
das Herz, -en *heart*
der Hintern *buttocks*
das Kinn, -e *chin*
das Knie, - *knee*
der Kopf, ̈e *head*
der Mund, ̈er *mouth*
die Nase, -n *nose*
das Ohr, -en *ear*
der Rücken, - *back*
die Schulter, -n *shoulder*
die Stirn, -en *forehead*
der Zahn, ̈e *tooth*
der Zeh, -en *toe*

*Der-*Wörter
alle, *pl. all*
dieser/dieses/diese *this, that
  (pl. these, those)*
jeder/jedes/jede *each, every*
welcher?/welches?/welche? *which?*

Dativpronomen
dir *(to/for) you (informal)*
euch *(to/for) you (plural)*
ihm *(to/for) him/it*
ihnen *(to/for) them*

Ihnen *(to/for) you (formal)*
ihr *(to/for) her*
mir *(to/for) me*
uns *(to/for) us*
wem? *(to/for) whom?*

Dativpräpositionen
aus *from; out of*
außer *except for*
bei *at; by; near; with*
mit *with*
nach *after; past; to*
seit *since, for*
von *from, of, by*
zu *to*

Dativverben
danken (hat gedankt) + *dat. to
  thank*
gefallen (gefällt, hat gefallen) +
  dat. to please, to appeal to
gehören (hat gehört) + *dat. to
  belong to*
helfen (hilft, hat geholfen) + *dat.
  to help*
schmecken (hat geschmeckt) +
  dat. to taste good
weh•tun (hat wehgetan) *to hurt*

Andere Verben
dauern (hat gedauert) *to last
  (a length of time)*
**nieder•schlagen (hat
  niedergeschlagen)** *to be reflected in*
rauchen (hat geraucht) *to smoke*
schenken (hat geschenkt) *to give (a
  gift)*
eine Frage stellen (hat gestellt)
  to ask a question
teilen (hat geteilt) *to share*

Andere Ausdrücke
alles in Ordnung *everything's in order/
  okay*
Alles klar! *Okay!, Great!*
Bis gleich! *See you soon!*
(Der Arm) tut mir weh. *My (arm)
  hurts.*

durchschnittlich *on average*
Es/Das tut mir leid. *I'm sorry.*
Entschuldigung. *Excuse me.*
gleich neben *right next to*
Guck mal! *Look!*
günstig *favorable, affordable*
(einen) Kater haben *to have a
  hangover*
meiner Meinung nach *in my
  opinion*
na ja *oh well*
öffentlich *public*
Schwein haben *to be really lucky*
Vielen Dank. *Thanks a lot.*
einen Vogel haben *to be crazy, nuts*
Wie geht es Ihnen/dir? *How are you?,
  How's it going?*

Andere Wörter
das Ding, -e *thing*
die Möglichkeit, -en *possibility*
die Reihenfolge, -n *sequence, order*
die Sache, -n *thing*
allein *alone*
alles *everything, all*
egal *no difference*
endlich *finally*
eng *narrow*
eventuell *possibly, by chance*
gerade *just now, directly*
hoffentlich *I/we hope*
klar *sure, all clear*
manchmal *sometimes*
nett *nice*
schwer *hard, difficult; heavy*
vor + *dat. before; in front of;
  (of time) ago*

Meine eigenen Wörter

_____
_____
_____
_____
_____

Literarisches Deutsch: Zwei Liebesgedichte

GEDICHT 1

Track 1-15

Ein Liebesgedicht
Autor unbekannt, ca. 1200

1 dû bist mîn, ich bin dîn,
2 des solt dû gewis sîn.
3 dû bist beslozzen
4 in mînem herzen;
5 verlorn ist daz slüzzelîn
6 dû muost immer drinne sîn.

1 Modern gesagt Die Sprache in diesem Gedicht° ist aus dem Mittelalter°. Welche Zeile° im Gedicht sagt das Gleiche wie diese Satze?

poem / Middle Ages
line

Satz	Zeile im Gedicht
1. In meinem Herzen	___
2. Dessen sollst du gewiss° sein	___
3. Verloren ist das Schlüsselein°	___
4. Du bist mein, ich bin dein	___
5. Du bist eingeschlossen°	___
6. Du musst immer drinnen sein	___

certain
little key

locked inside

2 Die Bedeutung Wovon erzählt das Gedicht?

1. Jemand hat seinen Hausschlüssel verloren.
2. Jemand hatte einen Herzanfall°.
3. Jemand hat sich schwer verliebt.
4. Jemand kann nicht aus dem Haus.

heart attack

3 Die Sprache Die deutsche Sprache im Mittelalter war anders. Man hat zum Beispiel keinen Unterschied° zwischen Großbuchstaben° und Kleinbuchstaben gemacht. Die Laute° waren auch anders als heute (z. B. **sl →schl, î →ei, zz →ss, uo →u** usw.). Wie heißen die folgenden Wörter vom Gedicht im modernen Deutschen?

difference / capital letters
sounds

mîn • dîn • sîn • beslozzen • mînem • slüzzelîn • muost

GEDICHT 2

Ein Jüngling liebt ein Mädchen
Heinrich Heine, 1797–1856

Harry Heine was born into a Jewish family on December 13, 1797, in Düsseldorf, but was later baptized as a Protestant to promote his career, a decision about which he remained ambivalent throughout his life. Following the baptism he was known as Heinrich Heine. Although he earned his doctorate in law, he chose a career as a writer and spent most of his life in financial straits. In 1831, Heine moved to Paris where he died in 1856. First associated with German Romanticism, his later writings became increasingly political and many were banned in Prussia, Austria, and other states in the German Confederation.

Bettmann/CORBIS

Heinrich Heine

4 **Eine unglückliche Liebesgeschichte** Das Gedicht „Ein Jüngling liebt ein Mädchen" endet mit dieser Zeile: „dem bricht das Herz entzwei°."

in two

expects

1. Klingt das optimistisch oder pessimistisch?
2. Erwartet° man das in einem Liebesgedicht?
3. Was erwartet man normalerweise von Liebe?
4. Ein Mädchen heiratet „den nächsten besten Mann". Ist das eine gute Motivation? Kennen Sie ein Beispiel aus den Hollywood-Zeitungen dafür?

🔊 Ein Jüngling° liebt ein Mädchen

Track 1-16

1 Ein Jüngling liebt ein Mädchen,
2 Die hat einen anderen erwählt°;
3 Der andre liebt eine andere.
4 Und hat sich mit dieser vermählt°.
5 Das Mädchen heiratet aus Ärger°
6 Den nächsten besten Mann,
7 Der ihr in den Weg gelaufen°;
8 Der Jüngling ist übel dran°.
9 Es ist eine alte Geschichte,
10 Doch bleibt sie immer neu;
11 Und wem sie just passiert°,
12 Dem bricht das Herz entzwei.

young man

chose

hat sich vermählt: *wed*
aus ... : *out of annoyance*

der ... : *who crosses her path*
ist ... : *is upset about it*

just ... : *happens this way*

> The original poem had these spellings: *andern* (2), *eine andre* (3), *passieret* (11).

5 **Was ist passiert?** Was passiert im Gedicht zuerst und was dann später? Nummerieren Sie die Sätze von **1** bis **5**.

___ ein junger Mann liebt und heiratet ein Mädchen

___ ein Mädchen heiratet einen jungen Mann, aber sie liebt ihn nicht

___ ein junger Mann liebt ein Mädchen, aber sie liebt ihn nicht

___ ein Mädchen liebt einen jungen Mann, aber er liebt sie nicht

___ ein junger Mann ist unglücklich

6 **Was glauben Sie?** Diskutieren Sie die folgenden Fragen mit der Klasse oder mit einem Partner/einer Partnerin mithilfe der Grafik.

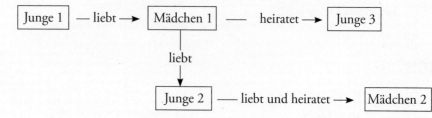

1. Wer kennt wen und wer kennt wen nicht? Wer heiratet wen zum Schluss?
2. Welche Ehe ist (un)glücklich? Warum?
3. Kennen Sie diese Geschichte aus einem Film, aus einem Buch oder aus dem wirklichen Leben?
4. Das mittelalterliche Gedicht ist optimistisch. Heines Gedicht ist pessimistisch. Welches ist Ihrer Meinung nach realistisch? Wie ist Liebe wirklich?

Owen Franken/CORBIS

Frisches Obst und Gemüse vom Wochenmarkt in Freiburg schmeckt super.

Man kann alles in der Stadt finden

In this chapter you will learn where to do errands and where to spend free time in a city, how to ask for and give directions, and how to talk about shopping, sports, travel, transportation, and destinations in town.

Kommunikative Funktionen

> Expressing location and destination
> Giving directions
> Talking about when events happen
> Talking about means of transportation
> Expressing time, manner, place
> Expressing the purpose for an action

Strukturen

> Two-case prepositions and verbs used with them
> **Wo?** and **wohin?**

> The prefixes **hin** and **her**
> Prepositions indicating location
> Verbs with two-case prepositions
> Verbs of destination vs. location
> Time expressions in the dative and accusative
> The preposition **mit** with means of transportation
> Word order: time, manner, place
> The subordinating conjunction **damit**

Vokabeln

> Wo gehst du gern hin? Wie kommt man dahin?
> Wo macht man das in der Stadt?

Kulturelles

> Studentenermäßigungen
> Einkaufen
> Stuttgart
> München
> Fußball und Profi-Sport in Mitteleuropa

Barbara muss ein Konto eröffnen

Barbara, die neue Studentin aus Dresden, sucht° eine Bank, denn sie will in Tübingen ein Konto eröffnen. Auf dem Weg zur Bushaltestelle° trifft sie Stefan und Karl. Zusammen fahren sie mit dem Bus in die Stadt. Karl und Stefan geben Barbara ein paar gute Tipps, zum Beispiel, wo sie eine gute Buchhandlung° finden kann und wo sie ein Semesterticket für den Bus kaufen kann.

is looking for
bus stop

bookstore

Vorschau

1 Thematische Fragen Beantworten Sie die folgenden Fragen auf Deutsch.

1. Wie kommen Sie zur Universität: mit dem Auto, mit dem Rad, mit dem Bus oder zu Fuß?
2. Was für Verkehrsmittel° gibt es in Ihrer Stadt – Busse, eine U-Bahn, Privatautos?
3. Wie kaufen Sie Ihre Bücher für die Uni: mit Bargeld°, mit einem Scheck, mit einer Bankkarte oder Kreditkarte?
4. Kaufen Sie Bücher lieber in einer Buchhandlung oder online?
5. Wie bekommen Sie Bargeld, wenn Sie es brauchen: von den Eltern, von Freunden, vom Bankautomaten, direkt von der Bank?
6. Wie viel Geld brauchen Sie pro Woche? Wie viel pro Monat?

means of transportation
cash

2 Satzdetektiv Welche Sätze bedeuten ungefähr das Gleiche?

1. Karl will auf der Bank Geld **abheben.**
2. Barbara muss auf der Bank ein **Konto eröffnen.**
3. Könnt ihr mir eine Bank **empfehlen?**
4. Die Sparkasse hat eine **Filiale** ganz in der Nähe von der Uni.

a. Bei der Uni gibt es auch eine Sparkasse.
b. Karl möchte von der Bank Geld holen°.
c. Barbara braucht ein neues Bankkonto.
d. Kennt ihr eine gute Bank?

pick up

5. Ich hab' ein **Semesterticket.**
6. Wo kann ich mir ein Semesterticket **besorgen?**
7. Am **Kiosk** gibt es Semestertickets.
8. Dann kann ich praktisch alles in der Stadt **erledigen.**

e. Wo kann ich mir ein Semesterticket für den Bus kaufen?
f. Ich habe für dieses Semester einen speziellen Buspass für Studenten.
g. Fast alles, was ich brauche, kann ich in der Stadt machen.
h. Semestertickets kann man an einem Stand für Zigaretten, Zeitschriften usw. kaufen.

Kulturnotiz. A **Kiosk** offers a variety of items, such as sweets, stamps, magazines, newspapers, stationery, cigarettes, and lottery and bus tickets.

Brennpunkt Kultur Web Search · Web Link

Studentenermäßigungen°

student discounts

In the German-speaking countries, all students receive a student identification card (**der Studentenausweis** for university students and **der Schülerausweis** for high school students and apprentices). With this ID, students are entitled to receive discounts for museums, theaters, movie theaters, ballet, and classical music

Teich/Caro/ullstein bild/The Image Works

Studenten und Schüler reisen billig mit der Bahn und mit dem Bus.

> **Kulturnotiz.** German speakers distinguish between university students (**Studenten, Studierende**) and all elementary and secondary school pupils (**Schüler**). Similarly, when a person says **ich gehe zur Schule,** he/she refers to a primary or secondary school. Attending university is called **auf die Universität gehen/zur Universität gehen** or simply **studieren.**

performances, but not popular music concerts. Students may also purchase a **Semesterkarte** (called a **Semesterticket** in Tübingen), which is a discounted ticket for use on public transportation in cities with a subway (**die Untergrundbahn** or **U-Bahn**), trains, or busses during the semester. Students also pay low rates for rooms in university residence halls, and the mandatory usage fees for television and radio may be waived for financially-strapped students. The federal government subsidizes many of these benefits.

Kulturkreuzung

Bekommen Sie als Student/Studentin Ermäßigungen? Wann? Wo? In Europa haben Studenten einen relativ hohen Status und die Finanzierung des Studiums ist eine soziale Verantwortung°. Ist das auch der Fall° in Ihrem Land? Warum? Warum nicht?

responsibility / case

Hören Sie gut zu.

Sprache im Alltag: **Wo** or **wohin?**

In English, *Where are you going?* is used to mean *Where are you going to?* In German, however, the distinction between location and destination in questions is strictly observed by using **wo** or **wohin.**

Wo sind Karl und Stefan?	*Where are Karl and Stefan?*
Wohin geht ihr?	*Where are you guys going?*

It is also common in spoken German to split the interrogative **wohin** into two parts and place the **hin** at the end of the sentence:

Wo geht ihr **hin?**	*Where are you guys going?*

An old English equivalent of German **wohin** is the question word *whither.*

Complete the **Ergänzen Sie** activity in the Student Activities Manual before starting activity 4.

valid

rivers

Rückblick

3 Stimmt das? Stimmen diese Aussagen zum Text? Wenn nicht, was stimmt?

	Ja, das stimmt.	Nein, das stimmt nicht.
1. Stefan muss auf die Post.	○	○
2. Karl braucht Geld von seinem Bankkonto.	○	○
3. Barbara sucht ein Buch, und dann will sie auch ein Bankkonto eröffnen.	○	○
4. Stefan und Karl empfehlen Barbara die Kreissparkasse.	○	○
5. Die Kreissparkasse hat keine Filiale ganz in der Nähe von der Universität.	○	○
6. Karl und Stefan fahren immer mit dem Bus in die Stadt.	○	○
7. In der Kreissparkasse kann Barbara ein Semesterticket für den Bus kaufen.	○	○
8. Gleich gegenüber von der Sparkasse ist der Hauptbahnhof.	○	○

4 Kurz gefragt Beantworten Sie diese Fragen auf Deutsch.

1. Warum fahren Karl und Stefan in die Stadt?
2. Was will Barbara alles in der Stadt erledigen?
3. Warum empfiehlt Karl die Kreissparkasse?
4. Wie fährt Karl meistens in die Stadt?
5. Warum fährt Stefan meistens mit dem Bus?
6. Wo kann Barbara ein Semesterticket kaufen?
7. Wo gibt es eine gute Buchhandlung?

5 Das Semesterticket Lesen Sie die Informationen über das Semesterticket für Tübingen und schreiben Sie die Sätze unten fertig.

1. Das Semesterticket ist gültig° von April bis _____.
2. Mit welchen Infos müssen Studenten das Ticket ausfüllen?
3. Der Preis ist _____.
4. Die Klasse ist _____.
5. Naldo steht für drei Namen. Welche drei? Sind das Städte, Flüsse° oder Menschen?
6. Was bedeutet wohl „Nicht übertragbar"?
   a. not transferable
   b. not useable
   c. not returnable

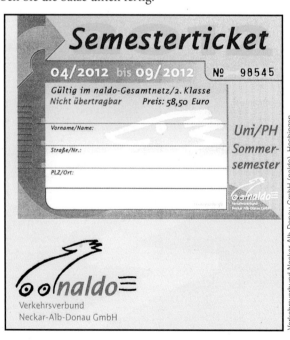

6 Textdetektiv: **Anlauftext.** Use the *Anlauftext* to recognize important aspects of German structure and usage.

1. Look at the following examples from the *Anlauftext* and indicate whether the boldface forms are in dative or the accusative case. Then write the verb that is used (or implied) in the correct column, depending on whether motion or location is expressed.

	D = Dative A = Accusative	Verb expressing motion	Verb expressing location
a. Wir fahren runter **in die Stadt.**	_____	_____	_____
b. Ich muss **auf die Post.**	_____	_____	_____
c. Ich muss **in die Buchhandlung**.	_____	_____	_____
d. Die Kreissparkasse hat eine Filiale **in der Nähe** von der Uni.	_____	_____	_____
e. **In der Sparkasse** kann ich mir ein Semesterticket besorgen.	_____	_____	_____
f. Fahrt ihr immer mit dem Bus **in die Stadt?**	_____	_____	_____
g. **Am Hauptbahnhof** kann ich mir ein Semesterticket besorgen.	_____	_____	_____
h. Dann kann ich praktisch alles **in der Stadt** erledigen.	_____	_____	_____

2. In the examples above, which case (dative or accusative) is used with verbs showing motion?

3. The title of the chapter is *Man kann alles **in der Stadt** finden*. Which is the more exact translation of the boldface phrase in the title?

    a. in town   b. into town

Barbara geht in die Buchhandlung und kauft sich ein Buch.

Strukturen

I Expressing Location and Destination

Two-case prepositions: wo? versus wohin?

A. Two-case prepositions

> Two-case prepositions are also known as two-way prepositions.

In **Kapitel 6,** you learned that the two-case preposition (**Wechselpräposition**) **in,** when used with the dative case, expresses location. The preposition **an** is also used frequently in the dative case to show location.

Wie muss sich Fabian **an** dieser Kreuzung verhalten?

When used with the accusative case and a verb of forward motion, however, these prepositions express destination. Location or destination is not expressed by the preposition itself but rather by the case ending of the article that follows.

Sie steht **an der** Tafel. *She is standing at the chalkboard.*
Sie geht **an die** Tafel. *She is going to the chalkboard.*

To ask about location, German speakers use **wo?** (*where?*). To ask about destination, they use **wohin?** (*where . . . to?*). In both situations, a two-case preposition with the appropriate case is commonly part of the answer.

Wo stehen sie? —**An der** Haltestelle. *Where are they standing? —At the bus stop.*
Wohin fahren sie? —**In die** Stadt. *Where are they driving to? —(In) to town.*

German has nine two-case prepositions.

> English has only two preposition pairs that are comparable to the German two-case prepositions: *in/into* and *on/onto.*

an	*at, on; to*	in	*at, in; into; to*	vor	*in front of*
auf	*at, on; onto; to*	neben	*beside, next to*	zwischen	*between*
hinter	*behind, to/in the back of*	über	*above, over*		
		unter	*under, underneath*		

Wohin? Wo?

an

Barbara geht **an die** Ampel.
Barbara walks up to the traffic light.

Das Auto steht **an der** Ampel.
The car is stopped at the traffic light.

auf

Die Kinder laufen **auf den** Spielplatz.
The children are running (on)to the playground.

Das Kind spielt **auf dem** Spielplatz.
The child is playing on the playground.

	Wohin?	**Wo?**

hinter Der Tankwart fährt den Wagen **hinter die Tankstelle.**
The station attendant is driving the car to the back of the gas station.

Der Tankwart wäscht den Wagen **hinter der** Tankstelle.
The station attendant is washing the car behind the gas station.

in Die Familie steigt **ins (in das)** Auto.
The family is getting into the car.

Die Familie sitzt **im (in dem)** Auto.
The family is in the car.

neben Er hängt den Fahrplan **neben das** Poster.
He is hanging the train schedule next to the poster.

Der Fahrplan hängt **neben dem** Poster.
The train schedule is hanging next to the poster.

über Der Bus fährt **über die** Brücke.
The bus is driving over the bridge.

Über der Bäckerei ist ein China Restaurant.
There's a Chinese restaurant above the bakery.

The following contractions are mandatory:

am = an dem
im = in dem
ins = in das

You have already used
ins Kino/Konzert/Theater/Museum/Schloss gehen in **Kapitel 3**.

Illustrations © Cengage Learning 2014

	Wohin?	**Wo?**

unter Der Ball rollt **unter das** Auto.
The ball is rolling under the car.

Der Ball ist **unter dem** Auto.
The ball is underneath the car.

vor Der BMW fährt **vor den**
Hoteleingang vor.
*The BMW is driving up to the
hotel entrance.*

Der Mercedes steht **vor dem**
Hoteleingang.
*The Mercedes is standing in front
of the hotel entrance.*

zwischen Der Ball rollt **zwischen die**
Autos.
*The ball is rolling between the
cars.*

Der Kiosk ist **zwischen dem** Theater
und **der** Bank.
*The kiosk is between the theater and
the bank.*

↩ **7** Wo sind die Bücher? Anna sucht ihre Bücher in ihrem Zimmer. Wo
sind sie alle? Benutzen Sie diese Wörter: **das Bett, der Schreibtisch, die
Lampe, der Spiegel, der Schrank, der Laptop, der Stuhl, die Tür, der
Tennisschläger** (*tennis racket*), **die Bettdecke** (*bedspread*).

BEISPIEL *Ein Buch ist unter dem Bett.*

B. *More about* an, auf, *and* in

An, auf, and **in** are the three most common two-case prepositions. **An** is often used for objects on vertical surfaces, such as a wall or a door, or the edge of something, such as a body of water. **Auf** is used for objects on horizontal surfaces such as a table or the floor. **Auf** is also used for certain locations (**die Post, der Fußballplatz, der Markt, die Uni**) and events (**das Fest, die Fete, die Party**). **In** is used for an enclosed space, such as a room or car, or a very defined space, such as a store or a city.

Dative of location

at   Uwe sitzt **an der** Tür (**am** Fenster).

   *Uwe is sitting at the door
   (at the window).*

   Bert arbeitet **auf der** Post.
   Bert works at the post office.

on   Die Nummer ist **an der** Tür.
   The number is on the door.

   Das Buch liegt **auf dem** Tisch.
   The book is on (top of) the table.

in   Er sitzt **in der** Küche.
   He's sitting in the kitchen.

   Er sitzt **im** Kino.
   He's sitting in the movie theater.

Accusative of destination

to   Uwe geht **an die** Tür (**ans** Fenster).

   *Uwe is going to the door
   (to the window).*

   Bert geht **auf die** Post.
   Bert is going to the post office.

on(to)   Er schreibt die Nummer **an die** Tür.
   He's writing the number on(to) the door.

   Sie legt das Buch **auf den** Tisch.
   She puts the book on(to) the table.

in(to)   Er geht **in die** Küche.
   He's going in(to) the kitchen.

   Er geht **ins** Kino.
   He's going to the movies.

> The preposition **in** is used for country names that have an article, **Wir fahren in die Schweiz** *We're driving to Switzerland.*

Brennpunkt Kultur   Web Search / Web Link

Einkaufen

While **der Supermarkt** has found its niche for one-stop grocery shopping throughout German-speaking Europe, many customers prefer the higher quality and personal service available in smaller specialty shops. Shoppers often make daily trips to their local stores to purchase fresh goods. Since shops and residential housing are well integrated, many people walk to stores and carry their groceries home. Many customers use their own bag (**die Einkaufstasche**), a mesh shopping bag (**das Einkaufsnetz**), or a basket (**der Einkaufskorb**) for shopping, since stores charge for each plastic bag (**die Plastiktüte/Tragetasche**). Customers also bag their own groceries and a deposit is charged for a shopping cart (**der Einkaufswagen**). While these frequent shopping trips reduce the need to purchase large quantities of groceries at one time, the higher cost and effort required have also given rise to the growth of discount marketers like Aldi, Netto Marken-Discount, and Lidl. Full-service retail supermarket chains like Edeka, Rewe, and Tengelmann are present all across Germany and often provide areas where customers can remove groceries from packaging and recycle it on the spot.

Bloomberg/Getty Images

Kulturkreuzung

Wie oft gehen Sie einkaufen? Gehen Sie zu Fuß oder fahren Sie zum Supermarkt? Warum? Was meinen Sie: Ist es eine gute Idee, dass man die eigene Tragetasche zum Einkaufen mitbringt? Machen Sie das? Warum (nicht)? Packen Sie Ihre Sachen selber im Supermarkt, oder tun das andere?

Wissenswerte Vokabeln: Wo gehst du gern hin?

Talking about where you like to go in your free time

in die Kirche (Synagoge, Moschee) gehen

ins Konzert gehen

ins Museum gehen

in den Jazzkeller gehen

in die Oper gehen

ins Theater gehen

ins Kino gehen

ins Schwimmbad gehen

ins Stadion gehen

ins Fitnessstudio gehen

in den Club gehen

in die Kneipe gehen

ins Restaurant gehen

auf eine Party (Fete) gehen

BEISPIEL   *Wohin gehst du (nicht) gern?*

8 Wohin gehen Karl und Stefan? Finden Sie für jede Situation einen passenden Ort°.

place

BEISPIEL *Wenn Karl und Stefan Durst haben, gehen sie in die Kneipe.*

1. Wenn sie Durst haben, gehen sie
2. Wenn sie billig° essen wollen, gehen sie
3. Wenn sie gut essen wollen, gehen sie
4. Wenn sie einen Film sehen wollen, gehen sie
5. Wenn sie ein Buch suchen müssen, gehen sie
6. Wenn sie Fußball spielen wollen, gehen sie
7. Wenn Karl kochen will, geht er
8. Wenn Stefan Musik von Wagner hören will, geht er
9. Wenn sie eine Vorlesung haben, gehen sie
10. Wenn sie auf eine Hochzeit° gehen, gehen sie

a. auf den Fußballplatz.
b. in den Hörsaal.
c. in die Mensa.
d. in die Oper.
e. in die Kneipe.
f. ins Kino.
g. ins Restaurant.
h. in die Bibliothek.
i. in die Küche.
j. in die Kirche.

cheaply

wedding

 9 Interview Stellen Sie einem Partner/einer Partnerin die folgenden Fragen.

1. Wohin gehst du, wenn du lernen willst?
2. Wohin gehst du, wenn du mit jemandem° ausgehst?
3. Wohin gehst du am Freitag, am Samstag, am Sonntag?
4. Wohin gehst du, wenn es im Sommer sehr heiß ist?
5. Wohin gehst du, wenn du Sport treiben° willst?
6. Wohin gehst du, wenn du einen Kurs oder ein Seminar hast?

someone

Sport treiben: *to do sports*

Sprache im Alltag: Names of cities with **an/am**

A few prominent German cities indicate their location on a major river (**der Fluss**) by using the preposition **an/am** and the name of the river in their name. The two Frankfurts rely on this designation to distinguish between them.

Frankfurt am Main	Fluss: der Main
Frankfurt an der Oder	Fluss: die Oder
Marburg an der Lahn	Fluss: die Lahn
Neustadt an der Donau	Fluss: die Donau
Ludwigshafen am Rhein	Fluss: der Rhein

Christian Colista/Shutterstock.com

Marburg an der Lahn

Wo macht man das in der Stadt?

Talking about where to run errands

Am Bahnhof kauft man Fahrscheine.

An der Haltestelle wartet man auf den Bus.

zahlt ein: deposits

Auf der Post kauft man Briefmarken und gibt Pakete auf.

Auf der Bank (Auf der Sparkasse) zahlt man Geld ein°, oder man hebt es ab.

Am Kiosk (Am Zeitungsstand) kauft man Zeitungen, Zeitschriften und Studentenpässe.

In der Buchhandlung kauft man Bücher.

Essen

Im Reformhaus (Im Bioladen) bekommt man gesunde, natürliche Kost°.

In der Bäckerei kauft man Brot, Brötchen und Brezeln.

Illustrations © Cengage Learning 2014

In der Konditorei kauft man Kuchen
und Torten.

Im Supermarkt hat man eine große
Auswahl°.

Illustrations © Cengage Learning 2014

selection

In der Fleischerei (In der Metzgerei)
bekommt man Fleisch, Wurst und
Geflügel.

Auf dem Markt kauft man alles
frisch vom Lande: Obst, Gemüse,
Käse, Eier.

BEISPIEL *Wo kauft man Bücher?*

↩ **10** Wo treffen sie sich? Lesen Sie die Liste von Stefan und die von Barbara
und fragen Sie dann einen Partner/eine Partnerin, wo die beiden sich treffen.
Wählen Sie Orte aus der **Wo?**-Liste.

die Tasche = die Tüte

Wo?

auf _____ Markt	auf _____ Post	in _____ Konditorei
in _____ Bäckerei	in _____ Metzgerei	in _____ Bank
an _____ Kiosk		

BEISPIEL S1: *Stefan holt Briefmarken und Barbara muss ein Paket schicken. Wo treffen
sie sich?*
S2: *Sie treffen sich auf der Post.*

Stefans Liste

1. Briefmarken holen°
2. Geld abheben
3. frische Landeier kaufen
4. eine Zeitung kaufen
5. Fleisch kaufen
6. Brot kaufen
7. einen Apfelkuchen kaufen

Barbaras Liste

1. ein Paket schicken
2. ein Konto eröffnen
3. Gemüse kaufen
4. einen Studentenpass kaufen
5. Wurst kaufen
6. Brötchen holen
7. eine Schokoladentorte kaufen

pick up, get

← **11**

Wohin müssen sie gehen? Klaus, Barbara und Anna müssen vieles erledigen. Stellen Sie einem Partner/einer Partnerin Fragen über Klaus, Barbara und Anna.

Wohin müssen sie gehen?

in _____ Bäckerei	in _____ Bibliothek	auf _____ Post
in _____ Supermarkt	in _____ Konditorei	auf _____ Markt
in _____ Bank	in _____ Metzgerei	in _____ Apotheke°

BEISPIEL S1: *Klaus muss Briefmarken kaufen. Wohin muss er gehen?*
S2: *Er muss auf die Post (gehen).*

Klaus muss ...
    a. Briefmarken kaufen.
    b. eine EC-Karte holen.
    c. Medikamente kaufen.
Anna muss ...
    d. Kuchen holen.
    e. Brot kaufen.
    f. frische Eier kaufen.
Barbara muss ...
    g. Kaffee und Käse kaufen.
    h. Bücher zurückgeben.
    i. Wurst und Fleisch kaufen.

← **12** **Rätsel: Wo ist die Buchhandlung?** Lesen Sie die Sätze und bestimmen° Sie, wo die Buchhandlung ist.

Rechts neben der Bäckerei ist die Metzgerei.
Direkt gegenüber von der Metzgerei ist die Konditorei.
Die Buchhandlung ist zwischen dem Zeitungskiosk und der Apotheke.
Die Bank ist an der Ecke°.
Rechts von der Buchhandlung ist die Apotheke.
Die Buchhandlung ist nicht an der Ecke.
Die Post ist zwischen der Bank und der Bäckerei.
Quer gegenüber von° der Post ist der Zeitungskiosk.

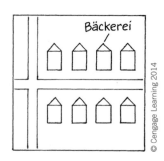

← **13** **Stuttgart** Anna, Barbara, Karl und Stefan besuchen Stuttgart. Helfen Sie Anna und Barbara, die folgenden Sehenswürdigkeiten in Stuttgart zu finden. (Siehe Seite 259.)

BEISPIEL *Der zentrale Omnibusbahnhof ist nebe dem Hauptbahnhof.*

1. Der zentrale Omnibusbahnhof	a. am Karlsplatz.
2. Der Schlossplatz	b. am Marktplatz.
3. Die Universitätsbibliothek	c. hinter dem Staatstheater.
4. Das Alte Schloss	d. im Stadtgarten.
5. Das Rathaus	e. neben dem Hauptbahnhof.
6. Die Markthalle	f. vor dem Postamt.
7. Die Staatsgalerie	g. zwischen dem Alten Schloss und dem Rathaus.

Wohin müssen sie gehen?
Note that you are talking about destinations. Therefore, the two-case prepositions require the accusative case.

pharmacy

determine

corner

Quer …: *diagonally across from*

Kulturnotiz. An **EC-Karte** is a debit card that can be used to access cash and make purchases in Europe.

© Cengage Learning 2014

STUTTGART

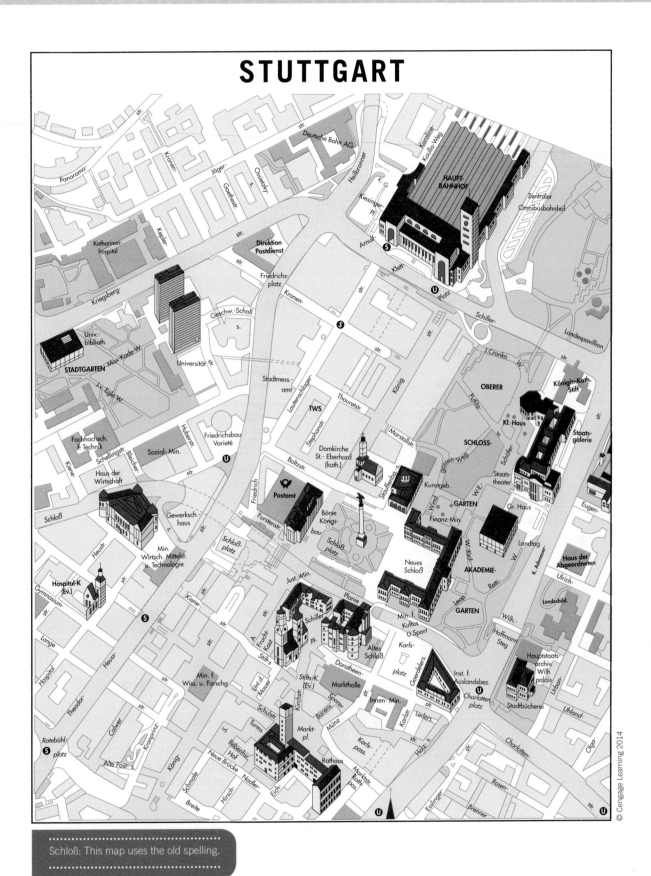

Schloß: This map uses the old spelling.

Stuttgart

Baden-Württemberg, bordering on France to its west and Switzerland to its south, is Germany's southwestern-most state. The city of Stuttgart, located an hour north of Tübingen, is the capital (**die Landeshauptstadt**) of Baden-Württemberg and cultural center of the dialect region called Swabia (**Schwaben**), noteworthy for its industrious, ingenious, and thrifty people. With a population of 581,092, Stuttgart ranks as Baden-Württemberg's largest city. It is home to two of the world's most famous carmakers, Daimler AG and Porsche, and to automobile parts manufacturer Robert Bosch. The city's fame in the automotive industry is further enhanced by the Porsche and Mercedes-Benz Museums.

Largely destroyed in World War II, Stuttgart has since emerged as an attractive regional metropolis with distinctly southern charms and a leisurely pace of life. Nestled in the Neckar River valley, the city exudes a sense of calm that is created by the surrounding forests and hills, many of which were home to working vineyards through the 19th century. Climbing the stairways (**die Weinbergstäffele**) through these old vineyards is one of the best ways to discover Stuttgart's romantic charm. Downtown Stuttgart maintains the calm of nature with its massive **Schlossgärten** and **Schlossplatz,** dominated by the majestic baroque **Neues Schloss,** located adjacent to Stuttgart's main shopping area, **Königstraße.** Culturally, Stuttgart has gained international fame for its ballet troupe, **Stuttgarter Ballett,** for its outstanding theater, **Staatstheater Stuttgart,** and for the architecture and art collections of **die Staatsgalerie.** The outstanding opera company, **Staatsoper Stuttgart,** was named "opera house of the year" six times between 1994 and 2006, and **die Internationale Bachakademie Stuttgart** and **Gächinger Kantorei** under the direction of Helmuth Rilling have achieved worldwide recognition for authentic performances of Bach's music. Stuttgarters also love sports, and none more passionately than their soccer team, **VfB Stuttgart.** The city's **Stuttgart 21** project aims to modernize the rail system by constructing a subterranean station under the historic Hauptbahnhof plus two additional stations, adding 60 kilometers of rail to the system.

Jürgen Fälchle/Fotolia LLC

Im Sommer kann man gemütlich auf dem Schlossplatz vor dem Neuen Schloss sitzen.

Kulturkreuzung

Stuttgart ist eine bekannte deutsche Auto-Stadt. Welche deutschen Autos kommen aus Stuttgart? Welche deutschen Automarken kommen nicht aus Stuttgart? Wie ist die Qualität von diesen Autos? Welche US-Städte und Staaten assoziiert man mit Autos?

14 Wohin gehen sie in Stuttgart? Anna und Karl machen Pläne. Hier sind ihre Interessen. Wohin gehen sie wahrscheinlich in Stuttgart?

BEISPIEL   S1: *Anna möchte Obst finden. Wohin möchte sie gehen?*
　　　　　 S2: *Sie möchte in die Markthalle gehen.*

1. Anna: Obst finden, einen Picasso sehen, Bücher finden, ein Schloss sehen
2. Karl: ein Theaterstück sehen, Briefmarken kaufen, den Bürgermeister suchen
3. du: ?

Strukturen

II Giving Directions

Prepositional phrases; *hin* and *her*

A. Prepositional phrases indicating location

German speakers frequently use two-case prepositions with the accusative when giving directions how to get somewhere.

> Gehen Sie **über die Brücke in die Stadt.**   *Go over the bridge into town.*

Other prepositions, such as **um** and **zu,** are common, too. Here are some useful prepositional phrases for asking for and giving directions.

Wie komme ich zur/zum …?	*How do I get to . . . ?*
bis zur Kreuzung/Ampel	*as far as (up to) the intersection/traffic light*
links/rechts ab•biegen	*turn left/right*
die Straße entlang	*down the street*
über die Straße	*across the street*
geradeaus	*straight ahead*
(gleich) um die Ecke	*(right) around the corner*
an der Ecke	*at the corner*

> Note that the preposition **zu** (e.g., **bis zur Kreuzung**) always occurs with the dative, while the preposition **um** (e.g., **um die Ecke**) always occurs with the accusative.

15 Wie kommt Anna zur Staatsgalerie? Anna ist in Stuttgart und möchte vieles sehen. Welche Wegbeschreibung° ist richtig?

direction

Anna ist …

1. am Hauptbahnhof und möchte zur Staatsgalerie.
2. am Marktplatz und möchte zum Karlsplatz.
3. am Postamt und möchte zum Hauptbahnhof.
4. in der Markthalle und möchte zum Karlsplatz.
5. im Neuen Schloss und möchte zum Königsbau.
6. am Marktplatz und möchte zum Rathaus.

Ein Stuttgarter/Eine Stuttgarterin sagt:

a. „Sie stehen doch direkt vor dem Rathaus!"
b. „Gehen Sie über den Schlossplatz."
c. „Gehen Sie die Münzstraße entlang."
d. „Nehmen Sie die Boltzstraße bis zur Königstraße, dann gehen Sie nach links und immer geradeaus."
e. „Gehen Sie die Schillerstraße entlang bis zur Konrad-Adenauer-Straße und dann nach rechts."
f. „Gehen Sie über die Dorotheenstraße."

> Use the map on page 259.

16 Wie komme ich zum Bahnhof? Sie sind in Stuttgart am Schlossplatz vor dem Neuen Schloss. Ein Tourist/Eine Touristin fragt nach dem Weg. Beschreiben Sie, wie man dahin kommt. Benutzen Sie den Stadtplan von Stuttgart.

> Use the map on page 259.

BEISPIEL   S1 (TOURIST/TOURISTIN): *Entschuldigung, wie komme ich zum Bahnhof?*
           S2   (SIE): *Gehen Sie die Königstraße entlang.*

S1 (*Tourist/Touristin*):
zum Bahnhof • zum Schillerplatz • zum Staatstheater • zur Markthalle

B. *The prefixes* hin *and* her

You have already encountered **hin** and **her** in the question words **wohin** *(where to)* and **woher** *(where from)*.

> Wo**her** kommst du? – Ich komme aus Berlin.
> Wo**hin** fährst du? – Ich fahre in die Stadt.

Both **hin** and **her** also occur as separable prefixes on verbs of motion to express origin, (e.g., **her•kommen**) and destination (e.g., **hin•fahren**).

Komm mal **her!**	*Come over here!*
Möchtest du dort **hin**fahren?	*Would you like to go (drive) there?*
Wo soll ich das Buch **hin**legen?	*Where should I put the book?*

---

nosy, curious

 17 Der neugierige° Zimmernachbar Karls Nachbar im Studentenwohnheim möchte alles ganz genau wissen. Welche Fragen hat er gestellt und was hat Karl geantwortet? Verbinden Sie seine Fragen mit den passenden Antworten von Karl und lesen Sie sie dann laut mit einem Partner/einer Partnerin.

BEISPIEL   S1 (NACHBAR): *Woher hast du deine Bankkarte?*
              S2   (KARL): *Von der Sparkasse bei der Uni.*

1. Woher hast du deine Bankkarte?
2. Woher hast du das gute Brot?
3. Wohin gehst du, wenn du eine Semesterkarte brauchst?
4. Woher hast du das Magazin?
5. Wohin bringst du das Geld?
6. Wohin gehst du, wenn du schnell einige Brötchen brauchst?

a. Vom Kiosk bei der Kreuzung.
b. Zum Kiosk bei der Kreuzung.
c. Auf die Sparkasse bei der Uni.
d. Von der Sparkasse bei der Uni.
e. Aus der Bäckerei gleich um die Ecke.
f. In die Bäckerei gleich um die Ecke.

C. Verbs commonly used with two-case prepositions

1. Verbs with prepositions followed by the accusative

Verbs expressing movement toward a destination often occur with two-case prepositions. In such instances, the preposition is followed by the accusative case: **Stefan geht in den Park.** (*Stefan is going into the park.*) Such sentences answer the question **wohin?** Commonly used verbs of this type include: **gehen, fahren, fallen, fliegen, laufen,** and **springen** (*to jump*).

Wohin gehen Stefan und Karl?	Sie gehen **in die Bank**.
	They are going to the bank.
Wohin fahren sie?	Sie fahren **in die Stadt**.
	They are driving into town.
Wohin ist Anna gefahren?	Anna ist **an die Nordsee** gefahren.
	Anna drove to the North Sea.
Wohin springt das Kind?	Das Kind springt **ins Wasser.**
	The child is jumping into the water.

2. Verbs with prepositions followed by the dative

Verbs that express location are used with two-case prepositions followed by the dative case.

> Wo **wohnt** Cornelia? – Sie wohnt **in der** Stadt.
> *Where does Cornelia live? – She lives in town.*

> Note that if the movement is *not* directed towards a destination, but is rather limited to a confined area, the dative case is used: **Stefan läuft im Park.** (*Stefan is running inside the park.*)

> These verbs may also occur with prepositions other than two-case prepositions, e.g., **ich fahre zum Bahnhof** (**zu** = dative preposition).

> **Sein** and **wohnen** are among the verbs that frequently trigger the dative after two-case prepositions.

3. The verbs *hängen/hängen; legen/liegen; setzen/sitzen; stellen/stehen.*

To show location, the verb **hängen (hat gehangen)**, **liegen (hat gelegen)**, **sitzen (hat gesessen)**, or **stehen (hat gestanden)** is used with the dative case. To show movement toward a destination, the verb **hängen (hat gehängt)**, **legen (hat gelegt)**, **setzen (hat gesetzt)**, or **stellen (hat gestellt)** is used with the accusative case. Notice that the four verbs showing location are all irregular (strong), while the verbs showing movement are regular (weak). The four regular verbs all essentially mean *to put*.

legen   to lay or put something (e.g., a newspaper) in(to) a horizontal position
setzen   to seat, set, or put someone (e.g., a person, a child, a doll) down
stellen   to put something (e.g., a bottle or suitcase) in(to) an upright position

One use of **stellen** is idiomatic: **Er stellt** (*not* legt) **den Teller auf den Tisch.**

Accusative of destination   *Dative of location*

Er **hängt** den Fahrplan an die Wand.

Der Fahrplan **hängt** an der Wand.

Er **legt** die Zeitung auf den Sitz.

Die Zeitung **liegt** auf dem Sitz.

Er **setzt** das Kind auf die Bank.

Das Kind **sitzt** auf der Bank.

The verbs **stehen** and **liegen** both mean *is* when describing locations. **Stehen** is used with buildings; **liegen** is used to state the location of streets, cities, states, and countries. **Das Haus steht an der Ecke.** *The house is on the corner.* **Heidelberg liegt am Neckar.** *Heidelberg is on the Neckar.* **Deutschland liegt im Herzen Europas.** *Germany is in the heart of Europe.*

Sie **stellt** den Koffer in den Bahnhof.

Der Koffer **steht** im Bahnhof.

Illustrations © Cengage Learning 2014

18 Mein Zimmer Machen Sie eine Zeichnung von Ihrem Zimmer und beschreiben Sie es dann für einen Partner/eine Partnerin. Der Partner/Die Partnerin soll Ihr Zimmer zeichnen. Stimmt die Zeichnung? Wechseln Sie die Rollen.

BEISPIEL   S1: *Das Bett steht an der Wand.*

Das	Bett	steht	in der/dem	Ecke.
	Poster	liegt	auf der/dem	Tisch.
		hängt	am	Boden.
Der	Schreibtisch	ist	an der	Stuhl.
	Stuhl	sind	neben der/dem	Fenster.
	Laptop	stehen	vor der/dem	Wand.
	Kleiderschrank			Tür.
Die	Lampe			
	Stereoanlage			
	Bücher			

messy
clean up

19 Annas Zimmer In Annas Zimmer ist alles durcheinander°. Was muss Anna machen? Helfen Sie Anna, das Zimmer aufzuräumen°.

BEISPIEL   Die Papiere liegen auf dem Boden. Sie liegen nicht auf dem Tisch.
Sie muss die Papiere auf den Tisch legen.

1. Die Papiere liegen auf dem Boden. Sie liegen nicht auf dem Tisch.
2. Das Poster liegt auf dem Bett. Es hängt nicht an der Wand.
3. Die Zeitung liegt unter dem Stuhl. Sie liegt nicht auf dem Stuhl.
4. Der Stuhl steht an der Tür. Er steht nicht am Tisch.
5. Das Radio steht neben dem Bett. Es steht nicht auf dem Nachttisch.
6. Die Uhr liegt auf dem Teppich. Sie hängt nicht über dem Bett.
7. Die Pflanze steht in der Ecke. Sie steht nicht am Fenster.
8. Die Schuhe liegen neben dem Stuhl. Sie stehen nicht im Schrank.

20 Freie Kommunikation: **Rollenspiel: Zimmer frei.** Sie haben ein Zimmer in einer Wohngemeinschaft frei und suchen einen Mitbewohner/eine Mitbewohnerin. Eine Person ruft an und möchte mehr über das Zimmer wissen. Beschreiben Sie dieser Person das Zimmer, die Wohnung und die anderen Menschen in der WG. Dann finden Sie von der Person heraus, was sie sucht und was sie von einer WG erwartet.

21 Schreibecke: **An meinen Lehrer/meine Lehrerin.** Schreiben Sie eine Postkarte an Ihren Deutschlehrer/Ihre Deutschlehrerin. Beschreiben Sie, was Sie schon alles in Tübingen gemacht haben: Wo und was haben Sie eingekauft? Wie haben Sie Ihr Zimmer eingerichtet? Was haben Sie schon alles gesehen? Wen haben Sie schon kennengelernt? Schreiben Sie in einem sehr positiven Ton.

Fußball und Profi-Sport in Mitteleuropa

Regardless of nationality, German-speaking **Mitteleuropäer** share their love of the world's most popular sport – soccer (**der Fußball**). Called football everywhere outside of North America, it is played by over 250 million players in more than 200 countries. Soccer has mass appeal because it doesn't involve complicated or expensive equipment. It can be played on any flat, open surface, and in most weather other than snow. As long as the players are able to run and kick a ball, there can be a soccer match. School-age children who are interested in developing their skills and playing real games join the town soccer club (**der Fußballverein**). There is no interscholastic play of any sort. As children increase in age and ability, they work their way up the league structure and can continue to play on adult teams all the way to semi-professional regional leagues. In larger cities, the clubs sponsor professional teams for national-level competition. In Germany these are called the **Bundesliga 1** and **2**.

European fans are rabidly loyal to their teams. On nights when important matches are broadcast, streets and restaurants are virtually empty as friends and families crowd around the television to cheer on their team. The pinnacle of international play in soccer is the World Cup (**die Weltmeisterschaft**, **die WM**), which takes place every four years. Germany was world champion (**Weltmeister**) in the 1974 World Cup under the leadership of Franz Beckenbauer, who later became the coach (**Trainer**) of the national team and a national celebrity and hero. Germany won the World Cup again in 1990. The nation hosted the 2006 World Cup. Women's soccer (**Frauenfußball**) is also very strong in Germany, with the German team winning the bronze medal at the 2008 Olympics. Other sports, both team and individual, are very popular in Central Europe, but all of them require membership in the local athletic club (**Sportverein**) to play. Gymnastics clubs (**Turnvereine**), highly popular in the 19th century, continue to exist in many towns, as do clubs for sports as diverse as judo (**Judo**), fencing (**Fechten**), and volleyball (**Volleyball**). Many of these clubs post schedules and game results on the Internet.

Professional **Basketball** has a huge following, especially with the success of seven-footer Dirk Nowitzki as power forward for the Dallas Mavericks and his recognition as MVP for the 2006-7 NBA season and the 2011 finals. German basketball has a national league, as do **Eishockey** and **Football**, all especially popular in areas that once housed U.S. military personnel. The interest in **Tennis** skyrocketed in the 1980s and 1990s with the international success of German players Boris Becker and Steffi Graf, a tradition carried on today by Swiss tennis master Roger Federer, who has won a record 16 Grand Slam singles titles and is ranked one of the top players in the world. In automobile racing, Germany is home to the famous Nürburgring race track and one of the world's most

© Cengage Learning 2014. Adapted from Deutscher Olympischer Sportbund.

Die beliebtesten Sportarten
(2008, in Millionen Mitgliedern)

Fußball	6,6
Turnen	5,0
Tennis	1,6
Schützen	1,5
Leichtathletik	0,9

successful Formula I race car drivers, seven-time world champion Michael Schumacher. The German-speaking nations of Germany, Austria, and Switzerland are all powerhouses of **Wintersport** and consistently place in the top ten at the Winter Olympics.

Kulturkreuzung

Was hält man hier für Nationalsport? Was ist hier wichtiger: Vereinssport oder Schulsport? Warum ist das so? Inwiefern° ist Studentensport wichtig im Studentenleben auf Ihrem Campus? Was sind die Möglichkeiten für Studenten/Studentinnen, die sich nicht für den „Leistungssport°"interessieren, aber trotzdem gern aktiv bleiben wollen? Welche Unis sind die traditionellen Rivalen Ihrer Uni? Europäische Unis haben normalerweise keine eigenen Sportmannschaften. Was halten Sie davon?

to what extent

competitive sport

Freiburgs Trainer Robin Dutt: „Bei uns lebt Multikulti"

unternehmen: what activities they can do

schlägt ...: suggests

Anna, Barbara und Karl fragen einander, was sie am Wochenende unternehmen können. Stefan hat gerade einen Artikel über den ehemaligen Freiburger Trainer Robin Dutt gelesen und schlägt vor°, dass sie alle nach München fahren, wo sie ein Heimspiel von FC Bayern gegen den SC Freiburg sehen können. Für leidenschaftliche Fans wie Stefan und Karl ist ein Fußballspiel ideal und alle freuen sich über ein Wochenende in der bayerischen Hauptstadt.

Vorschau

 22 Sportarten: Was halten Sie davon? Identifizieren Sie 5 bis 10 Sportarten, die Sie interessieren. Fragen sie dann einen Partner/eine Partnerin, ob er/sie diese Sportart auch interessant findet.

Sportarten:
amerikanischer Football • Angeln • Baseball • Basketball • Boxen • Eishockey • Feldhockey • Fußball • Golf • Lacrosse • Mountain-Bike-Fahren • Schwimmen • Segeln • Skifahren • Surfen • Tennis • Volleyball • Wandern • Wasserskifahren

Aussagen:
Positiv: ... finde ich toll.
Neutral: ... finde ich so lala.
Negativ: ... gefällt mir gar nicht.

BEISPIEL   S1: *Ich finde Eishockey wirklich toll. Und du? Wie findest du Eishockey?*
S2: *Eishockey gefällt mir gar nicht. Ich spiele lieber Lacrosse. Und du?*
S1: *Lacrosse finde ich so lala.*

Kulturnotiz: Turnvereine started by German immigrants in the United States during the 19th century introduced the sport of gymnastics to North America. Cities like San Antonio still have old buildings designated **Turnverein** or **Turner Halle.**

Findest du Turnen interessant?

→ **23** Thematische Fragen

1. Bewerten Sie diese Merkmale°. Wie wichtig finden Sie die folgenden Merkmale, wenn Sie andere Menschen treffen?

characteristics

1 = total unwichtig ... 5 = sehr wichtig

Merkmal	Unwichtig oder wichtig (1-5)
a. die Religion	_____
b. die Haarfarbe	_____
c. das Alter	_____
d. das Geschlecht (Mann oder Frau)	_____
e. die Nationalität	_____
f. die Hautfarbe	_____
g. einen Akzent (beim Sprechen)	_____
h. die Nationalität	_____
i. Hobbys und Talente	_____
j. die Schulausbildung°	_____

education

2. Wie wichtig finden Sie die folgenden Gründe für Sport?

1 = total unwichtig ... 5 = sehr wichtig

Gründe für Sport	Unwichtig oder wichtig? (1–5)
a. Man kann Erfolg° erleben.	_____
b. Man kann Teamgeist erleben.	_____
c. Man lernt neue Dinge von dem Trainer und den Mitspielern.	_____
d. Man kann Leute treffen, die anders sind als man selbst.	_____
e. Sport macht einfach Spaß.	_____
f. Sport ist gesund.	_____
g. Wenn man Sport macht, hat man keine Zeit für dumme Dinge.	_____
h. Man herausfinden, wer besser und wer schlechter dabei ist.	_____
i. Sport verbessert den Charakter.	_____
j. Wenn man Sport macht, kann man auch viel lesen.	_____

success

3. Wie wichtig finden Sie es, dass die folgenden Leute gut Deutsch sprechen?

1 = total unwichtig ... 5 = sehr wichtig

Leute, ...	Unwichtig oder wichtig? (1–5)
a. die° in Deutschland geboren sind.	_____
b. die nach Deutschland immigrieren.	_____
c. die in Deutschland professionell Sport machen.	_____
d. die in Deutschland Urlaub machen.	_____
e. die in Deutschland studieren.	_____

who

Lesestrategien

 24 Die Textstruktur verstehen The way a text is structured can offer important cues about its content. At the same time, prior knowledge of writing conventions and the language is required in order to appreciate the text and to exploit it for your own better understanding. Answer the following questions about the structure of the *Absprungtext* on page 271.

1. A first glance at the text suggests it is ...
   a. a novel.
   b. a poem.
   c. a newspaper article.

2. The heading **(der Titel)** names ...
   a. the topic or person about whom the text was written.
   b. the person who wrote the text.
   c. the person who is intended to read the text.

3. The direct quote in the title suggests that this text will be about ...
   a. an implausible story.
   b. an interview from which quotes have been taken.
   c. a daydream.

4. As is customary in German newspaper articles, the first paragraph of the text (shown in boldface) ...
   a. explains why the topic is interesting.
   b. summarizes the gist of the content.
   c. provides solutions to problems described in the text.

5. Throughout the text, there are questions in boldface. They represent ...
   a. the interview questions that coach Dutt was answering.
   b. the questions that coach Dutt was asking.
   c. the questions that were not asked but should have been.

Fußball ist in Deutschland sehr beliebt.

25 Den Hintergrund verstehen Texts do not just share new information. They also make assumptions about the reader's background knowledge, both of the cultural (geographic, historical, social) context and, more generally, of how the world works. To understand foreign language texts it is particularly important to remember or acquire the appropriate cultural knowledge and to use common sense. Answer the following questions to activate your common good sense and to consider cultural context. These reflect the basic questions **Wer? Wo? Was? Wann?** and help establish the background for understanding the text.

1. Freiburg is a city in which German state **(Bundesland)?** What dialect is spoken there?
   a. Schleswig-Holstein (**Plattdeutsch**/Low German)
   b. Baden-Württemberg (**Schwäbisch**/Swabian around Stuttgart)
   c. Bayern (**Bairisch**/Bavarian)

2. The man's first name Robin is not a common German name. Which of the following options probably best captures the author's choice to profile Robin Dutt for an article on soccer and multiculturalism in Germany?
   a. Robin is the first name of a former famous German soccer coach.
   b. Robin is associated with soccer players who steal or "rob" the ball from their opponents.
   c. Robin suggests that the coach himself may not be what one would assume to be a typical German.

3. Why would a reporter choose the example of athletes to discuss multiculturalism?
   a. People are more accepting of multiculturalism among athletes.
   b. Athletes love to talk about their multi-ethnic background.
   c. Multiculturalism is only an issue in professional sports not everyday life.

4. From the perspective of a soccer club, the most important concern is to ...
   a. assemble an ethnically diverse team.
   b. win games and championships.
   c. maintain a common religion among teammates.

5. Understanding that this text is based on an interview, the text's language likely seeks to replicate which style?
   a. spoken language   b. academic papers   c. an advertisement

6. Examples of this style are (mark all that apply) ...
   a. words that look like English words (cognates such as **Kommunikation**).
   b. the contraction of words (**fürs**) and abbreviations (**Multikulti**).
   c. the use of questions within the text.
   d. the use of quotes and direct speech.

7. In an interview about diversity and assimilation of a German sports team, one would probably discuss (mark all the apply) ...
   a. how diversity affects performance.
   b. religious diversity of film stars.
   c. how language plays a role in team cohesion.
   d. which uniform colors flatter a variety of complexions.
   e. how long it takes to integrate players.
   f. that players have integration challenges when they join a new team.

26 Wörter und Phrasen erraten Good readers do not necessarily know more words, but they are adept at guessing the meaning of new words. The following guessing strategies used so far in *Vorsprung* will help you when reading.

a. The new word reminds you of a familiar English word, i.e., it's a cognate word.
b. You already know many words in the phrase and you can guess the meaning of the other word(s).
c. You recognize part of the word and can infer the rest of the word from it.
d. You know the literal meaning of a word and can guess a figurative meaning.

Suggest a translation for the boldfaced words or parts of words below. Then think about which of the strategies above (a. through d.) were helpful to come up with a translation. Sometimes more than one strategy is useful.

1. Sohn eines **Inders:** ____*Indian; a,b*____
2. **schwäbischer** Akzent: _____
3. Fußball**mannschaft:** _____
4. **Kommunikation:** _____
5. Was **bedeutet** Integration für Sie? : _____
6. der **Schlüssel** für alles: _____
7. Team**geist:** _____
8. In meinem **täglichen** Leben: _____

27 Was bedeuten diese Ausdrücke? Using the strategies above, find the location of the German versions of the following English expressions in the text. Give the matching line number(s).

Beispiele aus dem Text, Zeilen 1–13	Zeile
1. otherwise he allows time to integrate – even for Germans	_____
2. between people who are already here (on the team) and people who are just joining	_____
3. he would find it funny if it were said of him that …	_____
4. He uses it (English) as needed.	_____

Beispiele aus dem Text, Zeilen 14-29	Zeile
5. How long does something like this take?	_____
6. Team building requires communication.	_____
7. last as long as you see development/progress	_____
8. I do not make it a topic in individual conversations.	_____

28 Phrasendetektiv Welche Phrasen bedeuten ungefähr das Gleiche?

1. Das oberste Ziel ist der sportliche Erfolg.
2. ab dem ersten Tag verpflichtend Deutschunterricht
3. wenn sich einer weigert, die Sprache des Teams zu sprechen

a. from the first day on (they have) obligatory German lessons
b. The most important goal is athletic success.
c. if someone refuses to speak the language

4. der Akzent verrät nichts über
5. Teamgeist, Respekt und Disziplin sind Begriffe, auf die Dutt besonderen Wert legt.
6. Woran merkt man, dass ein Spieler angekommen ist?

d. Team spirit, respect, and discipline are concepts on which Dutt places special value.
e. How do you know a player has made it?
f. the accent reveals nothing about

Freiburgs Robin Dutt arbeitet mit Spielern aus zwölf Nationen: Fürs Teambuilding braucht er Kommunikation. Ansonsten gewährt er Integrationszeit auch für Deutsche.

Der leicht schwäbische Akzent verrät nichts über Robin Dutts Migrationshintergrund°. Der Trainer des SC Freiburg ist der Sohn einer Deutschen und eines Inders, der in den sechziger Jahren zum Studium nach Deutschland gekommen ist. Dutt sagt, er fände es komisch, wenn es über ihn hieße: „Den hat man gut integriert." Er sei schließlich° in Deutschland geboren: in Köln, 1965. Teamgeist, Respekt und Disziplin sind Begriffe, auf die Dutt besonderen Wert legt, wenn er über seine Arbeit redet. Der Schlüssel für all das heißt: Kommunikation. Neben Deutsch spricht Dutt noch Englisch – und setzt es nach Bedarf auch als Trainer ein.

Was bedeutet Integration für Sie?° Der Trainer weiß: „Teambuilding erfordert Kommunikation." Dass man auf einem natürlichen Weg in einem optimalen Tempo ein Wohlbefinden herstellt° zwischen Menschen, die schon da sind, und Menschen, die dazukommen. In meinem täglichen Leben mit einer Fußballmannschaft ist Multikulti nicht tot, da lebt Multikulti.

Muss man als Trainer die Religionen seiner Spieler kennen? Ich weiß, welchen Glauben die Spieler haben, aber ich thematisiere das nicht im Einzelgespräch. Die Integration ist ja nicht das oberste Ziel. Das oberste Ziel ist der sportliche Erfolg.

Welche Rolle spielt Sprache? Die größere Herausforderung° ist: Wie integriere ich einen Spieler aus menschlicher Sicht° in unseren Kreis? Und da ist die Sprache das Wichtigste. Die Spieler haben bei uns ab dem ersten Tag verpflichtend Deutschunterricht, zwei- oder dreimal in der Woche. Das Teambuilding, das man braucht, erfordert Kommunikation. Wenn sich einer weigert, die Sprache des Teams zu sprechen – und da gehört natürlich die Landessprache dazu –, dann hat er bei uns keine Chance.

Woran merkt man, dass ein Spieler angekommen ist – und wie lange dauert so etwas? Wenn ich nicht mehr über ihn nachdenken muss. Selbst bei deutschen Spielern haben wir festgestellt°, dass es manchmal sechs Monate dauert, bis sie integriert sind. Wenn es dann mal sieben, acht Monate dauert, dann dauert es eben so lange. Und wenn es ein Spieler ist, der erst 19 ist, der nicht nur ein anderes Land, eine andere Mentalität, sondern auch eine andere Art, Fußball zu spielen, kennenlernen muss, dann kann es auch zwei Jahre dauern. Es darf so lange dauern, wie man eine Entwicklung sieht.

Freiburgs Trainer Robin Dutt: Bei uns lebt Multikulti." Christian Kamp, FAZ.NET, 29.10.2010. Reprinted by permission.

immigrant background

sei ...: was after all

Was bedeutet... What does integration mean to you?

ein ...: creates a sense of well-being

die...: the greater challenge

aus...: from a human perspective

haben...: we have determined

SC Freiburg (Schwarz-Rot) im Spiel gegen Köln

Rückblick

29 Stimmt das? Stimmen die folgenden Aussagen zum Text? Wenn nicht, was stimmt?

	Ja, das stimmt.	Nein, das stimmt nicht.
1. Robin Dutt kommt aus Indien.	○	○
2. Robin Dutt spricht Deutsch mit einem schwäbischen Akzent.	○	○
3. Robin Dutt kann Englisch und spricht es manchmal in seinem Beruf.	○	○
4. Robin Dutt findet Kommunikation besonders wichtig.	○	○
5. Robin Dutt spricht mit jedem Spieler über Religion.	○	○
6. Robin Dutt findet es wichtig, dass alle Spieler gut Deutsch sprechen.	○	○
7. Spieler, die nicht Deutsch sprechen, müssen es lernen.	○	○
8. Auch deutsche Spieler brauchen eine Integrationsphase.	○	○
9. Die Integration darf nicht länger als sechs Monate dauern.	○	○
10. Robin Dutt weiß, dass Spieler integriert sind, wenn sie ihm keine Sorgen mehr machen.	○	○
11. Kulturelle Unterschiede gibt es nicht nur in der Sprache und in der Religion, sondern auch im Fußballspielen.	○	○

sportclubfreiburg

Complete the **Ergänzen Sie** activity in the Student Activities Manual before doing the next activity.

most important

30 Kurz gefragt Beantworten Sie die folgenden Fragen auf Deutsch.

1. Aus wie vielen Nationen kommen die Spieler in der Freiburger Mannschaft?
2. Wo wurde Trainer Dutt geboren?
3. Wie hat Trainer Dutt einen mulitkulturellen Hintergrund?
4. Welche Region kann man in Trainer Dutts Sprache hören?
5. Was findet Trainer Dutt am allerwichtigsten° im Sport?
6. Wofür ist Deutsch für die Mannschaft wichtig?
7. Wie lange darf die Integration für die Spieler dauern?
8. Wie ist die Situation anders für neue Spieler auf dem Ausland als für neue Spieler aus Deutschland? Wie ist sie ähnlich?
9. Wann weiß der Trainer, dass ein Spieler mit den Herausforderungen klarkommt?
10. Wie weiß der Trainer, dass ein ausländischer Spieler sich nicht integrieren will?

31 Textdetektiv: **Absprungtext.** The following examples from the *Absprungtext* all contain dative forms. Identify the preposition in each example. Mark whether it is a two-case preposition or a preposition that always requires the dative. Finally, identify any dative articles, endings, or pronouns that follow that preposition. The first one is done as a model.

Example from Absprungtext	Preposition	Two-case or dative?	Dative forms following the preposition (if applicable)
1. Robin Dutt arbeitet mit Spielern	*mit*	*dative*	*Spielern*
2. ein Inder, der zum Studium gekommen ist	_____	_____	_____
3. auf einem natürlichen Weg	_____	_____	_____
4. im täglichen Leben	_____	_____	_____
5. mit einer Fußballmannschaft	_____	_____	_____
6. aus menschlicher Sicht	_____	_____	_____
7. bei uns	_____	_____	_____
8. ab dem ersten Tag	_____	_____	_____
9. dreimal in der Woche	_____	_____	_____

Courtesy of Sport-Club Freiburg e.V.

32 Interview: Sport in Ihrem Leben Stellen Sie einem Partner/einer Partnerin die folgenden Fragen.

1. Was ist Ihr Lieblingssport°? Spielen Sie gern aktiv mit oder sind Sie lieber Zuschauer°?

2. Haben Sie als Kind viel Sport gemacht? Zu welchen Jahreszeiten haben Sie gespielt? Wenn nicht, warum nicht? Welche anderen Interessen haben Sie gehabt?

3. Was für Sport werden Sie wohl treiben können, wenn Sie älter sind?

4. Welche Sportarten kann man als Nationalsport betrachten°? Welche Sportarten sind regional besonders populär? Spielen Sie diese Sportarten gern?

5. Wie heißen die professionellen Sportmannschaften in Ihrer Gegend? Sind Sie ein Anhänger°/eine Anhängerin von diesen Teams? Wie zeigen loyale Fans ihre Treue°?

6. Was sind die populärsten Sportarten auf Ihrem Campus? Was kosten die Eintrittskarten für die Spiele? Wie oft gehen Sie selber hin?

favorite sport / spectator

view

fan / loyalty

Strukturen

III Talking about when events happen

Time expressions in the dative and accusative case

A. Time expressions in the dative case

German speakers use the two-case prepositions **in/im, am,** and **vor** with the dative case to express a time when an event occurs. **In/im** is used when referring to years, seasons, months, and weeks. **Am** is used when referring to days, dates, and weekends. These expressions answer the question **wann?** *(when?).*

> **Wann** hast du Geburtstag? – **Im** Mai.
> *When is your birthday? – In May.*
> **Wann** kommen die Schmidts? – **In einer** Stunde.
> *When are the Schmidts coming? – In an hour.*
> **Wann** hast du Geburtstag? – **Am** 11. Mai. (**Am** elften Mai.)
> *When is your birthday? – On the 11th of May. (On the eleventh of May.)*
> **Wann** hast du in Zürich studiert? – **Vor einem** Jahr.
> *When did you study in Zurich? – A year ago.*

The preposition **in/im** can be used several ways.

1. It can define the point in time of an event happening.

   Ich bin **im Jahre** *1986 geboren.*   *I was born in the year 1986.*

2. It can also define the length of time before which an event occurs.

   Er kommt **in einem Monat.**   *He's coming in one month.*

3. It can be used to designate a decade with the ending **-er** on the end of a decade number.

   Er ist der Sohn einer Deutschen und   *He is the son of a German woman and*
   eines Inders, der **in den Sechzigerjahren**   *an Indian man who came to*
   nach Deutschland gekommen ist.   *Germany in the sixties.*

German speakers use **am** to describe an event that happens on a specific day or date or on the weekend.

> **Am Wochenende** spielen wir Fußball.   *We're going to play soccer on the weekend.*

The preposition **vor** expresses time in the past in the way that *ago* does in English.

> Ich habe die Karten **vor einer**   *I picked up the tickets a week ago.*
> **Woche** abgeholt.

Remember to use the accusative preposition **um** when referring to hours and minutes to talk about clock time: **um zwei Uhr; um drei Minuten nach zwei.**

B. Time expressions in the accusative case

The accusative case without a preposition may also be used in a time expression to express definite time in German. These time expressions often correspond to an expression with the preposition *for* in English. For emphasis of duration, speakers sometimes add **lang: ein Jahr lang, einen Tag lang.**

> **Diesen Samstag** fahren wir nach Stuttgart.   *We are driving to Stuttgart this Saturday.*
> Ich habe **ein Jahr** in Heidelberg gewohnt.   *I lived in Heidelberg for one year.*
> Er bleibt **eine Woche** bei uns.   *He's staying with us for one week.*

Sprache im Alltag: Expressing regularity

German speakers use the expressions **einmal** (*once*), **zweimal** (*twice*), **dreimal** (*three times*), etc. before non-specific time expressions (e.g., **im Sommer, im Jahr, am Tag, am Wochenende, in der Woche**) to tell how often they do an activity.

Karl wäscht sein Auto **einmal im Monat.**   *Karl washes his car once a month.*

> For special emphasis or to express their exasperation, speakers use the expressions **hundertmal** (*a hundred times*), **zigmal,** or **x-mal** (*umpteen times*): **Das habe ich dir schon x-mal gesagt.** *I've told you that umpteen times.*

33 **Wann ist Barbara zu Hause gewesen?** Fragen Sie einen Partner/ eine Partnerin nach einer Aktivität mit einem Fragezeichen. Beantworten Sie dann eine Frage von Ihrem Partner/Ihrer Partnerin.

BEISPIEL   S1: *Wann ist Stefan zu Hause gewesen?*
S2: *Stefan ist vor einer Woche zu Hause gewesen.*
S1: *Wann bist du zu Hause gewesen?*
S2: *Ich bin am Wochenende zu Hause gewesen.*

Tabelle A (S1):

	Barbara	Stefan	Partner(in) 2
zu Hause gewesen	am Freitag	?	?
Freunde in Berlin besucht	?	vor einem Jahr	?
in die Stadt gefahren	?	vor einer Stunde	?
ein gutes Buch gelesen	vor einem Monat	?	?
ein Konto eröffnet	?	vor zwei Wochen	?
auf die Post gegangen	gestern	?	?
an der Uni gewesen	heute Morgen	?	?
einen Film gesehen	?	am Samstag	?
mit dem Rad gefahren	dieses Wochenende	?	?

Tabelle B (S2):

	Barbara	Stefan	Partner(in) 1
zu Hause gewesen	?	vor einer Woche	(am Wochenende)
Freunde in Berlin besucht	im Sommer	?	?
in die Stadt gefahren	vor 25 Minuten	?	?
ein gutes Buch gelesen	?	am Wochenende	?
ein Konto eröffnet	gestern	?	?
auf die Post gegangen	?	vor zehn Minuten	?
an der Uni gewesen	?	um zehn Uhr	?
einen Film gesehen	gestern Abend	?	?
mit dem Rad gefahren	?	am Sonntag	?

Oft oder nie? In sentences referring to both a time and a place, Germans mention the time *before* the place. **Ich fahre um sieben Uhr nach Hause.**

†† 34 Oft oder nie? Notieren Sie, wie oft Sie die folgenden Aktivitäten machen: **einmal (zweimal** usw.**) am Tag (in der Woche, im Monat, im Jahr)** oder **nie?** Fragen Sie dann einen Partner/eine Partnerin, wie oft er/sie das macht.

BEISPIEL   S1: *Wie oft gehst du in eine Buchhandlung?*
S2: *Ich gehe (einmal in der Woche) in eine Buchhandlung.*

	Ich	Partner(in)
1. in eine Buchhandlung gehen	_____	_____
2. ins Restaurant gehen	_____	_____
3. ins Kino gehen	_____	_____
4. zu Fuß zur Uni gehen	_____	_____
5. auf eine Party gehen	_____	_____
6. in die Kneipe gehen	_____	_____
7. ins Fitnessstudio gehen	_____	_____
8. auf die Bank gehen	_____	_____
9. in die Kirche (Synagoge, Moschee) gehen	_____	_____

Interview. Remember that **wenn** (*if*) is a subordinating conjunction in German. The verb always occurs at the end of the subordinate clause.

†† 35 Interview Stellen Sie einem Partner/einer Partnerin die folgenden Fragen.

BEISPIEL   S1: *Wohin gehst du am Montag, wenn du Bücher ausleihen willst?*
S2: *Ich gehe am Montag in die Bibliothek, wenn ich Bücher ausleihen will.*

1. Wohin gehst du am Montag, wenn du Bücher ausleihen willst?
2. Wohin gehst du am Freitagabend, wenn du einen neuen Film sehen willst?
3. Wohin gehst du am Wochenende, wenn du ein Theaterstück sehen willst?
4. Wohin gehst du am Samstag, wenn du tanzen willst?
5. Wohin gehst du im Sommer, wenn du ein Bier trinken willst?
6. Wohin gehst du am Freitagabend, wenn du gute Musik hören willst?
7. Wohin gehst du am Sonntagabend, wenn du Jazz hören willst?
8. Wohin gehst du im August, wenn du schwimmen willst?
9. Wohin gehst du im Winter, wenn du Bodybuilding machen willst?

Strukturen

IV Talking about means of transportation

The preposition *mit* with the dative case

German speakers use the dative preposition **mit** (*with, by*) to talk about means of transportation.

Stefan kommt **mit dem Auto** nach Hause.   *Stefan is driving his car home.*

To ask about means of transportation German speakers use the question words **wie?** *(how?)* or **womit?** *(with what?)*.

Wie kommst du nach Hause?   – Mit dem Taxi.
Womit fährt Stefan in die Stadt?   – Mit dem Fahrrad.

To talk about travel on foot, speakers most commonly use the expression **zu Fuß** with the verbs **gehen** or **laufen**.

Wir gehen **zu Fuß**.   *We walk (are walking).*

Wissenswerte Vokabeln: Wie kommt man dahin?

Talking about means of transportation

mit dem Fahrrad
(Rad)

mit dem Auto
(Wagen, Pkw)

mit dem Bus

mit der Bahn
(dem Zug)

mit der Straßenbahn

mit der U-Bahn
(Untergrundbahn)

mit dem Schiff

mit dem Flugzeug

mit dem Taxi

mit dem Motorrad

Inline-Skaten

zu Fuß

Illustrations © Cengage Learning 2014

BEISPIEL Womit fährst du? *Ich fahre mit dem Bus.*
Wie kommst du? *Ich komme mit dem Taxi.*

36 Interview Stellen Sie einem Partner/einer Partnerin die folgenden Fragen.

BEISPIEL S1: *Wie kommst du am Vormittag zur Uni?*
S2: *Ich fahre mit dem Rad. Und du?*
S1: *Ich fahre mit dem Bus.*

	Ich	Partner(in)
1. Wie kommst du am Vormittag zur Uni?	_____	_____
2. Wie kommst du im Winter zur Uni?	_____	_____
3. Wie kommst du nach Hause?	_____	_____
4. Wie kommt man am besten° nach Europa?	_____	_____
5. Wie fährst du lieber: mit der Straßenbahn oder mit der U-Bahn?	_____	_____

am ... : the best way

37 Fahren Sie am besten mit dem Taxi Sie arbeiten in einem Luxushotel in Köln und geben den Hotelgästen Rat, womit sie fahren sollen.

BEISPIEL S1: *Wir müssen in fünf Minuten im Stadttheater sein. Aber das ist am anderen Stadtende. Wie kommen wir am schnellsten dahin?*

S2: *Dann fahren Sie am besten mit dem Taxi.*

1. Wir wollen den Kölner Dom besuchen. Aber mit kleinen Kindern können wir nicht den ganzen Weg laufen. Wie kommen wir dahin?
2. Heute Nachmittag muss ich in Düsseldorf sein, aber ich habe kein Auto. Das ist aber nicht so weit – weniger als eine Stunde von hier. Wie fährt man dahin?
3. Ich möchte so gern die Schlösser und die Weinberge am Rhein sehen!
4. Wir suchen ein kleines Café oder eine Konditorei hier gleich in der Nähe.
5. Wie kommt man von Köln nach Bonn?
6. In drei Stunden muss ich in London sein! Was soll ich machen?

Der Kölner Dom gilt als das Wahrzeichen Kölns.

Strukturen

V Expressing time, manner, and place

Word order for time, manner, and place

References to time in German often occur at the beginning of a main clause, followed by the conjugated verb and the subject.

>   *time*   *verb*   *subject*
> **Heute fahren wir** in die Stadt.   *We are going (driving) into town today.*

Such time references may also appear after the verb in the interior of the sentence.

> Wir fahren **heute** in die Stadt.

Information about how an action occurs (the manner) follows the time reference.

>   *1*   *2*
>   ***time***   ***manner***
> Wir fahren **heute mit dem Auto** in die Stadt. (*or* **Heute** fahren wir **mit dem Auto** in die Stadt.)

Information about where an action occurs follows the references to time and manner. In summary, information in a German sentence follows the sequence: (1) time, (2) manner, (3) place.

1	2	3
time	*manner*	*place*

Wir fahren **heute mit dem Auto in die Stadt**.

The sequence of information in an English sentence is organized in the opposite order: (1) place, (2) manner, (3) time: We are driving *to town by car today*.

↩ **38** Wann, wie und wo lesen Sie das? Wählen Sie aus jeder Spalte° ein Element und formulieren Sie eine passende Antwort.

column

BEISPIEL S1: *Liest du dein Deutschbuch?*
S2: *Ja, ich lese mein Deutschbuch so oft wie möglich laut in meinem Zimmer.*

eine deutsche Zeitung • *Vorsprung* • eine Wirtschaftszeitung (z. B. *Money Magazine*) • ein Mathematikbuch • eine Lokalzeitung • eine Frauenzeitschrift (z. B. *Cosmopolitan*) • ein Automagazin • ein Physikbuch • einen Roman von David Sedaris • einen Krimi von Agatha Christie • Gedichte von Goethe • einen Roman von J.K. Rowling • eine Tratschzeitschrift° (z. B. *People Magazine*) • Comics-Hefte • ein Nachrichtenmagazin (z. B. *Time Magazine*)

gossip magazine

Wann?	Wie?	Wo?
jeden Abend	leise°	im Wohnzimmer
jeden Tag	laut	auf der Post
am Morgen	im Kopf	im Bett
einmal im Monat	mit den Kindern	vor dem Fernseher
nie	allein	in meinem Zimmer
immer	mit großem Interesse	an der Uni
jede Woche	ohne großes Interesse	im Schwimmbad
einmal am Abend	mit dem Lehrer	im Café
?	?	?

quietly

↩ **39** Schreibecke: **Eine Postkarte schreiben.** Sie sind in München und vermissen Ihren Deutschlehrer/Ihre Deutschlehrerin sehr. Schreiben Sie ihm/ihr wieder eine Postkarte. Verwenden Sie die folgenden Vokabeln und Ausdrücke.

Letzte Woche	bin	ich		Auto		
Gestern	ist	mein Freund	mit dem	Bus	ins Museum	gegangen.
Heute Morgen	sind	meine Freundin	mit der	Fuß	ins Theater	gefahren.
Heute		meine Freunde	zu	Straßenbahn	in die Kneipe	
		meine Freundinnen		Taxi	in die Oper	
				U-Bahn	auf die Uni	

---

†† **40** Freie Kommunikation: **In die Sprechstunde gehen.** Ihr Partner/Ihre Partnerin möchte nach der Stunde mit dem Deutschlehrer/der Deutschlehrerin sprechen. Erklären Sie ihm/ihr, wie man vom Klassenzimmer zum Büro von dem Deutschlehrer/der Deutschlehrerin kommt.

Strukturen

VI Expressing the purpose for an action

The subordinating conjunction *damit*

A clause introduced by the subordinating conjunction **damit** *(so that)* stresses one's intent or purpose in carrying out an action. This differs somewhat from **weil** *(because)*, which stresses the reason for the action.

faule Säcke: *"lazy bones," "couch potatoes"*

> Barbara geht in die Buchhandlung, **damit** sie *Fitness für faule Säcke*° kaufen kann.
> *Barbara is going to the bookstore so that she can buy* Fitness für faule Säcke.

> Barbara geht in die Buchhandlung, **weil** sie *Fitness für faule Säcke* sucht.
> *Barbara is going to the bookstore because she is looking for* Fitness für faule Säcke.

---

41 Lesen nur zum Spaß? Warum lesen Sie das? Benutzen Sie **weil** oder **damit** in Ihrer Antwort.

BEISPIEL   *Ich lese eine deutsche Zeitung, weil ich sie gern lese.*

Ich lese …

1. eine deutsche Zeitung,	damit ich gute Noten bekomme.
2. mein Deutschbuch,	weil es mich interessiert.
3. das Mathematikbuch,	weil ich (sie/es) gern lese.
4. die Lokalzeitung,	weil ich neue Ideen suche.
5. Frauenzeitschriften (z. B. Cosmopolitan),	damit ich neue Informationen finden kann.
6. ein Automagazin,	weil ich Stephen Kings (Danielle Steeles usw.) Romane liebe.
7. Wirtschaftszeitschriften (z. B. Money Magazine),	weil es lustig ist.
	weil es mir gefällt.
8. Romane° von Stephen King (Danielle Steele usw.),	weil …
	damit …
9. das Horoskop,	
10. Gedichte° von Goethe,	
11. eine Geschichte von Agatha Christie,	
12. Nachrichtenmagazine (z. B. Time Magazine),	

novels

poems

Warum lesen Sie die Nachrichten?

†† 42 Freie Kommunikation: **Rollenspiel: In die Stadt fahren.** Es ist Samstag. Sie müssen vieles erledigen (z. B. Bücher und Lebensmittel einkaufen, Geld abheben), aber Ihr Auto funktioniert momentan nicht. Sie brauchen Hilfe und möchten auch nicht allein in die Stadt fahren. Ihr Partner/Ihre Partnerin möchte nicht mitkommen, denn es sind immer so viele Leute in der Stadt und es ist zu hektisch **(Ich will nicht kommen, weil ...).** Versuchen Sie, Ihren Partner/Ihre Partnerin zu überreden°, dass er/sie mitkommt oder dass er/sie Sie im Auto mitnimmt. Sagen Sie, wohin Sie gehen.

persuade

← 43 Schreibecke: **Meine Biografie/Autobiografie.** Beschreiben Sie Ihre Biografie/Autobiografie für einen Buchkatalog.

1. Was ist der Titel?
2. Was ist die Länge?
3. Wie heißt der Autor/die Autorin? (Schreiben Sie selbst? Wenn nicht, wer schreibt? Warum?)
4. Was ist der Preis?
5. Was steht in der Biografie/Autobiografie?
6. Was ist passiert? Wann? Wie oft?
7. Wohin sind Sie (oft, selten) gefahren? Womit?

MEIN LEBEN

PixAchi/Shutterstock.com

> **Schreibecke.** Provide basic information such as where and when you were born, how and where you spent your early years, etc. Use the conversational past.

ZIEL

🌐 **Endspurt:** Online Listening Text & Activities.

mmaxer / Shutterstock.com

See **Wissenswerte Vokabeln: Literatur und Film** online on the *Vorsprung* website.

lacht ...: *laughs himself/herself silly* (literally, *nearly dead*) / *cartoon, animated film*

Mein Leben als Film
Zielaktivitäten

44 Mein Leben als Film Machen Sie die folgenden Aufgaben.

1. Denken Sie an einen normalen Tag in Ihrem Leben. Was erledigen Sie? Machen Sie eine detaillierte Liste. Beschreiben Sie chronologisch, wie und wo Sie alles machen.

BEISPIEL

> um sechs Uhr morgens: ich wache langsam in meinem Bett auf
> um sechs Uhr fünf: ich mache in der Küche Kaffee
> um sechs Uhr zehn: ich finde heraus, dass im Kühlschrank keine Milch ist
> um sechs Uhr elf: ich trinke den Kaffee schwarz

2. Hollywood will aus Ihrem normalen Tag einen tollen Film machen. Welche Art von Film passt gut? Wie soll der Film wirken?

Filmart	Filmwirkung
ein Abenteuerfilm	Das Publikum ...
ein Actionfilm	findet den Film spannend.
ein Märchenfilm	kann nach dem Film drei Tage lang nicht schlafen.
eine Komödie	lacht sich fast tot.°
ein Zeichentrickfilm°	weiß jetzt, dass das Gute immer gewinnt.
ein Krimi (Kriminalfilm)	weiß jetzt, dass manchmal auch das Schlechte gewinnt.
?	findet den Film zu brutal.
	findet die Filmkostüme ganz toll.
	findet Sie sehr sympathisch.
	findet Ihr Leben stressig.
	?

Und wie soll der Film heißen? _____

3. Welche Filmart haben Sie gewählt? Schauen Sie sich Ihre Liste von Nummer 1 oben an. Korrigieren Sie die Liste, damit sie zu Ihrem Film passt. Was muss von der alten Liste weg? Was muss in die neue Liste rein? Machen Sie eine korrigierte Liste.

BEISPIEL   Filmart: Komödie

> um ~~sechs~~ *zehn* Uhr morgens: ich wache langsam ~~in meinem Bett~~ *unter dem Tisch* auf
> ~~um sechs Uhr fünf: ich mache in der Küche Kaffee~~
> ~~um sechs Uhr zehn: ich finde heraus, dass im Kühlschrank keine Milch ist~~
> um ~~sechs~~ *zehn* Uhr elf: ~~ich trinke den Kaffee schwarz~~ *Der Hund bringt mir Kaffee mit Milch, zwei Brötchen - eines für ihn, eines für mich - und die Hamburger Morgenpost.*

4. Schreiben Sie jetzt eine Zusammenfassung von Ihrem Film in drei Teilen:

Teil 1: Der Anfang

BEISPIEL Der Zeichentrickfilm *Zwischen den Seen in Madison* zeigt einen Tag im
Leben von Monika Chavez.

Teil 2: Die Filmbeschreibung

Verwenden Sie die neue Liste oben und beschreiben Sie damit, was im Film passiert.
Verwenden Sie auch Konjunktionen, damit Sie die Handlung° besser beschreiben
können. Geben Sie neue Informationen an, damit der Film interessanter wird.

action

Die Konjunktion	... erklärt, ...	Ideen... Ich mache Kaffee, ...
weil	warum man etwas macht.	... weil ich müde bin.
denn	warum man etwas macht.	... denn ich bin müde.
damit	was das gewünschte Resultat ist.	... damit ich aufwache.
und	was man auch macht.	... und esse ein Brötchen.
oder	was man alternativ macht.	... oder ich mache Tee.
aber	was man auch machen kann, aber nicht wirklich macht	... aber ich habe keine Milch für den Kaffee.

BEISPIEL Ich wache um zehn Uhr morgens langsam unter dem Tisch auf und
mir tut der Kopf weh. Der Hund bringt mir Kaffee mit Milch, zwei Brötchen (eines
für ihn, eines für mich) und die Hamburger Morgenpost, weil wir am Morgen gern
zusammen Zeitung lesen. ...

Teil 3: Das Ende

Lesen Sie die Beschreibung (Teil 1 und Teil 2) einem Partner/einer Partnerin vor. Er/
Sie schreibt den letzten Satz: Wie hat der Partner/die Partnerin auf den Film reagiert?
Ideen kann man unter Teil 2 oben finden.

BEISPIEL Jeremy findet den Film brutal, aber er hat sich fast totgelacht.

 45 **Auf ins Münchner Stadion!** Sie besuchen München mit Freunden.
Heute Abend wollen Sie alle zusammen in die Stadt fahren und etwas machen.
Besprechen Sie, ob Sie ins Stadion gehen, ins Theater oder sonstwohin. Besprechen Sie auch, wie Sie in die Stadt kommen – mit dem Bus, mit dem Auto
usw. Besprechen Sie auch Ihre persönlichen Interessen. Hier sind einige Ideen
für München: **ins Hofbräuhaus, ins Museum, ins Theater, ins Konzert, in
die Neue Pinakothek gehen.**

> S1: Hallo Andy. Was machen wir heute Abend in München?
> S2: Gute Frage. Ich möchte ein Fußballspiel sehen.
> S1: Wer spielt denn heute Abend?
> S2: Bayern München.
> S1: Wann spielen sie und wo?
> S2: Um 17 Uhr im Fußballstadion.
> S1: OK, dann gehen wir heute ins Stadion, aber wie kommen wir dahin?
> S2: …

Refer to the **Brennpunkt
Kultur** about Munich on
p. 284 for more ideas of
things to do.

München

Munich (**München**), a city with a population of over 1,410,000 and third largest in the country, is officially the capital of the Free State of Bavaria (**der Freistaat Bayern**), the largest of Germany's 16 **Bundesländer** in land mass and second largest in population. But to many non-Bavarians, it's considered "**die heimliche Hauptstadt**" of the nation. Graced with a gentle climate and a location near the Alps, Munich is a historic city of great charm and ambience while also being a first-class center of business development and the service industry. With 26 universities and other **Hochschulen** and many research institutions, such as eleven Max Planck Institutes and seven Fraunhofer Gesellschaft institutions, Munich is very science- and technology-friendly, attracting talented young people from all over Germany and the world, who are drawn to its outstanding quality of life. Munich maintains a uniquely Bavarian atmosphere: cozy, comfortable, inviting, exciting.

The city's three 14th-century gates still stand, creating the connection to Munich's past. On the central **Marienplatz** square, the **Altes Rathaus** is within sight of the **Neues Rathaus,** whose 260-foot tower and **Glockenspiel** attract hoardes of visitors. Along with the new City Hall, Munich's most recognizable building is the **Frauenkirche,** whose twin onion-domed towers are the symbol (**das Wahrzeichen**) of the city. Nearby, **das Hofbräuhaus** draws locals and tourists with its traditional Bavarian cuisine, oom-pah bands, and its famous beer, and the 900-acre **Englischer Garten** provides respite for busy city-dwellers with its walking paths, ponds, and four beer gardens. Sports-minded Münchners may be split in their loyalty to soccer teams FC Bayern-München and TSV 1860, but they all enjoy easy access to abundant winter sports in the nearby Alps. Museum lovers will find a treasure trove in Munich, with everything from the science and technology collections of the **Deutsches Museum** and the automotive history at the **BMW-Museum** to the extraordinary art collections of the **Alte und Neue Pinakothek.** But for many visitors, Munich's greatest attraction will always be **das Oktoberfest,** a mixture of county fair and traditional costume festival celebrated beginning each September on the **Theresienwiesen,** fondly known to locals as **die Wies'n.** Each brewery headquartered in Munich sets up an immense beer tent (**das Bierzelt**) that can hold thousands of patrons who come to savor a one-liter **Maß** of beer and sway in harmony to traditional Bavarian bands.

Courtesy of J. Douglas Guy.

Am Marienplatz im Herzen Münchens steht das Neue Rathaus mit dem Glockenspiel quer gegenüber vom Alten Rathaus.

Kulturkreuzung

München liegt in Bayern und für viele Amerikaner und Kanadier ist München oder Bayern „typisch deutsch". Was assoziieren Sie mit München? Vieles aus Bayern ist nur ein Klischee, d. h.°es ist nicht repräsentativ für ganz Deutschland. Welche Aspekte vom Leben in den USA oder in Kanada dienen als° Klischees für Europäer? Wie finden Sie das? Haben Sie etwas Neues über München aus **Brennpunkt Kultur** gelernt?

das heißt
dienen ...: serve as

WORTSCHATZ

Tutorial Quiz
Audio Flashcards

Das Studentenleben

der Mitbewohner, -/die Mitbewohnerin, -nen *roommate, apartment mate, cohabitant*

der Schüler, -/die Schülerin, -nen *school pupil*

das Semesterticket, -s *semester pass (for city transportation)*

der Studentenausweis (Schülerausweis), -e *student ID*

Wechselpräpositionen

an *at, on; to*

auf *at, on; onto, to*

hinter *behind, to/in the back of*

in *at, in; into; to*

neben *beside, next to*

über *above, over*

unter *under, underneath*

vor *in front of; ago*

zwischen *between*

Wo gehst du gern hin?

der Club / Klub, -s *club*

die Fete, -n *party*

das Fitnessstudio, -s *health club*

der Fluss, ̈e *river*

der Jazzkeller, - *jazz club*

die Moschee, -n *mosque*

die Oper, -n *opera*

das Stadion, *pl.* **Stadien** *stadium*

die Synagoge, -n *synagogue*

Noch einmal: **die Disko(thek), das Kino, die Kirche, die Kneipe, das Konzert, das Museum, die Party, das Restaurant, das Schwimmbad, das Theater**

auf /in … gehen *to go to . . .*

Wo macht man das in der Stadt?

die Apotheke, -n *pharmacy*

die Bäckerei, -en *bakery*

die Bank, -en *bank*

der Bioladen, ̈ *health food store*

die Buchhandlung, -en *bookstore*

das Büro, -s *office*

die Fleischerei, -en *butcher shop*

die Haltestelle, -n *bus stop*

der Kiosk, -s *kiosk, stand*

die Konditorei, -en *pastry shop*

der Markt, ̈e *market*

die Metzgerei, -en *butcher shop*

die Post *post office*

das Reformhaus, ̈er *health food store*

die Sparkasse, -n *savings bank*

der Zeitungsstand, ̈e *newspaper stand*

Noch einmal: **der Bahnhof, der Supermarkt**

Verkehrsmittel

das Motorrad, ̈er *motorcycle*

der Pkw (Personenkraftwagen), -s *car*

die Rollerblades *pl. in-line skates*

das Schiff, -e *boat*

die Straßenbahn, -en *streetcar*

das Taxi, -s *taxi*

die U-Bahn (Untergrundbahn), -en *subway*

Noch einmal: **das Auto, die Bahn, der Bus, das Fahrrad (Rad), das Flugzeug, der Wagen, der Zug**

zu Fuß *on foot*

Der Sport

der Football *American-style football*

das Eishockey *ice hockey*

das Feldhockey *field hockey*

das Lacrosse *lacrosse*

Noch einmal: **der Baseball, der Basketball, der Fußball, das Golf, das Tennis, der Volleyball**

Sport treiben (hat getrieben) *to do sports*

Noch einmal: **angeln, schwimmen, segeln, surfen, wandern**

die Disziplin *discipline*

der Erfolg, -e *success; winning*

die Herausforderung, -en *challenge*

der Kreis, -e *circle*

die Mannschaft, -en *team*

der Profi, -s *professional*

die Sicht, -en *perspective, view*

der Spielplatz, ̈e *playground*

das Team, -s *team*

der Teamgeist *team spirit*

das Tempo, -s *speed*

der Trainer, - *coach*

der Verein, -e (Sportverein, Turnverein, Fußballverein usw.) *club (sports club, gymnastics club, soccer club, etc.)*

das Ziel, -e *goal*

der Zuschauer, - *fan, spectator*

oberst *upper-most*

sportlich *athletic*

täglich *daily*

verpflichtend *mandatory, required*

an•kommen (ist angekommen) *to arrive; meet expectations*

dauern (hat gedauert) *to last*

ein•stellen (hat eingestellt) *to implement, utilize*

fest•stellen (hat festgestellt) *to determine*

her•stellen (hat hergestellt) *to create*

merken (hat gemerkt) *to notice*

nach•denken über + *Akkusativ* **(hat nachgedacht)** *to think about, worry about*

sich weigern (hat sich geweigert) *to refuse*

tot•lachen *to laugh yourself silly*

Wert legen auf + *Akkusativ* **(hat gelegt)** *to emphasize*

Der Multikulturalismus

die Art, -en *style, type*

der Akzent, -e *accent*

der Bedarf *need*

der Begriff, -e *concept*

die Chance, -n *chance*

die Entwicklung, -en *development*

der Glaube, [-n], -n *faith, belief*

die Integration *integration*

die Kommunikation *commuication*

die Mentalität, -en *mentality*

der Migrationshintergrund *ethnic background*

die Nation, -en *nation*

die Religion, -en *religion*

der Respekt *respect*

die Sprache, -n *language*

der Unterricht *instruction, lesson*

das Wohlbefinden *well-being*

menschlich *human*

erfordern (hat erfordert) *to require, demand*

verraten (verrät, hat verraten) *to reveal, betray*

In welcher Richtung?

die Richtung *direction*

Wie komme ich zur/zum … ? *How do I get to . . . ?*

an der Ecke *at/on the corner*

bis zur Ampel *as far as (up to) the traffic light*

bis zur Kreuzung *as far as (up to) the intersection*

die Straße entlang *down the street*

gegenüber (von + dat.) *across from*

geradeaus *straight ahead*

(gleich) um die Ecke *right around the corner*

links/rechts ab•biegen (ist abgebogen) *to turn to the left/right*

näher *nearer, closer*

quer gegenüber von *diagonally across from*

Auf der Post

die Briefmarke, -n *postage stamp*

das Paket, -e *package*

Beim Einkaufen

das Einkaufsnetz, -e *mesh shopping bag*

die Kasse, -n *check-out counter; cash register*

der Kunde, [-n], -n/die Kundin, -nen *customer*

die Quittung, -en *receipt*

die Tragetasche, -n *plastic store bag*

die Tüte, -n/die Plastiktüte, -n *sack, bag*

billig *inexpensive, cheap*

teuer *expensive*

Auf der Bank

das Bargeld *cash*

das Konto, pl. Konten *bank account*

das Girokonto, -konten *checking/debit account*

das Sparkonto, -konten *savings account*

der Scheck, -s *check*

Noch einmal: **die Bankkarte, die Kreditkarte**

ab•heben (hat abgehoben) *to withdraw (money)*

(ein Konto) eröffnen (hat eröffnet) *to open (an account)*

ein•zahlen (hat eingezahlt) *to deposit (money)*

Die Meinung geben

(Das) finde ich so lala. *I find (that) so-so.*

(Das) finde ich toll. *I think (that) is great/fantastic.*

(Das) gefällt mir gar nicht. *I don't like (that) at all.*

Zeitausdrücke

einmal, zweimal, dreimal usw. *once, twice, three times, etc.*

zigmal (x-mal) *umpteen times*

Eigenschaften

bemerkenswert *noteworthy*

gesund *healthy*

hochaktuell *very current, very timely*

neugierig *nosy, curious*

praktisch *practical; practically*

unhöflich *impolite*

zufrieden *happy, satisfied*

Andere Verben

empfehlen (empfiehlt, hat empfohlen) *to recommend*

entdecken (hat entdeckt) *to discover*

erklären (hat erklärt) *to explain*

erledigen (hat erledigt) *to take care of*

hängen (hat gehangen) *to be hanging*

hängen (hat gehängt) *to hang (something) up*

hoffen (hat gehofft) auf + acc. *to hope for*

holen (hat geholt) *to fetch, get, pick up*

lachen (hat gelacht) über + acc. *to laugh about, at*

legen (hat gelegt) *to lay (something) down, put down*

liegen (hat gelegen) *to be lying down, lie*

reisen (ist gereist) *to travel*

schauen (hat geschaut) *to look at, watch*

setzen (hat gesetzt) *to set (something) down*

sitzen (hat gesessen) *to be sitting*

springen (ist gesprungen) *to jump*

stehen (hat gestanden) *to stand, be standing*

steigen (ist gestiegen) *to climb*

stellen (hat gestellt) *to stand (something), put*

suchen (hat gesucht) *to look for*

vor•schlagen (schlägt vor, hat vorgeschlagen) *to suggest*

Noch einmal: **beschreiben, denken an, gehen in/auf/an, fahren in/nach, fallen auf, fliegen, laufen in/nach, schreiben an, sein in/an/auf, sprechen über, warten auf, wohnen in**

Andere Wörter

damit *with it/that; so that*

her *here*

hin *there*

Meine eigenen Wörter

_____

_____

_____

_____

_____

Viele Studenten fahren mit dem Fahrrad zur Uni.

An der Uni studieren

In this chapter you will learn to talk about your daily routine, about issues of personal health, and what you will do in the future. You will also learn to talk about university-related activities.

Kommunikative Funktionen

> Talking about activities we do for ourselves
> Talking about daily hygiene routines
> Talking about future events
> Expressing probability
> Specifying additional information about actions

Strukturen

> Reflexive verbs
> Reflexive pronouns

> Future time and time expressions
> The verb **werden + wohl**
> Verbs with prepositional objects
> **Da-** and **wo-**compounds

Vokabeln

> Die tägliche Routine
> Im Badezimmer
> Krank sein

Kulturelles

> Universitätskurse
> Das deutsche Universitätssystem

> Wie Studierende ihr Studium finanzieren
> Das deutsche Schulsystem

Ein Gruppenreferat°

group presentation

Karl und Stefan sind Partner in einem Betriebswirtschaftsproseminar. Ihre Arbeitsgruppe soll nächste Woche ein Referat halten; sie müssen im Proseminar ihr gemeinsames° Projekt präsentieren, aber sie haben noch gar nichts geschrieben. Karl geht zu seiner Dozentin°, Frau Dr. Osswald, in die Sprechstunde°und erfindet Ausreden°, warum er und Stefan noch nicht viel gemacht haben.

joint
college instructor
office hours / excuses

Vorschau

 1 Thematische Fragen Beantworten Sie die folgenden Fragen auf Deutsch.

1. Mit wem sprechen Sie zuerst, wenn Sie Probleme in einem Kurs haben?
   a. mit Freunden
   b. mit Kommilitonen°
   c. mit dem Professor/der Professorin (dem Dozenten/der Dozentin)
   d. mit den Eltern
   e. mit dem Dekan°
   f. mit dem Institutsleiter/der Institutsleiterin°

college classmates

dean
department chairperson

2. Besuchen Sie Professoren/Professorinnen in der Sprechstunde? Warum? Warum nicht? Wie oft haben Ihre Professoren/Professorinnen Sprechstunde?
3. Haben Sie schon mal ein Gruppenprojekt gemacht? Was ist passiert? Was war gut? Was war schlecht?
   a. Wir haben nicht genug Zeit für das Projekt gehabt.
   b. Manche Leute haben mehr gearbeitet als andere.
   c. Wir haben viele gute Ideen gehabt.
   d. Wir haben viele Talente in der Gruppe gehabt.
   e. Wir haben verschiedene° Interessen gehabt.
   f. Wir haben Konflikte gehabt.
   g. Wir haben alles in der letzten Minute gemacht, aber wir haben es geschafft.

different

Kulturnotiz. A **Dozent/ Dozentin** is a tenured university professor with a Ph.D. who is not yet a full professor **(Professor/ Professorin)**. The number of full professors is limited in Germany to the number of positions determined for the country.

Studenten arbeiten an einem Gruppenprojekt.

Andresr/Shutterstock.com

2 Die Seminararbeit° Was muss man machen, wenn man eine gute Seminararbeit schreiben will? Ordnen Sie die Faktoren nach ihrer Wichtigkeit von 1 (sehr wichtig) bis 10 (unwichtig).

term paper

	Wichtigkeit
ein Thema wählen°	_____
einen Partner/eine Partnerin finden	_____
Notizen machen	_____
in die Bibliothek gehen	_____
im Internet recherchieren°	_____
Bücher und Artikel lesen	_____
ein paar Versionen schreiben	_____
mit dem Professor/der Professorin bzw. dem Dozenten/der Dozentin sprechen	
Handouts vorbereiten	_____
eine PowerPoint-Präsentation oder einen Podcast zusammenstellen	_____
eine Tabelle° oder eine Grafik zeichnen	_____

select

research

table, chart

→ **3** Satzdetektiv Welche Sätze bedeuten ungefähr das Gleiche?

1. Schön, dass Sie **sich** endlich **melden**.
2. Wie sieht es mit Ihrem **Referat** aus?
3. Ich habe **mich** schwer **erkältet**.
4. Sie haben wirklich **Pech gehabt!**

a. Es ist gut, dass Sie jetzt zu mir gekommen sind.
b. Ich war krank – ich habe eine schlimme Erkältung gehabt.
c. Das war wirklich eine schlechte Situation für Sie!
d. Wie weit sind Sie mit Ihrem Projekt?

5. Haben Sie **sich** überhaupt **für** ein Thema **entschieden**?
6. Wie lange wird das Referat **dauern**?
7. Ich **freue mich** schon **auf** Ihr Referat.
8. Wir müssen unser **Referat** schon nächste Woche **halten**.
9. Das werden wir bis nächste Woche nie **schaffen**.

e. Das können wir bis nächste Woche nicht zu Ende machen!
f. Nächste Woche müssen wir unsere Arbeit mündlich° präsentieren.
g. Wie viel Zeit werden Sie für das Referat brauchen?
h. Wissen Sie schon, über welches Thema Sie sprechen werden?
i. Ich bin auf Ihren Vortrag° gespannt.

orally

presentation

Hören Sie gut zu.

Ja, herein, bitte.

Guten Tag. Sie haben heute Sprechstunde, nicht?

Ja. Schön, dass Sie sich endlich melden. Wie sieht es mit Ihrem Referat aus? Kann Ihre Arbeitsgruppe nächste Woche das Referat halten?

Ja, deswegen bin ich da. Wir haben ein paar Probleme gehabt.

Ja?

Ja, ich habe mich schwer erkältet und habe drei Tage im Bett gelegen.

Ja, und Ihr Partner?

Tja, er hat sich das Bein gebrochen.

Soso. Sie haben wirklich Pech gehabt! Haben Sie sich überhaupt für ein Thema entschieden?

Ja. Haben wir das nicht angemeldet?

Ich kann mich jedenfalls nicht daran erinnern. Wie heißt Ihr Thema noch mal?

"Kulturmanagement: Koordinierung vom Spielplan"

Schön. Das ist ein wirklich aktuelles Thema. Wie lange wird das Referat dauern?

Das wissen wir noch nicht so genau.

Vergessen Sie nicht: Sie haben maximal fünfundvierzig Minuten. Konzentrieren Sie sich auf das Wichtigste.

Sprache im Alltag: Interjections, Rejoinders, and Particles

German speakers use a wide range of interjections, rejoinders, and particles to express attitudes and emotions towards what is being said. These words appear at the beginning of a response and are frequently followed by a slight pause.

Tja, er hat sich das Bein gebrochen.	*Well, he broke his leg.*
Soso. Sie haben wirklich Pech gehabt.	*You don't say. You really had bad luck.*
Na, Karl, wie war's?	*So, Karl, how'd it go?*
Ach, Stefan, wir müssen unser Referat schon nächste Woche halten.	*Oh, Stefan, we have to make our presentation next week already.*

Tja generally indicates hesitation based on embarrassment or misfortune. **Soso** expresses irony or disbelief. **Na** is used in informal conversation to initiate a hopeful question or positive statement. **Ach** is an expression of surprise, frustration, or pain. Rejoinders such as **ja, schön,** or **fein** provide positive confirmation of what has just been said.

Rückblick

4 Stimmt das? Stimmen diese Aussagen zum Text? Wenn nicht, was stimmt?

	Ja, das stimmt.	Nein, das stimmt nicht.
1. Karl und Stefan sind Partner in einer Arbeitsgruppe.	○	○
2. Stefan sagt, er hat sich erkältet.	○	○
3. Karl und Stefan haben Glück gehabt.	○	○
4. Frau Dr. Osswald kann sich nicht an das Thema für Karls Arbeitsgruppe erinnern.	○	○
5. Das Thema für das Referat ist „Kulturmanagement: Koordinierung vom Spielplan".	○	○
6. Karl weiß noch nicht, wie lange das Referat dauern wird.	○	○
7. Die Arbeitsgruppe soll sich auf die Details konzentrieren.	○	○
8. Dr. Osswald bringt ihren Laptop mit.	○	○
9. Dr. Osswald freut sich auf das Referat.	○	○
10. Stefan und Karl haben das Referat schon geschrieben.	○	○

Complete the **Ergänzen Sie** activity in the Student Activities Manual before doing the next activity.

5 Kurz gefragt Beantworten Sie die Fragen auf Deutsch.

1. Welche Probleme haben Karl und Stefan angeblich° gehabt?
2. Was ist das Thema von ihrem Gruppenreferat?
3. Warum gefällt der Dozentin das Thema?
4. Warum will die Dozentin wissen, wie lange das Referat dauern wird?
5. Warum will Karl wissen, ob es einen Beamer im Seminarraum gibt?
6. Wie wird die Dozentin Karls Arbeitsgruppe helfen?
7. Was haben Karl und Stefan angeblich schon für das Referat vorbereitet?
8. Warum fühlt sich Karl nach dem Gespräch krank?

supposedly

evaluate

6 Ausreden bewerten° Sie sind der Dozent/die Dozentin. Ein Student/Eine Studentin kann heute sein/ihr Referat nicht halten. Hier sind einige typische Ausreden. Bewerten Sie die Ausreden als **sehr glaubhaft, akzeptabel** oder **Unsinn.**

	Sehr glaubhaft	Akzeptabel	Unsinn
1. Mein Hund hat mein Referat gefressen°.	○	○	○
2. Ich habe es zu Hause vergessen.	○	○	○
3. Der Bus hat Verspätung° gehabt.	○	○	○
4. Ich habe verschlafen,° weil mein Wecker nicht richtig funktioniert.	○	○	○
5. Ich kann nicht zur Uni kommen. Mein Auto ist kaputt.	○	○	○
6. Ich habe mir das Bein gebrochen.	○	○	○
7. Ich habe Probleme mit meinem Drucker gehabt.	○	○	○
8. Meine Oma ist gestorben.	○	○	○

eaten

delay
overslept

7 Textdetektiv: **Anlauftext.** Use the *Anlauftext* to recognize important aspects of German structure and usage.

1. Identify the word on the right that is being referred to by the boldface personal pronoun in the examples from the *Anlauftext* on the left.

Example from the Anlauftext	*Boldface personal pronoun refers to ...*	
1. Schön, dass Sie **sich** bei mir melden.	a. Sie	b. bei mir
2. Ich hab **mich** schwer erkältet.	a. ich	b. im Bett
3. Mein Partner hat **sich** das Bein gebrochen.	a. mein Partner	b. das Bein
4. Haben Sie **sich** überhaupt für ein Thema entschieden?	a. Sie	b. für ein Thema
5. Ich kann **mich** jedenfalls nicht daran erinnern	a. ich	b. daran
6. Ich freue **mich** schon auf Ihr Referat.	a. ich	b. Ihr Referat

2. Based on these examples, we can conclude that the highlighted pronouns ...
   a. reflect back on the subject (agent, doer) of the sentence.
   b. introduce new information into the sentence.

3. An appropriate name for these pronouns would be ...
   a. introductory pronouns   b. reflexive pronouns

4. What is the case of the highlighted pronouns in examples 1 & 2 above?
   a. nominative   b. accusative   c. dative

5. For each of the four rows below compare the boldface forms in the example sentences in all three columns. Then answer the question that follows.

Third person singular (er/sie/es)	*Third person plural/formal address (sie/Sie)*	*First person singular (ich)*
Mein Partner hat **sich** schwer erkältet.	Sie haben **sich** schwer erkältet.	Ich habe **mich** schwer erkältet.
Mein Partner meldet **sich** bei mir.	Sie melden **sich** bei mir.	Ich melde **mich** bei dir.
Mein Partner hat **sich** das Bein gebrochen.	Sie haben **sich** das Bein gebrochen.	Ich habe **mir** das Bein gebrochen.
Mein Partner muss **sich** unbedingt hinlegen.	Sie müssen **sich** unbedingt hinlegen.	Ich muss **mich** unbedingt hinlegen.

Which observations are correct? Mark all that apply.

a. The third person singular **(er/sie/es)** and the third person plural/formal address **(sie/Sie)** have the same reflexive pronoun.

b. The reflexive pronoun for third person singular **(er/sie/es)** and plural/formal address **(sie/Sie)** looks different than a 'regular' personal pronoun.

c. The reflexive pronoun for first person **(ich)** singular looks different than a 'regular' personal pronoun in the accusative.

d. The dative and accusative forms of the reflexive pronoun in the first person singular **(ich)** look identical.

e. The dative and accusative forms of the reflexive pronouns for the third person singular **(er/sie/es)** and the third person plural/formal address **(sie/Sie)** look identical.

← **8** Unsere Universität Diskutieren Sie die folgenden Sätze in kleinen Gruppen, bis Sie alle dieselbe Meinung haben. Teilen° andere Gruppen Ihre Meinung?

share

1. An dieser Universität muss man _____ schreiben.
   a. sehr viel   b. viel   c. nicht sehr viel

2. Dozenten/Dozentinnen an dieser Universität verbringen viel Zeit _____.
   a. mit Studenten   b. beim Forschen°   c. im Unterricht

research

3. Es ist _____, mit Lehrkräften° auf diesem Campus zu sprechen.
   a. leicht   b. schwierig   c. undenkbar°

instructors
unthinkable

4. Der beste Fachbereich° auf diesem Campus ist _____.

department

5. In diesem Deutschkurs müssen wir viel _____.
   a. sprechen   c. lesen   e. schreiben
   b. zuhören   d. Grammatik lernen

6. In diesem Kurs müssen wir zu viele _____.
   a. Hausaufgaben machen
   b. Prüfungen schreiben
   c. Referate halten

7. Unsere Bibliothek ist _____.
   a. nicht besonders gut   b. recht gut   c. ausgezeichnet

8. Wer° hier abends im Studentenwohnheim lernen will, _____.
   a. muss sich sehr intensiv konzentrieren
   b. muss extrem unfreundlich sein
   c. wird keine Probleme haben

Whoever

9. Assistenten (und nicht Professoren und Dozenten) unterrichten bei uns _____.
   a. nie   b. nicht sehr oft   c. oft

10. Wer hier Schwierigkeiten° in einem Kurs hat, _____.
    a. hat einfach Pech°
    b. muss sich selber Hilfe suchen
    c. kann ohne Probleme Hilfe bekommen

difficulties
Probleme

11. Studenten hier meinen, Pflichtkurse° sind _____.
    a. nervig°   b. akzeptabel   c. wertvoll

required courses
irritating

9 Freie Kommunikation: **Rollenspiel: Ausreden.** Spielen Sie die folgende Situation mit einem Partner/einer Partnerin.

S1: Sie sind in einer Arbeitsgruppe, aber Sie haben gar nichts gemacht. Sie müssen heute mit den anderen Studierenden in der Arbeitsgruppe sprechen. Besprechen Sie mit ihnen so viele Ausreden wie möglich°.

S2: Sie sind auch in der Arbeitsgruppe. Stellen Sie viele Fragen über diese Ausreden und versuchen° Sie, eine gute Lösung° zu finden.

so … : as many excuses as possible

try / solution

Universitätskurse

Students in Germany pursuing an undergradute degree program **(das Grundstudium)** go through a three-part modular system. The introductory module **(das Basismodul)** provides students with a general overview of the discipline in lecture courses, seminars, and practical courses. A lecture course **(die Vorlesung)** may have as many as 600 students. There are no tests and few opportunities for interaction between instructor and students. In an introductory seminar **(das Basisseminar, das Proseminar)**, students are introduced to the discipline and practice with basic concepts. They are evaluated on the basis of class discussions, an oral presentation **(das Referat)**, summary notes **(das Protokoll)**, and group work **(die Gruppenarbeit)**. In the more practical courses **(die Übung)**, students complete assignments and take tests. Students continue to build skills through the intermediate module **(das Aufbaumodul)** and advance to the advanced module **(das Vertiefungsmodul)**. Students must collect credits **(Leistungspunkte)** or certificates of completion **(Scheine)**, which they need to be able to take the test **(die Klausur)** that admits them to the next module, and finally for the exams that earn them a degree **(das Vordiplom** or **die Zwischenprüfung)**. A thesis **(die Bachelorarbeit)** serves as a capstone project for the bachelor's degree.

Students who successfully complete their **Grundstudium** can attend graduate school **(das Hauptstudium)** where they take advanced-level **Hauptseminare**. Programs leading to a master's degree **(der Master)** last two or four semesters and require a thesis and oral exams. For a Ph.D. **(die Promotion)**, students must complete course-work, advanced seminars, colloquia, and even part-time employment in **Graduiertenkollegs** as well as conduct original research and produce a dissertation **(die Dissertation)**.

Universität Tübingen Campus-Portal für Studium und Lehre				
Einführung in die NDL[1] (Prosa)				
Veranstaltungsart: Proseminar				
Semester: SS 12				
Tag	**Zeit**	**Rhythmus**	**Dauer**	**Raum**
Di.	10 c.t. – 12	wöch.	24.04.2018 bis 24.07.2018	Neuphilologicum - 315 - 315
Zugeordnete Person: Thums, Barbara, apl. Prof., Dr. phil.				
Abschluss	**Studiengang**		**Semester**	**Prüfungsversion**
Bachelor	Germanistik Deutsch. Sem.		-	2005
Magister	Neuere deutsche Literatur Magister		-	96
Kommentar	Anhand ausgewählter Prosatexte vom 18. Jahrhundert bis zur Gegenwart (u.a. E.T.A. Hoffmann, Büchner, Stifter, Kafka, Fleißer, Seghers) wird in literaturwissenschaftliches Arbeiten eingeführt. Erörtert werden Kategorien der Erzähltextanalyse, literaturgeschichtliche Kontexte, zentrale literaturtheoretische Probleme sowie grundlegende Arbeitstechniken unseres Faches.			

[1] **NDL = Neue Deutsche Literatur:** *Modern German Literature*

Kulturkreuzung

Haben Sie viele Vorlesungen? Wie finden Sie das, wenn der Professor oder die Professorin wortwörtlich° aus den eigenen° Notizen vorliest? Was machen viele Studierende in den Vorlesungen? Welcher Kurs hat die meisten Studierenden? Wie viele sind das? Wo lernen Sie besser – in einer großen Vorlesung oder in einem kleinen Kurs oder Seminar? Warum?

word for word / his or her own

Strukturen

 Talking about activities we do for ourselves

Reflexive verbs with accusative reflexive pronouns

A. Reflexive and non-reflexive usage of verbs

In both German and English, many action verbs may be followed by a direct object that refers to another person, animal, or object.

> Ich wasche **das Kind**.   *I wash/am washing the child.*

The direct object may also refer back to the subject of the sentence.

> Ich wasche **mich**.   *I wash/am washing myself.*

To describe activities people do for themselves, German speakers use a verb with a reflexive pronoun (**das Reflexivpronomen**). The reflexive pronoun refers back to the subject of the sentence, which is performing the action indicated by the verb. A verb that has a reflexive pronoun as the direct object is called a *reflexive verb* (**das Reflexivverb**). Many German verbs require a reflexive pronoun where in English the reflexive pronoun *self/selves* is never required.

> Ich ziehe **mich** an.   *I get/am getting (myself) dressed.*
> Karl rasiert **sich**.   *Karl shaves/is shaving (himself).*
> Ich fühle **mich** jetzt schon krank.   *I feel/am feeling sick already.*

Here are some more reflexive verbs from the previous **Anlauftext**.

> **sich erinnern** an *(to remember)*
>   Ich kann **mich** nicht daran **erinnern**.   *I can't remember it.*
>
> **sich entscheiden** für *(to decide on)*
>   Für welches Thema haben Sie **sich**
>   **entschieden?**   *Which topic did you decide on?*
>
> **sich fühlen** *(to feel)*
>   Ich **fühle mich** jetzt schon krank.   *I feel/am feeling sick already.*
>
> **sich hinlegen** *(to lie down)*
>   Ich muss **mich** unbedingt **hinlegen**.   *I absolutely have to lie down.*
>
> **sich melden** *(to report, get in touch)*
>   Schön, dass Sie **sich** endlich **melden**.   *It's good that you're finally getting in touch.*

Here are the accusative forms of the reflexive pronouns. Note that the only new reflexive pronoun you need to learn is **sich**.

> Note that the reflexive pronouns look like direct object pronouns (**mich, dich**) except in the singular and plural forms of the 3rd person, and the 2nd person formal (**sich**). Verbs that require a reflexive pronoun appear in the *Vorsprung* vocabulary lists and glossary preceded by the reflexive pronoun **sich** (e.g., **sich beeilen**). In commercial dictionaries, these reflexive verbs are followed by the abbreviation *vr* (e.g., **beeilen** *vr*).

	Singular						Plural			
	1st	**2nd**		**3rd**			**1st**	**2nd**		**3rd**
Nom.	ich	du	Sie	er	sie	es	wir	ihr	Sie	sie
Acc.	**mich**	**dich**	**sich**	**sich**	**sich**	**sich**	**uns**	**euch**	**sich**	**sich**
	myself	*yourself*	*yourself*	*himself/ itself*	*herself/ itself*	*itself*	*ourselves*	*yourselves*	*yourselves*	*themselves*

B. Verbs that always require a reflexive pronoun

At the beginning of this section you learned that some German verbs may or may not be used with a reflexive pronoun (e.g., **waschen** vs. **sich waschen**). Some German verbs and verb + preposition expressions always require a reflexive pronoun and cannot be used without one. You have already encountered a few of these reflexive verbs in this and earlier chapters.

sich beeilen *(to hurry)*
sich freuen auf *(to look forward to)*
sich freuen über *(to be happy about)*
sich konzentrieren auf *(to concentrate on)*

sich trennen von *(to break up with, separate from)*
sich verlieben in *(to fall in love with)*
sich verloben mit *(to get engaged to)*

C. Word order in sentences with reflexive pronouns

1. Statements

In main clauses, the reflexive pronoun follows the conjugated verb. When the noun subject and verb are transposed, the reflexive pronoun tends to precede the noun subject, but always follows a pronoun subject.

Dr. Osswald <u>freut</u> **sich** auf das Referat.

Dr. Osswald is looking forward to the oral presentation.

Natürlich <u>freut</u> **sich** Dr. Osswald auf das Referat.

Of course Dr. Osswald is looking forward to the oral presentation.

Natürlich <u>freut</u> sie **sich** auf das Referat.

Of course she is looking forward to the oral presentation.

In subordinate clauses, the reflexive precedes a noun subject but follows a pronoun subject.

Ich glaube, dass **sich** <u>Dr. Osswald</u> auf das Referat freut.

I believe that Dr. Osswald is looking forward to the oral presentation.

Ich glaube, dass <u>sie</u> **sich** auf das Referat freut.

I believe that she is looking forward to the oral presentation.

2. Questions

In questions, the reflexive pronoun can precede or follow a noun subject. If the subject is a pronoun, the reflexive pronoun must follow it immediately.

Beeilt **sich** <u>Inge</u>?   OR   Beeilt <u>Inge</u> **sich**?   *Is Inge hurrying up?*

Beeilt <u>sie</u> **sich**?   *Is she hurrying up?*

↩ **10 In der Sprechstunde** Barbara spricht mit ihrem Professor in seiner Sprechstunde. Schreiben Sie die richtigen Reflexivpronomen in die Lücken°.

PROFESSOR: Guten Tag, Frau Müller. Setzen Sie _____! Was kann ich für Sie tun?

BARBARA: Ich habe _____ für das Examen im Dezember angemeldet und ich habe einige Fragen.

PROFESSOR: Dezember? Das überlegen° wir _____ besser. Warum beeilen Sie _____ so? Ist das nicht etwas früh?

BARBARA: Ich glaube nicht. Ich habe _____ schon für meine Schwerpunkte° entschieden.

PROFESSOR: Ja, wenn Sie meinen. Aber ich rate° Ihnen, konzentrieren Sie _____ auf das Wichtigste, ja?

BARBARA: Ja, natürlich. Ich freue _____ eigentlich schon auf das Examen.

blanks

consider

major topics

advise

Wissenswerte Vokabeln: die tägliche Routine

Talking about your daily routine and personal hygiene

Volker bereitet sich auf den Tag vor.

Ich ziehe mich aus und dusche (mich). — Ich trockne mich ab. — Ich rasiere mich. — Ich ziehe mich an und beeile mich.

Sabine bereitet sich auf den Abend vor.

Sie badet. — Sie wäscht sich. — Sie trocknet sich ab. — Sie zieht sich an. — Sie schminkt sich.

Illustrations © Cengage Learning 2014

BEISPIEL *Was machst du morgens?*

11 **Am Morgen** In welcher Reihenfolge machen Sie diese Aktivitäten? Benutzen Sie die Zahlen 1 bis 7.

___ Ich trockne mich ab.   ___ Ich beeile mich.
___ Ich ziehe mich an.   ___ Ich rasiere mich.
___ Ich dusche mich.   ___ Ich schminke mich.
___ Ich stehe auf.

12 Was hast du heute schon gemacht? Sagen Sie, was Sie heute schon gemacht haben, und fragen Sie dann einen Partner/eine Partnerin.

BEISPIEL   S1: *Ich habe mich heute schon rasiert. Und du?*
             S2: *Ich habe mich heute auch schon rasiert. (oder)*
                 Ich habe mich heute noch nicht rasiert.

angezogen • ausgezogen • gebadet • geduscht • geschminkt • gewaschen • abgetrocknet • rasiert • beeilt • hingelegt • gesetzt

13 **Minidialog** Ingo wohnt in einer Wohngemeinschaft mit fünf anderen Studenten. Er ist gerade° aufgestanden und ist jetzt im Badezimmer. Holger wohnt auch in der Wohngemeinschaft und möchte auch ins Badezimmer. Schreiben Sie das richtige Reflexivpronomen (**dich, mich**) in die Lücken.

just

Holger klopft an die Tür zum Badezimmer.

HOLGER: Ingo, bist du's?

INGO: Ja.

HOLGER: Kannst du _____ beeilen? Ich muss _____ rasieren.

INGO: Du, zieh _____ erstmal an. Ich habe _____ gerade geduscht. Ich muss _____ noch abtrocknen.

HOLGER: Ich habe _____ schon angezogen. Ich muss _____ schnell waschen, denn ich muss in die Stadt.

INGO: Gut. Ich bin gleich fertig.

Im Badezimmer

Talking about bathroom objects

Kulturnotiz. Beware! There may not be a **Toilette** in the **Badezimmer**. If German speakers need to go to the bathroom, they say: **Ich muss auf die Toilette gehen.** In a more informal setting they may say: **Ich muss aufs Klo.**

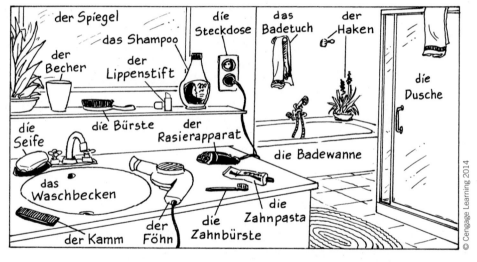

der Spiegel / das Shampoo / die Steckdose / das Badetuch / der Haken / der Becher / der Lippenstift / die Dusche / die Seife / die Bürste / der Rasierapparat / die Badewanne / das Waschbecken / der Kamm / der Föhn / die Zahnbürste / die Zahnpasta

© Cengage Learning 2014

BEISPIEL *Wo machst du das?* — *Ich trockne mich im Badezimmer ab.*
Womit° machst du das? — *Ich trockne mich mit dem Badetuch ab.*

With what

14 **Was wollen sie machen?** Erklären Sie, was Karl und Inge mit diesen Gegenständen im Badezimmer machen.

BEISPIEL S1: *Was will Karl machen, wenn er den Rasierapparat hat?*
S2: *Er will sich rasieren.*

Was will Karl machen, ...
1. wenn er den Rasierapparat hat?
2. wenn er das Badetuch nimmt?
3. wenn er die Seife hält?
4. wenn er unter die Dusche geht?

Was will Inge machen, ...
5. wenn sie in den Spiegel schaut?
6. wenn sie in die Badewanne steigt?
7. wenn sie sich eine frische Bluse holt?

↩ **15** Wo und womit macht man das? Erklären Sie, wo oder mit welchem Gegenstand im Badezimmer man diese Aktivitäten machen kann.

BEISPIEL   S1: *Wo kann man baden?*
S2: *In der Badewanne. Womit kann man sich waschen?*
S1: *Mit Seife.*

1. Wo kann man baden?
2. Wo kann man sich duschen?
3. Wo kann man sich rasieren?

4. Wo kann man Wasser trinken?
5. Wo kann man sich abtrocknen?
6. Wo kann man sich waschen?

Strukturen

II Talking about daily hygiene routines

Reflexive verbs with dative reflexive pronouns

You have already learned some of the reflexive verbs that German speakers use to talk about personal hygiene activities (e.g., **sich waschen, sich duschen, sich rasieren, sich anziehen**).

Ich rasiere **mich**.	*I'm shaving.*
Hast du **dich** gewaschen?	*Did you wash (yourself)?*
Er zieht **sich** an.	*He's getting dressed.*

When a part of the body (teeth, hair, legs, etc.) or an article of clothing (shirt, socks, coat, etc.) is specified, the reflexive pronoun is in the dative case and the direct object (the part of the body or clothing) is in the accusative case.

Dative

Ich rasiere	**mir**	die Beine.	*I'm shaving my legs.*
Hast du	**dir**	die Hände gewaschen?	*Did you wash your hands?*
Er zieht	**sich**	die Jacke an.	*He's putting his jacket on.*

Wir putzen **uns** die Zähne.

Du rasierst **dir** die Beine.

Sie wäscht **sich** die Haare.

Er föhnt **sich** die Haare.

Kämmst du **dir** die Haare?

Habt ihr **euch** die Haare gebürstet?

Illustrations © Cengage Learning 2014

Dative reflexive pronouns also designate the beneficiary of actions other than grooming.

Ich backe **mir** einen Kuchen.	*I'm baking a cake for myself.*
Er hat **sich** einen BMW gekauft.	*He bought himself a BMW.*
Mach **dir** keine Sorgen.	*Don't worry (yourself).*

English speakers say *I'm combing my hair.* German avoids using possessive pronouns. Instead it uses the definite article along with a dative reflexive object: *Ich kämme mir die Haare.*

Here are the dative forms of the reflexive pronouns.

| | Singular | | | | | | Plural | | | |
	1st	**2nd**		**3rd**			**1st**	**2nd**		**3rd**
Nom.	ich	du	Sie	er	sie	es	wir	ihr	Sie	sie
Acc.	mich	dich	sich	sich	sich	sich	uns	euch	sich	sich
Dat.	**mir**	**dir**	**sich**	**sich**	**sich**	**sich**	**uns**	**euch**	**sich**	**sich**
	myself	*yourself*	*yourself*	*himself/ itself*	*herself/ itself*	*itself*	*ourselves*	*yourselves*	*yourselves*	*themselves*

16 **Am Morgen** In welcher Reihenfolge machen Sie diese Aktivitäten? Benutzen Sie die Zahlen 1 bis 10.

___ Ich kämme (bürste) mir die Haare.
___ Ich stehe auf.
___ Ich putze mir die Zähne.
___ Ich ziehe mich an.
___ Ich föhne mir die Haare.
___ Ich gehe aufs Klo.
___ Ich setze mich hin und frühstücke.
___ Ich rasiere mich. (Ich schminke mich.)
___ Ich wasche mir die Haare.
___ Ich dusche (bade).

> Note that the only dative reflexive forms that are different from the accusative forms are those for **ich** (**mich** vs. **mir**) and **du** (**dich** vs. **dir**). All other reflexive pronouns are identical in the accusative and dative.

17 **Was haben Sie heute gemacht?** Sagen Sie, was Sie heute gemacht haben, und fragen Sie dann einen Partner/eine Partnerin.

BEISPIEL   S1: *Ich habe mir heute die Zähne geputzt. Und du?*
S2: *Ja, ich habe mir heute auch die Zähne geputzt.* (oder)
Nein, ich habe mir die Zähne noch nicht geputzt.

die Zähne geputzt • geduscht • die Haare gewaschen • die Haare geföhnt • die Haare gekämmt • die Haare gebürstet • die Beine/den Bart rasiert • die Hände gewaschen • (eine lange Hose) angezogen

18 **Barbaras Morgen** Barbara macht jeden Morgen immer dasselbe! Schreiben Sie die richtigen Reflexivpronomen (**mich** oder **mir**) in die Lücken.

Ich stehe jeden Morgen um 7.00 Uhr auf. Zuerst gehe ich auf die Toilette. Dann ziehe ich _____ aus und gehe unter die Dusche. Heute ist Freitag und ich wasche _____ die Haare. Dann trockne ich _____ ab und föhne _____ die Haare. Dann ziehe ich _____ an. Meistens° ziehe ich _____ Jeans und ein T-Shirt an. Dann kämme ich _____ die Haare und putze _____ die Zähne. Jetzt muss ich _____ beeilen. Schließlich° gehe ich in die Küche und mache _____ schnell Frühstück.

Most of the time

Finally

checkmark
paragraph

19 Wie oft machst du das? Kreuzen Sie mit **x** an, wie oft Sie diese Aktivitäten machen. Fragen Sie dann einen Partner/eine Partnerin, wie oft er/sie das macht, und markieren Sie das mit einem Haken°. Benutzen Sie diese Informationen, um einen kurzen Absatz° über das Morgenritual von Ihrem Partner/Ihrer Partnerin zu schreiben. Benutzen Sie die Sätze in Aktivität 18 als Beispiel.

BEISPIEL sich die Haare waschen
S1: *Wie oft wäschst du dir die Haare?*
S2: *Ich wasche mir einmal am Tag die Haare.*

	Zweimal am Tag	Einmal am Tag	Alle zwei Tage	Einmal die Woche	Nie
1. sich die Haare waschen	○○	○○	○○	○○	○○
2. sich die Haare föhnen	○○	○○	○○	○○	○○
3. sich anziehen	○○	○○	○○	○○	○○
4. sich ausziehen	○○	○○	○○	○○	○○
5. sich die Zähne putzen	○○	○○	○○	○○	○○
6. sich duschen	○○	○○	○○	○○	○○
7. baden	○○	○○	○○	○○	○○
8. sich rasieren	○○	○○	○○	○○	○○
9. sich schminken	○○	○○	○○	○○	○○

> To prepare for this writing assignment, ask your partner about his/her daily habits and find out in what order your partner does them: **Was machst du zuerst? Und dann?**

20 Ja, aber was brauche ich? Sie sind im Badezimmer. Sie wissen, was Sie tun wollen, aber Sie haben nicht den Gegenstand, den Sie brauchen. Ihr Partner/Ihre Partnerin hilft Ihnen mit einer Frage.

BEISPIEL *sich das Gesicht waschen*
S1: *Ich will mir das Gesicht waschen.*
S2: *Brauchst du die Seife?*
S1: *Ja, bitte.*

1. sich das Gesicht waschen
2. sich abtrocknen
3. sich die Haare trocknen
4. sich rasieren
5. sich die Hände waschen
6. sich die Zähne putzen
7. sich die Haare waschen
8. sich die Haare bürsten

21 Was wollen sie damit machen? Bilden Sie Sätze mit einem Reflexivverb.

BEISPIEL Inge / den Föhn in der Hand halten
S1: *Inge hält den Föhn in der Hand. Was will sie damit machen?*
S2: *Sie will sich die Haare föhnen.*

1. Inge / den Föhn in der Hand halten
2. Oliver / den Kamm in der Hand halten
3. Annegret / die Zahnbürste haben
4. Michael / den Rasierapparat haben
5. Werner / die Seife halten
6. Monika / den Rasierapparat haben
7. Torsten / das Badetuch haben
8. Liselotte / den Taschenspiegel und den Lippenstift in der Hand halten

†† 22 Freie Kommunikation: **Rollenspiel: Ein Badezimmer teilen.** Sie wohnen mit vier Personen in einem Haus mit nur einem Badezimmer. Zu viele Leute wollen das Badezimmer zur selben Zeit benutzen. Formulieren Sie einen Plan für die Benutzung des Badezimmers. Benutzen Sie Ausdrücke aus der Liste.

Um wie viel Uhr? • Wann? • Von wann bis wann? • Wie oft? • Wie lange? • baden • duschen • sich die Haare waschen • sich die Zähne putzen • sich rasieren • sich die Haare föhnen • sich schminken

Wissenswerte Vokabeln: krank sein

Talking about illnesses

Ich habe Fieber. Meine Temperatur ist über 38 Grad.

Ich habe mich in den Finger geschnitten. Ich brauche ein Heftpflaster.

Ich habe mir das Bein gebrochen. Ich habe einen Gips.

Ich lege mich hin. Ich liege im Bett. Ich ruhe mich aus. Ich erhole mich.

Ich fühle mich nicht wohl.

Ich muss mich übergeben.

Ich habe Durchfall.

Ich habe (einen) Muskelkater.

Ich habe Zahnschmerzen. Mir tut der Zahn weh.

Ich habe Halsschmerzen. Mir tut der Hals weh.

Ich habe Kopfschmerzen. Mir tut der Kopf weh.

Ich nehme Schmerztabletten.

Ich habe mich erkältet. Ich habe eine Erkältung. Ich habe (einen) Schnupfen.

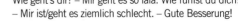
Wie geht's dir? – Mir geht es so lala. Wie fühlst du dich? – Mir ist/geht es ziemlich schlecht. – Gute Besserung!

Illustrations © Cengage Learning 2014

BEISPIEL *Wie geht es dir? Ich habe eine Erkältung.*

dentist

claim / in any case

das Handgelenk: *wrist*

36.6°C is considered normal body temperature.

language laboratory
nicht ...: *couldn't any more*
chews
pretzel sticks / nuts
typing

beklagt sich: *is complaining*
Wechseln ...: *Switch roles*

stiff

wisdom tooth
tissue

23 Ursache° und Wirkung° Bilden Sie Sätze, die Ursache und Wirkung beschreiben.

1. Wer Zahnschmerzen hat,
2. Wer Kopfschmerzen hat,
3. Wer zu viel Sport treibt,
4. Wer sich in den Finger schneidet,
5. Wer im Winter im Meer schwimmen geht,
6. Wer viel zu viel Alkohol trinkt,

a. bekommt am nächsten Tag einen Muskelkater.
b. braucht ein Heftpflaster.
c. muss sich übergeben.
d. soll eine Schmerztablette nehmen.
e. wird sich erkälten.
f. soll zum Zahnarzt° gehen.

24 Studentenkrankheiten Kann ein Deutschstudium krank machen? Diese Studenten/Studentinnen behaupten° es jedenfalls°. Besprechen Sie mit einem Partner/einer Partnerin, wie sich die Kommilitonen und Kommilitoninnen fühlen. Dann erklären Sie, was sie jetzt machen sollen.

Augenschmerzen • Bauchschmerzen • Handgelenkschmerzen° • Kopfschmerzen • Ohrenschmerzen

BEISPIEL S1: *John hat die ganze Nacht ohne viel Licht sein Deutschbuch gelesen.*
S2: *Und wie fühlt er sich jetzt?*
S1: *Er hat Augenschmerzen. Ihm tun die Augen weh.*

1. John hat die ganze Nacht ohne viel Licht sein Deutschbuch gelesen.
2. Susie hat das ganze Wochenende intensiv gelernt. Jetzt ist ihr ganz heiß und sie kann sich nicht konzentrieren. Sie nimmt Aspirin.
3. Daniel war den ganzen Samstag im Sprachlabor° und hat sich Deutsch-CDs angehört, bis er nicht mehr konnte°.
4. Philip hat morgen ein Referat und ist ziemlich nervös. Er kaut° an seinen Fingernägeln, isst Chips, Salzstangen° und Nüsse° und trinkt viel.
5. Joan hat die Nacht beim Tippen° am Computer durchgemacht und hat gerade ihre Seminararbeit mit 30 Seiten abgegeben.

25 Was ist passiert? Ein Freund/Eine Freundin beklagt sich°. Was ist wahrscheinlich passiert? Stellen Sie Fragen. Wechseln Sie sich ab°.

BEISPIEL S1: *Ich habe Schmerztabletten genommen.*
S2: *Hast du Kopfschmerzen gehabt?*
S1: *Ja, ich habe Kopfschmerzen gehabt.*

sich den Arm gebrochen • sich in den Finger geschnitten • Durchfall / Kopfschmerzen / Zahnschmerzen / einen Muskelkater gehabt • sich erkältet • sich ausgeruht

1. Ich habe Schmerztabletten genommen.
2. Ich habe jetzt einen Gips am Arm.
3. Ich trage jetzt ein Heftpflaster am Finger.
4. Ich komme von der Massage zurück und fühle mich nicht mehr so steif°.
5. Ich komme von der Toilette zurück, aber der Bauch tut mir noch weh.
6. Der Zahnarzt hat mir einen Weisheitszahn° gezogen.
7. Ich brauche ein Taschentuch°.
8. Ich bin nicht mehr müde.

26 Wie fühlst du dich, wenn …? Wann fühlen Sie sich nicht wohl? Kreuzen Sie Ihre Antworten an. Fragen Sie dann einen Partner/eine Partnerin.

BEISPIEL   S1: *Ich fühle mich nicht wohl, wenn ich zu viel Alkohol trinke. Und du?*
S2: *Ich fühle mich auch nicht wohl, wenn ich zu viel Alkohol trinke.* (oder)
Ich fühle mich nicht wohl, wenn ich zu viel esse. Wie fühlst du dich, wenn du zu viel isst?

	Ich	Partner(in)
Ich fühle mich nicht wohl,		
1. wenn ich zu viel Alkohol trinke.	○	○
2. wenn ich zu viel esse.	○	○
3. wenn ich eine Prüfung in Physik habe.	○	○
4. wenn ich sehr früh° aufstehen muss.	○	○
5. wenn ich mit meinem Professor sprechen muss.	○	○
6. wenn ich am Telefon Deutsch sprechen muss.	○	○
7. wenn ich jeden Tag das Essen in der Mensa essen muss.	○	○

early

27 Freie Kommunikation: **Rollenspiel: Den Notarzt° anrufen.** Spielen Sie die folgende Situation mit einem Partner/einer Partnerin.

emergency room doctor

S1: Sie sind sehr krank. Es ist Samstag. Rufen Sie Dr. Meiser, den Notarzt/die Notärztin, an und beschreiben Sie ihm/ihr Ihre Symptome. Sagen Sie auch, was Sie gemacht haben, bevor Sie diese Symptome bekommen haben.

S2: Sie sind Dr. Meiser. Ihr Patient/Ihre Patientin ist sehr krank. Fragen Sie, wie er/sie sich fühlt, was er/sie gemacht hat und warum er/sie diese Symptome hat. Geben Sie ein paar Tipps.

DR. MEISER: *Dr. Meiser. Guten Tag.*
PATIENT(IN): *Guten Tag. Hier ist …*

28 Schreibecke: **Eine Entschuldigung.** Sie sollen heute ein Referat halten, aber es ist noch nicht fertig, und Sie wollen deshalb nicht zum Unterricht gehen. Schreiben Sie per E-Mail oder SMS eine Entschuldigung° an Ihren Dozenten/Ihre Dozentin. Schreiben Sie, dass Sie sehr krank sind und nicht kommen können. Beschreiben Sie drei Symptome, warum Sie diese Symptome haben und warum sie es unmöglich machen, zum Unterricht zu kommen. Dann schreiben Sie Ihren Plan, das Referat an einem anderen Tag zu halten.

excuse

Die beste Uni für mich

college preparatory high school
pass

Wer in Deutschland studieren will, muss zuerst auf dem Gymnasium° schriftlich sowie mündlich ein großes Examen, das Abitur, ablegen°. Die Noten auf dem „Abi" bestimmen, was und wo man studieren darf. Nach dem Abi kann man sich an verschiedenen Unis bewerben°.

sich bewerben: *apply*

frightening

gather

chosen
*decision / **ein Mädchen, das***
das Abitur ablegen muss

Für manche jungen Leute sind das furchterregende° Fragen: Was will ich studieren? Wo soll ich studieren? College-Berater wie in den USA gibt es nicht. Man muss allein Informationen sammeln° und hoffen, dass man die richtige Universität und das richtige Fach ausgewählt° hat. Wie trifft man so eine wichtige Entscheidung°? Im folgenden Text erzählt Jessie, eine junge Abiturientin°, von ihrer Reise durch die deutsche Uni-Landschaft.

filmfoto/Shutterstock.com

Vorschau

⊃ 29 Thematische Fragen Beantworten Sie die folgenden Fragen auf Deutsch.

1. An wie vielen Universitäten (Colleges) haben Sie sich beworben?
2. Warum studieren Sie an dieser Universität? Nennen Sie drei wichtige Faktoren.
3. Haben Sie ein Hauptfach? Wenn ja, wann haben Sie gewusst, dass Sie sich für dieses Fach interessieren? Im ersten Jahr? Später? Haben Sie ein Nebenfach oder ein zweites Hauptfach?
4. Wie früh sollen Studierende ihr Hauptfach wählen: in der Schule? Im ersten Jahr an der Uni? Später?
5. Wie sind die Dozenten und Dozentinnen und die Studierenden an Ihrer Uni?
6. Ist Ihre Unistadt für Studierende interessant? Was kann man da in der Freizeit machen?

Sprache im Alltag: **Studieren** vs. **lernen**

German distinguishes between **Schule** (*primary or secondary school*) and **Universität** (*post-secondary*) and between **Schüler/Schülerin** (*school pupil*) and **Student/ Studentin** (*university/college student*). In recent years it has become commonplace to refer to college students as **der** or **die Studierende** in the singular, and **Studierende/ die Studierenden** in the plural to avoid the necessity to specify masculine or feminine endings in the plural. The German verb **studieren** refers to university and college studies only: **Ich studiere Deutsch**. *I'm studying German* and implies that one is majoring in the field. **Lernen** refers to the acquisition of skills, e.g., **Ich lerne Deutsch** (*I'm studying German* [*for a test tomorrow or to just learn the language outside a college setting*]).

→ **30** Meine ideale Universität Wie wichtig waren Ihnen die folgenden Faktoren, als Sie eine Universität oder ein College gesucht haben?

	Sehr wichtig	Mittel- wichtig	Unwichtig	
1. ein gutes Ranking in meinem Fach	◯	◯	◯	
2. niedrige Studiengebühren°	◯	◯	◯	*niedrige* …: *low tuition*
3. die Stadt	◯	◯	◯	
4. eine gute Bibliothek	◯	◯	◯	
5. gute und nette Professoren	◯	◯	◯	
6. zufriedene Studierende	◯	◯	◯	
7. einfache Vorlesungen und Seminare	◯	◯	◯	
8. ein interessantes Sozialleben auf dem Campus	◯	◯	◯	
9. gutes Mensaessen	◯	◯	◯	
10. bequeme° und moderne Wohnheime	◯	◯	◯	*comfortable*
11. die Sportmannschaften	◯	◯	◯	
12. Multikulturalismus	◯	◯	◯	
13. moderne Einrichtungen° in den Klassenzimmern	◯	◯	◯	*equipment*
14. gute Praktika° in den Ferien	◯	◯	◯	*internships*
15. Studienmöglichkeiten im Ausland°	◯	◯	◯	*abroad*

Lesestrategien

→ **31** Den Kontext verstehen Finden Sie im Text Antworten auf die folgenden Fragen.

1. Was sind die Namen von drei Universitätsstädten in Deutschland?
2. Woher kommt Jessie?
3. Wie alt ist Jessie?
4. Was möchte sie studieren – Soziologie, Psychologie oder Englisch?

→ **32** Neue Wörter lernen: Erster Versuch „Die beste Uni für mich" handelt von Jessie, einer Schülerin, die eine Universität auswählen muss. Können Sie die Bedeutung von den folgenden Ausdrücken erraten°?

guess

1. die Abiturientin
2. das Fachwissen
3. der Lehrstuhl
4. das Praktikum (*pl.* Praktika)
5. die Studiendauer
6. sich einschreiben
7. Professoren und Studenten empfehlen die Uni.

33 Neue Wörter lernen: Drei Strategien Unten sind die Zitate° aus dem Text. Erraten Sie die fett gedruckten Wörter mithilfe von den drei folgenden Strategien. Beantworten Sie die Fragen.

quotes

world knowledge

Weltwissen°

1. „Nur noch wenige Monate bis zur **Einschreibung.** Der Countdown läuft."

   Neue Studierende an einer Universität müssen sich einschreiben, bevor sie offiziell studieren dürfen. Was ist wohl die **Einschreibung?**

2. „Professoren und Studenten empfehlen die Uni, die **Studiendauer** ist kurz und die **Ausstattung** top."

   • Die **Studiendauer** kann lang oder kurz sein. Was kann lang oder kurz sein: Geld? Zeit? Fächer?
   • Eine Universität braucht gute und neue Gegenstände im Labor, im Hörsaal und im Wohnheim. Was gehört wohl zur **Ausstattung:** die Professoren oder die Geräte und die Technologie im Klassenzimmer?

3. „Wie gut ist die **Betreuung** durch die Professoren?"

   Professoren unterrichten und halten Vorlesungen, aber sie sprechen auch mit Studierenden und helfen ihnen. Sie geben ihnen Tipps, Informationen und Ratschläge. Was heißt **Betreuung?**

4. „Welche Spezialisierungen gibt es am **Lehrstuhl?**"

   has

   Deutsche Universitäten haben Lehrstühle. Das sind keine richtigen Sitzplätze. Wer besitzt° einen **Lehrstuhl** an einer Uni: ein Professor oder ein Student?

Wortformen

1. „Die 20-Jährige hat sich nach dem Abi ein Jahr **Auszeit** genommen, um nachzudenken."

   Nach dreizehn Jahren Schule ist man oft müde. **Auszeit = aus + Zeit.** Was hat Jessie wahrscheinlich ein Jahr lang nach der Schule gemacht? Warum?

2. „Eigentlich hatte Jessie gar **keine große Lust …**"

   Das Wort **Lust** im Deutschen ist neutral und nicht stigmatisiert wie im Englischen. Hat Jessie viel oder wenig Interesse?

3. „Ein Studium ist keine **Einbahnstraße.**"

   direction
   change

   Städte haben Einbahnstraßen **(ein + Bahn + Straße),** d. h. alle Autos fahren in die gleiche Richtung°. Wie ist das Studium für viele Leute? Kann man die Richtung wechseln°?

4. „Und oft sind **Praktika** viel wichtiger für den **Berufseinstieg** als irgendwelches **Fachwissen.**"

   • Ein Universitätsstudium kann sehr theoretisch sein. Das, was man studiert, heißt „Fach". Ist Fachwissen **(Fach + wissen)** spezialisiertes oder generelles Wissen?
   • Viele Studierende arbeiten im Sommer, um Geld zu verdienen, aber nicht jede Sommerarbeit ist ein Praktikum. Was bedeutet wohl ein **Praktikum?**
   • Nach dem Studium muss man sicher praktisch sein und Geld verdienen. Ist der **Berufseinstieg** der Beginn von einem neuen Job oder der Beginn von Freizeit?

Kontext

1. „Nach zwölf oder dreizehn vorgezeichneten° Jahren sollen sie plötzlich **selbst entscheiden**, was zu ihnen passt. Von der Schule dürfen sie dabei keine Hilfe erwarten.“ *geplant, unflexibel*

   Auf der Schule sagen die Eltern und die Lehrer, was ein Kind machen soll. Wer sagt, was man machen soll, wenn man an die Uni geht? Was heißt **selbst entscheiden?**

2. „Weiter nach Jena. In der thüringischen Stadt fühlt sich Jessie gleich **wohl**. Jessie ist **beeindruckt** von der Vielfalt° des Faches Psychologie.“ *great variety*

   - Hat das Fach Psychologie einen positiven oder negativen Einfluss° auf Jessie? Was heißt **beeindruckt?** *influence*
   - Ist Jessie zufrieden in Jena? Was heißt **wohl?**

3. „Berlin ist Jessies Lieblingsstadt; Passau und Jena haben im Ranking **gut abgeschnitten**.“

   Wenn eine Uni unter anderen Unis **gut abschneidet**, hält man sie für eine gute oder eine nicht so gute Uni?

George Burba/Shutterstock.com

Die Universität Jena schneidet im Ranking gut ab.

34 Wichtige Wörter finden: deutsche Umgangssprache° *slang, colloquial speech*
Erraten Sie die Bedeutung von den folgenden Wörtern in den Ausdrücken von jungen Studierenden.

1. Der **Countdown** läuft.
   a. die letzte Phase
   b. die erste Phase

2. Nie mehr **büffeln**, was der Lehrplan vorschreibt°. *stipulates*
   a. kurz vor einer Prüfung intensiv lernen
   b. durch das ganze Semester diszipliniert lernen

3. Passau ist **ein Flop**.
   a. sehr gut
   b. sehr schlecht

4. Das Essen schmeckt **fade**.
   a. sehr interessant
   b. sehr uninteressant

5. Den Leuten fehlt° der **Pep**. *is lacking*
   a. die Energie
   b. die Müdigkeit

6. Sie findet es hier **spießig**.
   a. zu progressiv
   b. zu konservativ

7. Sie findet die Hauptstadt **klasse**.
   a. sehr gut
   b. sehr schlecht

Lesen Sie jetzt den Text.

Nur noch wenige Monate bis zur Einschreibung. Der Countdown läuft. Bald geht das Leben richtig los, bald kommt die große Freiheit. Ausziehen, weggehen, sich jeden Tag neu erfinden°! Nie mehr büffeln, was der Lehrplan vorschreibt – endlich lesen, denken, ausprobieren°, was einen wirklich interessiert. Jessie, Abiturientin aus München, freut sich auf „wilde
5 Diskussionen und neue Lebenswelten". Sie möchte „was mit Menschen machen". Sicher weiß sie nur eins: Sie will studieren. Die große Freiheit – für viele Abiturienten ist sie erst mal eine große Zumutung°. Nach zwölf oder dreizehn vorgezeichneten Jahren sollen sie plötzlich selbst entscheiden, was zu ihnen passt. Von der Schule dürfen sie dabei keine Hilfe erwarten.

„Ich will mit so vielen Menschen wie möglich reden, um mir am Ende aus vielen Meinungen
10 und Ansichten die eigene Wahrheit zu basteln°", sagt Jessie. Die 20-Jährige hat sich nach dem Abi ein Jahr Auszeit genommen, um nachzudenken. Eine Uni-Hopping-Tour soll Klarheit bringen. Passau, Jena, Berlin: Die Route bestimmen° Jessies Studienwünsche – und das Hochschulranking von *stern* und CHE (Centrum für Hochschulentwicklung), das größte und fundierteste Ranking, das jemals in Deutschland erhoben wurde°. Berlin ist
15 Jessies Lieblingsstadt°; Passau und Jena haben im Ranking gut abgeschnitten°. Jessie will sich in Vorlesungen und Seminare setzen, Professoren und Studenten befragen und natürlich auch Mensa und Nachtleben testen.

Passau ist ein Flop.
Beim Ranking im Fach
20 Betriebswirtschaft schneidet die Passauer Uni gut ab°: zufriedene Studenten, schnelles Studium. Dafür steht man an der Mensa
25 lange an°, das Essen schmeckt fade, und auch den Leuten fehlt der Pep, findet Jessie. Die Jungs da drüben tragen alle rosa Hemden. Und
30 die Mädchen neben ihnen, mit Stöckelschuhen° und Seidentüchern° – wie ihre eigenen Großmütter. Jessie schüttelt sich°. Irgendwie findet sie es hier eng°, spießig, konservativ.

Die Universitätsstadt Passau

Weiter nach Jena. In der thüringischen Stadt fühlt sich Jessie gleich wohl. Jessie ist
35 beeindruckt von der Vielfalt des Faches Psychologie. Und von den netten Dozenten: „Ich will Sie verfüüühren° – zum Studium der Psychologie!", ruft Professor Rainer Silbereisen und sieht ihr tief in die Augen. Jessie blinkert zurück: „Ich bin auf einmal sehr sicher, dass Psychologie richtig sein könnte° für mich", sagt sie.

Eigentlich hatte Jessie gar keine große Lust, nach Jena zu kommen, erst das gute
40 Abschneiden des Fachbereichs Psychologie im Hochschulranking hat sie überzeugt°: Professoren und Studenten empfehlen die Uni, die Studiendauer ist kurz und die Ausstattung top. Nicht nur Jessie reist mit dem Ranking im Rucksack. Immer mehr Abiturienten orientieren sich an den Ergebnissen.

Marginal glossary (left column):

sich neu erfinden: *to reinvent oneself / to try out*

burden

to create, construct

determine

jemals erhoben wurde: *was ever conducted / favorite city /* **haben gut abgeschnitten**: *fared well*

gut abschneiden: *to place well*

steht an: *stands in line*

high-heel shoes

silk scarves / **schüttelt sich:** *is horrified; literally: shakes herself / confining*

verführen: *to entice, tempt*

could

positiv beeinflusst

Wenn Jessie das Ranking verfassen würde°, würde sie zusätzliche Kriterien einführen: die
45 besten Cafés, die besten Bars, die besten Clubs am Studienort.

verfassen ... : were to write

Mag ja sein, dass die Humboldt-Uni im Fachbereich Psychologie nicht immer in der
Spitzengruppe landet – aber Berlin macht vieles wett°. Nicht nur Jessie findet die Hauptstadt
klasse: Weil alle nach Berlin wollen, ist der Numerus clausus für Psychologie hier besonders
hoch. Zwischen 1,2 und 1,5 lag er in

macht ... : makes up for that

50 den letzten Semestern. Trotzdem ist sie
zufrieden mit ihrer Uni-Tour: „Die Reise
hat mir super geholfen. Ich weiß jetzt,
worauf ich achten muss: Wie gut ist die
Betreuung durch die Professoren? Gibt
55 es Möglichkeiten, ins Ausland zu gehen?
Welche Spezialisierungen gibt es am
Lehrstuhl? Fühle ich mich in der Stadt
und unter den Mitstudenten wohl?"
Vor allem eins ist ihr klar geworden: Ein
60 Studium ist keine Einbahnstraße. Man ist
nicht auf eine Richtung festgelegt, sondern
kann ganz unterschiedliche Schwerpunkte
setzen. Und oft sind Praktika viel
wichtiger für den Berufseinstieg als
65 irgendwelches Fachwissen. Wer zum
Beispiel später Manager auf Auslandsein-
sätze vorbereiten° will, kann das mit einem
Psychologiestudium machen – oder mit
einem Wirtschaftsstudium. Nichts ist plan-
70 bar°: Jessies Vater hat Literatur studiert –
heute betreibt er einen Holzhandel°. Ihre
Mutter wollte Kunstlehrerin werden – als
sie das erste Mal vor einer Klasse stand,
merkte sie: „Ich kann das nicht!" Heute ist
75 sie Kunsttherapeutin°.

Christian Bach - ullsteinbild/The Granger Collection

Am Haupteingang der Humboldt-Universität zu Berlin

von Nikola Sellmair in **stern**, *16/2002*

prepare

capable of being planned
lumber business

art therapist

Rückblick

⊡ 35 Stimmt das? Stimmen diese Aussagen zum Text? Wenn nicht, was stimmt?

	Ja, das stimmt.	Nein, das stimmt nicht.
1. Jessie will studieren, und sie weiß, was und wo sie studieren will.	○	○
2. Nicht alle Abiturienten/Abiturientinnen freuen sich, alles selbst zu entscheiden.	○	○
3. Jessie will direkt vom Gymnasium zur Uni gehen und ihr Studium beginnen.	○	○
4. Jessie will die Unis in Passau und in Jena besuchen, weil sie im Ranking weit oben liegen.	○	○
5. Das Ranking vom Fachbereich Psychologie in Jena hat Jessie sehr interessiert.	○	○
6. Passau gefällt Jessie, weil das Mensa-Essen prima° schmeckt und die Studierenden so ambitioniert sind.	○	○
7. Jena findet Jessie langweilig und die Professoren im Fachbereich Psychologie aggressiv.	○	○
8. Die Humboldt-Universität in Berlin gefällt Jessie, weil der Fachbereich Psychologie zu den Besten gehört.	○	○
9. Für Jessie ist ein Programm mit Möglichkeiten für Praktika und Auslandsstudium wichtig.	○	○

top-notch

⊡ 36 Kriterien Welche „typischen" und welche persönlichen Kriterien sind für Jessie wichtig, wenn sie eine Universität wählt?

1. eine Stadt, wo sie sich „wohl" fühlt
2. die Ausstattung der Universität
3. Studenten, die „modern" sind
4. Spezialisierungen am Lehrstuhl
5. Professoren, die berühmt° sind
6. billige Wohnmöglichkeiten
7. Möglichkeit, im Ausland zu studieren
8. Betreuung durch die Professoren
9. gutes Essen
10. gut im Fach Psychologie
11. kurze Studiendauer
12. viel Sport an der Uni
13. Cafés, Bars, Clubs
14. Studenten mit Energie
15. Möglichkeit für Praktika
16. in der Nähe von München

famous

Complete the Ergänzen Sie activity in the Student Activities Manual before doing the next activity.

plans
future

⊡ 37 Kurz gefragt Beantworten Sie diese Fragen kurz auf Deutsch.

1. Was finden viele Abiturienten so schwierig?
2. Wie will Jessie die beste Entscheidung treffen?
3. Für welche drei Unis interessiert sich Jessie am Anfang? Warum?
4. Was gefällt Jessie an Berlin und was ist eigentlich nicht so gut für Jessies Pläne°?
5. Wie wichtig findet Jessie ihr Studium für ihre Zukunft°?
6. Welche Beispiele kennt Jessie persönlich, warum man sich nicht immer auf einen Beruf vorbereiten kann?

→ **38** Textdetektiv: **Absprungtext.** Use the *Absprungtext* to recognize important aspects of German structure and usage.

1. Check the *Absprungtext* for the following features and determine whether the style of the text is on balance formal or informal.

Text feature	Formal	Informal
Focus	on groups and the abstract	on individuals and examples
Perspective	objective, third person, reporting	subjective, first person, direct speech
Sentence structure	long, complex sentences	short, simple sentences
Word choice	specialized vocabulary intended for experts	common words used in everyday conversations
Text structure	linear structure that builds logically toward a conclusion	cyclical structure that recycles ideas

   The text is primarily _____ in style.   a) formal   b) informal

2. Which words from the list below are intended to reflect language used by youth?

   Countdown • Hochschulranking • klasse • Flop • Fachbereich • Betriebswirtschaft • Uni-Hopping-Tour • basteln

3. Which sentences reflect a third person perspective?
   a. Ich will mit so vielen Menschen wie möglich reden.
   b. Dafür steht man an der Mensa lange an.
   c. Irgendwie findet sie es hier eng, spießig, konservativ.
   d. Die Reise hat mir super geholfen.

4. For whom do you think this text was written?
   a. for professors wanting to know just how good their university is
   b. for parents seeking to advise their children on a good choice for their studies
   c. for students trying to decide what and where to study
   d. for retailers wanting to determine what to sell to students

5. This text best serves to ...
   a. offer serious advice on how to select a university.
   b. address the agony of choice from a personal perspective.
   c. provide an objective overview of German universities.
   d. push students toward the study of psychology.

6. Which of these examples from the text contain reflexive pronouns?

Example from the text	Yes, a reflexive.	No, not a reflexive.
a. Die 20-Jährige hat **sich** nach dem Abi ein Jahr Auszeit genommen.	○	○
b. Jessie will **sich** in Vorlesungen und Seminare setzen.	○	○
c. Fühle ich **mich** in der Stadt und unter den Mitstudenten wohl?	○	○
d. Immer mehr Abiturienten orientieren **sich** an den Ergebissen.	○	○
e. Die Reise hat **mir** super geholfen.	○	○

Das deutsche Universitätssystem

To limit the number of students to the number of university spots (**Studienplätze**) available, universities have established maximum enrollments (**Numerus clausus**, literally "closed number") in many high-demand subject areas, such as business administration, biochemistry, international relations, law, and psychology. Selection for these spots depends primarily on a student's grade on the **Abitur** (**das Abiturergebnis**), and secondarily on the number of semesters the student has waited for admission. Die **Stiftung für Hochschulzulassung** in Dortmund is a clearinghouse for students applying nationally for admission in medicine, veterinary science, dentistry, or pharmacology. A new national admisions service (**Dialogorientiertes Serviceverfahren**) for other **Numerus clausus** subjects is forthcoming. In general students need to apply to each university individually.

Passing the **Abitur** signals the completion of a German student's liberal arts education. There are no general education requirements at German universities. First-year students typically begin taking classes in their majors – for example, business administration, law, medicine – in their first semester at college.

Globalization and the need for standardization within the European Union prompted German universities to introduce 3- to 4-year bachelor's degree programs and an internationally recognized master's degree program by 2010. Some uniquely German degree programs remain in place like **das Staatsexamen** for teachers and lawyers, which require a first and second exam after a period of on-the-job training, and the advanced **Diplom** for engineers, economists, artists, and musicians.

GESAMTWERTUNG

Rangplätze in den Einzelfächern
● Spitzengruppe ○ Mittelfeld ● Schlussgruppe

GESAMTERGEBNIS RANG	UNIVERSITÄT	PUNKTZAHL	Betriebs-wirtschaft	Chemie	Germa-nistik	Informatik	Maschinen-bau	Medizin	Politologie	Psycho-logie
1	München, TU	3,0	●	●		●	●	●		
2	Freiburg, U	2,9		●	●	●		●	●	●
3	Leipzig, U	2,7	○	●	●	●		●	●	●
4	Berlin, Humboldt-U	2,6	○	●	●	●		●	●	○
4	Konstanz, U	2,6		●	○	●		●	●	●
4	München, U	2,6	●	●	●	●		●	●	●
7	Heidelberg, U	2,5		●	●	●		●	●	○
7	Stuttgart, U	2,5	●	○	●	●	●	●		
7	Tübingen, U	2,5	○	●	●	●		●	●	●
10	Augsburg, U	2,4	○		●	●		●		
10	Mannheim, U	2,4	●		●	●		●	○	
12	Kaiserslautern, TU	2,3	○	○		●	●			
12	Würzburg, U	2,3	○	●	●	●		●	○	○
14	Jena, U	2,2	●	●	●	●		○	○	○
14	Münster, U	2,2	○	○	○	●		●	○	○
16	Berlin, FU	2,1	●	●	○	○		●	○	○
16	Bonn, U	2,1	○	●	○	●		●	○	○
16	Darmstadt, TU	2,1	○	●		●	●		○	●

Reprinted by permission of Spiegel.

Im Ranking können Abiturienten erkennen, welche Unis gut sind.

Kulturkreuzung

general education / take

Deutsche Studierende müssen keine allgemeinbildenden° Kurse belegen°, denn sie haben das meiste schon in der Schule gehabt. Wie finden Sie das? Möchten Sie an der Uni nur Kurse in Ihrem Hauptfach belegen und dafür schon an der *High School* schwierige allgemeinbildende Kurse machen? Welches System finden Sie besser? Warum?

39 Zum Überlegen Denken Sie über die folgenden Fragen nach. *Achtung:* Sie können sie nicht direkt aus dem Text beantworten.

1. Welche von Jessies Ranking-Kriterien finden Sie auch wichtig?
2. Jessie scheint° geografisch sehr flexibel zu sein. Glauben Sie, dass auch andere Schüler so flexibel sind? Warum? Warum nicht?
3. Wo möchten Sie eventuell° in Deutschland studieren? Warum?
4. Wie wichtig sind Praktika, Erfahrung im Ausland oder Fremdsprachen für Ihren zukünftigen Beruf?
5. Wir wissen, dass Jessie 20 Jahre alt ist. Wie stellen Sie sich Jessie sonst noch vor? Wie sieht sie aus? Welche Kleidung trägt sie gern? Welche Musik hört sie gern? Was macht sie in ihrer Freizeit? Arbeitet sie? Hat sie Geschwister° – und wenn ja, ist sie die Älteste oder vielleicht die Jüngste? Wird sie eine gute Studentin sein? Begründen Sie Ihre Antworten.

seems

perhaps

Brüder oder Schwestern

40 Die Vor- und Nachteile von meinem Studium Welche Aspekte von Ihrem Studium finden Sie positiv? Welche negativ? Vergleichen Sie Ihre Liste mit der Liste von einem Partner/einer Partnerin.

	Positiv	Negativ
1. die Dozenten und Professoren	○	○
2. die Kontaktmöglichkeiten	○	○
3. die Kurse	○	○
4. meine Kommilitonen/Kommilitoninnen	○	○
5. die Arbeitsatmosphäre	○	○
6. die Bibliothek	○	○
7. die Arbeitsmöglichkeiten	○	○
8. die Studienberatung°	○	○
9. die Ausstattung der Klassenräume und Labors	○	○

Studienberatung: academic advising

S.Borisov/Shutterstock.com

Die Universität Salzburg in Österreich. Im Hintergrund sieht man die Festung Hohensalzburg.

Interview: Mein Studentenleben Beantworten Sie die folgenden Fragen zuerst für sich. Stellen Sie sie dann einem Partner/einer Partnerin.

	Ich	Partner(in)
1. Was studierst du?	_____	_____
2. Welche Kurse belegst du?	_____	_____
3. Wie viele Kurse mit Lehrassistenten° hast du?	_____	_____
4. Wo lernst du normalerweise? In der Bibliothek? Zu Hause?	_____	_____
5. Wie viele Stunden lernst du jeden Tag?	_____	_____
6. Wie viele Stunden verbringst du pro Woche in der Bibliothek? Online?	_____	_____
7. Wie viele Referate oder Klassenarbeiten schreibst du dieses Semester?	_____	_____
8. Wie oft schreibst du eine Prüfung?	_____	_____
9. Hast du dieses Semester einen Nebenjob?	_____	_____
10. Hast du noch Zeit für Sport oder andere Hobbys?	_____	_____

teaching assistants (glosses for items 3)

👥 42 **Wie es bei uns ist** Das Studium in den USA und in Kanada ist in vielen Aspekten ganz anders als das Studium in deutschsprachigen Ländern. Wie unterscheidet° sich Ihr Studium von einem mitteleuropäischen Studium? Besprechen Sie diese Fragen in einer kleinen Gruppe von drei bis fünf Personen. Berichten Sie dann der Klasse Ihre Ergebnisse.

differs

1. Haben Sie auch eine Uni-Hopping-Tour gemacht und viele Unis besucht? Welche Unis haben Sie besucht?
2. Gibt es auch hier wie in Deutschland keine Diskussionen und keine Prüfungen in Vorlesungen?
3. Halten Sie lieber ein Referat oder schreiben Sie lieber eine Prüfung? Warum?
4. Was sind die Vor- und Nachteile von Gruppenreferaten oder Einzelreferaten?
5. Ist es hier typisch, Dozenten/Dozentinnen in der Sprechstunde zu besuchen? Warum?
6. Wie finden Sie Ihre Studiengebühren? Wie finanzieren Sie Ihr Studium: mit Darlehen° von der Bank, mit einem Stipendium° von der Uni oder mit Nebenjobs?

loans / scholarship

Viele Studierende haben einen Nebenjob.

Wie Studierende ihr Studium finanzieren

College in Germany has traditionally been tuition-free. Students only paid nominal adminstration and social fees. However, by 2005 a number of **Bundesländer** – including Baden-Württemberg, Bavaria, Hamburg, Lower Saxony and North Rhine-Westphalia – had introduced semester tuition fees of € 300 to € 500. Baden-Württemberg has since eliminated the fees. In the other **Bundesländer,** college remains tuition-free. Students pay for their own living expenses, books, and supplies. Residence halls and meals in the university cafeteria are subsidized by the government. Students can receive monthly financial aid through a national loan system known as **BAföG (Bundesausbildungsförderungsgesetz),** named after the law that provides for it. Half of **BAföG** is a grant-in-aid; the other half is an interest-free loan that gets repaid only after the student has completed his degree program. Regardless of the total **BaföG** received, no one is required to repay the government more than € 10,000.

Because of the relatively low cost of education, German students historically did not need to hold part-time jobs during the academic year. However, student habits are changing. Many take on short-term or part-time work, but they are not allowed to work more than 20 hours a week or more than 50 days during semester vacations (**Semesterferien**) to keep their income tax-free.

Oberhaeuser/Caro/ullstein bild/The Image Works

Diese Studentin verdient relativ viel Geld als Kellnerin.

Due to several influences, e.g., the European Union, widespread use of the English language, and the growth of international business, Germany has seen an increase in prestigious private universities to over 100 accredited institutions, among them 12 private universities, 87 **Fachhochschulen** and colleges, and two academies for art and music. Many of them teach classes in English to an international study body. Tuition for some fields of study may be as much as 30,000 Euros per year, but because of better study conditions students may be able to complete their degree programs a year earlier than their public school counterparts.

Kulturkreuzung

In Europa kostet ein Universitätsstudium generell weniger Geld als in den USA oder in Kanada. In Europa meint man, dass alle Bürger von guten Universitäten profitieren, nicht nur die Studierenden selbst. Darum zahlt der Staat die meisten Kosten und die Studierenden zahlen keine oder nur niedrige Studiengebühren. In den USA und in Kanada sind die meisten Universitäten und Colleges ziemlich teuer. Finden Sie das akzeptabel? Wie finanzieren Studierende das Studium in Ihrem Land?

Strukturen

 Talking about future events

Future time

A. The present tense with a time expression

You have already learned that German speakers commonly express the future with a present tense verb and a future time expression, such as **morgen, nächste Woche, im Sommer.**

> Morgen fliege ich nach Berlin.   *I'm going to fly to Berlin tomorrow.*

Time expressions (**Zeitausdrücke**) frequently begin German sentences. This helps organize the sequence of events chronologically in a narrative. Once a future time expression establishes the time frame, other future time expressions are not necessary in subsequent sentences.

> Morgen um 7.00 Uhr stehe ich auf.   *I'll get up at 7 A.M. tomorrow.*
> (Morgen) Um 8.00 Uhr fahre ich   *I'll drive to the airport at 8 A.M.*
>   zum Flughafen.   *(tomorrow).*

Remember that expressions of time always precede expressions of place.

>   *verb   time   place*
> Ich <u>fliege</u> <u>morgen</u> <u>nach Berlin</u>.   *I'm going to fly to Berlin tomorrow.*

Here are some time expressions German speakers frequently use. All of them can be used to talk about the future. Some of them will already be familiar to you.

heute	*today*
heute Morgen (Nachmittag, Abend)	*this morning (afternoon, evening/tonight)*
morgen	*tomorrow*
morgen früh (Nachmittag, Abend)	*tomorrow morning (afternoon, evening)*
übermorgen	*the day after tomorrow*
später	*later*
am Wochenende (am Freitag, am Abend)	*on the weekend (on Friday, in the evening / at night)*
im Sommer (im Juli)	*in the summer (in July)*
in zwei Tagen (Wochen, Monaten, Jahren)	*in two days (weeks, months, years)*
diese Woche (dieses Wochenende, diesen Freitag)	*this week (this weekend, this Friday)*
nächste Woche (nächstes Wochenende, nächsten Freitag)	*next week (next weekend, next Friday)*
jede Woche (jedes Wochenende, jeden Freitag)	*every week (every weekend, every Friday)*

Time expressions with **an** and **in** occur in the dative case and express specific points in time.

> **Am Montag** haben wir Deutsch.   *We have German on Monday.*
> **Im Sommer** arbeiten viele Studenten.   *A lot of students work in the summer.*

Time expressions that take the accusative don't need a preposition. They can also express specific points in time.

> **Nächsten** Freitag haben wir eine Prüfung.   *We have a test next Friday.*

†† 43 Wann machst du das? Fragen Sie einen Partner/eine Partnerin, wann diese Situationen in der Zukunft stattfinden°. Benutzen Sie Zeitausdrücke aus der Liste oben.

take place

> S1: *Wann bringst du die Bücher in die Bibliothek zurück?*
> S2: *Morgen früh bringe ich die Bücher zurück.*

1. Wann lernst du mit Freunden für die Prüfung?
2. Wann gehst du zu deinem Dozenten/ deiner Dozentin in die Sprechstunde?
3. Wann triffst du Freunde in der Mensa?
4. Wann musst du zum Zahnarzt gehen?
5. Wann ist die nächste Deutschprüfung?
6. Wann fährst du nach Hause?
7. Wann treibst du Sport?
8. Wann gehst du in die Bibliothek?
9. Wann putzt du dir die Zähne?
10. Wann beginnen die Semesterferien?

wavebreakmedia ltd/Shutterstock.com

B. The future tense: *werden* + infinitive

Besides using the present tense with a future time expression, German speakers also use the future tense (**das Futur**) to describe events in the future. The **Futur** consists of the auxiliary or helping verb **werden** with an infinitive at the end of the clause. The **Futur** may be used with or without a future time adverbial.

Wie lange **wird** das Referat dauern?	*How long will the presentation last?*
Bei diesem Wetter **wirst** du dich erkälten!	*You'll catch a cold in this weather!*

The word **Futur** is only a grammatical term and is not used in conversation to refer to the future (**die Zukunft**).

Note the spelling changes in the verb **werden: e > i** in the 2nd, informal, and 3rd persons (**wirst, wird**) and the loss of **d** in the 2nd, informal person (**wirst**).

werden bauen: *will (be going to) build*	
Singular	**Plural**
ich **werde** bauen	wir **werden** bauen
du **wirst** bauen	ihr **werdet** bauen
Sie **werden** bauen	Sie **werden** bauen
er/sie/es **wird** bauen	sie **werden** bauen

When used with the first-person pronouns, the future tense with **werden** can express a mild promise if directed toward another person.

Ich **werde** einen Beamer für Sie **bestellen.**	*I will/am going to order a data projector for you.*

With a reflexive verb in the future tense, the reflexive pronoun occurs immediately after **werden** or after the subject if it is positioned midsentence: **Du wirst dich bei diesem Wetter erkälten.**

Be careful not to confuse the modal verb **wollen** (*to want to*) with English *will*.

Ich **will** nach Deutschland fliegen.	*I **want** to fly to Germany.*
Ich **werde** nach Deutschland fliegen.	*I **will** fly to Germany.*

44 Meine Pläne nach dem Studium Kreuzen Sie zuerst an, was für Sie stimmt. Fragen Sie dann einen Partner/eine Partnerin.

distinction

BEISPIEL S1: *Ich werde mein Diplom mit Auszeichnung° machen.*
Wirst du auch dein Diplom mit Auszeichnung machen?
S2: *Ja, ich werde auch mein Diplom mit Auszeichnung machen. (oder)*
Nein, ich werde es nicht mit Auszeichnung machen.

	Ich	Partner(in)
Ich werde ...		
1. mein Diplom mit Auszeichnung machen.	○	○
2. andere Kontinente sehen, bevor ich mir meine erste Arbeitsstelle suche.	○	○
3. in einer neuen, unbekannten Großstadt leben.	○	○
4. in meine Heimatstadt zurückkehren°.	○	○
5. promovieren und meinen Doktor machen.	○	○
6. ein Haus kaufen.	○	○
7. Präsident/Präsidentin von den USA werden.	○	○
8. eine große Familie mit vielen Kindern haben.	○	○
9. mich auf meine Karriere° konzentrieren.	○	○

in ... : go back to my home-town

career

45 Feste Termine machen Ein Freund/Eine Freundin fragt, ob Sie oder andere diese Dinge machen werden. Antworten Sie affirmativ mit **werden** und geben Sie eine Zeit an. Benutzen Sie Zeitausdrücke wie **heute, heute Abend, später, morgen, nächste Woche, nächstes Jahr** usw.

BEISPIEL S1: *Kannst du mir bei den Hausaufgaben helfen?*
S2: *Ja, sicher. Morgen werde ich dir bei den Hausaufgaben helfen.*

1. Kannst du mir bei den Hausaufgaben helfen?
2. Schreibt dein Freund deine Seminararbeit?
3. Kannst du mit mir in die Sprechstunde gehen?
4. Möchtet ihr meine Vorlesung in Betriebswirtschaft besuchen?
5. Kann deine Freundin mit uns ins Seminar gehen?
6. Gibt uns der Professor den Schlüssel zum Hörsaal?
7. Kannst du mir deinen Computer leihen?
8. Können deine Freunde mit in die Bibliothek gehen?

promise
responsibly / act

46 Ja, ich verspreche° es! Bevor Sie nach Deutschland reisen, müssen Sie Ihren Eltern versprechen, dort verantwortungsvoll° zu handeln°. Sagen Sie, was Sie machen und was Sie nicht machen werden.

BEISPIEL S1 (VATER/MUTTER): *Gehst du immer in die Vorlesung?*
S2 (TOCHTER/SOHN): *Ja, ich verspreche es, ich werde immer in die Vorlesung gehen. (oder)*
Nein, ich werde nicht immer in die Vorlesung gehen.

1. immer in die Vorlesung gehen
2. viel Zeit an der Uni verbringen
3. jeden Abend ausgehen
4. viele Partys besuchen
5. keinen Alkohol trinken
6. jedes Wochenende nach Paris fahren
7. einen deutschen Freund/eine deutsche Freundin finden und gleich heiraten
8. ins Museum und in die Oper gehen
9. sich auf Seminare vorbereiten

Strukturen

IV Expressing probability

The verb *werden* + *wohl*

When used with the adverb **wohl** (*probably*) and an infinitive, **werden** expresses probability.

Er **wird wohl** krank sein.	*He is probably sick.*

You have now learned these three uses of the verb **werden:**

1. As a main verb, meaning *to become, get.*

   Ich **werde** müde.   *I am getting tired.*

2. As an auxiliary verb that, together with an infinitive, designates future tense.

   Das Referat **wird** 45 Minuten **dauern**.   *The presentation will last 45 minutes.*

3. As an auxiliary verb that, together with the adverb **wohl** and an infinitive, expresses probability in the present tense.

   Stefan **wird wohl** nach Moskau fahren.   *Stefan is probably going to Moscow.*

---

†† 47 Pläne für nächstes Jahr Was werden Sie nächstes Jahr machen? Wählen Sie **werde, werde wohl** oder **werde nicht.** Fragen Sie dann einen Partner/eine Partnerin, was er/sie nächstes Jahr bestimmt machen wird, was er/sie wohl machen wird und was er/sie bestimmt nicht machen wird.

BEISPIEL   S1: *Wirst du dir nächstes Jahr einen Nebenjob suchen?*
S2: *Ja, ich werde mir wohl einen Nebenjob suchen.* (oder)
Nein, ich werde keinen Nebenjob suchen.

	werde	werde wohl	werde nicht
1. sich einen Nebenjob suchen	○	○	○
2. viele Seminararbeiten schreiben	○	○	○
3. viel Zeit in der Bibliothek verbringen	○	○	○
4. jeden Abend ausgehen	○	○	○
5. oft in die Sprechstunde gehen	○	○	○
6. neue Freunde kennenlernen	○	○	○
7. sich ein Praktikum suchen	○	○	○
8. jedes Wochenende intensiv lernen	○	○	○

†† 48 Interview: Pläne für die nähere Zukunft Stellen Sie einem Partner/einer Partnerin die folgenden Fragen.

BEISPIEL   S1: *Was wirst du heute nach dem Deutschkurs machen?*
S2: *Ich werde wohl (in die Mensa gehen).*

1. Was wirst du heute nach dem Deutschkurs machen?
2. Was wirst du heute Abend machen?
3. Was wirst du morgen früh machen?
4. Was wirst du übermorgen machen?
5. Wohin wirst du am Wochenende fahren?
6. Wann wirst du mit Freunden ausgehen?
7. Was wirst du im Sommer machen?

ᵢᵢ 49 Freie Kommunikation **Rollenspiel: Das Gruppenreferat.** Spielen Sie mit einem Partner/einer Partnerin die folgende Situation.

> S1: Sie sind Professor/Professorin. Sie halten jetzt Ihre Sprechstunde und wollen mit Repräsentanten von jeder Arbeitsgruppe über das Gruppenreferat sprechen. Stellen Sie Fragen über das Thema, die Vorbereitungen und die anderen Studenten/Studentinnen in der Arbeitsgruppe.
>
> S2: Sie sind Student/Studentin und gehen in die Sprechstunde von Ihrem Professor/Ihrer Professorin. Ihre Arbeitsgruppe hat noch kein Thema für das Referat, aber das dürfen Sie dem Professor/der Professorin nicht sagen.

ᵢᵢ 50 Rollenspiel: Die Sommerreise Spielen Sie mit einem Partner/einer Partnerin die folgende Situation.

> S1: Sie sind der Sohn/die Tochter. Sie haben eine Sommerreise geplant und möchten für eine Rucksack-Tour nach Europa fliegen. Sie haben nicht sehr viel Geld, aber viele Ideen. Erklären Sie Ihren Eltern, was Sie machen möchten.
>
> S2: Sie sind der Vater/die Mutter. Ihr Sohn/Ihre Tochter erzählt Ihnen, dass er/sie nach Europa fliegen möchte. Sie machen sich Sorgen, denn er/sie hat nicht viel Geld. Stellen Sie viele Fragen (z. B. **Wo wirst du schlafen? Was wirst du alles machen?**).

◁ 51 Schreibecke: **Ein Brief an Jessie.** Sie werden zwei Semester an der Universität in Jena studieren. Jessie hat schon ein Jahr in Jena studiert. Schreiben Sie einen Brief an Jessie. Stellen Sie sich vor° und beschreiben Sie Ihre Pläne für das Jahr in Deutschland. Stellen Sie Jessie ein paar Fragen über Wohnen, Arbeiten und Studieren in Jena.

sich vorstellen: to introduce oneself

Strukturen

Specifying additional information about actions

A. Using verbs with prepositional objects

Some German verbs may be accompanied by a preposition and its object, which offer more specific information about the activity expressed by the verb.

> **Konzentrieren** Sie **sich auf** das Wichtigste.　　*Concentrate on the most important things.*

The meaning of a verb + prepositional object can change when the preposition changes.

> Wir freuen uns **auf** die Reise nach Spanien.　　*We're looking forward to the trip to Spain.*
>
> Wir freuen uns **über** die Universität.　　*We're happy about the university.*

The German preposition does not necessarily have an obvious English equivalent. It needs to be learned together with the verb and the required case.

Here are some important verb-preposition combinations grouped according to case and preposition.

1. Preposition + accusative case

an + *accusative*

denken an (hat gedacht)	*to think of*
sich erinnern an (hat sich erinnert)	*to remember*
glauben an (hat geglaubt)	*to believe in*

auf + *accusative*

achten auf (hat geachtet)	*to pay attention to*
sich freuen auf (hat sich gefreut)	*to look forward to*
gespannt sein auf (ist gespannt gewesen)	*to be excited about*
hoffen auf	*to hope for*
sich konzentrieren auf (hat sich konzentriert)	*to concentrate on*
sich vor•bereiten auf (hat sich vorbereitet)	*to prepare for, get ready for*
warten auf (hat gewartet)	*to wait for*

für + *accusative*

danken für (hat gedankt)	*to thank for*
sich entscheiden für (hat sich entschieden)	*to decide on, in favor of*
halten für (hält, hat gehalten)	*to consider/think (someone) is (something)*
sich interessieren für (hat sich interessiert)	*to be interested in*

in + *accusative*

sich verlieben in (hat sich verliebt)	*to fall in love with*

über + *accusative*

sich freuen über (hat sich gefreut)	*to be happy about*
lachen über	*to laugh about*
reden/sprechen über (redet/spricht, hat geredet/gesprochen)	*to talk about*
sich ärgern über (hat sich geärgert)	*to get angry about*

um + *accusative*

bitten um (hat gebeten)	*to ask for, request*

> **sich entscheiden gegen** means *to decide against*

2. Preposition + dative case

nach + *dative*

fragen nach (hat gefragt)	*to ask about*

von + *dative*

erwarten von (hat erwartet)	*to expect of*
erzählen von (hat erzählt)	*to tell a story about, talk about*
halten von (hält, hat gehalten)	*to think of, about*
handeln von (hat gehandelt)	*to be about*
sich trennen von (hat sich getrennt)	*to break up with, separate from*
etwas verstehen von (hat verstanden)	*to know something about*
wissen von (weiß, hat gewusst)	*to know about*

vor + *dative*

Angst haben vor (hat Angst gehabt)	*to be afraid of*

zu + *dative*

passen zu (hat gepasst)	*to fit, go with*

> **Handeln von** is used to talk about plots in stories, e.g., **Die Geschichte handelt von einem alten Mann.**

Als Tourist in Stuttgart Verbinden Sie die richtigen Satzteile.

1. Stuttgart erinnert mich ein bisschen …
2. Es regnet seit Tagen. Wir hoffen …
3. Vergiss nicht! Du sollst eine E-Mail …
4. Pass auf! Du musst besser …
5. Ich bin wirklich böse …
6. Wir warten noch fünf Minuten …
7. Unser Busfahrer bittet uns …
8. Gehen wir ins Hallenbad. Dann springe ich gleich …
9. Wenn ich dieses Foto wieder zu Hause sehe, werde ich immer …

a. auf die Verkehrszeichen achten.
b. ins warme Wasser.
c. an meine Heimatstadt – Pittsburgh.
d. um etwas Geduld.
e. auf ihn, dann laufen wir!
f. auf gutes Wetter.
g. an deinen Freund zu Hause schreiben.
h. an die schöne Zeit in Stuttgart denken.
i. auf unseren Reiseleiter°. Er kommt zu spät.

tour guide

→ **53** Annas Jahr in Deutschland Ergänzen Sie die Sätze mit der richtigen Präposition (**an, auf, für, in, über, um, von, vor**).

Anna Adler hat sich immer (1) _____ Deutschland interessiert. Am Anfang war sie sich nicht sicher, ob sie in Hamburg oder Tübingen studieren sollte°. Sie war natürlich gespannt (2) _____ das Jahr in Deutschland, aber sie hatte auch etwas Angst (3) _____ der Reise

should

Sie hat mit ihren Eltern und mit ihrer Deutschlehrerin in Ft. Wayne (4) _____ die Vorteile und die Nachteile von beiden Unis gesprochen. Ihre Eltern haben sehr viel Positives (5) _____ Hamburg erzählt. Sie hat auch ihre Deutschlehrerin gefragt, was sie (6) _____ Tübingen weiß. Dann hat sie sich (7) _____ Tübingen entschieden. Sie hält Tübingen (8) _____ die bessere Alternative.

even though / for that reason
had to

Anna hat sich gut (9) _____ das Jahr vorbereitet und profitiert sehr von der Erfahrung. Sie freut sich täglich (10) _____ ihre Entscheidung, in Tübingen zu studieren, obwohl° sie sich deshalb° für eine Zeit lang (11) _____ ihrer Familie und ihren Freunden trennen musste°. Bald ist das Jahr aber zu Ende und sie denkt wieder (12) _____ ihre Freunde und Familie in den USA. Jetzt freut sie sich natürlich auch (13) _____ ihre Heimkehr, aber sie wird sich immer (14) _____ ihr Jahr in Deutschland gern erinnern.

B. Using *da-* and *wo-*compounds

The prefix **da** is used with a preposition when the object of that preposition is a pronoun, e.g., **dafür, damit.** This **da**-compound only refers to objects that are things and not people.

Haben Sie etwas gegen dieses Thema?	*Do you object to this topic?*
—Nein, ich habe nichts **dagegen**.	*—No, I don't object to it.*
Haben Sie etwas gegen Carlos?	*Do you have something against Carlos?*
—Nein, ich habe nichts **gegen ihn**.	*—No, I don't have anything against him.*

Prepositions beginning with a vowel require that an **r** be inserted after **da,** e.g., **da+r+an.**

Ich kann mich nicht **daran** erinnern.	*I don't remember that.*
Er hat sich wochenlang **darauf** vorbereitet.	*He prepared himself for it for weeks.*
Ist schon Milch und Zucker **darin**?	*Is there already milk and sugar in it?*

In speech, **darum, daran,** and **darin** contract to **drum, dran,** and **drin.**

The prefix **wo-** is used with a preposition to form a question when the object is inanimate. Prepositions beginning with a vowel require that an **r** be inserted between **wo** and the preposition.

Wofür hat er sich entschieden?	*What did he decide on?*
Worauf freut ihr euch?	*What are you looking forward to?*

To refer to people, speakers use a preposition with **wen** (accusative) or **wem** (dative).

Woran erinnern Sie sich?	*What do you remember?*
An wen erinnern Sie sich?	*Whom do you remember?*
Wovon handelt das Buch?	*What is the book about?*
Von wem handelt das Buch?	*Whom is the book about?*

---

 54 Worauf wartet Anna? Beantworten Sie die folgenden Fragen.

BEISPIEL   Anna steht an der Bushaltestelle. Worauf wartet sie?
Sie wartet auf den Bus.

1. Anna steht an der Bushaltestelle. Worauf wartet sie?
2. Sie braucht Auskunft, wann der Bus abfährt. Worum bittet sie?
3. Im Bus muss sie eine dumme Hausaufgabe für Deutsch schreiben. Worüber ärgert sie sich?
4. Claudia will nächstes Jahr aufs Gymnasium gehen. Wofür hat sie sich entschieden?
5. Karl und Stefan haben heute eine Prüfung. Worauf bereiten sie sich vor?
6. Am Wochenende gibt Barbara eine Party. Worauf freut sie sich?
7. Karl hat seine Bücher vergessen. Woran hat er sich nicht erinnert?
8. Stefan versteht das Thema in Physik kaum. Wovon versteht er nicht viel?
9. Stefan muss einen Bericht für Physik schreiben. Wovor hat er Angst?
10. Nächste Woche hat Stefan zwei Prüfungen. Woran denkt er?

 55 Was macht Karl? Stellen Sie einem Partner/einer Partnerin eine Frage mit **wo(r)-** oder **wen/wem**.

BEISPIEL   Karl hat sich in Inge verliebt.
S1: *In wen hat er sich verliebt?*
S2: *Er hat sich in Inge verliebt.*

1. Karl hat sich in Inge verliebt.
2. Inge hat sich an Karls Geburtstag erinnert.
3. Karl ist gespannt auf die Party heute Abend.
4. Karl und Inge warten auf die Gäste.
5. Die Gäste reden über Karl.
6. Karl hält nicht viel von Rapmusik.
7. Die Gäste freuen sich über das leckere° Essen.
8. Inge hat auch an alkoholfreie Getränke gedacht.
9. Anna erzählt von ihrer Reise nach Mainz.
10. Karl achtet nicht auf die Zeit.

delicious

†† 56 Gespräch über das Studentenleben Stellen Sie einem Partner/einer Partnerin diese Fragen über das Studentenleben.

1. Warum hast du dich für Deutsch als Fremdsprache entschieden?
2. Worauf freust du dich am meisten im Herbst? Im Winter? Im Frühling?
3. Vor welchen Kursen (oder Professoren/Professorinnen) hast du Angst?
4. Auf welche Kurse (Professoren/Professorinnen) bist du gespannt?
5. Was hält man von den und den Kursen in deinem Hauptfach?
6. Worüber hast du dich in der letzten Zeit geärgert?
7. Wovon handelt dein Lieblingsfilm?
8. Über welche aktuellen Themen redet man auf diesem Campus?

academic advisor

†† 57 Freie Kommunikation: **Rollenspiel: Gespräch mit dem Studienberater°.** Spielen Sie die folgende Situation mit einem Partner/einer Partnerin.

awfully

> S1: Sie sind Student/Studentin. Ihre Noten sind dieses Semester schrecklich° schlecht, Sie haben Pech mit Ihrem Mitbewohner/Ihrer Mitbewohnerin, Sie haben Ihren Job verloren, und Sie sind frustriert. Sie überlegen sich, ob Sie mit dem Studium aufhören sollen. Sie melden sich bei Ihrem Berater und reden darüber.
>
> S2: Sie sind Berater/Beraterin. Sie halten diesen Studenten/diese Studentin für sehr talentiert, aber Sie verstehen auch die Frustration. Geben Sie ihm/ihr Rat. Stellen Sie Fragen, sagen Sie Ihre Meinung, machen Sie Vorschläge und helfen Sie dem Studenten/der Studentin, sich richtig zu entscheiden.

58 Schreibecke: **Interviews mit Prominenten.** Sie schreiben einen Zeitungsartikel über eine prominente Person. Nächste Woche machen Sie ein Interview mit dieser Person. Überlegen Sie sich jetzt schon, welche Fragen Sie stellen möchten. Schreiben Sie sieben bis zehn Fragen auf. Benutzen Sie die Ausdrücke aus der Liste.

Angst haben vor • glauben an • fragen nach • erzählen von • sich ärgern über • sich vorbereiten auf • warten auf • sich erinnern an • sich freuen auf • halten von • bitten um • erwarten von • passen zu • wissen von • gespannt sein auf

59 Julia wird wohl in den Kindergarten gehen Was werden diese Leute wohl nächstes Jahr machen? Wählen Sie eine Antwort von der Liste.

auf die Fachschule gehen • auf die Grundschule gehen • aufs Gymnasium gehen • auf die Hauptschule gehen • in den Kindergarten gehen • die Matura machen • auf die Musikhochschule gehen • auf die Realschule gehen

BEISPIEL Julia wird im Juli fünf Jahre alt.
> *Sie wird wohl im September in den Kindergarten gehen.*

1. Julia wird im Juli fünf Jahre alt.
2. Florian ist im Kindergarten.
3. Monika interessiert sich für Musik und möchte nach dem Gymnasium studieren.
4. Golo hat die Mittlere Reife gemacht.
5. Claudia ist in der sechsten Klasse und möchte auf die Universität gehen.
6. Frank ist in der Hauptschule und möchte eine Kfz°-Mechaniker-Lehre machen.
7. Gabriele ist Schülerin an einem Gymnasium in Wien.

Kfz = *Kraftfahrzeug:* *automotive*

Das deutsche Schulsystem

Germany and Switzerland have similar public school systems that are centrally administered, in Germany by each state Ministry of Education and the Arts (**das Kultusministerium**) and in Switzerland by the individual Cantonal Ministries. The Federal Ministry of Education in Austria oversees educational policy there.

In Germany, **der Kindergarten** is a private preschool. Thereafter, children typically enter the public school system (**die Grundschule**) through the fourth grade. In the orientation phase (**die Orientierungsstufe**) of fifth and six grades, teachers assess each pupil and recommend that they attend **die Hauptschule, die Realschule,** or **das Gymnasium.** All German students are required by law to attend school through the age of 18 (**die Schulpflicht**).

Roughly 20% of all German students are **Hauptschüler,** typically students of average ability. When they finish school (**die Hauptschule**), they may become an apprentice (**der Lehrling** or **der/die Auszubildende [Azubi]**) in a trade. In Germany's reknowned **duales Ausbildungssystem,** companies provide on-the-job training and pay for students to attend a **Berufsschule** part-time.

About 40% of all German students attend **die Realschule. Realschüler** learn a skill geared for practical applications in the work world. An intermediate diploma (**die Mittlere Reife**) is awarded upon successful completion of their training.

Schuljahr				
12 (17 J)	Berufsausbildung			
11 (16 J)				
10 (15 J)			Gymnasium	Gesamtschule
9 (14 J)				
8 (13 J)	Hauptschule	Realschule		
7 (12 J)				
6 (11 J)				
5 (10 J)				
4 (9 J)	Grundschule			
3 (8 J)				
2 (7 J)				
1 (6 J)				
	Kindergarten			

© Cengage Learning 2014

Gymnasiasten, making up the final 40% of German high school students, pursue the traditional college preparatory track at **das Gymnasium,** which customarily lasts through the 12th grade. These students usually take a variety of science and the humanities courses in nine subjects. To graduate and obtain a degree (**das Abitur** in Germany, **die Matura** in Austria, and **die Reifeprüfung** in Switzerland) students are tested in two major subjects. This diploma allows the student to attend a university, a technical university, or any other post-secondary educational institution, such as **die Musikhochschule, Kunsthochschule,** or a university of applied science, **die Fachhochschule.**

A fourth type of German school, **die Gesamtschule,** modeled on the comprehensive American high school, was a product of the reform movement of the 1960s. It incorporates the curricula of all three traditional German secondary schools, giving students a broad choice of programs and courses and making it easier to complete different degree programs.

Kulturkreuzung

Nicht alle Schüler müssen oder wollen auf die Universität gehen. Das deutsche Schulsystem bietet Schülern die Möglichkeit, einen guten Beruf zu erlernen, ohne zur Universität zu gehen. Das Schulsystem in den USA dagegen hat ein Universitätsstudium immer als Ziel im Auge. Was sind die Vorteile und Nachteile von beiden Systemen?

ZIEL

⊕ **Endspurt:** Online
Listening Text & Activities.

Ausreden im Deutschkurs
Zielaktivitäten

↩ **60** Eine super-gute Ausrede Sie haben heute Pech. Morgen sollen Sie ein Referat für Ihren Deutschkurs halten, aber Sie haben noch nicht einmal ein Thema! Was machen Sie jetzt? Schreiben Sie eine E-Mail an Ihren Dozenten/ Ihre Dozentin und erklären Sie, warum Sie morgen das Referat absolut nicht halten können. Beeindrucken° Sie Ihren Dozenten/Ihre Dozentin mit Ihrem exzellenten Deutsch!

impress

Planen Sie die E-Mail zuerst
Beantworten Sie diese Fragen.
1. Heute Morgen sind Sie aufgestanden und haben Sie sich *wie* gefühlt?
   a. miserabel   b. fantastisch   c. aufgeregt

BEISPIEL   *Heute Morgen bin ich aufgestanden und ich habe mich miserabel gefühlt.*

2. Woran haben Sie sich gleich beim Aufstehen erinnert?
   a. an Ihren Dozenten/Ihre Dozentin
   b. an Ihr Deutschreferat
   c. an Ihre Faszination für Deutsch

BEISPIEL   *Gleich beim Aufstehen habe ich mich …*

immediately

3. Worauf haben Sie sich sofort° nach dem Frühstück gefreut?
   a. auf das tolle Deutschbuch
   b. auf den interessanten Deutschkurs
   c. auf den freundlichen Deutschlehrer/die freundliche Deutschlehrerin

BEISPIEL   *Ich habe mich sofort nach dem Frühstück …*

did want

4. Und was wollten° Sie als nächstes gleich machen?
   a. Ihr Referat schreiben
   b. sich endgültig° für ein Thema entscheiden
   c. die PowerPoint-Präsentation vorbereiten

definitively

BEISPIEL   *Und dann wollte ich gleich als nächstes …*

suddenly

5. Was ist dann passiert?
   a. Ihr Computer hat plötzlich° nicht mehr funktioniert.
   b. Sie haben sich nicht für ein Thema entschieden. (Es gibt so viele interessante Themen im Deutschkurs!)
   c. Sie sind total nervös geworden und haben alles vergessen.
   d. Sie haben sich beim Rasieren geschnitten.

BEISPIEL   *Und dann hat plötzlich mein Computer nicht mehr funktioniert.*

JanVlcek/Shutterstock.com

6. Und jetzt möchten Sie sich mir dem Dozenten/der Dozentin treffen, ...
   a. um sich persönlich zu entschuldigen.
   b. um ein Thema für das Referat zu finden.
   c. um ein neues Datum für das Referat zu finden.
   d. um Ihre Probleme zu besprechen.

BEISPIEL   *Und jetzt möchte ich mich mit Ihnen treffen, um …*

7. Warum haben Sie aber heute Nachmittag keine Zeit für ein Treffen?
   a. weil Sie sich erst einmal ein paar Stunden hinlegen müssen
   b. weil Sie sich den ganzen Nachmittag auf Ihr Deutschbuch konzentrieren wollen
   c. weil Sie sich von Ihrem Hund nicht trennen können
   d. weil Sie sich erst einmal beruhigen° müssen

sich beruhigen: to calm down

BEISPIEL   *Aber heute Nachmittag habe ich keine Zeit für ein Treffen, weil …*

8. Was werden Sie jetzt machen?
   a. Sie werden sofort in die Bibliothek gehen.
   b. Sie werden nächste Woche das Referat halten.
   c. Sie werden ein neues Thema finden.
   d. Sie werden …

9. Was sagen Sie zum Schluss?
   a. Es wird Ihnen bald besser gehen.
   b. Der Dozent/Die Dozentin wird sehen, wie toll Ihr Referat sein wird.
   c. Sie werden Ihre Nerven stärken°.

strengthen

   d. Sie werden heute Abend im Bett das Deutschbuch lesen.
   e. Sie werden von Deutsch träumen ... keinen Albtraum! Nur gute Sachen!

Schreiben Sie jetzt die E-Mail

1. Fangen Sie mit einem Gruß an:
   a. Formell:
      Sehr geehrter Herr Professor [Schmidt]!
      Sehr geehrte Frau Professor [Schmidt]!
   b. Informeller:
      Lieber Professor [Schmidt]!
      Liebe Frau Professor [Schmidt]!
   c. Ganz informell:
      Lieber [Hans]!
      Liebe [Johanna]!

2. Schreiben Sie Ihre Nachricht. Verwenden Sie Ihre Antworten von oben und geben Sie auch noch neue Informationen dazu.

3. Wählen Sie eine Schlussformel:
   a. Sehr formell: Hochachtungsvoll° [Ihr Name]
   b. Formell: Mit freundlichen Grüßen [Ihr Name]
   c. Informell: Liebe Grüße [Ihr Name]

respectfully

61 Freie Kommunikation: **Rollenspiel: das Referat.** Sie müssen morgen ein Referat halten, aber es ist nicht fertig. Fragen Sie einen Freund, was Sie machen sollen. Erklären Sie ihm die Situation und bitten Sie um Rat. Zusammen besprechen Sie ein paar Ausreden.

> S1: Hallo, Herbert
> S2: Tag, Georg. Was gibt's?
> S1: Ich habe wirklich Pech. Ich habe mein Referat noch nicht fertig und ich muss es morgen halten. Was kann ich jetzt machen?
> S2: Tja, das ist wirklich schlecht. Erzähl mal. Was ist passiert?
> S1: Also, ich...

62 Schreibecke: **Ein Brief an die Günthers.** Barbara hat Anna den folgenden Brief von ihrer Freundin aus Dresden gezeigt. Anna will auch so einen Brief an die Günthers in Weinheim schreiben. Benutzen Sie den Brief von Barbaras Freundin Caroline als Beispiel für Annas Brief an die Günthers.

hardly

would

Meißener Straße 27
01069 Dresden
Dienstag, den 2. November

Liebe Barbara,

es tut mir leid, dass ich nicht geschrieben habe. Ich habe mich erkältet und war eine Woche lang krank. Jetzt geht's mir besser.

Wie geht es dir an der Uni in Tübingen? Mir gefällt die Uni hier in Dresden sehr gut. Ich habe in diesem Semester einen Kurs in Biologie. Er gefällt mir sehr, denn der Professor ist ausgezeichnet. Er ist sehr studentenfreundlich. Nur sind seine Sprechstunden immer überfüllt. Ich habe mich auch entschieden Medizin zu studieren. Ich warte jetzt nur noch auf einen Studienplatz.

Mir gefallen auch meine Vorlesungen hier. Sie sind nicht so voll, und ich habe andere Studenten kennengelernt.

Wie sind deine Kurse? Stimmt es, was man über Tübingen hört? Die Uni ist überfüllt und Kontakt mit Professoren hat man kaum? Schreib doch mal wieder!

Ich werde wohl nächste Woche mehr Zeit haben. Dann kann ich dich eventuell besuchen. Ich würde mich auf eine Antwort per E-Mail oder einen Anruf von dir sehr freuen.

Alles Liebe
deine Caroline

WORTSCHATZ

 Tutorial Quiz
Audio Flashcards

Universität und Schule

das Abitur, -e (das Abi, -s) *high school exit examination*

der Abiturient, [-en], -en/die Abiturientin, -nen *high school senior, soon-to-be graduate*

der/die Auszubildende, -n (der/die Azubi, -s) *apprentice, trainee*

der Bachelor *bachelor's degree*

das Diplom, -e *diploma*

der Dozent, [-en], -en/die Dozentin, -nen *assistant professor, lecturer*

das Ergebnis, -se *result*

die Grundschule, -n *elementary school*

das Gymnasium, *pl.* **Gymnasien** *college preparatory high school*

die Hauptschule, -n *technical-vocational secondary school*

die Hochschule, -n *college, university, post-secondary school*

der Kindergarten, ¨ *preschool*

der Kommilitone, [-n], -n/die Kommilitonin, -nen *fellow student, classmate*

die Lust *desire*

Lust haben *to have desire, to be interested in*

der Master *master's degree*

das Modul, -e *module*

das Praktikum, *pl.* **Praktika** *internship*

die Realschule, -n *middle-track secondary school*

die Schule, -n *school*

die Semesterferien *(pl.)* *semester break, holiday*

das Seminar, -e *seminar*

Basisseminar, Proseminar *introductory seminar*

Aufbauseminar *intermediate seminar*

Vertiefungsseminar *intensification seminar*

der/die Studierende, -n *(university level) student*

die Vorlesung, -en *lecture*

gut ab•schneiden (hat abgeschnitten) *to place well, do well*

sich ein•schreiben (hat sich eingeschrieben) *to register, enroll*

tippen (hat getippt) *to type*

mündlich *oral(ly)*

schriftlich *in writing*

Die Gruppenarbeit

die Arbeitsgruppe, -n *study group*

das Handout, -s *handout*

das Referat, -e *(seminar), oral presentation*

die Seminararbeit, -en *seminar project, paper*

die Sprechstunde, -n *office hour*

das Thema, *pl.* **Themen** *topic; theme*

Die tägliche Routine

sich ab•trocknen (hat sich abgetrocknet) *to dry oneself off*

sich an•ziehen (hat sich angezogen) *to get dressed*

sich (eine Jacke) an•ziehen *to put on (a jacket)*

sich aus•ziehen (hat sich ausgezogen) *to get undressed*

baden (hat gebadet) *to bathe*

sich beeilen (hat sich beeilt) *to hurry*

sich die Haare bürsten (hat sich die Haare gebürstet) *to brush one's hair*

(sich) duschen (hat [sich] geduscht) *to take a shower*

sich die Haare föhnen (hat sich die Haare geföhnt) *to blow-dry one's hair*

sich die Haare kämmen (hat sich die Haare gekämmt) *to comb one's hair*

sich die Zähne putzen (hat sich die Zähne geputzt) *to clean/brush one's teeth*

sich rasieren (hat sich rasiert) *to shave*

sich die Beine rasieren *to shave one's legs*

sich schminken (hat sich geschminkt) *to put on make-up*

sich waschen (wäscht sich, hat sich gewaschen) *to wash oneself*

sich die Haare waschen *to wash one's hair*

sich die Hände waschen *to wash one's hands*

Im Badezimmer

das Badetuch, ¨er *bath towel*

die Badewanne, -n *bathtub*

der Becher, - *cup*

der Föhn, -e *blow dryer*

der Haken, - *hook*

der Rasierapparat, -e *electric razor*

die Seife, -n *soap*

das Shampoo, -s *shampoo*

Krank sein

der Arzt, ¨e/die Ärztin, -nen *doctor, physician*

der Durchfall *diarrhea*

Durchfall haben *to have diarrhea*

die Erkältung, -en *head cold; chill*

das Fieber *fever*

Fieber haben *to have a fever*

der Gips *cast*

das Heftpflaster, - *adhesive bandage*

der Muskelkater, - *sore muscle*

der Schmerz, -en *pain*

Zahnschmerzen (Halsschmerzen, Kopfschmerzen) haben *to have a toothache (sore throat, headache)*

die Schmerztablette, -n *painkiller*

der Schnupfen, - *head cold, sniffles*

sich aus•ruhen (hat sich ausgeruht) *to rest*

sich (das Bein) brechen (bricht sich, hat sich gebrochen) *to break one's (leg)*

sich erholen (hat sich erholt) *to recuperate, get well*

sich erkälten (hat sich erkältet) *to catch a cold*

sich fühlen (hat sich gefühlt) *to feel*

sich nicht wohl fühlen *to feel unwell*

sich hin•legen (hat sich hingelegt) *to lie down*

sich in den Finger schneiden (hat sich geschnitten) *to cut one's finger*

sich melden (hat sich gemeldet) *to report, show up*

sich übergeben (übergibt sich, hat sich übergeben) *to vomit*

weh•tun (hat wehgetan) + *dat.* *to hurt, be painful (to someone)*

sich weh•tun (hat sich wehgetan) *to hurt oneself*

krank *sick*

wohl *fine, healthy; probably*

Gute Besserung! *Get well!*

Mir geht es so lala. *I'm so so.*

Mir geht es ziemlich schlecht. *I'm feeling pretty bad.*

Wie fühlst du dich? *How are you feeling?*

Zeitausdrücke

der Morgen, - *morning*

der Nachmittag, -e *afternoon*

der Abend, -e *evening*

früh *early*

in zwei Tagen (Wochen, Monaten) *in two days (weeks, months)*

jeden Tag *every day*

morgen früh *tomorrow morning*

nächste Woche *next week*

nächsten Samstag *next Saturday*

nächsten Sommer *next summer*

nächstes Jahr *next year*

übermorgen *the day after tomorrow*

Verben mit präpositionalem Objekt

achten auf + *acc.* (hat geachtet) *to pay attention to*

Angst haben vor + *dat.* (hat Angst gehabt) *to be afraid of*

sich ärgern über + *acc.* (hat sich geärgert) *to be angry about*

bitten um + *acc.* (hat gebeten) *to ask for, request*

sich entscheiden für/gegen + *acc.* (hat sich entschieden) *to decide for/against*

sich erinnern an + *acc.* (hat sich erinnert) *to remember*

erwarten von + *dat.* (hat erwartet) *to expect of*

sich freuen auf + *acc.* (hat sich gefreut) *to look forward to*

sich freuen über + *acc.* (hat sich gefreut) *to be happy about*

gespannt sein auf + *acc.* (ist gespannt gewesen) *to be excited about*

halten für + *acc.* (hält, hat gehalten) *to consider/think (someone) is (something)*

handeln von + *dat.* (hat gehandelt) *to be about*

sich interessieren für + *acc.* (hat sich interessiert) *to be interested in*

sich konzentrieren auf + *acc.* (hat sich konzentriert) *to concentrate on*

passen zu + *dat.* (hat gepasst) *to suit, fit*

sprechen über + *acc.* (spricht, hat gesprochen) *to talk about, discuss*

sich trennen von + *dat.* (hat sich getrennt) *to break up with, separate from*

sich verlieben in + *acc.* (hat sich verliebt) *to fall in love with*

sich verloben mit + *dat.* (hat sich verlobt) *to get engaged to*

sich vor•bereiten auf + *acc.* (hat sich vorbereitet) *to prepare (oneself) for, get ready for*

Noch einmal: **danken für** + *acc.*, **denken an** + *acc.*, **erzählen von** + *dat.*, **fragen nach** + *dat.*, **glauben an** + *acc.*, **halten von** + *dat.*, **reden über** + *acc.*, **etwas verstehen von** + *dat.*, **warten auf** + *acc.*, **wissen von** + *dat.*

Andere Verben

bestellen (hat bestellt) *to order*

dauern (hat gedauert) *to last*

ein Referat halten (hält, hat gehalten) *to give an oral report*

klingen *to sound*

Das klingt gut. *That sounds good.*

Sie klingt freundlich. *She sounds friendly.*

kopieren (hat kopiert) *to copy*

probieren (hat probiert) *to try*

schaffen (hat geschafft) *to succeed, get done*

statt•finden (hat stattgefunden) *to take place*

versuchen (hat versucht) *to try*

sich vor•stellen (hat sich vorgestellt) *to introduce oneself*

Darf ich mich vorstellen? *Allow me to introduce myself.*

wählen (hat gewählt) *to choose*

wechseln (hat gewechselt) *to change*

Adjektive und Adverbien

aktuell *current(ly)*

anders *different(ly)*

bekannt *familiar; famous*

berühmt *famous*

gemeinsam *shared, communal*

genau *exact(ly)*

kaum *hardly*

meistens *mostly*

natürlich *natural(ly)*

plötzlich *suddenly*

schließlich *finally*

schrecklich *awful(ly)*

selbst *oneself*

verschieden *different*

zusätzlich *additionally*

Andere Wörter

die Lösung, -en *solution*

die Schwierigkeit, -en *difficulty*

die Freiheit, -en *freedom, liberty*

die Wahrheit, -en *truth*

Andere Ausdrücke

deswegen *that's why*

ein paar *a few*

Herein (bitte). *Come in (please).*

klasse *great, cool*

noch mal *(once) again*

Pech haben *to have bad luck*

Muellek Josef/Shutterstock.com.

Wien bei Sonnenuntergang

Ein Praktikum in Wien

In this chapter you will continue to learn how to describe people, objects, and activities. You will talk and read about Vienna, music history, professions, job interviews, and job qualifications.

Kommunikative Funktionen

> Providing additional descriptive information about people and topics

> Proposing activities, making suggestions

> Describing people and things

> Comparing people and things

Strukturen

> Nominative, accusative, and dative case relative pronouns

> Present tense subjunctive with **würde, hätte, wäre**

> Endings on adjectives after **ein**-words, **der**-words, or neither

> Comparative and superlative forms of adjectives and adverbs

Vokabeln

> Berufe

> Eigenschaften von guten Bewerbern

> Österreichs Leute und Länder

Kulturelles

> Wien

> Österreich

> Berufswahl und Berufsausbildung in deutschsprachigen Ländern

Karl hat ein Vorstellungsgespräch° bei der Wiener Staatsoper

Anna und Stefan freuen sich für Karl: Karl hat gute Chancen, ein Praktikum im Kulturmanagement an der weltberühmten° Wiener Staatsoper zu bekommen. In einer Woche muss er zum Vorstellungsgespräch nach Wien reisen. Anna und Stefan wünschen° Karl viel Glück, aber dann beginnt Karl sehr nervös zu werden. Ist er wirklich für die Stelle qualifiziert? Kann er in der Praxis alles benutzen, was er an der Universität gelernt hat? Kann er die Fragen beantworten, die man ihm im Interview stellt? Anna und Stefan helfen Karl, sich auf das Vorstellungsgespräch vorzubereiten.

Vorschau

  1 Thematische Fragen Beantworten Sie die folgenden Fragen auf Deutsch.

1. Was versteht man als typische Studentenjobs an Ihrer Uni? Sagen Sie für jeden Job, ob er als Studentenjob typisch oder untypisch ist.

   a. Assistent/in im Studentenwohnheim
   b. Verkäufer/in im Einzelhandel° oder Discount-Laden
   c. Babysitter/in
   d. Forschungsassistent/in°
   e. Kellner/in

   f. Mitarbeiter/in an der Uni-Bibliothek
   g. Pizzazusteller/in
   h. Reinemachefrau°/Hausmeister°
   i. Tellerwäscher/in in der Mensa
   j. Barkeeper/in in einer Kneipe

2. Arbeiten Sie jetzt auf dem Campus oder in der Stadt? Als was? Gefällt Ihnen die Arbeit?
3. Was für Jobs haben Sie schon gehabt? Wie viele Stunden in der Woche haben Sie gearbeitet? Wie viel Geld haben Sie verdient?
4. Ein Praktikum ist praktische Arbeit, die man als Teil des Studiums macht, um Berufserfahrung zu sammeln. Man verdient nicht immer Geld dafür. Müssen Sie für Ihr Hauptfach ein Praktikum machen? Halten Sie das für gut oder nicht? Warum?

Karl macht ein Praktikum in der Wiener Staatsoper.

2 Autogrammspiel: Arbeiten und Geld verdienen

Finden Sie für jede Frage eine Person, die die Frage mit **Ja** beantworten kann. Bitten Sie die Person um ihre Unterschrift.

BEISPIEL Wer arbeitet nur in den Sommerferien?
    S1: *Arbeitest du nur in den Sommerferien?*
    S2: *Nein, ich arbeite auch während° des Semesters.*   during
    S1: *Arbeitest du nur in den Sommerferien?*
    S3: *Ja, das stimmt, ich arbeite nur in den Sommerferien.*
    S1: *OK, danke. Unterschreib bitte hier.*

1. Wer arbeitet nur in den Sommerferien?   _____
2. Wer arbeitet während des Semesters?   _____
3. Wer arbeitet nur abends?   _____
4. Wer arbeitet nur am Wochenende?   _____
5. Wer arbeitet das ganze Jahr durch?   _____
6. Wer muss gar nicht arbeiten?   _____

3 Satzdetektiv

Welche Sätze bedeuten ungefähr das Gleiche?

1. Gute **Nachrichten** von der Wiener Staatsoper.
2. Ich habe eine Einladung zum **Vorstellungsgespräch** in Wien!
3. **Hast du dich** um ein Praktikum **beworben?**
4. Das ist eine **großartige Stelle** in der **Betriebsleitung.**
5. Ich habe noch **keinen festen Termin.**
6. Das ist eine **einmalige Gelegenheit** für dich.

a. Es ist ein fantastischer Job in der Geschäftsführung°.   management
b. Ich weiß noch nicht genau, wann mein Interview ist.
c. Ich fahre nach Wien für ein Interview!
d. Du hast nur einmal im Leben eine solche° Chance.   *eine ... : such a*
e. Ich habe eine positive Antwort aus Wien bekommen.
f. Hast du die Papiere für eine Praktikantenstelle eingereicht?

7. Ich **drücke dir** ganz fest **die Daumen!**
8. Wie soll ich **mich** bloß im Vorstellungsgespräch **verhalten** und was soll ich tragen?
9. **Wie wäre es** mit einem Rollenspiel?
10. Aber was soll ich sagen, wenn sie fragen, welche **Arbeitserfahrung** ich schon habe?
11. **Beruhige dich** doch, Karl.
12. Warum **würdest du** sie nicht **beeindrucken?**

g. Warum sollst du keinen positiven Eindruck° auf die Leute machen?   impression
h. Sei nicht so nervös, Karl.
i. Ich wünsche dir viel Glück!
j. Was hältst du davon, wenn wir ein Rollenspiel machen?
k. Wie antworte ich, wenn sie fragen, ob ich schon im Kulturmanagement gearbeitet habe?
l. Was soll ich im Interview sagen und tun und was soll ich anziehen?

Karl hat ein Vorstellungsgespräch bei der Wiener Staatsoper

Track 2-2

Hören Sie gut zu.

Anna, Stefan! Gute Nachrichten von der Wiener Staatsoper.

Ich habe eine Einladung zum Vorstellungsgespräch in Wien!

In der Tat? Für das Praktikum, um das du dich beworben hast?

Ja, für die Stelle im Kulturmanagement, die ich im Internet gefunden habe.

Was für eine Stelle soll das sein?

Das ist ja wahnsinnig!

Das ist eine großartige Stelle in der Betriebsleitung.

Fantastisch! Fährst du gleich nach Wien?

Nee, das hat keinen Zweck. Ich habe noch keinen festen Termin.

Trotzdem, das ist eine einmalige Gelegenheit für dich. Ich drücke dir ganz fest die Daumen!

Aber was mache ich nun? Ich bin schon ganz nervös und aufgeregt.

Wie soll ich mich bloß im Vorstellungsgespräch verhalten, und was soll ich tragen?

© Cengage Learning 2014

Rückblick

4 Stimmt das? Stimmen diese Aussagen zum Text? Wenn nicht, was stimmt?

	Ja, das stimmt.	Nein, das stimmt nicht.
1. Karl hat einen permanenten Job an der Wiener Staatsoper bekommen.	○	○
2. Karl hat sich um ein Praktikum im Kulturmanagement beworben.	○	○
3. Karl muss schon heute nach Wien zum Vorstellungsgespräch fahren.	○	○
4. Karls Praktikum ist als Sänger im Chor von der Staatsoper.	○	○
5. Karl meint, er wird die Stelle sicher bekommen.	○	○
6. Stefan bringt Karl zum Friseur für einen anständigen° Haarschnitt.	○	○
7. Der neue Anzug soll einen guten Eindruck machen.	○	○
8. Anna schlägt vor, ein Rollenspiel mit Karl zu machen.	○	○
9. Karl hat Angst, dass er für diese Stelle nicht genug im Kulturmanagement gearbeitet hat.	○	○
10. Anna erinnert Karl daran, dass er mit fast allen Menschen arbeiten kann.	○	○
11. Karl gibt zu, dass er gern Theater spielt.	○	○

decent

Sprache im Alltag: Wishing someone luck

There are several expressions for wishing people luck in German:

Ich drücke dir ganz fest die Daumen!	*I'm crossing my fingers for you!*
Hals- und Beinbruch!	*Break a leg!*
Ich wünsch dir was!	*I'm hoping for you!*
Toi, toi, toi!	*Good luck (e.g., with the interview)!*

Instead of crossing their fingers, German speakers make a clenched fist enclosing the thumb on the left hand to gesture that they're wishing someone good luck.

> Complete the **Ergänzen Sie** activity in the Student Activities Manual before doing the next activity.

5 Kurz gefragt Beantworten Sie die folgenden Fragen auf Deutsch.

1. In welcher Abteilung° von der Wiener Staatsoper soll Karl sein Praktikum machen?
2. Warum ist Karl nervös und aufgeregt?
3. Wie reagieren Anna und Stefan auf Karls Situation?
4. Warum muss Karl nicht sofort° nach Wien reisen?
5. Was schlagen Anna und Stefan vor, um Karl zu helfen?
6. Was sind Karls Vorteile als Kandidat für das Praktikum?

department

sofort

6 Textdetektiv: **Anlauftext.** Use the *Anlauftext* to recognize important aspects of German structure and usage.

1. Look at the boldfaced words in the following examples from the *Anlauftext* and select the word or phrase to which they most likely refer.
   a. Für das Praktikum, um **das** du dich beworben hast?
      i. das Praktikum ii. du iii. dich
   b. Für die Stelle im Kulturmanagement, **die** ich im Internet gefunden habe.
      i. die Stelle ii. das Kulturmanagement iii. das Internet
   c. Stefan hilft dir, einen Anzug auszusuchen, **der** einen guten Eindruck macht.
      i. Stefan ii. einen Anzug iii. einen guten Eindruck

2. True or false: In example c above, the pronoun **der** agrees with the noun it refers back to in gender (masculine) and number (singular), but not case (accusative > nominative).

3. These article-like words most likely function . . .
   a. to relate information from one clause with another clause.
   b. to contradict information presented in another clause.
   c. to introduce clauses that present unrelated information.

4. A good name for these article-like words would be _____ pronouns.
   a. relative b. contradictory c. introductory

5. What is the case and the function of the relative pronoun in each of the following two examples?
   „Für das Praktikum, um **das** du dich beworben hast?"
   „Stefan hilft dir, einen Anzug auszusuchen, **der** einen guten Eindruck macht."
   a. accusative because it follows an accusative preposition
   b. accusative because it is the direct object
   c. nominative because it is the subject of the clause or sentence

6. Based on the answers in question 5, we can conclude that relative pronouns ...
   a. share the case of the noun or pronoun they refer back to.
   b. take the case that reflects their role in the clause in which they appear.
   c. take their case randomly.

7. A common English equivalent of German relative pronouns is:
   a. that b. so c. because

8. In clauses with relative pronouns, the conjugated verb is placed at/in the _____.
   a. beginning of the clause b. middle of the clause c. end of the clause

9. In this respect, relative pronouns act like . . .
   a. coordinating conjunctions (**und, oder, aber, denn**)
   b. subordinating conjunctions (**weil, damit, obwohl,** etc.)
   c. prepositions (**um, auf,** etc.)

7 Interview: Stundentenjobs und Praktika Stellen Sie einem Partner/einer Partnerin die folgenden Fragen.

1. Hast du im Moment einen Job? Ist er gut? Warum, oder warum nicht?
2. Welche Studentenjobs hältst du für gut? Welche hältst du für nicht gut? Warum?
3. Warum arbeiten viele Studierende? Hältst du das für gut oder schlecht?
4. Was findest du besser – ein interessantes Praktikum zu machen oder im Praktikum viel zu verdienen?
5. Wie kann man als Studierender/Studierende sehr viel Geld verdienen?
6. Würdest du ein unbezahltes Praktikum machen? Warum? Warum nicht?

Interview. Jot down notes as your partner answers each of these questions and be prepared to report your findings to the class.

Strukturen

⬛ Providing additional information about topics

Nominative, accusative, and dative case relative pronouns

A. Nominative case relative pronouns

A relative clause (**der Relativsatz**) allows writers and speakers to provide additional information about something mentioned in the main clause without the awkward repetition of a noun. The relative clause connects to a main clause through a shared common noun.

> Ich spiele **die Dame. Die Dame** interviewt dich.
> *I'll play the lady. The lady is interviewing you.*

> Ich spiele **die Dame**,
> *I'll play the lady who is interviewing you.*

A relative clause always has a relative pronoun (**das Relativpronomen**) at or near its beginning. The relative pronoun (e.g., **die**) refers back to a preceding noun in the sentence (e.g., **die Dame**). This noun is known as the antecedent (**das Bezugswort**). The gender and number of the relative pronoun are determined by the gender and number of the antecedent.

> *masculine, singular*
> Ich spiele **den Betriebsleiter. Der Betriebsleiter** wird dein neuer Chef.
> *I'll play the executive officer. The executive officer will be your new boss.*

> Ich spiele **den Betriebsleiter, der** dein neuer Chef wird.
> *I'll play the executive officer who'll be your new boss.*

The case is determined by the relative pronoun's use in the relative clause. When the relative pronoun is the subject of the relative clause, it occurs in the nominative case (**der, das, die** for singular, and **die** for plural).

> In English, relative clauses are formed with *which, who, whom,* or *that,* although sometimes the relative pronoun is omitted: *The job (that) I found is in Vienna. The person (whom) I met yesterday comes from Austria.*

Du brauchst einen Anzug,	*You need a suit that makes a good impression.*
Ich suche ein Auto,	*I'm looking for a car that is not too expensive.*
Das ist eine Gelegenheit,	*That is an opportunity that only comes once in a lifetime.*
Die anderen Bewerber, haben nicht mehr Erfahrung als du.	*The other applicants who want the position don't have any more experience than you.*

In written German, commas set off the relative clause from the main clause, and since a relative clause is a subordinate clause (**der Nebensatz**), the verb occurs at the end of the subordinate clause.

Die Stelle, ist in Wien.	*The job that I found on the Internet is in Vienna.*

8 Definitionen Definieren Sie die fett gedruckten Wörter. Verbinden Sie jeden Hauptsatz in der linken Spalte° mit einem passenden Relativsatz in der rechten Spalte.

1. Eine **Praktikumsstelle** ist eine Stelle,
2. Ein **Vorstellungsgespräch** ist ein Gespräch,
3. Ein **Betriebsleiter** ist ein Mann,
4. Eine **Seminararbeit** ist eine Arbeit,
5. Ein **Tellerwäscher** ist ein Mann,

a. das zwischen einem Bewerber° und einem Interviewer stattfindet.°
b. die für Studierende gedacht° ist.
c. der im Restaurant in der Küche arbeitet.
d. der der Chef von der ganzen Firma ist.
e. die Studierende in einem Proseminar schreiben.

column

applicant
occurs
intended

9 Was für ein Job ist das? Beschreiben Sie die Jobs der folgenden Personen mithilfe der Informationen in der rechten Spalte.

1. Ich habe einen Job,
2. Ich möchte eine Stelle haben,
3. Ich suche ein Praktikum,
4. Mein(e) Freund(in) hat eine Arbeit,
5. Mein Vater/Meine Mutter hat einen Job,

der
das
die

mir/ihm/ihr Spaß macht.
hart ist.
langweilig ist.
interessant ist.
Initiative verlangt°.
viel Flexibilität hat.

requires

Andrey_Popov/Shutterstock.com

Ein Vorstellungsgespräch zwischen einem Bewerber und einer Interviewerin.

Wissenswerte Vokabeln: Berufe

Talking about occupations

Andere Berufe

der Architekt / die Architektin
architect

der Arzt / die Ärztin
physician

der Bauer / die Bäuerin
farmer

der Beamte / die Beamtin
civil servant

der Berater / die Beraterin
advisor; consultant

der Filmemacher / die
Filmemacherin *filmmaker*

der Journalist / die
Journalistin *journalist*

der Krankengymnast /
die Krankengymnastin
physical therapist

der Künstler / die Künstlerin
artist

der Lehrer / die Lehrerin
school teacher

der Musiker / die Musikerin
musician

der Politiker / die Politikerin
politician

der Regisseur / die
Regisseurin *film or stage
director*

der Sänger / die Sängerin
singer

der Sekretär / die Sekretärin
secretary

der Apotheker
die Apothekerin

der Automechaniker
die Automechanikerin

der Bäcker
die Bäckerin

der Chef
die Chefin

der Fleischer
die Fleischerin
der Metzger
die Metzgerin

der Friseur
die Friseurin

der Geschäftsmann
die Geschäftsfrau

der Ingenieur
die Ingenieurin

der Kaufmann
die Kauffrau

der Koch
die Köchin

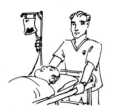
der Krankenpfleger
die Krankenschwester

der Makler
die Maklerin

der Programmierer
die Programmiererin

der Rechtsanwalt
die Rechtsanwältin

der Schauspieler
die Schauspielerin

der Schriftsteller
die Schriftstellerin

der Tierarzt
die Tierärztin

der Verkäufer
die Verkäuferin

der Wissenschaftler
die Wissenschaftlerin

der Zahnarzt
die Zahnärztin

BEISPIEL *Wer unterrichtet Deutsch?*   *Der Lehrer oder die Lehrerin.*

10 Berufe Was ist z. B. ein Kellner? Geben Sie zusammen mit einem Partner/ einer Partnerin Definitionen für die folgenden Berufe.

im Parlament sitzen • eine Rolle im Theaterstück spielen • Brot und Brötchen backen • Häuser verkaufen • etwas im Geschäft verkaufen • im Krankenhaus arbeiten • im Restaurant das Essen servieren • in einer Schule unterrichten • kranke Tiere behandeln • Romane und Krimis schreiben • Pläne für Häuser zeichnen • in Finanzfragen Rat geben

BEISPIEL   S1: *Was ist ein Kellner?*
S2: *Ein Kellner ist ein Mann, der im Restaurant das Essen serviert.*

1. Kellner	5. Ärztin	9. Tierarzt
2. Lehrerin	6. Maklerin	10. Verkäuferin
3. Bäcker	7. Schriftstellerin	11. Finanzberater
4. Schauspielerin	8. Architekt	12. Politikerin

> When naming a person's profession, German speakers generally omit the indefinite article **ein/eine,** e.g., **Er ist Arzt.** (*He's a doctor.*). When describing specifics about a person's professional skills, they use an article before the adjective, e.g., **Er ist mein neuer Arzt.** (*He's my new doctor.*).

11 Autogrammspiel: Was möchten Sie werden? Finden Sie für jede Frage eine Person, die mit **Ja** antwortet. Bitten Sie die Person um ihre Unterschrift.

BEISPIEL   *Lehrer/Lehrerin*
S1: *Möchtest du Lehrerin werden?*
S2: *Ja. Ich möchte Lehrerin werden*

1. Lehrer/Lehrerin _____
2. Architekt/Architektin _____
3. Arzt/Ärztin _____
4. Ingenieur/Ingenieurin _____
5. Geschäftsmann/Geschäftsfrau _____
6. Kaufmann/Kauffrau _____
7. Krankenpfleger/Krankenschwester _____
8. Rechtsanwalt/Rechtsanwältin _____
9. Programmierer/Programmiererin _____
10. Künstler/Künstlerin _____

B. Accusative case relative pronouns

In the preceding activities, you practiced the use of the relative pronoun in the nominative case, when it functions as the subject of the relative clause.

Ein Mann, **der** Brot bäckt/backt, ist ein Bäcker.

When a relative pronoun functions as a direct object in the relative clause, it is in the accusative case.

Der Mann kommt aus Algerien. Barbara hat **den Mann** bei der Arbeit kennengelernt.
The man is from Algeria. Barbara met the man at work.

Der Mann, den Barbara bei der Arbeit kennengelernt hat, kommt aus Algerien.
The man, whom Barbara met at work, is from Algeria.

C. Dative case relative pronouns

A relative pronoun may also replace a noun in the dative case. Frequently the relative pronoun functions as the indirect object of the relative clause.

> Der Mann ist Herr Kronemeyer. Wir geben **dem Mann** die Pläne.
> *The man is Mr. Kronemeyer. We are giving the plans to the man.*

> Der Mann, **dem** wir die Pläne geben, ist Herr Kronemeyer.
> *The man to whom we are giving the plans is Mr. Kronemeyer.* OR
> *The man we're giving the plans to is Mr. Kronemeyer.*

This is a summary chart of the relative pronouns.

	Masculine	Neuter	Feminine	Plural
Nominative	der	das	die	die
Accusative	den	das	die	die
Dative	dem	dem	der	denen

↩ **12** Im Büro Verbinden Sie die richtigen Satzteile.

BEISPIEL *Ist das der neue Kollege, den wir gestern in der Kantine getroffen haben?*

1. Ist das der neue Kollege,
2. Wo ist der neue Tablet-PC,
3. Herr Diehl, haben Sie das Inserat° geschrieben,
4. Frau Jahn, hier sind die Papiere,
5. Frau Anders, geben Sie mir bitte den Brief,
6. Ich suche das kleine Päckchen,
7. Wie heißt denn dieser Mann,

a. den Herr Tingelmann gestern bei Apple gekauft hat?
b. das wir in die Zeitung setzen wollen?
c. die wir heute losschicken müssen.
d. das gerade angekommen ist.
e. den Sie gestern getippt haben.
f. den wir gestern in der Kantine getroffen haben?
g. dem wir den Auftrag° gegeben haben?

classified ad

contract, order

D. Relative pronouns after prepositions

You have learned that a relative pronoun can function as a subject, a direct object, or an indirect object in a relative clause. A relative pronoun can also replace a noun after a preposition and then appears in the case required by that preposition.

Accusative prepositions (durch, für, gegen, ohne, um):
> Ist es für das Praktikum, **um das** du dich beworben hast?
> *Is it for the internship that you applied for?*

Dative prepositions (aus, außer, bei, mit, nach, seit, von, zu):
> Das sind die Leute, **mit denen** Karl arbeiten soll.
> *Those are the people with whom Karl is supposed to work.*

Two-case prepositions (an, auf, hinter, in, neben, über, unter, vor, zwischen):
> Das ist eine Karriere, **an die** ich gedacht habe.
> *That's a career (that) I've thought about.*

The interrogative **wo** can replace a preposition and relative pronoun that express location.

> Das ist ein Job, **bei dem** man viel Trinkgeld bekommt.
> Das ist ein Job, **wo** man viel Trinkgeld bekommt.
> *That's a job in which (where) one gets a lot of tips.*

→ **13 Das Wort, das ich suche** Hier sind vier Abbildungen mit Relativsätzen. Identifizieren Sie das Relativpronomen und das Bezugswort.

BEISPIEL Der einzige Arztroman, bei dem das Publikum mitbestimmen kann.

Relativpronomen: _dem_
Bezugswort: _Arztroman_

Der einzige Arztroman, bei dem das Publikum mitbestimmen kann:

Praxis Dr. Berger

die interaktive Komödie in der
*ufa*fabrik
4. März–15. März, 20.30 Uhr
Viktoriastr. 10-18, U6 Ullsteinstraße
Karten & Infos: 75 50 30
www.praxis-dr-berger.com

UFA Fabrik, Fotos: Tom Wagner

lofoto/Shutterstock.com

Suchen Sie einen Partner, mit dem Sie Ihr Leben verbringen können.

1. Relativpronomen: _____
   Bezugswort: _____

Endlich eine Zeitschrift, bei der für Sie richtig was rausspringt!

Guter Rat

Jetzt neu! Für nur 2€

Die besten Reise-Angebote der Saison

Digital-Kamera

Schauen Sie doch mal rein

Guter Rat, Berlin

2. Relativpronomen: _____
   Bezugswort: _____

Jason X Pacheco/Shutterstock.com

Kaufen Sie sich einen neuen Anzug, den man nicht alle Tage sieht.

3. Relativpronomen: _____
   Bezugswort: _____

Ich suche einen Job, in dem ich viel lernen kann.

nakamasa/Shutterstock.com

4. Relativpronomen: _____
   Bezugswort: _____

14 Definitionen Definieren Sie die fett gedruckten Wörter. Verbinden Sie jeden Hauptsatz in der linken Spalte mit einem passenden Relativsatz in der rechten Spalte.

1. Ein **Vorstellungsgespräch** ist ein Gespräch,
2. Ein **Bäcker** ist ein Mann,
3. Wien ist eine **Stadt,**
4. Kulturmanagement ist ein **Beruf,**
5. Eine Tierärztin ist eine **Frau,**
6. Ein Studienberater ist eine **Person,**

a. bei dem man Brot kauft.
b. in dem man Schauspieler kennenlernen kann.
c. in dem man sich bei einer Firma vorstellt.
d. in der man viel Kultur erleben kann.
e. mit der Studierende sprechen, wenn sie Fragen zum Studium haben.
f. zu der wir unseren Hund bringen, wenn er krank ist.

Brennpunkt Kultur   Web Search / Web Link

Berufswahl und Berufsausbildung in deutschsprachigen Ländern

Students in Germany, Austria, and Switzerland are trained in a profession that they will most likely have for life. Occupational choices come early in school. During the third and fourth grades in Germany, parents and teachers decide if students will go to **die Hauptschule, die Realschule,** or **das Gymnasium.**

German businesses, government, and schools collaborate closely to provide vocational and academic training in manual trades for **Hauptschüler,** or training for administrative positions for **Realschüler**. This close collaboration ensures a skilled workforce and streamlines vocational education.

In an on-the-job apprenticeship (**die Lehre** or **die Ausbildung**) an apprentice from the **Hauptschule (der Lehrling** or **der/die Auszubildende, Azubi**) learns a trade in three years. Apprentices are paid a trainee wage while they attend academic classes at a school (**die Berufsschule**) one or two days a week. They take courses in their specialty along with courses in German, history, economics, and other subjects. Apprentices must pass an exam given by a board of teachers, employer-trainers, and representatives of the appropriate trade guild.

Stephan Goerlich/Alamy

Ein Azubi bei der Ausbilding

Students who are interested in technical professions or careers in business, administration, or civil service attend **die Realschule** for six years and participate in short-term internships (**die Praktikantenstellen** or **Praktika**). Upon passing **die Mittlere Reife** at the end of the 10th grade, these students may start an apprenticeship in areas such as banking, business, or office administration or attend a technical college (**die Fachschule**) or a special school (**die Fachoberschule**). Increasingly, graduates from a **Gymnasium** who do not go on to college compete with **Realschüler** for apprenticeships and often win out.

Kulturkreuzung

Wissen Sie schon, was Sie später beruflich machen werden? Haben Sie das schon gewusst, als Sie zehn Jahre alt waren? Wie lernt man in Ihrem Land, Mechaniker, Bäcker oder Krankenpfleger zu werden? Was sind die Vorteile und Nachteile vom deutschen Bildungssystem?

Strukturen

II Proposing activities, making suggestions

Present tense subjunctive with *würde, hätte, wäre*

The *mood* (**der Modus**) of a verb expresses the speaker's attitude toward what is being said, e.g., certainty, doubt, probability, impossibility, politeness, or hypothetical state. Mood is reflected in the form of the verb.

Factual statements use the indicative mood (**der Indikativ**).

> Ich **habe** morgen ein Vorstellungsgespräch.   *I have an interview tomorrow.*

Commands use the imperative mood (**der Imperativ**).

> **Mach** schnell!   *Be quick! (Hurry up!)*

To express possibility, hypothetical situations, and politeness, German speakers can use the subjunctive mood (**der Konjunktiv**).

A. The present subjunctive of *werden*

The most common way to express the present subjunctive in speaking is to use the auxiliary verb **würde** (*would*) with an infinitive at the end of the main clause.

> Was **würdest** du **tun?**   *What would you do?*

Here are the forms of **würde** combined with the infinitive **sagen.**

würde sagen: *would say*	
Singular	**Plural**
ich **würde** sagen	wir **würden** sagen
du **würdest** sagen	ihr **würdet** sagen
Sie **würden** sagen	Sie **würden** sagen
er/sie/es **würde** sagen	sie **würden** sagen

Würde is the subjunctive form of the verb **werden**.

---

15 Das Vorstellungsgespräch Was würden Sie in einem Vorstellungsgespräch tun oder nicht tun? Markieren Sie die relevanten Punkte und fragen Sie dann einen Partner/eine Partnerin.

BEISPIEL   einen Anzug tragen
S1: *Würdest du einen Anzug tragen?*
S2: *Ja, ich würde einen Anzug tragen. Und du?*
S1: *Nein, ich würde keinen Anzug tragen.*

	Ich	Mein Partner/ Meine Partnerin
1. einen Anzug tragen	_____	_____
2. vorher zum Friseur gehen	_____	_____
3. alte Turnschuhe tragen	_____	_____
4. über Religion sprechen	_____	_____
5. zu spät zum Vorstellungsgespräch kommen	_____	_____
6. über meine (deine) Probleme sprechen	_____	_____
7. meine (deine) Dokumente mitbringen	_____	_____
8. fragen, wie viel man verdient	_____	_____

B. The present subjunctive of *haben* and *sein*

The present subjunctive of **haben** (**hätte**) and **sein** (**wäre**) can be used to express possibility.

Hättest du jetzt schon Zeit?	*Would you have time now?*
Ja, das **wäre** gut.	*Yes, that would be good.*

The expression **Wie wäre es mit ... ?** is used to make a suggestion.

Wie wäre es mit einem Kaffee?	*How about a cup of coffee?*
Wie wäre es mit einem Rollenspiel?	*How would it be if we did a role play?*

Here are the forms of **hätte** and **wäre**.

hätte: *would have*		
Singular		**Plural**
ich **hätte**	wir **hätten**	
du **hättest**	ihr **hättet**	
Sie **hätten**	Sie **hätten**	
er/sie/es **hätte**	sie **hätten**	

wäre: *would be*		
Singular		**Plural**
ich **wäre**	wir **wären**	
du **wärest**	ihr **wäret**	
Sie **wären**	Sie **wären**	
er/sie/es **wäre**	sie **wären**	

> The expressions **Das wäre interessant (klasse, prima, schön, super, toll**, etc.**)** and **Ich hätte Lust dazu (Interesse daran**, etc.**)** are used to respond positively to suggestions.

> In conversation, many speakers glide over the **-e-** in the **du-** and **ihr-**forms of **wäre**, so that those forms sound like **du wärst** and **ihr wärt**.

 16 Die Einladung Stefan möchte Anna einladen. Spielen Sie in Paaren, was Stefan und Anna sagen. Bilden Sie Fragen nach dem Beispiel. Benutzen Sie Ausdrücke aus der Liste.

interessant sein • klasse sein • schön sein • super sein • toll sein • Geld dafür haben • Interesse daran haben • Lust dazu haben • Zeit dazu haben

BEISPIEL   heute Abend ins Kino gehen

> S1 (STEFAN): *Ich gehe heute Abend mit Barbara und Karl ins Kino. Hättest du Zeit (Lust) dazu?*
>
> S2 (ANNA): *Au, ja! Ich hätte schon Zeit (Lust) ins Kino zu gehen.* (oder) *Au, ja! Das wäre super, mit euch ins Kino zu gehen.*

1. heute Abend ins Kino gehen
2. morgen Abend essen gehen
3. am Wochenende nach Heidelberg fahren
4. später auf eine Party gehen
5. zusammen eine Pizza essen
6. mit Karl und Barbara in die Kneipe gehen
7. am Wochenende einen Spaziergang machen
8. ein Schloss am Rhein besichtigen

17 Freie Kommunikation: **Jeopardy.** Teilen Sie die Klasse in zwei Gruppen auf. Jede Person in der Gruppe spielt abwechselnd° für die Gruppe. Der Dozent/Die Dozentin sagt ein Kompositum°, und ein Spieler/eine Spielerin aus jeder Gruppe meldet sich, wenn er/sie das Kompositum mit einem Relativsatz definieren kann. Die richtige Antwort muss eine Frage sein.

taking turns
compound noun

BEISPIEL   lehr er(in): *Tageszeitung*

> S1: *Wie heißt eine Zeitung, die man jeden Tag liest?*

⊙ 18 Schreibecke: **Die Übersetzung.**° Sie arbeiten als Englischübersetzer/-übersetzerin in einer Werbeagentur°. Ihr Kollege Herr Neumeier hat Sie gebeten, die folgenden englischen Ausdrücke auf Deutsch zu erklären. Schreiben Sie ihm eine Mitteilung°, in der Sie kurze, einfache Definitionen geben.

An: Herrn Neumeier
Anbei sind die Definitionen der englischen Ausdrücke, die Sie mir gestern geschickt haben.

BEISPIEL   *laptop computer:* Das ist ein Computer, der …

laptop computer: (der Computer)
freeware: (die Software)
color monitor: (der Monitor)
high-speed modem: (das Modem)
computer nerd: (die Person)
help line: (die Telefonnummer)

⊙ 19 Als Azubi … Wie wäre es, wenn Sie Azubi wären? Bilden Sie Sätze mit den folgenden Elementen.

1. Als Azubi würde ich _____.
   a. nur Englisch sprechen
   b. Deutsch und Englisch sprechen
   c. Deutsch, Englisch und eine dritte Sprache sprechen
2. Als Azubi wäre ich _____.
   a. unmotiviert und faul
   b. motiviert und flexibel
   c. motiviert und unflexibel
3. Als Azubi würde ich _____.
   a. ungern Überstunden° machen
   b. gern früh nach Hause gehen
   c. gern Überstunden machen
4. Als Azubi hätte ich _____.
   a. viel Geld
   b. nicht viel Geld
5. Als Azubi würde ich viel _____.
   a. von den Mitarbeitern lernen
   b. vom Beruf lernen
   c. von meiner Freundin lernen
6. Als Azubi wäre ich _____.
   a. der Tech-Profi im Team
   b. der Fußballfan im Team
   c. der Chef im Team
7. Als Azubi hätte ich _____.
   a. bessere Chancen für einen Vollzeitjob
   b. kein Problem viel Geld zu verdienen
   c. keine Möglichkeit im Beruf aufzusteigen.

jede Menge: *a large amount*

Wiener Musikleben und Musiker-Gedenkstätten

Bevor Karl nach Wien zum Vorstellungsgespräch abreist, will er sich schnell über die Wiener Musikszene informieren. Online gibt es jede Menge° Infos auf der Website vom Wiener Fremdenverkehrsverein, Wien Tourismus.

Vorschau

20 Thematische Fragen Beantworten Sie die folgenden Fragen auf Deutsch.

1. Welche österreichischen Städte kennen Sie? Was assoziieren Sie mit Österreich? Wen assoziieren Sie mit Österreich?
2. Gibt es Stereotype über Österreich oder Österreicher? Wissen Sie mehr über das historische oder mehr über das moderne Österreich? Warum vielleicht?
3. Wien ist sehr bekannt für Musik. Welche berühmten Komponisten haben in Wien gelebt?
4. Gehen Sie gern in die Oper? Ins Konzert? Würden Sie in Wien in die Oper oder ins Konzert gehen? Würden Sie sich ein Ballett ansehen? Warum? Warum nicht?
5. Interessieren Sie sich für Architektur? Haben Sie jemals von den folgenden Stilen gehört: vom Barock, vom Jugendstil, vom Biedermeier?

Das Dreimädlerhaus: Ein Beispiel für den Wiener Biedermeier-Stil.

Das Schloss Belvedere: Ein Beispiel für den Wiener Barock.

Die Secession: Ein Beispiel für den Wiener Jugendstil.

Lesestrategien

Benutzen Sie die folgenden Lesestrategien, um den Absprungtext über Wien zu verstehen.

➲ 21 **Den Kontext verstehen** Finden Sie im Absprungtext Antworten auf die folgenden Fragen.

1. Für welche Gruppe hat man diesen Text geschrieben? Für Menschen aus Wien? Für Touristen, die Wien besuchen? Für Kinder? Für Studierende aus den USA?
2. Welche Menschen erwähnt° der Text?
3. Welche Gebäude° erwähnt der Text?
4. Wie ist der Text organisiert? Nach der Zeit (chronologisch)? Nach Themen? Nach Lokalitäten? Nach Personen?

mentions
buildings

➲ 22 **Neue Wörter lernen: Drei Strategien** Erraten° Sie die fett gedruckten Wörter mithilfe der drei folgenden Strategien. Beantworten Sie die Fragen.

guess

Weltwissen°

world knowledge

1. „Die Wiener Staatsoper ist eines der Top-Opernhäuser der Welt° und die **Bühne** der internationalen Opern-**Elite**."

   world

   Im Theater ist die Bühne vorne, wo die Schauspieler singen, tanzen und sprechen. Was heißt **Bühne?**

> The construction **werden/ wurde** + participle is used to express the passive and will be explained in **Kapitel 11.**

2. „... wo neben Opern auch schwungvolle Operetten und Musicals inszeniert und erstklassige Ballett**aufführungen** gezeigt werden."

   Eine Aufführung findet auf der Bühne statt. Ist **Aufführung** ein Synomym für **Programm, Schuhe** oder **Karten?**

3. „Entsprechend zahlreich sind hier die Gelegenheiten, auf den **Spuren der Meister zu wandeln,** zu sehen, wie sie lebten, und Erinnerungsstücke an sie zu bewundern."

   Wenn man im Sand geht, sieht man leicht die Spuren im Sand. Weltberühmte Musiker lassen auch ihre Spuren zurück, aber nicht im Sand. Was für **Spuren** haben Meister wie Beethoven und Mozart hinterlassen: politische Spuren? Musikalische Spuren? Philosophische Spuren?

> The narrative past tense is introduced in **Kapitel 10.**

4. „Das Mozarthaus Vienna, in dem Wolfgang Amadeus Mozart ‚Die Hochzeit des Figaro' **komponierte**..."
   „... wo Ludwig van Beethoven u. a. seine 4. Symphonie ... **schrieb** ..."
   „Hier, im Haydn-Haus, **schuf** er die großen Oratorien ‚Die Schöpfung' und ‚Die Jahreszeiten ...'"

   Sie kennen sicherlich die Namen Mozart, Beethoven und Haydn. Die Verben **komponierte, schrieb** und **schuf** sind „Synonyme". Stehen sie hier für **Musik gemacht, Musik gehört** oder **Musik gern gehabt?**

Wortformen

5. „Ein **abwechslungsreiches** Programm bietet auch die Wiener Volksoper, …"

   • Die Sprache bildet oft Wortkombinationen (Komposita) wie **Spielplan (Spiel + Plan)**. Das Wort **abwechslungsreich** besteht aus **Abwechslung + s + reich**. Sie wissen schon die Bedeutung von **wechseln**. Hat ein abwechslungsreiches Programm viele oder nur zwei oder drei Aufführungen im Jahr?

   • Hier sind andere Wortkombinationen. Können Sie ihre Bedeutungen erraten?

   der Mittelpunkt • erstklassig • zahlreich • die Welthauptstadt • die Ballettaufführung • der Kopfhörer • weltberühmt • das Konzertleben • die Zwölftonmusik • die Volksoper

Kontext

6. Manchmal kann man erraten, was neue Wörter im Satz bedeuten, wenn man darüber nachdenkt, was die anderen Wörter im Satz sind.

   „Seine musikalische Bandbreite umfasst nicht nur das klassische Repertoire, sondern **reicht vom Mittelalter** bis zu progressivsten Tönen der **Gegenwart.**"

   • Ist die **Gegenwart** die Zeit jetzt oder die Zeit früher?
   • Ist das **Mittelalter** die Zeit jetzt oder die Zeit früher?
   • Was heißt wohl das Verb **reicht von … bis …?**

7. „In Wiens **Musikergedenkstätten** – als Museen gestaltete Wohnungen, in denen berühmte Komponisten lebten …"

   Der Text gibt eine Definition für **Musikergedenkstätte** durch das Synomym **Museum**. Sehen die Museen aus wie Wohnungen oder wie Klassenzimmer?

8. „**Raritäten** des Musiktheaters setzt die Wiener Kammeroper in Szene: selten gezeigte Operetten, Musicals und Singspiele sowie barocke und moderne Opern."

   • Raritäten kommen selten auf die Bühne. Sieht man Raritäten oft oder nicht sehr oft?
   • Der Text definiert das Wort **Raritäten**. Bedeutet **Raritäten** „selten gezeigte" oder „barocke und moderne" Opern?

23 Satzdetektiv Verbinden Sie die Sätze mit der besten Bedeutung.

1. In Wiens Musikergedenkstätten … sehen Sie neben **Mobiliar und Gegenständen aus dem persönlichen Besitz** der Künstler auch Faksimiles von Partitur-Autographen, Gemälde und Fotos.

2. Walzer und Operette sind hier zu Hause, auch Musicals „made in Vienna" **haben** das internationale Publikum **erobert.**

3. Besuchen Sie jenes Haus, wo Ludwig van Beethoven … sein überaus berührendes „Heiligenstädter Testament" schrieb, in dem er der **Verzweiflung** über seine **Taubheit** Ausdruck verlieh.

4. Es **beherbergt** nicht nur den **Nachlass** des Erfinders der Zwölftonmusik und Begründers der „Neuen Wiener Schule" – Manuskripte, Ölbilder, Zeichnungen, Tagebücher und Musikinstrumente …

a. Die leichte Wiener Pop-Musik des 19. und 20. Jahrhunderts sowie moderne Musicals haben in Wien und anderswo triumphiert.

b. Es gibt im Museum persönliche Dinge wie Tische und Stühle, Faksimiles, Bilder und Fotos.

c. Das Haus zeigt die Original-Dokumente, Kunstwerke und Instrumente von Schönberg, der für die Zwölftonmusik berühmt ist.

d. Sehen Sie die Wohnung, in der Beethoven ein Testament über seine Frustration über die Gehörlosigkeit geschrieben hat.

Wien

Vienna (**Wien**) is the capital of modern Austria and
the former capital of the Austro-Hungarian Empire
(**Österreich-Ungarn**), which comprised portions of
Bulgaria, the Czech Republic, Slovakia, Italy, Poland,
Romania, Slovenia, Ukraine, and Yugoslavia, as well
as Austria and Hungary. In the 19th century, Austro-
Hungary was ruled by the Hapsburgs, and Vienna
was home to the emperor or empress (**der Kaiser/die
Kaiserin**) and his/her court. As such, Vienna was the
showplace of the empire. Absorbing and assimilating
peoples of diverse nationalities and their customs,
art forms, language, and tastes, Vienna developed
an atmosphere conducive to intellectual and artistic
creativity. Over the centuries, Vienna has been home
to such well-known figures as the psychoanalyst
Sigmund Freud, the composers Haydn, Mozart,
Beethoven, Schubert, Brahms, Mahler, Schönberg,
and Strauß, the filmmakers Otto Preminger, Fritz Lang,
and Billy Wilder, actors Christoph Waltz, and the painters Friedensreich Hundertwasser, Egon Schiele, and
Gustav Klimt. Vienna is also closely associated with numerous writers, e.g., the playwrights Franz Grillparzer
(1791–1872) and Arthur Schnitzler (1862–1931) as well as Ingeborg Bachmann (1926–1973), and the
2004 Nobel Prize winner Elfriede Jelinek (b. 1946).

**In der Hofburg erkennt man die Größe und die
Schönheit vom kaiserlichen und königlichen
Österreich-Ungarn.**

Courtesy of J. Douglas Guy.

Downtown Vienna is a compelling mix of the historic and the modern. The inner city (**die Innenstadt**) is
Vienna's oldest part. At its heart is **der Stephansdom**, the seat of the cardinal of Austria and Austria's national
cathedral, dating back to 1147 with distinctly Gothic influences from the early 14th century. **Die Ringstraße,**
with buildings dating to the mid-19th century, surrounds the **Innenstadt** and reflects the glory days of the
Hapsburg empire. One particular building, **das Secessionsgebäude** or **die Secession,** for short, was completed
in 1898. It served as the home base of the artistic movement of the same name, led by the painter Gustav
Klimt, most well known for his painting **Der Kuss.** The impact of the Hapsburg emperors is seen in their former
residences, the **Hofburg**, as well as **der Burggarten, der Heldenplatz, die Österreichische Nationalbibliothek**,
and **die Spanische Reitschule** with its famous Lipizzaner horses. In the summer the royal family retreated to its
country residence, **Schloss Schönbrunn**, a spectacular rococo palace with expansive baroque gardens.

Visitors to Vienna today encounter both old-world elegance and international engagement with the
contemporary world. In a Viennese **Kaffeehaus**, visitors can savor a rich cup of coffee or enjoy a world-
famous Viennese pastry such as **Apfelstrudel** and **Sachertorte**. Viennese cuisine is renowned for **Wiener
Schnitzel**, a breaded veal cutlet, and **Tafelspitz,** lean boiled beef served with horseradish sauce. Tourists and
locals enjoy visiting **der Prater,** the world's oldest amusement park, and riding its gigantic Ferris wheel (**das
Riesenrad**). On the other hand, Vienna is also home to institutions such as OPEC, as well as to **UNO-City**, the
site of the United Nations headquarters.

Kulturkreuzung

Welche Länder in und außerhalb von Europa haben noch einen König oder eine Königin? Sind diese
Monarchien auch Demokratien? Was ist die Funktion von einem König oder einer Königin in einer modernen
Demokratie? Was meinen Sie? Hat das Königtum heute noch einen Wert und eine wichtige Funktion?
Vergleichen Sie den historischen österreichischen Begriff von Multikulturalismus mit dem heutigen Begriff
davon in Ihrem Land. Was sind die Ähnlichkeiten? Was sind die Unterschiede?

Track 2-3

Lesen Sie jetzt den Text.

Wiener Musikleben

Willkommen in der Welthauptstadt der Musik! Hier haben mehr berühmte Komponisten gelebt als in irgendeiner anderen Stadt, und Musik liegt in Wien förmlich in der Luft: Walzer und Operette sind hier zu Hause, auch Musicals „made in Vienna" haben das internationale Publikum erobert. Die Wiener Staatsoper ist eines der Top-Opernhäuser der Welt und die Bühne der internationalen Opern-Elite. Hier genießen° Sie Abwechslung auf höchstem Niveau: Rund 50 Opern und 20 Ballettwerke werden an 300 Tagen im Jahr aufgeführt°, und zwar bei täglich wechselnden Vorstellungen.

enjoy

performed

Im Theater an der Wien wurde Musikgeschichte geschrieben°: Emanuel Schikaneder, der geniale Textautor von Mozarts „Zauberflöte"°, war dort Direktor, Beethoven wohnte° eine Zeit lang in dem Gebäude und seine Oper „Fidelio" wurde dort uraufgeführt°. Nun gibt es hier monatlich eine Premiere, von Mozart über Barockoper bis zur Moderne.

wurde geschrieben: was written / Magic Flute

lived

wurde uraufgeführt: was premiered

Die Wiener Staatsoper: Eines der Top-Opernhäuser der Welt

Jim Zuckerman/CORBIS

Ein abwechslungsreiches Programm bietet auch die Wiener Volksoper, wo neben Opern auch schwungvolle Operetten und Musicals inszeniert und erstklassige Ballettaufführungen gezeigt werden°.

gezeigt werden: are shown

Raritäten des Musiktheaters setzt die Wiener Kammeroper in Szene: selten gezeigte Operetten, Musicals und Singspiele sowie barocke und moderne Opern.

Wiens klassisches Konzertleben wird von zwei großen Häusern dominiert: Millionen Musikfreunde auf der ganzen Welt kennen den Wiener Musikverein als traditionsreichen Veranstaltungsort. Denn aus seinem Goldenen Saal wird alljährlich das Neujahrskonzert der Wiener Philharmoniker international im Fernsehen übertragen.

Ein weiterer Mittelpunkt des Konzertlebens ist das Wiener Konzerthaus im stimmungsvollen Jugendstil-Ambiente. Seine musikalische Bandbreite° umfasst nicht nur das klassische Repertoire, sondern reicht vom Mittelalter bis zu progressivsten Tönen der Gegenwart. Neben diesen beiden renommierten° Häusern gibt es ein gutes Dutzend von Konzertsälen, wo man ebenfalls den guten Ton trifft.

scope, range

renowned

Musiker-Gedenkstätten

In keiner anderen Stadt haben so viele weltberühmte Komponisten gelebt wie in Wien. Entsprechend zahlreich° sind hier auch die Gelegenheiten, auf den Spuren der Meister zu wandeln, zu sehen, wie sie lebten°, und Erinnerungsstücke an sie zu bewundern.

Entsprechend ...: equally numerous / lived

In Wiens Musikergedenkstätten – als Museen gestaltete Wohnungen, in denen berühmte Komponisten lebten – sehen Sie neben Mobiliar und Gegenständen aus dem persönlichen Besitz° der Künstler auch Faksimiles von Partitur-Autographen, Gemälde und Fotos. Die wichtigsten Werke der Meister genießt man dort in historischen oder besonders prominent besetzten Einspielungen über Kopfhörer.

possession

Herwig Prammer/Reuters/CORBIS

Die Wiener Philharmoniker spielen das Neujahrskonzert im Goldenen Saal des Wiener Musikvereins.

Das „Mozarthaus Vienna", in dem Wolfgang Amadeus Mozart „Die Hochzeit des Figaro" komponierte und geradezu herrschaftlich logierte°, finden Sie mitten in der Altstadt hinter dem Stephansdom. Besonders viele Erinnerungsstücke sind von Walzerkönig Johann Strauß erhalten und in jenem Haus ausgestellt, wo ihm sein größter Hit, der Donauwalzer, gelang°.

Besuchen Sie jenes Haus, wo Ludwig van Beethoven u. a.° seine 4. Symphonie und sein überaus berührendes°„ Heiligenstädter Testament" schrieb, in dem er der Verzweiflung über seine Taubheit Ausdruck verlieh°. Auch die letzte Wohnung von Joseph Haydn ist erhalten geblieben. Hier, im Haydnhaus, schuf er die großen Oratorien „Die Schöpfung" und „Die Jahreszeiten", und das heutige Museum ist ein Muss für Haydn-Fans.

Ebenso lädt das Haus, in dem der „Liederfürst"° Franz Schubert geboren wurde, zum Besuch ein. In dem heute malerisch anmutenden Häuschen lebten damals 16 Familien – jede in einer nur aus Zimmer und Küche bestehenden Wohnung.

Mehr als nur Gedenkstätte ist das Arnold-Schönberg-Center: Es beherbergt nicht nur den Nachlass des Erfinders der Zwölftonmusik und Begründers° der „Neuen Wiener Schule" – Manuskripte, Ölbilder, Zeichnungen, Tagebücher und Musikinstrumente –, sondern zeigt auch Sonderausstellungen und ist ein vitales Forschungszentrum°.

Reprinted by permission of Vienna Tourism Board.

herrschaftlich logierte: *lodged in grand style*

ihm sein größter Hit gelang: *he achieved his greatest success /* ***unter anderen:*** *among others / moving*

Ausdruck ...: *gave expression to*

prince of song

founder

research center

gary718/ Shutterstock.com

Die goldene Statue des Walzerkönigs Johann Strauß

Rückblick

24 Stimmt das? Stimmen die folgenden Aussagen zum Text? Wenn nicht, was stimmt

	Ja, das stimmt.	Nein, das stimmt nicht.
1. Wien ist für Musik sehr bekannt.	○	○
2. Die Wiener Staatsoper ist eine kleine, unbekannte Bühne.	○	○
3. An fast 300 Tagen im Jahr kann man Oper oder Ballett in der Wiener Staatsoper besuchen.	○	○
4. Wer sich mehr für Operetten und Musicals interessiert, geht am besten in die Wiener Volksoper.	○	○
5. In der Wiener Kammeroper kann man weniger bekannte Stücke sehen.	○	○
6. Zu Neujahr kann man die Wiener Philharmoniker im Fernsehen hören.	○	○
7. In den Gedenkstätten kann man über Kopfhörer Musik von den Komponisten hören.	○	○
8. Johann Strauß ist der Komponist, den man als den Liederfürsten kennt.	○	○
9. Franz Schubert war so arm, dass er im eigenen Geburtshaus leben musste, das heute seine Gedenkstätte bleibt.	○	○
10. Das Haus, in dem Wolfgang Amadeus Mozart in Wien wohnte, ist da, wo heute die Neustadt ist.	○	○

Complete the **Ergänzen Sie** activity in the Student Activities Manual before doing the next activity.

25 Textdetektiv: **Absprungtext.** Use the *Absprungtext* to recognize important aspects of German structure and usage.

1. Circle the relative pronoun and identify its antecedent in the following two examples.
„In Wiens Musikergedenkstätten – als Museen gestaltete Wohnungen, in denen berühmte Komponisten lebten – sehen Sie neben Mobiliar und Gegenständen aus dem persönlichen Besitz° der Künstler ...“

possession

    a. Gedenkstätten   b. Wohnungen   c. Mobiliar und Gegenständen

„Das ‚Mozarthaus Wien‘, in dem Wolfgang Amadeus Mozart ‚Die Hochzeit des Figaro‘ komponierte ...“

    a. das Mozarthaus   b. die Stadt „Wien“   c. die Oper „Figaro“

2. What is the antecedent of **wo** in the example below?
„Besuchen Sie jenes Haus, **wo** Ludwig van Beethoven u. a. seine 4. Symphonie und sein überaus berührendes°, Heiligenstädter Testament‘ schrieb.“

moving

    a. Haus   b. Ludwig van Beethoven   c. Testament

3. Which statement below is true?
    a. **Wo** can refer to people or locations.
    b. **Wo** changes its form like other relative pronouns.
    c. **Wo** occurs at the front of the relative clause.

4. What is the best alternative for **wo**?
    a. in das   b. in was   c. in dem

26 Kurz gefragt Beantworten Sie die folgenden Fragen auf Deutsch.

1. Welches von den drei Wiener Opernhäusern möchten Sie besuchen? Warum?
2. Haben Sie Lieblingskomponisten? Welche Art von Musik hören Sie – klassische Musik, Jazz oder Rock?
3. Warum hat eine Stadt wie Wien wohl drei Opernhäuser? Haben Sie eine Oper in Ihrer Stadt? Was halten Sie und Ihre Freunde von der Oper?
4. Haben Sie jemals das Geburtshaus oder die Wohnung von einem Komponisten, Schriftsteller oder Künstler besucht? Warum oder warum nicht?
5. Haben Sie Musikunterricht gehabt, ein Instrument gelernt oder im Chor gesungen? Ist es wichtig, Musikunterricht zu bekommen?

27 Schreibecke: **Klassiker-Tour von Wien.** Sie arbeiten bei einer Firma in Wien, die sich auf Musikfreunde spezialisiert und Sondertouren° von Wien anbietet. Sie wollen einen einminütigen° Werbe-Spot° für Ihre deutschsprachigen Kunden machen. Beschreiben Sie die Attraktionen von Ihrer Tour für Fans von Ludwig van Beethoven, Josef Haydn, Wolfgang Amadeus Mozart, Franz Schubert, Arnold Schönberg und Johann Strauß.

specialty tours
one-minute / commercial

28 Freie Kommunikation: **Sondertouren für Musikfreunde.** Rufen Sie diese Firma in Wien an und fragen Sie, ob sie Sondertouren für Musikfreunde von Mozart, Strauß oder Haydn haben. Fragen Sie, wann die Führung ist, wie lange sie dauert, wo sie beginnt und was man sieht.

Miguel Cabezónc/Shutterstock.com

Die Mozartstatue im Burggarten in Wien

Strukturen

 Describing people and things (I)

Endings on adjectives after *ein*-words, *der*-words, or neither

A. Endings on adjectives after *ein*-words: nominative case

Adjectives are words that describe the nature or quality of nouns and occur in one of two positions in a sentence:

1. as a predicate adjective after the verbs **sein, werden,** or **bleiben**
   Der Job ist **toll**. *The job is great.*

2. before a noun
   Das ist ein **toller** Job! *That's a great job!*

In German, only adjectives that occur before a noun have an ending. When an adjective follows an **ein**-word, the ending reflects the gender, the number, and the case of the noun that follows that adjective. Remember that the **ein**-words include the possessive adjectives **mein, dein, sein, ihr, unser, euer, ihr,** and **Ihr,** as well as the negative article **kein.**

> Remember that **ein** (*a, an*) cannot be used with plural nouns.

Er ist **ein** sehr nett**er** Typ.	*He's a really nice guy.*
Das ist **kein** gut**es** Praktikum.	*That's not a good internship.*
Unsere neu**en** Opern sind sehr populär.	*Our new operas are very popular.*

In the nominative case, the adjective following the **ein**-word has one of these endings.

Gender			Nominative singular adjective endings			Nominative plural adjective endings	
Masc	der Typ	**-er**	ein nett**er** Typ	*a nice guy*	**-en**	keine nett**en** Typen	*no nice guys*
Neut.	das Praktikum	**-es**	ein gut**es** Praktikum	*a good internship*	**-en**	keine gut**en** Praktika	*no good internships*
Fem.	die Stelle	**-e**	eine toll**e** Stelle	*a great job*	**-en**	keine toll**en** Stellen	*no good jobs*

> The last letter on the singular definite article is the same as the last letter on the adjective following the **ein**-word: *masc. sing.* **de**r → ein nette**r** Typ; *neut. sing.* **da**s → ein gute**s** Praktikum; *fem. sing.* **di**e → eine toll**e** Stelle.

Adjectives that end in **-el** and many that end in **-er** drop the internal **e** when an ending is added.

miserabel:	Das ist ein **miserabler** Job.	*That is a terrible job.*
teuer:	Das ist ein **teures** Auto.	*That is an expensive car.*

The adjective **hoch** (*high, tall*) has a special form, **hoh-**, to which endings are added.

Das ist ein **hohes** Gebäude. *That is a tall building.*

→ 29 **Was ist das?** Erklären Sie, was diese Begriffe° bedeuten.

> *terms*

> **AG=Aktiengesellschaft:** *corporation*

BEISPIEL S1: *Was ist die Volkswagen AG°?*
S2: *Das ist eine deutsche Autofirma.*

1. die Volkswagen AG
2. ein BMW
3. Dresden
4. der Neckar
5. Bayern
6. der Intercity/ICE

a. Das ist eine deutsche Stadt.
b. Das ist ein deutsches Auto.
c. Das ist ein deutscher Express-Zug.
d. Das ist ein deutscher Fluss.
e. Das ist ein deutsches Bundesland.
f. Das ist eine deutsche Autofirma.

⊖ 30 **Was für eine Arbeit ist das?** Wählen Sie für jeden Beruf ein passendes Adjektiv und schreiben Sie es auf. Geben Sie dann Ihre Meinung zu den folgenden Berufen.

Was für eine Arbeit ist das? The words **relativ** and **ziemlich** are adverbs modifying **gut** and do not have adjective endings.

BEISPIEL Kellner/Kellnerin
Das ist eine gute Arbeit (ein guter Beruf, ein gutes Leben)

+	+/–	–	
gut	relativ gut	schlecht	
fantastisch	ziemlich gut	blöd°	*dumb*
interessant	anständig	langweilig	
toll		hart	
		stressig	
		dreckig°	*filthy*

	Die Arbeit	Der Beruf	Das Leben
1. Kellner/Kellnerin	_____	_____	_____
2. Taxifahrer/Taxifahrerin	_____	_____	_____
3. Professor/Professorin	_____	_____	_____
4. Automechaniker/Automechanikerin	_____	_____	_____
5. Pilot/Pilotin	_____	_____	_____
6. Tellerwäscher/Tellerwäscherin	_____	_____	_____
7. Schauspieler/Schauspielerin	_____	_____	_____
8. Rechtsanwalt/Rechtsanwältin	_____	_____	_____

⊖ 31 **Ein Spiel: Trivialwissen** Was wissen Sie über Deutschland und Österreich? Bilden Sie zwei Teams und stellen Sie einander Fragen. Antworten Sie in ganzen Sätzen.

BEISPIEL eine / österreichisch- / Stadt
S1 (TEAM 1): *Nennen Sie eine österreichische Stadt.*
S2 (TEAM 2): *Salzburg ist eine österreichische Stadt.*

Team 1

1. eine / österreichisch- / Stadt
2. ein / deutsch- / Basketballspieler in der NBA
3. eine / deutsch- / Stadt im Osten Deutschlands
4. ein / deutsch- / Bundesland im Norden Deutschlands
5. ein(e) / österreichisch- / Schauspieler(in) und Oscar-Preisträger(in)
6. ?

Team 2

1. eine / deutsch- / Autofirma in München
2. ein(e) / österreichisch- / Musiker(in) aus Salzburg
3. ein / deutsch- / Komponist aus Bonn
4. ein / deutsch- / Fluss in Bayern
5. ein(e) / deutsch- / Politiker(in)
6. ?

Wissenswerte Vokabeln: Eigenschaften von guten Bewerbern

Talking about characteristics of good job applicants

analytisch

begabt

diszipliniert

dynamisch

gründlich

kollegial

kontaktfreudig

motiviert

pünktlich

qualifiziert

selbstständig

zuverlässig

BEISPIEL   *Soll ein Bäcker analytisch sein?*   *Nein, er soll (zuverlässig) sein.*

32 Stellensuche: Beschreibung in einem Inserat Welche von den folgenden Adjektiven findet man wahrscheinlich in einem Jobinserat°? Welche nicht?

help-wanted ad

kontaktfreudig • intelligent • dynamisch • faul • langsam • selbstständig • interessiert • unpünktlich • flexibel • passiv • zuverlässig • schüchtern • aggressiv • begabt • desorganisiert

2. Einkommen bis zu 1.200 Euro pro Monat, durch seriöse Nebentätigkeit (Büro). Hervorragende Zukunfts-Perspektiven.

33 Wie heißt eine Person, die … ? Stellen Sie einem Partner/einer Partnerin Fragen über die folgenden Personen und ihre Eigenschaften. Benutzen Sie die Adjektive.

BEISPIEL Eine Person, die gern neue Leute kennenlernt, ist eine …
S1: *Wie nennt man eine Person, die gern neue Leute kennenlernt?*
S2: *Eine Person, die gern neue Leute kennenlernt, ist eine kontaktfreudige Person.*

kollegial • kontaktfreudig • pünktlich • qualifiziert • selbstständig

1. Eine Person, die gern neue Leute kennenlernt, ist eine …
2. Ein Arbeiter, der allein gut arbeiten kann, ist ein …
3. Eine Ärztin, die nie zu spät kommt, ist eine …
4. Ein Friseur, der gern mit Kollegen arbeitet, ist ein …
5. Eine Lehrerin, die gute Qualifikationen hat, ist eine …

begabt • diszipliniert • dynamisch • gründlich • motiviert

6. Ein Sekretär, der viel Talent hat, ist ein …
7. Ein Kaufmann, der hohe Motivation hat, ist ein …
8. Eine Architektin, die an alle Details denkt, ist eine …
9. Ein Rechtsanwalt, der viel Energie hat, ist ein …
10. Eine Person, die viel Disziplin bei der Arbeit zeigt, ist eine …

B. Endings on adjectives after *ein*-words: accusative and dative case

These are the nominative, accusative, and dative case adjective endings following an **ein**-word.

	Masculine	Neuter	Feminine	Plural (all genders)
Nominative	ein nett**er** Mann	ein neu**es** Inserat	eine gut**e** Idee	keine gut**en** Ideen
Accusative	einen nett**en** Mann	ein neu**es** Inserat	eine gut**e** Idee	keine gut**en** Ideen
Dative	mit einem nett**en** Mann	in einem neu**en** Inserat	von einer gut**en** Idee	keinen gut**en** Ideen

	Accusative	*Dative*
Masculine:	Sie hat einen neu**en** Job.	Sie ist glücklich mit ihrem neu**en** Job.
Neuter:	Sie verkauft ihr alt**es** Auto.	Sie fährt in unserem alt**en** Auto nach München.
Feminine:	Sie hat eine neu**e** Mitarbeiterin.	Sie gibt ihrer neu**en** Mitarbeiterin einen Brief.
Plural:	Die Firma hat keine frei**en** Stellen.	Man spricht heute mit keinen neu**en** Bewerbern.

34 Neue Jobs Barbara und Stefan sprechen über ihre neue Arbeit. Barbara ist immer sehr positiv, aber Stefans Situation ist nicht so rosig.

> **BEISPIEL** S1 (BARBARA): *Ich habe einen guten Job. Und du?*
> S2 (STEFAN): *Ich habe einen schlechten Job.*

<table>
<thead>
<tr><th></th><th>Barbara</th><th>Stefan</th></tr>
</thead>
<tbody>
<tr><td>1. einen … Job</td><td>gut</td><td>schlecht</td></tr>
<tr><td>2. von meinem … Chef viel gelernt</td><td>neu</td><td>ehemalig°</td></tr>
<tr><td>3. heute eine … Aufgabe gehabt</td><td>interessant</td><td>langweilig</td></tr>
<tr><td>4. heute einen … Auftrag° erfüllt°</td><td>wichtig</td><td>unwichtig</td></tr>
<tr><td>5. ein … Interview für eine Beförderung°</td><td>leicht</td><td>stressig</td></tr>
<tr><td>6. eine … Sporthalle in der Firma</td><td>herrlich</td><td>furchtbar</td></tr>
<tr><td>7. einen … Tag gehabt</td><td>fantastisch</td><td>miserabel</td></tr>
<tr><td>8. einen … Laptop bekommen</td><td>nagelneu°</td><td>uralt°</td></tr>
<tr><td>9. eine … Kantine in der Firma</td><td>preiswert</td><td>teuer</td></tr>
</tbody>
</table>

former

assignment / completed
promotion

sehr neu / sehr alt

Strukturen

IV Describing people and things (II)

Endings on adjectives after definite articles

A. Adjectives preceded by a definite article: nominative, accusative, and dative case endings

Note that adjectives following a **der**-word have only one of two endings: **-e** or **-en.** The ending in the dative or plural is always **-en.** All nominative singular endings are **-e.**

Like adjectives that follow **ein**-words, adjectives that follow the definite article also take endings that change according to the gender, the number, and the case of the noun that follows. Here are the nominative, accusative, and dative endings of adjectives that follow **der**-words.

	Masculine	Neuter	Feminine	Plural
Nominative	der neu**e** Beruf	das neu**e** Büro	die neu**e** Stelle	die neu**en** Berufe/Büros/Stellen
Accusative	den neu**en** Beruf	das neu**e** Büro	die neu**e** Stelle	die neu**en** Berufe/Büros/Stellen
Dative	dem neu**en** Beruf	dem neu**en** Büro	der neu**en** Stelle	den neu**en** Berufen/Büros/Stellen

These adjective endings appear with any **der**-word (e.g., **dieser, jeder,** and **welcher**).
> Nominative: Dieser neu**e** Computer hat kein Kabel.
> Accusative: Angelika findet jedes neu**e** Gesprächsthema langweilig.
> Dative: Welchem jung**en** Mann haben Sie den Schlüssel gegeben?

	Masculine	Neuter	Feminine	Plural
Nominative	**ein** neu**er** Chef	**ein** neu**es** Büro	**eine** neu**e** Stelle	**meine** neu**en** Kollegen
	der neu**e** Chef	**das** neu**e** Büro	**die** neu**e** Stelle	**die** neu**en** Kollegen
Accusative	**einen** neu**en** Chef	**ein** neu**es** Büro	**eine** neu**e** Stelle	**meine** neu**en** Kollegen
	den neu**en** Chef	**das** neu**e** Büro	**die** neu**e** Stelle	**die** neu**en** Kollegen
Dative	**einem** neu**en** Chef	**einem** neu**en** Büro	**einer** neu**en** Stelle	**meinen** neu**en** Kollegen
	dem neu**en** Chef	**dem** neu**en** Büro	**der** neu**en** Stelle	**den** neu**en** Kollegen

35 Das neue Praktikum Karl beginnt ein neues Praktikum. Er beantwortet die Fragen, die seine Freundin stellt. Spielen Sie die Rollen. Wechseln Sie sich ab.

BEISPIEL   das Praktikum / interessant
S1: *Sag mal, Karl, wie gefällt dir das Praktikum? Ist es interessant?*
S2: *Ja, mir gefällt das interessante Praktikum sehr!*

1. das Praktikum / interessant
2. der Chef / tolerant
3. das Büro / groß
4. die Praktikantin / freundlich
5. die Sekretärin / hilfsbereit

6. das Gehalt° / schön   *salary*
7. der Firmenwagen / komfortabel
8. das Smartphone / neu
9. der Internet-Anschluss / schnell
10. das Arbeitsklima° / kollegial   ***Arbeitsatmosphäre***

36 Wie kann Karl das machen? Verbinden Sie ein Element in der linken Spalte mit einer Funktion in der rechten Spalte.

1. Mit dem schnellen Internet-Anschluss
2. Mit dem komfortablen Firmenwagen
3. Mit dem toleranten Chef
4. Mit der freundlichen Praktikantin
5. Von der hilfsbereiten Sekretärin
6. Mit dem schönen Gehalt
7. In dem großen Büro
8. Mit dem neuen Smartphone

a. kann Karl effektiv zusammenarbeiten.
b. kann Karl schnell Videos und Fotos herunterladen°.   *download*
c. hat Karl Platz für einen großen Schreibtisch
d. kann Karl Schauspieler am Wiener Flughafen abholen.
e. kann Karl Geld für sein Studium verdienen.
f. kann Karl simsen° und Fotos machen.   *text*
g. kann Karl über Studentenprobleme sprechen.
h. kann Karl wichtige Informationen über das Praktikum online bekommen.

Auch hinter der Bühne in der Wiener Staatsoper gibt es wichtige Arbeit zu tun.

†† 37 Was macht Karl lieber? Beantworten Sie die folgenden Fragen zusammen mit einem Partner/einer Partnerin.

BEISPIEL   mit dem fleißigen/faulen Mitarbeiter arbeiten
S1: *Arbeitet Karl lieber mit dem fleißigen oder mit dem faulen Mitarbeiter?*
S2: *Er arbeitet lieber mit dem fleißigen Mitarbeiter.*
S1: *Und du?*
S2: *Ich arbeite (auch) lieber mit einem fleißigen Mitarbeiter.*

1. mit dem fleißigen/faulen Mitarbeiter arbeiten
2. den neuen/alten Wagen fahren
3. mit dem schnellen/langsamen Computer schreiben
4. mit der kollegialen/unfreundlichen Praktikantin zusammenarbeiten
5. den schweren/leichten Laptop tragen
6. in der bekannten/unbekannten Oper arbeiten

B. Endings on unpreceded adjectives

An attributive adjective that is preceded by neither an **ein**-word nor a **der**-word has the same ending as a **der**-word.

Unser Chef trinkt ungern kalt**en** Kaffee.	*Our boss doesn't like to drink cold coffee.*
Die Volksoper bietet schwungvoll**e** Operetten und Musicals	*The **Volksoper** offers lively operettas and musicals.*
Wir haben schön**es** Wetter.	*We're having nice weather.*

38 Persönliches Profil Sie bewerben sich um eine Stelle in diesen Berufen. Sie haben ein Vorstellungsgespräch. Beantworten Sie diese Fragen für jeden von diesen Berufen in der Liste.

Geschäftsperson • Künstler(in) • Professor(in) • Verkäufer(in)

BEISPIEL   S1: *Was für Kleidung tragen Sie normalerweise am Arbeitsplatz?*
S2 (GESCHÄFTSPERSON): *Ich trage normalerweise formelle Kleidung.*

1. Was für Kleidung tragen Sie normalerweise am Arbeitsplatz? (formell / informell / schick / modisch)
2. Was für Essen bestellen Sie bei einem Geschäftstreffen°? (deutsch / chinesisch / französisch / exotisch / vegetarisch)
3. Was für Bier trinken Sie auf einer Geschäftsparty? (alkoholfrei / bayerisch / deutsch / dunkel)
4. Was für Computerkenntnisse° haben Sie? (gut / mäßig° / schlecht)
5. Mit was für Leuten arbeiten Sie gern? (tolerant / kreativ / intelligent / interessant)

business meeting

computer skills
moderate

Österreich

Austria (**Österreich**) is about the size of Iowa and is bordered by Germany, the Czech Republic, Slovakia, Hungary, Slovenia, Italy, Switzerland, and Liechtenstein. Its rich history and geographic location in Europe have produced a true multicultural and cosmopolitan society. Austria first became a democracy with the resignation of the Hapsburg **Karl der Erste** on November 11, 1918 after the close of World War I (**der Erste Weltkrieg**). In 1938 Hitler annexed Austria in an action known as **der Anschluss**. After the defeat of Nazi Germany in World War II, the Allies divided Austria into four occupation zones (**Besatzungszonen**), and democracy returned to Austria in 1945. Its constitution requires Austria to be a neutral nation. In 1995 Austria became the second German-speaking country to join the European Union (**die Europäische Union**).

The country is divided into nine states (**Bundesländer**): Burgenland, **Kärnten, Niederösterreich, Oberösterreich, Salzburg, Steiermark, Tirol, Vorarlberg,** and **Wien.** The Danube River (**die Donau**) flows eastward in the north through Linz and Vienna. The Alpine regions in the west and south, which make up about 62% of the total land area, have given Austria its reputation as a country of high mountains.

Although the economy of Austria suffered greatly during and after World War II, it is strong and vibrant today, with a very low unemployment rate.

In addition to the capital Vienna (**Wien**), Austria's major cities include **Graz, Innsbruck**, and **Salzburg. Graz,** the second largest city, is an industrial center producing chemicals, iron and steel products, mathematical instruments, and more. It has a university dating from 1586. **Innsbruck** is a rail and marketing center, as well as a historic resort town known more recently for hosting the 1964 and 1976 Winter Olympics. **Salzburg,** the birthplace of Wolfgang Amadeus Mozart, holds world-famous music and theater festivals every year.

S Lubenow/Getty Images

In der Getreidegasse in Salzburg findet man viel Charme und viele Menschen.

Kulturkreuzung

Städte oder Länder zwischen zwei Welten spielen eine besondere Rolle. Die Städte New York, Miami oder Los Angeles, zum Beispiel, integrieren Einwanderer in die USA. Welche Rolle, glauben Sie, spielt das Land Österreich für Menschen aus Osteuropa und welche Rolle für Menschen aus westeuropäischen Ländern?

Wissenswerte Vokabeln: Österreichs Leute und Länder

Talking about Austria

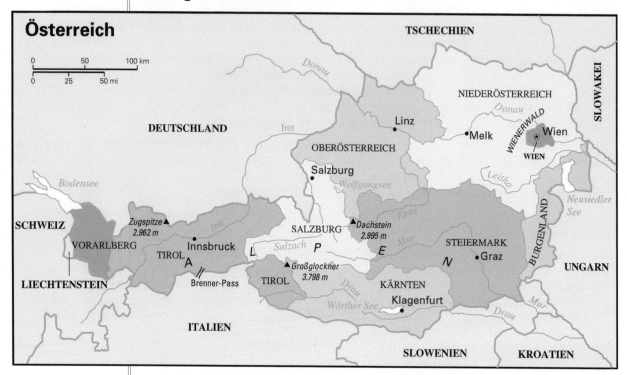

Fläche: 83 855 km2

Bevölkerung: rund 8,4 Millionen

Geburtsrate: 8,9 / 1 000 Personen

Sterberate: 9,56 / 1 000 Personen

Sprachzugehörigkeit: 88,5% deutsch; *andere:* slowenisch, kroatisch, ungarisch, tschechisch

Hauptstadt: Wien

neue Immigranten: 10% aus der Türkei, Bosnien, Serbien, Kroatien

Religionszugehörigkeit: 73,6% römisch-katholisch; 4,7% protestantisch; 4,2% Muslime; 17,4% keine Religion

39 Fragen über Österreich Stellen Sie einem Partner/einer Partnerin die folgenden Fragen über Österreich.

1. Wie viele Bundesländer hat Österreich?
2. Wie viele Einwohner hat Österreich? Sind das mehr oder weniger als Deutschland?
3. Findet man wohl mehr Priester oder Pastoren in Österreich? Warum?
4. Welche Sprachen hört man in Österreich außer Deutsch?
5. Ist das Land Österreich so groß wie Kalifornien oder wie Iowa?
6. Welches Bundesland ist gleichzeitig die Hauptstadt von Österreich?
7. Was unterscheidet wahrscheinlich Oberösterreich von Niederösterreich? Was meinst du?
8. Welches Bundesland möchtest du am liebsten besuchen? Warum?

Strukturen

 Comparing people and things

Comparative and superlative forms of adjectives and adverbs

A. Comparative forms

1. Regular adjectives and adverbs

To compare two or more people, objects, animals, or activities, German speakers use the comparative form (**der Komparativ**) of an adjective (**das Adjektiv**) or adverb (**das Adverb**). Adjectives modify nouns; adverbs modify verbs.

Most German adjectives and adverbs are identical in form, while English adverbs are generally distinguished from the adjective by the ending *-ly: happy, happily.*

> Das klingt schon **besser.** *That sounds better.*

Most adjectives and adverbs with an **e** or **i** in the stem form the comparative by adding **-er.** To express inequality, speakers use a comparative form with **als.**

Adjective:	Ein VW ist **schnell.**	*A VW is fast.*
Comparative:	Ein BMW ist **schneller als** ein VW.	*A BMW is faster than a VW.*
Adverb:	Ein VW fährt **schnell.**	*A VW goes fast.*
Comparative:	Ein BMW fährt **schneller als** ein VW.	*A BMW goes faster than a VW.*

To express equality in a comparison, German speakers use the construction **so ... wie** (*as . . . as*).

> Ein Porsche ist **so** teuer **wie** ein Mercedes. *A Porsche is as expensive as a Mercedes.*

Here are the base and comparative forms of some regular adjectives and adverbs.

Base	Comparative		Base	Comparative
bekannt	**bekannter**		schnell	**schneller**
interessant	**interessanter**		schön	**schöner**

Many adjectives that end in **-el** or **-er** drop the last internal **e** in the comparative form.

teue̶r:	Das Benzin wird **teurer.**	*Gasoline gets more expensive.*
flexibe̶l:	Ihre Arbeitszeit ist **flexibler** als meine.	*Her work hours are more flexible than mine.*

Other regular adjectives include: neu, **neuer**; billig, **billiger**; schwer, **schwerer**; wenig, **weniger**

 40 Frau Günthers VW und Herrn Günthers BMW Frau Günther möchte ein neues Auto kaufen. Sie hat mit Herrn Günther diese Informationen über ihre Autos aufgeschrieben. Vergleichen° Sie ihre Autos.

Compare

BEISPIEL billig sein
S1: *Frau Günthers VW ist billiger als Herrn Günthers BMW.*
S2: *Herrn Günthers BMW ist ...*

Use your own ideas for sentences where you see a question mark; e.g., **Herrn Günthers BMW hat mehr Prestige als Frau Günthers VW.**

	Frau Günthers VW Golf	Herrn Günthers BMW 530
billig (teuer) sein:	30 000 €	70 000 €
neu sein:	2011	2013
schnell fahren:	140 km/h°	220 km/h
schwer sein:	1 740 kg°	2 055 kg
schön sein:	?	?
Prestige haben:	?	?

Stundenkilometer
Kilogramm

2. Adjectives and adverbs that add an umlaut

Many one-syllable adjectives and adverbs with an **a, o,** or **u** in the stem add an umlaut in the comparative form. Shown below are some common ones.

Ich bin **älter** als mein Bruder.   *I am older than my brother.*

	Base	Comparative			Base	Comparative
a > ä	alt	**älter**		o > ö	groß	**größer**
	kalt	**kälter**			oft	**öfter**
	lang	**länger**				
	stark	**stärker**		u > ü	jung	**jünger**
	warm	**wärmer**			kurz	**kürzer**

3. Irregular adjectives and adverbs

Some adjectives and adverbs are irregular in German.

Remember that **hoch** drops the **c** in the comparative.

Positive	Comparative	Examples	
gut	**besser**	Siehst du jetzt **besser?**	*Do you see better now?*
hoch	**höher**	Dieses Gebäude ist **höher.**	*This building is taller.*
viel	**mehr**	Wir verdienen jetzt **mehr** Geld.	*We're earning more money now.*
gern	**lieber**	Ich gehe **lieber** ins Kino.	*I prefer to go to the movies.*

4. Using comparative adjectives

Like all adjectives, comparative adjectives can be placed before a noun (attributive position) or after the verb **sein** or **bleiben** (predicate adjectives). Like any adjective, comparative adjectives that precede a noun must also have an ending that shows the gender, number, and case of the noun. Adverbs and adjectives after **sein** or **bleiben** have no ending.

der älter**e** Bruder	das schneller**e** Auto	die lustiger**e** Dame
mein älter**er** Bruder	mein schneller**es** Auto	eine lustiger**e** Dame

---

↩ **41** Freiburg ist kleiner als Berlin Stellen Sie Vergleiche an.

BEISPIEL   Freiburg(–) / Berlin(+) / klein
Freiburg ist kleiner als Berlin. (oder: Freiburg *ist die kleinere Stadt.*)

Dresden(+) / Tübingen(+) / groß
Dresden ist so groß wie Tübingen.

1. Freiburg(–) / Berlin(+) / klein
2. Dresden(+) / Tübingen(+) / groß
3. die Uni in Tübingen(+) / die Uni in Bochum(–) / alt
4. Garmisch-Partenkirchen(+) / Stuttgart(–) / hoch liegen
5. der Mercedes 500 SL(+) / der VW Golf(–) / teuer
6. ein Motorrad(+) / ein Fahrrad(–) / schnell
7. Norddeutschland im Winter(–) / Süddeutschland im Winter(+) / viel Schnee haben
8. der deutsche Weißwein(+) / der deutsche Rotwein(+) / gut
9. Bockbier(+) / Exportbier(–) / stark
10. der Nürnberger Christkindlesmarkt(+) / der Bremer Weihnachtsmarkt(–) / bekannt

ii 42 Interview Stellen Sie einem Partner/einer Partnerin die folgenden Fragen.

1. Wer ist kontaktfreudiger, dein Vater oder deine Mutter?
2. Ist deine Mutter älter oder jünger als dein Vater?
3. Verdient deine Mutter mehr als dein Vater?
4. Wer arbeitet länger, deine Mutter oder dein Vater?
5. Wer ist intelligenter, du oder deine Schwester (dein Bruder, dein Cousin)?
6. Bist du stärker als dein Bruder (deine Schwester, dein Cousin)?
7. Wer ist selbstständiger, du oder dein bester Freund/deine beste Freundin?
8. Wer ist sportlicher, du oder dein bester Freund/deine beste Freundin?
9. Wer studiert disziplinierter, du oder dein bester Freund/deine beste Freundin?
10. Wer ist zuverlässiger, du oder dein bester Freund/deine beste Freundin?

B. Superlative forms

1. Regular adjectives and adverbs

German speakers form the superlative by adding **-st** to the adjective or adverb stem and adding the appropriate adjective ending.

- When preceding a noun, superlative adjectives must have the proper ending to reflect the gender, number, and case of the noun.

- Superlative adjectives in the predicate after **sein** and superlative adverbs that modify the verb are expressed with the construction **am** + adjective/adverb + **-sten** (e.g., **am schnellsten).**

Ein Porsche ist/fährt **am schnellsten.**	*A Porsche is/goes the fastest (of all).*
Ein Porsche ist das **schnellste** Auto.	*A Porsche is the fastest car (of all).*
Ich studiere an der **ältesten** Universität Deutschlands.	*I'm studying at the oldest university in Germany.*

Stems that end in **-t** and **-z** form the superlative with **-est.** Many one-syllable adjectives and adverbs with an **-a**, **-o**, or **-u** in the stem add an umlaut in the superlative forms.

In dem großen Konzerthaus war es **am lautesten.**	*It was the loudest in the big concert hall.*
Herr Müller ist unser **ältester** Mitarbeiter.	*Mr. Müller is our oldest employee*

Here are the superlative forms of some regular adjectives and adverbs.

Base	Predicate superlative	Attributive superlative (nominative case)
bekannt	**am bekanntesten**	das **bekannteste** Schloss in Deutschland
billig	**am billigsten**	der **billigste** Käse
interessant	**am interessantesten**	der **interessanteste** Kurs
neu	**am neuesten**	die **neuesten** Musicals
schlecht	**am schlechtesten**	der **schlechteste** Tag
schnell	**am schnellsten**	die **schnellste** Mitarbeiterin
schön	**am schönsten**	das **schönste** Geschenk
schwer	**am schwersten**	die **schwersten** Fragen
teuer	**am teuersten**	die **teuersten** Autos
wenig	**am wenigsten**	die **wenigsten** Leute

2. Adjectives and adverbs with an umlaut

These are some adjectives and adverbs that add an umlaut in the superlative form. Stems that end in **-ss, -ß, -t,** or **-z** also insert an **-e-** before the **-st.**

	Base	Superlative
a > ä	alt	**am ältesten**
	kalt	**am kältesten**
	lang	**am längsten**
	stark	**am stärksten**

	Base	Superlative
o > ö	groß	**am größten**
	oft	**am öftesten**
u > ü	jung	**am jüngsten**
	kurz	**am kürzesten**

3. Irregular adjectives and adverbs

Here are the superlative forms of some common irregular adjectives and adverbs.

Base	Comparative	Superlative	Examples
gut	besser	**best-**	**Der beste** Weißwein kommt aus Deutschland.
		am besten	Dieser Wein ist **am besten**.
hoch	höher	**höchst-**	**Der höchste** Berg heißt Everest.
		am höchsten	Everest ist **am höchsten**.
viel	mehr	**meist-**	**Die meisten** Kinder spielen Fußball.
		am meisten	Henning spielt **am meisten** Tennis.
gern	lieber	**Lieblings-**	Sein **Lieblings**essen ist Brot.
		am liebsten	Er isst **am liebsten** Brot.

The superlative of **gern** (**liebst-**) is not typically used as an adjective. Instead, the term **Lieblings-** (*favorite*) is added to the beginning of the noun to form a compound noun: **Lieblingssport, Lieblingsfilm,** etc.

4. Using superlative adjectives

German speakers most frequently use the superlative forms with the definite articles **der, das,** and **die.**

Herr Wimmer ist **der beste** Chef.   *Mr. Wimmer is the best boss.*
Die höchsten Gebäude stehen im Stadtzentrum.   *The highest buildings are downtown.*

---

 43 Studienzeiten Beantworten Sie die folgenden Fragen mit Informationen aus der Tabelle.

1. Wo sind die Studenten am jüngsten, wenn sie mit dem Studium fertig sind?
2. In welchem Land sind die Studenten am ältesten?
3. Sind Studenten in den USA am Ende des Studiums jünger oder älter als Studenten in Italien?
4. Studenten aus den ____ sind genau so alt (22) wie Studenten aus ____ am Ende des Studiums.

Später Abschluss
Abschlussalter von Hochschulabsolventen 2007

Deutschland	24 bis 26 Jahre
Österreich	22 bis 24
Griechenland	22 bis 23
Norwegen	22 bis 23
Italien	23
Niederlande	21 bis 23
Frankreich	20 bis 23
USA	22
Großbritannien	20 bis 22
Spanien	20

Quelle: OECD

44 Fakten über Deutschland Sie arbeiten im Fremdenverkehrsamt in Frankfurt und müssen eine Tourismusbroschüre über Deutschland schreiben. Bilden Sie Aussagen im Superlativ.

BEISPIEL die Gebäude / hoch = in Frankfurt
Die höchsten Gebäude sind in Frankfurt.

1. die Gebäude / hoch = in Frankfurt
2. das Bundesland / klein = die Hansestadt Bremen
3. der Fluss / lang = der Rhein
4. die Universität / alt = in Heidelberg
5. der Kirchturm° / hoch = in Ulm
6. die Bierbrauereien / viel = in Bayern
7. die Autos / schnell = Porsche und BMW
8. die Stadt in Deutschland / nördlich = Flensburg

church steeple

45 Freie Kommunikation: **Verkäufer/in gesucht.** Hier sind drei Personen, die sich für die Stelle bei Foto-Kirsch interessieren. Lesen Sie die Informationen über jede Person und besprechen Sie, wer für die Stelle besser (am besten) geeignet ist

	Fabian	Carlos	Jutta
Alter	20 Jahre	19 Jahre	18 Jahre
selbstständig	+ + +	+ + +	+ + +
dynamisch	+	+ +	+ +
kollegial	+ +	+ +	+ +
zuverlässig	+ + +	+ +	+
flexibel	+	+ + +	+ +
motiviert	+ +	+	+ + +

Junge(r), dynamische(r) Verkäufer(in)
mit Führerschein für unsere Filiale in Seemarn gesucht.
(Gewerbegebiet B 93).
Sie sollten selbstständig arbeiten können und Spaß am Umgang mit Menschen haben.
Bewerbungen mit Bild an
Foto-Kirsch
Arnoldstraße 13
09702 Seltz, Telefon 03941-14 79

© Cengage Learning 2014

46 Schreibecke: **Ein Stellengesuch-Inserat schreiben.** Sie suchen eine neue Stelle. Schreiben Sie ein Stellengesuch-Inserat. Sie dürfen maximal 50 Wörter benutzen. Nennen Sie mindestens zwei Eigenschaften. Benutzen Sie die folgenden Inserate als Beispiele.

Sekretärin (21)
zuverlässig und flexibel, sucht dringend neuen Wirkungskreis im Raum FG/BED, PC-Kenntnisse und Führerschein Klasse 3 vorhanden.

© Cengage Learning 2014

Einsatzfreudiger junger Mann,
36 Jahre, sucht Tätigkeit als Kraftfahrer im Fern- oder Nahverkehr, FS Kl. 1 bis 5 vorhanden.

© Cengage Learning 2014

ZIEL

Endspurt: Online Listening Text & Activities

Vorbereitung auf ein Jobinterview
Zielaktivitäten

47 Jobmöglichkeiten Besprechen Sie mit einem Partner/einer Partnerin die folgenden Jobmöglichkeiten. Ist das ein guter/stressiger/realistischer Job für Sie? Warum (nicht)?

Tierarzt/Tierärztin • Deutschprofessor/in • Babysitter/in • Kellner/in • Internetprogrammierer/in • Koch/Köchin • Fußballspieler/in • Bankmanager/in • ?

48 Erfolg? Denken Sie nach: Wollen Sie den Job bekommen und im Jobinterview erfolgreich° sein? Oder wollen Sie den Job nicht und das Jobinterview verpatzen°? Warum?

49 Im Interview Überlegen Sie sich Folgendes und machen Sie Notizen.

1. Was würden Sie im Jobinterview tragen, wenn Sie den Job haben wollen? Was tragen Sie, wenn Sie ihn *nicht* wollen?

BEISPIEL *Ich würde einen Anzug tragen, in dem man sich gut bewegen kann.*
Ich würde Schuhe tragen, die mindestens acht Zentimeter hohe Absätze haben.

Männer: Ich würde ... tragen.

a. keinen Anzug

b. einen Anzug, | der altmodisch /teuer/schmutzig ist
in dem man nicht schmutzig werden darf
in dem man sich (nicht) gut bewegen kann
?

c. keine Krawatte

d. eine Krawatte, | die viele bunte Farben hat
die sehr modisch ist
die zu kurz ist
auf der Flecken sind
?

e. keine Schuhe

f. Schuhe, | die sauber/schmutzig sind
in denen man Sport machen kann
in denen man bequem gehen kann
?

successful

mess up, ruin

Ist das ein guter Job für Sie?

shock/Shutterstock.com

Frauen: Ich würde ... tragen.

a. kein Kostüm°   *women's suit*

b. ein Kostüm,   das altmodisch ist
                   das teuer und elegant ist
                   das Löcher° hat   *holes*
                   in dem man nicht schmutzig werden darf
                   in dem man sich nicht bewegen kann
                   ?

c. ein T-Shirt,   das Information über ein Rockkonzert hat
                   das einen radikalen Text hat
                   ?

d. eine Bluse,   die mindestens 10 Jahre alt ist
                   die meiner Urgroßmutter gehört hat
                   in der man auch in einem Nachtklub tragen kann
                   in der man gut Fußball spielen kann
                   ?

e. keine Schuhe

f. Schuhe,   die mindestens acht Zentimeter hohe Absätze° haben.   *heels*
                die schmutzig sind
                die man auch in einem Nachtklub tragen kann
                in denen man gut Fußball spielen kann
                ?

Worüber würden Sie im Jobinterview *nicht* sprechen?

2. Was würden Sie zum Jobinterview mitbringen?
   a. einen Lebenslauf°
   b. Empfehlungsbriefe°
   c. ein Kurs-Transkript von der Uni
   d. eine beste Freundin/meinen besten Freund
   e. ?

3. Was würden Sie in der Tasche tragen?
   a. einen roten/keinen Lippenstift
   b. mein Handy
   c. ein volles/leeres/kein Portmonnaie
   d. einen organisierten/chaotischen/keinen Terminkalender
   e. ein frisches/altes/kein Taschentuch
   f. eine Tüte von McDonald's
   g. ?

4. Worüber würden Sie im Jobinterview sprechen?
   a. über Geld
   b. über Ferien und Urlaub
   c. über mein Privatleben
   d. über meine Qualifikationen
   e. über meine Deutschkenntnisse
   f. über Religion
   g. ?

5. Was würden Sie fragen?
   a. ob ich nette/doofe/gutaussehende Kollegen hätte
   b. ob die Arbeitszeit kurz/entspannend/stressig wäre
   c. ob ich wenig/viel/kein Talent für den Job haben müsste
   d. ob ich wenig/viel/nichts verdienen würde
   e. ob ich einen interessanten/gefährlichen/langweiligen Job hätte
   f. ?

50 Zusammenfassung Schreiben Sie eine kurze Beschreibung davon, was Sie im Jobinterview machen würden. Benutzen Sie diese Struktur:

1. Beschreiben Sie den Job, für den Sie sich bewerben.
2. Sagen Sie, was Sie tragen würden und in Ihrer Tasche hätten.
3. Beschreiben Sie, was Sie zum Jobinterview mitnehmen würden.
4. Erklären Sie, worüber Sie im Jobinterview sprechen würden.
5. Sagen Sie, was Sie (nicht) fragen würden.

51 Rat geben Geben Sie Ihrem Partner/Ihrer Partnerin, was Sie geschrieben haben. Der Partner/Die Partnerin sagt Ihnen, was er/sie denkt, zum Beispiel, ob Sie im Interview erfolgreich sind, was Sie sich (nicht) anziehen sollen, etc. Der Partner/Die Partnerin sagt auch, was er/sie machen würde.

WORTSCHATZ

Tutorial Quiz
Audio Flashcards

Die Ausbildung

die Ausbildung, -en *education; apprenticeship*

der Praktikant, [-en], -en/die Praktikantin, -nen *intern, apprentice*

Noch einmal: **der/die Auszubildende (Azubi), das Gymnasium, das Praktikum**

Das Vorstellungsgespräch

der Anzug, ⸚e *suit*

die Arbeitserfahrung, -en *work experience*

der Bewerber, -/die Bewerberin,-nen *applicant*

der Bewerbungsbrief, -e *letter of application*

der Eindruck, ⸚e *impression*

die Empfehlung, -en *recommendation*

das Formular, -e *form (to be filled out)*

die Gelegenheit, -en *opportunity*

die Kenntnis, -se *knowledge; skill*

der Lebenslauf, ⸚e *résumé, CV*

die Nachricht, -en *news*

die Praxis, *pl.* **Praxen** *practice, doctor's office*

die Stelle, -n *position, job*

der Termin, -e *appointment*

die Theorie, -n *theory*

die Vorstellung, -en *introduction; image, idea*

das Vorstellungsgespräch, -e *interview*

beeindrucken (hat beeindruckt) *to impress*

sich bewerben (bewirbt sich, hat sich beworben) um/für + acc. *to apply for*

sich verhalten (verhält sich, hat sich verhalten) *to behave, act*

Noch einmal: **die Erfahrung, sich vor•bereiten, sich vor•stellen**

Hochachtungsvoll *Respectfully (at end of a letter)*

unbezahlt *unpaid*

Eigenschaften von guten Bewerbern

analytisch *analytical*

anständig *decent, respectable*

begabt *talented*

diszipliniert *disciplined*

dynamisch *dynamic*

flexibel *flexible*

gründlich *thorough, detail-oriented*

kollegial *cooperative*

kontaktfreudig *sociable*

motiviert *motivated*

pünktlich *punctual*

qualifiziert *qualified*

selbstständig *self-reliant, independent*

zuständig *responsible*

zuverlässig *reliable*

Die Arbeit

die Aushilfe, -n *part-time worker*

das Gehalt, ⸚er *salary*

der Kollege, [-n], -n/die Kollegin, -nen *colleague, co-worker*

der Termin, -e *meeting, appointment*

Noch einmal: **die Aufgabe**

führen (hat geführt) *to lead, direct*

gut aus•kommen (ist gut ausgekommen) mit + dat. *to get along with*

Berufe

der Beruf, -e *occupation*

der Apotheker, -/die Apothekerin, -nen *pharmacist*

der Bäcker, -/die Bäckerin, -nen *baker*

der Chef, -s/die Chefin, -nen *boss*

der Fleischer, -/die Fleischerin, -nen *butcher*

der Friseur, -e/die Friseurin, -nen *hairdresser, barber*

der Geschäftsmann, ⸚er/die Geschäftsfrau, -en *businessman/-woman*

der Kaufmann, ⸚er/die Kauffrau, -en *dealer, merchant*

der Komponist, [-en], -en/die Komponistin, -nen *composer*

der Krankenpfleger, -/die Krankenschwester, -n *nurse, orderly*

der Lehrer, -/die Lehrerin, -nen *school teacher*

der Makler, -/die Maklerin, -nen *real estate agent*

der Metzger, -/die Metzgerin, -nen *butcher*

der Musiker, -/die Musikerin, -nen *musician*

der Rechtsanwalt, ⸚e/die Rechtsanwältin, -nen *lawyer, attorney*

der Schauspieler, -/die Schauspielerin, -nen *actor/actress*

der Schriftsteller, -/die Schriftstellerin, -nen *author*

der Tierarzt, ⸚e/die Tierärztin, -nen *veterinarian*

der Verkäufer, -/die Verkäuferin, -nen *salesman/-woman*

der Wissenschaftler, -/die Wissenschaftlerin, -nen *scientist*

der Zahnarzt, ⸚e/die Zahnärztin, -nen *dentist*

Kognate: **der Architekt/die Architektin, der Automechaniker/die Automechanikerin, der Babysitter/die Babysitterin, der Filmemacher/die Filmemacherin, der Ingenieur/die Ingenieurin, der Journalist/die Journalistin, der Koch/die Köchin, der Politiker/die Politikerin, der Programmierer/die Programmiererin, der Sänger/die Sängerin, der Sekretär/die Sekretärin**

Noch einmal: **der Arzt/die Ärztin, der Kellner/die Kellnerin**

Kultur und Architektur

die Aufführung, -en *performance*
das Ballett, -e *ballet*
der Begründer, - *founder*
die Bühne, -n *stage*
der Erfinder, - *inventor*
das Erinnerungsstück, -e *keepsake*
das Gebäude, - *building*
das Geburtshaus, -häuser *birthplace*
der Gegenstand, ¨e *object*
die Gegenwart *present*
das Gemälde, - *painting*
der Konzertsaal, -säle *concert hall*
der Kopfhörer, - *headphones*
der Meister, - *master*
das Mittelalter *Middle Ages*
das Musical, -s *musical*
der Nachlass *estate*
die Premiere, -n *premiere*
das Programm, -e *program*
die Spur, -en *track, trace*
die Taubheit *deafness*
die Verzweiflung *desperation*
die Vorstellung, -en *presentation, performance*
Noch einmal: **die Oper, das Stück**
auf•führen (hat aufgeführt) *to perform*
aus•stellen (hat ausgestellt) *to exhibit*
bauen (hat gebaut) *to build*
bewundern (hat bewundert) *to admire*
erobern (hat erobert) *to conquer*
dominieren (hat dominiert) *to dominate*
gelingen + *Dativ* (ist gelungen) *to succeed*
genießen (hat genossen) *to enjoy*
gestalten (hat gestaltet) *to create, form*
inszenieren (hat inszeniert) *to stage, produce*
komponieren (hat komponiert) *to compose*
schaffen (hat geschaffen) *to create*
üben (hat geübt) *to practice, rehearse*
abwechslungsreich *varied, entertaining*
klassisch *classical*
kulturell *cultural*
schwungvoll *lively*
stimmungsvoll *full of atmosphere*
weltberühmt *world-famous*
zahlreich *numerous*

Komparative und Superlative

gern / lieber / Lieblings-, am liebsten *with eagerness / preferably / favorite, most preferably*
gut / besser / best-, am besten *good, well / better / best*
hoch / höher / höchst-, am höchsten *high / higher / highest; tall / taller / tallest*
höchstens *at the most*
viel / mehr / meist-, am meisten *much, many / more / most*
Noch einmal: **meistens**

Relativpronomen

der/den/dem; das/das/dem; die/die/der; die/die/denen *relative pronouns*

Andere Verben

sich beruhigen (hat sich beruhigt) *to calm down*
bieten (bietet, hat geboten) *to offer*
merken (hat gemerkt) *to notice*
recht haben (hat recht gehabt) *to be right*
reichen (hat gereicht) von … bis *to stretch from . . . to*
wünschen (hat gewünscht) *to wish*

Andere Substantive

die Hochzeit, -en *wedding ceremony*
der Typ, -en *guy*
die Welt, -en *world*
Noch einmal: **das Beispiel, die Einladung, die Leute**

Andere Adjektive

andere *other*
aufgeregt *excited, agitated, anxious*
einmalig *unique*
einzig *only*
fest *firm, solid, fixed; steady*
fremd *foreign, strange*
großartig *great, fabulous, fantastic*
hart *hard*
hilfsbereit *helpful*
klasse *cool, great*
letzt *last*
möglich *possible*
nett *nice*
stark *strong*
toll *great*
wahnsinnig *crazy, insane*
weitere *further; additional*
Noch einmal: **nervös, schwierig**

Andere Wörter

als *as; than*
gewöhnlich *usually*
niemals *never*
nun *now*
trotzdem *nevertheless*
Noch einmal: **gleich, sicher, trotzdem**

Andere Ausdrücke

Das hat keinen Zweck. *There's no point in it.*
Hals- und Beinbruch! *Break a leg!*
heute in acht Tagen *a week from today*
Ich drücke dir (Ihnen) ganz fest die Daumen! *I'll really be crossing my fingers for you.*
ich hätte *I would have*
ich wäre *I would be*
Ich wünsch' dir was! *I'm hoping for you! Good luck!*
ich würde *I would*
Toi, toi, toi! *Lots of luck!*
was für ein(e)? *what kind of?*
Wie wäre es mit …? *How would . . . be? How about . . . ?*
Noch einmal: **und so weiter (usw.), zum Beispiel (z.B.)**

Meine eigenen Wörter

_____
_____
_____
_____
_____

The Internet is a valuable resource for locating job opportunities. Stefan went to www.monster.de to find a part-time job that would take advantage of his studies and his English-speaking abilities. He found a job entitled **Praktikum Event Management.**

(Referenz-Nr. 10068112)   Eingang 19.02

Praktikum Event Management   **Die Firma**

Firma:	<u>Global Competence Forum</u>
Abteilung:	Event-Management
Dienstsitz:	72070 Tübingen
Beschreibung des Unternehmens:	Global Competence Forum vermittelt Wissen und Inspiration auf höchstem Niveau. Wir veranstalten Top-Trainings zu aktuellen Managementthemen sowie internationale Seminare im Bereich der Außenwirtschaft.
Anzahl der Plätze:	1

Das Praktikum

Berufsfeld(er) des Praktikums:	• Aus- und Weiterbildung • Sonstige - Weitere Berufsfelder • Organisation • Assistenz/Sekretariat • Sachbearbeitung • Sonstige verwaltende Berufe • Sonstige - Hotelservice/Tourismus • Sonstige - Gastronomie
Gesuchte Studienfächer:	sonstige Fachrichtung
Aufgaben:	Aufgaben- und Terminplanung für die Seminar- und Konferenzorganisation Suche und Auswahl geeigneter Tagungsstätten und sonstiger Partner Kommunikation & Management Abstimmung und Produktion von Seminardokumentationen Organisation von Rahmenprogrammen und Ausstellungen Organisation und Durchführung von An- und Abreise Nachbereitung von Veranstaltungen inklusive Qualitätsmanagement
Anforderungen:	Ausbildung oder Studium Tourismus-/oder Eventbereich Organisiert, zuverlässig und belastbar. Außerdem teamorientiert und bereit zu überdurchschnittlichem Einsatz.
Erforderliche Sprachkenntnisse für das Praktikum:	• Deutsch • Englisch
Frühester Beginn:	01.09.
Dauer:	6 Monate
Vergütung:	400-600 Euro
Sonstige Informationen:	Eine vielseitige Tätigkeit in einem internationalen Umfeld mit Vorgesetzten und Mitarbeitern, die etwas bewegen wollen. Ein leistungsorientiertes Team mit Dynamik, flachen Hierarchien und freundlicher Atmosphäre. Einen Arbeitsplatz in Süddeutschland in der reizvollen Universitätsstadt Tübingen.

Die Bewerbung

Kontakt:	Global Competence Forum Kontaktperson: <u>Frau Claudia Weisser</u> Abteilung: Personalwesen Schlossbergstr. 10 72070 Tübingen Fax: 07071 559730
Bitte bewerben Sie sich per:	E-Mail

Beantworten Sie die folgenden Fragen zum Inserat von Global Competence Forum.

Die Firma

1. In welcher Stadt ist die Firma?
2. Wie viele Personen sucht die Firma?

Das Praktikum

3. Was sind drei Berufsfelder des Praktikums?
4. Welche Sprachen sind wichtig?
5. Wie viel Geld verdient man?

Die Bewerbung

6. Wie heißt die Kontaktperson?
7. Wie soll man sich bewerben?

Sie suchen eine Stelle bei der Firma Global Competence Forum. Schreiben Sie eine kurze E-Mail an die Kontaktperson und stellen Sie sich vor. Stellen Sie auch einige Fragen über das Team, die Arbeitsatmosphäre und den Arbeitsplatz.

wavebreakmedia ltd/Shutterstock.com

GoSeeFoto/Alamy

Der Rosenmontagsumzug in Mainz: Den Karneval feiert man auf der Straße!

Feste, Feiertage und Ferien

In this chapter you will continue to learn how to relate events in the past. You will read and discuss fairy tales and explore vacationing in Switzerland and elsewhere.

Kommunikative Funktionen

> Narrating past events
> Talking about consecutive events in the past
> Talking about concurrent events in the past
> Saying when events occur
> Expressing ownership

Strukturen

> The narrative past
> The past perfect
> Word order in sentences beginning with a subordinate clause
> The subordinating conjunctions **als, nachdem, ob, wann,** and **wenn**
> The genitive case
> Genitive prepositions

Vokabeln

> Märchen
> Die Schweiz: geografische Daten

Kulturelles

> Die Brüder Grimm und ihre Kinder- und Hausmärchen
> Karneval, Fasching, Fastnacht
> Die Schweiz
> Fest- und Feiertage

ANLAUF

Cinderella

fools, carnival participants
parades

Did you enjoy reading fairy tales as a child? Why or why not? Which ones were your favorites?

Kulturnotiz. Märchen are tales in which a hero/heroine survives an ordeal or injustice but is rewarded for perseverance, hope, and faith, where good triumphs over evil, and where there is often retribution for the evil-doer. Irrational forces play a significant role—animals talk, the forest hides witches and dwarves, and princes become enchanted frogs— but the hero/heroine, subjected to endless trial, learns to trust innate abilities, and soon overcomes these evil forces to reach a happy ending. On the surface, **Märchen** are fantastic and antiquated tales but they speak to the unarticulated, unsophisticated fears of children with vivid imagery and a clear delineation between good and evil, helping them process their fears in a productive manner. Although long sometimes, **Märchen** generally contain many recurring expressions.

Aschenputtel°: Ein Märchen nach den Brüdern Grimm

Anna und ihre Freunde wollen zum Karneval ein langes Wochenende in Köln verbringen. Tagsüber gibt es viele kostümierte Narren° auf den Straßen und endlose Umzüge°. Und abends können sie auf einen Karnevalsball gehen, wo man bis spät in die Nacht tanzt und trinkt … und sich vielleicht verliebt. Wer weiß? Vielleicht lernt Anna dort ihren Prinzen kennen, wie Aschenputtel …

Vorschau
Wissenswerte Vokabeln: Märchen

Talking about fairy tales

„Es war einmal ein König ...“

der Königssohn, die Königin, der König, die Königstochter
der Prinz   die Prinzessin

die Stiefmutter

der Jäger

der Wald

die Hexe

ein giftiger Apfel

der Zwerg

die gute Fee

der Frosch

der Zauberer

der Spiegel

Illustrations © Cengage Learning 2014

„... und wenn sie nicht gestorben sind, dann leben sie noch heute.“

BEISPIEL   *Was gibt die alte Hexe Schneewittchen?*

1 Schneewittchen „Schneewittchen" ist ein sehr bekanntes Märchen von den Brüdern Grimm. Lesen Sie die Sätze und setzen Sie die richtigen Wörter ein.

1. Eine böse _____ will ihre Stieftochter Schneewittchen von einem _____ erschießen lassen°.
2. Er erschießt Schneewittchen nicht und sie läuft allein weg in den dunklen _____ hinein.
3. Schneewittchen wohnt bei sieben _____en.
4. Die Königin schaut jeden Tag in einen _____ und findet heraus, dass sie nicht die Schönste ist.
5. Die Königin verkleidet° sich als _____.
6. Die Königin gibt Schneewittchen einen giftigen _____ und Schneewittchen scheint zu sterben.
7. Die Zwerge legen Schneewittchen in einen Glassarg°. Ein _____ bekommt Schneewittchens Glassarg von den Zwergen, und auf dem Heimweg fällt der Apfel aus ihrem Hals. Sie wird wieder lebendig.
8. Er heiratet Schneewittchen und sie wird schließlich die neue _____.

erschießen lassen: have shot to death

Märchen: singular and plural forms are the same.

disguises

glass coffin

Brennpunkt Kultur

Web Search
Web Link

Die Brüder Grimm und ihre Kinder- und Hausmärchen

There has been no single work of children's literature more important to Western culture than the **Kinder- und Hausmärchen,** an anthology of folk (fairy) tales **(Volksmärchen)** published by the Brothers Grimm, Jacob (1785–1863) and Wilhelm (1786–1859). The Brothers Grimm spent many years collecting these oral **Märchen,** which had previously existed only in the memory of the people who told and retold them. The Grimms did not write the fairy tales themselves, but instead wrote down and edited the tales they were told. They published the first volume of their anthology in 1812; a second volume, including contributions from other collectors of folk tales, was printed in 1814. Because of their research and their fascination with the German language, the Grimm brothers are regarded as the founders of modern German studies **(Germanistik).** This reputation was enhanced by Jacob Grimm's **Deutsche Grammatik** and by their efforts to publish the first comprehensive **Deutsches Wörterbuch,** a project that lasted from 1852 to its completion in 1961.

rook76/Shutterstock.com

Wilhelm und Jacob Grimm

Kulturkreuzung

Haben Sie als Kind gern gelesen? Was für Geschichten haben Sie am liebsten° gehört oder gelesen? Hatten Sie eine Heldenfigur, die Sie verehrt° haben? Warum hatten Sie diese Figur so gern? Welche Märchen haben Ihnen besonders gut gefallen? Gibt es Unterschiede zwischen Märchenfiguren, die Jungen und Mädchen am besten gefallen?

like the most
cherished

2 Berühmte Märchensprüche Welches Zitat stammt aus welchem Märchen?

Aschenputtel • Die Bremer Stadtmusikanten • Hänsel und Gretel • Rapunzel • Rumpelstilzchen • Rotkäppchen • Schneewittchen

1. „Ei, Großmutter, was hast du für ein entsetzlich großes Maul!" „Dass ich dich besser fressen kann!"
2. „Heute back ich, morgen brau ich, übermorgen hol ich der Königin ihr Kind; ach, wie gut, dass niemand weiß, dass ich _____ heiß!"
3. „Zieh lieber mit uns fort, wir gehen nach Bremen; etwas Besseres als den Tod° findest du überall."
4. „Rüttel dich und schüttel dich, wirf Gold und Silber über mich."
5. „Rapunzel, Rapunzel, lass dein Haar herunter."
6. „Spieglein, Spieglein an der Wand, wer ist die Schönste im ganzen Land?"
7. „Knusper, knusper, knäuschen, wer knuspert an meinem Häuschen?" – „Der Wind, der Wind, das himmlische Kind."

death

Bäumchen, Bäumchen schüttle dich: Wirf Lack und Leder° über mich!

3 Thematische Fragen Beantworten Sie die folgenden Fragen auf Deutsch.

1. Was passiert in der Version von „Aschenputtel", die wir in Nordamerika kennen? Lebt die Mutter noch? Lebt der Vater noch?
2. Wie ist das Leben für Aschenputtel? Was muss sie alles machen?
3. Wer hilft Aschenputtel: eine Fee, ein Zauberer oder zwei Vögel?
4. Hat Aschenputtel Stiefbrüder oder Stiefschwestern? Wie sind sie?
5. Wohin geht Aschenputtel?
6. Was verliert Aschenputtel auf dem Ball?

Courtesy of Matthias Schwoerer, www.schwoe.net.

4 Zeitdetektiv Hier sind siebzehn Sätze im Präteritum°. Welche Sätze im Präsens bedeuten ungefähr das Gleiche?

1. Aschenputtels Mutter **starb.**
2. Eine schlimme Zeit **begann.**
3. Der König **lud** zu einem Fest° **ein.**
4. Der Königssohn **hielt** Aschenputtel für eine fremde Königstochter.

a. Der Königssohn hält Aschenputtel für eine fremde Königstochter.
b. Der König lädt zu einem Fest ein.
c. Aschenputtels Mutter stirbt.
d. Eine schlimme Zeit beginnt.

Aschenputtels Vater …
5. … **heiratete** eine neue Frau.
6. … **sollte** für Aschenputtel einen Zweig zurückbringen.
7. … **brachte** für Aschenputtel einen Haselzweig°.

Aschenputtels Vater …
e. … heiratet wieder.
f. … bringt für Aschenputtel einen Haselzweig.
g. … soll für Aschenputtel einen Zweig zurückbringen.

Aschenputtel …
8. … **sah** schmutzig **aus.**
9. … **ging** jeden Tag zum Baum und **weinte.**
10. … **zog** das Kleid **an.**
11. … **rannte** schnell davon.
12. … **verlor** auf der Treppe ihren linken Schuh.
13. … **wollte** auch zum Tanz mitgehen.

Aschenputtel …
h. … rennt° schnell davon.
i. … will auch zum Tanz mitgehen.
j. … zieht das Kleid an.
k. … geht jeden Tag zum Baum und weint°.
l. … verliert auf der Treppe ihren linken Schuh.
m. … sieht schmutzig aus.

Die Stiefschwestern …
14. … **nannten** sie Aschenputtel.
15. … **riefen** Aschenputtel **zu:** „Wir gehen auf das Schloss des Königs."
16. … **erkannten** Aschenputtel nicht.
17. … **schnitten** sich die Zehe und die Ferse **ab.**

Die Stiefschwestern …
n. … erkennen° Aschenputtel nicht.
o. … nennen° sie Aschenputtel.
p. … schneiden sich die Zehe und die Ferse ab.
q. … rufen Aschenputtel zu: „Wir gehen auf das Schloss des Königs."

5 Wortfelder Welches Wort gehört zum gleichen Wortfeld wie das Wort in der linken Spalte? Unterstreichen Sie es.

BEISPIEL das Messer:	<u>schneiden</u>	schwer arbeiten	tanzen
1. der Herd:	waschen	kochen	schlafen
2. die Asche:	schön	blau	schmutzig
3. Edelsteine:	Diamanten	Kleider	Essen
4. der Baum:	passen	bringen	pflanzen
5. der liebe Gott:	beten°	schütteln°	studieren
6. das Vögelchen:	fliegen	schwimmen	heiraten
7. der Ball:	arbeiten	tanzen	studieren
8. der Schuh:	weinen	anprobieren	trinken
9. der Fuß:	das Haar	die Zehe	die Nase

narrative past

party, celebration

Zeitdetektiv. You will learn about the narrative past (**Präteritum**) in this chapter.

hazelnut branch

Kulturnotiz. The Disney animation *Cinderella* is based on Charles Perrault's French version of the tale.

runs
cries

recognize
name

to pray / to shake

Lesen Sie eine deutsche Version von „Aschenputtel".

whose
pious, devout

Es war einmal ein hübsches Mädchen, dessen° Mutter krank wurde. Als die Frau fühlte, dass sie sterben musste, rief sie ihre Tochter zu sich: „Liebes Kind, bleib fromm° und gut, so wird dir der liebe Gott immer helfen, und ich will vom Himmel auf dich herabblicken." Dann starb die Frau.

Nach einem Jahr heiratete der reiche Vater eine neue Frau, die zwei Töchter mit ins Haus brachte. Diese Schwestern waren schön von Gesicht, aber böse von Herzen. Nun musste das Mädchen von morgens bis abends schwer arbeiten. Abends musste sie sich neben den Herd in die Asche legen. Und weil sie darum immer schmutzig aussah, nannten die Stiefschwestern sie Aschenputtel.

Eines Tages machte der Vater eine Reise. Er fragte, was er den Mädchen mitbringen sollte. „Schöne Kleider!", „Perlen und Edelsteine", sagten die Stiefschwestern. Aber Aschenputtel sagte: „Vater, bring mir einfach den ersten Zweig von einem Baum, den du auf dem Heimweg findest."

es=das Mädchen=Aschenputtel

Der Vater brachte Kleider und Edelsteine für die Stiefschwestern und einen Haselzweig für Aschenputtel. Aschenputtel dankte ihm und pflanzte den Zweig auf dem Grab ihrer Mutter. Er wuchs zu einem schönen Haselnussbaum. Aschenputtel ging jeden Tag dreimal darunter, weinte und betete. Jedes Mal kam ein weißes Vögelchen auf den Baum und gab dem Mädchen alles, was es° sich wünschte.

Illustrations courtesy of Margret Rettich.

Eines Tages lud der König alle Mädchen im Land zu einem Fest ein. Der Königssohn suchte eine Braut. Die zwei Stiefschwestern riefen Aschenputtel zu: „Wir gehen auf das Schloss des Königs." Aschenputtel wollte auch gern zum Tanz mitgehen. Die Stiefmutter aber erlaubte es nicht: „Du hast keine Kleider und Schuhe und willst tanzen? Du kommst nicht mit!" Darauf ging sie mit ihren beiden Töchtern fort.

shake
schüttel ...: *shiver*

Aschenputtel ging zum Grab ihrer Mutter unter den Haselbaum und rief: „Bäumchen, rüttel° dich und schüttel dich° – wirf Gold und Silber über mich!" Da warf ihr der Vogel ein Kleid aus Gold und Silber herunter. Aschenputtel zog das Kleid an und ging zum Fest. Ihre Schwestern und Stiefmutter erkannten sie nicht. Der Königssohn hielt sie für eine fremde Königstochter und tanzte nur mit ihr. Als Aschenputtel nach Hause gehen wollte, sprach der Königssohn: „Ich begleite° dich!" Aber Aschenputtel lief schnell fort.

accompany

Am zweiten Tag wiederholte sich alles. Am dritten Tag brachte das Vögelchen ein glänzendes Kleid und Schuhe aus Gold. Wieder tanzte der Königssohn nur mit ihr, wieder lief Aschenputtel schnell fort. Aber diesmal verlor sie auf der Treppe ihren linken Schuh.

Der Königssohn proklamierte: „Die Frau, deren° Fuß in diesem Schuh passt, soll meine Braut werden!" Da freuten sich die Schwestern. Die älteste Stiefschwester nahm den Schuh mit in ihr Zimmer und probierte ihn an. Aber der Schuh war zu klein. Da sagte ihr die Mutter: „Schneid die Zehe ab! Wenn du Königin bist, so brauchst du nicht mehr zu Fuß zu gehen." Da schnitt die Schwester die Zehe ab.

whose

Der Königssohn nahm sie als seine Braut aufs Pferd. Als sie am Grab von Aschenputtels Mutter vorbeiritten°, riefen zwei Täubchen° vom Haselbaum: „Rucke di guh, rucke di guh, Blut ist im Schuh. Der Schuh ist zu klein. Die rechte Braut sitzt noch daheim°." Da sah der Königssohn das Blut und brachte sie zurück.

rode past / little doves
at home

Da probierte die andere Schwester den Schuh an, aber die Ferse° war zu groß. Da nahm sie ein Messer und schnitt die Ferse ab. Die Schwester und der Königssohn ritten am Grab vorbei und wieder riefen die Täubchen: „Rucke di guh, rucke di guh, Blut ist im Schuh ..." Da brachte der Königssohn die falsche Braut wieder nach Hause zurück.

heel

Er fragte den Vater: „Haben Sie noch eine andere Tochter?" „Nein", sagte der, „nur das schmutzige Aschenputtel. Sie kann nicht die Richtige sein." Der Königssohn wollte sie aber sehen. So probierte Aschenputtel den goldenen Schuh an, und er passte wie angegossen°. Dann nahm der Königssohn Aschenputtel aufs Pferd und ritt mit ihr fort. Diesmal riefen die Täubchen: „Rucke di guh, rucke di guh, kein Blut ist im Schuh. Der Schuh ist nicht zu klein, die rechte Braut, die führt er heim." Dann flogen die beiden Täubchen auf Aschenputtels Schultern, eines rechts, das andere links.

poured on

40
45
50
55
60
65

Rückblick

6 Stimmt das? Stimmen diese Aussagen zum Text? Wenn nicht, was stimmt?

	Ja, das stimmt.	Nein, das. stimmt nicht
1. Aschenputtels Vater war krank und starb.	○	○
2. Aschenputtel musste in der Küche schwer arbeiten und in der Asche neben dem Herd schlafen.	○	○
3. Aschenputtels Vater brachte ihr Perlen und Edelsteine von seiner Reise zurück.	○	○
4. Der König lud alle Mädchen im Land zu einem Fest ein, weil sein Sohn eine Braut suchte.	○	○
5. Die Stiefmutter nahm Aschenputtel zum Ball mit.	○	○
6. Aschenputtel rief zum Haselbaum: „Rüttel dich und schüttel dich, wirf Gold und Silber über mich!"	○	○
7. Am dritten Abend brachte der Vogel Aschenputtel das schönste Kleid und Schuhe aus Glas.	○	○
8. Aschenputtel verlor einen Schuh beim Tanzen.	○	○
9. Der Königssohn wollte die Frau heiraten, deren Fuß in den goldenen Schuh passte.	○	○
10. Aschenputtel musste sich die Ferse und die Zehe abschneiden, damit der Schuh passte.	○	○
11. Die Stiefmutter und die Stiefschwestern freuten sich, dass der Königssohn Aschenputtel als seine Braut erkannte.	○	○

Complete the **Ergänzen Sie** activity in the Student Activities Manual before doing the next activity.

änderte ...: changed

Kurz gefragt. These questions are in the simple past.

7 Kurz gefragt Beantworten Sie diese Fragen auf Deutsch.

1. Was sagte Aschenputtels Mutter zu ihrer Tochter, bevor sie starb?
2. Wie änderte sich° Aschenputtels Leben, nachdem ihre Mutter starb?
3. Warum nannten die Stiefschwestern das Mädchen „Aschenputtel"?
4. Was wünschte sich Aschenputtel von ihrem Vater und was machte sie damit?
5. Warum hielt der König ein Fest?
6. Warum wollten die Stiefschwestern (und auch Aschenputtel) zum Fest gehen?
7. Was machte das Vögelchen, als Aschenputtel zum Grab ging?
8. Wen nahm die Stiefmutter mit zum Fest?
9. Wie fand der Königssohn Aschenputtel wieder?
10. Wie wusste der Königssohn, dass Aschenputtel wirklich die richtige Braut war?

8 Kurz interpretiert Beantworten Sie diese Fragen auf Deutsch.

1. In vielen Märchen hat die Zahl 3 eine symbolische Funktion. Zählen Sie alle Elemente in „Aschenputtel", die in Dreiergruppen passieren. Was symbolisieren sie wohl?
2. Aschenputtels Liebe zu ihrer Mutter ist sehr wichtig. Wie zeigt Aschenputtel diese Liebe? Hält die verstorbene Mutter ihr Versprechen ein, und passt sie auf Aschenputtel auf? Wenn ja, wie tut sie das?
3. Welche Zauberelemente oder unwahrscheinlichen Episoden gibt es in diesem Märchen? Was sind sie und warum sind sie wichtig?
4. In dieser Geschichte spielt Aschenputtels Vater praktisch keine Rolle. Warum ist die Figur des Vaters so neutral, aber die Figuren der Stiefmutter und Stiefschwestern sind so böse und negativ?

9 **Textdetektiv: Anlauftext.** Use the *Anlauftext* to recognize important aspects of German structure and usage.

1. Fairy tales are written in the past tense. This is shown in the form of the verb. Look at the following examples from the *Anlauftext* and decide if the verb shows the past tense with or without a **-te** ending and mark the appropriate column. Then find the infinitive for that verb in the word bank.

gehen • kommen • machen • müssen • sagen • sehen • tanze

	-te ending	no ending	infinitive
a. Nun **musste** das Mädchen schwer arbeiten.	○	○	_____
b. Eines Tages **machte** der Vater eine Reise.	○	○	_____
c. Jedes Mal **kam** ein weißes Vögelchen.	○	○	_____
d. Aschenputtel **ging** zum Grab ihrer Mutter.	○	○	_____
e. Wieder **tanzte** der Köngissohn mit ihr.	○	○	_____
f. Da **sagte** ihr die Mutter ...	○	○	_____
g. Da **sah** der Königssohn das Blut.	○	○	_____

2. True or False: What conclusions concerning past tense in German are correct?
   a. Strong verbs like **gehen** show the past tense with a **-te** ending.
   b. Weak verbs like **machen** have the same stem vowel in the infinitive and the past tense.
   c. Strong verbs like **kommen** have a **-t** ending in the past tense in the third person singular (**er/sie/es**) form.
   d. Modal verbs like **müssen** change their stem vowel from the infinitive to the past tense form.
   e. Some past tense forms in German (**sah, kam, war**) look very much like English forms.

10 **Freie Kommunikation: Rollenspiel: Der Prinz und Aschenputtel.** S1 ist der Prinz und S2 ist seine Mutter, die Königin. Sprechen Sie miteinander über Aschenputtel. Was haben Sie auf dem Fest gemacht? Wie war Aschenputtel? Was möchten Sie jetzt machen?

11 **Interview: Märchen** Stellen Sie einem Partner/einer Partnerin die folgenden Fragen.

1. Hast du als Kind „Aschenputtel" gelesen? Was war damals deine Reaktion?
2. Was sollen Kinder von „Aschenputtel" lernen?
3. Welche Märchen findest du sexistisch? Warum?
4. Hast du als Kind gern Märchen gelesen? Hast du sie immer noch gern?
5. Welches sind deine Lieblingsmärchen? Beschreib die Hauptfiguren in deinen Lieblingsmärchen.
6. In den meisten Märchen passiert ein großes Unglück. Was ist das Unglück in deinen Lieblingsmärchen?
7. Welche Zauberkräfte helfen der Hauptfigur in deinen Lieblingsmärchen?
8. Welche Märchen aus anderen Ländern, Kontinenten und Kulturen kennst du?

Hänsel und Gretel

Rotkäppchen

© Cengage Learning 2014

Strukturen

 Narrating past events

The narrative past

In **Kapitel 5** you learned that the conversational past tense (**das Perfekt**) is used in informal contexts, in speaking, and in letter writing to talk about events in the past.

> Tante Uschi **hat** als Kellnerin **gearbeitet.**

German speakers use the narrative past (**das Präteritum**), also called the simple past, to recount past events in written texts, such as novels, stories, news articles, and occasionally in speaking, especially when telling a long, uninterrupted story.

> Da **begann** eine schlimme Zeit.   *With that began a difficult time.*

A. Narrative past: regular (weak) verbs

Regular (weak) verbs (**schwache Verben**) add a **-te** as a narrative past tense marker. All forms except the **ich-** and **er/sie/es-**forms add the same endings as in the present tense (e.g., **-st, -t,** or **-n**).

machen: *to do, make*	
Singular	**Plural**
ich mach**te**	wir mach**ten**
du mach**test**	ihr mach**tet**
Sie mach**ten**	Sie mach**ten**
er/sie/es mach**te**	sie mach**ten**

Regular verbs with a stem ending in **-t, -d, -fn, -gn, -chn,** or **-kn** insert an additional **e** before the **-te** to facilitate pronunciation, e.g., **arbeiten, beten, reden,** and **öffnen.**

> Aschenputtel weinte und bet**e**te.   *Cinderella cried and prayed.*

These are the narrative past forms of **arbeiten** showing the inserted **-e-.**

arbeiten: *to work*	
Singular	**Plural**
ich arbeit**e**te	wir arbeit**e**ten
du arbeit**e**test	ihr arbeit**e**tet
Sie arbeit**e**ten	Sie arbeit**e**ten
er/sie/es arbeit**e**te	sie arbeit**e**ten

As in the present tense, regular verbs with separable prefixes place the prefix at the end of the sentence, leaving the conjugated narrative past form of the verb in the second position.

> **an•probieren**
>
> Aschenputtel **probierte** den goldenen Schuh **an.** *Cinderella tried on the golden slipper.*

Remember that regular (weak) verbs have a letter **-t** in both the narrative past tense and the conversational past tense: **sagen, ich sagte, ich habe gesagt.**

Many North German speakers prefer the narrative past over the conversational past even in conversation.

Some of these forms look very much like the English simple past forms and should present few problems in reading.

Notice that the ich-form and the er/sie/es-forms of the narrative past are identical, as are the wir- and sie/Sie-forms.

Other verbs that insert an additional e include regnen, rechnen, and **trocknen.**

12 Hannelores Kindheit° in Deutschland Erzählen Sie Hannelores Geschichte im Präteritum mit den angegebenen schwachen Verben.

childhood

Hannelore
1. in Weinheim leben
2. oft auf der Straße spielen
3. 1975 ihren fünften Geburtstag feiern
4. mit ihren Eltern im Wald Pilze° suchen
5. von amerikanischen Soldaten Englisch lernen

mushrooms

Oma Kunz
6. jeden Tag einkaufen
7. für die ganze Familie kochen
8. Opa heiraten
9. in der Stadt arbeiten
10. jeden Sonntag in der Kirche beten

Ihre Nachbarn
11. einen Tante-Emma-Laden° gründen°
12. Brot, Käse und Wurst verkaufen
13. den Laden morgens um halb sieben aufmachen
14. den Laden abends um sechs zumachen
15. ein gutes Einkommen verdienen

family-run shop / establish

13 Verliebt, verlobt, verheiratet Erzählen Sie die Liebesgeschichte von Hannelore und Bob Adler mit den angegebenen schwachen Verben im Präteritum.

Hannelore
1. die Universität in Heidelberg wählen
2. zu Hause bei den Eltern wohnen und Geld sparen°
3. mit dem Zug von Weinheim nach Heidelberg pendeln°
4. Englisch und Volkswirtschaft studieren
5. mit Nachhilfestunden° in Deutsch und Englisch Taschengeld verdienen
6. mit Schülern und mit amerikanischen Soldaten arbeiten
7. eines Tages einen Deutsch sprechenden namens Bob Adler kennenlernen

save

commute

tutoring

Bob
8. der Hannelore lustige Witze° erzählen
9. einen guten Eindruck auf sie machen
10. als Ingenieur in der Armee dienen°
11. sich auf die Wochenenden in Heidelberg freuen
12. die Studentin nach ihrer Telefonnummer fragen
13. sich schnell in die Hannelore verlieben
14. eine Weile warten und sich dann den Eltern in Weinheim vorstellen
15. sich nach einem romantischen Jahr in Heidelberg mit der Hannelore verloben
16. in Bad Krozingen die Hannelore heiraten

jokes

serve

sprinter81/Shutterstock.com

Karneval, Fasching, Fastnacht

The "crazy" days **(Die tollen Tage)** of the **Karneval** season are some of the most popular holidays of the calendar in German-speaking countries. The name changes with location—**Karneval** in the Rhineland, **Fasching** in Bavaria and Austria, **Fastnacht** in Southwestern Germany, and **Fasnacht** in Switzerland—as do customs and actual dates, but it is generally regarded as the high point of the winter season. These are the days of revelry and merrymaking that precede the beginning of Lent **(die Fastenzeit)**, the period in which Catholics have been traditionally required to fast in preparation for Easter.

In the Rhineland, the Karneval season always opens on November 11th at 11:11 A.M., while in the south the season traditionally begins on Epiphany, January 6 **(Dreikönigstag)**. On the last Thursday before Ash Wednesday **(Fetter Donnerstag, or Altweiberfastnacht)** women customarily chase men with scissors and try to cut off a piece of their neckties. This marks the start of the six-day celebration: social taboos are relaxed, romances blossom, and the partying begins. Schools either go on vacation or suspend classes, while students hold costumed dance parties and small towns and city neighborhoods put on their own parades. In and around the Rhineland, special "fools' guilds" **(Narrengesellschaften)** hold balls and "roasts" **(Kappensitzungen)** presided over by a **Narrenkönig** and **Narrenkönigin**. On **Rosenmontag**, two days before Ash Wednesday, Cologne and Mainz host their famous parades with marching bands, costumed participants, dancing spectators, and decorated floats. On **Karnevalsdienstag** final parades, parties, and costume balls signal the conclusion of the holiday season, which traditionally ends with a fish dinner and a ritualistic "funeral of the **Karneval**" on Ash Wednesday **(Aschermittwoch)**.

Gernot Huber/laif/Redux

Die Tanzpaare von den Blauen Funken gehören zum Kölner Karneval wie der Dom zu Köln.

Kulturkreuzung

Viele Kulturen haben einen Feiertag, an dem die Menschen ein Kostüm oder eine Verkleidung tragen. An welchem Tag ist das in den USA und in Kanada? Welche religiöse oder nicht-religiöse Funktion haben die Kostüme an diesem Feiertag? Feiert man in den USA und Kanada Karneval? Wo?

B. Narrative past: irregular (strong) verbs

Strong verbs **(starke Verben)** show a vowel change from the infinitive to the narrative (simple) past. In English these verbs are referred to as *irregular verbs* (e.g., *see > saw, eat > ate*). You should learn to recognize these forms in German texts and be able to recall the infinitive.

> sehen > sah
>> Da **sah** der Königssohn das Blut.   *Then the king's son saw the blood.*

Some verbs change consonants as well as the vowel in the narrative past.

> **geh**en > g**ing**
>> Aschenputtel **ging** zum Grab ihrer Mutter.   *Cinderella went to her mother's grave.*

Verbs with separable prefixes position the prefix at the end of the sentence.

> an•zieh**en** > zog an
>> Aschenputtel **zog** das Kleid **an.**   *Cinderella put the dress on*

Irregular verbs have no ending in the **ich-** and the **er/sie/es**-forms. The endings of all other forms are the same as the present tense endings.

<table>
<tr><th colspan="2">sehen: to see</th></tr>
<tr><th>Singular</th><th>Plural</th></tr>
<tr><td>ich sah</td><td>wir sahen</td></tr>
<tr><td>du sahst</td><td>ihr saht</td></tr>
<tr><td>Sie sahen</td><td>Sie sahen</td></tr>
<tr><td>er/sie/es sah</td><td>sie sahen</td></tr>
</table>

Here are some common strong verbs in the narrative and conversational past. Use your knowledge of English irregular verbs to remember the German forms (e.g., *sing/sang, eat/ate*.) For a complete list see the appendix of this book.

Infinitive	Narrative past	Conversational past	
	ich/er/sie/es	**er/sie/es**	
beg**i**nnen	beg**a**nn	hat begonnen	*began*
essen	**a**ß	hat gegessen	*ate*
f**i**nden	f**a**nd	hat gefunden	*found*
g**e**ben	g**a**b	hat gegeben	*gave*
g**e**hen	g**ing**	ist gegangen	*went*
k**o**mmen	k**a**m	ist gekommen	*came*
schl**a**fen	schl**ief**	hat geschlafen	*slept*
schr**ei**ben	schr**ie**b	hat geschrieben	*wrote*
s**e**hen	s**a**h	hat gesehen	*saw*
s**i**tzen	s**a**ß	hat gesessen	*sat*
spr**e**chen	spr**a**ch	hat gesprochen	*spoke*
st**e**hen	st**a**nd	hat gestanden	*stood*
tr**i**nken	tr**a**nk	hat getrunken	*drank*
z**ie**hen	z**o**g	hat gezogen	*pulled*

Strong verbs with stems ending in **-t** or **-d** generally insert an additional **e** in the narrative past forms for **du** and **ihr** (e.g., **du standest, ihr standet**). Those with stems ending in an **s**-sound generally insert an **e** for **du** (e.g., **du lasest, du aßest**).

Here are the infinitives and narrative past forms of some more common verbs: **anfangen, fing … an** *to begin;* **bekommen, bekam** *to get;* **bitten, bat** *to ask for;* **bleiben, blieb** *to remain;* **einladen, lud … ein** *to invite;* **fahren, fuhr** *to drive;* **fangen, fing** *to catch;* **fliegen, flog** *to fly;* **halten, hielt** *to stop;* **helfen, half** *to help;* **laufen, lief** *to run, walk;* **lesen, las** *to read;* **nehmen, nahm** *to take;* **reiten, ritt** *to ride;* **rufen, rief** *to call;* **schneiden, schnitt** *to cut;* **schwimmen, schwamm** *to swim;* **singen, sang** *to sing;* **steigen, stieg** *to climb;* **sterben, starb** *to die;* **tragen, trug** *to wear, carry;* **treffen, traf** *to meet;* **werfen, warf** *to throw.*

14 Der gestiefelte Kater° Kennen Sie das Märchen vom gestiefelten Kater? Ein Müller° hatte drei Söhne. Der Müller starb, und der jüngste Sohn bekam kein Geld, sondern nur einen Kater. Schreiben Sie das richtige Verb in die Lücken und erzählen Sie das Märchen vom gestiefelten Kater nach.

Der ...: Puss-in-Boots
miller

aß • bat • begann • bekam • trug

Der jüngste Müllerssohn _____ nach dem Tod seines Vaters nichts als einen Kater. Doch plötzlich _____ dieser Kater zu sprechen und bat den Müllerssohn um ein Paar Stiefel. Bald _____ der Kater wunderbare° rote Stiefel. Dann jagte° er Rebhühner°, brachte° sie zu dem König und sagte: „Die hat Ihnen mein Herr, der Graf°, geschickt!" Das freute den König sehr, weil er sehr gern Rebhühner _____, und er schenkte dem Kater einen Sack voll Gold. Der Müllerssohn war erstaunt°, als ihm der Kater das Gold brachte und ihn _____: „Tu, was ich dir sage, und so wirst du reich!"

wonderful
hunted / partridges / brought
count, earl

astounded

fuhr • hörte • lief • lud ... ein • saß • schenkte • schwamm

Ein paar Tage später _____ der Müllerssohn im Fluss und der Kater versteckte° seine Kleider. Als der König in seiner Kutsche° vorbei _____, rief der Kater: „Hilfe, jemand° hat meinem Herrn, dem Grafen, die Kleider gestohlen!!!" Der König _____ dem Müllerssohn schöne Kleider und _____ ihn _____ mitzufahren. In der Kutsche _____ die schöne Tochter des Königs, die Prinzessin. Der Kater _____ voraus und befahl° den Leuten in den Feldern: „Gleich wird der König vorbeifahren. Wenn er fragt, so sagt, das ganze Land gehört dem Grafen!" Als der König dies _____, meinte er, der Müllerssohn sei ein reicher Edelmann°.

hid
coach
someone

ordered

nobleman
devoured (as an animal eats)

ankam • fragte • fraß° • bekam • kam • sprang

Bald _____ der Kater ins Schloss des großen Zauberers. Der Kater _____: „Also, Zauberer, kannst du dich in jedes Tier verwandeln°?" „Ja, natürlich," sagte er! Kaum hatte der Zauberer sich in eine Maus verwandelt, _____ der Kater auf und _____ sie. So wurde der Müllerssohn der Besitzer° des großen Schlosses. Als die Kutsche am Schloss _____, begrüßte der Kater den König: „Willkommen im Schloss meines Herrn!" Der arme° Müllerssohn _____ die Prinzessin zur Frau und wurde selbst König.

transform

owner

poor

15 Der Mann im Smoking° Helene hat einen „Prinzen" im Smoking getroffen, aber leider hat ihr „Märchen" kein Happyend. Ergänzen Sie die Geschichte mit der richtigen Präteritumform.

tuxedo

| (an)kommen | (an)rufen | (auf)schreiben | beginnen | essen | finden |
| sagen | sitzen | sprechen | tragen | treffen | trinken |

Gestern Abend ging Helene auf einen Fastnachtsball in der Tübinger Stadthalle. Der Ball _____ um 20.00 Uhr, aber sie _____ erst um 21.00 Uhr an. Dort _____ sie einen jungen Mann. Er _____ einen eleganten Smoking. Sie _____ lange miteinander, _____ Wein und tanzten. Sie _____ auch Pizza und Kuchen. Um 24.00 Uhr _____ Helene, dass sie gehen musste. Er _____ ihre Adresse auf. Am nächsten Tag _____ er ihre Adresse nicht mehr und war sehr traurig darüber. Helene _____ den ganzen Tag in ihrem Zimmer und wartete auf den Mann im Smoking, aber er _____ sie nicht an.

C. Narrative past: *sein, haben,* and the modal verbs

German speakers frequently use the auxiliary verbs **haben** and **sein** in the narrative (simple) past—in speaking as well as in writing. These are their forms.

sein: *to be*				haben: *to have*		
Singular		**Plural**		**Singular**		**Plural**
ich	**war**	wir	**waren**	ich	**hatte**	wir	**hatten**
du	**warst**	ihr	**wart**	du	**hattest**	ihr	**hattet**
Sie	**waren**	Sie	**waren**	Sie	**hatten**	Sie	**hatten**
er/sie/es	**war**	sie	**waren**	er/sie/es	**hatte**	sie	**hatten**

The modal verbs form their past tense like the regular (weak) verbs with the **-te** past tense marker. In the narrative past, the umlaut is dropped. Note that the **g** in **mögen** changes to **ch** in the narrative past.

Infinitive	Narrative past	Meaning
dürfen	d**u**rfte	*was allowed to*
können	k**o**nnte	*was able to, could*
mögen	m**o**chte	*liked*
müssen	m**u**sste	*had to*
sollen	sollte	*was supposed to*
wollen	wollte	*wanted to*

16 Als Kind durfte ich nicht rauchen Was durften (konnten usw.) Sie als Kind nicht machen? Beantworten Sie die folgenden Fragen mit einem Partner/einer Partnerin. Benutzen Sie das passende Modalverb im Präteritum.

BEISPIEL S1: *Was durftest du als Kind nicht machen?*
S2: *Als Kind durfte ich nicht rauchen.*

weit zur Schule fahren	mein Zimmer sauber° machen	Sport treiben
Gemüse essen	schnell laufen	spät ins Kino gehen
früh aufstehen	(sich) baden	rauchen
Auto fahren	in die Schule gehen	Schlittschuh° laufen
Alkohol trinken	Deutsch sprechen	Klavier üben

clean

ice skate

1. Was durftest du als Kind nicht machen?
2. Was konntest du als Kind nicht machen?
3. Was musstest du als Kind nicht machen?
4. Was wolltest du als Kind nicht machen?
5. Was solltest du als Kind zu Hause nicht machen?

Losevsky Pavel/Shutterstock.com

Remember: **ich durfte nicht** = *I wasn't allowed to, was forbidden to*; **ich musste nicht** = *I didn't have to*; **ich sollte nicht** = *I wasn't supposed to.*

↩ **17** Was wollte Aschenputtel? Beschreiben Sie mithilfe von den Modalverben alles, was Aschenputtel **wollte, sollte, musste, konnte** oder **durfte**.

BEISPIEL fromm und gut bleiben   *Aschenputtel sollte fromm und gut bleiben.*

1. fromm und gut bleiben
2. nicht mehr in einem Bett schlafen
3. neben dem Herd in der Asche schlafen
4. einen Zweig als Andenken von ihrem Vater bekommen
5. auch zum Fest des Königs mitgehen
6. ohne Kleid und Schuhe nicht zum Fest mitgehen
7. allein zu Hause bleiben
8. als einzige mit dem Königssohn tanzen
9. erst als Letzte den Schuh anprobieren

Courtesy of Tom Lovik.

Frosch oder Prinz?

D. Narrative past: mixed verbs

Mixed verbs (**gemischte Verben**) combine the past tense marker **-te** that is added to the stem of regular (weak) verbs with the vowel change of irregular (strong) verbs when forming the narrative (simple) past.

Infinitive: **denken**
Der Vater **dachte**: „Kann das   *The father thought, "Can that*
   Aschenputtel sein?"   *be Cinderella?"*

Here are some of the most common mixed verbs. The consonant clusters **nk** and **ng** in the infinitive change to **ch** in the narrative past.

The English verbs *bring/ brought, think/thought* are mixed verb forms in English as well.

	Infinitive	Narrative past	Conversational past	
e > a	br**e**nnen	br**a**nn**te**	hat gebrannt	*burned*
	d**e**nken	d**a**ch**te**	hat gedacht	*thought*
	erk**e**nnen	erk**a**nn**te**	hat erkannt	*recognized*
	k**e**nnen	k**a**nn**te**	hat gekannt	*knew (person or place)*
	n**e**nnen	n**a**nn**te**	hat genannt	*named*
	r**e**nnen	r**a**nn**te**	ist gerannt	*ran*
i > a	br**i**ngen	br**a**ch**te**	hat gebracht	*brought*
	verbr**i**ngen	verbr**a**ch**te**	hat verbracht	*spent time*

Similarly, the verbs **wissen** and **werden** also mix both strong and weak verb narrative past tense markers. Note that **werden** has a **-d** instead of a **-t.**

Infinitive	Narrative past	Conversational past	
wissen	**wuss**te	hat gewusst	*knew (a fact)*
werden	**wur**de	ist geworden	*became*

18 Aus „Aschenputtel" Ergänzen Sie die folgenden Sätze aus „Aschenputtel" mit einer passenden Verbform aus der Liste.

brachte (3×)   hatte   rannte   waren
erkannten   nannten   war   wurde

1. Es war einmal ein hübsches Mädchen, dessen Mutter krank _____ und starb.
2. Nach einem Jahr nahm sich der Mann eine neue Frau, die zwei Töchter mit ins Haus _____.
3. Diese Schwestern _____ schön von Gesicht, aber böse von Herzen.
4. Selbst ein Bett _____ das Mädchen nicht mehr, es musste neben dem Herd in der Asche liegen.
5. Und weil sie darum immer schmutzig aussah, _____ die Stiefschwestern sie „Aschenputtel".
6. Als der Vater zurückkam, _____ er Kleider und Edelsteine für die Stiefschwestern.
7. Ihre Schwestern und Stiefmutter _____ Aschenputtel nicht auf dem Fest.
8. Das Vögelchen _____ ihr ein noch viel schöneres Kleid.
9. Wieder _____ Aschenputtel schnell davon.
10. Da ging die andere Schwester in das Zimmer und probierte den Schuh an, aber die Ferse _____ zu groß.

19 Freie Kommunikation: **Ein erlebnisreicher° Abend.** Erzählen Sie einer Gruppe von drei bis vier Studenten von einem erlebnisreichen Abend auf einem Fest, einer Hochzeit oder einem anderen Tanzabend (z. B. *senior prom*). Was passierte dort? Was machten Sie? Beschreiben Sie fünf bis sechs Details im Präteritum (**z. B. Ich ging/aß/trank/tanzte ...**).

eventful

20 Schreibecke: **Ein neues Märchen.** Schreiben Sie Ihr eigenes Märchen mithilfe der Sätze unten.

1. Es war einmal ... ein Prinz/eine Prinzessin • ein Student/eine Studentin • ein Zauberer/eine Hexe • ein Deutschlehrer/eine Deutschlehrerin
2. Er/Sie war sehr ... schön/hässlich • intelligent/dumm • gut/böse
3. Er/Sie lebte ... auf einem Schloss • in einem Wald • an der Uni
4. Dort hatte er/sie ... viele Freunde/Feinde • Bücher • wilde Tiere • giftige Äpfel • Edelsteine
5. Er/Sie wollte ...
6. Da kam ein/eine ...
7. Der/Die war ...
8. Und wenn sie nicht gestorben sind, dann ...

Braunwald autofrei: Ein Wintermärchen ... hoch über dem Alltag

Anna und ihre Freunde haben von Mitte Februar bis Mitte April Semesterferien und planen seit Wochen einen Skiurlaub°. Sie haben Broschüren von bekannten Wintersportorten bestellt und jetzt diskutieren sie alle Möglichkeiten. Für Anna klingt Braunwald in der Schweiz wirklich ideal: viel Schnee und viele Pisten° zum Skilaufen in den Alpen und keine Autos! Die Gruppe muss sich entscheiden, ob sie sich einen Skiurlaub in der Schweiz leisten° kann oder ob er einfach zu teuer ist.

skiing vacation

ski runs

afford

Braunwald Klausenpass
Tourismus AG, Switzerland

Alexander Chaikin/Alamy

Sprache im Alltag: **Urlaub oder Ferien?**

German has two separate words for vacation, **der Urlaub** and **die Ferien** (pl). **Ferien** are school-free vacation days that are scheduled into a school year and observed by students and teachers alike (**Schulferien, Semesterferien, Weihnachtsferien**). German university students have two long vacation breaks: **Winterferien** from mid-February to mid-April and **Sommerferien** from mid-July to mid-October. **Urlaub,** on the other hand, is active vacation time taken to relax and recuperate from work, and in most instances, to travel. However, the Swiss often use the term **Ferien** where Germans would use **Urlaub.**

Vorschau

⊕ **21** Thematische Fragen Beantworten Sie die folgenden Fragen auf Deutsch.

1. Wann machen Sie lieber Urlaub: im Winter, Frühling, Sommer oder Herbst?
2. Wann haben Sie als Kind meistens mit der Familie Urlaub gemacht: im Winter, Frühling, Sommer oder Herbst?
3. Sind Sie als Kind weit gefahren oder sind Sie in der Nähe geblieben?
4. Was wollten Ihre Eltern damals° im Urlaub erleben und was sind heute Ihre Ziele   *at that time*
   für den Urlaub? Kreuzen Sie die passend Antworten an.

	Meine Eltern damals	Ich heute
a. viele Sehenswürdigkeiten sehen	○	○
b. Tiere und Natur erleben	○	○
c. Verwandte besuchen	○	○
d. Ruhe und Entspannung° haben	○	○
e. viele Aktivitäten planen	○	○
f. eine fremde Kultur und Sprache kennenlernen	○	○
g. so wenig Geld wie möglich ausgeben	○	○
h. viel Geld ausgeben und tolle Andenken kaufen	○	○
i. viel Zeit mit Freunden verbringen	○	○
j. gut essen und trinken	○	○

relaxation

5. Mit wem reisen Sie jetzt am liebsten, wenn Sie Urlaub machen? Oder fahren Sie lieber allein?
6. Was ist Ihr Traum-Urlaubsland? Warum? Was möchten Sie dort machen, sehen, hören, lernen? Wann wollen Sie dorthin reisen?

Lesestrategien

Benutzen Sie die folgenden Strategien, um den Text „Braunwald autofrei" zu verstehen.

⊕ **22** Den Kontext verstehen Suchen Sie im Text die Information unten.

1. Wie heißt der Ort?
2. Welche Jahreszeit (Sommer, Herbst usw.) sieht man in der Broschüre dargestellt?
3. Warum kommen Menschen dahin? Was kann man dort machen?
4. Schauen Sie sich die Bilder an. Suchen Sie die Wörter **einen Schlitten, schlittelnde Kinder, Millionen von Menschen, die Autos.**

Braunwald Klausenpass Tourismus AG, Switzerland

23 Neue Wörter lernen: erster Versuch Erraten Sie die Bedeutung von den Ausdrücken aus dem Kontext.

1. „Glauben Sie, dass es die kleinen **Winterferienwunder** noch gibt?"

   Was sind die drei Wörter im Kompositum? Ist ein Wunder etwas Normales?

2. „Unten sind **gestresste Stadtmenschen** eingestiegen, oben steigen **gutgelaunte Ferienmenschen** aus."

   Welchen Kontrast zwischen Menschen sieht man hier im Satz?

3. „Gutgelaunte Spaziergänger in einer echten **Postkartenlandschaft.**"

   Was hat die Landschaft mit einer Postkarte zu tun?

4. „Nach der Schussfahrt auf der Piste, Aufwärmen auf der **Sonnenterrasse** der **Bergwirtschaft** oder beim Kaffeefertig unten **im Dorf.**"

   In einer Wirtschaft kauft man etwas zu essen und trinken. Wo sind die zwei Wirtschaften in diesem Satz?

5. „Eine herzliche, unkomplizierte **Gastfreundschaft.** Ein gutes Gefühl, **Gast** in einem **gastlichen** Haus zu sein."

   Ein Gast ist eine Person, die zu Besuch kommt und kurze Zeit bleibt. Sollte man Gäste nett und freundlich behandeln°?

treat

24 Neue Wörter lernen: Drei Strategien Erraten Sie die fett gedruckten Wörter mithilfe der drei Strategien. Wählen Sie die korrekte Antwort.

Weltwissen

1. „Hier bringt der **Postbote** ... auf seinem Schlitten gerade die Morgenzeitung."
   ○ Der Briefträger bringt die Zeitung.   ○ Ein Boot bringt die Zeitung.

2. „**Gutgelaunte** Spaziergänger in einer echten Postkartenlandschaft."
   ○ in schlechter Stimmung   ○ in guter Stimmung

3. „Nach der Schussfahrt auf der **Piste** ..."
   ○ Man fährt Ski auf einer Piste.   ○ Man fährt Auto auf einer Piste.

4. „Pisten für Anfänger und **Fortgeschrittene** ..."
   ○ für Leute, die schon sehr gut Ski laufen.   ○ für Leute, die nicht gut Ski laufen.

Kontext

1. „Es [das Bähnli] **rüttelt und schüttelt sich** und **klettert** durch den Schnee hinauf auf die Sonnenterrasse."
   ○ Es fährt sehr schnell hinauf.   ○ Es fährt langsam und mit Mühe° hinauf.

effort

2. „Das Wunder des Wandels **findet** im Bähnli **statt** ... Unten sind gestresste Stadtmenschen eingestiegen, oben steigen gutgelaunte Ferienmenschen aus."
   ○ Etwas Wunderbares passiert im Bähnli   ○ Man findet die Stadt im Bähnli.

3. „Einfach keine Autos! Da **fehlt das Dröhnen** der Motoren."
   ○ Man hört keine Motoren.   ○ Man hört laute Motoren.

Lesen Sie jetzt den Text.

Wach' uf liäbs Bruunwald

Das Bähnliwunder im Wunderbähnli

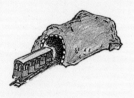

Braunwald Klausenpass Tourismus AG, Switzerland

Glauben Sie, dass es die kleinen Winterferienwunder noch gibt? Wir aus Braunwald glauben daran, denn Winter für Winter erleben wir eine seltsame Geschichte ...

Nach Braunwald führt keine Strasse – nur ein Bähnli in die Zukunft. In dieses Bähnli steigen unten im Tal täglich Menschen aus dem Unterland. Müde vom Alltag, den grauen Wolken und langen Nebeltagen. Eben Leute von heute. Gestresst, überarbeitet und ferienreif.

Dann setzt sich das rote Bähnli in Bewegung[1]. Es rüttelt und schüttelt sich und klettert durch den Schnee hinauf auf die Sonnenterrasse.

Braunwald Klausenpass Tourismus AG, Switzerland

Das Bähnli steigt und steigt. Jetzt noch der kleine Tunnel und schon ist das alltägliche Bähnliwunder von Braunwald perfekt.

Das Wunder des Wandels findet im Bähnli statt. Ob Millionär oder Tellerwäscher – am Bähnli kommt keiner vorbei. Unten sind gestresste Stadtmenschen eingestiegen, oben steigen gutgelaunte Ferienmenschen aus. Jeden Winter täglich neu: das kleine Bähnliwunder von Braunwald.

Illustrations © Cengage Learning 2014

[1]**Bewegung:** *motion*

Text reprinted by permission of Braunwald-Klausenpass Tourismus AG.

> **Kulturnotiz.** Note that in this Swiss text **ss** is used instead of standard German **ß** following long vowels, e.g., **Straße–Strasse, Spaß–Spass, Fuß–Fuss, Genießer–Geniesser.**

Guätä Morgä liäbs Bruuwald

Gut geschlafen, lieber Gast? Hier bringt der Postbote – den wir in Braunwald „Pöschtler" nennen – auf seinem Schlitten gerade die Morgenzeitung. Der "Pöschtler" geht zu Fuss, weil er kein Auto hat.

Das ist normal hier oben. Denn in Braunwald gibt es keine Autos. Braunwald ist autofrei. Zuerst ist es ein richtiger Schock. Einfach keine Autos! Da fehlt das Dröhnen der Motoren. An die saubere Luft muss man sich zuerst gewöhnen. Hier ist eben schon alles etwas anders als anderswo. Gast bedeutet nicht nur Gastfreundschaft. GAST heisst auch Gemeinschaft Autofreier Schweizer Tourismusorte.

Persönlichkeit ist alles – Prestige ist gar nichts. Eine herzliche, unkomplizierte Gastfreundschaft. Ein gutes Gefühl, Gast in einem gastlichen Haus zu sein.

Gutgelaunte Spaziergänger in einer echten Postkartenlandschaft. Schlittelnde Kinder, die keine Angst vor Autos haben. Hier sagt man sich noch „Grüezi", wenn man sich begegnet. Man kennt sich eben in Braunwald.

Braunwald Klausenpass Tourismus AG, Switzerland

Guätä Tag liäbs Bruuwald

Der sanfte[1] Tourismus findet auch im Winter statt. Auch wer nicht Ski fährt, ist hier Erstklassgast. Was für ein Spass, im Pferdeschlitten durch das verschneite Wintermärchenland zu fahren!

Was den Winter attraktiv und sportlich macht, ist in Braunwald zu finden. Ein Schlittelparadies, eine Langlaufloipe und eine Schweizer Skischule.

Das Skifahren ist noch Spass und weniger aggressiv als anderswo. Pisten für Anfänger und Fortgeschrittene und auch Pisten zum gemütlichen Bergrestaurant. Sonnige Pisten auf der Südseite und Pulverschnee an den Nordhängen.

Für die ehemaligen Skistars und die ewigen Anfänger, die gar nie Pistenraser[2] werden wollen.

Nach der Schussfahrt auf der Piste, Aufwärmen auf der Sonnenterrasse der Bergwirtschaft oder beim Kaffeefertig unten im Dorf. Eine ehrliche Gastronomie der kleinen Familienbetriebe.

Illustrations © Cengage Learning 2014

Guät Nacht liäbs Bruuwald

Abendliches Wintermärchen Braunwald: Zauberstimmung. Was ist schon Glück? Vielleicht die Stille eines Bergabends, eine nächtliche Schlittelfahrt, ein Kinoabend oder ein Schlummertrunk[3] an einer Hotelbar? „Hoch über dem Alltag" finden Sie noch Naturschönheit, Herzlichkeit und Lebensfreude. Millionen von Menschen kommen Gott sei Dank gar nie nach Braunwald.

Braunwald ist nichts für die Massen, sondern für echte Geniesser[4]. Braunwald ist etwas ganz Besonderes. Die wesentlichen[5] Dinge sind in Braunwald sichtbar[6] – mit den Augen und dem Herzen.

[1]**sanfte:** *relaxing* [2]**Pistenraser:** *speed demons* [3]**Schlummertrunk:** *nightcap* [4]**Geniesser:** *connoisseur* [5]**wesentlichen:** *essential* [6]**sichtbar:** *visible*

Text reprinted by permission of Braunwald-Klausenpass Tourismus AG.

Rückblick

⟳ **25** **Stimmt das?** Stimmen die folgenden Aussagen zum Text? Wenn nicht, was stimmt?

	Ja, das stimmt.	Nein, das stimmt nicht.
1. Nur mit dem „Bähnli" kommt man nach Braunwald, weil keine Straße dahin führt.	○	○
2. Es kann tagelang dauern, bis man in Braunwald gutgelaunt und in Ferienstimmung ist.	○	○
3. Im Winter bringt der Postbote die Post mit seinem Fahrrad.	○	○
4. Es ist ein Schock, dass man in Braunwald keine Motoren hört.	○	○
5. Die Leute in Braunwald sagen „Grüezi", wenn sie einander treffen.	○	○
6. Wer gern Ski läuft, kann hier Pisten für Anfänger oder Fortgeschrittene finden.	○	○
7. Für die Nicht-Skifahrer gibt es in Braunwald nichts zu tun.	○	○
8. Essen kann man in der Bergwirtschaft.	○	○
9. Abends gibt es wilde Après-Ski-Partys°, laute Diskomusik und viel Bier.	○	○
10. Braunwald ist nicht für jedermann°, sondern nur für echte Genießer.	○	○

Complete the **Ergänzen Sie** activity in the Student Activities Manual before doing the next activity.

after-ski parties

everyone

⟲ **26** **Kurz interpretiert** Beantworten Sie die folgenden Fragen auf Deutsch.

1. Was für eine Atmosphäre will diese Broschüre erzeugen°? Warum?
2. Was assoziiert der Normalmensch mit dem Wort „Märchen"? Ist das für einen Tourismusort positiv?
3. Welche Assoziationen mit einem Märchen hat man, wenn man die Broschüre liest? Erklären Sie die Wörter **Wunder, rüttelt und schüttelt, Postkartenlandschaft.**
4. In welcher Hinsicht° ist Braunwald märchenhaft?
5. Wie ist das Skifahren in Braunwald in der Broschüre beschrieben? Klingt das langweilig, normal, attraktiv?
6. Welche Attraktionen gibt es in Braunwald für Leute, die nicht Alpinski fahren?
7. Wie ist das Nachtleben in Braunwald? Welche Aktivitäten nennt man hier?

create

way, respect

⟳ **27** **Die Schweiz** Was assoziieren Sie *nicht* mit der Schweiz? Streichen Sie in jeder Zeile einen Begriff durch°.

1. die Schokolade, der Käse, das Wiener Schnitzel, das Müesli
2. der Atlantik, die Alpen, der Genfer See, der Rhein
3. Deutsch, Spanisch, Italienisch, Französisch, Rätoromanisch
4. das Rote Kreuz, die chemische Industrie, Banken, Popmusik
5. die Demokratie, die Diktatur, die Neutralität
6. Wandern, Surfen, Bergsteigen, Ski laufen

*durchstreichen: **to cross out***

Sprache im Alltag: Diminutives

The Swiss German dialects form diminutives by adding the suffix **-li** to nouns instead of the standard German **-chen** and **-lein**.

Original	*Standard*	*Schweizerdeutsch*
die Bahn	das Bähnchen	das Bähnli
	das Bähnlein	

These diminutives change the gender of the noun to **das,** and add an umlaut (e.g., **die Bahn > das Bähnli**).

⮌ 28 Textdetektiv: **Absprungtext**. Use the *Absprungtext* to recognize important aspects of German structure and usage.

1. Which of the words below are written in the Swiss German dialect?
   täglich • (das) Bähnli • überarbeitet • Guätä Morgä! •
   Pöschtler • liäbs Bruuwald • Guät Nacht! • Wach uf! •
   (das) Dröhnen • Grüezi! • aufwärmen • Guätä Tag!

2. Find the Swiss German equivalents above for the following English greetings.
   a. good morning
   b. good day
   c. good night
   d. greetings/hello

3. Match these Swiss German words with standard German equivalents.

Swiss German	**Standard German**
a. Bähnli	Postler/Postbote (*letter carrier*)
b. liäbs Bruuwald	Wach auf! (*Wake up!*)
c. Pöschtler	liebes Braunwald (*dear Braunwald*)
d. Wach uf!	Bähnlein (*little train*)

4. Be a linguist. Match each Swiss German word on the left to the standard German sound equivalency that it illustrates.

Swiss German word	**Standard German sound equivalency**
a. liäbs	li = lein
b. guätä	sch = s
c. uf	uä = u
d. Pöschtler	iä = ie
e. Bähnli	u = au

5. The text contains Swiss German . . .
   a. so that Swiss readers may understand the text better.
   b. because there is no other way to say these things.
   c. because it serves the advertising aspect well by lending the text local flavor.

6. The intended audience for this text is most likely . . .
   a. English-speaking tourists.
   b. German-speaking tourists from outside of Switzerland.
   c. German Swiss tourists.

Die Schweiz

Switzerland (**die Schweiz**, officially **Confœderatio Helvetica**) is a small, multilingual nation of approximately 7.9 million people located in the heart of central Europe. Bordered by Germany, France, Italy, Austria, and Liechtenstein, the country has four national languages: German, the native language of nearly two-thirds (63.7%) of all Swiss, French (spoken by 20.4% of the population), Italian (6.5%), and Rhaeto-Romanic (0.5%). Each of these languages is spoken in regional dialects. Because all students in Swiss schools are required to develop fluency in a second national language, the Swiss are generally considered bilingual, and many are multilingual. Important German-speaking cities are Bern, the capital of Switzerland; Zürich, the business and banking center; and Basel, the center of the Swiss chemical and pharmaceutical industry. Geneva (called **Genf** in German and **Genève** in French), the chief French-speaking city, is headquarters for the International Red Cross and one of two European headquarters for the United Nations.

Switzerland is one of Europe's oldest democracies, dating from an alliance signed in 1291 by the cantons of Uri, Schwyz, and Unterwalden that guaranteed the traditional autonomy of the communes and their citizens. This loose confederation was later replaced with a federation of 26 individual Swiss states (**Kantone**). Since then, the Swiss have maintained a reputation of tolerance and respect for the rights and autonomy of individuals, although ironically, Swiss women did not acquire the right to vote until 1971. Switzerland has maintained a policy of diplomatic neutrality since 1515. It is not a member of the European Union or NATO and it only joined the United Nations in 2002 when a referendum approved membership. The official currency of Switzerland is the Swiss franc (**der Schweizer Franken**).

Blaine Harrington/Age Fotostock

Die Altstadt der Schweizer Hauptstadt Bern: In der Schweiz verliert man die Berge nie aus den Augen.

Although the country has relatively few natural resources and nearly 70% of its land mass is covered by the Alps and Jura Mountains, the Swiss economy is robust and its service industries are world-famous. In banking, insurance, and tourism, Switzerland has few peers. In addition, Swiss industries such as chemicals, pharmaceuticals, watchmaking, textiles, and metal-, machine-, and instrument-making have helped establish a per capita income that surpasses that of Germany, France, the U.S.A., Canada, and Sweden. Gruyère and Swiss cheese (**Emmenthaler**), cheese fondue (**Käsefondue**), raclette, **Rösti** potatoes, and high quality chocolates number among Switzerland's top culinary contributions.

Kulturkreuzung

Spricht man mehrere Sprachen in Ihrer Stadt? In Ihrem Staat oder Ihrer Provinz? In Ihrem Land? Wenn ja, welche Sprachen? Sind diese Sprachen offizielle Sprachen? Warum hat Kanada zwei offizielle Sprachen? Warum haben die USA keine offizielle Sprache?

Wissenswerte Vokabeln: die Schweiz – geografische Daten

Talking about Switzerland

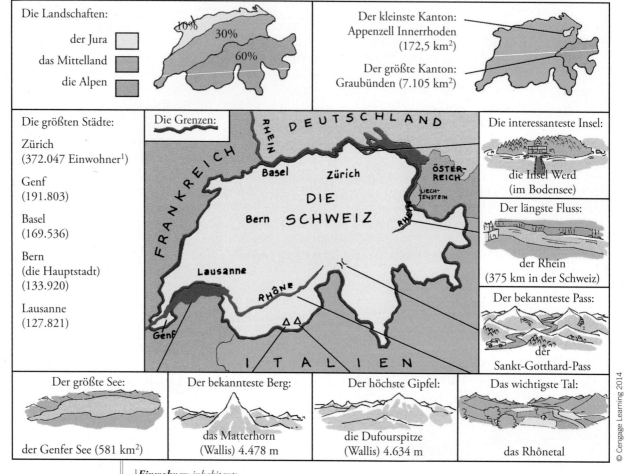

Die Landschaften:

der Jura
das Mittelland
die Alpen

10%
30%
60%

Der kleinste Kanton:
Appenzell Innerrhoden
(172,5 km²)

Der größte Kanton:
Graubünden (7.105 km²)

Die größten Städte:

Zürich
(372.047 Einwohner[1])

Genf
(191.803)

Basel
(169.536)

Bern
(die Hauptstadt)
(133.920)

Lausanne
(127.821)

Die Grenzen:

RHEIN · DEUTSCHLAND
FRANKREICH
Basel   Zürich   ÖSTER-REICH
LIECHTENSTEIN
DIE SCHWEIZ
Bern   RHÔN
Lausanne
RHÔNE
Genf
I T A L I E N

Die interessanteste Insel:

die Insel Werd
(im Bodensee)

Der längste Fluss:

der Rhein
(375 km in der Schweiz)

Der bekannteste Pass:

der
Sankt-Gotthard-Pass

Der größte See:

der Genfer See (581 km²)

Der bekannteste Berg:

das Matterhorn
(Wallis) 4.478 m

Der höchste Gipfel:

die Dufourspitze
(Wallis) 4.634 m

Das wichtigste Tal:

das Rhônetal

© Cengage Learning 2014

[1]**Einwohner:** *inhabitants*

BEISPIEL   *Wie heißt der längste Fluss in der Schweiz?*

↩ **29** Geografie-Jeopardy Sie wissen die Antwort schon, aber wie heißt die Frage? Fragen Sie nach Superlativen in der Schweiz.

BEISPIEL   S1: *Zürich*
S2: *Welches ist die größte Stadt in der Schweiz?*

1. Zürich
2. Dufourspitze
3. Appenzell Innerrhoden
4. Graubünden
5. die Alpen

6. das Rhônetal
7. der Genfer See
8. der Sankt-Gotthard
9. der Rhein

30 Freie Kommunikation: **Rollenspiel: Braunwald besuchen.**

> S1: Sie planen eine Winterreise und suchen Informationen im Reisebüro. Sie fahren nicht gern Ski, sind aber gern draußen, mögen den Massentourismus nicht und sind etwas snobbistisch.

> S2: Sie arbeiten im Reisebüro und erzählen, warum Braunwald Touristen so gut gefällt oder was Touristen dort ärgert. Versuchen Sie den Kunden/ die Kundin (S1) zu überzeugen, in Braunwald Urlaub zu machen oder Braunwald fernzubleiben° und einen besseren Urlaubsort zu finden.

stay away from

31 Schreibecke: **Reisetagebuch.** Sie haben in Braunwald eine Woche Urlaub gemacht. Schreiben Sie ein Reisetagebuch im Präteritum. Machen Sie für jeden Tag einen Eintrag°, in dem Sie beschreiben, was Sie machten und sahen.

entry

Brennpunkt Kultur   🌐   Web Search / Web Link

Fest- und Feiertage

Germans celebrate numerous holidays (**Fest- und Feiertage**) throughout the year. New Year's Eve (**Silvester**) is celebrated with parties, dances, and fireworks, and New Year's Day (**Neujahr**) with a festive dinner. **Karneval** season precedes the beginning of Lent. On Easter Sunday (**Ostern**), many children hunt for chocolates and colored eggs hidden by the Easter bunny (**der Osterhase**). Trade unions organize public rallies on May 1st, International Labor Day (**Tag der Arbeit**). Throughout the summer, cities and towns stage local fairs and festivals (**der Jahrmarkt, die Kirmes**) parades, rides, food and drink booths, contests, concerts, and dancing. Munich's **Oktoberfest** runs for two weeks in September, ending on the first Sunday in October.

Germans observe the Day of German Unity (**Tag der deutschen Einheit**) on October 3rd to commemorate the date in 1990 when the German Democratic Republic was dissolved and officially united with the Federal Republic of Germany. Muslims celebrate the month-long **Ramadan** fast period, ending with a three-day **Ramadanfest.**

Jewish citizens celebrate **Chanukka** for eight days late in the year. Candles are lit on the menorah, festive holiday foods are enjoyed, and children receive **Chanukkageld** as a reward for good deeds. Open-air Christmas markets (**Weihnachtsmärkte**) are held in many cities in December. Families bake seasonal treats such as gingerbread (**der Lebkuchen**) and fruit cakes called **Christstollen.** On December 6th **Sankt Nikolaus** puts candy in children's shoes. Sometimes he is accompanied by his assistant **Knecht Ruprecht,** known by a variety of other names. On Christmas Eve (**der Heilige Abend**), parents put up the Christmas tree and decorate it, often with real candles. Christmas presents are left by the Christ Child (**das Christkind**) or by **der Weihnachtsmann.** Families exchange gifts on Christmas Eve. Christmas Day (**Weihnachten**) is a holiday, as is the day after Christmas.

Sankt Nikolaus und der Krampus

Kulturkreuzung

Hat Ihre Familie religiöse Feste gefeiert, als Sie ein Kind waren? Welche? Welche Feste sind Familienfeste und welche nicht? Kommen Familien immer am Feiertag zusammen? Warum? Warum nicht?

Strukturen

II Talking about consecutive events in the past

The past perfect

A. Using the conjunction *nachdem* with the past perfect

German speakers use the past perfect tense (**das Plusquamperfekt**) to refer to the earlier of two or more events that occurred in the past. It frequently occurs with the subordinating conjunction **nachdem** (*after*). The past perfect consists of a form of **haben** or **sein** in the narrative past and a past participle.

> Nachdem Aschenputtels Vater ihr den Haselzweig **gebracht hatte**, pflanzte sie ihn auf dem Grab ihrer Mutter.
>
> *After Cinderella's father had brought her the hazelnut branch, she planted it on her mother's grave.*

In colloquial speech, Germans frequently prefer to use the conversational past instead of the past perfect. In these cases, the word **nachdem** alone signals the sequence of events.

> Wohin bist du gegangen, nachdem wir uns **gesehen haben**?
>
> *Where did you go after we saw each other?*

B. Word order in sentences beginning with a subordinate clause

A German complex sentence frequently begins with a subordinate clause. It is followed by a main clause, which begins with the verb and is followed by the subject. This sequence results in two conjugated verbs appearing side by side. The subordinate clause is always separated from the main clause by a comma.

> Nachdem Aschenputtel zum Grab ihrer Mutter **gegangen war,** **bekam** sie ein schönes Kleid.
>
> *After Cinderella had gone to her mother's grave, she received a beautiful dress.*

→ **32** Was passierte den Märchenfiguren nachher? Finden Sie für jeden Hauptsatz den Nebensatz, der erklärt, was später im Märchen passierte.

BEISPIEL *Nachdem Aschenputtel die kranke Mutter besucht hatte, starb die Mutter.*

1. Nachdem Aschenputtel die kranke Mutter besucht hatte,
2. Nachdem der Wolf Rotkäppchen gefressen hatte,
3. Nachdem der gestiefelte Kater die Kleider seines Herrn genommen hatte,
4. Nachdem Schneewittchen in den vergifteten Apfel gebissen hatte,
5. Nachdem Schneewittchen eingeschlafen war,
6. Nachdem die böse Hexe Hänsel und Gretel ins Pfefferkuchenhaus eingeladen hatte,
7. Nachdem die Hexe ein Feuer im Ofen gemacht hatte,

a. ging er zum König und sagte, dass Diebe die Kleider gestohlen hatten.
b. schloss sie Hänsel in einen Käfig° ein.
c. schob Gretel die Hexe in den Ofen und sie verbrannte.
d. fiel sie wie tot um.
e. starb die Mutter.
f. legten die sieben Zwerge sie in einen Glassarg.
g. kam der Jäger, schnitt dem Wolf den Bauch auf und rettete Rotkäppchen.

Just as in English, the German narrative past tense is frequently substituted for the past perfect in spoken German.

Courtesy of Margret Rettich.

cage

33 Meine Zeittafel° Unten ist Annas Zeittafel. Schreiben Sie Ihre eigene. Stellen Sie sich dann gegenseitig Fragen über Ihre Zeittafel.

time line

> **BEISPIEL** S1: *Was hast du gemacht, nachdem du die Schule angefangen hattest?*
> S2: *Nachdem ich die Schule angefangen hatte, lernte ich schwimmen.*

1998–die Schule anfangen
2003–eine Reise nach Florida machen
2005–nach Kanada fahren

2007–im Softballtournier in Ohio spielen
2010–das Studium in Michigan beginnen
2012–nach Deutschland fliegen

Meine Zeittafel. The most commonly used narrative past forms in speaking are **war, hatte, ging, kam,** and the modal verbs (**konnte, wollte, musste, sollte, durfte, mochte**).

Strukturen

III Talking about concurrent events in the past

Using the conjunction *als*

German speakers use the subordinating conjunction **als** (*when*) with the narrative (simple) past or the conversational past to talk about two or more past events that happened at the same time.

> **Als** sie am Grab vorbeiritten, riefen zwei Täubchen vom Haselbaum.
> *When they rode past the grave, two doves called out from the hazelnut tree.*

 34 Als Kind Was machte Barbara in Dresden, als Anna in den USA Kind war? Stellen Sie einem Partner/einer Partnerin mithilfe der Tabellen Fragen.

> **BEISPIEL** S1: *Was machte Anna, als Barbara Fußball spielte?*
> S2: *Als Barbara Fußball spielte, spielte Anna Softball.*

Tabelle A (S1):

Anna	Barbara
?	Fußball spielen
Orangensaft zum Frühstück trinken	?
jeden Sonntag in die Kirche gehen	?
bis spät nachmittags in der Schule bleiben	?
?	den Nachmittag frei haben
?	nach Italien fahren wollen

Tabelle B (S2):

Anna	Barbara
Softball spielen	?
?	Kaffee zum Frühstück trinken
?	jeden Sonntag spazieren gehen
?	um 13.00 Uhr nach Hause gehen
täglich nach der Schule Sport haben	?
alle Länder besuchen können	?

35 Autogrammspiel: Als ich zehn Jahre alt war, ... Bilden Sie Fragen im Präteritum. Finden Sie für jede Frage eine Person, die mit **Ja** antwortet. Bitten Sie die Person um ihre Unterschrift.

BEISPIEL S1: *Hattest du schon lange Haare, als du zehn Jahre alt warst?*
S2: *Ja. Als ich zehn Jahre alt war, hatte ich schon lange Haare.*

1. 10 Jahre alt: lange Haare haben   _____
2. 11 Jahre alt: groß sein   _____
3. 12 Jahre alt: ein Instrument spielen können _____
4. 13 Jahre alt: Hausarbeit machen müssen   _____
5. 14 Jahre alt: einen Computer haben   _____
6. 15 Jahre alt: Deutsch sprechen können   _____
7. 16 Jahre alt: Auto fahren dürfen   _____
8. 17 Jahre alt: zur Uni gehen wollen   _____

Strukturen

IV Saying when events occur

Using *wenn* vs. *wann* vs. *ob*

As you learned in **Kapitel 6**, **wenn** (*if*) also expresses a condition. The presence of **so** or **dann** in the second clause often signals that, e.g., „... **und** *wenn* sie nicht gestorben sind, *dann* leben sie noch heute. ("... *and if they haven't died, then they are still living today.*"); *Wenn* du Königin bist, *so* brauchst du nicht mehr zu Fuß zu gehen. (*If you are the queen, you do not need to walk anymore.*)

The subordinating conjunction **wenn** (*whenever, if*) points to an event that occurs (or occurred) repeatedly. It may be used with the present tense or any past tense. German speakers often use it in the expression **immer wenn** (*always when, whenever*).

Hier sagt man sich noch „Grüezi", **wenn** man sich begegnet.	*Here, people still greet each other with "Grüezi" whenever they meet.*
Immer wenn ich nachmittags nach Hause komme, habe ich Hunger.	*Whenever I come home in the afternoon, I'm hungry.*

The interrogative pronoun **wann** (*when*) occurs in questions about when something happened or will happen. It establishes a specific point of time.

Wann ist der Winterball?   *When is the winter ball?*

Wann can also be embedded into a sentence as an indirect question. In this case, the conjugated verb moves to the end of the subordinate clause.

Sie weiß nicht, **wann** der Ball stattfindet.   *She doesn't know when the ball is taking place.*

In complex sentences, embedded yes/no questions start with the subordinating conjunction **ob** (*if, whether*).

Sie weiß nicht, **ob** der Ball stattfindet.   *She doesn't know if the ball will take place.*

You can always determine whether you should use **wenn, wann,** or **ob** by reconstructing the original question or statement.

Statement	*Question*
Der Ball findet um 20.00 Uhr statt.	*Wann* findet der Ball statt? (*um 20.00 Uhr*)
Question	*Statement*
Findet der Ball Sonnabend statt?	Sie möchte wissen, *wann* der Ball stattfindet. (am *Sonnabend*)
	Sie möchte wissen, *ob* der Ball Sonnabend stattfindet.

36 Als, wenn, wann oder ob? Ergänzen Sie die Sätze mit **als, wenn, wann** oder **ob**.

1. ANNA: _____ kommst du morgen Abend vorbei? Um 19.00 Uhr?
   BARBARA: _____ ich Zeit habe, komme ich kurz vor 19.00 Uhr vorbei.

2. KARL: Weißt du, _____ der Film beginnt?
   STEFAN: Nein. Aber sag mir doch bitte, _____ du's herausfindest.
   KARL: Ich weiß nicht, _____ ich die Zeit dazu habe. Mal sehen.

3. ANNA: Immer _____ ich müde bin, bekomme ich Hunger.
   BARBARA: _____ ich Hunger habe, will ich schlafen.
   ANNA: _____ hast du zuletzt gegessen?
   BARBARA: _____ ich an der Uni war.

4. ANNA: _____ ist meine Mutter in die USA gegangen?
   OMA: _____ sie 23 Jahre alt war.
   OPA: Damals haben wir nicht gewusst, _____ wir die Hannelore je wiedersehen.
   OMA: Aber natürlich ist sie dann immer gekommen, _____ sie die Familie sehen wollte.
   ANNA: Und _____ kommt ihr endlich zum Besuch nach Fort Wayne?
   OPA: Ach, Anna! Vielleicht, _____ ich endlich Englisch verstehen kann.

37 Interview: Fest- und Feiertage Stellen Sie einem Partner/einer Partnerin die folgenden Fragen.

1. Auf welchen Feiertag hast du dich am meisten gefreut, als du ein Kind warst? Warum? Und jetzt?
2. Kannst du dich an einen besonderen Feiertag aus deiner Kindheit erinnern?
3. Welche Feiertage feierst du, wenn du bei deiner Familie zu Hause bist?
4. Welche Feiertage feierst du mit Freunden?
5. Welche Feiertage feierst du gar nicht? Warum?
6. Wie feierst du deinen Geburtstag am liebsten?
7. Was hast du als Kind zu Halloween gemacht?
8. Welche deutschen Feiertage kennt man in Amerika und Kanada nicht?

Strukturen

V Expressing ownership

The genitive case

The primary function of the genitive case (**der Genitiv**) is to show ownership.

Wir gehen auf das Schloss **des Königs**.   *We are going to the king's castle.*

The genitive can express a relationship between things as indicated by *of* in English

Das Wunder **des Wandels** findet im Bähnli statt.   *The miracle of transformation takes place in the little train.*

Da fehlt das Dröhnen **der Motoren**.   *The roar of engines is missing.*

The genitive is also used for indefinite time phrases, such as **eines Tages** (*one day*), **eines Abends** (*one evening*), **eines Morgens** (*one morning*), and **eines Nachts** (*one night*).

English speakers express ownership by adding *'s* to the person who possesses the object or who is related to the person mentioned: *Is that really **your friend's** car? Of* can also be used: *What's the name **of** that French restaurant?*

The genitive case frequently occurs in answers to the question **wessen?** (*whose?*).

> **Question**
> **Wessen** Auto ist das?   *Whose car is that?*
>
> **Answer**
> Das ist das Auto **der Studentin.**   *That is the student's car (car of the student).*

Note the word order: In German, the person who possesses something follows the object being possessed. In English, the possessor precedes the item possessed.

> das Auto **der Studentin**   *the student's car*

A. Masculine and neuter nouns

Articles that precede masculine and neuter nouns in the genitive case end in **-es** (e.g., **des, eines**). The masculine and neuter nouns themselves also add **-s** or **-es** in the genitive singular.

- Most nouns of one syllable add **-es** (e.g., **eines Tages, des Buches**).
- Most nouns of more than one syllable add **-s** (e.g., **des Königs, meines Professors**).
- Nouns ending in **-s, -ss, -ß, -tsch, -tz, -x, -z,** and **-zt** add **-es** (e.g., **des Schlosses, meines Arztes**).

B. Feminine and plural nouns

Articles that precede all feminine and plural nouns in the genitive case end in **-er** (e.g., **meiner Mutter**). The feminine and plural nouns themselves have no special genitive endings.

C. Masculine N-nouns

Nouns like **der Student, der Herr, der Mensch** that add **-(e)n** in the accusative and dative singular also have the ending **-(e)n** instead of **-(e)s** in the genitive singular (e.g., **des Studenten, des Herrn, des Prinzen**) and in the genitive plural (e.g., **der Studenten**).

D. Adjective endings

The ending on adjectives used with genitive nouns preceded by any article or possessive is always **-en**.

> Eine ehrliche Gastronomie der klein**en**   *An honest catering trade of small family*
> Familienbetriebe.   *businesses.*

These are the genitive case forms.

Masculine	Neuter	Feminine	Plural
des König**s**	**des** Zimmer**s**	**der** Person	**der** Könige/Zimmer/Personen
ein**es** Tag**es**	ein**es** Märchen**s**	ein**er** Frau	kein**er** Tage/Märchen/Frauen
sein**es** Professor**s**	sein**es** Buch**es**	sein**er** Tochter	sein**er** Professoren/Bücher/Töchter
dies**es** Herr**n**	dies**es** Schloss**es**	dies**er** Stadt	dies**er** Herren/Schlösser/Städte

The genitive case relative pronouns are **dessen** (*m.* and *n.*) and **deren** (*f.* and all *pl.*).

> Es war einmal ein hübsches Mädchen,   *Once upon a time there was a beautiful girl,*
> **dessen** Mutter krank wurde.   *whose mother became ill.*

E. Proper names

In standard German, proper names of people and countries simply add an **-s** without an apostrophe to show possession. An apostrophe is used when the name ends in –s or –z.

Er übernachtet in **Roberts (Hans')** Ferienwohnung.	*He's staying overnight in Robert's (Hans's) vacation home.*

However, when additional descriptive information is present, the genitive case is required.

Er übernachtet in der Ferienwohnung **meines Freundes Robert.**	*He's staying overnight in my friend Robert's vacation home.*

In non-standard German the use of the apostrophe is on the rise.

F. The dative preposition *von*

As you learned in **Kapitel 6,** German speakers frequently express ownership with the preposition **von** + *dative*. The word **von** is increasingly replacing the genitive case in spoken German.

Wie heißt die Adresse **deines Hotels?** Wie heißt die Adresse **von deinem Hotel?**	*What's the address of your hotel?*

Mich interessieren die Bücher **dieser italienischen Journalistin** sehr. Mich interessieren die Bücher **von dieser italienischen Journalistin** sehr.	*I am very interested in the books by this Italian journalist.*

---

38 **Wessen Sachen sind das?** Ihre Freunde fragen dauernd°, wessen Sachen Sie benutzen. Antworten Sie mit den passenden Genitivformulierungen.

continuously

BEISPIEL S1: *Wessen Wagen fährst du in der Schweiz? (mein Freund Tom)*
S2: *Ich fahre den Wagen meines Freundes Tom.*

1. In wessen Haus hast du übernachtet? (meine Freunde Willi und Maria)
2. Wessen Skier hast du benutzt? (Willi)
3. Wessen Gastfreundschaft hast du genossen°? (mein guter Freund Willi) *enjoyed*
4. Wessen Sonnenbrille hast du getragen? (meine gute Freundin Maria)
5. Wessen Anorak° hast du zum Skilaufen getragen? (Maria) *parka*
6. In wessen Sauna hast du den Nachmittag verbracht? (meine neue Bekannte Jutta)
7. Wessen Bier hast du getrunken? (mein lieber alter Freund Jörg)
8. Wessen Weingläser hast du eben kaputt gemacht? (meine lieben Freunde)

G. Genitive prepositions

German speakers also use the genitive case after certain prepositions.

(an)statt	*instead of*	**trotz**	*in spite of, despite*
außerhalb	*outside of*	**während**	*during*
innerhalb	*inside of*	**wegen**	*on account of, because of*

Trotz ihrer Stiefmutter ist Aschenputtel zum Ball gegangen.	*In spite of her stepmother, Cinderella went to the ball.*
Während des Balls hat der Prinz viel mit Aschenputtel getanzt.	*During the ball, the prince danced a lot with Cinderella.*

---

39 Wo übernachten Anna und Barbara während ihrer Semesterferien? Wählen Sie für jeden Satz die richtige Genitivpräposition.

außerhalb • innerhalb • trotz • (an)statt • während • wegen

1. _____ der Semesterferien wollen Anna und Barbara in die Schweiz fahren.
2. _____ der hohen Preise in der Schweiz möchten sie in Braunwald Urlaub machen.
3. _____ eines Jugendhotels buchen sie Zimmer in einem Familien-Hotel.
4. _____ der besseren Preise buchen sie Zimmer im Bänningerhaus und nicht im teuren Bellevue.
5. _____ des Dorfes gibt es wenige Schlafmöglichkeiten.
6. _____ der sagenhaften Preise im Bänningerhaus können sie ein paar Tage länger bleiben.
7. _____ der Woche wollen sie Ski fahren und snowboarden gehen.
8. _____ der zwei Sterne ist die Pension Ahorn relativ preiswert.
9. _____ der RehaClinic kann man eine Internet-Ecke finden.

40 Interview: Das Leben eines Studenten/einer Studentin Stellen Sie einem Partner/einer Partnerin die folgenden Fragen und beantworten Sie sie. Benutzen Sie den Genitiv.

BEISPIEL S1: *Mit wessen Geld finanzierst du dein Studium?*
S2: *Ich finanziere mein Studium mit dem Geld meiner Eltern.*

1. Mit wessen Geld finanzierst du dein Studium?
2. In wessen Zimmer verbringst du mehr Zeit: in deinem eigenen Zimmer oder im Zimmer deiner Freundin (deines Freundes)?
3. Mit wessen Computer arbeitest du auf dem Campus? Zu Hause?
4. Was heißt der Titel deines Lieblingskurses?
5. Wessen Auto leihst du dir für eine Verabredung?
6. Wessen Job möchtest du eines Tages haben? Warum?
7. Die Musik von welchem Sänger/Rapper oder von welcher Sängerin/Rapperin gefällt dir am besten?

41 Freie Kommunikation: **Rollenspiel: Italien oder die Schweiz?** Es ist März und Sie können zwei Wochen Urlaub machen. Fahren Sie lieber nach Italien oder in die Schweiz? Besprechen Sie mit einem Partner/einer Partnerin die zwei Reisemöglichkeiten. Versuchen Sie, die andere Person mit Argumenten aus den folgenden Listen zu überzeugen°. S1 fährt gern im Auto, möchte in der Sonne liegen und etwas Exotisches erleben. S2 ist sehr aktiv, fährt gern mit dem Zug und hat Massentourismus nicht gern.

convince

Italien	*die Schweiz*
die Sonne genießen	Ski fahren
schwimmen gehen	eine Bergwanderung machen
relativ billig	relativ teuer
weit fahren	nicht so weit fahren
mit dem Auto fahren	mit dem Auto/Zug fahren
Italienisch hören	Deutsch, Französisch oder Italienisch sprechen
viele Touristen	wenige Touristen
viele Sehenswürdigkeiten besuchen	aktiv sein, Sport treiben
gutes Essen	gutes Bier, guter Käse

42 Schreibecke: **Schönen Gruß aus der Schweiz!** Sie kommen gerade vom Skilaufen zurück und haben ein paar Minuten Zeit. Schreiben Sie Ihren Freunden/Freundinnen oder Ihrer Familie zu Hause, wie Ihnen der Winterurlaub in der Schweiz gefällt. Erzählen Sie im Präteritum, was Sie schon alles gemacht haben. Dann adressieren Sie die Postkarte an den Empfänger/die Empfängerin°. Die folgende Liste enthält° ein paar Ideen.

recipient / contains

Ski laufen • Schlitten fahren • Gastfreundschaft • Spaß machen • autofrei • Postkartenlandschaft • märchenhafte Landschaft • Zauberstimmung • fehlen° • gute Pisten • hoch über dem Alltag • Spaziergänger • Touristen • Grüezi!

to be missing, lacking

Tomas Sereda/Shutterstock.com

43 Was sind die Kosten pro Person?

Anna, Barbara und ihre Freunde haben vor, im März nach Braunwald in die Schweiz zu fahren, aber jetzt müssen sie eine preiswerte Unterkunft finden. Die Schweiz ist ja bekanntlich teuer. Lesen Sie die Anzeigen auf Seite 415 und stellen Sie Fragen über die Kosten. Benutzen Sie **von** in der Frage.

two meals per day

BEISPIEL

S1 (ANNA): *Was sind die Kosten pro Person von einer Übernachtung mit Halbpension° im Hotel Bellevue im Winter?*

S2 (BARBARA): *Die Kosten einer Übernachtung mit Halbpension im Hotel Bellevue sind zwischen 210 und 295 Franken pro Person im Winter.*

1. eine Übernachtung mit Halbpension im Hotel Bellevue im Winter
2. ein Doppelzimmer mit Halbpension im Hotel Cristal
3. eine Übernachtung mit Frühstück im Alexander's Tödiblick
4. das 5-Gang-Diner im Alexander's Tödiblick
5. ein Schlafplatz ohne Frühstück im adrenalin backpackers hostel
6. das Frühstück im adrenalin backpackers hostel

44 Allwissende° Anna

all-knowing

Die Gruppe ist schon in Braunwald angekommen. Anna muss die Fragen ihrer Freunde mithilfe der Broschüre beantworten. Spielen Sie die Rollen von Anna und ihren Freunden. Anna benutzt den Genitiv und ihre Freunde benutzen **von**. Wechseln Sie die Rollen.

BEISPIEL

S1 (FREUND/FREUNDIN): *Sag mal, Anna. Was sind die Ruhetage von der Apotheke?*

S2 (ANNA): *Die Ruhetage der Apotheke sind Samstag und Sonntag.*

1. die Ruhetage / die Apotheke
2. der Name / der einzige Zahnarzt im Dorf
3. die Telefonnummer / das Fundbüro
4. der Name / ein Ski- und Snowboardvermieter
5. die Länge / die Langlaufloipe auf dem Grotzenbüel
6. die Spielzeit / das Kino
7. der Preis / eine Stunde in der Internet-Ecke von der RehaClinic
8. die Öffnungszeiten / das Hallenbad
9. die Telefonnummer / die Wäscherei im Dorf
10. die Öffnungszeiten / der Braunwald-bahnen-Schalter

Apotheke
RehaClinic Braunwald. Montag-Freitag, 9.00-12.00 und
13.00-17.00 Uhr.
Nur Medikamente, keine Drogerieartikel
Tel. 055 643 22 55

Braunwaldbahnen
Schalteröffnungszeiten Berg- und Talstation:
Jeweils 10 Minuten vor Abfahrt
SBB Schalter: 7.00-19.00 Uhr

Fundbüro
Braunwald Tourismus
Tel. 055 643 65 85

Hallenbad
Mittwoch von 14.00-16.00 Uhr (übrige Zeit auf Anfrage)

Internet-Ecke / Internet Café
Internet-Ecke: Bibliothek der RehaClinic
Braunwald. Öffnungszeiten wie Bibliothek, CHF 4,- pro Stunde.
Internet Café: Hotel Alpenblick. Öffnungszeiten auf Anfrage
Tel. 055 643 15 44

Kino
Aktuelles Filmangebot. Mittwoch um 21.15 Uhr im Saalkino Hotel Alpenblick
Tel. 055 643 15 44

Langlauf
Langlaufloipe auf dem Grotzenbüel bis zu vier Kilometer je nach Schneeverhältnissen.
Mittelschwere Strecke (Klassisch und Skating gespurt). Umkleidekabine und Dusche bei der Bergstation der Gondelbahn.

Ski-, und Snowboardmiete, Service
Vermietung von Ski- und Snowboardausrüstungen in Braunwald bei Regula Sport
Tel. 055 643 22 22
Im Schwettiberg bei Glarner Sport
Tel. 055 643 35 69

Wäscherei
Wäscherei Braunwald, Tel. 055 643 14 68
Wäscherei Schwettiberg, Tel. 055 643 10 86

Zahnarzt
Med. dent. F. Christensen, Linthal
Tel. 055 643 18 55
Mo-Di 8.00-12.00 und 13.30-17.30 Uhr
Mi 8.00-12.00 Uhr, Nachmittag geschl.
Do 8.00-12.00 und 13.30-17.30 Uhr
Fr 8.00-15.00 Uhr durchgehend

Zeichenerklärung für Unterkünfte

⌃⋆⋆	Klassifikation von hotelleriesuisse	⌙	Eisfeld
✳✳✳	Klassifikation des STV	⇅	Lift
⊛	Familienfreundliches Hotel	✕	Öffentliches Restaurant
⊘	Ferienhotel	▥	Terrassen-/Gartenrestaurant
⊘	Seminarhotel	⇚	Aussichtsrestaurant
⬢Q	Qualitäts-Gütesiegel, Stufe 1	✎	Vegetarisches Restaurant
⬡F	Familiengütesiegel	☺	Schonkost/Diät
⋈	Anzahl Betten	⸙	Vollwertküche
♂	Öffnungszeiten	⊖	Nichtrauchertische
☎	Telefon in allen Zimmern	⛾	Bar
TV	TV in allen Zimmern	♫	Dancing, Night Club, Discothek
▤	Radio in allen Zimmern	▦	Spezialisiert für Tagungen/Seminare
▭	Modem in allen Zimmern	⊞	Saal, Säli, Sitzungszimmer
⋔	Minibar in allen Zimmern	✕	Keine Haustiere
⊙	Zentrale Lage	⤬	Nichtraucherbetrieb
⮐	Nichtraucherzimmer	⸸	Reservation durch Reisebüros möglich
⬧	Rollstuhlgängig		**Zahlungsmittel**
⚘	Besonders ruhige Lage	AE	American Express
♣	Garten, Parkanlage	VISA	Visa
☺	Speziell geeignet für Familien	MasterCard	MasterCard
⊠	Kinderbetreuung	⊙	Diners Card
✎	Tennisplätze	JCB	JCB Card
🏛	Hallenbad	reka	Reka-Checks
♨	Wellness-Anlage	Postcard	Postcard
♨	Sauna	Maestro	Maestro

Hotels in Braunwald

Märchenhotel Bellevue

★★★★ ⌃⋆⋆ ⬢Q ⬡F ⊛ ☺

Familie Nadja und Patric Vogel
CH-8784 Braunwald
Telefon +41 (0)55 653 71 71
Fax +41 (0)55 643 10 00
info@maerchenhotel.ch
www.maerchenhotel.ch

Sommer: Fr. 144.– bis 205.–
Winter: Fr. 210.– bis 295.–
Winter-Nachsaison:
Fr. 153.– bis 195.–
pro Person
inkl. Gourmet-Halbpension

54 Zimmer/⋈100/
♂6–10, 12–4

☎ TV ▤ ⋔ ♣ ⚘ ☺ ⊠ ✎ ♨
♨ 🏛 ⇅ ✕ ⇚ ⊙ ⛾ ✕ ⤬
VISA MasterCard reka Postcard MasterCard €

Geniessen Sie den Komfort des einzigen 4-Stern-Hotels in der Region. Geschmackvolle Designer- und Familienzimmer. Kinder erwartet viel Spass und Abenteuer mit oder ohne Betreuung. Luftschloss, Hallenbad mit Tarzankletterparcours, Rutschbahn von Stock zu Stock, Spielplatz, Aquarium-Lift mit Unterwasserwelt. Die allabendliche Märchenstunde mit dem Märchenonkel ist nicht wegzudenken. Erwachsene schätzen die Relax-Oase «Wellness on the top», die hervorragende Küche und den Charme des stilvoll renovierten Grand Hôtel. Speisesaal mit einer traumhaften Aussicht und elegante Bar.
Neu: Familiensuiten und Loftsuiten mit fantastischem Blick auf den Tödi.

Planquadrat F5/Nr. 10

Hotel Cristal

⌃⋆⋆ ⬢Q ⬡F ☺

Familie
Magdi und Hans Schilling
und Ursina Kappeler
CH-8784 Braunwald
Telefon +41 (0)55 643 10 45
Fax +41 (0)55 643 12 44
info@hotel-cristal.ch
www.hotel-cristal.ch

Nebensaison: Fr. 90.– bis 130.–
Sommer: Fr. 100.– bis 140.–
Winter: Fr. 120.– bis 165.–
Preise pro Person
inkl. Halbpension

19 Zimmer/⋈35/
♂5–10, 12–3

☎ TV ▤ ⋔ ♣ ⚘ ☺ ✕ ▥
⇚ ✎ ☺ ⊙ ⊞
AE VISA MasterCard ⊙ reka Postcard
MasterCard €

Der gepflegte Familienbetrieb für erholsame und erlebnisreiche Ferien. Ideale Lage bei der Station Hüttenberg der Gondelbahn Grotzenbüel und neben dem Sammelplatz der Schweizer Schneesportschule. Komfortable und wohnlich ausgestattete Zimmer mit schöner Aussicht. Appartements. Speisesaal und Aufenthaltsraum mit Spielecke. TV/Video. Gemütliches Restaurant mit Terrasse. Gute, neuzeitliche Küche mit marktfrischem Angebot. Abholservice des Gepäcks. Ihr persönliches Wohl liegt den Gastgebern am Herzen.

Planquadrat B5/Nr. 12

Alexander's Tödiblick

⬡F ⊛ ☺

Familie Stuber
CH-8784 Braunwald
Telefon +41 (0)55 653 63 63
Fax +41 (0)55 653 63 66
toediblick@bluewin.ch
www.holidayswitzerland.com
www.toediblick.ch

Nebensaison: Fr. 65.– bis 118.–
Sommer: Fr. 75.– bis 143.–
Winter: Fr. 85.– bis 158.–
pro Person inkl. Frühstück
5-Gang-Dîner: + Fr. 40.–

22 Zimmer/⋈40/
♂ Ganzjährig geöffnet

☎ TV ▤ ⊞ ♣ ⚘ ☺ ⊙ ⇅
✕ ▥ ✎ ⊙ ⊞ ▦
AE ⊙ VISA MasterCard reka
MasterCard €

Hoch über dem Alltag, mit grandiosem Blick auf die Glarner Alpen, steht seit über 100 Jahren ein kleines, feines Familienhotel, in dritter Generation geführt von der Familie Stuber. Herzliche Gastfreundschaft und höchste Qualität sowie die herausragende Marktküche sind unser Markenzeichen. Die individuellen Räume bieten Geborgenheit, eine einmalige Ruhe – und eine Aussicht, die uns noch immer jeden Tag von neuem verzaubert. Ob Sie alleine oder zu zweit reisen, mit Ihren Kindern oder Ihren Eltern – unser Haus ist das perfekte Feriendomizil. Wir holen als einziges Braunwalder Hotel unsere Gäste mit dem Pferde-Hoteltaxi an der Bahnstation ab.

Planquadrat D4/Nr. 13

Familien- und Jugendunterkünfte in Braunwald

adrenalin backpackers hostel

⬢Q ⬡F

Familie Brigitte und Markus
Zweifel-Schumacher
CH-8784 Braunwald
Telefon +41 (0)79 347 29 05
info@adrenalin.gl
Neu: online buchbar unter
www.adrenalin.gl

Basispreis
(im eigenen Schlafsack,
ohne Frühstück): ab Fr. 29.–
Frühstück: + Fr. 8.–
Bettwäsche: + Fr. 5.–
Preise pro Person und Nacht

28 Zimmer/⋈60/♂1–12

⊙ ⮐ ♣ ⊙ 🏛 ⇅ ✎ ⊙ ⛾ ♫
▦ ⊞

VISA MasterCard JCB reka Postcard MasterCard
€/Bargeld

Das zentral gelegene Hostel verfolgt folgende Philosophie: Low-Budget-Tourismusangebot für junge und jung gebliebene Gäste, denen Erlebnis und das Knüpfen von Kontakten wichtiger ist als Komfort und Luxus. Saubere und sehr einfach eingerichtete Zimmer. Frühstückservice. Bar/Dorfbeiz täglich ab 16.00 Uhr geöffnet. Cordon-bleu-Festival, einfache Menüs und Snacks. Dazu während des Sommers: feinste Grilladen. Play-Arena mit Billard, Airhockey und anderen Spieltischen. **Besonderes:** Empfehlenswert für Vereine und Gruppen. Selbstkocherküche, Handyguthaben laden (Voucher-Service).

Planquadrat E6/Nr. 18

Bauernhaus Burstberg

Familie Gisler
CH-8784 Braunwald
Telefon +41 (0)55 643 11 12
famgisler5@bluewin.ch
www.gislerferien.ch

Pro Person und Nacht
Fr. 17.– bis 23.–, exkl. Kurtaxen

7 Zimmer/⋈12/♂1–12

♣ ⚘ ☺

reka €/auf Rechnung

Gemütliches, über 100-jähriges frei stehendes Schindeln-Bauernhaus. Viehbestand. Einfach eingerichtete Zimmer. 1 Badezimmer und 2 WC zur gemeinsamen Benützung. Gemeinschaftsküche und Aufenthaltsraum. Sitzplatz.

Planquadrat A5/Nr. 16

🌐 **Endspurt:** Online Listening Text & Activities.

Ein Schweizer Märchen
Zielaktivitäten

↩ **45** Ein Schweizer Märchen Stellen Sie sich vor, Sie waren in der Schweiz und erzählen Ihren Freunden eine ganz tolle (vielleicht nicht ganz wahre°) Geschichte von Ihren Erlebnissen°. Planen Sie zuerst die Geschichte, indem Sie diese Fragen beantworten.

true
experiences

1. Mit wem waren Sie in der Schweiz?
   a. mit _____
   b. allein

BEISPIEL *Ich war mit meinen besten zehn Freunden in der Schweiz.*

2. Wie waren Sie in die Schweiz gekommen?
   a. mit der Bahn / dem Flugzeug / dem Schiff / dem Rad / ?
   b. zu Fuß
   c. auf einem Pferd° / auf einem Esel° / auf ?
   d. ?

horse / donkey

BEISPIEL *Wir waren auf einem Esel in die Schweiz gekommen.*

3. Wann war das?
   a. mitten im Sommer / Herbst / Winter / Frühling
   b. am Ende eines Sommers / Herbstes / Winters / Frühlings
   c. in einer dunklen Nacht / bei hellem Tageslicht / in der Abenddämmerung°
   d. ?

dusk

BEISPIEL *Es war am Ende eines Sommers.*

4. Was wollten Sie in der Schweiz machen?
   a. mich/uns entspannen
   b. Ski fahren
   c. spazieren gehen
   d. eine Uhr kaufen
   e. ?

BEISPIEL *Wir wollten uns entspannen.*

5. Wo übernachteten Sie?
   a. in einem luxuriösen Hotel / einem billigen Hotel / einer Jugendherberge
   b. bei reichen / verrückten / alten / neuen Freunden
   c. in einem kleinen / dunklen Stall°
   d. im Auto / in der Bahn / auf dem Schiff
   e. ?

barn

BEISPIEL *Wir übernachteten in einem luxuriösen Hotel.*

6. Was lag auf dem Bett / auf dem Boden / in einer Ecke, als Sie in Ihr Zimmer / in Ihr Zelt / in Ihren Stall kamen?
   a. ein großer Hund / eine große Spinne° / eine giftige Schlange°
   b. eine langhaarige Katze
   c. ein teures Geschenk / ein langer Brief / ein Deutschbuch
   d. ?

BEISPIEL   *Als wir ins Zimmer kamen, lag ein langer Brief auf dem Bett.*

7. Wer hatte Ihnen den _____ (Hund) / die _____ (Katze) / das _____ (Geschenk) geschickt?
   a. eine Hexe   c. mein Deutschlehrer / meine Deutschlehrerin
   b. ein Zauberer   d. ?

BEISPIEL   *Eine Hexe hatte uns den Brief geschickt.*

8. Was machten Sie mit dem _____ (Hund, Geschenk usw.) / der _____ (Katze usw.)?
   a. Ich fasste ihn / sie / es (nicht) an°.
   b. Ich machte nichts damit.
   c. Ich/wir ?

BEISPIEL   *Wir fassten ihn nicht an.*

9. Was passierte dann? Benutzen Sie Ihre Fantasie!

10. Was passierte zum Schluss?
    a. Wir fuhren / Ich fuhr einfach wieder nach Hause.
    b. _____ starb.
    c. _____ verwandelte/n sich in° ein/einen/eine _____
    d. _____ war nie wieder der-/die-/dasselbe°.

11. Was ist ein gutes Motto für Ihre Erlebnisse?
    a. Was für eine interessante/tolle/schöne/verrückte/_____ Reise!
    b. Die magische/idyllische/gefährliche/_____ Schweiz!
    c. Meine Freunde sind / ich bin extrem intelligent/entspannt/dumm/ risikofreudig!
    d. ?

12. Schreiben Sie jetzt Ihr Märchen.

46   **Das Publikum**   Für welche Leser ist Ihre Geschichte (nicht) geeignet°?

Leser	Geeignet	Nicht geeignet
1. kleine Kinder	○	○
2. Jugendliche unter 13	○	○
3. Jugendliche unter 18	○	○
4. Erwachsene	○	○

Wenn nicht geeignet, warum nicht?
   a. zu gewalttätig°   c. zu intellektuell   e. zu kindisch
   b. zu komplex   d. zu (un)realistisch   f. zu ?

spider / snake

anfassen = to touch

verwandelte sich in: turned into / war ...: was never again the same

suited

violent

47 Dramatisches Erzählen Erzählen Sie der Gruppe von 3–5 Personen Ihr Schweizer Märchen. Die anderen Leute stellen Fragen. Machen Sie auch dramatische Gesten° und arbeiten Sie mit Ihrer Stimme°. Fangen Sie mit der typischen Märchenstruktur an.

gestures / voice

> **BEISPIEL** *Es war einmal ein Student / eine Studentin aus …*

48 Schreibecke: **Anekdoten aus dem Urlaub.** Jeder von uns hat komische oder traurige Erinnerungen an den Urlaub. Was ist Ihnen mal im Urlaub passiert, das Sie in einer kurzen Geschichte erzählen können? Schreiben Sie eine kleine Erzählung von mindestens zehn Sätzen im Präteritum. Beschreiben Sie, wo Sie waren, mit wem Sie da waren, was Sie machen wollten and was dann passierte.

Schneewittchen und die sieben Zwerge.

49 Freie Kommunikation: **Ein altes Märchen erzählen.** Bilden Sie eine Gruppe von fünf Personen und erzählen Sie der Gruppe Ihr Lieblingsmärchen. Wenn Sie möchten, benutzen Sie beim Sprechen das Perfekt (z. B. hat **gewohnt, hat geheiratet**). Die anderen Studenten/Studentinnen müssen den Titel Ihres Märchens erraten. Geben Sie Ihrem Märchen einen typischen Anfang und ein typisches Ende.

> **BEISPIEL** Sie: *Es war einmal ein(e) …*
>
> *…*
>
> *… Und wenn sie nicht gestorben sind, dann leben sie noch heute.*

50 Das ist zu grausam°! Lesen Sie die folgende Schlussszene aus der ursprünglichen° Grimmschen Version von „Aschenputtel". Mehrere Eltern in der Schule halten diese Version für zu brutal für Kinder. Teilen Sie die Klasse in drei Gruppen auf: **Pro, Kontra** und **Revisionisten**. Die Kontra-Gruppe will diese Schlussszene verbieten°. Die Revisionisten finden die Schlussszene auch unakzeptabel und schlagen Änderungen vor. Die Pro-Gruppe argumentiert gegen eine Zensur°. Die Mitglieder von allen Gruppen erklären, warum sie für oder gegen die Schlussszene sind.

gruesome, cruel
original

ban, prohibit

censorship

Als die Brautleute zur Kirche gingen, war die ältere Schwester zur rechten Seite und die jüngere zur linken Seite der Braut. Da pickten die Tauben° einer jeden° ein Auge aus. Danach, als sie aus der Kirche kamen, war die jüngere Schwester zur rechten Seite und die ältere zur linken Seite der Braut. Da pickten die Tauben einer jeden das andere Auge aus. So war Blindheit die Strafe° für ihre Bosheit° und Falschheit.

pigeons
einer …: *from each one*

punishment / mean-spiritedness

Märchen

die Asche, -n *ash, cinder*
der Ball, ̈e *ball, dance*
der Baum, ̈e *tree*
das Blut *blood*
die Braut, ̈e *bride*
der Edelstein, -e *jewel*
die Fee, -n *fairy*
die Ferse, -n *heel*
der Frosch, ̈e *frog*
der giftige Apfel, ̈ *poison apple*
das Gold *gold*
das Grab, ̈er *grave*
die Handlung, -en *plot* (*of a story*)
der Herd, -e *stove, hearth*
die Hexe, -n *witch*
der Himmel *heaven*
der Jäger, - *hunter*
der König, -e *king*
die Königin, -nen *queen*
der Königssohn, ̈e *prince*
die Königstochter, ̈ *princess*
das Messer, - *knife*
der Prinz, [-en], -en *prince*
die Prinzessin, -nen *princess*
das Silber *silver*
die Stiefmutter, ̈ *stepmother*
die Stieftochter, ̈ *stepdaughter*
die Treppe, -n *stair*
der Wald, ̈er *forest, woods*
der Zauberer, - *sorcerer, magician*
die Zehe, -n *toe*
der Zweig, -e *branch*
der Zwerg, -e *dwarf*
Noch einmal: **das Märchen, der Spiegel, das Tier**
arm *poor*
fromm *religious, faithful*
grausam *gruesome; cruel*
hässlich *ugly*
schmutzig *dirty*

ab•schneiden (schnitt ab, hat abgeschnitten) *to cut off*
erlauben (hat erlaubt) *to allow*
passen (hat gepasst) *to fit*
pflanzen (hat gepflanzt) *to plant*
sterben (stirbt, starb, ist gestorben) *to die*
suchen (hat gesucht) *to seek, look for*
sich verkleiden (hat sich verkleidet) *to disguise oneself*
verlieren (verlor, hat verloren) *to lose*
verstecken (hat versteckt) *to hide, conceal*
wachsen (wächst, wuchs, ist gewachsen) *to grow*
Es war einmal ein … *Once upon a time there was a . . .; There once was a . . .*
eines Tages (Morgens, Abends, Nachts) *one day (morning, evening, night)*
Und wenn sie nicht gestorben sind, dann leben sie noch heute. *And they lived happily ever after.*

Die Schweiz

der Anfänger, - *beginner*
der Berg, -e *mountain*
der/die Fortgeschrittene, [-n], -n *advanced student*
der Gast, ̈e *guest*
der Genießer, - *connoisseur, fan*
der Gipfel, - *peak*
die Grenze, -n *border*
die Hauptstadt, ̈e *capital city*
die Insel, -n *island*
der Kanton, -e *canton* (*Swiss state*)
die Landschaft, -en *landscape*
der Pass, ̈e *pass* (*through a mountain*)
der Postbote, [-n], -n *mail carrier*
der See, -n *lake*
die Stimmung, -en *mood*
das Tal, ̈er *valley*

der Wandel *change, transformation*
die Wirtschaft, -en *tavern*
das Wunder, - *miracle*
die Zukunft *future*
Noch einmal: **der Fluss, die Stadt**
ehemalig *former*
seltsam *strange, odd, unusual*
verschneit *snowy*
sich gewöhnen (hat sich gewöhnt) an + acc. *to get used to*
steigen (stieg, ist gestiegen) *to rise, climb*
   ein•steigen (stieg ein, ist eingestiegen) *to get on*
   aus•stiegen (stieg aus, ist ausgestiegen) *to get off*

Urlaub, Ferien und Festtage

das Andenken, - *souvenir*
die Entspannung *relaxation*
der Feiertag, -e *holiday*
das Fest, -e *party, celebration, festival, feast*
   der Festtag, -e *holiday*
das Hotel, -s *hotel*
die Jugendherberge, -n *youth hostel*
der Reiseleiter, - / die Reiseleiterin, -nen *tour guide*
die Sehenswürdigkeit, -en *sightseeing attraction*
der Umzug, ̈e *parade*
der Urlaub, -e *vacation taken by a person to relax (often involves travel)*
Chanukka *Chanukah*
Karneval, Fasching, Fastnacht *celebration before Lent, Mardi Gras*
das Neujahr *New Year's Day*
Ostern *Easter*
Ramadan *Ramadan*
Silvester *New Year's Eve*
Weihnachten *Christmas*

Noch einmal: **die Erfahrung, die Ferien** *(pl.)*, **die Pension**

erleben (hat erlebt) *to experience*

feiern (hat gefeiert) *to celebrate, have a party*

genießen (genoss, hat genossen) *to enjoy*

Schlittschuh laufen (läuft, lief, ist gelaufen) *to ice-skate*

verreisen (ist verreist) *to take a trip*

Noch einmal: **verbringen**

gestresst *stressed*

gut gelaunt *easy-going*

preiswert *reasonably priced, well worth the money*

Noch einmal: **fremd, wunderbar**

Skiurlaub, Ski fahren

der Anorak, -s *parka*

das Dorf, ̈-er *village*

die Piste, -n *(downhill)* *ski run, ski slope; track*

Andere Verben

an•probieren (hat anprobiert) *to try on*

beten (hat gebetet) *to pray*

brennen (brannte, hat gebrannt) *to burn*

erkennen (erkannte, hat erkannt) *to recognize*

fangen (fängt, fing, hat gefangen) *to catch*

fehlen (hat gefehlt) *to be missing, lacking*

kosten (hat gekostet) *to cost*

nennen (nannte, hat genannt) *to name, call (someone something)*

rennen (rannte, ist gerannt) *to run*

rufen (rief, hat gerufen) *to call*

sparen (hat gespart) *to save (money)*

überzeugen (hat überzeugt) *to convince*

verbieten (verbat, hat verboten) *to ban, prohibit*

weinen (hat geweint) *to cry*

werfen (wirft, warf, hat geworfen) *to throw*

ziehen (zog, hat gezogen) *to pull*

Noch einmal: **schneiden, statt•finden, wünschen**

Andere Substantive

die Art, -en *type, kind*

der Feind, -e *enemy, adversary*

die Kindheit *childhood*

der Lack *cenamel*

der Leder *leather*

der Unterschied, -e *difference*

der Witz, -e *joke*

Andere Adjektive

echt *true, real*

eigene *own*

erstaunt *astounded*

erwachsen *grown-up, adult*

sauber *clean*

ursprünglich *original*

Andere Adverbien

damals *at that time, back then*

insgesamt *all in all*

Andere Wörter

wessen? *whose?*

dessen/dessen/deren *whose*

jedermann *everyone*

jemand *someone*

als *when*

nachdem *after*

ob *if, whether*

von + *dat.* *of (possession)*

wann *when*

wenn *whenever; if*

immer wenn *always when, whenever*

Andere Ausdrücke

ohne es zu sagen *without telling*

Meine eigenen Wörter

_____

_____

_____

_____

_____

_____

Seitz/ullstein bild/The Image Works

Das Brandenburger Tor ist seit 1990 wieder das Zentrum der Stadt „Bärlin".

Geschichte und Geografie Deutschlands

In this chapter you will learn to talk about what you might do, make polite suggestions and requests, describe actions as a process, and state what you could or should have done. You will also learn to talk about German history.

Kommunikative Funktionen

> Speculating about activities, making suggestions

> Talking about unreal situations

> Talking about actions as a process

Strukturen

> The subjunctive mood

> Role reversal statements (*If I were you, . . .*)

> The double-infinitive construction

> **Wenn**-clauses for unreal conditions

> The passive voice

Vokabeln

> Sehenswürdigkeiten in Berlin

Kulturelles

> Deutschland: von der Monarchie zur Demokratie (I, II, III)

> Freistaat Sachsen: Leipzig und Dresden

Was würdest du dann vorschlagen?

In den Ferien fährt Anna nach Berlin, wo sie ihren Onkel Werner besucht. Beim Abendessen erzählt Anna Onkel Werner von ihrem ersten Tag in Berlin. Anna wollte den Reichstag und die Mauer sehen. Aber zu viele Leute haben vor dem Reichstag Schlange gestanden° und später konnte sie Reste von der Mauer nirgendwo° finden. Anna und Onkel Werner machen Pläne für die nächsten Tage und besprechen, was Anna sehen möchte und was sie zusammen machen könnten. Heute Abend gehen sie ins Konzert, und danach will Anna noch jemanden treffen.

Schlange stehen: to stand in line / nowhere

Vorschau

🔁 **1** Thematische Fragen Beantworten Sie die folgenden Fragen auf Deutsch.

1. Wie lernen Sie am ersten Tag eine neue Stadt kennen?
   - a. auf einer Stadtrundfahrt°
   - b. auf einer Führung°
   - c. durch eine Powerpoint-Präsentation
   - d. allein
   - e. mit Freunden
   - f. durch ein Video

city bus tour
walking tour

2. Wo informieren Sie sich über eine neue Stadt?
   - a. bei Freunden
   - b. bei Verwandten
   - c. bei jungen Leuten
   - d. beim Verkehrsbüro
   - e. bei Facebook
   - f. beim Fremdenführer/bei der Fremdenführerin
   - g. beim Telefondienst
   - h. im Internet

3. Was möchten Sie als Tourist/Touristin als Erstes in Berlin erleben?
   - a. die Museen
   - b. die Disko- und Clubszene
   - c. die Architektur
   - d. die tollen Parks und Seen
   - e. die Musikszene
   - f. die Kunstszene

Seit der Vereinigung ist der Potsdamer Platz ein Symbol für das neue Berlin geworden.

© Visum/Meisel/The Image Works

Wissenswerte Vokabeln: Sehenswürdigkeiten in Berlin

Talking about sights in and around Berlin

der Kurfürstendamm

die Kaiser-Wilhelms-Gedächtniskirche

die Philharmonie

die Museumsinsel

der Potsdamer Platz

Unter den Linden

das Brandenburger Tor

der Alexanderplatz

das Schloss Charlottenburg

die Humboldt-Universität

Berlin-Mitte

der Reichstag

die Spree

die Mauer

das neue Regierungsviertel

der Prenzlauer Berg

Illustrations © Cengage Learning 2014

Kulturnotiz. Five museums in the heart of Berlin-Mitte on **die Museumsinsel** form the nucleus of Berlin's art exhibition space: **(1) die Alte Nationalgalerie,** with German art of the 19th and 20th centuries; **(2) das Bode-Museum,** with its collections of sculpture, Byzantine art, and Old Masters paintings; **(3) das Pergamonmuseum** with its famous Greek Pergamon altar and collections of Near Eastern and Islamic art; **(4) Altes Museum,** with its core collections of classical antiquities from Greek, Etruscan, and Roman art; and **(5) Neues Museum,** with sections for pre- and early-history and Egyptian art and culture.

BEISPIEL   *Was würdest du in Berlin machen?   Ich würde gern die Mauer besichtigen°.*

visit, look at

→ **2** Lernen Sie Berlin kennen Wählen Sie die beste Beschreibung für jede Sehenswürdigkeit in **Wissenswerte Vokabeln.**

1. Hier spielt das berühmteste Orchester Deutschlands.
2. Diese Kirche – im Krieg bombardiert – steht heute noch als Ruine.
3. Das ist der große Einkaufsplatz im ehemaligen Ostberlin; er hat die Internationale Weltzeituhr.
4. Das ist eine lebendige Einkaufsstraße° im westlichen Teil Berlins mit dem Warenhaus Ka-De-We: Kaufhaus des Westens.
5. Hier ist der Sitz des deutschen Bundestages ab 1999.
6. Diese neuen Gebäude stehen in Berlin-Mitte um den Reichstag und sind für die Ministerien.
7. Hier findet man den Stadtteil, der bei jungen Leuten „in" ist, mit vielen Szene-Clubs und Kneipen.
8. Diese Barriere stand als Symbol des Kalten Krieges zwischen Ost und West. Sie existiert nicht mehr als Ganzes.
9. Das ist ein Sommerpalast mitten in Berlin, der für Sophie Charlotte, die Frau von König Friedrich I, gebaut wurde.
10. Das ist die elegante Hauptstraße im östlichen Teil Berlins.
11. Dies ist das Wahrzeichen Berlins und steht am Anfang von Unter den Linden.
12. Das ist der berühmteste Fluss Berlins.
13. Hier gibt es fünf Museen: die Alte Nationalgalerie, das Bode-Museum, das Pergamonmuseum, das Alte Museum und das Neue Museum.
14. Hier ist der historische Mittelpunkt Berlins.
15. Dieser Platz mit dem Sony Center ist ein architektonisches Wunder.
16. Das ist die älteste Universität Berlins.

← **3** Würdest du das machen? Was würden Sie als Tourist/Touristin in einer fremden Stadt machen? Kreuzen Sie die Aktivitäten an. Fragen Sie dann einen Partner/eine Partnerin, was er/sie machen würde.

BEISPIEL   S1: *Würdest du in ein Konzert gehen?*
            S2: *Ja, das würde ich machen.* (oder)
                Nein, das würde ich nicht machen.

	Ich		Mein(e) Partner(in)	
	Ja	Nein	Ja	Nein
1. in ein Konzert gehen	○	○	○	○
2. historische Denkmäler° anschauen	○	○	○	○
3. eine historische Kirche oder einen Dom° besichtigen	○	○	○	○
4. einen Park oder einen Platz im Freien° besuchen	○	○	○	○
5. eine berühmte Sehenswürdigkeit anschauen	○	○	○	○
6. durch die Altstadt bummeln°	○	○	○	○
7. ein Museum besuchen	○	○	○	○
8. die Clubszene ausprobieren	○	○	○	○
9. einen Geschäftsbummeln machen	○	○	○	○
10. eine berühmte Universität besichtigen	○	○	○	○

shopping street

The **Kurfürstendamm,** West Berlin's main boulevard and shopping street, has its name because it was originally constructed by Berlin's imperial electors (**Kurfürsten**).

The **Humboldt-Universität** was founded in 1809 and named for Wilhelm von Humboldt (1767–1835) and his brother Alexander (1769–1859). It has been home to 29 Nobel Prize winners.

After doing this activity, determine which things both of you find interesting and report to the class what you could do together (e.g., **Wir könnten zusammen in ein Konzert gehen.**).

monuments

cathedral

im ...: outdoors

stroll

Hören Sie gut zu.

1 Grüß dich, Onkel Werner. Entschuldige die Verspätung.

Komm, erzähl mal von deinem ersten Tag in Berlin.

2 Haben wir Zeit?

Klar. Die Philharmonie fängt erst um 20 Uhr an. Wir essen erst eine Kleinigkeit.

3 Also, es war recht interessant, aber frustrierend. Ich wollte die Kuppel des Reichstags besichtigen, aber ich hätte stundenlang anstehen müssen.

Und dafür muss man sich jetzt vorher anmelden.

Und dann bin ich zum Brandenburger Tor gelaufen, weil ich die Mauer sehen wollte, aber da war nichts. Ich hätte sie so gern gesehen!

4 Oje, ich hätte dich warnen sollen! In Berlin-Mitte sind Mauerreste kaum noch zu finden. Wir könnten ja morgen oder übermorgen zur East Side Gallery, zum Mauerpark oder zur Bernauer Straße gehen. Dort stehen noch Mauerreste.

Gut. Das würde mich schon interessieren.

5 Abgemacht. Und was hast du für morgen vor?

Tja, ich würde gern Potsdam sehen. Vielleicht morgen Nachmittag …

6 Nee, nee pass mal auf. Allein für den Park Sanssouci braucht man einen ganzen Tag! Wir sollten damit bis Samstag warten. Dann hätte ich mehr Zeit.

7 Klingt gut. Aber was würdest du dann für morgen vorschlagen?

© Cengage Learning 2014

8 An deiner Stelle würde ich am Vormittag einen Bummel über den Kurfürstendamm machen, die Gedächtniskirche besuchen und ins Ka-De-We gehen. Und am Nachmittag könnten wir zusammen Unter den Linden entlang spazieren und Berlin-Mitte sehen — die Humboldt-Universität, den Berliner Dom und die Museumsinsel.

9 Das wäre schön. Und ich würde gern sehen, wo das neue Regierungsviertel ist, und das jüdische Mahnmal und der Potsdamer Platz auch.

Hm, vom Brandenburger Tor aus könnten wir das machen.

10 Fantastisch! Und, Onkel Werner, ich hätte noch einen Wunsch: Könnten wir nach der Philharmonie in den Prenzlauer Berg fahren?

Was willst du denn dort um diese Zeit?

11 Tja, ich habe heute jemanden kennengelernt, der dort wohnt. Und der hat von der Clubszene im Prenzlauer Berg geschwärmt.

Am Wochenende wäre es aber lebendiger …

12 Aber ich bin für heute Abend verabredet!

Aha. Das hätte ich gleich ahnen sollen!

Kulturnotiz. After years of intense debate, the memorial for the Jewish victims of the Holocaust (**das Mahnmal für die ermordeten Juden Europas**) was opened in 2005 on a site just a short walk from the **Brandenburger Tor.** (See 9 above.)

Rückblick

→ **4** Stimmt das? Stimmen die folgenden Aussagen zum Text? Wenn nicht, was stimmt?

	Ja, das stimmt.	Nein, das stimmt nicht.
1. Annas erster Tag in Berlin war frustrierend.	○	○
2. Der Reichstag war geschlossen.	○	○
3. Anna hat das Brandenburger Tor gesehen, aber die Mauer hat sie nicht finden können.	○	○
4. Für morgen hat Anna keine festen Pläne.	○	○
5. Werner meint, dass man für Potsdam und den Park Sanssouci nur ein paar Stunden braucht.	○	○
6. Werner schlägt Anna vor, dass sie am Vormittag den Kurfürstendamm allein besuchen soll.	○	○
7. Am Nachmittag könnten sie zusammen eine Schifffahrt auf der Spree machen.	○	○
8. Heute Abend gehen sie zusammen in ein Rockkonzert.	○	○
9. Nachher will Anna in den Prenzlauer Berg fahren.	○	○
10. Werner versteht endlich, dass Anna noch heute mit einem jungen Mann im Prenzlauer Berg verabredet ist.	○	○

← **5** Kurz gesagt Vervollständigen Sie diese Sätze. Benutzen Sie Ihre eigenen Worte.

1. Werner und Anna sind heute Abend in Eile°, weil …
2. Anna soll noch eine Kleinigkeit essen, bevor …
3. Anna hat die Kuppel vom Reichstag nicht besichtigt, weil …
4. Werner meint, er hätte Anna warnen sollen, dass …
5. Werner schlägt Anna vor, morgen nicht nach Potsdam zu fahren, weil …
6. Werner sagt, dass er an Annas Stelle morgen Vormittag …
7. Am Nachmittag meint Werner, dass …
8. Anna möchte in den Prenzlauer Berg fahren, weil …

Complete the **Ergänzen Sie** activity in the Student Activities Manual before doing the next activity.

sind … in Eile: are in a hurry

Sprache im Alltag: Confirming what someone said

In informal conversation, the expressions below are used for the following purposes.

- to seek confirmation: **nicht wahr?, ne?**
- to give confirmation: **fantastisch, fein, klar, Das wäre schön, Das klingt gut, Das hört sich gut an.** Sometimes **das** is abbreviated or dropped in these expressions: **'S wäre schön, Klingt gut, Hört sich gut an.**
- to agree with an opinion: **Du hast vollkommen recht.**
- to agree with or accept a proposal: **Abgemacht!**
- to express hesitation: **aha, ach so, na ja**

👥 6 **Was möchtest du in Berlin sehen?** Sie verbringen ein paar Tage in Berlin. Was möchten Sie machen? Planen Sie mit einem Partner/einer Partnerin den ersten Tag. Benutzen Sie die Sehenswürdigkeiten in **Wissenswerte Vokabeln: Sehenswürdigkeiten in Berlin.**

BEISPIEL S1: *Was möchtest du in Berlin machen?*
S2: *Ich möchte den Ku-Damm sehen, und du?*
S1: *Ich möchte auch gern den Ku-Damm sehen.* (oder)
  Na ja, ich möchte lieber in den Prenzlauer Berg gehen.
S2: *(Das) Klingt gut!*

7 Textdetektiv: **Anlauftext.** Use the *Anlauftext* to recognize important aspects of German structure and usage.

1. The verb **würde** is a subjunctive verb form that was introduced in **Kapitel 9.** Many other subjunctive verb forms are also marked by the vowels **ä, ö,** or **ü.** Which *Anlauftext* sentence in each pair below contains a subjunctive verb form?
   a. ○ Es war recht interessant.   ○ Das wäre schön.
   b. ○ Könnten wir nach der Philharmonie   ○ Ich wollte als erstes die Kuppel
        in den Prenzlauer Berg fahren?   des Reichstags besichtigen.
   c. ○ Das würde mich schon interessieren.   ○ Klingt gut.
   d. ○ Ich habe heute jemanden   ○ Ich hätte dich warnen sollen.
        kennengelernt.
   e. ○ Und ich hätte die Mauer so gern   ○ Und was hast du für
        gesehen.   morgen vor?

2. Which *Anlauftext* sentence in each pair below contains the past time subjunctive helping verb **hätte?**
   a. ○ Wir sollten damit bis Samstag   ○ Ich hätte dich warnen sollen.
        warten.
   b. ○ Ich hätte sie so gern gesehen.   ○ Ich habe heute jemanden
                                                       kennengelernt.
   c. ○ An deiner Stelle würde ich am   ○ Das hätte ich gleich ahnen sollen.
        Vormittag einen Bummel über den
        Kurfürstendamm machen.
   d. ○ Vom Brandenburger Tor aus   ○ Ich hätte stundenlang anstehen
        könnten wir das machen.   müssen.

3. Choose the correct English translation of each German example from the *Anlauftext.*
   a. Was würdest du für morgen vorschlagen?
      ○ *What will you propose for tomorrow?*
      ○ *What would you propose for tomorrow?*
   b. Wir sollten damit bis Samstag warten.
      ○ *We shall hold off with it until Saturday.*
      ○ *We should hold off with it until Saturday.*
   c. Ich hätte dich warnen sollen.
      ○ *I had been warning you.*
      ○ *I should have warned you.*

d. Und am Nachmittag könnten wir zusammen Unter den Linden entlang spazieren.
  ○ *And in the afternoon we could walk along Unter den Linden together.*
  ○ *And in the afternoon we can walk along Unter den Linden together.*
e. Das wäre schön.
  ○ *That was nice.*
  ○ *That would be nice.*
f. Weil ich die Mauer sehen wollte.
  ○ *Because I want to see the Wall.*
  ○ *Because I wanted to see the Wall.*

4. How are the modal verbs in the examples above marked to show the subjunctive?

	true	*false*
a. Modal verbs with **ö** in the infinitive (**können**) also have **ö** in the subjunctive.	○	○
b. Modal verbs with **o** in the infinitive (**sollen, wollen**) also have **ö** in the subjunctive.	○	○

5. The example **Wir sollten damit bis Samstag warten** conveys a *hypothetical* and *NOT* a past event. This is the case even though:
  a. The verb **sollten** is identical when used in the narrative past and in a hypothetical sense.
  b. All modal verbs convey hypothetical events.

6. Look at these past tense subjunctive examples from the *Anlauftext*. Mark the statements about them as true or false.

Ich hätte stundenlang anstehen müssen.
Ich hätte dich warnen sollen.
Das hätte ich gleich ahnen sollen.

	true	*false*
a. There is no past participle (**ge**-form) in the examples.	○	○
b. Two infinitives are used.	○	○
c. The last position in the sentence is occupied by a modal verb.	○	○

Strukturen

 Speculating about activities, making suggestions

The subjunctive mood

In **Kapitel 9,** you learned how to propose activities and make polite requests and suggestions using the present subjunctive of **werden (würde), haben (hätte),** and **sein (wäre).**

8 **Anna würde gern alles sehen** Anna hofft, alles in Berlin zu sehen, aber in der kurzen Zeit ist das unmöglich. Fragen Sie einen Partner/eine Partnerin, was Anna und ihr Onkel sehen würden. Fragen Sie dann, was Ihr Partner/Ihre Partnerin gern sehen würde.

BEISPIEL S1: *Würde Anna gern die Mauer sehen?*
S2: *Ja, sie würde gern die Mauer sehen. Würdest du gern die Mauer sehen?*
S1: *Ja (Nein), ich würde (nicht) gern die Mauer sehen.*

Tabelle A (S1)

	Anna	Onkel Werner	Partner(in)
die Mauerreste fotografieren	Ja	?	_____
den Reichstag besichtigen	Ja	?	_____
zum Potsdamer Platz fahren	Ja	?	_____
das Museum am Checkpoint Charlie besuchen	?	Nein	_____
in Kreuzberg türkisch essen	?	Ja	_____
ins Olympiastadion gehen	Nein	?	_____
die Gedächtniskirche besichtigen	?	Nein	_____

Tabelle B (S2):

die Gedächtniskirche besichtigen	Ja	?	_____
ins Olympiastadion gehen	?	Nein	_____
in Kreuzberg türkisch essen	Nein	?	_____
das Museum am Checkpoint Charlie besuchen	Nein	?	_____
zum Potsdamer Platz fahren	?	Ja	_____
den Reichstag besichtigen	?	Nein	_____
die Mauerreste fotografieren	?	Nein	_____
	Anna	Onkel Werner	Partner(in)

👥 9 Das wäre wirklich interessant! Ihr Freund hat viele Vorschläge. Reagieren Sie auf seine Vorschläge mit einer passenden Antwort aus der Liste.

BEISPIEL   S1 (IHR FREUND): *Ich habe eine Idee: Gehen wir heute Abend ins Konzert!*
S2 (SIE): *Das wäre aber wirklich langweilig.*

Positiv: Das wäre … (ganz toll / prima / echt spitze / super gut!)
Ich hätte schon … (Lust° dazu / Interesse daran.)

Negativ: Das wäre aber … (wirklich langweilig / zu gefährlich / viel zu teuer.)
Nein, ich hätte … (gar keine Lust dazu / überhaupt kein Interesse daran.)

1. heute Abend ins Konzert gehen
2. zum Konzentrationslager Sachsenhausen fahren
3. in die Nationalgalerie gehen
4. in die Disko gehen
5. die Neue Synagoge in der Oranienburger Straße besuchen
6. mit der U-Bahn zum Olympiastadion fahren
7. die Clubszene im Prenzlauer Berg erleben
8. das neue Regierungsviertel besuchen

Lust zu etwas haben: to want to do something, to feel like doing something

A. The present subjunctive of *können* and the other modal verbs

To express the possibility or the potential of an action, German speakers frequently use the present subjunctive of modal verbs. The infinitive appears at the end of the main clause.

Könnten wir nach der Philharmonie   *Could we go to Prenzlauer Berg after*
in den Prenzlauer Berg **fahren?**   *the concert at the* Philharmonie?

These are the present subjunctive forms of **können.**

könnte: *could*			
Singular		**Plural**	
ich	**könnte**	wir	**könnten**
du	**könntest**	ihr	**könntet**
Sie	**könnten**	Sie	**könntet**
er/sie/es	**könnte**	sie	**könnten**

The other modal verbs follow the same pattern as **können/könnte** in the present subjunctive. Modals with an umlaut in the infinitive (e.g., **müssen**) lose the umlaut in the narrative past (e.g., **musste**) but regain it in the subjunctive (e.g., **müsste**). The narrative past and the present subjunctive of modals without an umlaut in the infinitive (e.g., **sollen, wollen**) are identical (e.g., **sollte, wollte**).

Infinitive	Subjunctive	
mögen	ich **möchte**	*I would like to*
dürfen	ich **dürfte**	*I would be allowed to*
müssen	ich **müsste**	*I would have to*
sollen	ich **sollte** *(no umlaut)*	*I should, ought to*
wollen	ich **wollte** *(no umlaut)*	*I would want to*

↩ 10 Das könntest du machen! Anna hilft Onkel Werner eine Party zu planen. Was sagt Anna?

BEISPIEL S1 (ONKEL WERNER): *Tanja hat viele CDs.*
      S2 (ANNA): *Sie könnte die Musik organisieren.*

1. Tanja hat viele CDs.
2. Margit und Waltraud haben ein Auto.
3. Andreas kennt die Nachbarn relativ gut.
4. Ich habe heute Geld bekommen.
5. Klaus-Peter arbeitet im Supermarkt.
6. Karl und ich kochen gern.
7. Claudia möchte helfen, aber sie hat vor der Party überhaupt keine Zeit.
8. Wir haben morgen relativ viel Zeit.

a. zwei Kästen° Bier mitbringen
b. nachher abwaschen
c. die anderen anrufen
d. die Nachbarn auch einladen
e. alles bezahlen
f. die Musik organisieren
g. Brot und Käse mitbringen
h. einen Obstsalat machen

↩ 11 Aber ich könnte das machen! Onkel Werner sieht immer Probleme. Anna hat immer eine Lösung. Benutzen Sie den Konjunktiv von **können** in Annas Antwort.

BEISPIEL S1 (WERNER): *Ich kann nicht mit dem Hund spazieren gehen. (die Nachbarin)*
      S2 (ANNA): *Die Nachbarin könnte mit dem Hund spazieren gehen.*

1. Ich kann nicht mit dem Hund spazieren gehen. (die Nachbarin)
2. Wir können heute nicht in die Neue Nationalgalerie. (wir / übermorgen)
3. Ich will morgen frische Brötchen vom Bäcker holen. (ich / noch heute)
4. Wir können keine Theaterkarten für Freitagabend kriegen. (du / zwei Karten / für Sonnabend reservieren)
5. Wir können erst nächste Woche zu Erich und Veronika hinausfahren. (sie / diese Woche zu uns kommen)
6. Ich soll dir das neue Jüdische Museum von Daniel Libeskind zeigen, aber mein Auto ist in der Reparatur. (wir / mit dem Bus fahren)

B. Making polite requests and suggestions

To make polite requests and suggestions (**höfliche Bitten und Vorschläge**), German speakers often use the present subjunctive. The subjunctive makes a request or suggestion sound less explicit or demanding than the indicative or imperative. Compare the tone in the following statements.

© Cengage Learning 2014

Imperative (Commands)	*Subjunctive (Requests, Suggestions)*
Bringen Sie mir bitte die Speisekarte!	**Könnten (Würden)** Sie mir bitte die Speisekarte **bringen?**
Kauf nicht bei Müller ein!	Du **solltest** nicht bei Müller **einkaufen.**
Indicative (Neutral)	*Subjunctive (Polite)*
Haben Sie einen Tisch frei?	**Hätten** Sie einen Tisch frei?
Ich **trinke** ein Bier.	Ich **würde gern** ein Bier trinken.
Ich **will** bezahlen.	Ich **wollte gern** bezahlen.
Können Sie mir sagen, wo die U-Bahn-Haltestelle ist?	**Könnten** Sie mir sagen, wo die U-Bahn-Haltestelle ist?

→ **12** **Anna will höflich sein** Onkel Werner hat viele Vorschläge für Anna. Anna sagt nicht direkt, was sie denkt, denn sie will eine höfliche Antwort geben. Was sagt Anna?

BEISPIEL WERNER SAGT: *Wir könnten ins Ägyptische Museum gehen.*
ANNA DENKT: *Das finde ich nicht so interessant.*
ANNA SAGT: *Das würde ich nicht so interessant finden.*

Das würde ich nicht so interessant finden. • Das könnte sehr schön sein. • Das wäre eine großartige Idee. • Das würde viel Spaß machen. • Dazu hätte ich nicht so viel Lust. • Ich hätte wirklich kein Interesse daran.

1. WERNER SAGT: Wir könnten ins Ägyptische Museum gehen.
   ANNA DENKT: Das finde ich nicht so interessant.
   ANNA SAGT: _____

2. WERNER SAGT: Wir könnten Kaffee bei meinen Nachbarn trinken.
   ANNA DENKT: Dazu habe ich nicht so viel Lust.
   ANNA SAGT: _____

3. WERNER SAGT: Wir könnten Checkpoint Charlie besuchen.
   ANNA DENKT: Das ist eine großartige Idee.
   ANNA SAGT: _____

4. WERNER SAGT: Wir könnten die alternative Kunstszene aufsuchen.
   ANNA DENKT: Das macht viel Spaß.
   ANNA SAGT: _____

5. WERNER SAGT: Wir könnten einfach zu Hause fernsehen.
   ANNA DENKT: Ich habe wirklich kein Interesse daran.
   ANNA SAGT: _____

6. WERNER SAGT: Wir könnten eine Stadtrundfahrt machen.
   ANNA DENKT: Das kann sehr schön sein.
   ANNA SAGT: _____

Deutschland: von der Monarchie zur Demokratie (I)

Germany's evolution to a peaceful democratic republic has been slow and painful. Until the early 19th century, the German landscape was divided into a number of separate principalities. It took until 1871 to unify Germany as a nation (**das Deutsche Reich**). The Prussian king became Emperor (**Kaiser**) Wilhelm I, and Otto von Bismarck was his chancellor (**Kanzler**).

ullstein bild/The Granger Collection

Kaiser Wilhelm I im Gespräch mit Kanzler Otto von Bismarck

After the defeat of the Germans in World War I (**der Erste Weltkrieg**) in 1918, Germany formed a democracy, the Weimar Republic (**die Weimarer Republik**). Radical forces on both the left and the right, most notably the Nazi party, officially known as **die Nationalsozialistische Deutsche Arbeiterpartei (NSDAP),** did not support it, however. The stability of the Weimar government was further undermined by immense war reparations to France, the post-war occupation of German territory by foreign troops, large-scale unemployment, astronomical inflation, and the stock market crash and world economic crisis of 1929.

The Nazi party promised to create jobs, fix social chaos and economic misery, and eliminate the purported root causes of these problems, which they blamed on world Jewry. By 1933, Adolf Hitler (referred to as **der Führer,** the leader) and the Nazi party had assumed power and established a one-party dictatorship. Establishment of the Third Reich (**das Dritte Reich**) followed shortly thereafter. The Nazis broke up trade unions, repressed the freedom of the press, and abolished most human and civil rights. Jews and other minority groups were denied their German citizenship and basic protection under the law and were forced into labor camps and concentration camps. Although open dissent was eliminated, there were still pockets of resistance (**der Widerstand**) in Germany that were always in grave danger and therefore operated in secrecy. Meanwhile, the German military set its sights on new territories throughout Europe and northern Africa. Hitler's 1939 attack on Poland signaled the beginning of World War II (**der Zweite Weltkrieg**), which would last over five years, engulf the continent in war, and lead to the Holocaust during which Jews and others were systematically killed by the Nazis. The war in total claimed an estimated 55 million lives.

Kulturkreuzung

Die Nazizeit ist eine sehr problematische Epoche für die Deutschen heute. Wie war es möglich, dass mitten in Europa im zwanzigsten Jahrhundert eine Diktatur entstehen konnte? Besteht diese Gefahr noch heute in der Welt, oder ist der Mensch dafür zu intelligent und tolerant geworden?

AP Photo

Adolf Hitler auf dem Parteitag der NSDAP in Nürnberg

13 **Nicht so direkt!** Sie sitzen in einem Café. Formulieren Sie Ihre Gedanken höflicher. Benutzen Sie **hätte gern** oder **würde (gern)** + Infinitiv.

BEISPIELE *Ich will ein Bier haben.*   *Ich hätte gern ein Bier.*
         Wir wollen jetzt bestellen.   *Wir würden jetzt gern bestellen.*

1. Ich will ein Bier haben.
2. Ich will die Speisekarte sehen.
3. Wir wollen jetzt bestellen.
4. Bringen Sie uns die Vorspeisen!
5. Wir wollen eine Pizza mit Salami essen.
6. Wir wollen gleich zahlen.

C. Making role-reversal statements with *an deiner* (*Ihrer*, etc.) *Stelle* ... **and the present subjunctive**

A common expression to introduce a hypothetical suggestion in German is

An deiner/Ihrer Stelle würde ich ...   *In your position, I would . . . /*
                                          If I were you, I'd . . .

---

14 **An deiner Stelle** ... Geben Sie Ihrem Partner/Ihrer Partnerin Rat.

BEISPIEL   S1: *Du, ich habe ein Problem. Ich muss morgen mein Referat abgeben°, aber* ***hand in***
               ich bin damit noch nicht fertig.
           S2: *An deiner Stelle würde ich mich auf die Arbeit konzentrieren und sie*
               schnell zu Ende schreiben.

1. Ich muss morgen mein Referat abgeben, aber ich bin damit noch nicht fertig.
2. Ich möchte morgen Abend ins Brecht-Theater gehen und „Die Dreigroschenoper" sehen.
3. Ich muss einen Brief per Express nach New York schicken.
4. Ich weiß nicht, was ich meiner Mutter zum Geburtstag schenken soll.
5. Ich habe meine Miete nicht bezahlt, und die Vermieterin will mich auf die Straße setzen.

a. die Theaterkasse anrufen und Karten bestellen
b. schnell die Miete° zahlen und der Vermieterin Blumen bringen   ***rent***
c. einen Expressdienst anrufen und den Brief abholen lassen°   ***abholen lassen:** to have picked up*
d. einfach fragen, was sie zum Geburtstag möchte
e. mich auf die Arbeit konzentrieren und sie schnell zu Ende schreiben

15 **An seiner Stelle würde ich** ... Besprechen Sie mit einem Partner/ einer Partnerin, was diese Personen in Annas Studentenwohnheim machen sollen. Was würden Sie an ihrer Stelle machen?

BEISPIEL   S1: *Tina trinkt zu viel Kaffee und kann nachts nicht schlafen.*
           S2: *An ihrer Stelle würde ich nicht so viel Kaffee trinken.*

1. Tina trinkt zu viel Kaffee und kann nachts nicht schlafen.
2. Jennifer fährt übers Wochenende nach Berlin. Was soll sie dort machen?
3. Johnny und Dagmar haben zu viele Hausaufgaben.
4. Katja ist mit ihrem Job nicht zufrieden.
5. Karin hat neue Arbeitsangebote° in München und in Basel bekommen.   ***job offers***
6. Ulf braucht einen neuen Computer, aber er hat nicht genug Geld.
7. Sascha hat Karten für die Philharmonie, aber er will nicht hingehen.
8. Ingo will einen Urlaub machen, aber er möchte nicht viel Geld ausgeben.

D. The past-time subjunctive

The past-time subjunctive (**der Vergangenheitskonjunktiv**) expresses events that might have taken place in the past but did not. The past-time subjunctive is formed with **hätte** or **wäre** + past participle.

Anna **hätte** die Mauer **gesehen.**	*Anna would have seen the Wall.*
Ich **hätte** die Antwort **gewusst.**	*I would have known the answer.*
Wir **wären** nach Potsdam **gefahren.**	*We would have gone to Potsdam.*

The past-time subjunctive looks like the past perfect, except for the umlaut on **hätte** and **wäre** and the **-e** ending on **wäre.**

Infinitive	Past perfect	Past-time subjunctive
sehen	hatte gesehen	hätte gesehen
fahren	war gefahren	wäre gefahren

The past-time subjunctive is used for all three forms of the past tense indicative.

Indicative

Conversational past
Er **hat** das **gewusst.**
Er **ist** nach Hause **gefahren.**

Narrative past
Er **wusste** das.
Er **fuhr** nach Hause

Past perfect
Er **hatte** das **gewusst.**
Er **war** nach Hause **gefahren.**

Subjunctive

Past
Er **hätte** das **gewusst.**
Er **wär**e nach Hause **gefahren.**

👥 16 **Ich hätte es anders gemacht** Ein reicher Freund/Eine reiche Freundin erzählt von einer luxuriösen Europareise. Sie haben nicht so viel Geld. Was hätten Sie anders gemacht? Benutzen Sie den Vergangenheitskonjunktiv.

BEISPIEL   S1 (FREUND/IN): *Ich habe überall in Luxushotels gewohnt.*
S2 (SIE): *Ich hätte in Jugendherbergen übernachtet.*

der reiche Freund/die reiche Freundin

1. überall in Luxushotels gewohnt
2. jeden Abend in die Oper gegangen
3. ein Auto gemietet°
4. in den besten Restaurants gegessen
5. tagsüber in Museen und alte Kirchen gegangen
6. nach Baden-Baden in die Casinos gefahren

Sie

a. auf dem Land oder im Wald wandern gegangen
b. mein Essen bei Lidl gekauft
c. an die Nordsee an den Strand gefahren
d. mit dem Zug gefahren
e. in Jugendherbergen übernachtet
f. den Abend mit jungen Leuten in der Stadt verbracht

rented

Kulturnotiz. Lidl is a large European discount grocery chain based in Germany.

E. The double-infinitive construction

Sometimes German speakers use a special construction called the *double infinitive* (**der Doppelinfinitiv**) to express the past time in statements with a modal verb. The term *double infinitive* refers to the presence of two infinitives (verb + modal) at the end of the clause that replace the past participle and may occur in the indicative or subjunctive.

Wir haben die Mauer **sehen wollen.**   *We wanted to see the Wall.*

To express the past-time subjunctive with a double-infinitive, **hätte** (never **wäre**) is always used as the auxiliary verb.

> Ich **hätte** es gleich **ahnen sollen.**   *I should have guessed it right away.*

In subordinate clauses following **weil, dass,** etc., the auxiliary **hätte** occurs <u>before</u> the double infinitive, not at the end of the clause.

> Onkel Werner hat gesagt, dass er es **hätte** <u>ahnen</u> **sollen.**

The double-infinitive construction (in the subjunctive) can be used with any modal verb, e.g., **hätte machen können (dürfen, müssen, sollen, wollen)** = *could have done (would have been allowed to, would have had to, should have, would have wanted to).*

  17 Wir hätten das machen sollen! Onkel Werner und Anna sprechen über ihren gemeinsamen Tag. Anna sagt, was (nicht) passiert ist, und Onkel Werner sagt, was (nicht) hätte passieren sollen. Drücken Sie seine Gedanken im Vergangenheitskonjunktiv mit einem Doppelinfinitiv aus.

BEISPIEL   S1 (ANNA): *Wir sind nicht ins Schloss Charlottenburg gegangen.*
        S2 (ONKEL WERNER): *Wir hätten ins Schloss Charlottenburg gehen sollen.*

1. Wir sind nicht ins Schloss Charlottenburg gegangen. (Wir …)
2. Ich habe die Kaiser-Wilhelms-Gedächtniskirche vergessen. (Du …)
3. Wir haben die Aufführung von Brechts „Dreigroschenoper" verpasst. (Wir …)
4. Wir haben den Reichstag nicht besichtigt. (Wir …)
5. Wir sind in Kreuzberg nicht türkisch essen gegangen. (Wir …)
6. Du hast mir das neue Regierungsviertel nicht gezeigt. (Ich …)

Strukturen

 Talking about unreal situations

In Section I you used the subjunctive mood to propose activities, to make polite requests and suggestions, and to express possibility and potential. This subjunctive form is called the subjunctive II (**Konjunktiv II**).

A. Expressing unreal conditions: *Wenn*-clauses

A conditional sentence (**der Konditionalsatz**) may express a hypothetical, unreal speculative, or contrary-to-fact situation (**irrealer Konditionalsatz**). In this case the subjunctive II is always used.

> Anna **würde** mehr machen, wenn   *Anna would do more if she had more time.*
>   sie mehr Zeit **hätte.**   *(But she has no time, so she can't do more.)*

The **wenn**-clause with the conjugated verb in final position frequently introduces the conditional sentence, followed by the conjugated verb in the main clause. This results in two conjugated verbs occurring side by side.

> Wenn er netter **wäre, würde**
> ich ihn öfter anrufen.

If he were nicer, I would call him more often.
(But he's not nice, so I won't call him.)

Informal German allows the use of **würde** in **wenn**-clauses while more formal German requires the single subjunctive II verb form.

> *Formal German:* Es wäre toll, wenn
> du uns **besuchtest**.

It would be great if you visited us.

> *Informal German:* Es wäre toll, wenn
> du uns **besuchen würdest.**

It would be great if you visited us.

To express hypothetical past-time events, German uses the past tense of the subjunctive II.

> Wenn Anna nicht nach Tübingen
> **gekommen wäre, hätte** sie Stefan
> nicht **kennengelernt.**

If Anna had not come to Tübingen,
she would not have met Stefan.

B. Present Tense Subjunctive II forms of regular, irregular, and mixed verbs

In **Kapitel 9** you learned that the subjunctive II forms for **haben, sein,** and **werden** are formed by adding an umlaut to the narrative past form.

Infinitive	Narrative past	Subjunctive II
haben	ich hatte	ich hätte
sein	ich war	ich wäre
werden	ich wurde	ich würde

German has another subjunctive form, the subjunctive I **(Konjunktiv I)**. The most common form is **sei (< sein)**. Speakers use it primarily for indirect speech, but since the subjunctive II frequently replaces the subjunctive I, it is not discussed in this book.

1. Regular (weak) verbs

Regular (weak) verbs look identical in the narrative past and in the present tense subjunctive II. To form the present tense subjunctive II, add **-te** to the present tense stem, followed by the endings **-st, -t,** or **-n**. These are the subjunctive II forms of **machen.**

Because of its high-frequency usage, only **würde** + infinitive will be practiced actively in this book.

machen: *to do; to make*

Singular		Plural	
ich	mach**te**	wir	mach**ten**
du	mach**test**	ihr	mach**tet**
sie	mach**ten**	Sie	mach**ten**
er/sie/es	mach**te**	sie	mach**ten**

To avoid confusion arising from the fact that the narrative past and present tense subjunctive II forms of regular verbs look identical, German speakers tend to use **würde** + infinitive instead of the subjunctive for many verbs except **sein, haben,** and **werden.**

> Wenn ich Zeit **hätte, machte** ich einen
> Bummel auf dem Kurfürstendamm.
> Wenn ich Zeit **hätte, würde** ich einen
> Bummel auf dem Kurfürstendamm **machen.**

If I had time, I would go for a stroll on the Kurfürstendamm.

↩ **18** Was würde Stefan (Anna) machen, wenn …? Fragen Sie einen Partner/eine Partnerin, was Anna oder Stefan in den folgenden Situationen machen würde. Fragen Sie dann, was Ihr Partner/Ihre Partnerin machen würde. Benutzen Sie **würde** + Infinitiv.

Was würde Stefan (Anna) machen, wenn … You should recognize the verbs in both **Tabellen** as the subjunctive II forms of common weak verbs.

BEISPIEL   S1: *Was würde Stefan machen, wenn er mehr Geld hätte?*
S2: *Wenn Stefan mehr Geld hätte, würde er eine Reise machen.*
S1: *Was würdest du machen, wenn du mehr Geld hättest?*
S2: *Ich würde (ins Ausland reisen).*

© Cengage Learning 2014

Tabelle A (S1):

Wenn er/sie …	Stefan	Anna	Partner(in)
mehr Geld hätte	?	kaufte sie ein neues Auto	_____
mehr Zeit hätte	besuchte er seine Eltern	?	_____
Lust hätte	schickte er Anna Blumen	?	_____
Freunde in Berlin hätte	?	wohnte sie ein Jahr lang dort	_____
mit dem Studium fertig wäre	?	bezahlte sie nichts mehr dafür	_____

Tabelle B (S2):

Wenn er/sie …	Stefan	Anna	Partner(in)
mehr Geld hätte	machte er eine Reise	?	_____
mehr Zeit hätte	?	besuchte sie die Günthers	_____
Lust hätte	?	lernte sie Spanisch	_____
Freunde in Berlin hätte	hörte er auf, in Tübingen zu studieren	?	_____
mit dem Studium fertig wäre	arbeitete er im Ausland	?	_____

2. Irregular (strong) verbs

The present tense subjunctive II forms of irregular (strong) verbs add the endings **-e, -est, -en,** or **-et** to the stem of the narrative past verb (**Präteritum**). Stems with **a, o,** and **u** also add an umlaut.

Infinitive	*Narrative past*	*Subjunctive II*	*Meaning*
kommen	er kam	er k**ä**m**e**	(*if*) *he came/would come*

These are the subjunctive II forms of **kommen**.

kommen: *to come*			
Singular		**Plural**	
ich	**käme**	wir	**kämen**
du	**kämest**	ihr	**kämet**
Sie	**kämen**	Sie	**kämen**
er/sie/es	**käme**	sie	**kämen**

The following chart lists the most frequently used irregular (strong) verbs in the subjunctive II.

The verb **stehen/stünde** follows the same pattern for the subjunctive II as **werden/ würde.**

Infinitive	Subjunctive II			Infinitive	Subjunctive II	
bleiben	ich	**bliebe**		kommen	ich	**käme**
fahren	ich	**führe**		nehmen	ich	**nähme**
finden	ich	**fände**		sprechen	ich	**spräche**
geben	ich	**gäbe**		stehen	ich	**stünde**
gehen	ich	**ginge**		tun	ich	**täte**

Wenn es etwas zu essen **gäbe, bliebe** ich hier.

If there were something to eat, I would stay here.

Es **ginge** mir besser, wenn wir nicht so weit **führen.**

I would feel better if we weren't driving so far.

Because some of these forms are infrequent or archaic, (e.g., **hülfe**), or because they sound like non-subjunctive forms (e.g., **nähme** vs. **nehme**), speakers tend to use **würde +** infinitive instead.

3. Mixed verbs

To form the present tense subjunctive II, mixed verbs add **-t** plus the endings **-e, -st, -t,** or **-n** to the stem like regular verbs. Some have a vowel change like irregular verbs, and others do not. The only mixed verb that is used with any frequency is **wüsste.** The others almost always occur with **würde,** e.g., **würde bringen, würde denken.**

Other verbs like **nennen** include **kennen, kennte** and **rennen, rennte.**

Infinitive	Subjunctive II		Infinitive	Subjunctive II
bringen	br**ä**chte		nennen	nennte
denken	d**ä**chte		wissen	w**ü**sste

→ **19** Annas Besuch in Berlin Verbinden Sie die richtigen Satzteile.

1. Wenn es nicht zu viel zu tun gäbe,
2. Wenn es nicht so viele Touristen gäbe,
3. Wenn es ihr besser ginge,
4. Wenn sie mehr Zeit hätte,
5. Wenn die Autofahrer nicht so schnell führen,
6. Wenn die Berliner nicht so schnell sprächen,

a. könnte Anna länger unterwegs sein, aber sie muss zum Arzt.
b. könnte Anna sie besser verstehen.
c. müsste Anna nicht so schnell überall hinfahren.
d. bliebe Anna länger in Berlin, aber sie muss zurück nach Tübingen.
e. wäre die Schlange nicht so lang.
f. würde Anna auch gern in Berlin Auto fahren, aber sie hat Angst.

†† 20 Freie Kommunikation: **Rollenspiel: Besuch aus Deutschland.** Sie haben einen Besucher/eine Besucherin aus Deutschland und Sie möchten ihm/ihr Ihre Stadt zeigen. Besprechen Sie, was Sie zusammen in Ihrer Stadt unternehmen können. Was würde diese Person interessieren? Stellen Sie Fragen und machen Sie Vorschläge.

BEISPIEL   S1 (SIE): *Wir könnten zusammen in den Zoo gehen.*
            S2 (BESUCHER/IN): *Das wäre O.K., aber ich würde lieber schwimmen gehen.*
            S1: *Schwimmen wäre auch möglich. Wir könnten auch zu einem Football-spiel gehen.*
            S2: *Das wäre …*

zum Strand fahren • wandern • ins Rockkonzert gehen • zum Rodeo gehen • zu einem Footballspiel gehen • Sehenswürdigkeiten ansehen • klettern° • ins Museum gehen • Baseball spielen • shoppen gehen

           climbing

↩ 21 Schreibecke: **Waltraud weiß Bescheid.** Frau Waltraud Bravermann schreibt für eine Zeitung und beantwortet Fragen der Leser/Leserinnen. Sie bekommt viele Briefe von Frauen und Männern, die Antworten auf ihre Probleme suchen. Lesen Sie die Probleme der folgenden Personen und schreiben Sie Frau Bravermanns Antwortbrief(e). Benutzen Sie den Konjunktiv (z. B. **An Ihrer Stelle würde ich …; An Ihrer Stelle hätte ich …**).

Waltraud Bravermann

Rosmarie T.: Rosmaries Tochter Susi hat noch keinen Mann und keinen festen Freund. Susi wohnt allein in Basel und schreibt intensiv an ihrer Doktorarbeit in Biochemie. Die Zeit, einen Mann zu finden, wird immer kürzer, meint Rosmarie, und sie möchte, dass Susi bald heiratet.

Marko H.: Marko ist 56 Jahre alt. Er schreibt, dass die meisten Frauen in seinem Alter nur junge Männer suchen. Seine Katze ist seine beste Freundin. Marko sucht eine Partnerin und die Liebe – schon seit Jahren!

Die Geschichte Berlins

seat of government

focal point

Berlin hat in der deutschen Geschichte eine wichtige Rolle gespielt. Zu verschiedenen Zeiten war Berlin Hauptstadt, Regierungssitz°, Kulturzentrum und auch das Hauptquartier Adolf Hitlers. Später wurde Berlin Brennpunkt° des Kalten Krieges und die Hauptstadt der Deutschen Demokratischen Republik, bevor es die Hauptstadt des vereinten Deutschlands wurde. In der Geschichte Berlins spiegelt sich die politische Geschichte Deutschlands wider°.

spiegelt sich wider: *is reflected*

Vorschau

22 **Was ist das?** Finden Sie für jede Definition in der linken Spalte den passenden Begriff oder Namen in der rechten Spalte.

1. das deutsche Parlament
2. moderner deutscher Regierungschef (wie z. B. der Premierminister in Kanada)
3. der Führer
4. moderne Staatsform in Deutschland
5. der deutsche Monarch von früher
6. das zeremonielle Oberhaupt° Deutschlands (wie z. B. die Königin in Großbritannien)
7. die erste deutsche Republik (1918–1933)
8. die Verfassung° der Bundesrepublik
9. nationalsozialistische Diktatur

a. das Dritte Reich
b. der Bundestag
c. die Republik
d. das Grundgesetz
e. der/die Bundeskanzler/in
f. Adolf Hitler
g. der Kaiser
h. die Weimarer Republik
i. der/die Bundespräsident/in

head of state

constitution

events

23 **Was wissen Sie schon?** Welche Daten gehören zu welchen Ereignissen°?

Daten	Ereignisse
1. 1918	a. Die Wende: Ex-DDR wird Teil der Bundesrepublik Deutschland.
2. 1933	b. Die DDR baut die Mauer um West-Berlin.
3. 1945	c. Der Erste Weltkrieg endet.
4. 1961	d. Der Zweite Weltkrieg endet.
5. 1989	e. Die Berliner Mauer fällt. DDR-Bürger dürfen in den Westen.
6. 1990	f. Hitler und die Nazis kommen an die Macht.

Kulturnotiz. The verb **wenden** means *to turn,* and the noun **die Wende** can refer to any significant turn of events or change. Today it generally refers to 1990, the time when East Germany was formally reunited with West Germany, the most profound change in postwar German history.

9. NOVEMBER 1989 FRIEDLICHER AUFBRUCH ZUR DEUTSCHEN EINHEIT

Manfred Gottschall/mit freundlicher Genehmigung des Bundesministeriums für Finanzen

BERLINER MAUER 1961 - 1989

Phoenix79/Shutterstock.com

Eine Sitzung des Bundestags im renovierten Reichstagsgebäude

ullstein bild/The Granger Collection, New York

24 Thematische Fragen Beantworten Sie die folgenden Fragen auf Deutsch.

1. Berlin ist jetzt die Hauptstadt Deutschlands. Wie hieß die Hauptstadt der Bundesrepublik im Jahre 1989?
2. Was assoziieren Sie mit Berlin?
3. Warum spielt Berlin so eine wichtige Rolle in der Weltgeschichte?
4. Kennen Sie den Namen Bismarck? Warum ist er eine wichtige Persönlichkeit der deutschen Geschichte?

Lesestrategien

Benutzen Sie die folgenden Strategien, um den Text zu verstehen.

25 Den Kontext verstehen Finden Sie im *Absprungtext* Antworten auf die folgenden Fragen.

1. Welche wichtigen Persönlichkeiten werden hier genannt?
2. In welchem Jahr sind die folgenden Ereignisse passiert?
   • die nationalsozialistische Machtergreifung (das Dritte Reich)
   • die Gründung° der Bundesrepublik Deutschland
   • die Gründung der Weimarer Republik
   • die Gründung des Zweiten Deutschen Reiches
   • der Beitritt der DDR zur Bundesrepublik Deutschland
   • die Gründung der Deutschen Demokratischen Republik
   • die Fußball-Weltmeisterschaft in Deutschland

founding

Deutschland: von der Monarchie zur Demokratie (II)

After the unconditional surrender of Nazi Germany on May 8, 1945 to the Allies, the U.S., Great Britain, France, and the Soviet Union agreed to disarm, demilitarize, and denazify Germany and divide the country into four occupation zones (**Besatzungszonen**) under their control. Berlin, which was located in the Soviet zone, was itself divided into four occupation sectors. Tensions immediately grew between the western Allies and the Soviets, leading to the Cold War (**der Kalte Krieg**).

Elf Monate lang versorgten die Alliierten ganz West-Berlin durch die Luftbrücke

The Soviets established hegemony throughout Eastern Europe and allowed the formation of Soviet-leaning political parties in their zones in 1945. This led to a pro-Communist regime ruled by the Socialist Unity Party (**Sozialistische Einheitspartei, SED**) in their zone. Wanting to respond with strong western political and economic systems and western values, the Allies pursued common political and economic structures in the three West German Zones. This essentially resulted in the formation of two separate Germanys, which lasted for forty years.

In 1948, in response to a currency reform in the west, the Soviets attempted to gain control of all of Berlin by blockading all roads from Western Germany to West Berlin. The Allies responded with a massive air transport of goods to West Berlin (**die Luftbrücke**) that lasted eleven months. It saved West Berlin and forced the Soviets to back down.

In 1949, the Federal Republic of Germany (**die Bundesrepublik Deutschland**) drew up its constitution (**das Grundgesetz**) for the territories of the three western zones. Shortly thereafter, the **SED** established a government in the Soviet zone, and the German Democratic Republic or GDR (**die Deutsche Demokratische Republik, die DDR**) came into being. Two completely different economic and political systems now existed: one a Western-oriented, capitalist-leaning, social-market economy in an elective democracy; the other a centrally planned economy in a one-party

Zu DDR-Zeiten war diese Gedenkstätte ein Mahnmal für die Opfer des Faschismus.

Marxist society. Berlin remained divided as well, West Berlin becoming a de facto state of the Federal Republic, while East Berlin became the capital of the **DDR**. American, British, French, and Russian troops remained stationed in Germany and Berlin for the next forty years.

Kulturkreuzung

Vierzig Jahre lang gab es zwei deutsche Staaten. Familien durften einander nicht besuchen. Das war sehr traumatisch für die Menschen. Hat es irgendwann in der US-Geschichte eine ähnliche Situation gegeben? Hat das heute noch Folgen in den USA?

Strategien verwenden Können Sie diese neuen Wörter ungefähr verstehen? Versuchen Sie, die fett gedruckten Wörter zu erraten. Benutzen Sie die Strategien, die Sie gelernt haben.

Strategie 1: Weltwissen

1. **die Machtergreifung:** Hitler ist auf legale Weise Reichskanzler geworden. Der Kanzler hat die **Macht** zu regieren. Hitler hat dann sehr schnell auf illegale Weise mehr Macht genommen oder **ergriffen.** Spricht man in den USA von einer **Machtergreifung** bei der Präsidentenwahl? Haben die Bolschewiken in Russland die Macht bekommen oder ergriffen?

2. **statt•finden:** Alle vier Jahre **finden** in den USA die Wahlen für die Präsidentschaft **statt.** Alle vier Jahre **finden** die Olympischen Spiele **statt.** Wie oft **findet** ein Test im Deutschkurs **statt?**

3. **besetzen:** Wenn man die Toilette nicht benutzen kann, weil jemand anders sie benutzt, sagt man: *Die Toilette ist besetzt.* Im militärischen Kontext ist ein Land **besetzt,** wenn ein ausländisches Militär die Macht hat. Welche Länder haben die Nazis im Krieg **besetzt?**

4. **Siegermächte:** Das sind die Mächte oder Länder, die einen Krieg gewinnen. Wer war im Jahr 1945 eine **Siegermacht** – die USA oder Nazi-Deutschland?

5. **verwalten:** Die Verwaltung ist der Staatsapparat oder die Bürokratie. Wer hat Deutschland nach dem Krieg **verwaltet?**

Strategie 2: Kontext

1. **zerstören:** Wenn man etwas **zerstört,** macht man es kaputt. Die Nazis haben viele jüdische° Geschäfte in der Kristallnacht zerstört. Haben die Nazis die Fenster mit einem Stein oder mit einem Wort zerstört? *Jewish*

2. **die Kriegserklärung:** Ein Krieg fängt nicht immer spontan an. Ein Staat macht den Krieg gegen einen anderen Staat. Ist eine **Kriegserklärung** das Ende oder der Anfang vom Krieg?

3. **teilen:** Das Verb **teilen** hat verschiedene Bedeutungen. In der Politik macht man aus einem Ganzen mehrere Komponenten, wenn man ein Land **teilt.** Hat 1961 die Berliner Mauer die Stadt **geteilt** oder zusammengebracht?

4. **vollenden:** Etwas ist nur dann **vollendet,** wenn man alle Ziele erreicht° und vielleicht sogar perfektioniert hat. Dann hat man nicht nur das Ende erreicht, man hat etwas **vollendet.** Hat Hitler seine Pläne für ein Drittes Reich **vollendet?** *reached*

5. **bei•treten** (+ *dat.*): Wenn man Mitglied bei einem Klub, einer Organisation oder einer Partei wird, **tritt** man der Organisation **bei.** Was bedeutet wohl **beitreten?**

Strategie 3: Wortformen

1. **erobern:** Sowjetische Soldaten kamen als erste nach Berlin. Die Sowjets hatten die Kontrolle. Die Nazis kapitulierten, und die Sowjets hatten Berlin **erobert.** Welches Land hat Japan im Zweiten Weltkrieg **erobert?**

2. **erhöhen:** Von welchem Adjektiv ist **höher** die Komparativform? Das Präfix **er-** findet man auch in **erhärten (hart werden)** und **erstarken (stark werden).** Was bedeutet wohl das Verb **erhöhen?**

3. **der Aufstand: Aufstand** stammt von **aufstehen.** Ein politischer **Aufstand** ist eine Aktion. Ist ein **Aufstand** freundlich oder aggressiv? Was wäre ein gutes Synonym für das Wort **Aufstand?**

4. **der Widerstand:** Wenn man aktiv gegen eine politische Struktur kämpft, die man für unmenschlich hält, leistet° man politischen **Widerstand.** Wogegen hat Dr. Martin Luther King **Widerstand** geleistet? *leisten: to undertake, put up*

Lesen Sie jetzt den Text.

1740   Friedrich II. (Friedrich der Große) wird König von Preußen. Berlin gewinnt als Hauptstadt Preußens europäischen Rang°.

status

1871   Gründung des Deutschen Reiches. Berlin wird Residenz des deutschen Kaisers (Wilhelm I.) und Reichshauptstadt. Berlin wird politisches, ökonomisches und wissenschaftliches Zentrum des Kaiserreichs.

1914–
1918   Während der Kriegsjahre wird die Versorgung der Millionenstadt immer schwieriger. Hunger und Kriegsmüdigkeit der Bevölkerung führen gegen Ende des Krieges in Berlin zu Massenstreiks.

1918   (9. November) Revolution in Berlin. Vom Balkon des Reichstages in Berlin ruft der Sozialdemokrat Philipp Scheidemann die „Deutsche Republik" aus°. Berlin ist Hauptstadt der Weimarer Republik.

ausrufen = proklamieren

1933   Machtergreifung der Nationalsozialisten. Hitler wird Reichskanzler. Berlin wird Zentrum der nationalsozialistischen Diktatur, aber auch des Widerstandes.

1936   Die XI. Olympischen Sommerspiele finden in Berlin statt.

1938   (9. November) In der „Reichskristallnacht" setzen SA- und SS-Männer neun der zwölf Berliner Synagogen in Brand und terrorisieren zahlreiche jüdische Bürger. Jüdische Geschäfte werden von den Nazis zerstört.

1939   (1. September) Mit der Kriegserklärung an Polen wird Berlin zum Ausgangspunkt des Zweiten Weltkriegs.

1945   Selbstmord Hitlers am 30. April. Berlin wird durch die Rote Armee erobert. Berlin wird von den vier Siegermächten (USA, UdSSR, Großbritannien, Frankreich) besetzt und verwaltet.

1948/49   Die Blockade Berlins: Die Stadt wird politisch geteilt. Die westlichen Alliierten reagieren mit der „Luftbrücke", dem größten Lufttransportunternehmen der Geschichte.

1949   Aus den westdeutschen Besatzungszonen wird die Bundesrepublik Deutschland mit Hauptstadt Bonn gegründet. Aus der sowjetischen Besatzungszone entsteht die Deutsche Demokratische Republik mit Hauptstadt Berlin (Ost).

1953   (17. Juni) Die Arbeitsnormen und auch die Preise für Lebensmittel werden in Ost-Berlin erhöht. Es entwickelt sich ein Volksaufstand gegen das SED-Regime und für freie Wahlen in ganz Deutschland. Der Aufstand wird von sowjetischen Truppen gewaltsam niedergeschlagen°.

suppressed

1961   (13. August) Die Stadt Berlin wird durch den Bau der Mauer geteilt.

1963   Berlin wird vom amerikanischen Präsidenten Kennedy besucht. („Ich bin ein Berliner.")

Kulturnotiz. In his famous 1963 speech, President Kennedy expressed the West's unflinching support for West Berlin by stating in German: **Ich bin ein Berliner.** Kennedy's visit to Berlin as the Cold War escalated demonstrated Allied resolve to keep West Berlin free.

AP Photo

Präsident Kennedy in Berlin

1972	Das Vier-Mächte-Abkommen regelt den Transit sowie Reisen und Besuche in die DDR.
1987	(12. Juni) US-Präsident Ronald Reagan hält seine berühmte Rede vor dem Brandenburger Tor. („Mr. Gorbachev, tear down this wall!")
1989	(9. November) Die Mauer fällt: Die Grenzen zu West-Berlin und zur Bundesrepublik Deutschland werden von der DDR geöffnet.
1990	(3. Oktober) Die DDR tritt der Bundesrepublik Deutschland bei. Die deutsche Einheit ist vollendet.
1999	Die Regierung siedelt offiziell nach Berlin um°.
2004	Am Olympiastadion werden die Umbaumaßnahmen° beendet.
2005	(10. Mai) Das zentrale Holocaust-Mahnmal der Bundesrepublik Deutschland wird in Berlin eingeweiht°.
2006	(26. Mai) Nach fast acht Jahren Bauzeit wird der Berliner Hauptbahnhof offiziell eröffnet. (7. Juni – 9. Juli) In Berlin und anderen deutschen Städten findet die Fußball-Weltmeisterschaft statt.
2011	Die FIFA Fußball-Frauen-Weltmeisterschaft wird mit dem Eröffnungsspiel im Berliner Olympiastadion gestartet.

Die Geschichte Berlins, 1740-2002, Berlin Tourism Brochure.

siedelt um: relocates
rebuilding efforts

dedicated

Das Olympiastadion in Berlin

Der Trabant

Das Ampelmännchen

Kulturnotiz. ***Das Leben der Anderen*** (2006), awarded the Oscar for Best Foreign Language Film, presents a sober depiction of GDR life in the 1980s when two party loyalists, a playwright and his actress girlfriend, are spied on round-the-clock by a Stasi officer who ends up sympathizing with their predicament. ***Good Bye Lenin!*** (2003) is a hugely popular comedy set in 1990 Berlin. It deals with a son's extraordinary efforts to keep the collapse of the GDR from his terminally ill mother.

Kulturnotiz. Since German unification there has arisen a longing for the "good old days" in the GDR, known as **Ostalgie** (*nostalgia for the East*). The most recognizable figure associated with **Ostalgie** is the **Ampelmännchen**, the little man depicted on East Berlin pedestrian cross-walk lights. He disappeared after Reunification but was reinstated on popular demand!

Rückblick

27 Was wissen Sie jetzt von Berlin? Wählen Sie die richtige Antwort.

1. Zur Zeit Friedrichs des Großen war Berlin die Hauptstadt von _____.
   a. Preußen   b. Weimar   c. der Bundesrepublik Deutschland

2. Der Reichstag steht _____.
   a. in Weimar   b. in Berlin   c. in Bonn

3. Berlin war die Hauptstadt der ersten deutschen Republik von _____.
   a. 1871–1918   b. 1918–1933   c. 1933–1945

4. Der Zweite Weltkrieg fing 1939 mit der Kriegserklärung an _____ an.
   a. Großbritannien   b. Polen   c. die Sowjetunion

5. Von 1949 bis 1990 war Berlin (Ost) die Hauptstadt von _____ .
   a. der Deutschen Demokratischen Republik
   b. der Bundesrepublik Deutschland
   c. dem Freistaat Bayern

6. Der afro-amerikanische Sportler Jesse Owens hat 1936 in Berlin an _____ teilgenommen.
   a. den Olympischen Spielen   b. der Kristallnacht   c. der Eroberung Berlins

7. Die Luftbrücke _____.
   a. ist eine Brücke über die Spree in Berlin-Mitte
   b. war der Transport von Gütern und Lebensmitteln für West-Berliner per Flugzeug
   c. war 1953 in Ost-Berlin

8. Die US-Präsidenten Kennedy und Reagan haben beide in Berlin _____.
   a. Urlaub gemacht
   b. an der Humboldt-Universität studiert
   c. während des Kalten Krieges eine sehr wichtige Rede gehalten

9. 1961 baute die DDR eine Mauer _____.
   a. um West-Berlin   b. durch die Mitte Ost-Berlins   c. um Ost-Berlin

10. Während des Kalten Krieges waren Truppen von _____ in Berlin stationiert.
    a. den USA, Frankreich, Großbritannien und der UdSSR
    b. den USA und der UdSSR
    c. der UNO

11. Seit Oktober 1990 gibt es _____.
    a. einen deutschen Staat
    b. die DDR
    c. das Holocaust-Mahnmal

12. Im Jahre 2011 fand in Berlin _____ statt.
    a. die Reichskristallnacht
    b. die Fußball-Meisterschaft
    c. die Fußball-Frauen-Weltmeisterschaft

Gilles Leimdorfer/AFP/Getty Images

Die deutsche Wiedervereinigung wird am Brandenburger Tor gefeiert.

Complete the **Ergänzen Sie** activity in the Student Activities Manual before doing the next activity.

28 Kurz gefragt/Kurz interpretiert Beantworten Sie diese Fragen auf Deutsch.

1. Liegt Berlin im Nordwesten, im Nordosten oder im Südwesten von Deutschland? Welchen Einfluss hat Berlins zentrale geografische Lage auf seine politische Rolle?
2. Für viele Ausländer ist Berlin das Symbol von Nazi-Deutschland. Ist dieses Image in Ordnung? Was meinen Sie?
3. Welche symbolische Rolle spielte Berlin zur Zeit des Kalten Krieges für die Siegermächte? Für die Ostdeutschen? Für die Westdeutschen?
4. Berlin hat eine negative und eine tragische Geschichte. Wie sehen Sie die Rolle Berlins in der Zukunft?
5. Für viele Touristen ist Berlin ein sehr attraktives Reiseziel geworden. Was hat Ihrer Meinung nach zu dieser Wende geführt? Was suchen junge Leute heutzutage in Berlin?

29 Textdetektiv: **Absprungtex**. Use the *Absprungtext* to recognize important aspects of German structure and usage.

1. Look at the following four example sentences from the *Absprungtext* and decide which of the two nouns or noun phrases is the grammatical subject in the nominative case in each sentence.
   a. Jüdische Geschäfte werden von den Nazis zerstört.
      ○ Jüdische Geschäfte ○ Nazis
   b. Die Stadt Berlin wird durch den Bau der Mauer geteilt.
      ○ Die Stadt Berlin ○ den Bau der Mauer
   c. Am Olympiastadion werden die Umbaumaßnahmen beendet.
      ○ Am Olympiastadion ○ die Umbaumaßnahmen
   d. Nach fast 8 Jahren Bauzeit wird der Berliner Hauptbahnhof offiziell eröffnet.
      ○ acht Jahren Bauzeit ○ der Berliner Hauptbahnhof
2. In each example above the subject is _____.
   a. a person   b. a thing   c. a person or a thing
3. What verbs are used in each example above? Pick the best answer.
   a. The helping verb **werden** and an infinitive.
   b. The helping verb **werden** and a participle.
   c. The helping verb **werden** by itself.
4. The structure in these examples is called the passive voice. Which English translation of the passive sentence below most likely captures its meaning?
   Der Berliner Hauptbahnhof wird offiziell eröffnet.
   a. The Berlin main train station was officially opened.
   b. The Berlin main train station is officially opened.
5. The person(s) or entity that carries out the action in a passive sentence is called the agent. Identify the agent in the following three sentences, if one is present.
   a. Jüdische Geschäfte werden von den Nazis zerstört.
      ○ Geschäfte   ○ Nazis   ○ no agent
   b. Die Grenzen zur Bundesrepublik Deutschland werden von der DDR geöffnet.
      ○ Grenzen   ○ DDR   ○ no agent
   c. Aus den westdeutschen Besatzungszonen wird die Bundesrepublik Deutschland gegründet.
      ○ Besatzungeszonen   ○ Bundesrepublik   ○ no agent

Strukturen

III Talking about actions as a process

The passive voice

A. The passive voice: present tense

In most sentences the grammatical subject performs the action described by the verb. This subject is called the *agent,* and it is the focus of the sentence. The verb in the following sentence uses the form of the *active* voice.

> <u>subject and agent</u>   <u>direct object</u>
> Die Rote Armee erobert <u>Berlin.</u>   *The Red Army conquers Berlin.*

Die Rote Armee is the grammatical subject as well as the agent in this sentence. Sometimes, however, it is important to focus on the process (**Vorgang**) and not on the agent. This occurs when the agent or performer of the action is not known at all or may simply not be as important as the action itself. In these sentences, the *passive* voice (**das Passiv**) is used. Frequently the agent is not even mentioned in the passive. When it is included, it appears after the verb **werden** with **von** in the dative case. The agent may also occur in the accusative case prepositional phrase with **durch.**

> <u>subject</u>   <u>agent</u>
> <u>Berlin</u> **wird** durch die <u>Rote Armee</u> **erobert.**   *Berlin is conquered by the Red Army.*

> <u>subject</u>   <u>agent</u>
> <u>Die Stadt</u> **wird** von den <u>Siegermächten</u>   *The city is occupied and governed*
> **besetzt** und **verwaltet.**   *by the Allied victors.*

> <u>subject</u>   <u>(agent)</u>
> <u>Jüdische Geschäfte</u> **werden** (von den <u>Nazis</u>)   *Jewish businesses are being*
> **zerstört.**   *destroyed (by the Nazis).*

The present tense of the passive voice (**das Passiv Präsens**) is formed with a conjugated form of the verb **werden** and a past participle, which expresses the meaning of the action. The grammatical subject is not the agent in a passive sentence. In main clauses, the conjugated form of **werden** occurs in second position and the past participle comes last.

geliebt werden: *to be loved*					
Singular			**Plural**		
ich	**werde geliebt**	*I am loved*	wir	**werden geliebt**	*we are loved*
du	**wirst geliebt**	*you are loved*	ihr	**werdet geliebt**	*you are loved*
Sie	**werden geliebt**	*you are loved*	Sie	**werden geliebt**	*you are loved*
er/sie/es	**wird geliebt**	*he/she/it is loved*	sie	**werden geliebt**	*they are loved*

The passive voice is often used in newspaper articles, instructions, and instances where the agent is unknown or unimportant.

Courtesy of K. Douglas Guy.

Die Kaiser-Wilhelm-Gedächtniskirche beim Sonnenuntergang

The present passive in German is the equivalent of two possible passive tenses in English—the simple present and the present continuous. For example, **Bücher werden jeden Tag in der Bibliothek gelesen.** (*Books are read every day in the library.*) and **Das Haus wird gebaut.** (*The house is being built.*)

30 Was wird hier gemacht? Verbinden Sie eine Sehenswürdigkeit in Berlin mit einer passenden Passiv-Konstruktion.

BEISPIEL   in der Bibliothek an der Humboldt-Universität
S1: *Was wird in der Bibliothek an der Humboldt-Universität gemacht?*
S2: *In der Bibliothek an der Humboldt-Universität werden viele Bücher gelesen.*

1. in der Bibliothek an der Humboldt-Universität
2. am Brandenburger Tor
3. auf dem Kurfürstendamm
4. in der Clubszene im Prenzlauer Berg
5. in den Cafés am Alexanderplatz
6. im Reichstag

a. Andenken von Berlin werden gekauft und verkauft.
b. Viele Bücher werden gelesen.
c. Neue Gesetze° werden erlassen°.
d. Musik wird gemacht.
e. Viele Fotos werden gemacht.
f. Kaffee wird getrunken.

laws / enacted

31 Das geht leider nicht Onkel Werner und Anna besprechen, was sie machen können. Leider können sie nicht alles machen, was sie machen wollen. Viele Sehenswürdigkeiten sind gerade geschlossen.

BEISPIEL   S1 (ANNA): *Wie wäre es mit dem Filmmuseum am Potsdamer Platz?*
S2 (WERNER): *Tja, das geht leider nicht. Das Filmmuseum am Potsdamer Platz wird momentan renoviert.*

1. das Filmmuseum am Potsdamer Platz / momentan renovieren
2. die Philharmonie / wegen Regenschaden° reparieren
3. das Schloss Charlottenburg / von oben bis unten putzen
4. die Gedächtniskirche / während des Gottesdienstes für Touristen schließen
5. die Antikensammlung der Staatlichen Museen / neu organisieren
6. das Schloss Sanssouci / wegen eines internationalen Programms / zumachen
7. die Kongresshalle / für eine wichtige Konferenz sauber machen

wegen ...: because of rain damage

B. The passive voice: narrative and conversational past

1. Narrative past tense

The narrative past tense of the passive voice (**das Passiv Präteritum**) is formed with the narrative past tense forms of **werden** and a participle at the end of the clause.

Die Grenzen **wurden** 1989 **geöffnet.**   *The borders were opened in 1989.*

wurde angerufen: *was called*			
Singular		**Plural**	
ich **wurde angerufen**	*I was called*	wir **wurden angerufen**	*we were called*
du **wurdest angerufen**	*you were called*	ihr **wurdet angerufen**	*you were called*
Sie **wurden angerufen**	*you were called*	Sie **wurden angerufen**	*you were called*
er/sie/es **wurde angerufen**	*he/she/it was called*	sie **wurden angerufen**	*they were called*

2. Conversational past and past perfect of the passive

In informal English, the passive is frequently formed with the verb *get*, e.g., *The car got hit by a bus.*

The conversational past of the passive voice (**das Passiv Perfekt**) is formed with the past participle of the verb expressing the action and the conversational past of the verb **werden**. The conversational past of the verb **werden** consists of a conjugated form of **sein** and a shortened past participle **worden.**

> Ich **bin** vor einer Stunde **angerufen worden.**   *I was/got called one hour ago.*

The past perfect passive is for recognition only.

The past perfect passive (**das Passiv Plusquamperfekt**) is formed with the past participle of the verb expressing the action and a form of the past perfect of the verb **werden**.

> Ich **war** schon **angerufen worden**.   *I had already been called.*

The conversational past passive and the past perfect passive always consist of three verbs:

1. a conjugated form of **sein** (e.g., **bin** in the conversational past or **war** in the past perfect)
2. the past participle of the verb expressing the action (e.g., **angerufen**)
3. **worden** (a shortened form of the past participle of **werden**), last in a main clause

Here is the conjugation of **an•rufen** in the conversational past passive.

angerufen worden: *was/have been called*		
Singular		**Plural**
ich **bin angerufen worden**	wir **sind angerufen worden**	
du **bist angerufen worden**	ihr **seid angerufen worden**	
Sie **sind angerufen worden**	Sie **sind angerufen worden**	
er/sie/es **ist angerufen worden**	sie **sind angerufen worden**	

Here is a summary chart of tenses in the passive voice.

Present	Er **wird angerufen.**	*He is (being) called.*
Narrative past	Er **wurde angerufen.**	*He was called.*
Conversational past	Er **ist angerufen worden.**	*He was/has been called.*
Past perfect	Er **war angerufen worden.**	*He had been called.*

---

 32 Wann ist das gemacht worden? Beschreiben Sie diese Ereignisse aus der deutschen Geschichte. Benutzen Sie das Passiv.

BEISPIEL   die Mauer / öffnen
S1: *Wann ist die Mauer geöffnet worden?*
S2: *Die Mauer ist 1989 geöffnet worden.*

1918 • 1938 • 1949 • 1953 • 1961 • 1972 • 1989 • 2005

1. die Mauer / öffnen
2. die Bundesrepublik Deutschland und die DDR / gründen
3. das Holocaust-Mahnmal / einweihen
4. die Berliner Mauer / bauen
5. der Volksaufstand in Ost-Berlin / niederschlagen
6. die Weimarer Republik / ausrufen
7. jüdische Geschäfte in der „Kristallnacht" / zerstören
8. der Transit zwischen Ost und West / regeln

33 **Eine Zeittafel für Ihre Heimatstadt** Schreiben Sie eine Zeittafel für Ihre Heimatstadt mit mindestens fünf wichtigen Ereignissen. Die folgende Liste enthält einige Ideen.

BEISPIEL das neue Schwimmbad   *Das neue Schwimmbad ist 2004 gebaut worden.*

das Schwimmbad	ist	gegründet	worden
das Einkaufszentrum°		erweitert°	
die Schule		gebaut	
unser Haus		abgerissen	
die Autobahn		zerstört	
das Autokino		renoviert	
die Innenstadt		geschlossen	
das Sportstadion		wieder aufgebaut	
die Kirche			

mall / expanded

34 **Das 20. Jahrhundert** Stellen Sie einem Partner/einer Partnerin Fragen mit **von**. Beantworten Sie die Fragen mit einem Passiv-Satz. Wechseln Sie sich ab.

BEISPIEL die Deutsche Republik ausrufen
S1: *Von wem ist die Deutsche Republik ausgerufen worden?*
S2: *Die Deutsche Republik ist von Philipp Scheidemann ausgerufen worden.*

die DDR • Philipp Scheidemann • der deutsche Kaiser • die Siegermächte • die Alliierten • John F. Kennedy • die Nazis • Adolf Hitler

1. die Deutsche Republik ausrufen
2. die jüdischen Geschäfte und Synagogen zerstören
3. Deutschland / nach dem Krieg besetzen
4. die Mauer bauen
5. die Macht ergreifen
6. Berlin im Jahre 1963 besuchen
7. die Luftbrücke organisieren
8. Preußen regieren

C. The impersonal passive

Both English and German allow passive sentences to be formed from an active sentence with a direct object.

Active

| direct object | direct object |
| Die DDR hat **die Grenze** geöffnet. | *The GDR opened **the border**.* |

Passive

| **Die Grenze** ist von der DDR geöffnet worden. | ***The border** was opened by the GDR.* |

Unlike English, however, German has passive constructions with no corresponding direct object in the active sentence. These expressions have only approximate equivalents in English. There are two frequently occurring types of passive sentences, formed with a dative or intransitive verb, that do not specify who is performing the action.

1. Intransitive verbs (e.g., **schwimmen, singen, sprechen, tanzen, rauchen**)

| Es wird hier nicht geraucht. | *No smoking allowed here. (No one is smoking here.)* |
| Es wird laut gesungen. | *Loud singing is going on. (People are singing loudly.)* |

2. Dative verbs (e.g., **helfen, danken**)

Dem Mann ist nicht geholfen worden.   *The man was not (being) helped.*

Since intransitive verbs and dative verbs do not have direct objects in the active voice, they cannot have a subject in the passive voice and are therefore termed *impersonal passive* or *subjectless passive.*

An impersonal passive construction frequently begins with **es**. This **es** is a placeholder, or dummy subject, and drops out whenever another element such as an adverb of location (e.g., **hier**), begins the sentence.

Es wird hier getanzt. }   *Dancing goes on/is going on here.*
Hier wird getanzt. }   *(People dance/are dancing here.)*

The corresponding active sentence uses **man**.

Man tanzt hier.   *One dances here.*

Dependent clauses that begin with a subordinate conjunction, such as **weil, als, dass,** and **wenn,** also omit the placeholder **es** in the passive.

Es wird heute gegrillt.   *There's barbecuing going on today.*
Wir haben gehört, **dass** heute gegrillt wird.   *We hear that there's barbecuing today.*

For impersonal passives, the verb is always in the third-person singular, because the subject of the sentence is **es**. The corresponding English sentence may have a plural verb.

Dem Mann **wird** (es) geholfen.   *The man **is** being helped.*
Den Männern **wird** (es) geholfen.   *The men **are** being helped.*

↩ **35** Was wird hier gemacht? Beschreiben Sie, was an jedem Ort gemacht wird.

BIESPIEL   in der Diskothek   *In der Diskothek wird getanzt.*

1. in der Diskothek   a. arbeiten
2. in der Oper   b. tanken
3. im Lesesaal   c. einkaufen
4. im Kaufhaus   d. lesen
5. im Büro   e. schwimmen
6. im Deutschkurs   f. singen
7. im Schwimmbad   g. Deutsch sprechen
8. an der Tankstelle   h. tanzen

↩ **36** Schreibecke: **Eine Seite aus dem Tagebuch.** Sie haben einen Wirbelsturm° in einem Keller überstanden°. Schreiben Sie in Ihr Tagebuch, was Sie während des Wirbelsturms erlebt haben. War es während des Tages oder der Nacht? Haben Sie die Sirenen gehört? Haben Sie Angst gehabt? Mit wem sind Sie in den Keller gegangen? Was ist im Keller passiert? Wie lange sind Sie im Keller gewesen? Wie sind Sie aus dem Keller gekommen? Wurde das Haus zerstört? Haben Sie alle Haushaltsgegenstände gefunden? Was hätten Sie anders machen sollen? Würden Sie das nächste Mal etwas anders machen?

tornado / survived

Deutschland: von der Monarchie zur Demokratie (III)

Throughout the Cold War (**der Kalte Krieg**), the tensions between East and West were nowhere more obvious than in Berlin. West Berlin became everything that East Berlin was not: affluent, colorful, free-spirited, and western. East Berlin and East Germany, in contrast, became a Marxist worker's state and socialist economy that was a model to Eastern Bloc countries.

Image copyright Markus Gann. Used under license from Shutterstock.com

Der Deutsche Bundestag hat seinen Sitz im renovierten Reichstagsgebäude.

As a so-called worker's state, where pro-communist, anti-fascist sentiment found a home, the **DDR** developed a strong economy and guaranteed full employment, inexpensive housing, universal health care, child care, and free education for all its citizens. Nevertheless, dissatisfaction with socialism existed at grassroots levels. In 1953, workers staged a revolt against productivity quotas and price hikes but were crushed by Soviet forces. As life in East Germany became more repressive, by the late 1950s up to 20,000 people per day were leaving for the West via Berlin, at a time when movement throughout the city was basically unrestricted. To end the drain on its workforce, the **DDR** began to construct a wall (**die Mauer**) encircling West Berlin during the night of August 13, 1961.

In 1989, the brave citizens of Leipzig in the **DDR** started weekly demonstrations against the state. That summer, East Germans vacationing in Czechoslovakia and Hungary stormed embassies and borders demanding access to the West. On November 9, 1989, fearing another mass flight of refugees to the West, East German authorities opened borders to the West for the first time in 28 years. East Berliners celebrated by climbing the Wall, partying on top of it, and visiting West Berlin, many for the first time. This was the beginning of the end for the **DDR**: within a year, the East German People's Parliament (**Volkskammer**) voted the socialist state out of existence (**die Wende,** the Turning Point). On October 3, 1990, the reunification of Germany (**die Wiedervereinigung**) was completed. In 1999, the parliament building (**der Reichstag**) was rededicated as the seat of the German Parliament (**der Bundestag**) in Berlin, the capital of unified Germany.

AP Photo

Der Reichstag am Ende des Zweiten Weltkriegs.

In national elections, voters select the political party of their choice. The majority party's leader becomes the federal chancellor (**der Bundeskanzler**). The president (**der Bundespräsident**) is the ceremonial head of the German state.

Kulturkreuzung

Manche Menschen haben Konflikte mit ihrem Staat. Wann würden Sie Ihre Heimat verlassen wollen, wie die Menschen in der ehemaligen DDR? Wann haben Sie das letzte Mal wegen Ihrer Nation ein Gefühl von Euphorie oder Schock gehabt?

ZIEL

🌐 **Endspurt:** Online
Listening Text & Activities.

Meine persönliche Zeittafel

Zielaktivitäten

Stellen Sie sich vor, es ist 20 Jahre in der Zukunft und Sie sind international berühmt. Im Internet wird Ihre persönliche Zeittafel veröffentlicht. Damit keine Fehler passieren (oder damit Sie die Wahrheit ein bisschen verbessern können), schreiben Sie Ihre eigene Zeittafel. Folgen Sie diesen Schritten.

37 Zeittafel Setzen Sie die fehlenden Informationen unten ein. Es muss nicht alles wahr sein! Schreiben

Jahreszahl	Verb im Infinitiv	Information
_____	gebären	Ich wurde in _____ [Stadt] als _____ [Ihr Name] geboren.
_____	beibringen°	Mir wurde _____ [Englisch / eine andere Sprache] beigebracht.
_____	ausbilden°	Ich wurde in der _____ [Name] Highschool ausgebildet.
_____	annehmen°	Ich wurde an der _____ [Name] Universität angenommen.
_____	auszeichnen°	Ich wurde mit dem _____ [Name]-Preis ausgezeichnet.
_____	anerkennen°	Ich wurde als der beste / die beste _____ [Beruf oder Talent] anerkannt.
_____	geben	Mir wurde für _____ [z. B. meine Musik / meine Forschung / ?] viel Geld gegeben.
_____	einladen	Ich wurde _____ [ins Weiße Haus / in den Buckingham Palast / ?] eingeladen.
_____	bitten	Ich wurde gebeten, meine Autobiografie zu schreiben.

to teach

to educate

to accept

to honor

to acknowledge

38 Ein intimes Gespräch mit Freunden Ihr Partner/Ihre Partnerin ist Ihr bester Freund/Ihre beste Freundin. Sagen Sie ihm/ihr, was Sie in Ihrem Leben gemacht haben – und was Sie hätten anders machen sollen oder lieber anders gemacht hätten. Ihr bester Freund/Ihre beste Freundin stimmt zu – oder auch nicht.

BEISPIEL   S1 (Sie): *Ich habe einen Ferrari gekauft, aber ...*
ich hätte lieber einen Volkswagen kaufen sollen. (oder)
ich wäre am besten ohne Auto gewesen.
S2 (Ihr bester Freund / Ihre beste Freundin):
Ja, du hast recht. Du hättest dir einen Volkswagen kaufen sollen. (oder)
Nein, ich hätte mir auch einen Ferrari gekauft. (oder)
Ohne Auto zu leben, wäre unmöglich gewesen. (oder)

39 Eine Autobiografie Die Zeittafel in Aktivität 37 zeigt nicht alle wichtigen Ereignisse in Ihrem Leben. Schreiben Sie Ihre Autobiografie mit neuen Informationen. Verwenden Sie die Antworten zu den folgenden Fragen, um neue Details anzugeben.

1. Wie heißen Ihre Eltern? Haben Sie Geschwister?
2. Hatten Sie als Kind ein Haustier (eine Katze, einen Hund, einen Vogel, ein Kaninchen usw.)? Wie hieß das Tier?
3. Wie hießen Ihre Freunde in der Highschool? Was machten Sie gern zusammen?
4. Was studierten Sie an der Uni? Welche Noten bekamen Sie an der Uni? Machten Sie an der Uni Sport?
5. Mussten Sie an der Uni Geld verdienen? Wie verdienten Sie Geld für das Studium?
6. Was war Ihr erster richtiger Job?
7. Verliebten Sie sich? Heirateten Sie diese Person? Wenn nicht, warum nicht?
8. Wo wohnen Sie heutzutage? Wohnen Sie allein?
9. Sind Sie glücklich? Un/zufrieden mit Ihrem Leben? Mit einem Partner / einer Partnerin, Ihrem Mann / Ihrer Frau, einem Haustier?
10. Haben Sie Hobbys? Was machen Sie so an einem typischen Tag?
11. Was sind Ihre Pläne für die Zukunft? Schreiben Sie ein paar Sätze.

BEISPIEL *Nächstes Jahr werde ich .... (einen Ferrari kaufen / nach Deutschland ziehen / viel Geld an karitative Organisationen spenden° / ...)*

donate

40 Der Tag nach der Maueröffnung Nehmen wir an°, Sie wohnen in Ost-Berlin. Es ist der 9. November 1989, und die Mauer ist gerade „gefallen", d. h. die Grenzen zum Westen sind geöffnet worden. Was hätten Sie zuerst gemacht? Was hätten Sie danach gemacht? Fragen Sie dann Ihren Partner/Ihre Partnerin.

Nehmen ...: *Let us assume*

BEISPIEL S1: *Hättest du Freunde oder Verwandte im Westen besucht?*
S2: *Ja, das hätte ich gemacht.* (oder)
   Nein, das hätte ich nicht gemacht.
S1: *Was hättest du zuerst gemacht? Und als Zweites?*

1. Freunde oder Verwandte im Westen besuchen
2. im Westen einkaufen gehen
3. im Westen bummeln gehen
4. Freunde in der DDR anrufen und mit ihnen feiern
5. zu Hause bleiben und nichts Besonderes machen
6. an eine westdeutsche Uni schreiben: vielleicht dort studieren
7. eine große Reise ins Ausland planen
8. eine Umsiedlung in die Bundesrepublik planen
9. vielleicht ins Ausland ziehen
10. ganz laut und offen meine politische Meinung ausdrücken
11. Souvenirs sammeln: ein Stück Mauer holen, eine Tageszeitung kaufen usw.
12. im Westen ins Kino gehen und West-Filme anschauen

© Cardaf/shutterstock.com

Mauerreste in Berlin.

Freistaat Sachsen: Leipzig und Dresden

Barbara's hometown, Dresden, is in the Free State of Saxony (**der Freistaat Sachsen**), which borders Poland and the Czech Republic. With a population of 4.5 million and a rapidly improving infrastructure, Saxony is well positioned to compete economically. Companies such as Audi, Zeiss, and Melitta Coffee, and inventions such as the washing machine, the tea bag, the coffee filter, and toothpaste all hail from Saxony. It is also the home of two of the most important and vibrant cities in eastern Germany, Leipzig and Dresden.

Leipzig, with 438,000 inhabitants, is located at the intersection of two important medieval trade routes, making it a natural center for the exchange of ideas and for East-West trade. Leipzig is also home to Germany's second oldest university. Famous graduates include the philosopher and mathematician Baron Gottfried Wilhelm von Leibnitz, the writer Gotthold Ephraim Lessing, and the philosopher Friedrich Nietzsche.

Johann Sebastian Bach served the city of Leipzig as choirmaster (**Kantor**) from 1723 until his death in 1750, directing the famous boys' choir, **der Thomanerchor**, at the **Thomaskirche**, and playing the organ at the Church of St. Nicholas (**die Nikolaikirche**). In 1989, the **Nikolaikirche** was the site of the "Monday demonstrations" which ultimately brought down the German Democratic Republic and led to unification with then West Germany

Dresden (pop. 480,000), the capital of Saxony (**Sachsen**), is located on the banks of the Elbe River and is known as **das deutsche Florenz** for the beauty of its art collections and architectural treasures. On February 13–14, 1945, Dresden was the target of Allied firebombing attacks. The bombing left more than 35,000 civilians dead and completely destroyed large parts of the city. In the decades after WWII, the East German government slowly reconstructed such architectural masterpieces as the Semper Opera House (**die Semperoper**), **die Brühlsche Terrasse** along the Elbe River, and **der Zwinger**, an elaborate complex of baroque pavilions, galleries, and gardens built by Saxony's ruler **August der Starke** (1670–1733). Today, the Zwinger is home to many art treasures and exhibits of the world-famous **Meißner Porzellan**. The ruins of the **Frauenkirche** served as a reminder of WWII for many years. The church has now been reconstructed.

Creative genius has always thrived in Dresden. The composers Carl Maria von Weber, Robert Schumann, and Richard Wagner were born there, as was the German Romantic painter Caspar David Friedrich. **Die Brücke,** the art movement (German Expressionist), was started here in 1905 by Ernst Ludwig Kirchner, Karl Schmidt-Rottluff, Fritz Bleyl, and Erich Heckel.

Kevin Galvin

Der Zwinger in Dresden

Kulturkreuzung

Dresden hat eine bekannte kulturelle Tradition, aber auch eine traurige Geschichte vom Krieg. Kennen Sie Städte in Ihrem Land, die auch eine traurige Geschichte haben?

WORTSCHATZ

Tutorial Quiz
Audio Flashcards

Eine Stadt erleben / Tourist sein

der Bummel, - *leisurely stroll, walk*

der Dom, -e *cathedral*

das Erlebnis, -se *experience*

das Zentrum, *pl.* Zentren *center*

    das Einkaufszentrum *mall*

Berlin

die (Kaiser-Wilhelms-) Gedächtniskirche (*Kaiser Wilhelm*) *Memorial Church*

der Kurfürstendamm (Ku'damm) *a main street of Berlin*

das Mahnmal, -e (¨er) *memorial*

die Mauer, -n *the Wall* (*in Berlin*); (*exterior*) *wall*

die Mitte, -n *middle; downtown*

    Berlin-Mitte *center of Berlin, formerly East Berlin*

die Museumsinsel *museum district of Berlin*

das Olympiastadion *Olympic Stadium*

die Philharmonie (*Berlin*) *Philharmonic Orchestra*

der Platz, ¨e *place, square*

der Reichstag *parliament building*

das Regierungsviertel *government quarter*

die Spree *river through Berlin*

die Stelle, -n *spot, place*

das Tor, -e *gate*

    das Brandenburger Tor *Brandenburg Gate*

das Viertel, - *quarter, district, neighborhood*

die Weltmeisterschaft, -en *world championship*

der Wunsch, ¨e *wish*

das Ziel, -e *goal, target, destination*

Regierung und Politik

der Bundeskanzler, - / die Bundeskanzlerin, -nen *Federal Chancellor*

das Bundesland, ¨er *federal state*

der Bundespräsident, [-en], -en / die Bundespräsidentin -nen *Federal President*

die Bundesrepublik Deutschland *Federal Republic of Germany*

der Bundestag *Federal Parliament*

das Gesetz, -e *law*

das Grundgesetz *basic law, constitution*

die Partei, -en *political party*

die Regierung, -en *government*

Die Geschichte Deutschlands

das Abkommen, - *treaty; agreement*

die Alliierten (*pl.*) *the Allies* (*in World War II*)

die Armee, -n *army*

der Aufstand, ¨e *uprising, revolt*

die Besatzungszone, -n *occupation zone*

die Blockade, -n *blockade*

die Deutsche Demokratische Republik (DDR) *German Democratic Republic (GDR)*

die Diktatur *dictatorship*

die Einheit *unity*

der Führer, - *leader (of Nazi Party)*

die Grenze, -n *border*

die Gründung *founding, establishment*

die Hauptstadt, ¨e *capital*

der Kaiser, - / die Kaiserin, -nen *emperor / empress*

    das Kaiserreich *empire*

der Kanzler, - / die Kanzlerin, -nen *chancellor*

der Krieg, -e *war*

    der Erste (Zweite) Weltkrieg *First (Second) World War*

    der Kalte Krieg *Cold War*

die Luftbrücke *airlift*

die Macht, ¨e *power, strength*

    die Machtergreifung, -en *coup, seizure of power*

das Reich, -e *empire; realm*

    das Deutsche Reich *German Empire*

    das Dritte Reich *Third Reich*

die Republik, -en *republic*

    die Weimarer Republik *Weimar Republic*

die Revolution, -en *revolution*

die Siegermacht, ¨e *victor, conquering power*

der Streik, -s *strike*

der Tag der Deutschen Einheit *German Unity Day*

die Vereinigung, -en *unification, union*

    die Wiedervereinigung *reunification*

die Wahl, -en *election*

die Wende *turning point*

der Widerstand *resistance*

das Zentrum, *pl.* Zentren *center*

Noch einmal: **das Schloss**

jüdisch *Jewish*

Positive Antworten

Abgemacht! *Agreed! It's a deal!*

Ach so. *I see. / Now I get it.*

Aha. *Oh.*

Das hört sich gut an. *That sounds good.*

Das klingt gut. *That sounds good.*

Das wäre schön. *That would be nice.*

Du hast vollkommen recht. *You're absolutely right.*

fantastisch *fantastic*

fein *fine, great, very nice*

klar *of course*

na? *well?*

nicht wahr? *right? no?*

Noch einmal: **na ja**

Die Stimmung

die Einstellung, -en *attitude*
das Gefühl, -e *feeling*
die Stimmung, -en, *atmosphere*
deprimierend *depressing*
drückend *depressing*
frustrierend *frustrating*
lebendig *lively, alive*
schlicht *simple*
überraschend *surprising(ly)*

Substantive

der Eindruck, ¨-e *impression*
die Frucht, ¨-e *fruit*
das Hausmittel, - *home remedy*
der Kasten, ¨ *case*
die Kleinigkeit, -en *trifle, little
something; detail*
die Miete, -n *rent*
der Rest, -e *rest, remainder*
das Unternehmen, - *undertaking,
project, operation*
der Wohnort, -e *home town, place of
residence*
die Vorstellung, -en *impression, image*

Adjektive und Adverbien

ausgeglichen *similar, balanced*
ehemalig *former*
gemeinsam *in partnership, together*
gewiss *certain*
konsumorientiert *materialistic,
consumer-oriented*
manche *several, some*
neulich *recently*
nirgendwo *nowhere*
stundenlang *for hours*
unbedingt *clearly*
vollkommen *completely*

Verben

ahnen (hat geahnt) *to guess, suspect, sense*
Das hätte ich ahnen sollen.
I should have guessed.
**an•kommen (kam an, ist
angekommen) auf** + *acc. to depend on*
an•melden (hat sich angemeldet)
to pre-register

**auf•fallen (fällt auf, fiel auf, ist
aufgefallen)** + *dat. to occur to s.o.*
Das fällt mir auf. *It occurs to me.*
**auf•wachsen (wächst auf, wuchs auf,
ist aufgewachsen)** *to grow up*
aus•rufen (rief aus, hat ausgerufen)
to proclaim, declare
**bei•treten (tritt bei, trat bei, ist
beigetreten)** + *dat. to join*
besetzen (hat besetzt) *to occupy*
besichtigen (hat besichtigt) *to visit,
look at*
bummeln (ist gebummelt) *to stroll*
ein•weihen (hat eingeweiht) *to
dedicate*
entschuldigen (hat entschuldigt) *to
excuse, pardon*
Entschuldige die Verspätung.
Sorry I'm late.
entstehen (entstand, ist entstanden)
to rise, result
erobern (hat erobert) *to defeat, conquer*
eröffnen (hat eröffnet) *to open*
erreichen (hat erreicht) *to reach*
gewinnen (gewann, hat gewonnen)
to win
gründen (hat gegründet) *to found,
establish*
interessieren (hat interessiert) *to interest*
klappen (hat geklappt) *to work out,
happen as planned*
merken (hat gemerkt) *to notice*
**nieder•schlagen (schlägt
nieder, schlug nieder, hat
niedergeschlagen)** *to repress*
reagieren (hat reagiert) *to react*
recht haben *to be right, correct*
regeln (hat geregelt) *to regulate*
renovieren (hat renoviert) *to
renovate, remodel*
**Schlange stehen (stand, hat
gestanden)** *stand in line*
spalten (hat gespalten) *to separate*
spüren (hat gespürt) *to feel, sense*
schwärmen (hat geschwärmt) von +
Dativ to rave about
teilen (hat geteilt) *to divide*

terrorisieren (hat terrorisiert)
to terrorize
um•siedeln (ist umgesiedelt)
to change residence, move
**sich verabreden (hat sich verabredet)
mit** + *dat. to make a date with*
verkünden (hat verkündet) *to announce*
verwenden (hat verwendet) *to use*
**vor•haben (hatte vor, hat
vorgehabt)** *to plan, have planned*
Was hast du vor? *What have you
got planned?*
**vor•schlagen (schlägt vor, schlug
vor, hat vorgeschlagen)** *to suggest*
warnen (hat gewarnt) *to warn*
wenden (hat gewendet) *to turn*
zerstören (hat zerstört) *to destroy*
Noch einmal: **statt•finden**

Andere Wörter und Ausdrücke

ab und zu *now and then*
**an deiner (Ihrer) Stelle würde ich
…** *in your place, I would . . . , if I
were you, I'd . . .*
deswegen *therefore*
einerseits *on the one hand*
Es spielt gar keine Rolle. *It plays no
role. It's not at all important.*
Ich hätte dich warnen sollen.
I should have warned you.
Ich kann mich noch erinnern. *I can
still remember.*
in Brand setzen *to set on fire*
im Freien *outdoors*
im Grunde *basically*
nicht unbedingt *not necessarily*
Pass mal auf! *Look here! Now listen
up!; Pay attention!*
und so *and stuff like that*
verabredet sein *to have a date*

Meine eigenen Wörter

_____
_____
_____
_____
_____

KAPITEL

12

Carly Rose Hennigan/Shutterstock.com

Hurra! Ende gut, alles gut!

Ende gut, alles gut!

In this chapter you will review Anna Adler's year in Germany. You will also learn about the importance of learning German, why many people choose to learn German, and how you might be able to use German in the future.

Strukturen
> Review of high-frequency structures, e.g., the conversational past, modal verbs, and the subjunctive

Kulturelles
> Der Einfluss der englischen und der deutschen Sprache aufeinander

> Amerikaner und amerikanische Kultur im deutschsprachigen Mitteleuropa

> Deutsche, österreichische und schweizerische Einflüsse auf Amerikas Kultur

Oh, Stefan, wenn du nur wüsstest!

Anna sitzt am Laptop in ihrem Zimmer und denkt über einiges nach: über einen Bericht über das Jahr in Tübingen, den sie schreiben soll, über die Leute, die sie in Tübingen kennengelernt hat, und besonders über Stefan, von dem sie sich bald verabschieden° muss.

sich verabschieden: say good-bye

1 Thematische Fragen Beantworten Sie die folgenden Fragen auf Deutsch.

1. Warum studieren Sie Deutsch? Haben Sie auch eine andere Fremdsprache° gelernt?

foreign language

2. Wenn Studierende im Ausland studieren, machen sie viele verschiedene Erfahrungen°, sowohl in ihrem Studium wie auch in ihrem Privatleben. Was könnte Ihrer Meinung nach ein ausländischer Student oder eine ausländische Studentin in Deutschland (oder in Österreich oder in der Schweiz) erleben und lernen?

experiences

3. Wer von Annas deutschen Freunden hat vielleicht ein romantisches Interesse an Anna? Glauben Sie, dass das die richtige Person für Anna ist? Was könnte in der Zukunft passieren?

4. Welche Erfahrungen in Deutschland, glauben Sie, waren für Anna besonders interessant? Besonders wichtig? Besonders stressig? Glauben Sie, dass das Studium in Deutschland Annas Leben verändert° hat oder verändern wird? Wenn ja, wie?

verändern: to alter

5. Würden Sie gern im Ausland studieren? Wo denn? Wie lange? Was würden Sie lernen oder erfahren wollen?

Ausländische Studierende in Deutschland

© J. Henning Buchholz/shutterstock.com

Vorschau

 2 Ratespiel Was denken Sie: Wie steht es mit Deutsch als Fremdsprache auf der Welt? Raten Sie.

1. Wie viele Menschen auf der Welt lernen Deutsch als Fremdsprache?
   a. 1 Million
   b. 10 Millionen
   c. mehr als 13 Millionen

2. Wie viele Universitätsstudenten auf der Welt lernen jedes Jahr Deutsch?
   a. 200 000
   b. 2 Millionen
   c. 20 Millionen

3. Wie viele Universitätsstudenten außerhalb Deutschlands haben Deutsch als Hauptfach?
   a. 7 000
   b. 70 000
   c. 700 000

> You will find the answers to these questions in the **Anlauftext**.

  Satzdetektiv Welche Sätze bedeuten ungefähr das Gleiche?

1. Wenn du nur **wüsstest**!
2. Oh, Entschuldigung, **störe** ich?
3. Ich **hätte** gern mal mit dir **was besprochen**.
4. Du wirst **mir fehlen**.
5. Mensch, bin ich aber **in einer Stimmung**!
6. Das hat mich **total umgeworfen**.

a. Wenn du nur eine Ahnung° hättest!
b. Ich werde dich sehr vermissen.
c. Pardon, unterbreche ich dich?
d. Ich möchte mit dir über etwas sprechen.
e. Das hat mich völlig überrascht.
f. Mensch, ich bin so verwirrt!

idea

---

7. Ich habe **gar nicht damit gerechnet**, dass ...
8. Das ist **ja Unsinn**!
9. Wir haben **uns** von Anfang an **sehr gut verstanden**.
10. Ich **kämpfe mit dem Gedanken**, dass ...
11. Das kann ich einfach nicht **ertragen**.
12. Wir **passen** wirklich prima **zusammen**.

g. Das ist ja verrückt!
h. Ich habe es nicht erwartet, dass ...
i. Ich werde traurig, wenn ich daran denke, dass ...
j. Das kann ich gar nicht akzeptieren.
k. Wir sind ein gutes Paar.
l. Wir haben uns von Anfang an gern gehabt.

Hören Sie gut zu.

Warum habe ich mit diesem Bericht nicht früher angefangen?

Oh, Mensch, Stefan, wenn du nur wüsstest …

Nee, nee, komm doch rein, Stefan. Ich denke gerade über die Zukunft nach — und auch über die Vergangenheit.

Hallo, Anna. Oh, Entschuldigung, störe ich? Ich hätte gern mal mit dir was besprochen. Schreibst du eine letzte Seminararbeit?

Oh Stefan, du wirst mir fehlen!

Und was schreibst du denn genau?

Einen Bericht über mein Jahr in Tübingen. Im ersten Teil soll ich über die Rolle der deutschen Sprache weltweit schreiben — wie viele Menschen zum Beispiel Deutsch lernen — und auch noch, was ich in meiner Zukunft mit Deutsch anfangen soll.

Hast du zum Beispiel gewusst, dass weltweit zirka 14 Millionen Menschen Deutsch als Fremdsprache lernen? Davon sind ungefähr 2 Millionen Universitätsstudenten, und über 700 000 haben Deutsch sogar als Hauptfach. Wahnsinn!

Aber was soll ich sonst noch schreiben? Mensch, bin ich aber in einer Stimmung!

Du hast uns, hmm, mich auch sehr …

© Cengage Learning 2014

Sprache im Alltag: **Etwas** and **nichts**

German uses the indefinite pronouns **etwas** or **nichts** followed by a capitalized adjective ending in **-es** to express a general idea.

Will er mir **etwas Persönliches** sagen?	*Does he want to tell me something personal?*
Stefan hat Anna endlich **etwas Romantisches** gesagt.	*Stefan finally said something romantic to Anna.*
Ich habe **nichts Neues** zu tragen.	*I've got nothing new to wear.*

Rückblick

4 Stimmt das? Stimmen die folgenden Aussagen zum Text? Wenn nicht, was stimmt?

	Ja, das stimmt.	Nein, das stimmt nicht.
1. Anna muss noch eine Seminararbeit fertig schreiben.	○	○
2. Anna will mit Stefan gar nicht sprechen.	○	○
3. Stefan muss auch eine Arbeit schreiben.	○	○
4. Stefan ist in Anna verliebt.	○	○
5. Anna versteht, worüber Stefan mit ihr sprechen will.	○	○
6. In ihrem Bericht muss Anna über das Deutschlernen weltweit schreiben.	○	○
7. Anna wird ein bisschen ungeduldig° mit Stefan.	○	○
8. Anna ist dankbar dafür, dass sie gute Freunde wie Barbara, Karl und Stefan kennengelernt hat.	○	○
9. Stefan hat Schwierigkeiten, die richtigen Worte zu finden.	○	○
10. Anna erklärt Stefan, dass sie ihn liebt.	○	○

impatient

....

Complete the **Ergänzen Sie** activity in the Student Activities Manual before doing the next activity.

....

5 Kurz gefragt Beantworten Sie die folgenden Fragen auf Deutsch.

1. Was haben Stefan und Anna vorher nicht klar gewusst? Warum haben sie das nicht gewusst?
2. Wie kann man die Beziehung zwischen Stefan und Anna beschreiben? Wie sehen Sie die Zukunft von Stefan und Anna?
3. Welche Fragen aus dem Ratespiel haben Sie richtig, welche falsch beantwortet? Haben Sie Zahlen unter- oder überschätzt°?
4. Glauben Sie, dass man in einem deutschsprachigen Land studieren oder arbeiten muss, um die Sprache gut zu lernen und besser über die Kultur Bescheid zu wissen?
5. Was würde Sie an einem Studium oder einem Praktikum in einem deutschsprachigen Land interessieren?

unter- ... : *under- or overestimated*

6 Interview Stellen Sie einem Partner/einer Partnerin die folgenden Fragen. Lassen Sie sich genug Zeit, Gedanken miteinander auszutauschen.

1. Warum hast du beschlossen, dieses Jahr Deutsch zu lernen?
2. Gefällt dir das Studium der deutschen Sprache? Warum? Warum nicht?
3. Was findest du besonders toll?
4. Was findest du besonders schwierig?
5. Willst du dein Studium der deutschen Sprache nächstes Jahr fortsetzen? In welchem Kurs? Wie lange willst du noch Deutsch studieren?
6. Würdest du gern ein Semester oder ein Jahr im Ausland studieren? Wie viele deiner Freunde und Kommilitonen haben solche Pläne? Was erwartest du davon? Was erwarten deine Freunde und Kommilitonen davon?
7. Findest du es wichtig, eine andere Sprache zu lernen? Hast du deine Meinung geändert? Erkläre deine Antwort.
8. Möchtest du noch mehr Sprachen lernen? Welche? Warum würdest du diese Sprache(n) lernen wollen?
9. Kannst du dir vorstellen, dass du deine Sprachkenntnisse in deinem zukünftigen Beruf oder Privatleben benutzen könntest? Erkläre deine Antwort.

Der Einfluss der englischen und der deutschen Sprache aufeinander

The German and English languages share many common features due to their common origin as Germanic languages. Some words are easily recognized as cognates, that is, words with similar forms and meanings, such as **Haus – house, Morgen – morning**, **Wasser – water, Apfel – apple**, or **Haar – hair**. Many others, however, have undergone sound changes that make them less transparent and more fascinating, for example, **Zaun** (*fence*) **– town, Zimmer – timber, gestern – yester(day), Garten – garden/yard** or **Weib – wife**.

Over the years, German has contributed many words to English, such as **Gesellschaft**, **Gemeinschaft** (in the field of sociology), **Angst, Gestalt** (in the field of psychology), **Kindergarten**, many military terms from World War II, for example, **Blitzkrieg, Luftwaffe**, and **Flak** (acronym of **Flugzeugabwehrkanone**), and the popular term **Schadenfreude**.

In modern times, English has been the source of many new words in German. In the realm of information technology, for example, English terms are everywhere in German (**klicken, dumpen, der Laptop, das Modem, die Software**) and are usually adapted to follow German grammar rules. Marketers exploit the attraction of English in their advertising campaigns based on key English terms (**Leasing, DriverLounge, Wellness, Shirts**). Since American movies and TV series are well-known worldwide, English expressions—often with a slightly different meaning (**Mister, Kids**)—have been borrowed into colloquial German, especially by the youth culture, and have had an impact on German culture.

Ilmagestate Media Partners Limited - Impact Photos/Alamy

Kulturkreuzung

Können Sie einige „deutsche" Wörter im Englischen nennen? Aus welchen Gebieten (z. B. Politik, Psychologie, Erziehung usw.) kommen diese Wörter? Kennen Sie auch einige Wörter aus dem Jiddischen, das von einem deutschen Dialekt abstammt°? Nicht alle Deutschsprechenden finden den Einfluss der englischen/amerikanischen Sprache auf ihre Sprache so gut. Warum wohl?

stems from

7 Rollenspiel: Das Gespräch zwischen Anna und Stefan
Spielen Sie Annas und Stefans Gespräch weiter. Anna will ihre Gefühle für Stefan klar ausdrücken und Stefan will Anna überzeugen, dass er es ernst meint und sie wirklich lieb hat.

8 Rollenspiel: Anna und ihr Enkelkind In **Kapitel 5** haben Sie die Geschichte von Tante Uschi und Onkel Hannes gelesen. Jetzt ist es vierzig Jahre her, seit Anna in Tübingen studiert hat. Spielen Sie die Rollen von Anna und ihrem Enkelkind mit einem Partner oder einer Partnerin. Das Enkelkind stellt Fragen über Annas Geschichte, die Anna beantwortet. Anna versucht, das Kind zu überzeugen, Deutsch zu lernen. Sprechen Sie nicht nur über Annas Zeit in Tübingen, sondern auch darüber, was später passiert ist, wo und wie sie gelebt hat und wie sie ihr Deutsch benutzt hat. Bevor Sie beginnen, besprechen Sie mit Ihrem Partner/mit Ihrer Partnerin, worüber Sie genau sprechen wollen.

9 Schreibecke: **Einen schwierigen Brief schreiben.** Im Gespräch haben Anna and Stefan Schwierigkeiten gehabt, die richtigen Worte zu finden. Es ist leichter für sie, ihre Gefühle in einem Brief zu beschreiben. Schreiben Sie Annas Brief an Stefan oder Stefans Brief an Anna. Erklären Sie Ihre Gefühle aus der Perspektive von Anna oder Stefan und wie Sie sich die Zukunft ohne oder mit einander vorstellen.

10 Meine Erfahrungen in Deutschland Schreiben Sie einen kurzen Bericht über Annas Erfahrungen in Deutschland. Was hat sie erlebt? Was hat sie gelernt? Wie hat es ihr gefallen? War es insgesamt eine gute oder eine schlechte Erfahrung? Welche Tipps kann Anna Studenten geben, die auch in Deutschland studieren wollen? Schreiben Sie zirka 100 Worte.

© Jens Ottoson/shutterstock.com

War Annas Jahr in Tübingen ein Traum oder ein Albtraum?

Warum Deutsch lernen?

Das *Sprachinstitut Treffpunkt* in Bamberg stellt die Frage „Warum Deutsch lernen?" auf seiner Website und stützt sich auf mehrere wissenschaftliche Arbeiten. Viele Menschen lernen Deutsch als Hobby, fürs Reisen, für Beruf und Karriere und noch mehr. Ihre Internetseite gibt eine ausführliche Antwort auf die Frage: „Warum Deutsch lernen?"

Vorschau

↩ **11** Thematische Fragen Beantworten Sie die folgenden Fragen auf Deutsch.

1. Haben Sie schon einmal mit einer Person aus Deutschland, Österreich oder der Schweiz gesprochen? Welche Sprache haben Sie verwendet? Konnten Sie gut miteinander kommunizieren?

2. Wie lange müssen Sie wahrscheinlich noch Deutsch lernen, bis Sie fließend° Deutsch können?

fluently

3. Glauben Sie, dass man eine fremde Sprache nur auf der Uni oder in der Schule lernen kann, oder muss man auch im Ausland leben oder studieren, um die Sprache gut zu lernen?

4. Was ist für Sie am wichtigsten: Deutsch gut verstehen, lesen, sprechen oder schreiben können? Warum?

5. Was ist wahrscheinlich der Grund dafür, dass das *Sprachinstitut Treffpunkt* eine Seite im Internet hat?

reasons

↩ **12** Meine Gründe° Deutsch zu lernen Warum haben Sie sich für Deutsch als Fremdsprache entschieden? Bewerten Sie jeden Grund mit einer Zahl: 0 = kein Grund; 1 = ein nicht so wichtiger Grund; oder 2 = ein wichtiger Grund.

Aktivität 12. Vergleichen Sie Ihre Antworten mit denen der anderen Studenten in der Klasse. Kann man sagen, dass es Gründe gibt, die viele Studenten wichtig finden?

Der Grund	Die Wichtigkeit
1. Deutsch ist eine schöne Sprache.	_____
2. Man kann im Deutschkurs leicht eine gute Note bekommen.	_____
3. Ich habe Verwandte aus/in einem deutschsprachigen Land.	_____
4. Deutschkenntnisse sind wichtig für meinen späteren Beruf.	_____
5. Die Kultur der deutschsprachigen Länder ist interessant.	_____
6. Ich möchte so viele Sprachen wie möglich lernen.	_____
7. Deutsch ist eine wichtige Sprache in Europa.	_____
8. Das Deutschprogramm an meiner Uni ist sehr gut.	_____
9. Ich möchte in einem deutschsprachigen Land studieren.	_____
10. Meine Freunde oder Verwandten lernen auch Deutsch.	_____

Das Rathaus in Bamberg

13 Satzdetektiv Welche Sätze bedeuten ungefähr das Gleiche?

1. Persönliche **Vorlieben** und Hobbys beinhalten ein weites Feld verschiedenster Themen, zu denen Kenntnisse in Deutsch **eine große Bereicherung** sein können.
2. Viele **wissenschaftliche Abhandlungen** werden nach wie vor° zuerst in Deutsch veröffentlicht.
3. Nicht wenige Menschen erzielen° einen **Informationsvorsprung**, indem sie **Originaltexte** auf Deutsch lesen.
4. **Erschließen° Sie sich** die berühmtesten Operetten und Opern neu, indem Sie die Originaltexte verstehen können.

a. Wenn Sie Deutsch verstehen, können Sie deutsche Operetten und Opern ganz neu interpretieren.
b. Viele Personen sind besser informiert, weil sie deutsche Texte in der Originalsprache lesen können.
c. Deutsch zu sprechen kann helfen, die eigenen Interessen und Hobbys noch interessanter zu machen.
d. Manche Wissenschaftsstudien erscheinen° zuerst auf Deutsch.

5. **Je dominanter** die englische Sprache … **desto wichtiger°** ist es für die **Englisch-Muttersprachler**, eine fremde Sprache zu lernen.
6. So werden Sie an den europäischen Urlaubsorten … sich häufig° besser auf Deutsch **verständlich machen** können als auf Englisch.
7. Nicht zuletzt verdeutlicht° auch **die bedeutende Anzahl** von deutschsprachigen Nobelpreisträgern den Stellenwert° der deutschen Sprache in der wissenschaftlich-kulturellen Welt.
8. Viele der Nachfahren° interessieren sich heute für **den Lebensraum** und **die Kultur** ihrer Großväter und Urgroßväter.

e. In vielen europäischen Ländern versteht man Deutsch besser als Englisch.
f. Viele Leute möchten sich über das Land und die Kultur ihrer Vorfahren° informieren.
g. Weil Englisch … die wichtigste Weltsprache ist, ist es noch wichtiger für Englischsprechende, eine Fremdsprache zu lernen.
h. Die hohe Anzahl von Nobelpreisträgern zeigt, dass Deutsch in der Wissenschaft und der Kultur sehr wichtig ist.

nach …: still

achieve

figure out, understand

appear

je … wichtiger: the more dominant the English language, the more important

oft / ancestors

makes clear

Status

descendants

I. Deutschlernen macht einfach Spaß

Deutsch ist eine lebendige Sprache – Deutsch lernen „aus Spaß an der Freude" und aus kulturellem, wirtschaftlichem und politischem Interesse! Persönliche Vorlieben und Hobbys beinhalten ein weites Feld verschiedenster Themen, zu denen Kenntnisse in Deutsch eine große Bereicherung sein können:

- Geschichte: Entdecken Sie die faszinierende Welt 2000-jähriger deutscher Geschichte von den Germanen über das Deutsche Reich bis in die jüngste Geschichte der Bundesrepublik Deutschland.
- Wissenschaft: Viele wissenschaftliche Abhandlungen werden nach wie vor zuerst in Deutsch veröffentlicht. Man betrachte dazu zum Beispiel auch die Publikationen im Internet: Deutsch ist die zweitwichtigste Sprache im Internet, und nicht wenige Menschen erzielen einen Informationsvorsprung, indem sie Originaltexte auf Deutsch lesen.
- Literatur: Die deutschsprachige Literatur ist berühmt und sehr reichhaltig. Viele der weltbekanntesten Autoren, wie Goethe, Kafka, Luther, Hegel, Nietzsche, Marx, Freud und die Nobelpreisträger/innen Thomas Mann (1929), Hermann Hesse (1946), Heinrich Böll (1972), Günter Grass (1999), Elfriede Jelinek (2004) und Herta Müller (2009) schreiben auf Deutsch.
- Popmusik: Musik von Falco, Kraftwerk, Nina Hagen, Nena, Herbert Grönemeyer oder Rammstein – um nur einige Namen zu nennen – stehen auch international ganz oben auf den Hitlisten.
- Klassische Musik: Mit Komponisten wie Bach, Beethoven, Mahler, Mozart, Strauß und Wagner nehmen die deutschsprachigen Komponisten eine dominierende Stellung innerhalb dieser Musikrichtung ein. Erschließen Sie sich die berühmtesten Operetten und Opern neu, indem Sie die Originaltexte verstehen können.
- Sprache und Kultur: Je dominanter die englische Sprache – nicht nur durch den vielschichtigen weltweiten Einfluss der Supermacht Amerika, sondern auch durch die Verbreitung des Internets –, desto wichtiger ist es für die Englisch-Muttersprachler, eine fremde Sprache zu lernen. In vielen Bereichen ist die deutsche Sprache besonders bedeutend: Architektur, Literatur, Malerei, Musik, Philosophie, Wissenschaft und Business. Sie werden erstaunt sein, wie viele der weltgeschichtlich bedeutendsten Werke im Original in deutscher Sprache verfasst sind.

Nationaldichter Johann W. von Goethe.

Nobelpreisträger Albert Einstein.

II. Deutschlernen für das Reisen

Lernen Sie Deutsch, um Ihre Reise durch Mitteleuropa zu einem intensiven, persönlichen Erlebnis zu machen.

Deutsch ist die in Europa am häufigsten und weitverbreitetsten gesprochene Sprache. Mit Kenntnissen der deutschen Sprache gestaltet sich das Reisen in Europa viel einfacher. So werden Sie sich an den europäischen Urlaubsorten in Italien, Frankreich, Spanien, Portugal, der Türkei oder Griechenland häufig besser auf Deutsch verständlich machen können als auf Englisch. Dazu trägt bei, dass viele Südeuropäer in den 60er- und 70er-Jahren als Gastarbeiter in Deutschland, der Schweiz oder Österreich tätig waren und dass die Deutschsprachigen als eifrige „Mittelmeertouristen" eine lange Tradition haben.

III. Deutschlernen zur Verbesserung der Berufs- and Karrierechancen

„Deutsch" ist die Muttersprache für mehr Europäer als etwa Englisch, Französisch, Spanisch oder Italienisch. In den Bereichen Wirtschaft, Tourismus und Diplomatie ist Deutsch – nach Englisch – heute die weltweit zweitwichtigste Sprache. In Mittel- und Osteuropa ist Deutsch die wichtigste Fremdsprache.

Mit Deutsch als Fremdsprache können Sie Ihre Berufschancen entscheidend verbessern. Besonders in den Bereichen Biologie, Diplomatie, Finanzen, Elektrotechnik, Maschinenbau, Chemie, Pharmazie, Sport, Fahrzeugbau, Tourismus und dem gesamten Bildungsbereich ist Deutsch – nach Englisch – die wichtigste Sprache zur Qualifikation junger Menschen weltweit.

Weltweit geben etwa 130 Millionen Menschen Deutsch als ihre Muttersprache an und etwa 14 Millionen lernen Deutsch.

Gemäß einer Studie, die 1994 im Auftrag der German American Chamber of Commerce durchgeführt wurde, gaben rund 65 % aller befragten Firmen an, dass bei der Suche nach neuen Mitarbeitern speziell bilinguale Fähigkeiten in Englisch und Deutsch ein wichtiges Auswahlkriterium sind. Deutsch ist die wichtigste Wirtschaftssprache in der Europäischen Union und eine Brücke zu den aufstrebenden Nationen Osteuropas. Innerhalb der europäischen Union sind die deutschsprachigen Länder mit rund 1/3 die größten Handelspartner.

Auch spielt die deutsche Sprache bei Wirtschaftskontakten in den aufstrebenden Märkten Osteuropas oftmals eine größere Rolle als Englisch: In vielen Gebieten Polens, Ungarns, Rumäniens, Russlands, der Ukraine und in den baltischen Staaten und der Tschechischen Republik ist Deutsch eine wichtige Sprache.

Nicht zuletzt verdeutlicht auch die bedeutende Anzahl von deutschsprachigen Nobelpreisträgern den Stellenwert der deutschen Sprache in der wissenschaftlich-kulturellen Welt: 30 Nobelpreise in Chemie, 25 in Medizin, 21 in Physik, 10 in Literatur und 8 Friedenspreise.

IV. Deutschlernen, um die Geschichte der Vorfahren kennenzulernen

Während der letzten vier Jahrhunderte sind aus Mitteleuropa besonders viele Menschen nach Nord- und Südamerika und auch nach Australien ausgewandert. Viele der Nachfahren interessieren sich heute für den Lebensraum und die Kultur ihrer Großväter und Urgroßväter. Wer dazu die alte Heimat besucht und wirklich kennenlernen will, kommt kaum daran vorbei, Deutsch zu lernen.

Reprinted by permission of Alexandra von Rohr.

Rückblick

14 Stimmt das? Stimmen die folgenden Aussagen zum Text? Wenn nicht, was stimmt?

	Ja, das stimmt.	Nein, das stimmt nicht.
1. Viele Studenten lernen Deutsch, weil es einfach Spaß macht.	○	○
2. Alle wissenschaftlichen Publikationen erscheinen heute nur auf Englisch.	○	○
3. Die deutsche Literatur spielt in der Weltliteratur eine große Rolle.	○	○
4. Die deutschsprachigen Autorinnen Elfriede Jelinek aus Österreich und Herta Müller aus Rumänien haben im Jahre 2004 und 2009 den Nobelpreis für Literatur gewonnen.	○	○
5. Es gibt keine gute Popmusik in Deutschland und schon gar keine Gruppe, die weltweit bekannt ist.	○	○
6. Deutschsprachige Komponisten haben in der klassischen Musik eine große Rolle gespielt.	○	○
7. Im Zeitalter von Englisch ist es nicht wichtig, die deutsche Kultur und Sprache zu verstehen.	○	○
8. Deutschkenntnisse helfen, wenn man in Südeuropa Urlaub macht.	○	○
9. Deutsch ist in der Wirtschaft, im Tourismus und in der Diplomatie wichtiger als Englisch.	○	○
10. Es gibt mehr Leute, die Deutsch als Fremdsprache lernen, als Leute, die Deutsch als Muttersprache sprechen.	○	○
11. Für weniger als die Hälfte aller befragten Firmen in den USA ist es wichtig, dass ihre Mitarbeiter nicht nur Englisch, sondern auch Deutsch sprechen.	○	○
12. Deutsch ist die wichtigste Wirtschaftssprache Europas.	○	○
13. In Osteuropa versteht und spricht man mehr Englisch als Deutsch.	○	○
14. Viele Leute in Nord- und Südamerika und in Australien haben deutsche Vorfahren.	○	○

Complete the **Ergänzen Sie** activity in the Student Activities Manual before doing the next activity.

surprised
areas

15 Kurz gefragt Beantworten Sie die folgenden Fragen auf Deutsch.

1. Aus welchen Gründen sollte man Deutsch lernen? Nennen Sie wenigstens zwei Gründe.
2. Welche Fakten und Zahlen haben Sie überrascht°? Warum?
3. In welchen Branchen und welchen geographischen Gebieten° ist Deutsch besonders wichtig?
4. Glauben Sie, dass Sie Deutsch in Ihrem Beruf und/oder Privatleben verwenden werden? Müssen Sie Ihr Deutsch dafür noch verbessern?
5. Kennen Sie deutsche Popmusikgruppen, die international bekannt sind? Warum sind sie wohl international bekannt? Was für Musik spielen sie?
6. Waren Sie schon einmal in einem deutschsprachigen Land? Wenn ja, erzählen Sie von Ihren Erfahrungen.
7. Sehen Sie Verbindungen mit Deutschkursen und Ihren anderen Kursen? Erklären Sie Ihre Antwort.
8. Warum sollte man Deutsch lernen, wenn so viele deutschsprachige Leute Englisch können?

Amerikaner und amerikanische Kultur im deutschsprachigen Mitteleuropa

Central Europe's interest in the United States started with the American Revolution and lasted through the 20th century, ultimately drawing wave after wave of immigrants from German-speaking areas well into the 1950s. But with the occupation of Germany and Austria after World War II, the American influence on German-speaking central European culture grew exponentially. In postwar Germany of the 50's, American GIs spent much-needed dollars in the community and spread interest in American popular culture, especially jazz and jitterbug music.

© ullstein bild/The Granger
Collection, New York

In Deutschland sowie in den USA war Elvis Presley ein großer Star.

Broadcasting in English for U.S. forces stationed in Germany from the 1960s to the 1980s, the American Forces Network (AFN) played the latest pop music, creating huge interest in American stars in Germany as well as Austria. Serving his stint in the U.S. Army in Friedberg, Germany, in 1958, Elvis Presley made German girls swoon just as much as he had the girls back home. Artists as diverse as Johnny Cash, Connie Francis, the Beatles, and Peter Gabriel recorded songs in German. German kids became aficionados of everything from soul, funk, hip-hop, and rap music to gospel and country music, and gradually adapted the musical styles to songs sung and performed in German. German hip-hop artists S.M.U.D.O. and Thomas D. honed their craft in the U.S. before launching their band, **Die fantastischen Vier,** back home in Stuttgart. Central European rockers like Falco, Milli Vanilli, Nena, Rammstein, and Tokio Hotel broadened their fan base by recording in English as well as German.

Texan theater director Robert Wilson became the darling of German theaters for his avant-garde productions and novel use of color and light. American film and television have had a profound impact on German cinema and television programming, resulting in TV spin-offs that mirror the very latest in American TV programming.

In the classical music world, the availability of jobs has drawn many talented American musicians, conductors, and dancers to the government-supported theaters of Europe. Brilliant young Americans became star players in groups such as **Concentus Musicus Wien.** James Levine became chief conductor of the **Münchner Philharmoniker** in 1999 and later chief conductor of the Metropolitan Opera and the Boston Symphony Orchestra. German-American violinist David Garrett has introduced the classical music tradition to a new generation of listeners with his rock band's adaptations of classical sonatas, pop songs, movie themes, and his own compositions.

Kulturkreuzung

Warum, glauben Sie, hat die amerikanische Kultur einen so starken Einfluss auf Europa und die ganze Welt? Sehen Sie das positiv oder negativ?

↩ **16** Warum Deutsch lernen? Schreiben Sie die fehlenden Informationen aus dem Text in die Grafik.

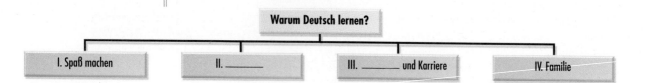

Warum Deutsch lernen?

- I. Spaß machen
- II. _____
- III. _____ und Karriere
- IV. Familie

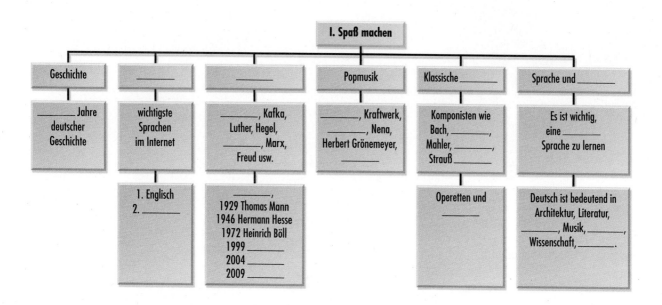

I. Spaß machen

Geschichte	_____	_____	Popmusik	Klassische _____	Sprache und _____
_____ Jahre deutscher Geschichte	wichtigste Sprachen im Internet	_____, Kafka, Luther, Hegel, _____, Marx, Freud usw.	_____, Kraftwerk, _____, Nena, Herbert Grönemeyer,	Komponisten wie Bach, _____, Mahler, _____, Strauß _____	Es ist wichtig, eine _____ Sprache zu lernen
	1. Englisch 2. _____	_____, 1929 Thomas Mann 1946 Hermann Hesse 1972 Heinrich Böll 1999 _____ 2004 _____ 2009 _____		Operetten und _____	Deutsch ist bedeutend in Architektur, Literatur, _____, Musik, _____, Wissenschaft, _____.

II. In Europa reisen

- Deutsch ist die in Europa am _____ und am weit verbreitesten gesprochene Sprache.
- Deutsch wird in den _____ in Südeuropa öfter als Englisch gesprochen.
- Viele Südeuropäer haben in Deutschland als _____ Deutsch gelernt.

IV. Familie und Vorfahren kennenlernen

- Während der letzten _____ sind viele Menschen nach Nord- und Südamerika und nach Australien ausgewandert.
- Die Nachfahren wollen die Heimat ihrer _____ besuchen.

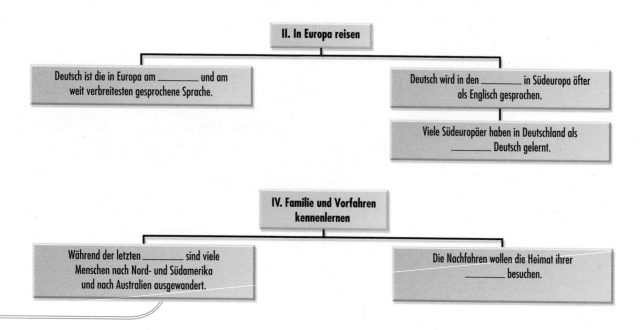

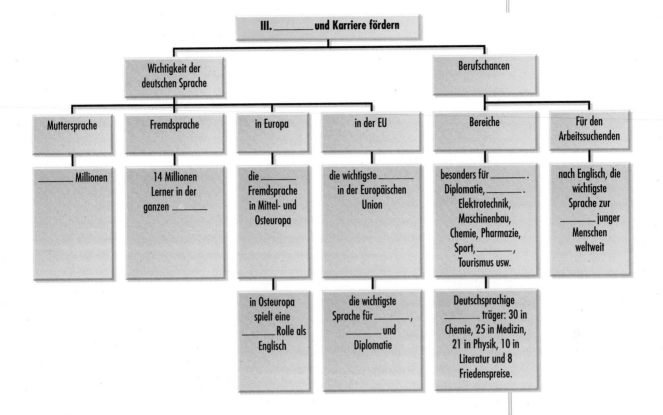

III. _____ und Karriere fördern

- **Wichtigkeit der deutschen Sprache**
  - **Muttersprache**
    - _____ Millionen
  - **Fremdsprache**
    - 14 Millionen Lerner in der ganzen _____
  - **in Europa**
    - die _____ Fremdsprache in Mittel- und Osteuropa
    - in Osteuropa spielt eine _____ Rolle als Englisch
  - **in der EU**
    - die wichtigste _____ in der Europäischen Union
    - die wichtigste Sprache für _____, _____ und Diplomatie
- **Berufschancen**
  - **Bereiche**
    - besonders für _____. Diplomatie, _____. Elektrotechnik, Maschinenbau, Chemie, Pharmazie, Sport, _____, Tourismus usw.
    - Deutschsprachige _____ träger: 30 in Chemie, 25 in Medizin, 21 in Physik, 10 in Literatur und 8 Friedenspreise.
  - **Für den Arbeitsuchenden**
    - nach Englisch, die wichtigste Sprache zur _____ junger Menschen weltweit

→ **17** Deutschsprachige Autoren Wer hat was geschrieben? Verbinden Sie einen berühmten Autor/eine berühmte Autorin mit den passenden Buchtiteln.

1. Heinrich Böll
2. Sigmund Freud
3. Johann Wolfgang von Goethe
4. Günter Grass
5. Georg Wilhelm Friedrich Hegel
6. Hermann Hesse
7. Elfriede Jelinek
8. Franz Kafka
9. Martin Luther
10. Thomas Mann
11. Karl Marx
12. Friedrich Nietzsche
13. Christa Wolf
14. Herta Müller

a. *Also sprach Zarathustra, Jenseits von Gut und Böse*
b. *Billard um halb zehn, Gruppenbild mit Dame*
c. *Das Ich und das Es, Die Traumdeutung*
d. *Das Kapital, Das Kommunistische Manifest*
e. *Der Große und der Kleine Katechismus*
f. *Der Zauberberg, Buddenbrooks, Der Tod in Venedig*
g. *Der geteilte Himmel, Nachdenken über Christa T.*
h. *Die Klavierspielerin, Die Kinder der Toten*
i. *Die Verwandlung, Der Prozess, Das Schloss, Amerika*
j. *Faust, Die Leiden des jungen Werther*
k. *Phänomenologie des Geistes*
l. *Steppenwolf, Das Glasperlenspiel*
m. *Die Blechtrommel, Katz und Maus*
n. *Atemschaukel, Herztier*

ii 18 Rollenspiel: Studienberater Suchen Sie sich einen Partner oder eine Partnerin. Eine Person ist ein Student oder eine Studentin und will wissen, warum er/sie Deutsch lernen soll. Diese Person meint, dass es gut genug ist, wenn man Englisch sprechen kann. Die andere Person ist ein Studienberater oder eine Studienberaterin und erklärt, warum es wichtig ist, Deutsch zu lernen.

draft

19 Schreibecke: **Annas Bericht.** Schreiben Sie die erste Fassung° von Annas Bericht über das Deutschlernen weltweit und die Gründe, warum es wichtig ist. Identifizieren Sie drei persönliche Gründe. Schreiben Sie 250–300 Worte.

20 Posterprojekt: **Warum Deutsch lernen?** Sie sollen eine Präsentation über das Deutschlernen machen. Das Ziel ist es, viele Studenten/Studentinnen zum Deutschlernen zu motivieren. Machen Sie ein Poster mit Bildern und Überschriften und zeigen Sie es den anderen Studenten/Studentinnen.

maintain

21 Annas Tipps für Deutsch Anna fragt sich, wie sie zu Hause in den USA ihre Deutschkenntnisse aufrechterhalten° kann. Markieren Sie alle Aussagen, die Sie auch relevant finden.

Annas Tipps für Deutschkenntnisse	Meine Tipps
1. Ich kann ab und zu einen deutschsprachigen Film anschauen.	○
2. Ich kann E-Mails an meine Freunde in Deutschland schicken.	○
3. Ich kann an meine Verwandten in Deutschland schreiben.	○
4. Ich kann deutschsprachige Nachrichten im Internet lesen.	○
5. Ich kann deutschsprachige Nachrichten im Radio oder Fernsehen hören.	○
6. Ich kann deutschsprachige Menschen in meiner Stadt finden und mit ihnen sprechen.	○
7. Ich kann an meiner Uni zur Kaffeestunde oder zum Deutschklub gehen.	○
8. Ich kann Städte in meiner Region besuchen, die deutschsprachige Einwohner haben.	○
9. Ich kann das nächste Goethe-Institut besuchen.	○
10. Ich kann in meinen Uni-Kursen deutsch-relevante Themen identifizieren.	○
11. Ich kann Beethoven-Konzerte besuchen.	○

© ruskpp/shutterstock.com

Deutsche und österreichische Einflüsse auf Amerikas Kultur

In the tumult of 20th century history, the immigration of countless German-speaking Europeans had a profound impact on American life, letters, science, culture, and business. The Nazi ban on Jewish artists, authors, and academics and their sympathizers forced a whole generation of creative talent to leave Germany for countries offering asylum. In 1933, the brilliant physicist **Albert Einstein** left Germany for the U.S., where he continued his work at the Institute for Advanced Study at Princeton University. After the war, German rocket scientist **Wernher von Braun** came to the U.S. and became the leading figure of NASA, leading the way to manned space flight. Nobel Prize laureate **Thomas Mann** spent the war years in exile in California. Theater revolutionary and author of the famous **Dreigroschenoper, Bertolt Brecht,** also moved to California, hoping to find work as a screenwriter. He only worked on one movie but spent his time completing his most important plays. Several German and Austrian actors left their mark in Hollywood: **Marlene Dietrich,** a fierce opponent of Hitler, became the romantic lead in numerous Hollywood films. The Austrian actress **Hedy Lamarr,** known as the "most beautiful woman in the world," became a Hollywood legend in the 30's and 40's. **Peter Lorre,** born in the Austro-Hungarian Empire, became a successful character actor, and **Billy Wilder** made familiar Hollywood movies from the 30's into the 90's. Brecht-collaborator **Kurt Weill** made a successful transition to Broadway, later penning memorable songs and musicals in English.

© Spauke, Bernd/Arte/Bavaria/WDR/ The Kobal Collection/Picture Desk

Der Film „Lola rennt" mit Franka Potente war ein weltweiter Filmerfolg.

The German impact in Hollywood has more recently been profound. After gaining worldwide attention for his groundbreaking film, **Das Boot,** German director **Wolfgang Petersen** moved on to Hollywood, directing films as diverse as **The NeverEnding Story** to **Troy** (2004). Director **Roland Emmerich**'s experience with special effects made him a natural choice to direct Will Smith in **Independence Day**. Actress **Franka Potente,** originally famous for running through Berlin as the punk Lola in **Lola rennt,** has made a name for herself in Hollywood films as well. German-Spanish actor **Daniel Brühl,** star of **Good Bye Lenin!,** is also expanding into an international career with Spanish- and English-language films **7 Days in Havana** and **Cargo**. Quentin Tarantino filmed his World War 2 fantasy **Inglourious Basterds** at Babelsberger Studios in Berlin, bringing fame in the English speaking world to established actors **Brühl, Diane Kruger, Til Schweiger,** and earning **Christoph Waltz** an Oscar. The aspirations and successes of Austrian bodybuilder-actor-politician, **Arnold Schwarzenegger,** moved from being the "Terminator" to becoming the governor of California. German models from **Claudia Schiffer** to **Heidi Klum** keep images of vivacious Germanic beauty alive for the world, while Austrian chef and actor **Wolfgang Puck** has built a dining dynasty in the U.S.

Kulturkreuzung

Zur Kultur gehört auch der Sport. Welche Sportarten werden mehr in den deutschsprachigen Ländern und welche werden mehr in den USA gespielt? Warum, glauben Sie, ist das so? Welche „amerikanischen" Sportarten spielt man aber jetzt auch in den deutschsprachigen Ländern, und umgekehrt, welche Sportarten, die typisch für die deutschsprachigen Länder sind, spielt man jetzt auch in den USA? Kennen Sie amerikanische Sportler, die in Deutschland leben?

Lernerbiografien

Sie sind jetzt am Ende von *Vorsprung* – leider! Reflektieren Sie nun ein bisschen über Ihre Erfolge und Ihre Zukunft mit Deutsch.

Zielaktivitäten

⇥ 22 Lernerbiografien analysieren Lesen Sie die folgenden Lernerbiografien der drei Textbuchautoren.

Ich habe relativ spät angefangen Deutsch zu lernen, obwohl die Eltern von meiner Mutter – meine Großeltern – aus Deutschland sind. Meine erste Fremdsprache in der Schule war Spanisch; danach kam Latein. Erst in der elften und zwölften Klasse habe ich Deutsch gehabt. Auf dem College habe ich weiterhin Deutsch gelernt. Im Januar 1970 bin ich zum ersten Mal nach Deutschland gereist – in die ehemalige DDR. Im akademischen Jahr 1970–1971 studierte ich an der Universität in Freiburg. Nach meinem Bachelor bin ich nach Israel gefahren, wo ich Archäologie machte. Von 1972 bis 1974 wohnte ich wieder in Freiburg, wo ich Student und Englischlehrer war. Ich habe danach in Berkeley promoviert. Zwischendurch war ich zwei Monate in Tübingen und ein Jahr in Heidelberg. Seit 1986 bin ich Professor in Michigan. Alle paar Jahre fahre ich mit Studenten nach Mayen in der Eifel.

Das Fremdsprachenlernen fing bei mir in der 9. Klasse in Whiting, Indiana an. Ich hatte die Wahl zwischen Französisch, Deutsch, Latein und Spanisch und entschied mich für Deutsch. Meine erste Lehrerin war gebürtige Deutsche, der das Unterrichten keinen besonderen Spaß machte, und die Bücher waren sehr alt. Aber in der 10. Klasse kamen neue Lehrbücher und eine tolle neue Lehrerin. Wir sprachen Deutsch und lasen und schrieben viel. In der 11. Klasse verbrachte ich sechs Wochen in Krefeld bei einer deutschen Familie. Den ganzen Sommer lang durfte ich kein Wort Englisch sprechen. Später studierte ich Germanistik, Slawistik und Pädagogik an der Indiana University. Das 11. und 12. Semester verbrachte ich an der Universität Hamburg. Später arbeitete ich eineinhalb Jahre bei der Deutschen Lufthansa in Frankfurt/Main. Meinen ersten Job als Lehrer bekam ich in Massachusetts, wo ich seit Jahrzehnten lebe und Deutsch unterrichte.

Ich wurde in einer kleinen Stadt in Österreich (Melk) geboren. In Österreich sprechen viele Leute Dialekt. Meine Eltern haben aber mit mir Standarddeutsch gesprochen, denn in der Schule muss man das sprechen und schreiben. Viele Kinder müssen Standarddeutsch in der Schule wie eine Fremdsprache lernen. So mit zehn oder elf Jahren durfte ich dann auch im Dialekt sprechen. Bis dahin hatte ich auch mit meinen Freundinnen hauptsächlich Standarddeutsch gesprochen – und die haben das sehr lustig gefunden! Sprachen haben mir immer Spaß gemacht. Ich habe in der Schule Englisch, Französisch, Latein und Italienisch „gelernt". Wirklich sprechen kann ich nur Deutsch und Englisch. An der Uni in Wien habe ich Deutsch und Geschichte studiert. Mit neunzehn hatte ich meinen ersten Studentenjob – als Deutschlehrerin für Ausländer! Ich bin in die USA gezogen und habe in Austin promoviert.

Julianna Lovik

Tom Lovik

Courtesy of Debra Graczyk.

Doug Guy

Courtesy of Franz Gabriel Lagler.

Monika Chavez

Welcher Autor spricht über welches Thema? Markieren Sie die passenden Antworten mit einem Häkchen.

	Tom	Doug	Monika
1. Wann er/sie Deutsch gelernt hat.	○	○	○
2. Welche Art von Deutsch er/sie gelernt hat.	○	○	○
3. Welche Sprache er/sie mit den Eltern gesprochen hat.	○	○	○
4. Welche Sprache er/sie mit den Freunden/Freundinnen gesprochen hat.	○	○	○
5. Woher die Eltern, Großeltern usw. gekommen sind.	○	○	○
6. Wo er/sie gewohnt hat.	○	○	○
7. Was er/sie studiert hat.	○	○	○
8. Wo er/sie gearbeitet hat.	○	○	○
9. Welche Sprachen er/sie gelernt hat.	○	○	○
10. Welche Sprachen er/sie sprechen kann.	○	○	○

↩ **23** Ihre Biografie schreiben Schreiben Sie jetzt Ihre persönliche Lernerbiografie. Beantworten Sie zuerst die folgenden Fragen in ganzen Sätzen. Wiederholen Sie in der Antwort die Frage und die Substantive aus der Frage.

BEISPIEL

FRAGE: *Wie alt waren Sie*, als Sie Ihr **erstes deutsches Wort** gesprochen haben?
ANTWORT: *Ich war elf Jahre alt*, als ich mein **erstes deutsches Wort** gesprochen habe.

1. Wie alt waren Sie, als Sie Ihr erstes deutsches Wort gesprochen haben?
2. Welche Sprachen haben Ihre Eltern und Großeltern gesprochen?
3. Welche Sprachen hat man an Ihrer High school unterrichtet? Welche Sprache(n) haben Sie gewählt und warum?
4. Wie hieß Ihr erster Sprachlehrer/Ihre erste Sprachlehrerin? Welche Sprache hat er/sie unterrichtet? Was hat Ihnen an Ihrem ersten Sprachunterricht besonders gut gefallen – und was hat Ihnen gar nicht gut gefallen?
5. Welche anderen Sprachen können Sie sprechen – und wie gut?
6. Warum haben Sie an der Uni Deutsch gewählt?
7. Verwenden Sie Deutsch auch außerhalb Ihrer Klasse, zum Beispiel im Internet, zum Chatten oder Internetsurfen? Kennen Sie persönlich Leute, die Deutsch sprechen? Sprechen Sie mit ihnen?

Courtesy of J. Douglas Guy.

Liebesschlösser an der Kölner Hohenzollernbrücke.

24 Umfrage Stellen Sie so vielen Leuten wie möglich die folgenden Fragen. Vergleichen Sie dann alle zusammen Ihre Resultate und berechnen° Sie für jede Antwortkategorie die Resultate für die ganze Klasse in Prozent.

1. Was findest du am schwierigsten, was am interessantesten beim Deutschlernen?
2. Was wären drei Tipps für Studenten, die gerade mit ihrem ersten Semester Deutsch anfangen?
3. Wie viele Wörter Deutsch hast du so in jeder Deutschstunde gesprochen?
4. Wie lange wirst du noch Deutsch studieren?
5. Was willst du am Ende können? (Beispiele: einen Roman lesen, mit Freunden über Weltpolitik diskutieren usw.)
6. Was kannst du jetzt schon auf Deutsch? (Beispiele: einkaufen gehen, mit dem Bus fahren, kleine Geschichten und Zeitungsartikel lesen usw.)

25 Interview Machen Sie ein Interview mit einem anderen Studenten/einer anderen Studentin.

1. Was waren deine Antworten in der Umfrage oben?
2. Möchtest du in einem deutschsprachigen Land studieren oder arbeiten oder ein deutschsprachiges Land besuchen? Wenn ja, wo? Wie lange und was genau?
3. Was ist dein Traumberuf?
4. Wo würdest du gern wohnen? Wie lange und warum?
5. Hast du deutschsprachige Bekannte, Freunde oder Familienmitglieder?
6. Wie kannst du Deutsch und andere Sprachen vielleicht im Privatleben oder im Beruf verwenden°? Nenne ein paar konkrete Dinge.

26 Schreiben Schreiben Sie die Lernerbiografie Ihres Partners/Ihrer Partnerin *aus der Perspektive der Zukunft.* Schreiben Sie im grammatischen Präsens oder Präteritum. Verwenden Sie Antworten aus Interviewfrage.

1. Erklären Sie, wie Ihr Partner/Ihre Partnerin heißt, wie alt er/sie jetzt ist, wo er/sie lebt und lebte und welchen Beruf er/sie hat oder hatte.

BEISPIEL   Erika ist jetzt 43 Jahre alt und lebt seit zwei Jahren in München. Vorher hat sie in Wien, Chicago und Mexico City gelebt. Von Beruf ist sie Architektin.

2. Erklären Sie, was Ihr Partner/Ihre Partnerin im Deutschkurs am schwierigsten und am interessantesten gefunden hat.

BEISPIEL   Wie die anderen Studenten in unserer Deutschklasse im Jahre 20XX hat Erika die Artikel besonders schwierig gefunden.

3. Erklären Sie, wie Ihr Partner/Ihre Partnerin zum Deutschstudium gekommen ist und welche anderen Sprachen er/sie oder seine/ihre Familie spricht.

BEISPIEL   Erika war elf Jahre alt, als sie ihr erstes deutsches Wort gesprochen hat. ...

4. Erklären Sie, wie Ihr Partnerin/Ihre Partner Deutsch und andere Sprachen im Privatleben oder im Beruf verwendet oder verwendet hat.

BEISPIEL   Erika lebt in ihrer Traumstadt München, wo sie jeden Tag Deutsch spricht. Als Architektin spricht Erika natürlich auch mit ihren Klienten Deutsch, aber auch Englisch, wenn sie mit ihrem Büro in Atlanta telefoniert. ...

WORTSCHATZ

Tutorial Quiz
Audio Flashcards

Persönliche Beziehungen

die Beziehung, -en *relationship*

das Gefühl, -e *feeling*

der Humor *humor*

die Spontaneität *spontaneity*

die Stimmung, -en *mood*

  in einer Stimmung sein *to be upset*

der Tipp, -s *tip, suggestion*

die Vergangenheit *past*

die Zukunft *future*

Noch einmal: **die Erfahrung**

berichten (hat berichtet) *to report*

besprechen (bespricht, besprach, hat besprochen) *to discuss*

erfahren (erfährt, erfuhr, hat erfahren) *to learn, find out, experience*

erklären (hat erklärt) *to explain*

erleben (hat erlebt) *to experience*

ertragen (erträgt, ertrug, hat ertragen) *to tolerate, bear*

fehlen (hat gefehlt) + *dat. to be missing, lacking*

fort•setzen (hat fortgesetzt) *to continue*

nach•denken (dachte nach, hat nachgedacht) + *acc. to consider something, think something over*

passieren (ist passiert) *to happen*

rechnen (hat gerechnet) *to count*

  mit etwas rechnen *to expect something*

stören (hat gestört) *to disturb*

überzeugen (hat überzeugt) *to convince*

um•werfen (wirft um, warf um, hat umgeworfen) *to knock over*

(sich) verabschieden (hat [sich] verabschiedet) von + *dat. to say goodbye to (someone)*

verändern (hat verändert) *to change*

vermissen (hat vermisst) *to miss (a person)*

(sich) verstehen (verstand, hat [sich] verstanden) *to understand (one another)*

  Wir haben uns sehr gut verstanden. *We got along very well with each other.*

zusammen•passen (hat zusammengepasst) *to fit together, belong together*

echt *real, authentic (with an adjective) really*

nett *nice*

  echt nett *really nice*

stressig *stressful*

toll *great*

  Ich finde es toll. *I think it's great.*

traurig *sad(ly)*

Ausdrücke

auf der Welt *in the world*

Das hat mich total umgeworfen! *That completely surprised me!*

Das ist ja Unsinn! *That's just nonsense!*

Das kann ich nicht ertragen. *I can't bear that.*

etwas Persönliches *something personal*

Ganz cool bleiben! *Keep cool! Stay calm!*

ich fürchte *I'm afraid*

mit dem Gedanken kämpfen *to struggle with the thought*

von Anfang an *from the very beginning*

was ich damit anfangen soll *what I should do with that*

Wenn du nur wüsstest! *If you only knew!*

Deutschlernen

der Aspekt, -e *aspect*

der Bereich, -e *area, region*

der Bericht, -e *report*

Deutsch als Fremdsprache *German as a foreign language*

der Dialekt, -e *dialect*

das Erlebnis, -se *experience*

die Fähigkeit, -en *ability*

das Gebiet, -e *area*

die Heimat, -en *home*

das Hobby, -s *hobby*

der Informationsvorsprung *information advantage*

das Institut, -e *institute*

  das Sprachinstitut, -e *language institute*

die Internetseite, -n *Internet page*

der Kurs, -e *course*

  der Kursteilnehmer, -/die Kursteilnehmerin, -nen *course participant*

der Lebensraum, -räume *habitat, living space*

der Nobelpreisträger, -/ die Nobelpreisträgerin, -nen *Nobel Prize winner*

die Note, -n *grade in a course*

der Originaltext, -e *original text*

die Sprachkenntnis, -se *linguistic competence*

der Stellenwert, -e *value, status*

die Stellung, -en *position, rank*

der Übersetzer, -/die Übersetzerin, -nen *translator*

der Urgroßvater, -väter *great grandfather*

der Vorfahr, [-en], -en/die Vorfahrin, -nen *forefather, ancestor*

die Website, -s *Website*

der Zusammenhang, ̈-e *connection*

Noch einmal: **die Kenntnis, der Komponist, der Laptop, die Seminararbeit**

aus•wandern (ist ausgewandert)
to emigrate

sich bedanken für (hat sich bedankt) + *acc. to thank for (something), express gratitude for (something)*

berichten (hat berichtet) *to report*

unterrichten (hat unterrichtet)
to teach

verbessern (hat verbessert)
to improve

veröffentlichen (hat veröffentlicht)
to publish

sich verständlich machen (hat sich verständlich gemacht) *to make oneself understood*

ausführlich *detailed*

erfolgreich *successful(ly)*

fließend *fluent(ly)*

lebendig *alive, lively*

tätig sein *to be active, working*

wissenschaftlich *scientific, scholarly*

Ausdrücke

ab und zu *now and then*

aus Spaß *for fun*

indem *(sub. conj.) by (doing something)*

je dominanter, desto wichtiger *the more dominant, the more important*

ohne im Ausland zu wohnen
without living abroad

Meine eigenen Wörter

_____

_____

_____

_____

_____

_____

GEDICHT 1

In der Frühe
Theodor Storm, 1817–1888

ullstein bild/The Granger Collection, New York

Theodor Storm

Theodor Storm was born on September 14, 1817 in Husum in the state of Schleswig-Holstein, then part of Denmark. He studied law and as a young married man, he fell violently in love with a 19-year old, whom he married after the death of his first wife. After his law career had taken him to Berlin for some time, he returned to Husum, where he died on July 4, 1888, of stomach cancer.

 1 Der poetische Student/die poetische Studentin Welche Wörter und Symbole würden Sie verwenden, wenn Sie ein Gedicht über den Morgen schreiben würden? Machen Sie eine Liste.

das Auto	horchen°	nun	sterben
das Bett	ein Kaffee	der Ort	die Sterne
das Dach	der Klang	schießen	wach
die Goldstrahlen	krähen	ein Schwein	
der Hahn	der Mondschein	der Sonnenschein	

listen, eavesdrop

 In der Frühe

Track 2-13

1 Goldstrahlen schießen übers Dach,
2 Die Hähne krähn den Morgen wach;
3 Nun einer hier, nun einer dort,
4 So kräht es nun von Ort zu Ort.
5 Und in der Ferne° stirbt der Klang –
6 Ich höre nichts, ich horche lang.
7 Ihr wackern° Hähne, krähet doch!
8 Sie schlafen immer, immer noch.

Notice that the **e** is missing in **krähen** (line 2). This reflects a colloquial variety of language as well as an attempt by Storm to maintain the meter or rhythm of the poem.

distance

valiant

 2 Die poetische Werkzeugkiste°. Hier ist eine Liste von möglichen poetischen Werkzeugen°. Welche von diesen Werkzeugen findet man in dem Gedicht „In der Frühe"? Und in welcher Zeile oder in welchen Zeilen im Gedicht? Es gibt mehr als eine richtige Antwort. Diskutieren Sie.

1. Symbolik
2. Reim
3. Rhythmus
4. Wörter, die für den Kontext ungewöhnlich sind
5. Wiederholung° von ähnlichen Wörtern
6. Wörter, die das Gegenteil° bedeuten

toolbox
tools

repetition
opposite

3 Das Gedicht in einem Satz Welcher von den fünf Sätzen unten fasst das Gedicht am besten zusammen°? Es gibt mehr als eine richtige Antwort. Diskutieren Sie.

1. Es wird Morgen
2. Die Tiere sind laut.
3. Die Menschen sind faul.
4. Ein schöner Tag fängt an.
5. Die Tiere begrüßen den Morgen

zusammenfassen: *to summarize*

The Granger Collection, New York

Rainer Maria Rilke

falling asleep

rock
accompany

would know

chiming

gently
stirs, moves

In his poetry, Rilke often invented words, and gave other words new meanings.

lover

GEDICHT 2

Zum Einschlafen zu sagen
Rainer Maria Rilke, 1875–1926

Rilke was born on December 4, 1875, in Prague. Educated at an Austrian military school, he later studied philosophy at the University of Munich (1896–1899). In 1920, he obtained Czech citizenship. He died of leukemia in a Swiss sanatorium on December 29, 1926.

4 Der poetische Student/die poetische Studentin Welche Wörter und Symbole würden Sie verwenden, wenn Sie ein Gedicht über das Einschlafen° schreiben würden? Machen Sie eine Liste.

| die Augen | das Dunkel | die Nacht | die Stille | der Wein |
| ein Bett | der Mondschein | die Sterne | eine Uhr | die Zeit |

Track 2-14

Zum Einschlafen zu sagen

1 Ich möchte jemanden einsingen,
2 bei jemandem sitzen und sein.
3 Ich möchte dich wiegen° und kleinsingen
4 und begleiten° schlafaus und schlafein.
5 Ich möchte der Einzige sein im Haus,
6 der wüsste°: die Nacht war kalt.
7 Und möchte horchen herein und hinaus
8 in dich, in die Welt, in den Wald.
9 Die Uhren rufen sich schlagend° an,
10 und man sieht der Zeit auf den Grund.
11 Und unten geht noch ein fremder Mann
12 und stört einen fremden Hund.
13 Dahinter wird Stille. Ich habe groß
14 die Augen auf dich gelegt;
15 und sie halten dich sanft° und lassen dich los,
16 wenn ein Ding sich im Dunkel bewegt°.

5 Der poetische Wortdetektiv Welche Ausdrücke und Sätze aus dem Gedicht von Rilke bedeuten ungefähr das Gleiche? Raten Sie!

1. jemanden einsingen
2. jemanden kleinsingen
3. schlafaus und schlafein
4. die Augen groß auf jemanden legen

a. in den Schlaf und aus dem Schlaf
b. für jemanden wie für ein Kind singen
c. jemanden ganz genau anschauen
d. für jemanden singen, bis er einschläft

6 Fragen zum Gedicht Beantworten Sie die folgenden Fragen.

1. An wen ist das Gedicht geschrieben – an ihn selbst? An einen Geliebten/eine Geliebte°?
2. Welche Stimmung oder welches Gefühl drückt das Gedicht Ihrer Meinung nach aus – Liebe? Freundschaft? Melancholie? Müdigkeit? Etwas anderes?

Reference

1. Personal pronouns

Nominative	Accusative	Accusative reflexive	Dative	Dative reflexive
ich	mich	mich	mir	mir
du	dich	dich	dir	dir
Sie	Sie	sich	Ihnen	sich
er	ihn	sich	ihm	sich
es	es	sich	ihm	sich
sie	sie	sich	ihr	sich
wir	uns	uns	uns	uns
ihr	euch	euch	euch	euch
Sie	Sie	sich	Ihnen	sich
sie	sie	sich	ihnen	sich

2. Interrogative pronouns

Nominative	wer	was
Accusative	wen	was
Dative	wem	
Genitive	wessen	

3. Relative pronouns

	Masculine	Neuter	Feminine	Plural
Nominative	der	das	die	die
Accusative	den	das	die	die
Dative	dem	dem	der	denen
Genitive	dessen	dessen	deren	deren

4. Definite articles and *der*-words

	Masculine	Neuter	Feminine	Plural
Nominative	der	das	die	die
	dieser	dieses	diese	diese
Accusative	den	das	die	die
	diesen	dieses	diese	diese
Dative	dem	dem	der	den
	diesem	diesem	dieser	diesen
Genitive	des	des	der	der
	dieses	dieses	dieser	dieser

Common **der**-words are **dieser, jeder, mancher, solcher,** and **welcher.**

5. Indefinite articles and *ein*-words

	Masculine	Neuter	Feminine	Plural
Nominative	ein	ein	eine	—
	kein	kein	keine	keine
	mein	mein	meine	meine
Accusative	einen	ein	eine	—
	keinen	kein	keine	keine
	meinen	mein	meine	meine
Dative	einem	einem	einer	—
	keinem	keinem	keiner	keinen
	meinem	meinem	meiner	meinen
Genitive	eines	eines	einer	—
	keines	keines	keiner	keiner
	meines	meines	meiner	meiner

The **ein**-words include **kein** and the possessive adjectives **mein, dein, sein, ihr, unser, euer, ihr,** and **Ihr.**

6. Plural of nouns

Type	Plural signal	Singular	Plural	Notes
1	(no change)	das Zimmer	**die Zimmer**	Masculine and neuter nouns
	⸚(umlaut)	der Garten	**die Gärten**	ending in **-el, -en, -er**
2	-e	der Tisch	**die Tische**	
	⸚e	der Stuhl	**die Stühle**	
3	-er	das Bild	**die Bilder**	Stem vowel **e, i** takes no umlaut
	⸚er	das Buch	**die Bücher**	Stem vowel **a, o, u** takes umlaut
4	-en	die Uhr	**die Uhren**	
	-n	die Lampe	**die Lampen**	
5	-nen	die Freundin	**die Freundinnen**	
6	-s	das Radio	**die Radios**	Mostly foreign words

7. Masculine *N*-nouns

	Nominative	Accusative	Dative	Genitive
Singular	der Herr	den Herrn	dem Herrn	des Herrn
Plural	die Herren	die Herren	den Herren	der Herren

Some other masculine *N*-nouns are **der Journalist, der Junge, der Kollege, der Komponist, der Kunde, der Mensch, der Nachbar, der Neffe, der Pilot, der Poet, der Präsident, der Praktikant, der Prinz, der Soldat, der Student, der Tourist.** Some add **-ns** in the genitive: **der Name → des Namens.**

8. Unpreceded adjectives

	Masculine	Neuter	Feminine	Plural
Nominative	kalt**er** Wein	kalt**es** Bier	kalt**e** Milch	alt**e** Leute
Accusative	kalt**en** Wein	kalt**es** Bier	kalt**e** Milch	alt**e** Leute
Dative	kalt**em** Wein	kalt**em** Bier	kalt**er** Milch	alt**en** Leuten
Genitive	kalt**en** Weines	kalt**en** Bieres	kalt**er** Milch	alt**er** Leute

9. Preceded adjectives

	Masculine	Neuter	Feminine	Plural
Nominative	der **alte** Tisch	das **alte** Buch	die **alte** Uhr	die **alten** Bilder
	ein **alter** Tisch	ein **altes** Buch	eine **alte** Uhr	keine **alten** Bilder
Accusative	den **alten** Tisch	das **alte** Buch	die **alte** Uhr	die **alten** Bilder
	einen **alten** Tisch	ein **altes** Buch	eine **alte** Uhr	keine **alten** Bilder
Dative	dem **alten** Tisch	dem **alten** Buch	der **alten** Uhr	den **alten** Bildern
	einem **alten** Tisch	einem **alten** Buch	einer **alten** Uhr	keinen **alten** Bildern
Genitive	des **alten** Tisches	des **alten** Buches	der **alten** Uhr	der **alten** Bilder
	eines **alten** Tisches	eines **alten** Buches	einer **alten** Uhr	keiner **alten** Bilder

10. Nouns declined like adjectives

• *Nouns preceded by definite articles or **der**-words*

	Masculine	Neuter	Feminine	Plural
Nominative	der Deutsch**e**	das Gut**e**	die Deutsch**e**	die Deutsch**en**
Accusative	den Deutsch**en**	das Gut**e**	die Deutsch**e**	die Deutsch**en**
Dative	dem Deutsch**en**	dem Gut**en**	der Deutsch**en**	den Deutsch**en**
Genitive	des Deutsch**en**	des Gut**en**	der Deutsch**en**	der Deutsch**en**

• *Nouns preceded by indefinite articles or **ein**-words*

	Masculine	Neuter	Feminine	Plural
Nominative	ein Deutsch**er**	ein Gut**es**	eine Deutsch**e**	keine Deutsch**en**
Accusative	einen Deutsch**en**	ein Gut**es**	eine Deutsch**e**	keine Deutsch**en**
Dative	einem Deutsch**en**	einem Gut**en**	einer Deutsch**en**	keinen Deutsch**en**
Genitive	eines Deutsch**en**	eines Gut**en**	einer Deutsch**en**	keiner Deutsch**en**

Other nouns declined like adjectives are **der/die Angestellte, Bekannte, Erwachsene, Fremde, Jugendliche, Studierende, Verwandte.**

11. Irregular comparatives and superlatives

Base form	bald	gern	gut	hoch	nah	viel
Comparative	eher	lieber	besser	höher	näher	mehr
Superlative	ehest-	liebst-	best-	höchst-	nächst -	meist-

12. Adjectives and adverbs taking umlauts in the comparative and superlative

alt	gesund (gesünder *or* gesunder)	kurz	schwach
arm	groß	lang	schwarz
blass (blasser *or* blässer)	jung	nass (nässer *or* nasser)	stark
dumm	kalt	oft	warm
fromm (frömmer *or* frommer)	krank	rot	

13. Prepositions

With accusative	With dative	With either accusative or dative	With genitive
durch, für, gegen, ohne, um	aus, außer, bei, mit, nach, seit, von, zu, gegenüber (von)	an, auf, hinter, in, neben, über, unter, vor, zwischen	(an)statt, außerhalb, innerhalb, trotz, während, wegen

14. Verbs and prepositions with special meanings

Accusative

achten auf	*to pay attention to*	hoffen auf	*to hope for*
bitten um	*to ask for*	lachen über	*to laugh about*
böse sein auf	*to be mad at*	reden über	*to talk about*
danken für	*to thank (s.o.) for*	schreiben an	*to write to*
denken an	*to think about*	schreiben über	*to write about*
erinnern an	*to remind (s.o.) of*	sprechen über	*to talk about*
gespannt sein auf	*to be excited about*	warten auf	*to wait for*
glauben an	*to believe in*	wissen über	*to know about*
halten für	*to think (s.o.) is*		

sich + Accusative

sich ärgern über	*to be angry about*	sich interessieren für	*to be interested in*
sich bewerben um	*to apply for*	sich konzentrieren auf	*to concentrate on*
sich entscheiden für/gegen	*to decide on/against*	sich unterhalten über	*to converse about*
sich erinnern an	*to remember*	sich verlieben in	*to fall in love with*
sich freuen auf	*to look forward to*	sich vor·bereiten auf	*to prepare for*
sich freuen über	*to be happy about*		

Dative

an·fangen mit	*to begin with*	handeln von	*to be about*
Angst haben vor	*to be afraid of*	sprechen mit	*to talk to*
arbeiten bei	*to work at (the business of)*	sprechen von	*to talk of*
beginnen mit	*to begin with*	suchen nach	*to look for*
erzählen von	*to tell about*	träumen von	*to dream of*
fahren mit	*to go/travel by*	etwas verstehen von	*to know something about*
fertig werden mit	*to come to grips with, accept*	wissen von	*to know about*
fragen nach	*to ask about*	wohnen bei	*to live at the home of*
halten von	*to think of; to value*		

sich + Dative

sich beschäftigen mit	*to keep busy with*	sich verabreden mit	*to make a date with*
sich trennen von	*to break up with*	sich versöhnen mit	*to reconcile with, make up with*
sich verabreden mit	*to make a date with*	sich verloben mit	*to get engaged to*

15. Dative verbs

antworten	gefallen	helfen	schaden
danken	gehören	leid·tun	schmecken
fehlen	glauben (*dat.* of person)	passen	weh·tun
folgen	gratulieren	passieren	

The verb **glauben** may take an impersonal accusative object: **ich glaube es.**

16. Guidelines for the position of *nicht*

1. **Nicht** always *follows* the finite verb.

   Hannes **arbeitet nicht.**
   Anna **kann nicht** gehen.

2. **Nicht** always *follows:*
   a. noun objects
   b. pronouns used as objects
   c. specific adverbs of time

   Ich glaube **Hannes nicht.**
   Ich glaube **es nicht.**
   Anna geht **heute nicht** mit.

3. **Nicht** *precedes* most other elements:
   a. predicate adjectives
   b. predicate nouns
   c. adverbs
   d. adverbs of general time
   e. prepositional phrases

   Dieter ist **nicht freundlich.**
   Dieter ist **nicht mein Freund.**
   Katrin spielt **nicht gern** Tennis.
   Katrin spielt **nicht oft** Tennis.
   Oliver geht **nicht ins Kino.**
   Ich gehe **nicht oft** ins Kino.

4. If several of the elements that are preceded by **nicht** occur in a sentence, **nicht** usually *precedes* the first one.

17. Verb conjugation

		Present	Narrative past	Subjunctive	Conversational past
Irregular (Strong)	*ich*	komme	kam	käme	bin gekommen
	du	kommst	kamst	kämest	bist gekommen
	er/sie/es	kommt	kam	käme	ist gekommen
	wir	kommen	kamen	kämen	sind gekommen
	ihr	kommt	kamt	kämet	seid gekommen
	sie, Sie	kommen	kamen	kämen	sind gekommen
Regular (Weak)	*ich*	mache	machte	machte	habe gemacht
	du	machst	machtest	machtest	hast gemacht
	er·sie/es	macht	machte	machte	hat gemacht
	wir	machen	machten	machten	haben gemacht
	ihr	macht	machtet	machtet	habt gemacht
	sie, Sie	machen	machten	machten	haben gemacht
Mixed	*ich*	weiß	wusste	wüsste	habe gewusst
	du	weißt	wusstest	wüsstest	hast gewusst
	er/sie/es	weiß	wusste	wüsste	hat gewusst
	wir	wissen	wussten	wüssten	haben gewusst
	ihr	wisst	wusstet	wüsstet	habt gewusst
	sie, Sie	wissen	wussten	wüssten	haben gewusst

		Present	Narrative past	Subjunctive	Conversational past
haben	ich	habe	hatte	hätte	habe gehabt
	du	hast	hattest	hättest	hast gehabt
	er/sie/es	hat	hatte	hätte	hat gehabt
	wir	haben	hatten	hätten	haben gehabt
	ihr	habt	hattet	hättet	habt gehabt
	sie, Sie	haben	hatten	hätten	haben gehabt
sein	ich	bin	war	wäre	bin gewesen
	du	bist	warst	wär(e)st	bist gewesen
	er/sie/es	ist	war	wäre	ist gewesen
	wir	sind	waren	wären	sind gewesen
	ihr	seid	wart	wär(e)t	seid gewesen
	sie, Sie	sind	waren	wären	sind gewesen
werden	ich	werde	wurde	würde	bin geworden
	du	wirst	wurdest	würdest	bist geworden
	er/sie/es	wird	wurde	würde	ist geworden
	wir	werden	wurden	würden	sind geworden
	ihr	werdet	wurdet	würdet	seid geworden
	sie, Sie	werden	wurden	würden	sind geworden

18. Modal auxiliaries

	dürfen	können	müssen	sollen	wollen	mögen	(möchte)
ich	darf	kann	muss	soll	will	mag	(möchte)
du	darfst	kannst	musst	sollst	willst	magst	(möchtest)
er/sie/es	darf	kann	muss	soll	will	mag	(möchte)
wir	dürfen	können	müssen	sollen	wollen	mögen	(möchten)
ihr	dürft	könnt	müsst	sollt	wollt	mögt	(möchtet)
sie, Sie	dürfen	können	müssen	sollen	wollen	mögen	(möchten)
Narrative past	durfte	konnte	musste	sollte	wollte	mochte	
Past participle	gedurft	gekonnt	gemusst	gesollt	gewollt	gemocht	

19. Imperative

	gehen	sehen	arbeiten	sein	haben
Familiar singular	geh	sieh	arbeite	sei	hab
Familiar plural	geht	seht	arbeitet	seid	habt
Formal	gehen Sie	sehen Sie	arbeiten Sie	seien Sie	haben Sie
Wir-form	gehen wir	sehen wir	arbeiten wir	seien wir	haben wir

20. Future

ich	werde		werde		
du	wirst		wirst		
er/sie/es	wird	sehen	wird	gehen	
wir	werden		werden		
ihr	werdet		werdet		
sie, Sie	werden		werden		

21. Passive voice

	Present passive		Narrative past passive		Conversational past passive	
ich	werde		wurde		bin	
du	wirst		wurdest		bist	
er/sie/es	wird	gesehen	wurde	gesehen	ist	gesehen worden
wir	werden		wurden		sind	
ihr	werdet		wurdet		seid	
sie, Sie	werden		wurden		sind	

22. Principal parts of irregular (strong) and mixed verbs

The following list contains the principal parts of most of the high-frequency irregular (strong) and mixed verbs that appear in the second edition of ***Vorsprung.*** Regular (weak) verbs and most other verbs with separable and inseparable prefixes that follow the pattern of corresponding verbs on this list are not included here. Some high-frequency verbs with separable prefixes, whose meanings differ substantially from the base verb, have also been included. All forms given here are in the third-person singular (**er, sie, es**).

Infinitive	Present	Narrative past	Conversational past	Meaning
an·fangen	fängt an	fing an	hat angefangen	*to begin*
an·rufen	ruft an	rief an	hat angerufen	*to call up, phone*
(sich) an·ziehen	zieht an	zog an	hat angezogen	*to put on, dress*
auf·fallen	fällt auf	fiel auf	ist aufgefallen	*to occur to*
aus·geben	gibt aus	gab aus	hat ausgegeben	*to spend (money)*
(sich) aus·ziehen	zieht aus	zog aus	hat ausgezogen	*to undress, get undressed*
befehlen	befiehlt	befahl	hat befohlen	*to command*
beginnen	beginnt	begann	hat begonnen	*to start, begin*
beschreiben	beschreibt	beschrieb	hat beschrieben	*to describe*
sich bewerben	bewirbt sich	bewarb sich	hat sich beworben	*to apply*
bieten	bietet	bot	hat geboten	*to offer*
bitten	bittet	bat	hat gebeten	*to request, ask for*
bleiben	bleibt	blieb	ist geblieben	*to stay, remain*
brechen	bricht	brach	hat gebrochen	*to break*
brennen	brennt	brannte	hat gebrannt	*to burn*
bringen	bringt	brachte	hat gebracht	*to bring*

Infinitive	Present	Narrative past	Conversational past	Meaning
denken	denkt	dachte	hat gedacht	*to think*
dürfen	darf	durfte	hat gedurft	*to be allowed to; may*
ein·laden	lädt ein	lud ein	hat eingeladen	*to invite*
empfehlen	empfiehlt	empfahl	hat empfohlen	*to recommend*
sich entscheiden	entscheidet sich	entschied sich	hat sich entschieden	*to decide*
erkennen	erkennt	erkannte	hat erkannt	*to recognize*
essen	isst	aß	hat gegessen	*to eat*
fahren	fährt	fuhr	ist gefahren	*to drive*
fallen	fällt	fiel	ist gefallen	*to fall*
fangen	fängt	fing	hat gefangen	*to catch*
fern·sehen	sieht fern	sah fern	hat ferngesehen	*to watch TV*
finden	findet	fand	hat gefunden	*to find*
fliegen	fliegt	flog	ist geflogen	*to fly*
geben	gibt	gab	hat gegeben	*to give*
gefallen	gefällt	gefiel	hat gefallen	*to please*
gehen	geht	ging	ist gegangen	*to go*
genießen	genießt	genoss	hat genossen	*to enjoy*
gewinnen	gewinnt	gewann	hat gewonnen	*to win*
haben	hat	hatte	hat gehabt	*to have to*
halten	hält	hielt	hat gehalten	*to stop; to hold*
hängen	hängt	hing	hat/ist gehangen	*to be hanging*
heben	hebt	hob	hat gehoben	*to lift*
heißen	heißt	hieß	hat geheißen	*to be named*
helfen	hilft	half	hat geholfen	*to help*
kennen	kennt	kannte	hat gekannt	*to know*
klingen	klingt	klang	hat geklungen	*to sound*
kommen	kommt	kam	ist gekommen	*to come*
können	kann	konnte	hat gekonnt	*to be able; can*
lassen	lässt	ließ	hat gelassen	*to let; to allow*
laufen	läuft	lief	ist gelaufen	*to run*
leihen	leiht	lieh	hat geliehen	*to lend*
lesen	liest	las	hat gelesen	*to read*
liegen	liegt	lag	hat gelegen	*to lie*
mögen	mag	mochte	hat gemocht	*to like*
müssen	muss	musste	hat gemusst	*to have to; must*
nehmen	nimmt	nahm	hat genommen	*to take*
nennen	nennt	nannte	hat genannt	*to name*
reiten	reitet	ritt	ist geritten	*to ride horseback*
rennen	rennt	rannte	ist gerannt	*to run, race*

Infinitive	Present	Narrative past	Conversational past	Meaning
rufen	ruft	rief	hat gerufen	*to call*
scheinen	scheint	schien	hat geschienen	*to shine; to seem*
schlafen	schläft	schlief	hat geschlafen	*to sleep*
schließen	schließt	schloss	hat geschlossen	*to close*
schneiden	schneidet	schnitt	hat geschnitten	*to cut*
schreiben	schreibt	schrieb	hat geschrieben	*to write*
schwimmen	schwimmt	schwamm	ist geschwommen	*to swim*
sehen	sieht	sah	hat gesehen	*to see*
sein	ist	war	ist gewesen	*to be*
singen	singt	sang	hat gesungen	*to sing*
sinken	sinkt	sank	ist gesunken	*to sink*
sitzen	sitzt	saß	hat gesessen	*to sit*
sollen	soll	sollte	hat gesollt	*to be supposed to; should*
sprechen	spricht	sprach	hat gesprochen	*to speak*
springen	springt	sprang	ist gesprungen	*to jump*
statt·finden	findet statt	fand statt	hat stattgefunden	*to take place, occur*
stehen	steht	stand	hat gestanden	*to stand*
steigen	steigt	stieg	ist gestiegen	*to climb*
sterben	stirbt	starb	ist gestorben	*to die*
stinken	stinkt	stank	hat gestunken	*to stink*
streiten	streitet	stritt	hat gestritten	*to argue*
tragen	trägt	trug	hat getragen	*to wear; to carry*
treffen	trifft	traf	hat getroffen	*to meet; to score*
treiben	treibt	trieb	hat getrieben	*to engage in*
treten	tritt	trat	ist getreten	*to step*
trinken	trinkt	trank	hat getrunken	*to drink*
tun	tut	tat	hat getan	*to do*
verbieten	verbietet	verbot	hat verboten	*to forbid*
verbringen	verbringt	verbrachte	hat verbracht	*to spend time*
vergessen	vergisst	vergaß	hat vergessen	*to forget*
verlieren	verliert	verlor	hat verloren	*to lose*
verstehen	versteht	verstand	hat verstanden	*to understand*
vor·schlagen	schlägt vor	schlug vor	hat vorgeschlagen	*to suggest*
wachsen	wächst	wuchs	ist gewachsen	*to grow*
waschen	wäscht	wusch	hat gewaschen	*to wash*
werden	wird	wurde	ist geworden	*to become*
werfen	wirft	warf	hat geworfen	*to throw*
wissen	weiß	wusste	hat gewusst	*to know*
wollen	will	wollte	hat gewollt	*to want*
ziehen	zieht	zog	hat gezogen	*to pull*

German-English Vocabulary

This German-English vocabulary is a comprehensive compilation of all active and receptive vocabulary used in *Vorsprung*. The information in brackets indicates the chapter in which the word was presented as active vocabulary. The symbol ~ represents the key word within an entry.

Nouns are preceded by the definite articles; the plural endings follow after a comma. Weak masculine nouns have the accusative, dative, and genitive endings in brackets before the plural ending, e.g., **[-en], -en.** If the plural form of a noun is rarely or never used, no plural ending is indicated. Adjectives and adverbs that take an umlaut in the comparative and superlative are shown: **alt (ä).**

Regular (weak) verbs are listed with conversational past tense forms only in parentheses, e.g., **spielen (hat gespielt).** Irregular (strong or mixed) verbs generally are listed with both the narrative and conversational past tense forms in parentheses, e.g., **ziehen (zog, hat gezogen);** if there is a present tense vowel change, the present tense will be listed before the other tenses, e.g., **geben (gibt, gab, hat gegeben).** Separable prefixes are indicated with a raised dot, e.g., **zurück·bringen.** Reflexive verbs are preceded by the reflexive pronoun **sich.**

The glossary uses the following abbreviations:

acc.	accusative
adj.	adjective
adv.	adverb
colloq.	colloquial
conj.	conjunction
dat.	dative
fam.	familiar
gen.	genitive
K.	Kapitel
pl.	plural
sing.	singular

A

ab und zu occasionally [K. 4, 11, 12]

ab·bauen (hat abgebaut) to reduce, decrease

ab·biegen (bog ab, ist abgebogen) to turn; **links/rechts ~** to turn to the left/right [K. 4]

ab·drehen (hat abgedreht) to turn off

der Abend, -e evening [K. 3, 8]; **eines Abends** one evening [K. 10]; **Guten ~!** Good Evening! [K. 1]; **der Heilige ~** Christmas Eve

das Abendbrot evening meal, supper [K. 3]

das Abendessen evening meal, supper [K. 3]

abendlich evening time

abends in the evening [K. 2]

der Abenteuerfilm, -e adventure film [K. 7]

aber but [K. 2]

ab·geben (gibt ab, gab ab, hat abgegeben) to turn in (a paper)

Abgemacht! Deal! Agreed! [K. 11]

der/die Abgeordnete, -n representative

abgetragen worn out

ab·hängen (hing ab, hat abgehangen) von + *dat.* to depend on

ab·hauen (ist abgehauen) to take off, scram [K. 10]

ab·heben (hob ab, hat abgehoben) to withdraw money [K. 7]

ab·holen (hat abgeholt) to pick up [K. 5]

das Abitur high school graduation exam [K. 8]

der Abiturient, [-en], -en/die Abiturientin, -nen high school senior, soon-to-be graduate [K. 8]

das Abkommen, - treaty [K. 11]

ab·lenken (hat abgelenkt) to divert

abnormal abnormal, unusual

die Abreise, -n departure

ab·reißen (riss ab, hat abgerissen) to tear down, demolish

der Absatz, ¨e paragraph

der Abschied farewell [K. 1]

die Abschiedsparty, -s bon voyage party

ab·schießen (schoss ab, hat abgeschossen) to shoot down

ab·schließen (schließt ab, schloss ab, hat abgeschlossen) to lock

der Abschluss, *pl.* Abschlüsse completion of program, degree

ab·schneiden (schnitt ab, hat abgeschnitten) to cut off [K. 10]; **gut ~** to place well, do well [K. 8]

ab·stammen (hat abgestammt) von + *dat.* to stem from

die Abstammung origin

ab·steigen to get off (a bike) [K. 4]

ab·stellen (hat abgestellt) to turn off

der Abstellraum, ¨e storage room [K. 6]

das Abteil, -e compartment

die Abteilung, -en department

ab·trocknen (hat abgetrocknet) to dry off [K. 8]

abwechselnd alternatingly

abwechslungsreich varied, entertaining [K. 9]

Ach so! Oh! I see! I get it! [K. 11]

acht eight [K. 1]

achten (hat geachtet) auf + *acc.* to pay attention to, watch for [K. 4, 8]

achtzehn eighteen [K. 1]

achtzig eighty [K. 1]

das Adjektiv, -e adjective

die Adresse, -n address

das Adressbuch, ¨er address book [K. 4]

der Advent Advent

das Adverb, -(i)en adverb

afrikanisch African

die AG: die Aktiengesellschaft, -en corporation

aggressiv aggressive

Aha. Oh. [K. 11]

ahnen (hat geahnt) to guess, suspect, sense [K. 11]

ähnlich similar, resembling

die Ahnung, -en foreboding, idea

die Akte, -n file

die Aktiengesellschaft, -en corporation

die Aktivität, -en activity [K. 2]

aktuell current, up-to-date [K. 8]

der Akzent, -e accent [K. 7]

akzeptabel acceptable

der Alarm alarm

der Albtraum, ¨e nightmare [K. 1]

der Alexanderplatz Alexander Square *(in Berlin)*

der Alkohol alcohol

alkoholfrei non-alcoholic

alle all, everybody [K. 6]; **aller Art** all kinds of; **vor allem** above all

allein alone [K. 2, 6]

allerdings nonetheless [AB 8]

alles everything, all [K. 6]; **~ Gute** all the best [K. 1]; **~ was du brauchst** everything you need; **~ in Ordnung** everything is in order [K. 6]; **Alles klar!** Okay!, Great! [K. 6]

die Alliierten *(pl.)* the Allies (in World War II) [K. 11]

der Alltag everyday life, routine [K. 2]; **hoch über dem ~** far beyond the everyday [K. 10]

allwissend all-knowing

die Alpen *(pl.)* the Alps

das Alphabet, -e alphabet [K. 1]

als as, than [K. 9]; when [K. 10]

also well, all right, OK *(conversation starter); well . . ., so . . . (for stalling)*

alt (ä) old [K. 1]

der Altar, ⸚e altar

das Alter age

die Altstadt historic part of town [K. 3]

am: ~ ersten Januar on the first of January [K. 2]; **~ liebsten** most of all, the most; **~ Sonntag** on (this) Sunday [K. 2]; **~ Wochenende** on the weekend [K. 2]

Amerika America [K. 11]

der Amerikaner, -/die Amerikanerin, -nen American [K. 1]

amerikanisch American; **der amerikanische Football** American football [K. 7]

die Ampel, -n traffic light; **bis zur Ampel** as far as (up to) the light [K. 7]

an at, on; to [K. 7]

analytisch analytical [K. 9]

an·bieten (bot an, hat angeboten) to offer

das Andenken, - souvenir [K. 4]

andere other [K. 9]; **unter anderem** among other things

andererseits on the other hand

ändern (hat geändert) to change

anders different(ly) [K. 8]; **~ als** different from

anderswo someplace else

die Anekdote, -n anecdote

der Anfang, ⸚e beginning; **von Anfang an** from the very beginning [K. 12]

an·fangen (fängt an, fing an, hat angefangen) to start, begin [K. 2, 3, 5]

der Anfänger, -/die Anfängerin, -nen beginner [K. 10]

angeblich supposedly

angegossen: wie ~ passen to have a perfect fit

an·gehören (hat angehört) + *dat.* to belong to

angeln to fish [K. 3]

angenehm pleasant; **Sehr ~!** Pleased to meet you! [K. 1]

der/die Angestellte, -n *(adj. as noun)* employee [K. 9]

der Anglist, [-en], -en/die Anglistin, -nen English major

die Anglistik English language and literature

an·glotzen (hat angeglotzt) to stare at

die Angst, ⸚e fear, anxiety [K. 2]

Angst haben (hat, hatte, hat gehabt) vor + *dat.* to be afraid of [K. 2, 4, 8]

an·halten (hält an, hielt an, hat angehalten) to stop [K. 4]

der Anhänger, -/die Anhängerin, -nen follower, supporter [K. 7]

sich an·hören (hat sich angehört) to sound like [K. 11]

an·kommen (kam an, ist angekommen) to arrive [K. 2], to meet expectations [K. 7]; **~ auf + *acc.*** to depend on [K. 11]

an·kreuzen (hat angekreuzt) to check (off)

die Ankunft, ⸚e arrival

der Anlauftext start-up text

an·melden (hat angemeldet) to announce, register [K. 8]

die Annonce, -n want ad

der Anorak, -s parka [K. 10]

an·pöbeln (hat angepöbelt) to pester

an·probieren (hat anprobiert) to try on [K. 10]

an·reden (hat angeredet) to address

die Anreise arrival

an·rufen (rief an, hat angerufen) to phone, call up [K. 2]

an·schauen (hat angeschaut) to (take a) look at [K. 6]; **schief ~** to look at (someone) funny [K. 6]

der Anschluss *pl.* **Anschlüsse** (train) connection

die Ansichtskarte, -n picture postcard

an·sprechen (spricht an, sprach an, hat angesprochen) to initiate a conversation

anspruchsvoll demanding; sophisticated

anständig decent, respectable [K. 9]

an·starren (hat angestarrt) to stare at

anstatt + *gen.* instead of [K. 8]

anstelle von instead of

die Antwort, -en answer

antworten (hat geantwortet) to answer [K. 1]

die Anweisung, -en direction

die Anzeige, -n ad

sich an·ziehen (zog sich an, hat sich angezogen) to put on clothes, get dressed [K. 8]

der Anzug, ⸚e suit [K. 4]

der Apfel, ⸚ apple [K. 3]

die Apfelsine, -n orange [K. 3]

die Apotheke, -n pharmacy, drug store [K. 7]

der Apotheker, -/die Apothekerin, -nen pharmacist [K. 9]

Appetit: Guten ~! Bon appetit!, Enjoy your meal! [K. 6]

der April April [K. 2]

das Äquivalent, -e equivalent

das Arabisch Arabic

die Arbeit, -en work [K. 9]

arbeiten (hat gearbeitet) to work [K. 5]

der Arbeiter, -/die Arbeiterin, -nen worker [K. 9]

das Arbeitsamt, ⸚er (un)employment agency

das Arbeitsangebot, -e job offer

das Arbeitsbuch, ⸚er workbook [K. 1]

die Arbeitserfahrung, -en work experience [K. 9]

die Arbeitsgruppe, -n study group [K. 8]

das Arbeitsklima work environment

arbeitslos unemployed

die Arbeitsnorm, -en work quota/standard

der Arbeitsplatz, ⸚e job; place of work

der Arbeitstag, -e work day [K. 2]

die Arbeitsvermittlung, -en job placement agency

das Arbeitszimmer, - workroom; study

der Architekt, [-en], -en/die Architektin, -nen architect [K. 9]

der Ärger annoyance

sich ärgern (hat sich geärgert) über + *acc.* to be angry about [K. 8]

der Arm, -e arm [K. 6]

arm (ä) poor [K. 10]

die Armbanduhr, -en wristwatch

die Armee, -n army [K. 11]; **die Rote ~** Red Army

die Art, -en kind, type [K. 7, 10]

der Artikel, - article; **der bestimmte ~** definite article; **der unbestimmte ~** indefinite article

der Arzt, ⸚e/die Ärztin, -nen physician [K. 8, 9]

die Asche, -n ash, cinder [K. 10]

Aschenputtel Cinderella; **der Aschermittwoch** Ash Wednesday

asiatisch Asian

der Aspekt, -e aspect [K. 12]

das Aspirin aspirin

der Assistent, [-en], -en/die Assistentin, -nen assistant

die Astronomie astronomy

attraktiv attractive (for females) [K. 1, 5]

auch also [K. 2]

auf on, onto [K. 7]; **~ dem Dachboden** in the attic; **~ Deutsch** in German

auf·bleiben (blieb auf, ist aufgeblieben) to stay up

auf·decken (hat aufgedeckt) to reveal [K. 11]

der Aufenthalt, -e stay, time spent in a place

auf·fallen (fällt auf, fiel auf, ist aufgefallen) + dat. to occur to s.o. [K. 11]

die Aufführung, -en performance [K. 9]

auf·führen (hat aufgeführt) to perform [K. 9]

die Aufgabe, -n assignment, task [K. 9]

auf·geben (gibt auf, gab auf, hat aufgegeben) to drop off, post; to give up [K. 5]

aufgeregt excited; tense, nervous [K. 4, 9]

aufgrund on the basis of

auf·hängen (hat aufgehängt) to hang up

auf·hören (hat aufgehört) to stop [K. 2]

auf·kriegen (hat aufgekriegt) to get open *(colloq.)* [K. 6]

auf·machen (hat aufgemacht) to open [K. 1]

auf·passen (hat aufgepasst) auf + acc. to watch out for, pay attention to [K. 4]; **Pass mal auf!** Look here! [K. 11]

auf·räumen (hat aufgeräumt) to pick up, clean up

aufrecht·erhalten (erhält aufrecht, erhielt aufrecht, hat aufrecht-erhalten) to maintain, preserve

sich auf·regen (hat sich aufgeregt) to get upset, nervous; to get excited

die Aufregung -en excitement; nervousness

auf·schauen (hat aufgeschaut) to look up

auf·schließen (hat aufgeschlossen) to unlock [K. 6]

der Aufschnitt cold cuts [K. 3]

auf·schreiben (schrieb auf, hat aufgeschrieben) to write down [K. 6]

der Aufstand, ¨e revolt, uprising [K. 11]

auf·stehen (steht auf, stand auf, ist aufgestanden) to get up, get out of bed [K. 1, 2] **Stehen Sie Auf!** Stand up.

der Auftrag, ¨e assignment

auf·wachen (ist aufgewacht) to wake up [K. 2]

auf·wachsen (wächst auf, wuchs auf, ist aufgewachsen) to grow up [K. 11]

auf·wärmen (hat aufgewärmt) to warm up

Auf Wiedersehen! Good-bye. [K. 1]

das Auge, -n eye [K. 1, 6]

die Augenbraue, -n eyebrow

der August August [K. 2]

aus + dat. from [K. 6]

die Ausbildung, -en education, job training [K. 9]

der Ausbildungsleiter, -/die Ausbildungsleiterin, -nen head trainer, lead teacher

der Ausdruck, ¨e expression

aus·fahren (fährt aus, fuhr aus, ist ausgefahren) to deliver

aus·fallen (fällt aus, fiel aus, ist ausgefallen) to be canceled

ausführlich detailed [K. 12]

aus·füllen (hat ausgefüllt) to fill out

aus·geben (gibt aus, gab aus, hat aus·gegeben) to spend (money) [K. 4]

ausgeglichen similar, uniform [K. 11]

aus·gehen (ging aus, ist ausgegangen) to go out [K. 5]

ausgesprochen decidedly

ausgezeichnet excellent

die Aushilfe, -n temporary, part-time worker [K. 9]

sich aus·kennen (hat sich ausgekannt) mit + dat. to know a lot about

aus·kommen (kam aus, ist ausgekommen) mit + dat. to get along with [K. 9]

das Ausland abroad; foreign country; **ohne im Ausland zu wohnen** without living abroad [K. 12]

der Ausländer, -/die Ausländerin, -nen foreigner [K. 6]

die Ausländerfeindlichkeit xenophobia [K. 6]

ausländisch foreign [K. 6]

aus·liegen (lag aus, hat ausgelegen) to be displayed

aus·machen (hat ausgemacht) to finalize, e.g., a date [K. 5]

die Ausnahme, -n exception

die Ausrede, -n excuse; **Ausreden machen (hat gemacht)** to make excuses

aus·rufen (rief aus, hat ausgerufen) to proclaim, announce [K. 11]

sich aus·ruhen (hat sich ausgeruht) to relax [K. 8]

aus·schalten (hat ausgeschaltet) to turn off [K. 5]

aus·schreiben (schrieb aus, hat ausgeschrieben) to advertise, announce

die Aussage, -n statement

das Aussehen appearance [K. 1]

aus·sehen (sieht aus, sah aus, hat ausgesehen) to appear, look (like) [K. 1, 5]

der Außenminister, -/die Außen-ministerin, -nen foreign minister

außer + dat. except for [K. 6]

außerdem besides, by the way

außerhalb + gen. outside of [K. 10]

die Aussicht, -en view [K. 3]; prospect, view

aus·steigen (stieg aus, ist ausgestiegen) to get out of, disembark [K. 10]

aus·stellen (hat ausgestellt) to exhibit [K. 9]

der Austausch exchange; **das Austauschprogramm, -e** study-abroad exchange program [K. 6]; **der Austauschstudent, [-en], -en/die Austauschstudentin, -nen** exchange student [K. 6]

aus·tragen (trägt aus, trug aus, hat ausgetragen) to deliver

(das) Australien Australia [K. 2]

aus·üben (hat ausgeübt): einen Beruf ~ to practice, pursue [a profession]

die Auswahl selection

aus·wählen (hat ausgewählt) to pick out, select

aus·wandern (ist ausgewandert) to emigrate [K. 12]

der Ausweis, -e identification card [K. 4]

auswendig by heart, memorized

die Auszeichnung award, recognition

sich aus·ziehen (zog sich aus, hat sich ausgezogen) to get undressed [K. 8]

der/die Auszubildende, -n (Azubi) (adj. as noun) apprentice [K. 8, 9]

authentisch authentic

das Auto, -s automobile, car [K. 4]; **~ fahren** to drive a car

die Autobahn, -en autobahn, superhighway [K. 4]

die Autobiografie, -n autobiography [K. 7]

der Autobus, -se bus [K. 4]

autofrei car-free

das Autogrammspiel, -e autograph game

der Automat, [-en], -en vending machine [K. 6]

der Automechaniker, -/die Automechanikerin, -nen car mechanic [K. 9]

der **Autor**, -en/die **Autorin**,
-nen author
der **Autoschlüssel**, - car key
der/die **Azubi**, -s apprentice

B

babysitten (hat gebabysittet) to
baby-sit
der **Babysitter**, -/die **Babysitterin**,
-nen baby-sitter [K. 9]
der **Bach**, ̈e brook
backen (bäckt/backt, backte, hat
gebacken) to bake
der **Bäcker**, -/die **Bäckerin**, -nen baker
[K. 9]
die **Bäckerei**, -en bakery [K. 7]
das **Bad**, ̈er bath [K. 6]
der **Badeanzug**, ̈e (woman's) bathing
suit [K. 4]
die **Badehose**, -n (man's) bathing suit
[K. 4]
sich baden (hat sich gebadet) to bathe
[K. 8]
das **Badetuch**, ̈er bath towel [K. 8]
die **Badewanne**, -n bathtub [K. 8]
das **Badezimmer**, - bathroom [K. 6]
das **BAföG** federal tuition assistance,
financial aid
die **Bahn**, -en railroad, train [K. 4] **mit
der ~ fahren** to travel by train [K. 4]
die **Bahncard** discount rail pass
der **Bahnhof**, ̈e train station [K. 3]; **~
verstehen** to not have a clue
das **Bähnli**, -s little train (Swiss dialect)
bald soon [K. 2, 5]
der **Balkon**, -s (-e) balcony [K. 6]
der **Ball**, ̈e ball, dance [K. 10]
das **Ballett**, -e ballet [K. 9]
die **Banane**, -n banana [K. 3]
die **Bandbreite** range
die **Bank**, -en bank [K. 7]
die **Bankkarte**, -n bank card, ATM
card [K. 4, 7]
der **Bankkredit**, -e bank loan [K. 10]
die **Bar**, -s bar [K. 6]
das **Bargeld** cash [K. 7]
das **Barock** Baroque
die **Barriere**, -n barrier
der **Baseball** baseball [K. 3]
der **Basketball** basketball [K. 3]
der **Bauch**, ̈e stomach [K. 6]
bauen (hat gebaut) to construct, build
[K. 9]
der **Bauer**, [-n], -n/die **Bäuerin**,
-nen farmer
der **Baum**, ̈e tree [K. 10]
(das) **Bayern** Bavaria

beachten (hat beachtet) to observe,
pay attention to [K. 4]
der **Beamer** computer projector [K. 1]
der **Beamte**, [-n] -n/die **Beamtin**,
-nen civil servant, official
der **Becher**, - cup ceramic, paper)
[K. 3, 8]
der **Bedarf** need [K. 7]
sich bedanken (hat sich bedankt) für
+ acc. to thank for (something)
[K. 12]
bedeckt overcast [K. 5]
bedeuten (hat bedeutet) to mean [K. 4]
das **Bedürfnis**, -se need
sich beeilen (hat sich beeilt) to hurry
[K. 8]
beeindrucken (hat beeindruckt) to
impress [K. 9]
beeindruckend impressive
der **Befehl**, -e command
befehlen (befiehlt, befahl, hat
befohlen) to command
die **Beförderung**, -en advancement,
promotion
begabt talented [K. 9]
begegnen (ist begegnet) + dat. to
meet, run into
begeistert enthusiastic, excited
beginnen (begann, hat begonnen) to
begin [K. 2, 5]
begleiten (hat begleitet) to accompany
begraben to bury; buried
begrenzen (hat begrenzt) to limit [K. 5]
begrenzt limited
der **Begriff**, -e concept, term [K. 7]
der **Begründer**, - founder [K. 9]
behalten (behält, behielt, hat
behalten) to keep [K. 7]
behandeln (hat behandelt) to treat
behaupten (hat behauptet) to claim,
maintain
beheizt heated
bei + dat. at, by, near, with [K. 6]
beide both [K. 5]
beige beige [K. 1]
das **Bein**, -e leg [K. 6]
das **Beispiel**, -e example [K. 2]; **zum ~
(z.B.)** for example [K. 2]
bei·treten (tritt bei, trat bei, ist
beigetreten) + dat. to join,
become a member [K. 11]
bekannt familiar, well-known [K. 8]
der/die **Bekannte**, -n (adj. as
noun) acquaintance [K. 5]
bekannt geben (gibt bekannt, gab
bekannt, hat bekannt gegeben) to
announce, reveal [K. 5]
die **Bekanntschaft**,
-en acquaintanceship

bekommen (bekam, hat
bekommen) to get, receive [K. 5]
belegen (hat belegt) to enroll in
(das) **Belgien** Belgium
beliebt popular
bemerkenswert noteworthy
die **Bemerkung**, -en observation
benachrichtigen (hat
benachrichtigt) to inform
das **Benehmen** behavior
sich benehmen (benimmt sich, benahm
sich, hat sich benommen) to
behave
benötigen (hat benötigt) to require, need
benutzen (hat benutzt) to use [K. 4]
das **Benzin** gasoline [K. 4]
bequem comfortable
der **Berater**, -/die **Beraterin**,
-nen counselor, advisor
die **Beratung** counseling
der **Bereich**, -e area, region [K. 12]
bereit ready
der **Berg**, -e mountain [K. 10]
berg·steigen (ist berggestiegen) to go
mountainclimbing
die **Bergwirtschaft**, -en mountain
restaurant
der **Bericht**, -e report [K. 12]
berichten (hat berichtet) to report
[K. 12]
der **Beruf**, -e profession, job,
occupation [K. 9]
die **Berufsschule**, -n technical-
vocational high school
sich beruhigen (hat sich beruhigt) to
calm down [K. 9]
berühmt famous [K. 8]
die **Besatzungszone**, -n occupation
zone [K. 11]
Bescheid bekommen (hat Bescheid
bekommen) to get an answer, be
notified
beschreiben (beschrieb, hat
beschrieben) to describe [K. 4]
besetzen (hat besetzt) to occupy [K. 11]
besichtigen (hat besichtigt) to visit,
look at [K. 11]
besitzen (besaß, hat besessen) to own,
to have
der **Besitzer**, -/die **Besitzerin**,
-nen owner
besonders especially [K. 4]
besorgen (hat besorgt) to acquire, get
besprechen (bespricht, besprach, hat
besprochen) to discuss [K. 12]
die **Besprechung**, -en discussion
besser better [K. 2, 3]
Besserung: Gute ~! Speedy recovery!
[K. 8]

best- best; **am besten** best of all [K. 9]

die Bestandsaufnahme assessment

das Beste the best (thing)

bestellen (hat bestellt) to order [K. 5]

bestimmen (hat bestimmt) to determine

bestimmt undoubtedly [K. 3]

bestrafen (hat bestraft) to punish

der Bestseller, - bestseller

besuchen (hat besucht) to visit [K. 2, 3]

der Besucher, -/die Besucherin, -nen visitor

beten (hat gebetet) to pray [K. 10]

betrachten (hat betrachtet) to view

betreuen (hat betreut) to take care of

der Betreuer, -/die Betreuerin, -nen person in charge

der Betrieb, -e business

die Betriebswirtschaft business administration [K. 2]

das Bett, -en bed [K. 3, 6]

bevor before [K. 3, 5]

die Bewegung, -en movement, motion

der Beweis, -e proof

beweisen (bewies, hat bewiesen) to prove

sich bewerben (bewirbt sich, bewarb sich, hat sich beworben) an to apply to [K. 9]; ~ um/für + acc. to apply for [K. 9]

der Bewerber, -/die Bewerberin, -nen applicant [K.9]

die Bewerbung, -en application

der Bewerbungsbrief, -e letter of application [K. 9]

das Bewerbungsformular, -e application form

bewerkstelligen (hat bewerkstelligt) to manage, take care of

bewerten (hat bewertet) to evaluate

bewirtet meals included

bewölkt cloudy, overcast [K. 5]

bewundern (hat bewundert) to admire [K. 9]

bezahlbar payable

bezahlen (hat bezahlt) to pay [K. 4]

beziehen (bezog, hat bezogen) to move in

die Beziehung, -en contact, relationship, relation [K. 5, 12]; **internationale Beziehungen** (pl.) international relations [K. 2]

Bezug: in ~ auf in regard to [K. 12]; **auf etwas ~ nehmen** to refer to

das Bezugswort, ¨er antecedent

die Bibliothek, -en library [K. 3]

der Bibliothekar, -/die Bibliothekarin, -nen librarian

das Bibliothekarswesen library science

das Bier beer [K. 3]

die Bierbrauerei, -en brewery

das Bierzelt, -e beer tent

bieten (bot, hat geboten) to offer [K. 9]

das Bild, -er picture [K. 6]

bilden (hat gebildet) to construct, form

billig cheap, inexpensive [K. 7]

die Biografie, -n biography [K. 7]

der Bioladen, ¨ health food store [K. 7]

die Biologie biology [K. 2]

bis until, as far as; ~ gleich! See you soon! [K. 6]; **bis zur Ampel** as far as the traffic light [K. 7]

bisschen: ein ~ a little [K. 2]

bitte please [K. 1], you're welcome; ~ schön! There you are!

die Bitte, -n request [K. 2]

bitten (bat, hat gebeten) um + acc. to ask for, request [K. 8]

das Blatt, ¨er page, sheet

blättern (hat geblättert) in + dat. to leaf through

blau blue [K. 1]

bleiben (blieb, ist geblieben) to stay, remain [K. 2]

der Bleistift, -e pencil [K. 1]

blitzen (hat geblitzt) to have lightning [K. 5]

das Blitzlicht, -er flash (for a camera)

die Blockade, -n blockade [K. 11]

blond blond [K. 1]

die Blume, -n flower [K. 6]

die Bluse, -n blouse [K. 4]

das Blut blood [K. 10]

der Boden (pl. Böden) floor, ground [K. 6]

der Bombenangriff, -e bombardment, bombing attack

die Bordkarte, -n boarding pass [K. 4]

die Börse stock market

böse angry [K. 5]; ~ sein (war, ist gewesen) auf + acc. to be upset with, mad at

die Bosheit, -en meanspiritedness

der Boss, pl. Bosse boss

boxen (hat geboxt) to box, hit

Brandenburg Brandenburg

das Brandenburger Tor Brandenburg Gate (in Berlin) [K. 11]

die Bratwurst, ¨e bratwurst, fried sausage [K. 3]

brauchen (hat gebraucht) to need [K. 4]; **ich brauche nicht** I don't have to [K. 4]

braun brown [K. 1]

die Braut, ¨e bride [K. 10]

sich etwas brechen (bricht sich, brach sich, hat sich gebrochen) to break [K. 8]

brennen (brannte, hat gebrannt) to burn [K. 10]

Brett: das schwarze ~ bulletin board [K. 6]

die Brezel, -n pretzel

der Brief, -e letter [K. 4]

die Briefmarke, -n stamp [K. 7]

die Brille, (sg) glasses [K. 1]

bringen (brachte, hat gebracht) to bring [K. 5]

die Brokkoli (pl.) broccoli

die Broschüre, -n brochure

das Brot, -e bread [K. 3]

das Brötchen, - hard roll [K. 3]; **ein belegtes ~** roll spread with cold cuts, slice of cheese, etc. [K. 3]

die Brücke, -n bridge [K. 3]

der Bruder, ¨ brother [K. 2]

die Brüderschaft brotherhood, fraternity

brüllen (hat gebrüllt) to yell, scream

die Brust, ¨e breast, chest [K. 6]

das Buch, ¨er book, textbook [K. 1]

das Bücherregal, -e bookcase [K. 6]

der Buchhalter, -/die Buchhalterin, -nen accountant

die Buchhandlung, -en bookstore [K. 7]

buchstabieren (hat buchstabiert) to spell

die Bude, -n student room (colloq.) [K. 6]

die Bühne, -n stage [K. 9]

der Bummel, - walk, leisurely stroll [K. 11]

bummeln (ist gebummelt) to stroll [K. 11]

der Bund alliance; Federal Government

der Bundeskanzler, -/die Bundeskanzlerin, -nen Federal Chancellor [K. 11]

das Bundesland, ¨er state, province [K. 3]

der Bundespräsident, (-en), -en/die Bundespräsidentin, -nen Federal President [K. 11]

der Bundesrat Federal Council

die Bundesregierung Federal Government

die Bundesrepublik Deutschland Federal Republic of Germany [K. 11]

der Bundestag Federal Parliament [K. 11]

der Bürger, -/die Bürgerin,
   -nen citizen
der Bürgermeister, -/die
   Bürgermeisterin, -nen mayor
das Büro, -s office [K. 7]
die Bürste, -n (hair)brush
sich bürsten (hat sich gebürstet): sich
   die Haare bürsten to brush one's
   hair [K. 8]
der Bus, -se bus
die Bushaltestelle, -n bus stop
die Butter butter [K. 3]

C

das Café, -s café [K. 3]
der Campingplatz, ̈-e campground
   [K. 3]
der Campus campus
die CD, -s CD [K. 4]
der CD-Player, - CD player [K. 4]
Celsius Centigrade
die Chance, -n chance [K. 7]
(die) Chanukka Chanukah [K. 10]
chaotisch chaotic
der Chef, -s/die Chefin, -nen boss
   [K. 9]
die Chemie chemistry [K. 2]
chinesisch Chinese [K. 2]
der Chor, ̈-e chorus, choir
das Christentum Christianity
das Christkind Christ child
die Christlich-Demokratische Union
   (CDU) Christian Democratic
   Union
die Christlich-Soziale Union
   (CSU) Christian Social Union
die Clique, -n clique, circle of friends
der Club, -s club
die Cola, -s cola [K. 3]
der Computer, - computer [K. 1, 6]
das Comicheft, -e comic book
Confoederatio Helvetica Switzerland
die Couch, -s (-en) couch [K. 6]
der Cousin, -s male cousin [K. 2]
die Cousine, -n female cousin [K. 2]

D

da there [K. 1]
dabei sein to participate in something
der Dachboden, ̈ attic [K. 6];
   auf dem ~ in the attic [K. 6]
dagegen against it
daheim at home
daher for that reason, that's why
damals back then [K. 10]

die Dame, -n lady
damit so that [K. 7]
danach afterwards [K. 3]
(das) Dänemark Denmark
der Dank thanks; **Vielen ~!** Thanks a
   lot! [K. 6]
danke thanks, thank you [K. 1]; **~**
   schön! Thanks a lot! [K. 1]
danken (hat gedankt) + *dat.* to thank
   [K. 6]; **~ für +** *acc.* to thank for
dann then
darf may, be permitted
darüber about it
das the *(neuter)* [K. 1]
das Date, -s date [K. 5]
das Datum, *pl.* **Daten** date
dass that *(conj.)* [K. 5]
dauern (hat gedauert) to last [K. 6, 7]
dauernd continuously
die Daumen drücken (hat gedrückt) +
   dat. to cross one's finger for [K. 9]
dazu·kommen (kam dazu, ist
   dazugekommen) to get to; to
   arrive at
der Deckel, - lid, top
dein your *(fam. sing.)* [K. 3]
der Dekan, -e dean
die Demokratie, -n democracy
denken (dachte, hat gedacht) to think
   [K. 4]; **~ an +** *acc.* to think of [K. 4]
das Denkmal, ̈-er monument [K. 9]
denn for, because; then [K. 3]
das Deo deodorant [K. 4]
deprimierend depressing [K. 11]
der the *(masc.)* [K. 1]
deren whose [K. 10]
deshalb that's (the reason) why
dessen whose [K. 10]
deswegen that's why, for that reason,
   therefore [K. 8, 11]
das Detail, -s detail
der Detektiv, -e detective
deutlich clear [K. 5]
(das) Deutsch the German language
   [K. 2]; **auf Deutsch** in German
   [K. 2]
der/die Deutsche, -n *(adj. as*
   noun) German [K. 1]
die Deutsche Demokratische Republik
   (DDR) German Democratic
   Republic (GDR) [K. 11]
das Deutsche Reich German Empire
der Deutschkurs, -e German language
   course
(das) Deutschland Germany [K. 1]
die Deutschprüfung, -en German test
der Deutschunterricht German class
der Dezember December [K. 2]
der Dialekt, -e dialect [K. 12]

dich you *(informal sing., acc.)* [K. 2]
der Dichter, -/die Dichterin,
   -nen poet [K. 9]
die the *(fem., plural)* [K.1]
die Diele, -n entrance hallway [K. 6]
dienen (hat gedient) to serve
der Dienstag, -e Tuesday [K. 2]
d.h. das heißt, that is
dieser, diese, dieses this, that *(pl.* these,
   those) [K. 6]
der Diktator, -en dictator [K. 11]
die Diktatur, -en dictatorship
das Ding, -e object, thing [K. 6]
der Dinosaurier, - dinosaur
das Diplom, -e diploma [K. 8]
dir (to, for) you *(informal sing., dat.)*
   [K. 6]
der Dirigent, [-en], -en/die Dirigentin,
   -nen orchestra conductor
die Diskothek, -en (die
   Disko) discotheque, disco
der Diskurs, -e discourse
die Diskussion, -en discussion
diskutieren (hat diskutiert) über +
   acc. to discuss [K. 5]
die Disziplin discipline [K. 7]
diszipliniert disciplined [K. 9]
doch go ahead and . . . *(persuasive*
   particle) [K. 2]; Oh, yes it is!
   (response to negative statement)
der Doktortitel,- doctorate, Ph.D.
der Dokumentarfilm, -e documentary
   film [K. 7]
der Dom, -e cathedral [K. 11]
dominieren (hat dominiert) to
   dominate [K. 9]
dominant dominant [K. 12]
die Donau Danube River
donnern (hat gedonnert) to thunder
   [K. 5]
der Donnerstag, -e Thursday [K. 2]
doof goofy [K. 4]
das Doppelbett, -en double bed
der Doppelinfinitiv, -e double
   infinitive
das Dorf, ̈-er village [K. 10]
dort there; **~ drüben** over there
der Dozent, [-en], -en/die Dozentin,
   -nen assistant professor, instructor
   [K. 8]
das Drama, *pl.* **Dramen** drama, play
   [K. 7]
dran sein: Sie sind dran. It's your turn.
der Dreck dirt, mud [K. 7]
drehen (hat gedreht): einen Film ~ über
   + *acc.* to make a movie about
drei three [K. 1]
dreißig thirty [K. 1]
dreizehn thirteen [K. 1]

dringlich urgent, pressing
drinnen inside
dröhnen (hat gedröhnt) to drone [K. 10]
der Druck pressure
drückend depressing [K. 11]
der Drucker, - printer [K. 6]
drunter (darunter) down below
du you *(informal sing.)* [K. 1]; Hey . . . *(used to introduce an utterance)*
dumm (ü) dumb, stupid [K. 4]
dunkel dark [K. 1]
dunkelgrau dark gray [K. 1]
durch + *acc.* through [K. 4];
durcheinander messy
der Durchfall diarrhea [K. 8]
durch·gucken (hat durchgeguckt) to look through, look over
durch·machen (hat durchgemacht) to stay up, get through
durchschnittlich on average [K. 6]
durch·streichen (strich durch, hat durchgestrichen) to cross out
dürfen (darf, durfte, hat gedurft) may; to be allowed to, permitted to [K. 4]; **ich darf nicht** I must not [K. 4]
der Durst thirst; **~ haben** to be thirsty [K. 4]
die Dusche, -n shower [K. 6]
(sich) duschen (hat sich geduscht) to shower [K. 8]
der Duschraum, ¨e shower room [K. 6]
die DVD, -s DVD
der DVD-Spieler, - DVD player [K. 1]
dynamisch dynamic [K. 9]

E

eben just
echt authentic, genuine; real(ly) [K. 10, 12] **echt nett** really nice [K. 12]
die Ecke, -n corner; **an der ~** at the corner; **um die ~** around the corner [K. 7]
der Edelmann, ¨er nobleman
der Edelstein, -e jewel, precious stone [K. 10]
egal no difference [K. 6]
ehemalig former(ly), previous(ly) [K. 10, 11]
eher rather; sooner
ehrlich honest
das Ei, -er egg [K. 3]; **weich (hart) gekochtes ~** softboiled (hard-boiled) egg [K. 3]
eifersüchtig jealous
eigen own [K. 10]

die Eigenschaft, -en personal trait, quality, characteristic [K. 4]
eigentlich actually [K. 5]
die Eile hurry; **~ haben** to be in a hurry
der Eilzug, ¨e fast train
ein, eine a, an [K. 1]
einander one another, each other [K. 5]
die Einbahnstraße, -n one-way street
der Eindruck, ¨e impression [K. 9, 11]
einerseits on the one hand [K. 11]
einfach simple, simply [K. 5]
die Einfahrt, -en entry
ein·fallen (fällt ein, fiel ein, ist eingefallen) + *dat.* to think of something, get an idea, occur to
einfallslos uncreative [K. 4]
das Einfamilienhaus, ¨er single-family house [K. 6]
der Einfluss, *pl.* **Einflüsse** influence
der Eingang, ¨e entrance, front door [K. 6]
eingestellt: ~ sein auf to be geared for, ready for
die Einheit, -en unity [K. 11]
einige a few, several
ein·kaufen (hat eingekauft) to shop [K. 2]
Einkaufs... *(in compounds)* shopping; **der Einkaufsbummel, -** shopping trip; **der Einkaufskorb, ¨e** shopping basket; **das Einkaufsnetz, -e** mesh shopping bag [K. 7]; **die Einkaufstasche, -n** shopping bag; **die Einkaufstüte, -n** shopping bag; **das Einkaufszentrum,** *pl.* **-zentren** shopping center, mall [K. 11]
ein·laden (lädt ein, lud ein, hat eingeladen) to invite; to take out [K. 5]
die Einladung, -en invitation [K. 5]
einmal once [K. 7]
einmalig unique [K. 9]
einminütig one-minute
die Einreise, -n arrival
ein·richten (hat eingerichtet) to set up, institute
eins one [K. 1]
einsam lonely [K. 5]
ein·schlafen (schläft ein, schlief ein, ist eingeschlafen) to fall asleep
ein·schlagen (schlägt ein, schlug ein, ist eingeschlagen) to strike, impact
ein·schließen (schloss ein, hat eingeschlossen) to include; to lock up
sich ein·schreiben (schrieb sich ein, hat sich eingeschrieben) to register, to enroll [K. 8]

ein·setzen (hat eingesetzt) to start
ein·steigen (stieg ein, ist eingestiegen) to get into a vehicle, board, climb in [K. 10]
ein·stellen (hat eingestellt) to hire, to implement, utlilize [K. 7]
die Einstellung, -en attitude, outlook [K. 11]
ein·tauschen (hat eingetauscht) to exchange
der Eintopf, ¨e stew
der Eintrag, ¨e entry
ein·weihen (hat eingeweiht) to dedicate [K. 11]
der Einwohner, -/die Einwohnerin, -nen inhabitant [K. 3]
ein·zahlen (hat eingezahlt) to deposit (money) [K. 7]
das Einzelzimmer, - single room [K. 6]
ein·ziehen (zog ein, ist eingezogen) to move in [K. 5, 6]; to deposit
einzig single; only [K. 9]
einzigartig unique, singular
der Einzug the move into a house/an apartment
das Eis ice; ice cream [K. 3]
die Eisenbahn railroad, train
der Eisenbahnzug, ¨e train
das Eishockey ice hockey [K. 7]
der Eiskunstlauf figure skating
der Eiskunstläufer, -/die Eiskunst-läuferin, -nen figure skater
das Eisstadion, *pl.* **-stadien** skating rink
die Elbe Elbe River
elegant elegant
elf eleven [K. 1]
der Ellenbogen, - elbow
die Eltern *(pl.)* parents [K. 2]
die E-Mail/Mail e-mail (message) **das E-Mail** e-mail (concept) [K. 2]
der Empfänger, - recipient
empfehlen (empfiehlt, empfahl, hat empfohlen) to recommend [K. 7]
die Empfehlung, -en recommendation [K. 9]
sich empören (hat sich empört) to become indignant
das Ende, -n end
endgültig final
endlich finally [K. 2, 6]
die »Endlösung« "final solution"
eng narrow [K. 6]
(das) England England [K. 1]
der Engländer, -/die Engländerin, -nen English person [K. 1]
(das) Englisch the English language [K. 2]
der Enkel, -/die Enkelin, -nen grandson/granddaughter [K. 2]

das Enkelkind, -er grandchild [K. 2]

entdecken (hat entdeckt) to discover [K. 7]

die Entdeckung, -en discovery

entfernt distant [K. 12]

enthalten (enthält, enthielt, hat enthalten) to contain

sich entscheiden (entschied sich, hat sich entschieden) für/gegen + *acc.* to decide on/against [K. 8]

die Entscheidung, -en decision

entschuldigen (hat entschuldigt) to excuse, pardon [K. 11]

die Entschuldigung, -en excuse **Entschuldigung!** Pardon! Excuse me! [K. 1, 6]

die Entspannung relaxation [K. 10]

entsprechend appropriate(ly)

entstehen (entstand, ist entstanden) to originate; to be built, to rise, result [K. 11]

enttäuscht disappointed [K. 5]

entweder... oder either . . . or

entwickeln (hat entwickelt) to develop

die Entwicklung, -en development [K. 7]

er he, it [K. 1]

erarbeiten (hat erarbeitet) to acquire, work out

die Erbse, -n pea [K. 3]

das Erdgeschoss, -e ground floor [K. 6]; **im~** on the ground floor [K. 6]

die Erdkunde geography

das Ereignis, -se event

erdrücken (hat erdrückt) to crush; to overwhelm

erfahren (erfährt, erfuhr, hat erfahren) to experience [K. 5, 12]

die Erfahrung, -en experience [K. 6]

erfinden (erfand, hat erfunden) to invent; **sich neu ~** to reinvent oneself

der Erfinder, - inventor [K. 9]

der Erfolg, -e success; winning [K. 7]

erfolgreich successful [K. 12]

erfordern (hat erfordert) to request, demand [K. 7]

erfüllen (hat erfüllt) to fulfill, complete [K. 6]

erfunden made-up, invented

ergänzen (hat ergänzt) to complete

sich ergeben (ergibt sich, ergab sich, hat sich ergeben) to materialize, result

das Ergebnis, -se result [K. 8]

erhöhen (hat erhöht) to raise, increase

sich erholen (hat sich erholt) to recuperate [K. 8]

sich erinnern (hat sich erinnert) an + *acc.* to remember [K. 8]

das Erinnerungsstück, -e keepsake [K. 9]

sich erkälten (hat sich erkältet) to catch cold [K. 8]

die Erkältung, -en common cold [K. 8]

erkennen (erkannte, hat erkannt) to recognize [K. 10]

erklären (hat erklärt) to explain [K. 7, 12]; **~für +** *acc.* to describe

erlauben (hat erlaubt) to permit, allow [K. 10]

erlaubt allowed, permitted

erläutern (hat erläutert) to explain

erleben (hat erlebt) to experience [K. 10, 12]

das Erlebnis, -se experience [K. 11]

erlebnisvoll eventful

erledigen (hat erledigt) to take care of, deal with [K. 7]

ernst serious [K. 4, 5]

erobern (hat erobert) to conquer, capture [K. 9, 11]

eröffnen (hat eröffnet) to open; **ein Konto ~** to open an account [K. 7]

erraten (errät, erriet, hat erraten) to guess

erreichen (hat erreicht) to reach [K. 11]

erschießen (erschoss, hat erschossen) to shoot to death

erschließen (erschloss, hat erschlossen) to figure out, understand

erst not until; first [K. 5]; **erst seit** just since [K. 5]

erstaunt astonished [K. 10]

ertragen (erträgt, ertrug, hat ertragen) to tolerate, bear [K. 12]

erträglich tolerable, manageable

erwachsen grown-up, adult [K. 10]

erwähnen (hat erwähnt) to mention

erwarten (hat erwartet) von + *dat.* to expect of [K. 8]

die Erwartung, -en expectation

erweitern (hat erweitert) to expand

erwünscht desired, sought

erzählen (hat erzählt) von + *dat.* to talk/tell a story about [K. 5]

die Erzählung, -en story [K. 7]

erzeugen (hat erzeugt) to create

erziehen (erzog, hat erzogen) to raise (children)

erzielen (hat erzielt) to strive for

es it [K. 2]

essen (isst, aß, hat gegessen) to eat [K. 3]

das Essen food

die Etage, -n floor; **die erste (zweite) ~** second (third) floor

etwas some, somewhat [K. 2]; some(thing) [K. 3]; **~ anderes** something else

euch (to, for) you *(informal pl. acc./ dat.)* [K. 2, 6]

euer your *(fam. pl.)* [K. 3]

der Euro, -s Euro *(European currency unit)*

(das) Europa Europe

europäisch European

die Europäische Union European Union

der Euroscheck, -s Euro check

eventuell perhaps, possibly; eventually [K. 6]

ewig eternal

exotisch exotic

der/die Ex, - former boyfriend/girlfriend [K. 5]

der Experte, [-n], -n/die Expertin, -nen expert

F

das Fach, ̈er academic subject; compartment [K. 6]

der Fachbereich, -e academic department

die Fachhochschule, -n specialized university [K. 6]

die Fachoberschule, -n technical college

die Fachschule, -n special school, technical college

das Fachwerk half-timbered architecture

die Fachzeitschrift, -en professional journal

die Fähigkeit, -en ability [K. 12]

fahren (fährt, fuhr, ist gefahren) to drive, ride [K. 3], **per Anhalter ~** to hitch-hike [K. 4]

der Fahrplan, ̈e schedule of transportation

die Fahrprüfung, -en driving test

das Fahrrad, ̈er bicycle [K. 4]

der Fahrradverleih bicycle rental [K. 3]

der Fahrschein, -e public transportation ticket

die Fahrschule, -n driving school, driver's education

die Fahrt, -en trip, journey

das Fahrzeug, -e vehicle

der Faktor, -en factor

der Fall, ̈e case, situation; **auf jeden ~** at any rate, in any case; **in diesem Fall(e)** in this case

fallen (fällt, fiel, ist gefallen) to fall
[K. 5]; **~ lassen** to drop

die Familie, -n family [K. 2]

der Familienbetrieb, -e family-owned business

der Familienstammbaum, ¨e family tree

das Familienverhältnis, -se family affair

der Fan, -s fan [K. 9]

fangen (fängt, fing, hat gefangen) to catch [K. 10]

die Fantasie, -n fantasy

fantastisch fantastic [K. 11]

die Farbe, -n color; [K. 1] **Welche Farbe hat... ?** What color is . . .? [K. 1]

der Fasching Carnival, Fasching [K. 10]

das Fass, *pl.* **Fässer** barrel [K. 3]

die Fassung, -en version; **die erste ~** first draft

fast almost, practically [K. 5]

die Fastenzeit Lent

die Fastnacht Carnival, Fasching [K. 10]

faul lazy [K. 4]

das Fax fax

der Februar February [K. 2]

das Fechten fencing

die Fee, -n fairy [K. 10]

fehlen (hat gefehlt) to be missing, be lacking [K. 10, 12]

feiern (hat gefeiert) to celebrate [K. 10]

der Feiertag, -e holiday [K. 10]

fein fine [K. 11]

der Feind, -e enemy, adversary [K. 10]

das Feldhockey field hockey [K. 7]

das Fenster - window [K. 1]

die Ferien *(pl.)* (school) vacation [K. 5]

der Ferienort, -e resort town

ferienreif ready for a vacation

die Ferienwohnung, -en vacation home

fern·bleiben (blieb fern, ist ferngeblieben) + *dat.* to stay away from

die Ferne distance

fern·sehen (sieht fern, sah fern, hat ferngesehen) to watch television [K. 2, 3]

der Fernseher, - television set [K. 1]

der Fernsehturm, ¨e television tower

die Ferse, -n heel [K. 10]

fertig finished [K. 5]; **~ werden (wird, wurde, ist geworden) mit +** *dat.* to come to grips with, accept [K. 5]

fest permanent; firm, solid [K. 9]

das Fest, -e festival, feast [K. 10]

das Festspiel, -e festival

fest·stellen (hat festgestellt) to determine [K. 7]

der Festtag, -e holiday [K. 10]

die Fete, -n party; **auf eine ~ gehen:** to go to a party [K. 7]

die Feuerwache, -n fire station

das Fieber fever, temperature [K. 8]

die Figur, -en figure; (story) character

die Filiale, -n branch office

der Film, -e movie, film [K. 7]

der Filmemacher, -/die Filmemacherin, -nen filmmaker [K. 9]

die Finanzen *(pl.)* finances

finden (fand, hat gefunden) to find [K. 2]

der Finger, - finger [K. 6]

der Fingernagel, ¨ fingernail

(das) Finnisch the Finnish language

(das) Finnland Finland

die Firma, *pl.* **Firmen** firm, company

der Fisch, -e fish [K. 3]

der Fischmarkt, ¨e fish market [K. 5]

das Fitnessstudio, -s health club [K. 7]

flach flat; low

die Fläche, -n land area [K. 3]

die Flak (Flugzeugabwehrkanone) flak, anti-aircraft weapon

die Flasche, -n bottle [K. 3]

das Fleisch meat [K. 3]

der Fleischer, -/die Fleischerin, -nen butcher [K. 9]

die Fleischerei, -en butcher shop [K. 7]

fleißig hardworking, industrious; busy [K. 4]

flexibel flexible [K. 9]

fliegen (flog, ist geflogen) to fly [K. 2]

fließen (floss, ist geflossen) to flow

fließend fluent(ly) [K. 12]

flirten (hat geflirtet) to flirt [K. 5]

die Flöte, -n flute [K. 3]

die Flötenmusik flute music

der Flug, ¨e flight [K. 4]

der Flughafen, ¨ airport [K. 4]

der Flugschein, -e plane ticket [K. 4]

das Flugticket, -s plane ticket

das Flugzeug, -e airplane [K. 4]

der Flur, -e hallway, corridor [K. 6]

der Fluss, ¨e river [K. 7]

der Föhn, -e blow dryer [K. 8]

sich die Haare föhnen (hat sich geföhnt) to blow-dry one's hair [K. 8]

die Fontäne, -n fountain

das Formular, -e form (to be filled out) [K. 9]

die Forschung, -en research

der Forschungsassistent, [-en], -en/ die Forschungsassistentin, -nen research assistant

der/die Fortgeschrittene, -n *(adj. as noun)* advanced student [K. 10]

fort·gehen (ging fort, ist fortgegangen) to go away

fort·setzen (hat fortgesetzt) to continue [K. 12]

das Fotoalbum, *pl.* **-alben** photo album

der Fotograf, [-en], -en/die Fotografin, -nen photographer

der Fotoapparat, -e photo camera

die Frage, -n question [K. 2]; **Fragen stellen (hat gestellt)** to ask questions [K. 9]

fragen (hat gefragt) to ask [K. 2]; **~ nach +** *dat.* to ask about

das Fragewort, ¨er question word, interrogative

(das) Frankreich France [K. 1]

der Franzose, [-n], -n/die Französin, -nen French person [K. 1]

(das) Französisch the French language [K. 2]

die Frau, -en woman; Mrs., Ms. [K. 1, 5]; wife, wives [K. 2, 5]

die Frauenzeitschrift, -en women's magazine

das Fräulein, - young girl; Miss (for young girls only) [K. 1]

frei free, open; allowed [K. 5]; **~ haben** to have time off [K. 2]; **im Freien** outdoors [K. 11]

die Freie Demokratische Partei (FDP) Free Democratic Party

die Freiheit, -en freedom [K. 3, 8]

das Frei(schwimm)bad, ¨er outdoor swimming pool

der Freitag, -e Friday [K. 2]

freiwillig voluntarily

die Freizeit free time, leisure time

die Freizeitaktivität, -en leisure activity [K. 3]

fremd foreign [K. 9]

der/die Fremde, -n *(adj. as noun)* foreigner

der Fremdenführer, -/die Fremdenführerin, -nen tour guide

der Fremdenhass xenophobia

die Fremdsprache, -n foreign language [K. 12]

fressen (frisst, fraß, hat gefressen) to eat *(said of animals)*

die Freude, -n joy

sich freuen (hat sich gefreut) to be happy; ~ **auf** + *acc.* to look forward to [K. 8]; ~ **über** + *acc.* to be happy about [K. 8]

der Freund, -e/die Freundin, -nen friend, boy-/girlfriend [K. 5]; **die Freunde** *(pl.)* a group of friends

der Freundeskreis, -e circle of friends; clique [K. 6]

freundlich friendly [K. 1]

die Freundschaft, -en friendship [K. 5]; **dicke ~** close, intimate friendship [K. 5]; ~ **schließen** to make friends [K. 5]

der Friedhof, ̈e cemetery [K. 9]

der Friseur, -e/die Friseurin, -nen/die Friseuse, -n hair dresser [K. 9]

froh happy [K. 5]

fromm (ö) pious, religious [K. 10]

der Frosch, ̈e frog [K. 10]

die Frucht, ̈e fruit [K. 11]

früh early [K. 8]

früher earlier, in the past [K. 5]

der Frühling spring [K. 5]

das Frühstück breakfast [K. 3]

frustrierend frustrating [K. 11]

sich fühlen (hat sich gefühlt) to feel [K. 8]; **sich krank ~** to feel sick; **sich nicht wohl ~** to feel unwell [K. 8]

führen (hat geführt) to lead [K. 9]

der Führer, - leader (used to refer to Adolf Hitler) [K. 11]

der Führerschein, -e driver's license [K. 4]

die Führung, -en leadership; tour [K. 11]

fünf five [K. 1]

fünfzehn fifteen [K. 1]

fünfzig fifty [K. 1]

für + *acc.* for [K. 4]

fürchten (hat gefürchtet) to be afraid of [K. 12]

Furcht erregend frightening

das Fürstentum, ̈er principality, kingdom

der Fuß, ̈e foot [K. 6]; **zu ~** on foot [K. 7]

der Fußball soccer [K. 3]; ~ **spielen** to play soccer [K. 3]

der Fußballplatz, ̈e soccer field [K. 7]

der Fußgänger, -/die Fußgängerin, -nen pedestrian [K. 4]

der Fußgängerbereich, -e pedestrian zone

die Fußgängerzone, -n pedestrian zone [K. 3]

der Fußweg, -e footpath [K. 4]

füttern (hat gefüttert) to feed

G

die Gabel, -n fork [K. 6]

der Gang, ̈e hall, hallway, corridor [K. 6]

ganz really, very; whole [K. 5]; ~ **nass** completely wet [K. 5]; ~ **schlimm** really bad [K. 5]; **die ganze Zeit** the whole time [K. 5]

gar nicht not at all [K. 3]

die Garage, -n garage [K. 6]

die Gardine, -n curtain(s) [K. 6]

der Garten, ̈ garden [K. 6]

der Gast, ̈e guest [K. 10]

das Gästezimmer, - guest room

die Gastfreundschaft hospitality

der Gastgeber, -/die Gastgeberin, -nen host

der Gasthof, ̈e inn [K. 3]

gastlich hospitable, friendly [K. 3]

das Gebäck pastry

das Gebäude, - building [K. 3, 9]

geben (gibt, gab, hat gegeben) to give [K. 3]; **es gibt (gab, hat gegeben)** there is, there are [K. 3]; **Was gibt es . . .?** What is (there)? **Was gibt's?** What's up? [K. 3]

das Gebiet, -e district, area [K. 12]

geboren born [K. 5]

gebraucht used

gebunden hard-bound

das Geburtshaus, ̈er birth place [K. 9]

der Geburtstag, -e birthday [K. 2]

die (Kaiser-Wilhelm) Gedächtniskirche (Kaiser Wilhelm) Memorial Church [K. 11]

gedacht sein für to be intended for

der Gedanke [-n], -n thought [K. 12]; **mit dem Gedanken kämpfen** to struggle with the thought [K. 12]

gedeckt set

das Gedicht, -e poem [K. 7]

die Geduld patience

gefährlich dangerous [K. 4]

gefallen (gefällt, gefiel, hat gefallen) + *dat.* to please; to like [K. 6]

das Geflügel poultry, fowl [K. 3]

der Gefrierpunkt freezing point [K. 5]

das Gefühl, -e feeling [K. 11, 12]

gegen + *acc.* against; around *(time)* [K. 4]

der Gegensatz, ̈e opposite

gegenseitig each other, reciprocal(ly)

der Gegenstand, ̈e object [K. 4, 9]

das Gegenteil, -e opposite; **im ~** in opposition, contrary to

gegenüber + *dat.* in regard to; ~ **(von)** + *dat.* across from [K. 7]

die Gegenwart present [K. 9]

der Gegner, -/die Gegnerin, -nen opponent

das Gehalt, ̈er salary, wage [K. 9]

die Gehaltsvorstellung, -en salary expectation

gehen (ging, ist gegangen) to go [K. 2, 7]; **nach Hause ~** to go home [K. 2]; **unter die Dusche ~** to take a shower; **Wie geht es Ihnen/dir?,** How are you? [K. 6]

gehören (hat gehört) + *dat.* to belong to [K. 6]

geil way cool *(slang)* [K. 1]

gelb yellow [K. 1]

das Geld money [K. 4]

die Gelegenheit, -en opportunity [K. 9]

der/die Geliebte, -n *(adj. as noun)* lover

gelingen + *dat.* **(ist gelungen)** to succeed [K. 9]

gelten (gilt, galt, hat gegolten) als to be considered (as) [K. 7]

das Gemälde, - painting [K. 9]

gemeinsam common, shared, in partnership [K. 8, 11]

die Gemeinschaft, -en association, group

das Gemeinschaftsbad, ̈er shared bathroom, floor bathroom [K. 6]

die Gemeinschaftsküche, -n shared kitchen [K. 6]

gemischt mixed

das Gemüse, - vegetable, vegetables [K. 3]

gemütlich cozy

genau exactly [K. 8]

genießen (genoss, hat genossen) to enjoy [K. 9, 10]

der Genießer, -/die Genießerin, -nen connoisseur [K. 10]

der Genitiv genitive case

genug enough, sufficient [K. 4]

genügend sufficient, enough

das Genus gender

das Gepäck luggage [K. 3]

gerade just now; directly [K. 6]

geradeaus straight ahead [K. 7]

das Gericht, -e dish

gering low, small, limited

die Germanistik German studies

gern + after a *verb* to like to . . . [K. 2]; ~ **geschehen!** Glad to help!, My pleasure! **~ haben** to like [K. 2]

die Gesamtschule, -n comprehensive secondary school

das Geschäft, -e store, business [K. 3]

die Geschäftsführung, -en business office

der Geschäftsmann, ¨er/die Geschäftsfrau, -en businessman/-woman [K. 9]

die Geschäftsreise, -n business trip

das Geschäftstreffen, - business meeting

das Geschenk, -e gift, present [K. 4]

die Geschichte, -n history [K. 2]; story

geschieden divorced

die Geschirrspülmaschine, -n dishwasher

geschlossen closed

der Geschmack, ¨e(r) taste

die Geschwister (pl.) siblings [K. 2, 8]

gesellig gregarious, sociable [K. 4]

die Gesellschaft, -en society

das Gesetz, -e law [K. 11]

das Gesicht, -er face [K. 6]

gespannt excited [K. 4]; ~ sein auf + acc. to be excited about [K. 2, 8]

das Gespräch, -e conversation [K. 8]; ins ~ kommen to strike up a conversation

gestalten (hat gestaltet) to create, form [K. 9]

gestern yesterday [K. 5]

gestresst stressed [K. 10]

gesund (ü) healthy [K. 7]

die Gesundheit health [K. 9]

das Getränk, -e beverage, drink [K. 3]

sich getrauen (hat sich getraut) to venture, dare

getrennt separate

die Gewalt violence

gewinnen (gewann, hat gewonnen) to win [K. 11]

gewiss certain [K. 5, 11]

das Gewitter thunderstorm [K. 5]

sich gewöhnen (hat sich gewöhnt) an + acc. to get used to, get accustomed to [K. 10]

gewöhnlich usually [K. 9]

das Ghetto, -s ghetto

das Gift, -e poison

giftig poisonous [K. 10]

der Gipfel, - mountain peak [K. 10]

der Gips, -e cast [K. 8]

das Girokonto, -konten checking/debit account [K. 7]

die Gitarre, -n guitar [K. 3]

glänzend gleaming

das Glas, ¨er glass [K. 3]

der Glassarg, ¨e glass coffin

glatt smooth, straight [K. 1]

der Glaube, -n faith, belief [K. 7]

glauben (hat geglaubt) to believe, think [K. 5]; ~ an + acc. to believe in

glaubhaft plausible, believable

gleich just, right away [K. 2]; similar, same [K. 4]

gleich neben right next to [K. 6]

gleichzeitig simultaneously, at the same time

das Glück good luck, fortune

glücklich happy [K. 4]

das Gold gold [K. 10]

der Golf golf [K. 3]

der Golfschläger, - golf club

der Gott, ¨er God [K. 1]; ~ sei Dank! Thank God!

das Grab, ¨er grave [K. 10]

der Grad degree [K. 5]

der Graf, [-en], -en count [K. 5]

das Gramm gram [K. 3]

die Grammatik grammar

die Graphik, -en graphics

grau gray [K. 1]; dunkelgrau dark gray [K. 1]; hellgrau light gray [K. 1]

grausam gruesome, cruel [K. 10]

die Grenze, -n border [K. 10, 11]

grenzen (hat gegrenzt) an + dat. to border on

(das) Griechenland Greece

grillen (hat gegrillt) to grill, barbeque

groß (ö) large, big, tall [K. 1]

großartig great, fantastic [K. 9]

der Großbuchstabe, -n capital letter

die Größe, -n size [K. 9]

die Großeltern (pl.) grandparents [K. 2]

die Großmutter, ¨ grandmother [K. 2]

die Großstadt, pl. Großstädte big city

der Großvater, ¨ grandfather [K. 2]

großzügig generous

Grüezi! Hello! (in Switzerland)

grün green [K. 1]

der Grund, ¨e reason; im Grunde basically [K. 11]

gründen (hat gegründet) to establish [K. 11]

das Grundgesetz Basic Law (Germany's constitution) [K. 11]

gründlich thorough, careful [K. 9]

die Grundschule, -n elementary school [K. 8]

die Gründung, -en foundation [K. 11]

die Grünen the Green Party

die Gruppe, -n group

der Gruppenleiter, -/die Gruppenleiterin, -nen group leader

das Gruppenreferat, -e group research paper

die Gruppenunterkunft, ¨e group lodging

der Gruß, ¨e greeting [K. 1]; Herzliche Grüße Sincerely yours (to close a letter) [K. 2]

grüßen: Grüßt euch! Grüß dich! Hi, you (guys)!; Grüß Gott! Hello! (in southern Germany) [K. 1]

gucken (hat geguckt) to look [K. 6]; Guck mal! Look! [K. 6]

gültig valid

günstig favorable, affordable [K. 6]

gut good [K. 1]; ~ aus·kommen to get along [K. 9]; ~ aussehend good looking (for males) [K. 1]; ~ gelaunt in a good mood [K. 10]

Gute Nacht! Good night. [K. 1]

Guten Abend! / 'n Abend! Good evening. [K. 1]

Guten Morgen! / Morgen! Good morning. [K. 1]

Guten Tag! / Tag! Good afternoon; Good day. [K. 1]

der Gymnasiast, [-en], -en/die Gymnasiastin, -nen college-track high school student

das Gymnasium, pl. Gymnasien college-track high school [K. 8]

H

das Haar, -e hair [K. 1, 6]

die Haarbürste, -n hairbrush [K. 4]

das Haarwaschmittel, - shampoo

haben (hat, hatte, hat gehabt) to have [K. 2]

Hab keine Angst! Don't be afraid [K. 4]

das Hackfleisch hamburger, chopped meat [K. 3]

der Hafen, ¨ harbor

das Hähnchen, - chicken [K. 3]

der Haken, - hook [K. 8]

halb half; ~ [zwei] half past [one] [K. 2]

das Hallenschwimmbad, ¨er indoor swimming pool

Hallo! Hello! [K. 1]

der Hals, ¨e throat [K. 6]; Hals- und Beinbruch! Break a leg! [K. 9]

die Halsschmerzen (pl.) sore throat [K. 8]

halt just

halten (hält, hielt, hat gehalten) to hold, to stop [K. 3]; ~ für + acc. to believe someone to be [K. 8]; ~ von + dat. to think of [K. 3]

die Haltestelle, -n bus stop [K. 7]

das Halteverbot no stopping (sign)

der Hamburger, - hamburger [K. 3]; ~/die Hamburgerin, -nen resident of Hamburg

die Hand, ¨e   hand [K. 6]
das Handgelenk, -e   wrist
das Handout, -s   handout [K. 8]
handeln (hat gehandelt) von + *dat.*   to be about [K. 8]
die Handlung, -en   dramatic action, plot [K. 10]
der Handschuh, -e   glove, mitten [K. 4]
die Handtasche, -n   handbag, purse [K. 4]
das Handy, -s   cell phone [K. 4]
hängen (hat gehängt)   to hang up [K. 7]
hängen (hing, hat gehangen)   to be hanging [K. 7]
hart (ä)   hard [K. 9]
hässlich   ugly [K. 10]
der Haufen, -   heap, pile
häufig   frequent
Haupt... *(in compounds)* main; der Hauptbahnhof, ¨e   main train station [K. 3, 4]; das Hauptfach, ¨er main subject, major Was haben Sie als Hauptfach? What's your major? [K. 2]; das Hauptgericht, -e   main course [K. 3]; der Hauptsatz, ¨e main clause
die Hauptschule, -n   equivalent to junior high school, technical-vocational school [K. 8]
der Hauptschüler, -/die Hauptschülerin, -nen   technical-vocational student
das Hauptseminar, -e   advanced seminar
die Hauptstadt, ¨e   capital city [K. 10, 11]
die Hauptstraße, -n   main street [K. 3]
das Haus, ¨er   house [K. 6]; nach Hause   (to) home [K. 2]; zu Hause   at home [K. 2]
die Hausaufgabe, -n   homework, assignment; die Hausaufgaben machen   to do homework [K. 2]
der Hauskamerad, [-en], -en/die Hauskameradin, -nen   housemate
die Hausleiter, -n   fire escape
der Hausmeister, -/die Hausmeisterin, -nen   custodian, superintendent
der Hauswart, -e   custodian
die Haut   skin [K. 6]
die Hautfarbe, -n   skin color
heben (hob, hat gehoben)   to lift, raise
das Heftpflaster, -   bandage [K. 8]
der Heilige Geist   Holy Ghost
die Heimat   home, hometown [K. 12]
die Heimatstadt, ¨e   hometown

heim·kommen (kam heim, ist heimgekommen)   to come home [K. 5]
das Heimweh   homesickness
heiraten (hat geheiratet)   to get married [K. 5]
heiß   hot [K. 5]
heißen (hieß, hat geheißen)   to be called Wie heißen Sie? What's your name? [K. 1]; das heißt (d.h.)   that is (to say) [K. 4]
heiter   funny, cheerful [K. 4]; sunny, clear [K. 5]
heizen (hat geheizt)   to heat
die Heizung, -en   heating system; heat
die Hektik   frenzy, fast pace
helfen (hilft, half, hat geholfen) + *dat.*   to help [K. 4, 6]; auf die Sprünge ~   to give a boost to
hell   light [K. 1]
hellgrau   light gray [K. 1]
hellwach   wide awake
(das) Helvetia   Switzerland *(Latin)*
das Hemd, -en   shirt [K. 4]
her   here *(from point of origin)* [K. 7]
herab·blicken (hat herabgeblickt)   to look down
heraus·finden (fand heraus, hat herausgefunden)   to find out, discover
die Herausforderung, -en   challenge [K. 7]
sich heraus·putzen (hat sich herausgeputzt)   to dress up, get decked out
der Herbst   autumn, fall [K. 5]
der Herd, -e   cooking stove [K. 6, 10]
Herein, bitte!   Please come in! [K. 8]
herein·kommen (kam herein, ist hereingekommen)   to come in
die Herkunft   origin [K. 6]
das Herkunftsland, ¨er   country of origin, home country
der Herr, [-n], -en   (gentle)man; Mr. [K. 1]
her·stellen (hat hergestellt)   to produce, make [K. 7]
das Herz, -en   heart [K. 6]; im Herzen   in the heart [K. 6]
der Herzanfall, ¨e   heart attack
herzlich   heartfelt, warm; ~ willkommen in ... !   Welcome to . . . !
die Herzlichkeit   warmth, heartfeltness, sincerity
Hessen   Hesse
heulen (hat geheult)   to cry; to howl
heute   today [K. 2]; ~ Abend   this evening; ~ in acht Tagen   a week from today [K. 9]; ~ Morgen   this

morning; ~ Nachmittag   this afternoon Was haben wir heute What day is it? Was ist heute? What day is today? [K. 2]
die Hexe, -n   witch [K. 10]
hier   here [K. 1]
die Hilfe, -n   help, aid [K. 9]
hilfsbereit   helpful
der Himmel   heaven, sky [K. 10]
hin   there *(point of destination)* [K. 7]; ~ und wieder   now and then [K. 4]
hinein   inside
hinein·gehen (ging hinein, ist hineingegangen)   to walk in [K. 1]
sich hin·legen (hat sich hingelegt)   to lie down [K. 8]
die Hinsicht   respect, regard
hinten   behind, in back
hinter   behind, in back of [K. 7]
hinterlassen (hinterlässt, hinterließ, hat hinterlassen)   to leave behind
der Hintern, -   rear, buttocks [K. 6]
historisch   historic
das Hobby, -s   hobby [K. 12]
der Hobbygärtner, -/die Hobbygärtnerin, -nen   amateur gardener
der Hobbyraum, ¨e   hobby room
hoch   high, up [K. 9]; am höchsten   highest [K. 9]; höchstens   at the most [K. 9]
hochachtungsvoll   respectfully [K. 9]
hochaktuell   very current, very timely [K. 7]
hoch·laufen (läuft hoch, lief hoch, ist hochgelaufen)   to walk up (a street)
die Hochschule, -n   college, university [K. 8]
die Hochzeit, -en   marriage, wedding [K. 9]
der Hochzeitstag, -e   wedding anniversary
hoffen (hat gehofft)   hope [K. 2] hoffen auf + *acc.*   to hope for [K. 7]
hoffentlich   hopefully, one hopes [K. 6]
höher   higher [K. 9]
holen (hat geholt)   to go get, fetch [K. 7]
das Holz, ¨er   wood
der Holzhandel   lumber business
der/die Homosexuelle, -n *(adj. as noun)*   homosexual
der Honig   honey [K. 3]
das Hoodie, -s   hooded sweatshirt [K. 4]
hören (hat gehört)   to hear, listen to [K. 2]
das Horoskop, -e   horoscope
der Horrorfilm, -e   horror movie [K. 7]

der Hörsaal, *pl.* **Hörsäle** lecture hall [K. 1]
die Hose, -n pants [K. 4]
das Hotel, -s hotel [K. 3, 10]
der Hoteleingang, ¨e hotel entrance
hübsch pretty (for females) [K. 1]
der Humor humor, sense of humor [K. 12]
humorvoll humorous
der Hund, -e dog [K. 2]
hundemüde dog-tired [K. 6]
hundert hundred [K. 1]
der Hunger hunger; ~ **haben** to be hungry [K. 2]
der Hypochonder, - hypochondriac
hypochondrisch hypochondriac(al)

I

ich I [K. 1]
die Idee, -n idea [K. 3]
sich identifizieren (hat sich identifiziert) mit + *dat.* to identify with
identisch identical
die Identität identity
ihm (to, for) him/it (*dat.*) [K. 6]
ihn him/it (*acc.*) [K. 2]
Ihnen (to, for) you (*dat.*) [K. 6]
ihnen (to, for) them (*dat.*) [K. 6]
ihr her; their [K. 3, 6]; you (*fam. pl.*) [K. 1]
Ihr your (*sg & pl formal*) [K. 3]
immer always [K. 3]; ~ **[beliebter]** more and more [popular]
imstande sein to be capable of
in at, in; into; to [K. 7]
indem (*sub. conj.*) by (doing something) [K. 12]
indes meantime, meanwhile
indianisch Native American
der Indikativ indicative mood
die Industrie, -n industry
die Info, -s information
die Informatik computer science [K. 2]
die Information, -en information
der Informationsvorsprung information advantage [K. 12]
sich informieren (hat sich informiert) über + *acc.* to inform oneself, educate oneself about
der Ingenieur, -e/die Ingenieurin, -nen engineer [K. 9]
das Ingenieurwesen engineering [K. 2]
der Inhalt, -e content [K. 8]
inklusive inclusive
innerhalb + *gen.* inside of [K. 8]
die Insel, -n island [K. 10]

das Inserat, -e newspaper advertisement
inszenieren (hat inszeniert) to stage, produce [K. 9]
insgesamt for a total of [K. 10]
das Institut, -e institute [K. 12]
die Integration integration [K. 7]
integriert integrated
intelligent intelligent [K. 4]
interessant interesting [K. 4]
das Interesse, -n interest
interessieren (hat interessiert) to interest [K. 8, 11]
Internationale Beziehungen (pl.) international relations [K. 3]
der Internetanschluss, ¨e Internet connection [K. 6]
die Internetseite, -n Internet page [K. 12]
interpretieren (hat interpretiert) to interpret
das Interview, -s interview
inwiefern to what extent
inzwischen in the meantime
der i-Pod, s iPod [K. 4]
irgendwas something, anything
(das) Irland Ireland
ironisch ironic
irritieren (hat irritiert) to irritate
irritierend irritating
der Islam Islam
(das) Island Iceland
(das) Italien Italy [K. 1]
der Italiener / die Italienerin (male/female) Italien person [K. 1]
italienisch Italian

J

ja yes [K. 1]
die Jacke, -n jacket [K. 4]
jagen (hat gejagt) to hunt
der Jäger, -/die Jägerin, -nen hunter [K. 10]
das Jahr, -e year [K. 2]; **schon seit Jahren** for years
die Jahreszeit, -en season [K. 5]
der Jahrmarkt, ¨e fair
jammern (hat gejammert) to whine, cry, lament
Jänner (*Austrian*) January
der Januar January [K. 2]; **am ersten** ~ on the first of January [K. 2]; **im** ~ in January [K. 2]
(das) Japan Japan [K. 1]
der Japaner, -/die Japanerin, -nen Japanese person [K. 1]
der Jazzkeller, - jazz club [K. 7]

die Jeans, - jeans [K. 4]
jedenfalls anyway, at any rate
jeder, jedes, jede each; every [K. 5, 6]
jedermann everyone [K. 10]
jederzeit anytime
jedoch however
jemand someone, somebody [K. 10]; **irgend~** somebody, anybody
jetzt now [K. 5]
das Jiddisch Yiddish
der Job, -s job
jobben (hat gejobbt) to work part-time
der/das Joghurt yogurt [K. 3]
der Journalist, [-en], -en/die Journalistin, -nen journalist [K. 9]
jubeln (hat gejubelt) to cheer [K. 7]
das Jubiläum, *pl.* **Jubiläen** anniversary
der Jude, [-n], -n/die Jüdin, -nen Jew
jüdisch Jewish [K. 11]
die Jugendherberge, -n youth hostel [K. 3, 10]
das Jugendhotel, -s budget youth hotel
die Jugendliteratur youth literature
der Jugendstil Art Nouveau
(das) Jugoslawien Yugoslavia
der Juli July [K. 2]
jung (ü) young [K. 1]
der Junge, [-n], -n boy [K. 2, 5]
die Jungs (*pl.*) boys, guys (*slang*) [K. 5]
der Juni June [K. 2]
der Jura Jura Mountains [K. 10]

K

der Kaffee coffee [K. 3]
das Kaffeehaus, ¨er coffee house
die Kaffeemaschine, -n coffee maker
der Käfig, -e cage
der Kaiser, -/die Kaiserin, -nen emperor, empress [K. 11]
das Kaiserreich empire [K. 11]
(das) Kalifornien California
kalt (ä) cold [K. 5]
die (digitale) Kamera, -s (digital) camera [K. 4]
der Kamin, -e fireplace
der Kamm, ¨e comb [K. 4]
kämmen (hat gekämmt) to comb; **sich die Haare** ~ to comb one's hair [K. 8]
kämpfen (hat gekämpft) to fight
(das) Kanada Canada [K. 1]
der Kanadier,-/die Kanadierin, -nen Canadian [K. 1]
der Kandidat, [-en], -en/die Kandidatin, -nen candidate
die Kantine, -n cafeteria, cantina

der Kanton, -e canton, state *(in Switzerland)* [K. 10]

der Kantor, -en choirmaster

der Kanzler, -/die Kanzlerin, -nen chancellor [K. 11]

die Kappensitzung, -en Carnival guild party, "roast"

der Karfreitag, -e Good Friday

der Karneval Carnival [K. 10]

die Karotte, -n carrot [K. 3]

die Karriere, -n career

die Karte, -n card; **Karten spielen** to play cards [K. 3]

die Kartoffel, -n potato [K. 3]

der Käse cheese [K. 3]

die Kasse, -n checkout counter, cash register [K. 7]

der Kasten, -, (¨) case [K. 11]

der Katalog, -e catalogue

die Katastrophe, -n catastrophe

der Kater, - tomcat; hangover *(slang)*; **der gestiefelte ~** Puss-in-Boots; **einen ~ haben** to have a hangover [K. 6]

die Katze, -n cat [K. 2]

kauen (hat gekaut) to chew

kaufen (hat gekauft) to buy, purchase [K. 2]

der Kaufmann, ¨er/die Kauffrau, -en clerk [K. 9]

der Kaugummi, -s chewing gum [K. 3]; **~ kauen** to chew gum

kaum hardly [K. 8]

kein, keine, *pl.* **keine** no, none, not one [K. 1] **kein ... mehr** no more

der Keller, - basement, cellar [K. 6]

der Kellner, -/die Kellnerin, -nen waiter/waitress [K. 5]

kennen (kannte, hat gekannt) to know (a city, person) [K. 3]

kennenlernen (hat kennengelernt) to meet, get to know [K. 2]

die Kenntnis, -se knowledge, skill [K. 9]

das Kilogramm kilogram [K. 3]

der Kilometer, - kilometer [K. 3]

das Kind, -er child, children [K. 2]

das Kinderbuch, ¨er children's book

der Kindergarten, ¨ preschool [K. 8]

das Kinderzimmer, - children's room, nursery [K. 6]

die Kindheit childhood [K. 10]

das Kinn -e chin [K. 6]

das Kino, -s movie theater, cinema; **ins ~ gehen** to go to the movies

der Kinoabend, -e night at the movies

der Kiosk, -e kiosk, stand [K. 7]

die Kirche, -n church [K. 3]

der Kirchturm, ¨e church tower, steeple

die Kirmes fair

die Kirsche, -n cherry [K. 3]

die Klamotten *(pl.)* clothes, duds [K. 6]

klappen (hat geklappt) to work out all right [K. 11]

klar clear; **Klar!** Sure! All clear! [K. 6, 11]

klasse cool, great [K. 8, 9]

die Klasse, -n class of students

die Klassengröße, -n class size

das Klassenzimmer, - classroom [K. 1]

klassisch classical [K. 9]

das Klavier, -e piano [K. 3]

das Kleid, -er dress [K. 4]

der Kleiderschrank, ¨e armoire, wardrobe [K. 6]

die Kleidung, -en clothing, clothes [K. 4]

das Kleidungsstück, -e piece of clothing

klein short [K. 1]

das Kleingeld pocket change

die Kleinigkeit, -en trifle, a little something; detail [K. 11]

klettern (ist geklettert) to climb

das Klima, *pl.* **Klimas** climate

klingen (klang, hat geklungen) to sound, ring [K. 8]

das Klo, -s (das Klosett, -e) toilet *(colloq.)* [K. 6]

klopfen (hat geklopft) to knock

klug (ü) smart, intelligent [K. 2]

knapp just barely, almost

die Kneipe, -n bar, pub [K. 5]

das Knie, - knee [K. 6]; **Knie- und Ellenbogenschutz** knee and elbow pads

der Koch, ¨e/die Köchin, -nen cook, chef [K. 9]

kochen (hat gekocht to cook [K. 3]

die Kochplatte, -n hotplate [K. 6]

der Koffer, - suitcase [K. 4]

der Kofferraum trunk of a car

der Kognat, -e cognate

die Kohle, -n coal

der Kollege, [-n], -n/die Kollegin, -nen colleague, co-worker [K. 9]

kollegial collegial [K. 9]

der Kölner Dom cathedral in Cologne

kombinieren (hat kombiniert) to combine

kommen (kam, ist gekommen) aus + *dat.* to come, be from [K. 2]

der Kommilitone, [-n], -n/die Kommilitonin, -nen fellow student [K. 8]

die Kommode, -n chest of drawers [K. 6]

die Kommunikation communication [K. 7]

der Kommunismus communism

der Kommunist, [-en], -en/die Kommunistin, -nen communist

die Komödie, -n comedy [K. 7]

kompliziert complicated

komponieren (hat komponiert) to compose [K. 9]

der Komponist, [-en], -en/die Komponistin, -nen composer [K. 9]

das Kompositum, *pl.* **Komposita** compound noun

die Konditorei, -en pastry shop [K. 7]

der Konflikt, -e conflict

konfus confused

die Kongresshalle, -n convention center

das Kongresszentrum, *pl.* **-zentren** convention center [K. 3]

der König, -e/die Königin, -nen king/queen [K. 10]

der Königssohn, ¨e prince [K. 10]

die Königstochter, ¨ princess [K. 10]

das Königtum, ¨er kingdom

die Konjunktion, -en conjunction

der Konjunktiv subjunctive mood

konkret concrete [K. 6]

können (kann, konnte, hat gekonnt) to be able to; can [K. 3, 4]

könnte could

konstruieren (hat konstruiert) to construct

konsumorientiert consumer-oriented [K. 11]

der Kontakt, -e contact, communication [K. 5]

Kontaktdaten contact information [K. 5]

kontaktfreudig outgoing, sociable [K. 9]

der Kontext, -e context

das Konto, *pl.* **Konten** bank account [K. 7]

der Kontrast, -e contrast

kontrollieren (hat kontrolliert) to check

kontrovers controversial

die Konversation, -en conversation

sich konzentrieren (hat sich konzentriert) auf + *acc.* to concentrate on [K. 8]

das Konzept, -e concept

der Konzern, -e company

das Konzert, -e concert [K. 3]

der Konzertsaal, -säle concert hall [K. 9]

der Kopf, ¨e head [K. 6]

der Kopfhörer, - headphones [K. 9]

die **Kopfschmerzen** (*pl.*) headache [K. 8]

kopieren (hat kopiert) to copy [K. 8]

der **Kopierer, -** photocopier

der **Kopierladen, ̈** copy shop

der **Körper, -** body

der **Körperteil, -e** body part [K. 6]

der **Korridor, -e** hall, corridor

die **Kost** food

die **Kosten** (*pl.*) expenses, costs

kosten (hat gekostet) to cost [K. 10]

kotzen (hat gekotzt) to throw up (*slang*)

der **Krach** argument, quarrel, noise [K. 5]; **~ haben** to have a fight, quarrel [K. 5]

krachen (hat gekracht) to crash

die **Kraftfahrstraße, -n** road for motorized vehicles

krank (ä) sick, ill [K. 8]

das **Krankenhaus, ̈er** hospital

der **Krankenpfleger, -/die Krankenschwester, -n** orderly, nurse [K. 9]

der **Krankenurlaub** sick leave, sick days

kraus tightly curled [K. 1]

die **Krawatte, -n** necktie [K. 4]

kreativ creative [K. 4]

die **Kreditkarte, -n** credit card [K. 4]

die **Kreide** chalk [K. 1]

der **Kreis, -e** circle [K. 7]

die **Kreuzung, -en** intersection, crossing [K. 4]; **bis zur ~** up to the intersection [K. 7]

der **Krieg, -e** war [K. 11]; **der Kalte ~** Cold War [K. 11]; **der Erste (Zweite) Weltkrieg** First (Second) World War [K. 11]

der **Krimi, -s** detective story

die **Kriminalität** crime, criminal activity

der **Kriminalroman, -e (der Krimi, -s)** detective story [K. 7]

der/die **Kriminelle, -n** (*adj. as noun*) criminal

die **Kriterien** (*pl.*) criteria

kritisieren (hat kritisiert) to criticize

(das) **Kroatien** Croatia

die **Küche, -n** kitchen [K. 6]; cuisine, food

der **Kuchen, -** cake [K. 3]

kühl cool [K. 5]

der **Kühlschrank, ̈e** refrigerator [K. 6]

der **Kuli, -s** ballpoint pen [K. 1]

die **Kultur, -en** culture; civilization

der **Kulturbeutel, -** shaving kit/cosmetic kit [K. 4]

kulturell cultural(ly) [K. 9]

das **Kulturzentrum,** *pl.* **-zentren** arts center, cultural center [K, 3]

das **Kultusministerium,** *pl.* **-ministerien** Ministry of Culture and Education

der **Kumpel, -s** buddy, pal [K. 5]

der **Kunde, [-n], -n/die Kundin, -nen** customer, client [K. 7]

die **Kunst** art [K. 2]

die **Kunsthalle, -n** art museum [K. 3]

die **Kunsthochschule, -n** art and design school

der **Künstler, -/die Künstlerin, -nen** artist

der **Kunstverein, -e** art association

der **Kurfürstendamm (Ku'damm)** *main street of West Berlin* [K. 11]

kurfürstlich electoral

die **Kurpfalz** Electoral Palatinate (until 1806, princes of the Palatinate region **[Pfalz]** helped select **[Kur]** German emperors)

der **Kurs, -e** course [K. 2, 12]

der **Kursteilnehmer, -/die Kursteilnehmerin, -nen** course participant [K. 12]

kurz (ü) short [K. 1]

die **Kurzgeschichte, -n** short story [K. 7]

die **Kusine, -n** female cousin [K. 2]

küssen (hat geküsst) to kiss [K. 5]

die **Kutsche, -n** coach, carriage

L

lächeln (hat gelächelt) to smile [K. 3]

lachen (hat gelacht) to laugh **Lachen Sie!** Laugh. [K. 1, 7]; **~ über +** *acc.* to laugh about, at

das **Lacrosse** lacrosse [K. 7]

die **Lade, -n** drawer

die **Lage, -n** position, situation

der **Lagerarbeiter, -/die Lagerarbeiterin, -nen** warehouse worker

lahm weak, boring, lame [ZT 8]

lala: (Das) finde ich so ~. I find (that) so-so. [K. 7]; **Mir geht es so ~.** I'm so-so. [K. 8]

die **Lampe, -n** lamp, light, light fixture [K. 1]

das **Land, ̈er** country [K. 1]

landen (ist gelandet) to land

die **Landeshauptstadt, ̈e** state capital

die **Landeskunde** geography [K. 3]

die **Landfläche, -n** land mass

die **Landkarte, -n** map [K. 1]

die **Landschaft, -en** landscape, scenery [K. 10]

lang (ä) (*adj.*) long; tall [K. 1]

lange (*adv.*) for a long time

die **Länge, -n** length

der **Langlauf** cross-country skiing

die **Langlaufloipe, -n** cross-country ski run [K. 10]

langsam slow(ly) [K. 4]

langweilig boring [K. 3]

der **Laptop, -s** laptop computer [K. 4]

lassen (lässt, ließ, hat gelassen) to let, allow; to leave [K. 5]

laufen (läuft, lief, ist gelaufen) to run; to walk [K. 3]

laut loud [K. 4]

der **Laut, -e** sound

leben (hat gelebt) to live [K. 5]

das **Leben, -** life

lebendig alive, lively [K. 11, 12]

die **Lebensfreude** joy of life

der **Lebenslauf, ̈e** resume, CV [K. 9]

die **Lebensmittel** (*pl.*) groceries

das **Lebensmittelgeschäft, -e** grocery store [K. 3]

der **Lebensraum, ̈e** habitat, living space [K. 12]

die **Leberwurst, ̈e** liverwurst, liver sausage

der **Lebkuchen, -** gingerbread

lecker delicious

die **Lederhose, -n** lederhosen

ledig single [K. 2]

leer empty

legen (hat gelegt) to lay down, put down [K. 7]

das **Lehrangebot, -e** course offering

der **Lehrassistent, [-en], -en/die Lehrassistentin, -nen** teaching assistant

die **Lehre, -n** apprenticeship

der **Lehrer, -/die Lehrerin, -nen** teacher [K. 9]

die **Lehrkraft, ̈e** instructor

der **Lehrling, -e** apprentice

die **Leiche, -n** corpse

leicht easy, light [K. 5]

leidenschaftlich passionately

leider unfortunately [K. 4]

leidtun (tat leid, hat leidgetan) + *dat.* to feel sorry for [K. 6]; **Es tut mir leid** I'm sorry

leihen (lieh, hat geliehen) to lend; to borrow [K. 6]

die **Leinwand, ̈e** projection screen [K. 1]

leise quiet(ly)

leisten (hat geleistet) to achieve, accomplish; **sich ~ (hat sich geleistet)** to afford

leiten (hat geleitet) to lead, be in charge of

lernen (hat gelernt) to learn; to study [K. 2]

lesbisch lesbian

lesen (liest, las, hat gelesen) to read [K. 3]

die Lesestrategie, -n reading strategy

letzte last [K. 9]

die Leute (*pl.*) people [K. 2, 5]

lieb dear; **Liebe ... /Lieber ...** Dear . . . (*used to begin a letter*)

die Liebe love [K. 5]

lieben (hat geliebt) to love [K. 5]

lieber (*comparative of* **gern**) preferably, rather [K. 9]; ~ **als** rather than; ~ + *verb* preferably; [I would] rather . . . [K. 3]

das Liebesgedicht, -e love poem

der Liebeskummer lovesickness; heartbreak [K. 5]

der Liebesroman, -e romance novel [K. 7]

der Lieblingssport favorite sport

liebsten: am ~ most preferably [K. 9]

Liechtenstein (principality of) Liechtenstein

der Liederfürst prince of songs

liegen (lag, hat gelegen) to lie, be located [K. 5, 7]; **es liegt daran, dass ...** that's because . . .

die Liga, *pl.* **Ligen** league [K. 7]

lila purple [K. 1]

links left, on the left [K. 4]

die Lippe, -n lip [K. 6]

der Lippenstift, -e lipstick [K. 4]

die List cunning

die Liste, -n list [K. 7]

der Liter, - liter [K. 3]

die Literatur literature [K. 7]

locken (hat gelockt) to entice, attract

locker relaxed, cool (*colloq.*) [K. 4]

der Löffel, - spoon [K. 6]

das Lokal, -e pub [K. 3]

die Lokalzeitung, -en local newspaper

der Lokalzug, ¨-e local commuter train

los off, loose; **Was ist ~?** What's the matter? [K. 5]; **Los!** Let's go!

lösen (hat gelöst) to solve

los·fahren (fährt los, fuhr los, ist losgefahren) to take off, leave, drive away [K. 5]

die Lösung, -en solution [K. 8]

die Lücke, -n blank

die Luft, ¨-e air

die Luftbrücke, -n airlift [K. 11]

die Lust desire [K. 8]; ~ **haben** to want, wish, have desire [K. 8]

lustig funny, jovial, comical [K. 4]

(das) Luxemburg Luxembourg [K. 12]

die Luxusbude, -n "luxury" student room (*colloq.*) [K. 6]

M

Mach dir keine Sorgen! Don't worry. [K. 4]

machen (hat gemacht) to make, do [K. 2]

die Macht, ¨-e power, strength [K. 11]

die Machtergreifung seizure of power [K. 11]

das Mädchen, - girl [K. 2, 5]

das Magazin, -e magazine

der Magister, - Master of Arts

Mahlzeit! (*at lunchtime*), Have a good meal. [K. 1]

das Mahnmal, -e (*selten:* **-mäler**) memorial [K. 11]

der Mai May [K. 2]

das Mail e-mail (the concept) [K. 2]

mailen (hat gemailt) to e-mail [K. 5]

der Makler, -/die Maklerin, -nen real estate agent [K. 9]

mal once (*emphatic particle*) [K. 4]

das Mal: zum ersten ~ for the first time [K. 5]

malerisch scenic

man (einen, einem) a person, anybody; you (*impersonal*), one [K. 3]

der Manager, -/die Managerin, -nen manager

manche several, some [K. 11]

manchmal sometimes [K. 6]

der Mann, ¨-er man; husband [K. 2, 5]

die Mannschaft, -en team [K. 7]

der Mantel, ¨- coat [K. 4]

das Märchen, - folk/fairy tale [K. 10]

das Märchenelement, -e fairy tale element

die Märchenfigur, -en fairy tale character

markieren (hat markiert) to mark

der Markt, ¨-e market [K. 7]

die Markthalle, -n market hall, indoor market

der Marktplatz, ¨-e market square [K. 3]

die Marmelade, -n marmalade, preserves [K. 3]

der Marsmensch, [-en], -en Martian

der März March [K. 2]

der Maschinenbau mechanical engineering

die Maß, -e one and a half liters; **die ~ Bier** one and a half liters of beer

die Massage, -n massage

die Masse, -n mass, crowd; **die Massen-Uni, -s** mega-university

der Master master's degree [K. 8]

das Material, -ien material

die Mathematik (die Mathe) mathematics [K. 2]

die Matura high school graduation exam (*in Austria*)

die Mauer, -n exterior wall; the Wall (in Berlin) [K. 11]

maximal maximally

die Medizin medicine [K. 2]

das Meer, -e sea

mehr more [K. 3]

das Mehrbettzimmer, - room with multiple beds

mein my [K. 3]

meinen (hat gemeint) to think, have an opinion [K. 2]

die Meinung, -en opinion; **meiner ~ nach** in my opinion [K. 6]

meisten: am ~ most (of all) [K. 9]

meistens usually, mostly [K. 8]

der Meister, - master [K. 9]

melancholisch melancholic

sich melden (hat sich gemeldet) to report, show up; to get in touch

die Menge, -n a bunch of, a lot of; crowd; **jede ~** (a) large amount

die Mensa, *pl.* **Mensen** student dining hall [K. 6]

das Mensa-Essen food in student dining hall

der Mensch, [-en], -en person, human being [K. 3]; **Mensch!** Man!

menschlich human [K. 7]

die Mentalität, -en mentality [K. 7]

merken (hat gemerkt) to notice [K. 7, 9, 11]

das Messer, - knife [K. 6, 10]

der Meter, - meter [K. 3]

der Metzger, -/die Metzgerin, -nen butcher [K. 9]

die Metzgerei, -en butcher shop [K. 7]

der Mexikaner, -/die Mexikanerin, -nen Mexican [K. 1]

(das) Mexiko Mexico [K. 1]

mich me (*acc.*) [K. 2]

mies rotten, lousy [K. 5]

die Miete, -n rent [K. 6, 11]

der Migrationshintergrund ethnic background [K. 7]

der Mikrowellenherd, -e microwave oven [K. 6]

die Milch milk [K. 3]

die Million, -en million

die Minderheit, -en minority

mindestens at least

das Mineralwasser, - mineral water [K. 3]

mir me (*dat.*) (to, for) [K. 6]

mischen (hat gemischt) to mix

miserabel miserable

missfallen (missfällt, missfiel, hat
   missfallen) + *dat.* to displease
das Missverständnis, -se
   misunderstanding
mit + *dat.* with [K. 2, 6]
der Mitarbeiter, -/die Mitarbeiterin,
   -nen co-worker
der Mitbewohner, -/die
   Mitbewohnerin, -nen roommate
   [K. 7]
mit·bringen (brachte mit, hat
   mitgebracht) to bring along, bring
   back [K. 3]
miteinander with one another
das Mitglied, -er member
mit·machen (hat mitgemacht) to join
   in, participate [K. 6, 10]
mit·nehmen (nimmt mit, nahm mit,
   hat mitgenommen) to take along
   [K. 4]
der Mittag noon [K. 2]
das Mittagessen, - lunch [K. 3]
die Mitte, -n middle [K. 11]; Berlin-
   Mitte center of Berlin [K. 11]
die Mitteilung, -en memo
das Mittelalter Middle Ages [K. 9]
(das) Mitteleuropa Central Europe
das Mittelland midlands, flatlands
der Mittelpunkt midpoint, center
die Mitternacht midnight [K. 2]
die Mittlere Reife 10th grade high
   school exam
mittlerweile meantime, meanwhile
der Mittwoch, -e Wednesday [K. 2]
das Möbel *(pl.)* furniture [K. 6]
möchte would like to [K. 2, 4]
das Modul, -e module [K. 8]
der Modus, *pl.* Modi mood
mögen (ich/er mag, mochte, hat
   gemocht) to like [K. 4]
möglich possible [K. 9]
die Möglichkeit, -en possibility [K. 6]
der Mokka mocha coffee
mollig chubby, plump [K. 1]
der Moment: - mal! Wait a minute!
momentan at the moment,
   momentarily
die Monarchie, -n monarchy [K. 11]
der Monat, -e month [K. 2]
der Montag, -e Monday [K. 2]
montags on Mondays
das Moped, -s moped [K. 4]
der Morgen, - morning [K. 8]; eines
   Morgens one morning [K. 10]
   Guten -! Good morning! [K. 1]
morgen tomorrow [K. 5]; - Abend
   (früh, Nachmittag) tomorrow
   evening (morning, afternoon) [K. 8]
morgens in the morning [K. 2]

die Moschee, -n mosque [K. 7]
das Motiv, -e motive
motiviert motivated [K. 9]
das Motorrad, ¨-er motorcycle [K. 7]
müde tired [K. 4]
das Müesli muesli, whole grain cereal
   [K. 3]
die Mühe, -n effort
mühselig with difficulty [K. 11]
der Müller, -/die Müllerin, -nen miller
der Multikulturalismus
   multiculturalism
multikulturell multicultural [K. 6]
der Mund, ¨-er mouth [K. 6]
mündlich oral(ly) [K. 8]
das Museum, *pl.* Museen museum [K. 3]
die Museumsinsel "Museum Island"
   (in Berlin) [K. 11]
das Musical, -s musical [K. 9]
die Musik music [K. 2]
musikalisch musical [K. 3]
der Musikant, [-en], -en/die
   Musikantin, -nen musician
der Musiker, -/die Musikerin,
   -nen musician [K. 9]
das Musikgeschäft, -e music store
   [K. 3]
die Musikhochschule, -n music
   conservatory
der Muskelkater,- sore muscle [K. 8]
müssen (muss, musste, hat
   gemusst) to have to, must; to
   be required to [K. 4]: ich muss
   nicht I don't need to [K. 4]
mutig brave, courageous
die Mutter, ¨ mother [K. 2]
die Muttersprache, -n native language
die Mutti, -s mom, ma, mommy
die Mütze, -n cap, hat

N

na well; - ja oh, well [K. 6]; -, wie
   auch immer ... yeah, whatever . . .
nach + *dat.* to *(countries, cities)*; past/
   after [K. 6]; - wie vor still
nachdem *(conj.)* after [K. 10]
nach·denken (dachte nach, hat
   nachgedacht) to consider
   something, to think something over
   [K. 12], - über + Akkusativ to
   think about, worry about [K. 7]
der Nachfahr, -en descendant
nachher *(adv.)* afterwards
die Nachhilfestunde, -n tutoring
   lesson
das Nachhinein: im - in retrospect
der Nachlass estate [K. 9]

der Nachmittag afternoon [K. 8]
die Nachricht, -en news, message
   [K. 9]
das Nachrichtenmagazin, -e news
   magazine
die Nachspeise, -n dessert [K. 3]
nächst-: nächste Woche next week
   [K. 8]; nächsten Samstag next
   Saturday [K. 8]
die Nacht, ¨-e night [K. 1]; eines
   Nachts one night [K. 10]; Gute -!
   Good night! [K. 1]
der Nachteil, -e disadvantage
der Nachtisch, -e dessert [K. 3]
nächtlich nighttime, nocturnal
nackt naked
der Nagellack nail polish [K. 4]
nagelneu brand-new
nah (ä) near
die Nähe vicinity; in der - von in the
   vicinity of, near [K. 3]
näher nearer, closer [K. 7]
der Name, [-n, -ns], -n name [K. 1]
namens by the name of
nämlich namely, that is
der Narr, [-en], -en fool
die Narrengesellschaft, -en fools' guild
die Nase, -n nose [K. 6]
nass (a/ä) wet, damp [K. 5]
die Nation, -en nation [K. 7]
die Nationalität, -en nationality [K. 1]
der Nationalsozialist, [-en], -en/
   die Nationalsozialistin,
   -nen National Socialist, Nazi
die Natur, -en nature
natürlich natural(ly) [K. 8]
die Naturschönheit, -en natural beauty
der Nebel, - fog [K. 5]
neben next to, beside [K. 7]
nebenan next door
nebendran adjacent, next to
nebeneinander next to each other
das Nebenfach, ¨-er minor *(area of
   study)* [K. 2]
nee nope, naw
der Neffe, [-n], -n nephew [K. 2]
nehmen (nimmt, nahm, hat
   genommen) to take [K. 3]; Platz
   - to have a seat
die Neigung, -en preference,
   inclination
nein no [K. 1]
nennen (nannte, hat genannt) to
   name, call someone something
   [K. 10]
der Neo-Nazi, -s Neo-Nazi
nervös nervous; irritable [K. 4]
nett nice [K. 6, 9, 12]
neu new [K. 4]

die Neuauflage, -n   reprint
der Neubau, -ten   new building
neugierig   curious, nosy [K. 7]
das Neujahr   New Year's Day [K. 10]
neulich   recently [K. 11]
neun   nine [K. 1]
neunzehn   nineteen [K. 1]
neunzig   ninety [K. 1]
neutral   neutral [K. 5]
die Neutralität   neutrality
nicht   not [K. 1]; ~ sehr   not very [K. 2];
     ~ so   not so [K. 2]; gar ~   not at all;
     Ich weiß ~.   I don't know. [K. 1] ~
     wahr?   Right? No? [K. 11]
die Nichte, -n   niece [K. 2]
nichts   nothing [K. 1, 3]
nicken (hat genickt)   to nod
nie   never [K. 4]; gar ~   never at all
nieder·brennen (brannte nieder, hat
     niedergebrannt)   to burn down
die Niederlande (pl.)   the Netherlands
(das) Niedersachsen   Lower Saxony
niederschlagen (hat niedergeschlagen)
     to be reflected in [K. 6] to repress
     [K. 11]
niemals   never [K. 9]
niemand (niemanden, niemandem)   no
     one, nobody [K. 4]
der Nikolaustag   St. Nicholas Day
nirgendwo   nowhere [K. 11]
das Niveau, -s   level
der Nobelpreisträger, -/die
     Nobelpreisträgerin, -nen   Nobel
     Prize winner [K. 12]
noch   still; again [K. 4]; ~ (ein)
     mal   once again [K. 4, 8]; Was ~?
     What else? [K. 5]
(das) Nordamerika   North America
der Nordosten   northeast
die Nordsee   North Sea [K. 3]
der Nordwesten   northwest
normalerweise   normally, usually
(das) Norwegen   Norway
der Notarzt, ¨e   emergency room
     physician
die Note, -n   grade in course [K. 12]
der Notendurchschnitt   grade point
     average
die Notiz, -en   note
notwendig   necessary
das Notwendigste   bare necessities
der November   November [K. 2]
der Numerus clausus   restricted
     enrollment
null   zero [K. 1]
die Nummer, -n   number
nun   now [K. 9]
nur   only, just [K. 2]
die Nuss, ¨e   nut

O

ob   whether, if [K. 5]
das Oberhaupt   head (of state)
oberst   upper-most [K. 7]
das Obst   fruit, fruits [K. 3]
oder   or [K. 2]
offen   open [K. 4, 5]
öffentlich   public(ly) [K. 6]
öffnen (hat geöffnet)   to open [K. 5]
die Öffnung, -en   opening
oft (ö)   often [K. 4]
ohne + acc.   without [K. 4]; ohne zu
     ...   without . . . -ing
das Ohr, -en   ear [K. 6]
Oje!   Geez! Oh boy!
ökologisch   ecological
der Oktober   October [K. 2]
das Öl, -e   oil
das Olympiastadion   Olympic Stadium
     in Berlin [K. 11]
die Olympiade, -n   Olympic Games
die Oma, -s   grandma [K. 2]
der Onkel, -   uncle [K. 2]
der Opa, -s   grandpa [K. 2]
die Oper, -n   opera; opera house [K. 7]
die Opposition, -en   opposition
optimistisch   optimistic
orange (adj.)   orange [K. 1]
die Orange, -n   orange [K. 3]
ordnen (hat geordnet)   to put in order,
     organize
die Ordnung   order; alles in
     ~ everything's in order [K. 6]; ~
     schaffen (hat geschafft)   to tidy up
die Organisation, -en   organization
organisieren (hat organisiert)   to organize
die Orientierung, -en   orientation
die Orientierungsstufe   orientation
     stage (5th and 6th grades)
der Originaltext, -e   original text [K. 12]
der Ort, -e   place
örtlich   local
der Osterhase, [-n], -n   Easter bunny
Ostern   Easter [K. 10]
(das) Österreich   Austria [K. 1]
der Österreicher, -/die Österreicherin,
     -nen   Austrian [K. 1]
die Ostsee   Baltic Sea [K. 3]
der Overheadprojektor, -en   overhead
     projector [K. 1]

P

paar: ein ~   a few, some [K. 8]; das
     Paar, -e   pair
packen (hat gepackt)   to pack [K. 4]

die Pädagogik   pedagogy, education [K. 2]
das Paket, -e   package [K. 7]
die Panik   panic
der Papa, -s   papa, dad
der Papierkorb, ¨e   wastepaper basket
     [K. 1]
das Paradies, -e   paradise
parken (hat geparkt)   to park
die Parkgebühr, -en   parking fee
das Parkhaus, ¨er   parking garage
der Parkplatz, ¨e   parking space,
     parking lot
der Parkschein, -e   parking stub, ticket
das Parlament, -e   parliament
die Partei, -en   political party [K. 11];
die Party, -s   party [K. 6]; auf eine ~
     gehen   to go to a party
der Pass, pl. Pässe   passport [K. 4];
     mountain/ski pass [K. 10]
passen (hat gepasst) zu + dat.   to suit,
     fit [K. 8, 10]
passieren (ist passiert) + dat.   to
     happen [K. 5, 12]
der Pastor, -en   pastor
der Patient, [-en], -en/die Patientin,
     -nen   patient
die Pause, -n   break, recess
der Pazifist, [-en], -en/die Pazifistin,
     -nen   pacifist
Pech haben (hat Pech gehabt)   to have
     bad luck [K. 8]
peinlich   embarrassing
pendeln (ist gependelt)   to commute
der Pendler, -/Pendlerin,
     -nen   commuter
die Pension, -en   guesthouse [K. 3]
peppig   peppy
perfekt   perfect
das Perfekt   conversational past
die Perle, -n   pearl, bead
die Person, -en   person [K. 1]
die Personalabteilung, -en   personnel
     department [K. 9]
der Personalchef, -s/die Personalchefin,
     -nen   head of the personnel
     department
der Personenkraftwagen, -   car
persönlich   personal; etwas
     Persönliches   something personal
     [K. 12]
die Persönlichkeit, -en   personality
pessimistisch   pessimistic
die Pfanne, -n   pan
der Pfeffer   pepper [K. 6]
der Pfennig, -e   pfennig (1/100 of a
     Deutsche Mark)
das Pferd, -e   horse
der Pferdeschlitten, -   horse-drawn
     sleigh

(das) Pfingsten   Pentecost
die Pflanze, -n   plant [K. 6]
pflanzen (hat gepflanzt)   to plant [K. 10]
pflegen (hat gepflegt)   to maintain, keep up
der Pflichtkurs, -e   required course
das Pfund, -e   pound [K. 3]
die Pharmazie   pharmaceutics
die Philharmonie   (Berlin) Philharmonic Orchestra [K. 11]
die Philosophie, -n   philosophy [K. 2]
die Physik   physics [K. 2]
der Pilz, -e   mushroom
die Piste, -n   (downhill) ski run, track [K. 10]
der Pistenraser, -   speed demon
der PKW, -s (Personenkraftwagen)   car [K. 7]
der Plan, ˝e   plan
planbar   capable of being planned
das Planetarium, *pl.* **Planetarien**   planetarium
die Planung, -en   plan; planning
das Plattengeschäft, -e   record store
der Platz, ˝e   plaza, square; space, room; seat [K. 3]; ~ **nehmen**   to sit down
plaudern (hat geplaudert)   to chat
plötzlich   suddenly [K. 8]
der Pluspunkt, -e   advantage, plus
pochen (hat gepocht)   to pound, beat
der Poet, [-en], -en/die Poetin, -nen   poet [K. 9]
(das) Polen   Poland [K. 1]
die Politik   politics
der Politiker, -/die Politikerin, -nen   politician [K. 9]
die Politikwissenschaft   political science [K. 2]
die Popmusik   popular music [K. 2]
populär   popular
Das Portemonnaie, -s   wallet [K. 4]
die Portion, -en   portion
(das) Portugal   Portugal
das Porzellan   porcelain, china
positiv   positive
die Post   post office [K. 7]
der Postbote, [-n], -n/die Postbotin, -nen   mailman, letter carrier [K. 10]
das Poster, -   poster
das Postfach, ˝er   mailbox, P. O. box [K. 6]
die Postkarte, -n   postcard [K. 2]
der Praktikant, [-en], -en/die Praktikantin, -nen   intern, trainee [K. 9]
das Praktikum, *pl.* **Praktika**   internship [K. 8, 9]
praktisch   practical(ly) [K. 7]

praktizieren (hat praktiziert)   to practice (a profession)
sich präsentieren (hat sich präsentiert)   to present oneself
das Präteritum   narrative past
die Praxis, *pl.* **Praxen**   doctor's office; *(no pl.)* practice [K. 9]
der Preis, -e   price; prize
preiswert   reasonably priced [K. 10]
die Premiere, -n   premiere [K. 9]
das Prestige   prestige
(das) Preußen   Prussia
prima   top-notch
der Prinz, [-en], -en/die Prinzessin, -nen   prince/princess [K. 10]
das Privatbad, ˝er   private bath
die Privatstunde, -n   private lesson
pro   per
probieren (hat probiert)   to try [K. 8]
das Problem, -e   problem [K. 2, 5]
problemlos   without a problem, hassle-free
der Professor, -en/die Professorin, -nen   professor [K. 1]
der Profi, -s   professional [K. 7]
das Programm, -e   program [K. 9]
der Programmierer, -/die Programmiererin, -nen   programmer [K. 9]
das Projekt, -e   project
proklamieren (hat proklamiert)   to proclaim
der/die Prominente, -n *(adj. as noun)*   public figure
das Proseminar, -e   introductory seminar [K. 8]
die Prüfung, -en   test, examination [K. 4]
die Psychologie   psychology [K. 2]
der Pudding, -s   pudding
der Pullover, -   pullover, sweater [K. 4]
der Pulverschnee   powder snow
pünktlich   punctual, on time [K. 9]
die Puppe, -n   doll
das Puppenhaus, ˝er   doll house
die Pute, -n   turkey [K. 3]
putzen (hat sich geputzt): sich die Zähne ~   to brush one's teeth [K. 8]

Q

das Quadrat, -e   square
qualifiziert   qualified [K. 9]
der Quark   *special German dairy spread* [K. 3]
quer   diagonal, across; ~ **gegenüber von**   diagonally across from [K. 7]
die Quittung, -en   receipt [K. 7]

R

der Rabatt, -e   rebate
das Rad, ˝er   bicycle; **Rad fahren (fährt Rad, fuhr Rad, ist Rad gefahren)**   to bicycle [K. 3]
der Radfahrausweis   bicycle permit [K. 4]
das Radfahren   bicycle riding
der Radfahrer, -/die Radfahrerin, -nen   cyclist, bicycle rider [K. 4]; ~ **frei**   open to cyclists, bicycles allowed
das Radio, -s   radio [K. 6]
der Radweg, -e   bicycle path [K. 4]
der Ramadan   Ramadan [K. 10]
der Rang, ˝e   rank, standing
rar   rare
der Rasierapparat, -e   electric razor, shaver [K. 8]
sich rasieren (hat sich rasiert)   to shave [K. 8]
der Rat, *pl.* **Ratschläge**   advice
raten (rät, riet, hat geraten)   to advise
das Ratespiel, -e   guessing game
das Rathaus, *pl.* **Rathäuser**   city hall [K. 3]
(das) Rätoromanisch   the Romansh language
der Ratschlag, ˝e   advice, suggestion
das Rätsel, -   puzzle, riddle
der Ratskeller, -   ratskeller, town hall basement restaurant
rauchen (hat geraucht)   to smoke [K. 6]
der Raum, ˝e   room [K. 6]
raus   out
raus·kommen (kam raus, ist rausgekommen)   to come out
raus·springen (sprang raus, ist rausgesprungen)   to jump out
reagieren (hat reagiert)   to react [K. 11]
die Reaktion, -en   reaction
realistisch   realistic
die Realität, -en   reality
die Realschule, -n   non-college track high school [K. 8]
der Realschüler, -/die Realschülerin, -nen   high school student
das Rebhuhn, ˝er   partridge
rechnen (hat gerechnet)   to count [K. 12]; ~ **mit** + *dat.*   to count on, reckon with, expect [K. 12]
der Rechtsanwalt, ˝e/die Rechtsanwältin, -nen   lawyer
recht haben (hat recht gehabt)   to be right [K. 3]; **Du hast vollkommen recht.**   You are absolutely right. [K. 11]

recht sein (ist, war, ist gewesen) + *dat.* to be all right with someone; **wenn es dir recht ist** if it's all right with you

rechtfertigen (hat gerechtfertigt) to justify

rechts right, on the right [K. 4]

der Rechtsanwalt, ⸚e/die Rechtsanwältin, -nen lawyer, attorney [K. 9]

der/die Rechtsradikale, -n *(adj. as noun)* right-wing extremist

der Rechtsradikalismus right-wing extremism

rechtzeitig on time

das Recycling recycling

reden (hat geredet) über + *acc.* to talk about [K. 5]

das Referat, -e seminar paper, presentation [K. 8]; **ein ⸚ halten** to make an oral presentation [K. 8]

das Reformhaus, ⸚er health food store [K. 7]

das Regal, -e shelf, shelving [K. 6]

die Regel, -n rule, regulation [K. 4]

regeln (hat geregelt) to regulate [K. 11].

der Regen rain [K. 5]

der Regenmantel, ⸚ raincoat

der Regenschaden rain damage

der Regenschirm, -e umbrella

die Regierung, -en government [K. 11]

der Regierungsantritt, -e taking office

das Regierungsviertel, - area of federal government buildings [K. 11]

der Regisseur, -e/die Regisseurin, -nen film or play director [K. 9]

regnen (hat geregnet) to rain [K. 5]

das Reich, -e empire; realm [K. 11]; **das Deutsche ⸚** German Empire [K. 11]; **das Dritte ⸚** Third Reich [K. 11]

reichen (hat gereicht) to be enough, suffice, last; to hand, give; **⸚ von . . . bis** to stretch from . . . to [K. 9]

der Reichstag parliament [K. 11] building

die Reifeprüfung, -en high school exam *(Switzerland)*

die Reihenfolge, -n order, sequence [K. 6]

die Reinemachefrau, -en cleaning lady

rein·stellen (hat reingestellt) to put in

der Reis rice

die Reise, -n trip, journey, travel [K. 2]

der Reisekoffer, - suitcase

der Reiseleiter, -/die Reiseleiterin, -nen tour guide, courier, group leader [K. 10]

reisen (ist gereist) to travel [K. 7]

der Reiseplan, ⸚e travel itinerary

das Reisetagebuch, ⸚er travel log, diary

das Reiseunternehmen, - travel agency

reißen (riss, hat gerissen): aus den Angeln ⸚ to tear off its hinges

reiten (ritt, ist geritten) to ride horseback [K. 3]

rekonstruieren (hat rekonstruiert) to reconstruct

relativ relative(ly)

das Relativpronomen, - relative pronoun

der Relativsatz, ⸚e relative clause

die Religion, -en religion [K. 7]

rennen (rannte, ist gerannt) to run, race [K. 10]

renovieren (hat renoviert) to renovate, remodel [K. 11]

die Rente, -n pension

die Rentenversicherung, -en pension insurance, social security

die Republik, -en republic [K. 11] **die Weimarer ⸚** Weimar Republic [K. 11]

der Republikaner, -/die Republikanerin, -nen member of the Republican Party

der Respekt respect [K. 5, 7]

respektieren (hat respektiert) to respect

die Ressource, -n resource

der Rest, -e rest, remainder [K. 11]

das Restaurant, -s restaurant [K. 3]; **im ⸚** in the restaurant [K. 3]

das Resultat, -e result

der Revisionist, [-en], -en/die Revisionistin, -nen revisionist

die Revolution, -en revolution [K. 11]

der Rhein Rhine

richtig correct [K. 1] right [K. 5]; authentic, really [K. 5]

das Richtige the right thing

die Richtung, -en direction [K. 7]

das Rindfleisch beef [K. 3]

das Risiko, pl. Risiken risk [K. 5]

riskant risky

riskieren (hat riskiert) to risk

der Rock, ⸚e skirt [K. 4]

der Rocksänger, -/die Rocksängerin, -nen rock singer

rodeln (ist gerodelt) to sled

die Rolle, -n role, part

die Rollerblades *(pl.)* in-line skates [K. 7]

der Rollladen, ⸚ roll-top shutters [K. 6]

der Rollschuh, -e roller skates

der Roman, -e novel [K. 7]

romantisch romantic [K. 1]

römisch Roman

rosa pink [K. 1]

die Rose, -n rose

rot (ö) red [K. 1]

das Rotkäppchen Little Red Riding Hood

die Routine, -n routine

der Rückblick review

der Rücken, - back [K. 6]

der Rucksack, ⸚e backpack [K. 4]

der Ruf reputation

rufen (rief, hat gerufen) to call [K. 10]

ruhig quiet, peaceful [K. 4]

das Rumpelstilzchen Rumpelstiltskin

rund approximately, roughly; **⸚ um** all around

die Runde, -n round

(das) Russisch the Russian language [K. 2]

rütteln (hat gerüttelt) to shake

S

die Sache, -n thing, object, item [K. 6]

die Sachertorte, -n Sacher chocolate layer cake

(das) Sachsen Saxony

der Saft, ⸚e juice [K. 3]

die Sage, -n myth, legend

sagen (hat gesagt) to say [K. 5]

die Saison, -s (travel) season

der/das Sakko, -s sport coat [K. 4]

der Salat, -e salad; lettuce [K. 3]

das Salz salt [K. 6]

die Salzstange, -n pretzel stick

der Samstag, -e Saturday *(in Southern Germany)* [K. 2]

die Sandale, -n sandal [K. 4]

sanft gentle, soft

der Sänger, -/die Sängerin, -nen singer [K. 9]

der Satz, ⸚e sentence

sauber clean [K. 10]

sauber machen (hat sauber gemacht) to clean

die Sauna, -s sauna

sausen (hat gesaust) to whistle

schade too bad, unfortunate [K. 5]

schaden (hat geschadet) + *dat.* to harm, hurt

schaffen (schuf, hat geschaffen) to create [K. 9]

schaffen (hat geschafft) to accomplish [K. 9]

der Schal, -s scarf, shawl [K. 4]

der Schatz, ⸚e treasure

schauen (hat geschaut) to look at, to watch [K. 7]; **Schau mal!** Look!

der Schauer, - shower; shivers [K. 5]

der Schauspieler, -/die Schauspielerin, -nen actor/actress [K. 9]

das Schauspielhaus, ¨-er theater

der Scheck, -s check [K. 7]

die Scheibe, -n slice [K. 3]

der Schein, -e paper money, bill; course credit certificate

scheinbar apparently, seemingly

scheinen (schien, hat geschienen) to shine; to appear to be [K. 5]

schenken (hat geschenkt) to give a gift [K. 6]

das Scheunenviertel former Jewish neighborhood in Berlin [K. 11]

schicken (hat geschickt) to send [K. 4]

schief·gehen (ging schief, ist schiefgegangen) to fail, go wrong

schießen (schoss, hat geschossen) to shoot [K. 7]

das Schiff, -e boat [K. 7]

die Schifffahrt, -en boat trip [K. 3]

das Schild, -er sign

schildern (hat geschildert) to portray, describe (an action)

der Schirm, -e umbrella

die Schlacht, -en battle, fight

schlafen (schläft, schlief, hat geschlafen) to sleep [K. 2]

schlafen gehen (ging schlafen, ist schlafen gegangen) to go to sleep [K. 2]

das Schlafzimmer, - bedroom [K. 6]

die Schlange, -n waiting line; snake; [in der] ~ stehen to stand/wait in line [K. 11]

schlank slim, slender [K. 1]

schlecht bad [K. 5]

der Schleier, - veil [K. 5]

schlicht simple [K. 11]

schließlich finally [K. 8]

schlimm bad, nasty [K. 5]

die Schlittelfahrt, -en toboggan run, sleighride (Swiss dialect)

schlittelnd sledding, by sled (Swiss dialect)

der Schlitten, - sled, sleigh

Schlittschuh laufen (läuft, lief, ist gelaufen) to skate [K. 10]

das Schlittschuhlaufen skating [K. 10]

das Schloss, pl. Schlösser castle, palace [K. 3]

der Schlossgarten, ¨- palace grounds, castle garden

der Schlossplatz, ¨-e castle square

der Schlummertrunk, ¨-e bedtime drink, nightcap

der Schluss, ¨-e conclusion, finish, end

der Schlüssel, - key [K. 6]

schmecken (hat geschmeckt) + dat. to taste good [K. 6]

der Schmerz, -en pain [K. 8]

die Schmerztablette, -n pain killer [K. 8]

sich schminken (hat sich geschminkt) to put on make-up [K. 8]

schmusen (hat geschmust) to cuddle, to make out [K. 5]

schmutzig dirty [K. 8]

der Schnee snow [K. 5]

das Schneewittchen Snow White

die Schneidemaschine, -n slicer

sich schneiden (schnitt sich, hat sich geschnitten) in + acc. to cut oneself in [K. 8]

schneien (hat geschneit) to snow [K. 5]

schnell fast, quickly [K. 4]

der Schnupfen head cold [K. 8]; einen ~ haben to have a head cold [K. 8]

der Schock, -s shock

die Schokolade, -n chocolate

schon already [K. 5]; ~ seit Jahren for years [K. 5]

schonen (hat geschont) to save, preserve

schön pretty, beautiful [K. 1]

die Schönheit, -en beauty

der Schrank, ¨-e closet, wardrobe [K. 6]

schrecklich awful(ly), terrible, terribly [K. 8]

schreiben (schrieb, hat geschrieben) to write [K. 2, 7]; ~ an + acc. to write to

die Schreibstube, -n office

der Schreibtisch desk [K. 1, 6]

schwarz black [K. 1]

die Schweiz Switzerland [K. 1]

der Schweizer / die Schweizerin Swiss person [K. 1]

schwer difficult, hard [K. 6]; heavy

schwerhörig hard-of-hearing

die Schwester, -n sister [K. 2]

schwierig difficult, hard [K. 5]

die Schwierigkeit, -en difficulty, problem [K. 8]

das Schwimmbad, ¨-er swimming pool [K. 3]

schwimmen (schwamm, ist geschwommen) to swim [K. 5]

schwul gay, homosexual (colloq.)

schwül humid [K. 5]

schwungvoll lively [K. 9]

sechs six [K. 1]

sechzehn sixteen [K. 1]

sechzig sixty [K. 1]

der See, -n lake [K. 10]

die See, -n sea [K. 11]

segeln (ist gesegelt) to sail [K. 3]

sehen (sieht, sah, hat gesehen) to see [K. 2]

die Sehenswürdigkeit, -en sightseeing attraction [K. 10]

sehr very [K. 2]; nicht ~ not very, not much [K. 2]

das Seidentuch, ¨-er silk scarf

die Seife, -n soap [K. 8]

die Seifenoper, -n soap opera sein his, its [K. 3]

sein (ist, war, ist gewesen) to be [K. 1]

seit + dat. since, for (+ time phrase) [K. 5, 6]

seitdem ever since

die Seite, -n page; side

der Sekretär, -e/die Sekretärin, -nen secretary [K. 9]

die Sekunde, -n second

selber self; oneself, myself, etc.

selbst self; (by) oneself, myself, etc. [K. 8]

selbstständig independent, selfreliant [K. 9]

selbstsicher self-assured, selfconfident [K. 4]

selten rare, seldom [K. 5]

seltsam strange, unusual [K. 10]

das Semester, - semester [K. 2]

die Semesterferien (pl.) semester break [K. 8]

die Semesterkarte, -n semester bus pass

das Semesterticket, -s semester pass (for city transportation) [K. 7]

das Seminar, -e seminar; academic department [K. 8]

die Seminararbeit, -en seminar paper [K. 8]

der Seminarraum, ¨-e seminar room

die Semmel, -n hard roll (in southern Germany and Austria) [K. 3]

senden (hat gesendet) to send

die Sendepause, -n non-broadcast time

der September September [K. 2]

die Serenade, -n serenade

Servus! Hello! (in Austria) [K. 1]

der Sessel, - armchair [K. 6]

setzen (hat gesetzt) to set down, put down [K. 7]; sich ~ (hat sich gesetzt) to sit (oneself) down [K. 1]

die Sexualität sexuality [K. 2]

das Shampoo, -s shampoo [K. 8]

sicher certain(ly), sure(ly) [K. 3]

die Sicherheit, -en safety, security

der Sicherheitshelm, -e safety helmet [K. 4]

sichtbar visible, clear to the eye

sie she, it; they [K. 1]; her, it, them *(acc.)* [K. 3]

Sie you *(formal)* [K. 1] *(formal nom. acc.)* [K. 3]

sieben seven [K. 1]

siebzehn seventeen [K. 1]

siebzig seventy [K. 1]

siegen (hat gesiegt) to win [K. 7]

die Siegermacht, ¨e victor, victorious foreign power [K. 11]

das Silber silver [K. 10]

das Silvester New Year's Eve [K. 10]

singen (sang, hat gesungen) to sing [K. 3]

sinken (sank, ist gesunken) to sink [K. 5]

sitzen (saß, hat gesessen) to be sitting, sit [K. 5, 7]

der Skandal, -e scandal

Ski laufen (läuft Ski, lief Ski, ist Ski gelaufen) to ski [K. 3]

der Skianorak, -s ski parka

die Skihütte, -n ski chalet

der Skistiefel, - ski boot

die Skizze, -n sketch

das Skript, -en lecture notes

die Slowakei Slovakia

(das) Slowenien Slovenia

der Smoking, -s tuxedo

so so; ~ **war das** that's the way it was

sobald as soon as

die Socke, -n sock [K. 4]

das Sofa, -s sofa

sofort at once

der Sohn, ¨e son

solange as long as [K. 4]

solche such

sollen (soll, sollte, hat gesollt) should, ought to; to be supposed to [K. 4]

der Sommer, - summer [K. 5]

das Sommerhäuschen, - summer cottage [K. 11]

der Sommerpalast, ¨e summer palace

sondern but, rather [K. 3]

die Sondertour, -en specialty tour

der Sonnabend, -e Saturday *(in northern Germany)* [K. 2]

die Sonne, -n sun [K. 5]

die Sonnenschutzcreme suntan lotion

die Sonnenterrasse, -n sunning deck

sonnig sunny [K. 5]

der Sonntag, -e Sunday [K. 2]

sonntags on Sundays [K. 2]

sonst otherwise; ~ **noch etwas?** Anything else?

Sonstiges other things

sonst wo (sonst irgendwo) somewhere else

sooft whenever

die Sorge, -n worry, concern; **sich Sorgen machen** to worry [K. 4]

sortieren (hat sortiert) to sort

die Sowjetunion (UdSSR) Soviet Union (USSR)

die Soziologie sociology [K. 2]

die Spalte, -n column

spalten (hat gespaltet) to separate [K. 11]

(das) Spanien Spain

der Spanier / die Spanierin Spanish person [K. 1]

das Spanisch the Spanish language [K. 2]

spannend exciting [K. 7]

sparen (hat gespart) to save [K. 10]

die Sparkasse, -n savings bank [K. 7]

das Sparkonto, -konten savings account [K. 7]

der Spaß, ¨e fun; **aus ~** for fun [K. 12]; ~ **machen** + *dat.* to be fun

spät late [K. 4]; **später** later [K. 5]; **spätestens** at the latest [K. 4]

spazieren gehen (ging spazieren, ist spazieren gegangen) to go for a walk [K. 2]

der Spaziergang, ¨e walk, stroll

der Spaziergänger, -/die Spaziergängerin, -nen walker, stroller

der Speisesaal, *pl.* -säle hotel dining room

der Spiegel, - mirror [K. 4]

das Spiel, -e game, match

spielen (hat gespielt) to play

der Spielkamerad, [-en] -en/die Spielkameradin, -nen playmate

der Spielplatz, ¨e playground [K. 7]

die Spielsache, -n toy

das Spielzeug, -e toy

das Spital, ¨er hospital *(in Austria)*

die Spitze, -n peak, summit

spontan spontaneous

die Spontaneität spontaneity [K. 12]

der Sport sports, athletics; ~ **treiben (hat Sport getrieben)** to do sports [K. 7]

der Sportler, -/die Sportlerin, -nen athlete

sportlich athletic [K. 2, 4, 7]

die Sportstätte, -n training field

die Sprache, -n language [K. 7]

das Sprachinstitut, -e language institute [K. 12]

die Sprachkenntnis, -se linguistic competence [K. 12]

das Sprachlabor, -s *(or* -e*)* language lab

die Sprachreise, -n language study tour

sprechen (spricht, sprach, hat gesprochen) to speak [K. 3]; ~ **für** + *acc.* to speak for, speak well of; to indicate; ~ **mit** + *dat.* to talk to; ~ **über** + *acc.* to talk about [K. 8]

die Sprechstunde, -n office hour [K. 8]

die Spree river through Berlin [K. 11]

das Sprichwort, ¨er proverb

springen (sprang, ist gesprungen) to jump [K. 7]

das Spülbecken, - kitchen sink

die Spur, -en track, trace [K. 9]

spüren (hat gespürt) to feel, to sense [K. 11]

der Staat, -en state, government

staatlich governmental, state-

das Staatsexamen, - state exam; teacher's degree

die Staatsgalerie, -n state gallery

das Stadion, *pl.* Stadien stadium [K. 7]

die Stadt, ¨e city [K. 3]

der Stadtplan, ¨e city map [K. 3]

der Stadtrand, ¨er outskirts of the city

die Stadtrundfahrt, -en city bus tour

der Stadtteil, -e city district

stark (ä) strong [K. 9]

statistisch statistically

statt + *gen.* instead of

statt·finden (fand statt, hat stattgefunden) to take place, occur [K. 8]

staub·saugen (hat gestaubsaugt; hat staubgesaugt) to vacuum

die Steckdose, -n electrical outlet [K. 1]

stecken (hat gesteckt) to stick

stehen (stand, hat gestanden) to stand [K. 7] **Stehen Sie still!** Stand still. [K. 1]

steif stiff, ill-at-ease [K. 4]

steigen (stieg, ist gestiegen) to climb; to rise [K. 5, 7, 10]

die Stelle, -n position, job [K. 9]; spot, place [K. 11]; **an deiner ~** if I were you [K. 11]

stellen (hat gestellt) to stand (something), put [K. 7]

der Stellenwert, -e value, status [K. 12]

die Stellung, -en position, rank [K. 12]

die Stellungnahme opinion

sterben (stirbt, starb, ist gestorben) to die [K. 5, 10]

die Stereoanlage, -n stereo set [K. 6]

der Stiefbruder, ¨ stepbrother

der Stiefel, - boot [K. 4]

die Stiefmutter, ¨ stepmother [K. 10]

die Stiefschwester, -n stepsister

die Stieftochter, ¨ stepdaughter [K. 10]

der Stift, -e pen or pencil

still still, quiet

die Stille   quiet, silence
still·stehen (stand still, hat stillge-
   standen)   to stand still
stimmen (hat gestimmt)   to be correct
   [K. 1]
die Stimmung, -en   atmosphere, mood
   [K. 10]; in einer ~ sein   to be upset
   [K. 12]
stimmungsvoll   full of atmosphere
   [K. 9]
stinken (stank, hat gestunken)   to
   stink
stinklangweilig   boring as heck
das Stipendium, pl. Stipendien
   scholarship, stipend
die Stirn, -en   forehead [K. 6]
der Stock, ¨e   stick
der Stock, pl. Stockwerke   floor, story
   [K. 6]; der erste ~   second floor
   [K. 6]; im zweiten ~   on the third
   floor [K. 6]; einen ~ höher   one floor
   up; einen ~ tiefer   one floor down
der Stöckelschuh, -e   high-heeled shoe
stolz   proud [K. 5]
stören (hat gestört)   to disturb [K. 12]
die Strafe, -n   punishment
der Strand, ¨e   beach
die Straße, -n   street; die ~
   entlang   down the street [K. 7]
die Straßenbahn, -en   streetcar [K. 7]
der Streit   argument [K. 5]
sich streiten (streitet, stritt, hat
   gestritten)   to argue, quarrel
stressen (hat gestresst)   to stress
stressig   stressful [K. 12]
die Strophe, -n   stanza
die Struktur, -en   structure
die Strumpfhose, -n   panty hose,
   stockings [K. 4]
das Stück, -e   piece [K. 3]
der Student, [-en], -en/die Studentin,
   -nen   student [K. 1]
der Studentenausweis, -e   student ID
   [K. 7]
die Studentenermäßigung, -en   student
   discount
die Studentenkneipe, -n   student bar,
   pub
das Studentenleben   student life
das Studentenwerk   student services
   [K. 6]
das Studenten(wohn)heim, -e
   dormitory [K. 6]
das Studentenzimmer, -   student room
   [K. 6]
der Studienberater, -/die Studienberaterin, -nen   academic adviser
das Studienbuch, ¨er   ledger of
   completed courses

das Studienfach, ¨er   academic subject
   [K. 2]
die Studiengebühr, -en   tuition
der Studienplatz, ¨e   place; university
   admission
studieren (hat studiert)   to study [K. 2]
der/die Studierende, -n   (adj. as
   noun)   (university-level) student
   [K. 8]
das Studium, pl. Studien   studies,
   college education
der Stuhl, ¨e   chair [K. 1]
die Stunde, -n   hour
stundenlang   for hours [K. 11]
der Stundenplan, ¨e   schedule
der Sturm, ¨e   storm [K. 5]
das Subjekt, -e   subject
die Suche, -n   search, hunt
suchen (hat gesucht)   to look for; ~
   nach + dat.   to search for, seek,
   look for [K. 7, 10]
südamerikanisch   South American
der Südwesten   southwest
südwestlich   southwestern
der Supermarkt, ¨e   supermarket [K. 3]
die Suppe, -n   soup [K. 3]
surfen (hat gesurft)   to surf [K. 5]
die Sympathie   likeability [K. 5]
sympathisch   likeable, pleasant, nice
   [K. 4]
das Symptom, -e   symptom
die Synagoge, -n   synagogue [K. 7]
systematisch   systematically [K. 7]
die Szene, -n   scene, "in-crowd" [K. 11]

T

die Tabelle, -n   table, chart
tabu   forbidden, taboo [K. 5]
die Tafel, -n   blackboard [K. 1]
der Tag, -e   day [K. 2]; ~ der deutschen
   Einheit   Day of German Unity
   [K. 11]; eines Tages   one day
   [K. 10]; Guten ~!   Good day!,
   Hello! [K. 1]; heute in acht Tagen
   a week from today; in zwei Tagen
   in two days [K. 8]; jeden ~   every
   day [K. 8]
der Tagesablauf   plan for the day, day's
   schedule
täglich   daily [K. 5, 7]
das Tal, ¨er   valley [K. 10]
die Tankstelle, -n   gas station
der Tankwart, -e/die Tankwärtin,
   -nen   gas station attendant
die Tante, -n   aunt [K. 2]
der Tante-Emma-Laden, ¨   family-run
   shop, "mom-and-pop" store

tanzen (hat getanzt)   to dance [K. 2]
der Tarif, -e   wage rate
die Tasche, -n   bag [K. 4]
das Taschengeld   pocket money,
   allowance
das Taschentuch, ¨er   tissue
die Tasse, -n   cup [K. 3]
tätig   active, involved [K. 12]
das Täubchen, -   pigeon, dove
die Taubheit   deafness [K. 9]
tausend   thousand [K. 1]
das Taxi, -s   taxi cab [K. 7]
das Team, -s   team [K. 7]
der Teamgeist,   team spirit [K. 7]
der Tee, -s   tea [K. 3]; ~ kochen   to
   make tea
der Teil, -e   part, portion [K. 9]
teilen (hat geteilt)   to share [K. 6];
   to divide [K. 11]; sich ~ (hat
   sich geteilt)   to share; to divide,
   split (up)
der Teilzeitjob, -s   part-time job
das Telefon, -e   telephone [K. 6]
telefonisch   by telephone
die Telefonnummer, -n   telephone
   number[K. 5]
die Telefonzelle, -n   telephone booth
   [K. 6]
der Teller, -   plate [K. 6]
die Temperatur, -en   temperature
   [K. 5]; Die ~ liegt um 10 Grad
   Celsius.   The temperature is
   around 10 degrees Celsius. [K. 5]
das Tempo, -s   speed [K. 7]
das Tennis   tennis [K. 3]
der Tennisball, ¨e   tennis ball
der Tennisschläger, -   tennis racket
der Teppich, -e   carpet, rug [K. 6]
der Termin, -e   appointment, date [K. 9]
terrorisieren (hat terrorisiert)   to
   terrorize [K. 11]
der Terrorismus   terrorism
teuer   expensive [K. 2, 7]
das Theater, -   theater [K. 3]
die Theaterkasse, -n   box office
das Theaterstück, -e   play [K. 7]
das Thema, pl. Themen   topic, theme
   [K. 8]
thematisch   topical
die Theorie, -n   theory [K. 9]
(das) Thüringen   Thuringia
der Tiefflieger, -   low-flying (fighter)
   plane
das Tier, -e   animal [K. 9]
der Tierarzt, ¨e/die Tierärztin,
   -nen   veterinarian [K. 9]
der Tierpark, -s   zoo
der Tipp, -s   suggestion, tip [K. 12]
tippen (hat getippt)   to type [K. 8]

der Tisch, -e   table [K. 1]
die Tochter, ¨   daughter [K. 2]
der Tod   death
todmüde   dead-tired
Toi, toi, toi!   Lots of luck! [K. 9]
die Toilette, -n   toilet; bathroom [K. 6]
der Toilettenartikel, -   toiletry
tolerant   tolerant
toleriert   tolerated
toll   great, neat, cool [K. 2, 5, 9, 12] **Ich finde es toll.** I think it's great. [K. 12]
die Tomate, -n   tomato [K. 3]
die Tonne, -n   ton
der Topf, ¨e   pot [K. 6]
das Tor, -e   gate; goal [K. 11]; **das Brandenburger ~** Brandenburg Gate [K. 11]
die Torte, -n   layer cake
tot   dead [K. 4]
töten (hat getötet)   to kill
tot·lachen   to laugh yourself silly [K. 7]
der Tourismus   tourism
der Tourist, [-en], -en/die Touristin, -nen   tourist [K. 3]
tragen (trägt, trug, hat getragen)   to wear; to carry [K. 3]
die Tragetasche, -n   bag [K. 7]
der Trainer, -/die Trainerin, -nen   coach [K. 7]
der Transit   transit
das Transportunternehmen, -   transportation company
die Tratschzeitschrift, -en   gossip magazine
die Traube, -n   grape [K. 3]
der Traum, ¨e   dream [K. 1]
träumen (hat geträumt)   to dream
der Traumpartner, -/die Traumpartnerin, -nen   dream partner
traurig   sad [K. 5, 12]
treffen (trifft, traf, hat getroffen)   to meet, run into [K. 5]; to score (in a game) [K. 7]
treiben (trieb, hat getrieben)   to do, play; **Sport ~** to do sports
sich trennen (hat sich getrennt) von + dat.   to break up with, separate from [K. 8]
die Treppe, -n   stairs, stairway [K. 6, 10]
das Treppenhaus, ¨er   stairway
treten (tritt, trat, hat getreten)   to kick, step
treu   faithful, loyal, true [K. 5]
die Treue   loyalty [K. 5]
der Trimm-dich-Pfad, -e   exercise course
trinken (trank, hat getrunken)   to drink [K. 2]
das Trinkgeld, -er   tip, gratuity [K. 5]
trivial   trivial
trocken   dry [K. 5]

trotz + gen.   in spite of, despite [K. 8]
trotzdem   nevertheless, in spite of that [K. 5, 9]
(das) Tschechien, die Tschechische Republik   Czech Republic
die Tschechoslowakei   Czechoslovakia
Tschüss!   Bye! [K. 1]
das T-Shirt, -s   T-shirt [K. 4]
die Tulpe, -n   tulip
tun (tat, hat getan)   to do; put [K. 3]
der Tunnel, -s or -   tunnel
die Tür, -en   door [K. 1]
der Türke, [-n], -n/die Türkin, -nen   Turk
die Türkei   Turkey
der Turm, ¨e   tower [K. 3]
das Turnier, -e   tournament
der Turnschuh, -e   athletic shoe [K. 3]
der Turnverein, -e   athletic club [K. 7]
die Tüte, -n   sack, bag [K. 7]
der Tutor, -en/die Tutorin, -nen   tutor
der Typ, -en   type; guy, fellow (colloq.) [K. 9]
typisch   typical

U

die U-Bahn, -en   subway [K. 7]
üben (hat geübt)   to practice, rehearse [K. 9]
über   above, over [K. 7]
überarbeitet   overworked
überfüllt   overfilled, oversubscribed
sich übergeben (übergibt sich, übergab sich, hat sich übergeben)   to vomit [K. 8]
überhaupt   at all [K. 4]; **~ kein** none at all [K. 2]
überholen (hat überholt)   to pass (a vehicle)
überlegen (hat überlegt)   to consider, think about; **sich ~ (überlegt sich, hat sich überlegt)** to think over, consider
übermäßig   excessively
übermorgen   the day after tomorrow [K. 8]
überprüfen (hat überprüft)   to check
überraschen (hat überrascht)   to surprise
überraschend   surprising(ly) [K. 11]
überreden (hat überredet)   to persuade
überschätzen (hat überschätzt)   to overestimate
übersehen (übersieht, übersah, hat übersehen)   to oversee; to overlook
übersetzen (hat übersetzt)   to translate

der Übersetzer, -/die Übersetzerin, -nen   translator, interpreter [K. 12]
die Übersetzung, -en   translation
übertreiben (übertrieb, hat übertrieben)   to exaggerate
die Übertreibung, -en   exaggeration
überzeugen (hat überzeugt)   to convince [K. 10, 12]
üblich   usual, common
die Übung, -en   practice; exercise; discussion section
die Uhr, -en   clock, watch [K. 1]; time [K. 2]; **Wie viel ~ ist es?** What time is it? [K. 2]; **um (sechs) ~** at (six) o'clock [K. 2]
die Ukraine   Ukraine
um + acc.   around; at (time) [K. 4]
umarmen (hat umarmt)   to embrace, to hug [K. 5]
die Umbauarbeit, -en   renovation work, remodeling
um·bauen (hat umgebaut)   to renovate
sich um·drehen (hat sich umgedreht)   to turn (oneself) around [K. 2]
die Umgangssprache, -n   colloquial language
die Umgebung, -en   surroundings, area
umgekehrt   the other way around, vice versa
um·siedeln (ist umgesiedelt)   to change residence, move [K. 11]
um·steigen (steigt um, stieg um, ist umgestiegen)   to change (trains)
die Umwelt   environment
umweltbewusst   environmentally aware
um·werfen (wirft um, warf um, hat umgeworfen)   to knock over [K. 12]
der Umzug, ¨e   parade [K. 10]
um ... zu   in order to . . .
unattraktiv   unattractive [K. 1]
unbedeutend   unimportant
unbedingt   absolutely, really [K. 11]
unbezahlt   unpaid [K. 9]
und   and [K. 1]; **... ~ so** . . . and stuff like that [K. 11]; **~ so weiter (usw.)** et cetera (etc.) [K. 5]
undenkbar   unthinkable
unentbehrlich   indispensable
der Unfall, ¨e   accident
unfreundlich   unfriendly [K. 4]
(das) Ungarn   Hungary
ungeduldig   impatient
ungefähr   approximately [K. 4]
unglücklich   unhappy [K. 4]
unhöflich   impolite [K. 7]
die Uni, -s   university

die Universität, -en university [K. 1]; **an der ~** at college, at the university

unmusikalisch unmusical [K. 4]

die UNO United Nations Organization (UN)

unpersönlich impersonal

uns us *(acc., dat.)* [K. 2, 6]

unser our [K. 3]

unsicher unsure, insecure [K. 4]

der Unsinn nonsense [K. 12]

unsportlich unathletic [K. 4]

unsympathisch unlikeable, disagreeable [K. 4]

unten downstairs

unter under, underneath [K. 7]; **~ sich** among themselves; **~ Verschluss halten** to keep under lock and key

unterbezahlt underpaid

die Unterbrechung, -en interruption

unter·bringen (brachte unter, hat untergebracht) to house, put up overnight

sich unterhalten (unterhält sich, unterhielt sich, hat sich unterhalten) mit + *dat.* to converse with, talk to [K. 5]

unterhaltend entertaining K. 7]

die Unterhaltung, -en entertainment; conversation

unter·kommen (ist untergekommen) to find lodging

die Unterlage, -n form, document

das Unternehmen, - business, company; undertaking, project [K. 11]

der Unternehmer, -/die Unternehmerin, -nen entrepreneur, venture capitalist

unternehmungslustig active, eager to participate

der Unteroffizier, -e non-commissioned officer

der Unterricht instruction, lesson, class [K. 6, 7]

unterrichten (hat unterrichtet) to instruct, teach [K. 12]

unterschätzen (hat unterschätzt) to underestimate

der Unterschied, -e difference [K. 10]

unterstützen (hat unterstützt) to support

der Untertitel, - subtitle

die Unterwäsche underwear [K. 4]

unterwegs enroute, underway[K. 4]

der Urgroßvater, -väter great-grandfather [K. 12]

der Urlaub, -e vacation [K. 10]

der Urlaubsschein, -e leave permit, pass

die Ursache, -n cause

ursprünglich originally [K. 10]

die USA *(pl.)* U.S.A. [K. 1]

usw. (und so weiter) etc. (et cetera) [K. 5]

V

der Vater, ‥ father [K. 2]

der Vati, -s dad

vegetarisch vegetarian

sich verabreden (hat sich verabredet) mit + *dat.* to make a date with [K. 11]

verabredet committed; have a date

die Verabredung, -en date

(sich) verabschieden (hat [sich] verabschiedet) von + *dat.* to say good-bye to (someone) [K. 12]

verändern (hat verändert) to change [K. 12]

verantwortlich responsible

die Verantwortung, -en responsibility

verantwortungsvoll responsible, responsibly

verbessern (hat verbessert) to improve [K. 2, 12]

verbieten (verbot, hat verboten) to forbid [K. 10]

das Verbot, -e ban, prohibition [K. 4]; **~ für Fahrzeuge aller Art** closed to all vehicles; **~ für Radfahrer** no bicycles allowed

verboten forbidden, prohibited [K. 6]

verbrauchen (hat verbraucht) to consume, use

[Zeit] verbringen (verbrachte, hat verbracht) to spend [time] [K. 2]

verdeutlichen (hat verdeutlicht) to clarify

verdienen (hat verdient) to earn [K. 5]

sich verdoppeln (hat sich verdoppelt) to double

der Verein, -e association, organization, club [K. 7]

die Vereinigten Staaten *(pl.)* the United States (of America)

die Vereinigung, -en union, unification [K. 11]

verfassen (hat verfasst) to write

die Verfassung constitution [K. 11]

verführen (hat verführt) to tempt, entice

die Vergangenheit past [K. 12]

vergessen (vergisst, vergaß, hat vergessen) to forget [K. 3]

vergiften (hat vergiftet) to poison

vergleichen (verglich, hat verglichen) to compare

vergrößern (hat vergrößert) to enlarge, expand

sich verhalten (verhält sich, verhielt sich, hat sich verhalten) to behave, act [K. 9]

verheiratet married [K. 2]

verhüllen (hat verhüllt) to wrap, conceal

verkaufen (hat verkauft) to sell [K. 5]

der Verkäufer, -/die Verkäuferin, -nen salesperson [K. 9]

die Verkaufsabteilung, -en sales department

der Verkehr traffic [K. 4]

das Verkehrsmittel, - means of transportation

die Verkehrsregel, -n rule of the road, traffic regulation

das Verkehrsschild, -er traffic sign [K. 4]

der Verkehrsverein, -e tourist office

das Verkehrszeichen, - traffic sign [K. 4]

verkleiden (hat verkleidet) to disguise [K. 10]

verkünden (hat verkundet) to announce [K. 11]

verlangen (hat verlangt) to demand, require

verlassen (verlässt, verließ, hat verlassen) to leave

der Verleih, -e rental company

verleihen (verlieh, hat verliehen) to loan out

sich verletzen (hat sich verletzt) to hurt oneself, injure oneself

sich verlieben (hat sich verliebt) in + *acc.* to fall in love with [K. 8]

verliebt sein (ist verliebt gewesen) in + *acc.* to be in love with [K. 5]; **über beide Ohren verliebt in** + *acc.* head over heels in love with

verlieren (verlor, hat verloren) to lose [K. 5, 10]

sich verloben (hat sich verlobt) mit + *dat.* to get engaged to [K. 5]

der/die Verlobte, -n *(adj. as noun)* fiancé(e) [K. 5]

sich vermählen (hat sich vermählt) to wed

vermeiden (vermied, hat vermieden) to avoid [K. 5]

vermissen (hat vermisst) to miss [K. 12]

der Vermieter, -/die Vermieterin, -nen landlord/landlady

die Vermittlungsagentur, -en placement agency

vernünftig reasonable, logical

veröffentlichen (hat veröffentlicht) to publish [K. 12]

die Veröffentlichung, -en publication
die Verpflegung food, board
verpflichtend mandatory, required [K. 7]
verraten (verrät, hat verraten) to reveal, betray [K. 7]
verreisen (ist verreist) to go on a trip [K. 10]
verrückt crazy
verschieden different [K. 8]
verschlafen (verschläft, verschlief, hat verschlafen) to oversleep
sich verschließen (hat sich verschlossen) to close oneself off
der Verschluss, -e lock, clasp
verschneit snow-covered [K. 10]
verschüttet blocked in
die Versicherung, -en insurance
die Version, -en version
sich versöhnen (hat sich versöhnt) mit + dat. to make up, reconcile with [K. 5]
die Verspätung, -en delay, late arrival, tardiness [K. 11]
versprechen (verspricht, versprach, hat versprochen) to promise
die Versprechung, -en promise
der Verstand reason, logic
sich verständlich machen (hat sich verständlich gemacht) to make oneself understood [K. 12]
das Verständnis understanding, sympathy
verstecken (hat versteckt) to hide, conceal [K. 10]
verstehen (verstand, hat verstanden) to understand, comprehend [K. 2]; **sich ~** to understand (one another) [K. 12]; **~ von + dat.** to know something (anything) about
versuchen (hat versucht) to try, attempt [K. 8]
der Vertrag, -e contract
das Vertrauen trust [K. 5]
vertrauen fassen zu (+dat) to trust [K. 5]
vervollständigen (hat vervollständigt) to complete
verwalten (hat verwaltet) to administrate
verwandeln (hat verwandelt) to transform
der/die Verwandte, -n *(adj. as noun)* relative [K. 2]
die Verwandtschaft, -en relatives
verwenden (hat verwendet) to apply, use [K. 11]
verwitwet widowed
verwundert amazed
die Verzweiflung, -en desperation [K. 9]
der Videofilm, -e movie on video cassette

der Videoverleih, -e video store
viel a lot, much [K. 2]; **viele** many [K. 2]; **Vielen Dank!** Thanks a lot! [K. 6]; **zu viele** too many [K. 3]
die Vielfalt great variety
vielleicht perhaps, maybe [K. 3]
vier four [K. 1]
vierzehn fourteen [K. 1]
vierzig forty [K. 1]
das Vier-Mächte-Abkommen Quadripartite Treaty
das Viertel, - quarter; district, neighborhood [K. 11]; **~ nach** quarter past [K. 2]; **~ vor zwei** quarter to two [K. 2]; **drei viertel zwei** quarter of two, quarter to two
der Vogel, : bird; **Er hat einen ~** He's crazy. He's nuts. [K. 6]; **das Vögelchen, -** little bird
der Vogelkäfig, -e bird cage
die Vokabel, -n word
die Völkerverständigung international understanding [K. 6]
die Volkskammer People's Chamber of the GDR Parliament [K. 11]
der Volkswagen, - Volkswagen
die Volkswirtschaft, -en economics [K. 2]
vollendet completed
der Volleyball volleyball [K. 3]
vollkommen completely [K. 11]
vollständig complete(ly)
von + dat. of, from, by [K. 6]; **~ da an** from that point on; **~ wem?** from whom? ; **~ ... bis** from . . . until
vor + dat. before; in front of; *(of time)* ago [K. 7]
vorbei·reiten (ritt vorbei, ist vorbeigeritten) to ride by, ride past on horseback [K. 10]
vor·bereiten (hat vorbereitet) to prepare [K. 8]; **sich ~ (hat sich vorbereitet) auf + acc.** to prepare for, get ready for [K. 8]
die Vorbereitung, -en preparation
vorbildlich exemplary
der Vorfahr, [-en], -en/die Vorfahrin, -nen ancestor [K. 12]
die Vorfahrt right of way [K. 4]
vor·haben (hat vor, hatte vor, hat vorgehabt) to plan, have planned [K. 11]
vorher before, previously
vor·kommen (ist vorgekommen) + dat. to appear to be
vor·lesen (liest vor, las vor, hat vorgelesen) to read aloud; lecture

die Vorlesung, -en lecture [K. 6, 8]
das Vorlesungsverzeichnis, -se course catalogue
vor·machen (macht vor, hat vorgemacht) to fool, kid, delude
vormittags in the morning, A.M.
vorne up front [K. 1]; **da ~** over there
die Vorschau preview
der Vorschlag, -e suggestion
vor·schlagen (schlägt vor, schlug vor, hat vorgeschlagen) to suggest [K. 7, 11]
vor·schreiben (schrieb vor, hat vorgeschrieben) to stipulate
vorsichtig careful, cautious [K. 4]
der/die Vorsitzende, -n *(adj. as noun)* chairperson
die Vorspeise, -n appetizer [K. 3]
der Vorsprung lead; advantage
sich vor·stellen (hat sich vorgestellt) to imagine; to introduce oneself [K. 8]
die Vorstellung, -en presentation, performance; introduction; image [K. 9] impression, image [K. 11]
das Vorstellungsgespräch, -e job interview [K. 9]
der Vorteil, -e advantage
der Vortrag, -e presentation
das Vorurteil, -e prejudice
vor·ziehen (zog vor, hat vorgezogen) + dat. to prefer to
der VW, -s VW, Volkswagen

W

wachsen (wächst, wuchs, ist gewachsen) to grow [K. 10]
wackeln (hat gewackelt) to wobble
wacker honest, upright
wagen (hat gewagt) to dare, risk
der Wagen, - car [K. 4]
die Wahl, -en selection, choice; election
wählen (hat gewählt) to choose, select; elect [K. 8]
der Wähler, -/die Wählerin, -nen voter
der Wahnsinn insanity
wahnsinnig crazy, insane [K. 9]
wahr real, true [K. 5]
während + gen. during [K. 8]
die Wahrheit, -en truth [K. 8]
wahrscheinlich probably [K. 3]
das Wahrzeichen, - emblem, symbol
der Wald, -er forest, woods [K. 10]
die Wand, -e interior wall [K. 1]
der Wandel, - change, transformation [K. 10]
wandern (ist gewandert) to hike, go hiking [K. 2]

die Wanderung, -en hike [K. 4]
der Wanderweg, -e hiking path
wann? When? [K. 1]
warm (ä) warm [K. 5]
warnen (hat gewarnt) to warn [K. 11]
warten (hat gewartet) to wait [K. 3];
    to service; ~ auf + acc. to wait for
die Wartezeit, -en waiting period
warum? Why? [K. 1]
was? What? [K. 1]; Was für
    ein(e)? What kind of? [K. 9]; Was
    gibt's? What's up?; Was tut dir
    weh? Where do you hurt?
das Waschbecken, - sink [K. 6]
die Wäsche laundry
sich waschen (wäscht sich, wusch sich,
    hat sich gewaschen) to wash
    (oneself) [K. 8]; sich die Haare
    ~ to shampoo [K. 8]; sich die
    Hände ~ to wash one's hands [K. 8]
die Waschküche, -n laundry room
    [K. 6]
die Waschmaschine, -n washing
    machine
das Wasser water [K. 3]
die Wasserflasche, -n water bottle
der Wasserturm water tower [K. 3]
Wasserski fahren (fährt, fuhr, ist
    gefahren) to waterski
das Wasserspiel, -e trick fountains
der Wassersport water sports
der Wasserturm, ¨e water tower
das WC, -s toilet [K. 6]
die Website, -s Website [K. 12]
wechseln (hat gewechselt) to change
    [K. 8]
der Wecker, - alarm clock [K. 6]
weg away
der Weg, -e path [K. 4]; auf dem
    ~ on the way
die Wegbeschreibung, -en directions
wegen + gen. because of [K. 8]
weg·räumen (hat weggeräumt) to
    clear away
weg·ziehen (zog weg, ist
    weggezogen) to move away [K. 5]
weh·tun (tat weh, hat wehgetan) +
    dat. to hurt (someone) [K. 6,
    8]; sich ~ (tat sich weh, hat sich
    wehgetan) to hurt oneself
weigern sich (hat sich geweigert) to
    refuse [K. 7]
das Weihnachten Christmas [K. 10]
der Weihnachtsmann, ¨er Santa Claus
der Weihnachtsmarkt, ¨e Christmas
    market
weil because [K. 5]
die Weile a while
der Wein, -e wine [K. 3]
der Weinberg, -e vineyard

weinen (hat geweint) to cry [K. 10]
der Weisheitszahn, ¨e wisdom tooth
weiß white [K. 1]
weit far [K. 5]; ~ weg far away [K. 5]
weitere further, additional [K. 9]
weiter·gehen (geht weiter, ging weiter,
    ist weitergegangen) to continue
welcher, welches, welche which [K. 1, 6]
wellig wavy [K. 1]
die Welt, -en world [K. 9] auf der Welt
    in the world [K. 12]
weltberühmt world-famous [K. 9]
der Weltkrieg, -e world war [K. 11]
die Weltmeisterschaft (die
    WM) World Cup, world
    championship [K. 11]
wem (to) whom (dat.) [K. 2, 6]
wen whom (acc.) [K. 2]
die Wende turning point; time in East
    Germany from 1989 to unification
    [K. 11]
wenden (hat gewendet) to turn [K. 11]
wenig little [K. 2]; wenige a few
    [K. 2]; weniger fewer, less
wenigstens at least [K. 5]
wenn if, when [K.5, 10]; immer ~
    always when, whenever [K. 10]
wer? Who? (nom.) [K. 1]
die Werbeagentur, -en advertising
    agency
die Werbebroschüre, -n advertising
    brochure
der Werbespot commercial
der Werdegang, ¨e development; career
werden (wird, wurde, ist geworden) to
    become [K. 3]; will, shall (future
    tense) [K. 8]
werfen (wirft, warf, hat geworfen) to
    throw, toss [K. 10]
das Werk, -e (creative) work
das Werkzeug, -e tool
die Werkzeugkiste, -n toolbox
Wert legen auf + acc. (hat gelegt) to
    emphasize [K. 7]
wertvoll valuable
wesentlich essential
wessen whose [K. 10]
das Wetter weather [K. 5]
der Wetterbericht, -e weather report
wett·machen (hat wettgemacht) to
    make up for, compensate for
wichtig important [K. 4]
die Wichtigkeit, -en importance
das Wichtigste the most important
    thing
wider·spiegeln (hat widergespiegelt)
    to reflect
der Widerstand, ¨e resistance [K. 11]
widmen (hat gewidmet) + dat. to
    dedicate [K. 9]

wie? how?; what [K. 1]; ~ alt? how
    old?; ~ bitte? Please repeat that.
    [K. 1]; ~ heißen Sie? What's your
    name? [K. 1]; ~ viel how much
    [K. 1]; ~ viele how many [K. 1]
wieder again
wieder·aufbauen (hat wiederaufgebaut)
    to reconstruct
wiederholen (hat wiederholt) to
    repeat
die Wiederholung, -en repetition
Wiederhören: Auf ~! Good-bye! (on
    the phone)
wieder·kommen (ist wiedergekommen)
    to come back, return
Wiedersehen: Auf ~! Good-bye! [K. 1]
die Wiedervereinigung reunification
    [K. 11]
Wien Vienna
die Wiese, -n meadow
wie viel how much [K. 1]; ~ Uhr ist es?
    What time is it? [K. 2]
das Willkommen, - welcome;
    Herzlich willkommen in
    ... Welcome to . . .
der Wind, -e wind
windig windy [K. 5]
die Windpocken (pl.) chicken pox
der Winter, - winter [K. 5]
wir we [K. 1]
der Wirbelsturm, ¨e tornado
wirken (hat gewirkt) to have an effect,
    impact, make an impression [K. 5]
wirklich really [K. 5]
die Wirklichkeit, -en reality
die Wirkung, -en effect
der Wirt, -e/die Wirtin, -nen host (in
    a restaurant or bar)
die Wirtschaft, -en tavern [K. 10];
    economy
die Wirtschaftszeitung, -en business/
    economics newspaper
wissen (weiß, wusste, hat gewusst) to
    know (a fact) [K. 3]; ~ von +
    dat. to know about
der Wissenschaftler, -/die Wissenschaftlerin,
    -nen scientist [K. 9]
wissenschaftlich scientific [K. 12]
wissenswert worth knowing
der Witz, -e joke, wit [K. 10]
wo? where? [K. 1]
die Woche, -n week [K. 2]; nächste
    ~ next week [K. 8]; vor einer ~ a
    week ago [K. 6]
das Wochenende, -n weekend [K. 2];
    am ~ on the weekend [K. 2]
der Wochentag, -e day of the week
    [K. 2]
woher? from where? [K. 1]
wohin? where to? [K. 1]

wohl in all likelihood, no doubt, probably [K. 3]; well, healthy [K. 8]
das Wohlbefinden well-being [K. 7]
wohnen (hat gewohnt) to live [K. 2]; **in Untermiete ~** to live in a sublet room
die Wohngemeinschaft, -en (WG) shared apartment, cooperative living [K. 6]
der Wohnort, -e place of residence [K. 11]
die Wohnung, -en apartment [K. 6]
der Wohnungsmarkt, ¨e real estate market
das Wohnzimmer, - living room [K. 6]
die Wolke, -n cloud [K. 5]
wolkig cloudy [K. 5]
wollen (will, wollte, hat gewollt) to want to [K. 4]
womit with what
das Wort, ¨er word
das Wörterbuch, ¨er dictionary [K. 4]
wortwörtlich literally
das Wunder, - miracle, wonder [K. 10]
wunderbar wonderful [K. 2]
der Wunsch, ¨e wish, request [K. 11]
wünschen (hat gewünscht) to wish [K. 9]
die Wurst, ¨e sausage [K. 3]
die Wut rage

X

x-mal umpteen times

Z

die Zahl, -en number [K. 1]
zahlen (hat gezahlt) to pay
zahllos innumerable
zahlreich multiple, many, numerous [K. 9]
der Zahn, ¨e tooth [K. 6]
der Zahnarzt, ¨e/die Zahnärztin, -nen dentist [K. 9]
die Zahnbürste, -n toothbrush [K. 4]
die Zahnpasta, *pl.* **-pasten** toothpaste [K. 4]
die Zahnschmerzen *(pl.)* toothache [K. 8]
der Zauberer, - magician, sorcerer [K. 10]
die Zauberstimmung magical mood
z. B. zum Beispiel *for example*
der Zeh, -en *or* **die Zehe, -n** toe [K. 6, 10]
zehn, ten [K. 1]
das Zeichen, - sign, marker
der Zeichenblock, ¨e sketch pad
der Zeichentrickfilm, -e animated movie, cartoon [K. 7]

zeichnen (hat gezeichnet) to draw, sketch
die Zeichnung, -en drawing, sketch
zeigen (hat gezeigt) to show, point; **Zeigen Sie . . .!** Point to [K. 1]
die Zeile, -n line
die Zeit, -en time [K. 2]; **die ganze ~** the whole time
die Zeitschrift, -en magazine [K. 7]
die Zeittafel, -n timetable, time line
die Zeitung, -en newspaper [K. 5]
der Zeitungskiosk, -e newspaper stand
der Zeitungsstand, ¨e newspaper stand [K. 7]
das Zelt, -e tent
die Zensur, -en censorship
das Zentrum, *pl.* **Zentren** center [K. 3, 11]
zerbrechlich fragile, breakable
zerreißen (zerriss, hat zerrissen) to rip up, tear up
zerschlagen all beat up
zerschossen shot up, riddled with bullet holes
zerstören (hat zerstört) to destroy [K. 11]
der Zettel, - note, scrap of paper
das Zeug stuff, things
ziehen (zog, hat gezogen) to pull, raise [K. 10]
das Ziel, -e goal, target, destination [K. 7, 11]
ziemlich rather, pretty [K. 4]
zigmal umpteen times [K. 7]
das Zimmer, - room [K. 6]; **~ und Verpflegung** room and board; **die ~ und Wohungsvermittlung, -en** housing placement service
der Zimmerkamerad, [-en], -en/ die Zimmerkameradin, -nen roommate
die Zimmernummer, -n room number
der Zoll, ¨e customs
der Zoo, -s zoo [K. 3]
zu + *dat.* to [K. 6]; **~ Hause** at home [K. 6]; **~ zweit** as a couple, in twos [K. 5]; **~** + *inf.* to [K. 5]
zuerst first of all [K. 3]
der Zufall, ¨e coincidence
zufrieden satisfied, content [K. 7]
der Zug, ¨e train [K. 4]
die Zugverbindung, -en train connection
zu·hören (hat zugehört) + *dat.* to listen
der Zuhörer, -/die Zuhörerin, -nen listener
zu·knallen (hat zugeknallt) to slam shut
die Zukunft future [K. 10, 12]
zuletzt finally [K. 3]

zum to (the); for; **~ ersten Mal** for the first time [K. 5] **~ Spaß** for fun
zu·machen (hat zugemacht) to close
die Zumutung, -en unreasonable demand
zunächst first of all
die Zunge, -n tongue
zu·reden (hat zugeredet) + *dat.* to talk to
zurück·bringen (brachte zurück, hat zurückgebracht) to bring back, return
zurück·geben (gibt zurück, gab zurück, hat zurückgegeben) to give back, return
zurück·gehen (ging zurück, ist zurückgegangen) to go back
zurück·kehren (ist zurückgekehrt) to return
zurück·kommen (kam zurück, ist zurückgekommen) to come back, return, get back [K. 2]
die Zusage, -n commitment
zusammen together [K. 5]
die Zusammenarbeit, -en collaboration, joint project
der Zusammenbruch, ¨e collapse
zusammen·fassen (hat zusammengefasst) to summarize
der Zusammenhang, ¨e connection [K. 12]
zusammen·leben (hat zusammengelebt) to live together, cohabitate [K. 5]
zusammen·passen (hat zusammengepasst) to fit together, belong together [K. 12]
zusammen·stellen (hat zusammengestellt) to put together, organize
zusätzlich additionally [K. 8]
der Zuschauer, -/die Zuschauerin, -nen spectator [K. 7]
zu spat (too) late [K. 4]
zuständig responsible [K. 9]
zu·stimmen (hat zugestimmt) + *dat.* to agree with someone
zuverlässig dependable [K. 9]
zu viel(e) too much, too many
zwanzig twenty [K. 1]
zwar actually, in fact
der Zweck, -e purpose, point [K. 9]
zwei two [K. 1]
der Zweig, -e branch [K. 10]
zweit second; by two; **zu ~** as a couple [K. 5]; two at a time, in a pair
der Zwerg, -e dwarf [K. 10]
zwischen between [K. 5, 7]
der Zwischenfall, ¨e incident
zwölf twelve [K. 1]

The English-German vocabulary focuses on key words (highest frequency words) from the core texts and the **Wissenwerte Vokabeln** sections of the chapters. Definite articles and plural forms are given for nouns. Verbs are listed with their participles. Separable-prefix verbs are marked with a raised dot: **mit·bringen.** For the principal parts of irregular (strong) verbs, refer to pages 495 through 497.

A

a/an ein, eine
ability die Fähigkeit, -en
able: to be ~ to können (hat gekonnt)
above über
absolutely unbedingt
accident der Unfall, ¨e
achieve leisten (hat geleistet)
accompany begleiten (hat begleitet)
accomplish leisten (hat geleistet); schaffen (hat geschafft)
account: on ~ of wegen + *gen.;* **current (bank) ~** das Girokonto, *pl.* Girokonten
accountant der Buchhalter, - / die Buchhalterin, -nen
acquaintance der/die Bekannte, -n *(noun decl. like adj.)*
across from gegenüber von
active tätig; aktiv
activity die Aktivität, -en; **leisure ~** die Freizeitaktivität, -en
actor/actress der Schauspieler, - / die Schauspielerin, -nen
actually eigentlich; zwar
additionally zusätzlich
address book das Adressbuch, ¨er
administer verwalten (hat verwaltet)
admit zu·geben (hat zugegeben)
adult erwachsen *(adj.)*
advanced student der/die Fortgeschrittene, -n *(noun decl. like adj.)*
advantage der Pluspunkt, -e; der Vorteil, -e; der Vorsprung; **information ~** der Informationsvorsprung
adventure film der Abenteuerfilm, -e
advertisement die Annonce, -n; das Inserat, -e; die Anzeige, -n
advice der Rat, *pl.* Ratschläge
advisor der Berater, - / die Beraterin, -nen
after nach + *dat. (prep.)*; nachdem *(conj.)*
afternoon der Nachmittag, -e; **this ~** heute Nachmittag; **Good ~.** Guten Tag.; Tag.
afternoons nachmittags
afterwards nachher
afraid: to be ~ of Angst haben (hat gehabt) vor + *dat.;* fürchten (hat gefürchtet)

African afrikanisch
again wieder; noch (ein)mal
against gegen + *acc.*
ago vor + *dat.*
agree zu·stimmen (hat zugestimmt) + *dat.;* **Agreed!** Abgemacht!
air die Luft
airlift die Luftbrücke
airline ticket der Flugschein, -e; das Flugticket, -s
airplane das Flugzeug, -e
airport der Flughafen, ¨
alarm clock der Wecker, -
alcohol der Alkohol
alcoholic alkoholisch; **non- ~** alkoholfrei
all alle; *(noun)* alles, *(pl.)* alle; **at ~** überhaupt; **~ day** den ganzen Tag; **~ in ~** insgesamt
Allies die Alliierten *(pl.)*
allow erlauben (hat erlaubt); **~ me to introduce myself.** Darf ich mich vorstellen?
allowed: to be ~ dürfen (hat gedurft)
almost fast; beinahe
alone allein
Alps die Alpen *(pl.)*
already schon
also auch
although obwohl
always immer
America (das) Amerika; **United States of ~** die Vereinigten Staaten von Amerika
American amerikanisch *(adj.)*; der Amerikaner, -/ die Amerikanerin, -nen
among unter + *dat.;* **~ themselves** unter sich
analytical analytisch
ancestor der Vorfahr [e], [-en], -en / die Vorfahrin, -nen
and und; **~ so on** und so weiter (usw.); **~ stuff like that** und so; **~ you?** Und Sie?
angry böse; **to be ~ about** sich ärgern (hat sich geärgert) über + *acc.*

animal das Tier, -e
animated cartoon der Zeichentrickfilm, -e
animation der Zeichentrickfilm, -e
announce aus·rufen (hat ausgerufen); bekannt geben (hat bekannt gegeben); aus·schreiben (hat ausgeschrieben)
answer die Antwort, -en; **to ~** antworten + *dat.;* beantworten + *acc.*
any einige; etwas
anything irgendetwas, irgendwas; **~ else?** Sonst noch etwas?
anytime jederzeit
anyway jedenfalls
apartment die Wohnung, -en
appear scheinen (hat geschienen), erscheinen (ist erschienen); aus·sehen (hat ausgesehen); **to ~ to be** vor·kommen (ist vorgekommen) + *dat.*
appearance das Aussehen
appetizer die Vorspeise, -n
apple der Apfel, ¨; **~ juice** der Apfelsaft
applicant der Bewerber, - / die Bewerberin, -nen
application die Bewerbung, -en; **~ form** das Bewerbungsformular, -e; **~ letter** der Bewerbungsbrief, -e
apply sich bewerben (hat sich beworben) für/um + *acc.*
appointment der Termin, -e
apprentice der Lehrling, -e; der/die Auszubildende, -n *(noun decl. like adj.)*; der/die Azubi, -s
approximately ungefähr
April der April
architect der Architekt, [-en], -en/die Architektin, -nen
area die Umgebung; **in the ~** in der Nähe; in der Umgebung; **land ~** die Fläche
area code die Vorwahl, -en
argue with sich streiten (hat sich gestritten) mit + *dat.*
argument der Krach, ¨e; der Streit
arm der Arm, -e

armchair der Sessel, -

army die Armee, -n

around um + *acc.*; ~ [time] gegen + *acc.*

arrival die Ankunft, ⸚e; die Anreise, -n

arrive an·kommen (ist angekommen)

art die Kunst; ~ **association** der Kunstverein, -e; ~ **museum** die Kunsthalle, -n; ~ **school** die Kunsthochschule, -n

artist der Künstler, -/die Künstlerin, -nen

article der Artikel, -

as als; wie; ~ . . . ~ so ... wie; ~ **a couple** zu zweit; ~ **always** wie immer

Asian asiatisch

ask: to ~ **about** fragen (hat gefragt) nach + *dat.*; **to** ~ **for** bitten (hat gebeten) um + *acc.*; **to** ~ **a question** eine Frage stellen (hat gestellt)

aspect der Aspekt, -e

aspirin das Aspirin

assignment die Aufgabe, -n

association der Verein, -e; die Gemeinschaft, -en

astonished erstaunt

at an; auf; in; ~ **(someone's house)** bei + *dat.*; ~ [time] um + *acc.*

at all überhaupt; **not** ~ gar nicht

athlete der Sportler, -/die Sportlerin, -nen

athletic sportlich

atmosphere die Stimmung, -en; **full of** ~ stimmungsvoll

attempt versuchen (hat versucht)

attic der Dachboden, ⸚; **in the** ~ auf dem Dachboden

attractive attraktiv

August der August

aunt die Tante, -n

Austria (das) Österreich

Austrian österreichisch *(adj.)*; der Österreicher, -/die Österreicherin, -nen

authentic echt; authentisch; wahr

author der Autor, -en/die Autorin, -nen; der Schriftsteller, -/die Schriftstellerin, -nen

automobile das Auto, -s; der Wagen, -

autumn der Herbst, -e

away weg; ab; fort; **far** ~ weit weg

awful schrecklich

awhile eine Weile

B

babysitter der Babysitter, -/die Babysitterin, -nen

back der Rücken, -; *(adv.)* zurück

backpack der Rucksack, ⸚e

bad schlecht; schlimm; böse; **have** ~ **luck** Pech haben; **not** ~ ganz gut, nicht schlecht; **too** ~ schade

bag die Tasche, -n; die Tüte, -n

baggage das Gepäck

bake backen (hat gebacken)

baker der Bäcker, -/die Bäckerin, -nen

bakery die Bäckerei, -en; **at the** ~ beim Bäcker; **to the** ~ zum Bäcker, in die Bäckerei

balcony der Balkon, -s

ball der Ball, ⸚e

ballet das Ballett, -e

ballpoint pen der Kugelschreiber, -; der Kuli, -s *(colloq.)*

Baltic Sea die Ostsee

ban das Verbot, -e; **to** ~ verbieten (hat verboten)

banana die Banane, -n

band die Band, -s

Band-Aid das Heftpflaster, -

bank die Bank, -en; die Sparkasse, -n; ~ **account** das Konto, *pl.* Konten; ~ **card (ATM card)** die Bankkarte, -n

bar die Bar, -s; die Kneipe, -n; das Lokal, -e

barrel das Fass, *pl.* Fässer

baseball der Baseball

basement der Keller, -

basically im Grunde

basketball der Basketball

bath das Bad, ⸚er; ~ **towel** das Badetuch, ⸚er

bathe baden (hat gebadet)

bathing suit *(man's)* die Badehose, -n; *(woman's)* der Badeanzug, ⸚e

bathroom das Badezimmer, -; **to go to the** ~ auf die Toilette (aufs Klo, *colloq.*) gehen

bathtub die Badewanne, -n

be: to ~ sein (ist gewesen); **to** ~ **able to** können (hat gekonnt); **to** ~ **about** handeln (hat gehandelt) von + *dat.*; **to** ~ **all right with someone** recht sein (ist gewesen) + *dat.*; **to** ~ **enough** reichen (hat gereicht); **to** ~ **in charge** leiten (hat geleitet)

beautiful schön

because weil; denn *(conj.)*; ~ **of** wegen *(prep.)* + *gen.*

become werden (ist geworden)

bed das Bett, -en; ~ **room** das Schlafzimmer, -

beef das Rindfleisch; **ground** ~ das Hackfleisch

beer das Bier

before vor + *dat.*; vorher *(adv.)*; bevor *(conj.)*

begin an·fangen (hat angefangen); beginnen (hat begonnen)

beginner der Anfänger, -/die Anfängerin, -nen

beginning der Anfang, ⸚e

behave sich verhalten (hat sich verhalten)

behind hinter + *acc./dat.*

beige beige

believable glaubhaft

believe glauben (hat geglaubt); **to** ~ **in** glauben an + *acc.*

belong to gehören (hat gehört) + *dat.*

beside bei + *dat.*; neben + *acc./dat.*

besides außerdem; außer + *dat.*

best best-; ~ **of all** am besten

better besser

between zwischen + *acc./dat.*

beverage das Getränk, -e

bicycle das Fahrrad, ⸚er; das Rad, ⸚er; **to** ~ Rad fahren (ist Rad gefahren); **to ride a** ~ mit dem Fahrrad fahren

bicycle path der Radweg, -e

bicycle rider der Radfahrer, -/die Radfahrerin, -nen

big groß (ö); ~ **city** die Großstadt, ⸚e

bike das Rad, ⸚er

biography die Biografie, -n

biology die Biologie

bird der Vogel, ⸚; **little** ~ das Vögelchen, -

birdcage der Vogelkäfig, -e

birthday der Geburtstag, -e; **When is your** ~ **?** Wann hast du Geburtstag?; **for one's** ~ zum Geburtstag

black schwarz (ä)

blackboard die Tafel, -n

blockade die Blockade, -n

blood das Blut

blond blond

blouse die Bluse, -n

blow-dry föhnen (hat geföhnt)

blow dryer der Föhn, -e

blue blau

board das Brett, -er; **bulletin** ~ das schwarze Brett; **chalk**~ die Tafel, -n

boarding pass die Bordkarte, -n

body der Körper, -; ~ **part** der Körperteil, -e

bombed out zerbombt

book das Buch, ⸚er

bookcase das Bücherregal, -e

bookkeeper der Buchhalter, -/die Buchhalterin, -nen

bookstore die Buchhandlung, -en

boot der Stiefel, -

border die Grenze, -n

border on grenzen (hat gegrenzt) an + *acc.*

boring langweilig; ~ **as heck** stinklangweilig

born geboren

borrow leihen (hat geliehen)

boss der Chef, -s/die Chefin, -nen

both beide; beides

bother stören (hat gestört)

bottle die Flasche, -n

boy der Junge, [-n], -n; ~**friend** der Freund, -e; **boys** die Jungs *(slang)*

branch der Zweig, -e; ~ **office** die Filiale, -n

brave mutig

bread das Brot, -e

break brechen (hat gebrochen); ~ **a leg! (Good Luck!)** Hals- und Beinbruch!; **to ~ one's (leg)** sich (das Bein) brechen (hat sich gebrochen); **to ~ up with** sich trennen (hat sich getrennt) von + *dat.*

breakable zerbrechlich

breakfast das Frühstück; **for ~** zum Frühstück

brewery die Bierbrauerei, -en

bribe die Bestechung, -en

brick der Ziegelstein, -e; der Backstein, -e

bride die Braut, ¨e

bridge die Brücke, -n

bright hell

bring bringen (hat gebracht); ~ **along** mit·bringen (hat mitgebracht)

broken kaputt; ~ **to pieces** zerbrochen

brother der Bruder, ¨; **brothers and sisters** die Geschwister *(pl.)*

brown braun

brush die Bürste, -n; **hair**~ die Haarbürste, -n; **tooth**~ die Zahnbürste, -n; **to ~ one's hair** sich die Haare bürsten (hat sich gebürstet); **to ~ one's teeth** sich die Zähne putzen (hat sich geputzt)

build bauen (hat gebaut); konstruieren (hat konstruiert)

building das Gebäude, -

bulletin board das schwarze Brett, -er

burn brennen (hat gebrannt)

bus der (Auto)bus, -se; ~ **stop** die Bushaltestelle, -n

business das Geschäft, -e; der Betrieb, -e; ~ **administration** die Betriebswirtschaft; ~ **trip** die Geschäftsreise, -n

businessman/businesswoman der Geschäftsmann, ¨er/die Geschäftsfrau, -en

but aber; sondern

butcher der Metzger, -/die Metzgerin, -nen; der Fleischer, -/die Fleischerin, -nen; ~ **shop** die Metzgerei, -en; die Fleischerei, -en

butter die Butter

buttocks der Hintern

buy kaufen (hat gekauft)

by bei + *dat.,* an + *dat.,* von + *dat.;* ~ **[car]** mit [dem Auto]

C

café das Café, -s

cafeteria die Mensa, *pl.* Mensen

cake der Kuchen, -; **layer ~** die Torte, -n

call rufen (hat gerufen); an·rufen (hat angerufen), telefonieren (hat telefoniert); **to ~ someone something** nennen (hat genannt)

called: to be ~ heißen (hat geheißen)

calm ruhig; **to ~ down** (sich) beruhigen (hat beruhigt)

camera: digital ~ die digitale Kamera, -s; **movie ~** die Kamera, -s; **still ~** der Fotoapparat, -e

campground der Campingplatz, ¨e

campus der Campus

can (to be able to) können (hat gekonnt)

Canada (das) Kanada

Canadian kanadisch *(adj.);* der Kanadier, -/die Kanadierin, -nen

candidate der Kandidat, [-en], -en/ die Kandidatin, -nen

cancelled to be ~ aus·fallen (ist ausgefallen)

canton der Kanton, -e

cap die Mütze, -n

capital die Hauptstadt, ¨e

car das Auto, -s; der Wagen, -; der PKW, -s (Personenkraftwagen, -)

card die Karte, -n; **to play cards** Karten spielen (hat Karten gespielt)

cardboard die Pappe

care die Sorge, -n; **to take ~ of something** erledigen (hat erledigt)

careful vorsichtig

carpet der Teppich, -e

carrot die Karotte, -n

carry tragen (hat getragen)

case der Fall, ¨e; **(container)** der Kasten, ¨

cash das Bargeld; ~ **register** die Kasse, -n

cassette die Kassette, -n

cast der Gips

castle das Schloss, *pl.* Schlösser; ~ **garden** der Schlossgarten, ¨; ~ **square** der Schlossplatz, ¨e

cat die Katze, -n

catalogue der Katalog, -e

catastrophe die Katastrophe, -n

catch fangen (hat gefangen); **to ~ a cold** sich erkälten (hat sich erkältet)

cathedral der Dom, -e

cause die Ursache, -n; der Grund, ¨e

CD die CD, -s; ~ **player** der CD-Player, -; der CD-Spieler, -

celebrate feiern (hat gefeiert)

celebration die Feier, -n; das Fest, -e; ~ **before Lent** der Karneval, der Fasching, die Fastnacht

cell phone das Handy, -s

cellar der Keller, -

center die Mitte, -n; das Zentrum, *pl.* Zentren

century das Jahrhundert, -e

cereal (grain) das Müesli; die Cerealien pl.

certain(ly) bestimmt; gewiss; sicher

chair der Stuhl, ¨e; **easy ~** der Sessel, -

chalk die Kreide

chalkboard die Tafel, -n

chancellor der Kanzler, -/die Kanzlerin, -nen; **federal ~** der Bundeskanzler, -/die Bundeskanzlerin, -nen

change der Wandel; **to ~** wechseln (hat gewechselt); (sich) verändern (hat verändert); **pocket ~** das Kleingeld

Chanukah Chanukka

characteristic die Eigenschaft, -en

chat plaudern (hat geplaudert)

cheap billig

check der Scheck, -s; **traveller's ~** der Reisescheck, -s; **to ~** kontrollieren (hat kontrolliert)

check-out counter die Kasse, -n

cheer jubeln (hat gejubelt)

cheerful heiter

cheese der Käse

chemistry die Chemie

cherry die Kirsche, -n

chest: ~ of drawers die Kommode, -n; **clothes ~** der Kleiderschrank, ¨e

chew kauen (hat gekaut); **to ~ gum** Kaugummi kauen

chewing gum der Kaugummi, -s

chicken das Hähnchen, -

child das Kind, -er; ~ **care subsidy** das Kindergeld

childhood die Kindheit

children's book das Kinderbuch, ¨er

children's room das Kinderzimmer, -

chin das Kinn

chocolate die Schokolade, -n

choice die Wahl, -en

choose wählen (hat gewählt)

Christianity das Christentum

Christmas das Weihnachten; **Merry ~**! Fröhliche Weihnachten!

chubby mollig

church die Kirche, -n

cigarette die Zigarette, -n

Cinderella Aschenputtel

circle der Kreis, -e

citizen der Bürger, -/die Bürgerin, -nen

city die Stadt, ¨e; **old part of the ~** die Altstadt; **~ hall** das Rathaus, ¨er; **~ district** der Stadtteil, -e; das Stadtviertel; **~ map** der Stadtplan, ¨e; **~ outskirts** der Stadtrand, ¨er; **~ bus tour** die Stadtrundfahrt, -en

civil servant der Beamte, -n *(noun decl. like adj.)* /die Beamtin, -nen

class die Klasse, -n; der Unterricht; **~ size** die Klassengröße, -n

classical klassisch

classmate der Kommilitone, [-n], -n/ die Kommilitonin, -nen

classroom das Klassenzimmer, -

clean sauber; **to ~** sauber machen (hat sauber gemacht); **to ~ up** auf·räumen (hat aufgeräumt)

cleaning lady die Reinemachefrau, -en

clear klar; heiter; **to ~ away** weg·räumen (hat weggeräumt)

clearly unbedingt

climate das Klima

climb klettern (ist geklettert); steigen (ist gestiegen); **to ~ into a train, car, etc.** ein·steigen (ist eingestiegen); **to ~ out** aus·steigen (ist ausgestiegen)

clique die Clique, -n; der Freundes-kreis, -e

clock die Uhr, -en; **alarm ~** der Wecker, -

close eng; nah(e); **a ~ friendship** eine dicke Freundschaft; **~ to** in der Nähe von + *dat.;* **to ~** schließen (hat geschlossen), zu·machen (hat zugemacht)

closet der Schrank, ¨e

clothing die Kleidung; die Klamotten *(pl.)*

cloud die Wolke, -n

cloudy wolkig; bewölkt

club der Club, -s; der Verein, -e; der Klub, -s; **athletic ~** der Turnverein, -e

coach der Trainer, -/die Trainerin, -nen

coal die Kohle, -n

coat der Mantel, ¨; **rain~** der Regenmantel, ¨; **sport~** der/das Sakko, -s

coffee der Kaffee; **~house** das Kaffeehaus, ¨er; **~maker** die Kaffeemaschine, -n

coincidence der Zufall, ¨e

cola die Cola, -s

cold kalt (ä) *(adj.);* **~ cuts** der Aufschnitt, -e; **~ war** der Kalte Krieg; **~ *(noun)*** die Erkältung, -en; der Schnupfen, -; **to catch a ~** sich erkälten (hat sich erkältet)

collaboration die Zusammenarbeit, -en

collapse der Zusammenbruch; **to ~** ein·stürzen (ist eingestürzt)

collegial kollegial

colleague der Kollege, [-n], -n/die Kollegin, -nen

college die Universität, -en; die Hochschule, -n; **to go to ~** studieren (hat studiert), an die Universität gehen

color die Farbe, -n; **What ~ is ... ?** Welche Farbe hat . . . ?

comb der Kamm, ¨e; **to ~ one's hair** sich die Haare kämmen (hat sich gekämmt)

combine kombinieren (hat kombiniert)

come kommen (ist gekommen); **to ~ along** mit·kommen (ist mitgekommen); **to ~ back** zurück·kommen (ist zurückgekommen); **to ~ by** vorbei·kommen (ist vorbeigekommen); **to ~ from** aus ... kommen; **to ~ home** heim·kommen (ist heimgekommen); **to ~ out** raus·kommen (ist rausgekommen); **to ~ to grips (with)** fertig werden (ist fertig geworden) mit + *dat.;* **~ in!** Herein!; **Where are you coming from?** Woher kommst du?

comedy die Komödie, -n

comical lustig, komisch

command der Befehl, -e; befehlen (hat befohlen) + *dat.*

common gemeinsam; **~ bathroom** das Gemeinschaftsbad, ¨er

communism der Kommunismus

communist der Kommunist, [-en], -en/ die Kommunistin, -nen

commuter der Pendler, -

compact disc die CD, -s

company die Gesellschaft, -en; die Firma, *pl.* Firmen; der Konzern, -e

compare vergleichen (hat verglichen)

compartment das Fach, ¨er

complete ganz; voll; **to ~** vervollständigen (hat vervollständigt); ergänzen (hat ergänzt)

completed vollendet

completely vollkommen; **~ wet** ganz nass

complicated kompliziert

compose komponieren (hat komponiert)

composer der Komponist, [-en], -en/ die Komponistin, -nen

computer der Computer, -; **~ science** die Informatik

concentrate sich konzentrieren (hat sich konzentriert) auf + *acc.*

concert das Konzert, -e; **~ hall** der Konzertsaal (*pl.* -säle); **to go to a ~** ins Konzert gehen

concierge der Hausmeister, -/die Hausmeisterin, -nen

connection der Zusammenhang, ¨e

connoisseur der Genießer, -/die Genießerin, -nen

conquer erobern (hat erobert)

consider sich überlegen (hat sich überlegt); **to be considered as** gelten (hat gegolten) als

constitution die Verfassung, -en; **German ~** das Grundgesetz

consume verbrauchen (hat verbraucht)

consumer-oriented konsum- orientiert

contact der Kontakt, -e

contain enthalten (hat enthalten)

content der Inhalt, -e

continue fort·setzen (hat fortgesetzt)/ fort·fahren (ist fortgefahren); **~ walking** weiter·gehen (ist weitergegangen)

contradictory widersprüchlich

contrary: on the ~ sondern; doch

controversial kontrovers

conversation das Gespräch, -e; die Unterhaltung, -en; **initiate a ~** an·sprechen (hat angesprochen)

converse with sich unterhalten (hat sich unterhalten) mit + *dat.*

convince überzeugen (hat überzeugt)

cook der Koch, ¨e/die Köchin, -nen; **to ~** kochen (hat gekocht)

cool kühl; cool; locker; klasse

cooperative kollegial

copy die Kopie, -n; **~ shop** der Kopierladen, ¨; das Kopiergeschäft, -e; **to ~** kopieren (hat kopiert)

corner die Ecke, -n; **around the ~** um die Ecke

correct richtig; **that's ~!** das stimmt!

corridor der Flur, -e; der Gang, ¨e; der Korridor, -e

cosmetic case der Kulturbeutel, -
cost kosten (hat gekostet)
couch die Couch, -en *or* -s
could könnte
counsel beraten (hat beraten)
counseling die Beratung, -en
counselor der Berater, -/die Beraterin, -nen
count zählen (hat gezählt); **to ~ on** rechnen (hat gerechnet) mit + *dat.*
country das Land, ⸚er; der Staat, -en; **in the ~** auf dem Land(e)
coup die Machtergreifung, -en
courageous mutig
course der Kurs, -e; **~ catalogue** das Vorlesungsverzeichnis, -se; **main ~** das Hauptgericht, -e; **of ~** natürlich; klar; selbstverständlich; **What ~s are you taking?** Welche Fächer haben Sie?
courtyard der Hof, ⸚e
cousin: *(female)* **~** die Cousine, -n; *(male)* **~** der Cousin, -s
co-worker der Mitarbeiter, -/die Mitarbeiterin, -nen
cozy gemütlich
cramp der Muskelkater, -
crazy wahnsinnig; verrückt; **to be ~** einen Vogel haben (*colloq.*)
create schaffen (hat geschaffen)
creative kreativ
credit card die Kreditkarte, -n
crime die Kriminalität
criminal der/die Kriminelle, -n (*noun decl. like adj.*)
criteria die Kriterien (*pl.*)
criticize kritisieren (hat kritisiert)
cross-country skiing der Langlauf; **~ trail** die Langlaufloipe, -n
crossing die Kreuzung, -en
crowd die Masse, -n; die Menge, -n
cruel grausam
cry weinen (hat geweint)
cucumber die Gurke, -n
cuddle schmusen (hat geschmust)
cuisine die Küche, -n
culture die Kultur, -en
cultural kulturell; **~ center** das Kulturzentrum, *pl.* Kulturzentren
cunning die List
cup die Tasse, -n; der Becher, -
curious neugierig; gespannt
curly hair krause Haare
current aktuell
curtain die Gardine, -n
custodian der Hauswart, -e
customer der Kunde, [-n], -n/die Kundin, -nen

customs der Zoll; **~ agent** der Zöllner, -/die Zöllnerin, -nen; **to go through ~** durch den Zoll gehen
cut schneiden (hat geschnitten); **to ~ oneself** sich schneiden in + *acc.;* **to ~ back** kürzen (hat gekürzt); **to ~ off** ab·schneiden (hat abgeschnitten)
cyclist der Radfahrer, -/die Radfahrerin, -nen

D

dad der Vati, -s; **grand~** der Opa, -s
daily täglich
damp nass (a/ä), feucht
dance der Ball, ⸚e; **to ~** tanzen (hat getanzt)
dangerous gefährlich
dare wagen (hat gewagt); riskieren (hat riskiert)
dark dunkel; **~ gray** dunkelgrau
darling der Liebling, -e; der Schatz, ⸚e
data die Tatsachen, die Daten (*pl.*)
date das Date, -s; das Datum, *pl.* Daten; die Verabredung, -en; **on your first ~** beim ersten Date; **to make a ~** sich verabreden (hat sich verabredet) mit + *dat.*
daughter die Tochter, ⸚
day der Tag, -e; **~ after tomorrow** übermorgen; **~ of the week** der Wochentag, -e; **~'s schedule** der Tagesablauf; **all ~** den ganzen Tag; **one ~** eines Tages; **Good ~.** Guten Tag.; Tag.; **What ~ is today?** Was ist heute?
dead tot; **~ tired** todmüde
dear lieb (-er, -e, -es)
December der Dezember
decide sich entscheiden (hat sich entschieden); **to ~ on/against** sich entscheiden für/gegen + *acc.*
decidedly ausgesprochen
decision die Entscheidung, -en
declare bekannt geben (hat bekannt gegeben); erklären (hat erklärt) für + *acc.*; aus·rufen (hat ausgerufen)
decorate dekorieren (hat dekoriert); auf·decken (hat aufgedeckt)
dedicate widmen (hat gewidmet)
defeat erobern (hat erobert)
degree der Abschluss, *pl.* Abschlüsse; *(temperature)* der Grad
delicious lecker
dentist der Zahnarzt, ⸚e/die Zahnärztin, -nen
deodorant das Deo, -s

depart ab·fahren (ist abgefahren)
departure die Abreise, -n; die Abfahrt, -en; der Abflug, ⸚e
department die Abteilung, -en; **academic ~** der Fachbereich, -e; **~ store** das Kaufhaus, ⸚er
deposit ein·zahlen (hat eingezahlt)
depressing deprimierend, drückend
describe beschreiben (hat beschrieben)
desk der Schreibtisch, -e
dessert die Nachspeise, -n; der Nachtisch, -e
destination das Ziel, -e
destroy zerstören (hat zerstört)
detail die Kleinigkeit, -en; das Detail, -s; **~-oriented** gründlich
detailed ausführlich
detective story der Kriminalroman, -e; der Krimi, -s
dependable zuverlässig
develop entwickeln (hat entwickelt)
development die Entwicklung, -en; der Werdegang
diagonally across from quer gegenüber von + *dat.*
dialect der Dialekt, -e
diarrhea der Durchfall
dictator der Diktator, -en
dictatorship die Diktatur, -en
dictionary das Wörterbuch, ⸚er
die sterben (ist gestorben)
difference der Unterschied, -e; **no ~** egal
different verschieden; anders; **something ~** etwas anderes
difficult schwer; schwierig
difficulty die Schwierigkeit, -en
digital digital
dining hall die Mensa, *pl.* Mensen
dining room das Esszimmer, -; **hotel ~** der Speisesaal, *pl.* Speisesäle
dinner das Abendessen, -; **for ~** zum Abendessen
diploma das Diplom, -e
direction die Richtung, -en
dirt der Dreck
dirty schmutzig
disappointed enttäuscht
disciplined diszipliniert
discotheque die Diskothek, -en (die Disko, -s)
discover entdecken (hat entdeckt)
discuss diskutieren (hat diskutiert) über + *acc.*; besprechen (hat besprochen); sich unterhalten (hat sich unterhalten) über + *acc.*
discussion die Diskussion, -en; die Besprechung, -en
disguise oneself sich verkleiden (hat sich verkleidet)

dishes   das Geschirr
dishwasher: electric ~   die Geschirrspülmaschine, -n
diskette   die Diskette, -n
district   das Viertel, -; **city ~**   das Stadtviertel, -
disturb   stören (hat gestört)
divide   teilen; auf·teilen (hat aufgeteilt) in + *acc.*
divorced   geschieden
do   machen (hat gemacht); tun (hat getan); **to ~ homework**   Hausaufgaben machen; **to ~ sports**   Sport treiben (hat Sport getrieben)
doctor   der Arzt, ¨e/die Ärztin, -nen
documentary film   der Dokumentarfilm, -e
dog   der Hund, -e
done   fertig, erledigt
door   die Tür, -en
dormitory   das Studentenwohnheim, -e
doubt: no ~   wohl
dove   das Täubchen, -
downstairs   unten; **to go ~**   die Treppe hinunter·gehen (ist hinuntergegangen)
down the street   die Straße entlang
drama   das Drama, *pl.* Dramen
drawer   die Schublade, -n
dream   der Traum, ¨e; **to ~ of**   träumen (hat geträumt) von + *dat.*
dress   das Kleid, -er; **to ~, get dressed**   sich an·ziehen (hat sich angezogen)
drink   das Getränk, -e; **to ~**   trinken (hat getrunken)
drive   fahren (ist gefahren); **to ~ away**   weg·fahren (ist weggefahren)
driver   der Fahrer, -/die Fahrerin, -nen
driver's license   der Führerschein, -e
drug   die Droge, -n
dry   trocken; **to ~ off**   ab·trocknen (hat abgetrocknet); **to ~ hair**   föhnen (hat geföhnt)
dumb   dumm (ü); doof; **something ~**   etwas Dummes
during   während + *gen.*
DVD   die DVD, -s; **~ player**   der DVD-Spieler, -
dwarf   der Zwerg, -e
dynamic   dynamisch

E

each   jed- (-er, -es, -e); **~ other**   einander
ear   das Ohr, -en
earlier   früher
early   früh

earn   verdienen (hat verdient)
east   der Osten; **~ German**   ostdeutsch
Easter   Ostern
easy   einfach; leicht; **~ going**   gut gelaunt
eat   essen (hat gegessen); **to ~** *(said of animals)*   fressen (hat gefressen)
economics   die Volkswirtschaft
economy   die Wirtschaft
educate   aus·bilden (hat ausgebildet)
education   die Erziehung; die Ausbildung; die Pädagogik
effect   die Wirkung, -en; **to have an ~**   wirken (hat gewirkt)
effort   die Mühe
e.g.   z. B Zum Beispiel
egg   das Ei, -er; **soft-boiled ~**   das weich gekochte Ei
either . . . or   entweder ... oder
elbow   der Ellenbogen, -
election   die Wahl, -en
electrical: ~ outlet   die Steckdose, -n; **~ storm**   das Gewitter, -
else: what ~ ?   was noch?; **something ~?**   sonst noch etwas?
e-mail   die E-Mail, -s; *(concept)* das Mail; **to ~**   mailen (hat gemailt)
emblem   das Wahrzeichen, -
embrace   umarmen (hat umarmt)
emperor/empress   der Kaiser, -/die Kaiserin, -nen
empire   das Reich, -e
employed   berufstätig
employee   der/die Angestellte, -n *(noun decl. like adj.)* der Mitarbeiter, -/die Mitarbeiterin, -nen
employer   der Arbeitgeber, -/die Arbeitgeberin, -nen
empty   leer
end   das Ende, -n; **in/at the ~**   am Ende
enemy   der Feind, -e
energy   die Energie
engaged   verlobt; **to get ~ to**   sich verloben (hat sich verlobt) mit + *dat.*
engineer   der Ingenieur, -e/die Ingenieurin, -nen
engineering   das Ingenieurwesen; **mechanical ~**   der Maschinenbau
England   (das) England
English   englisch *(adj.);* **~ (language)**   (das) Englisch; **~ (person)**   der Engländer, -/die Engländerin, -nen
enjoy   genießen (hat genossen); **~ your meal!**   Guten Appetit!
enjoyment   die Lust; das Vergnügen; der Spaß
enlarge   vergrößern (hat vergrößert)
enough   genug; genügend
entertaining   unterhaltend

entrance   der Eingang, ¨e; **~ hall**   die Diele, -n; der Flur, -e
entry *(in a diary)*   der Eintrag, ¨e
environment   die Umwelt
environmental: ~ protection   der Umweltschutz
environmentally friendly   umweltfreundlich
especially   besonders
et cetera (etc.)   und so weiter (usw.)
eternal   ewig
Euro *(currency unit)*   der Euro, -s
Europe   (das) Europa
European   europäisch; **~ Union**   die Europäische Union
even   sogar; **~ if**   auch wenn
evening   der Abend, -e; **good ~**   Guten Abend., Abend.; **this ~**   heute Abend
evenings   abends
eventually   schließlich, endlich
every   jed- (-er, -es, -e)
everyone   jeder; alle; jedermann
everything   alles; **~ okay**   alles in Ordnung
exactly   genau
examination   die Prüfung, -en; das Examen, -; **high school graduation ~**   das Abitur
examine   überprüfen (hat überprüft)
example   das Beispiel, -e; **for ~**   zum Beispiel (z.B.)
excellent   ausgezeichnet
except   außer + *dat.*
exciting   spannend
excited   aufgeregt; **to be ~ about**   gespannt sein auf + *acc.*
excitement   die Aufregung, -en
excuse   die Ausrede, -n; die Entschuldigung, -en; **me!** Entschuldigung!; **to ~**   entschuldigen (hat entschuldigt)
expand   erweitern (hat erweitert)
expect   erwarten (hat erwartet)
expectation   die Erwartung, -en
expensive   teuer
experience   die Erfahrung, -en; das Erlebnis, -se; **to ~**   erleben (hat erlebt); erfahren (hat erfahren)
explain   erklären (hat erklärt)
explanation   die Erklärung, -en
expression   der Ausdruck, ¨e
expressway   die Autobahn, -en
eye   das Auge, -n

F

face   das Gesicht, -er
fairly   ganz; ziemlich

fairy die Fee, -n; **~ tale** das Märchen, -; **~ tale figure** die Märchenfigur, -en

fall der Herbst; **to ~** fallen (ist gefallen); **to ~ asleep** ein·schlafen (ist eingeschlafen); **to ~ in love with** sich verlieben (hat sich verliebt) in + *acc.*

false falsch

familiar bekannt

family die Familie, -n; **~ owned business** der Familienbetrieb, -e; **~ tree** der Familienstammbaum, ̈-e

famous bekannt; berühmt; **world-~** weltberühmt

fan (*sports*) der Fan, -s; der Anhänger, -

fantastic phantastisch; toll; prima; großartig

far weit; **~ away** weit weg

farewell der Abschied

farmer der Bauer, [-n], -n/die Bäuerin, -nen

fast schnell

fat dick; mollig

father der Vater, ̈-; **grand~** der Großvater, ̈-

favorite Lieblings-

fax das Fax; **to ~** faxen (hat gefaxt)

fear die Angst, ̈-e; **to ~** Angst haben (hat gehabt) vor + *dat.*; fürchten (hat gefürchtet)

feast das Fest, -e

February der Februar

Federal Republic of Germany die Bundesrepublik Deutschland

feel sich fühlen (hat sich gefühlt); spüren (hat gespürt); **to ~ like** Lust haben; **to ~ unwell** sich nicht wohl fühlen; **I'm ~ing pretty bad.** Mir geht's ziemlich schlecht.

feeling das Gefühl, -e

fetch holen (hat geholt)

fever das Fieber; **to have a ~** Fieber haben

few wenig(e); **a ~** ein paar

fiancé(e) der/die Verlobte, -n *(noun decl. like adj.)*

field hockey das Feldhockey

fight sich streiten (hat sich gestritten)

figure skater der Eiskunstläufer, -/die Eiskunstläuferin, -nen

film der Film, -e; **~ director** der Regisseur, -e/ die Regisseurin, -nen; **~maker** der Filmemacher, -/die Filmemacherin, -nen; **documentary ~** der Dokumentarfilm, -e

finally endlich, schließlich

finances die Finanzen (*pl.*)

find finden (hat gefunden); **to ~ out** heraus·finden (hat herausgefunden)

fine fein; gut; **I'm ~.** Es geht mir gut.

finger der Finger, -; **to cross one's ~s** ganz fest die Daumen drücken (hat gedrückt)

finished fertig; zu Ende

fireplace der Kamin, -e

firm die Firma, *pl.* Firmen; (*adj.*) fest

first erst; **~ name** der Vorname, [-n], -n; **~ of all** zuerst; zunächst; **for the ~ time** zum ersten Mal

fish der Fisch, -e; **~ market** der Fischmarkt, ̈-e; **to ~** angeln (hat geangelt)

fit passen (hat gepasst) zu + *dat.*; **to ~ together** zusammen·passen (hat zusammengepasst)

flash das Blitzlicht, -er

flexible flexibel

flight der Flug, ̈-e

flirt flirten (hat geflirtet)

floor der Boden, *pl.* Böden; der Stock, *pl.* Stockwerke; die Etage, -n; **first ~** das Erdgeschoss; **one ~ down** einen Stock tiefer

flow fließen (ist geflossen)

flower die Blume, -n

fluent fließend

fly fliegen (ist geflogen)

flute die Flöte, -n

fog der Nebel

follower der Anhänger, -/die Anhängerin, -nen

food das Essen; die Lebensmittel (*pl.*); die Kost

foot der Fuß, ̈-e; **~path** der Fußweg, -e; **to go on ~** zu Fuß gehen (ist gegangen); laufen (ist gelaufen)

football (*American*) der amerikanische Football

for für + *acc.*; denn (*conj.*); **~ (time)** seit/schon seit + *dat.*; **~ years** seit Jahren

forbid verbieten (hat verboten)

forbidden verboten

foreign fremd; ausländisch

foreigner der Ausländer, -/die Ausländerin, -nen; der/die Fremde, -n (*noun decl. like adj.*)

forest der Wald, ̈-er

forever ewig

forget vergessen (hat vergessen)

forehead die Stirn, -en

fork die Gabel, -n

form die Unterlage, -n; das Formular, -e

former ehemalig

formerly früher

fragile zerbrechlich

France (das) Frankreich

free frei; **~ time** die Freizeit

freedom die Freiheit

freeway die Autobahn, -en

freezing point der Gefrierpunkt

French französisch (*adj.*); **~ (language)** (das) Französisch

Frenchman der Franzose, [-n], -n; **Frenchwoman** die Französin, -nen

frequent häufig; oft

Friday der Freitag

friend der Freund, -e/die Freundin, -nen

friendliness die Freundlichkeit

friendly freundlich

friendship die Freundschaft, -en **make a ~ official** eine Freundschaft schließen

frog der Frosch, ̈-e

from von + *dat.*; **~ (native of)** aus + *dat.*; **~ where?** woher?

front: up ~ da vorne; **in ~ of** vor + *dat.*

fruit das Obst; die Frucht, ̈-e; **~ jam, preserves** die Marmelade

frustrating frustrierend

full voll

fun der Spaß; **That's ~.** Das macht Spaß. (hat Spaß gemacht)

funny lustig, heiter

furniture das Möbel, -

further weiter

future die Zukunft

G

game das Spiel, -e

garage die Garage, -n

garden der Garten, ̈-

gasoline das Benzin

gate das Tor, -e

generous großzügig

gentle sanft

gentleman der Herr, [-n], -en

genuine echt, authentisch

geography die Landeskunde; die Erdkunde

German deutsch (*adj.*); **~ (person)** der/die Deutsche (*noun decl. like adj.*); **~ (language)** (das) Deutsch; **in ~** auf Deutsch; **~ studies** die Germanistik; **~ Democratic Republic** die Deutsche Demokratische Republik (DDR); **~ Empire** das Deutsche Reich; **~ Unity Day** der Tag der Deutschen Einheit

Germany (das) Deutschland; die Bundesrepublik Deutschland

get bekommen (hat bekommen); kriegen (hat gekriegt); besorgen (hat besorgt); **to ~ along with** gut aus·kommen (ist gut ausgekommen) mit + *dat.;* **~ well!** Gute Besserung!; **to go ~** holen (hat geholt); **to ~ through** durch·machen (hat durchgemacht); **to ~ up** auf·stehen (ist aufgestanden); **to ~ used to** sich gewöhnen (hat sich gewöhnt) an + *acc.;* **to ~ to know** kennenlernen (hat kennengelernt); **to ~ in touch** sich melden (hat sich gemeldet)

gift das Geschenk, -e

girl das Mädchen, -

girlfriend die Freundin, -nen

give geben (hat gegeben); **to ~ (as a gift)** schenken (hat geschenkt); **to ~ up** auf·geben (hat aufgegeben)

glad froh; **to be ~** sich freuen (hat sich gefreut)

glass das Glas, ¨er

glasses die Brille, -n

gladly gern

glove der Handschuh, -e

go gehen (ist gegangen); **to ~ along** mit·gehen (ist mitgegangen); **to ~ by [train]** mit [der Bahn / dem Zug] fahren (ist gefahren); **to ~ away** fort·gehen (ist fortgegangen); weg·gehen (ist weggegangen); **to ~ on foot** zu Fuß gehen; **to ~ out** aus·gehen (ist ausgegangen); **to ~ to** auf/in . . . gehen

goal das Tor, -e; das Ziel, -e

God der Gott, ¨er

gold das Gold

golf der Golf; **~club** der Golfschläger, -

gone weg

good gut, **~-looking** gut aussehend

good-bye auf Wiedersehen; tschüss *(colloq.);* **to say ~** sich verabschieden (hat sich verabschiedet)

Good morning. Guten Morgen!

goofy doof

got to müssen (hat gemusst)

government die Regierung, -en; der Staat, -en; **~ district** das Regierungsviertel

grade die Note, -n; **[seventh] ~** [die siebte] Klasse

gram das Gramm

grammar die Grammatik

grand groß (ö); großartig

grandchild das Enkelkind, -er

granddaughter die Enkelin, -nen

grandfather der Großvater, ¨; der Opa, -s; **great-~** der Urgroßvater, -väter

grandmother die Großmutter, ¨; die Oma, -s

grandparents die Großeltern *(pl.)*

grandson der Enkel, -

grape die Traube, -n

grave das Grab, ¨er

gray grau; **dark ~** dunkelgrau; **light ~** hellgrau

great toll, ausgezeichnet, prima, klasse, großartig

Greece (das) Griechenland

green grün

greeting der Gruß, ¨e

groceries die Lebensmittel *(pl.)*

grocery store das Lebensmittel-geschäft, -e

ground der Boden, ¨; **~ floor** das Erdgeschoss; **on the ~ floor** im Erdgeschoss

group die Gruppe, -n; **~ leader** der Gruppenleiter; der Betreuer; **~ project** das Gruppenprojekt, -e; **~ research paper** das Gruppenreferat, -e; **study ~** die Arbeitsgruppe, -n

grow wachsen (ist gewachsen); **to ~ up** auf·wachsen (ist aufgewachsen)

gruesome grausam

guess ahnen

guest der Gast, ¨e; der Besucher, -/die Besucherin, -nen; **~ room** das Gästezimmer, -; **~ house** die Pension, -en; das Gasthaus, ¨er; der Gasthof, ¨e

guitar die Gitarre, -n

guy der Typ, -en; **a really nice ~** ein ganz netter Typ

H

habitat der Lebensraum

hair das Haar, -e; **~cut** der Haarschnitt, -e; **straight (tightly curled, wavy) ~** glatte (krause, wellige) Haare

hairbrush die Haarbürste, -n

hairdresser der Friseur, -e/die Friseurin, -nen/die Friseuse, -n

half past (one o'clock) halb (zwei)

hallway der Flur, -e; der Gang, ¨e; der Korridor, -e

hamburger der Hamburger, -

hand die Hand, ¨e; **on the one ~** einerseits

handbag die Handtasche, -n

handout das Handout, -s

hang: to ~ up hängen (hat gehängt)

hanging: to be ~ hängen (hat gehangen)

hangover: to have a ~ (einen) Kater haben *(colloq.)*

happen passieren (ist passiert); **What happened to you?** Was ist dir passiert?

happily: And they lived ~ ever after. Und wenn sie nicht gestorben sind, dann leben sie noch heute.

happy froh, glücklich; **to be ~ about** sich freuen (hat sich gefreut) über + *acc.*

harbor der Hafen, ¨

hard hart (ä); schwer

hardly kaum

hard-working fleißig

harm schaden (hat geschadet) + *dat.*

hatred der Hass; **~ of foreigners** der Ausländerhass; der Fremdenhass

have haben (hat gehabt); **to ~ to** müssen (hat gemusst); **I don't ~ to** ich brauche nicht zu

he er

head der Kopf, ¨e; **~ cold** der Schnupfen, die Erkältung

headache die Kopfschmerzen *(pl.)*

health die Gesundheit; **~ club** das Fitnessstudio, -s; **~ food store** der Bioladen, ¨; das Reformhaus, ¨er

healthy gesund (ü), wohl

heap der Haufen, -

hear hören (hat gehört)

heart das Herz, -en

hearth der Herd, -e

heaven der Himmel, -

heavy schwer

hello Guten Morgen/Tag/Abend; Grüß dich.; Hallo.

help die Hilfe, -n; **to ~** helfen (hat geholfen) + *dat.*

her *(pronoun)* sie *(acc.),* ihr *(dat.);* *(possessive)* ihr

here hier, da; *(toward the speaker)* her; **~ you are** bitte sehr

hey! du!; he!; Hallo!

hi! Tag! Grüß dich! Servus!

hide verstecken (hat versteckt)

high (higher, highest) hoch (höher, am höchsten)

high school das Gymnasium *(pl.* Gymnasien); **~ exit examination** das Abitur, -s (Abi); **~ senior** der Abiturient, [-en], -en/die Abiturientin, -nen

hike die Wanderung, -en; **to ~** wandern (ist gewandert)

him ihn *(acc.);* ihm *(dat.)*

hire   ein·stellen (hat eingestellt)

his   sein

history   die Geschichte

hitchhike   per Anhalter fahren (ist gefahren)

hobby   das Hobby, -s; ~ **room**   der Hobbyraum, ⸚e

hockey: ice ~   das Eishockey; **field** ~   das Feldhockey

hold   halten (hat gehalten)

holiday   der Feiertag, -e; der Festtag, -e

home: at ~   zu Hause; daheim; **to come** ~   heim·kommen (ist heimgekommen); **to go** ~   nach Hause gehen (ist gegangen);

homeland   die Heimat; das Herkunftsland, ⸚er

homesickness   das Heimweh

hometown   die Heimatstadt, ⸚e; der Wohnort, -e

homework   die Hausaufgaben (pl.); **to do** ~   die Hausaufgaben machen

homosexual   der/die Homosexuelle, -n (noun decl. like adj.); schwul

honest   ehrlich

honey   der Honig

hook   der Haken, -

hope   hoffen (hat gehofft); **to** ~ **for**   hoffen auf + acc.

hopefully   hoffentlich

horrible   furchtbar; fürchterlich; schrecklich

horror movie   der Horrorfilm, -e; der Gruselfilm, -e

horse   das Pferd, -e; ~**-drawn sleigh**   der Pferdeschlitten, -

hospital   das Krankenhaus, ⸚er; [Austrian] ~   das Spital, ⸚er

hospitality   die Gastfreundschaft

host   der Gastgeber, -/die Gastgeberin, -nen; (in a restaurant) der Wirt, -e/ die Wirtin, -nen

hot   heiß

hotel   das Hotel, -s

hour   die Stunde, -n; **for** ~**s**   stundenlang

house   das Haus, ⸚er

housekeeper   die Reinemachefrau, -en

how   wie; ~ **are you?**   Wie geht es Ihnen?/Wie geht's?; ~ **are you feeling?**   Wie fühlst du dich?; ~ **do I get to . . . ?**   Wie komme ich nach/zu ... ?; ~ **many?**   wie viele?; ~ **much?**   wie viel?; ~ **would . . . be?**   Wie wäre es mit ... ?

hug   umarmen (hat umarmt)

human being   der Mensch, [-en], -en

humid   schwül

hundred   hundert

hunger   der Hunger

hungry   hungrig; **to be** ~   Hunger haben (hat gehabt)

hunter   der Jäger, -

hurry   sich beeilen (hat sich beeilt)

hurt   weh·tun (hat wehgetan) + dat.; **(My arm)** ~**s.**   (Der Arm) tut mir weh.

husband   der Mann, ⸚er

I

I   ich

ice   das Eis; ~ **cream**   das Eis; ~ **hockey**   das Eishockey

idea   die Idee, -n; der Einfall, ⸚e; die Vorstellung, -en

if   wenn; ob; **even** ~   wenn auch

identify: to ~ **with**   sich identifizieren (hat sich identifiziert) mit + dat.

identity   die Identität

ill   krank

illness   die Krankheit, -en

image   das Bild, -er; die Vorstellung, -en

imagine   sich vor·stellen (hat sich vorgestellt) + dat.; ~ **that!**   Stell dir mal vor!

immediately   gleich

impatient   ungeduldig

impolite   unhöflich

important   wichtig; **the most** ~ **thing**   das Wichtigste

impress   beeindrucken (hat beeindruckt)

impression   der Eindruck, ⸚e

impressive   beeindruckend

improve   verbessern (hat verbessert)

in   in + acc./dat.; ~ **order to**   um ... zu; ~ **spite of**   trotz + gen.

in-line skates   die Rollerblades (pl.)

increase   erhöhen (hat erhöht)

industrious   fleißig

industry   die Industrie, -n

influence   der Einfluss, pl. Einflüsse; **to** ~   beeinflussen (hat beeinflusst)

inhabitant   der Einwohner, -/ die Einwohnerin, -nen

injure   verletzen (hat verletzt)

inn   der Gasthof, ⸚e

innumerable   zahllos

inquire about   fragen (hat gefragt) nach + dat.

insane   wahnsinnig

insecure   unsicher

inside   innerhalb + gen.

instead of   (an)statt + gen.

instrument   das Instrument, -e

insurance   die Versicherung, -en

intelligent   intelligent, klug (ü)

intend to   vor·haben (hat vorgehabt)

interest   das Interesse, -n; **to** ~   interessieren (hat interessiert)

interested: to be ~ **in**   (sich) interessieren für + acc.

interesting   interessant

intern   der Praktikant, [-en], -en/die Praktikantin, -nen

international   international; ~ **relations**   internationale Beziehungen (pl.)

Internet   das Internet; ~ **connection**   der Internet-Anschluss, ⸚e; ~ **page**   die Internetseite, -n

intersection   die Kreuzung, -en

internship   das Praktikum, pl. Praktika; die Praktikantenstelle, -n

interview   das Interview, -s; das Vorstellungsgespräch, -e

into   in + acc.; hinein

introduce   vor·stellen (hat vorgestellt)

introduction   die Vorstellung, -en

invitation   die Einladung, -en

invite   ein·laden (hat eingeladen)

irritate   irritieren (hat irritiert); nerven (hat genervt)

Islam   der Islam

is   ist; **isn't it?**   nicht?; nicht wahr? (tag question)

island   die Insel, -n

it   er/sie/es

Italian   italienisch (adj.); ~ **(language)**   (das) Italienisch

J

jacket   die Jacke, -n

January   der Januar

Japanese   (das) Japanisch; ~ **(person)**   der Japaner, -/die Japanerin, -nen

jazz   die Jazzmusik; ~ **club**   der Jazzkeller, -

jeans   die Jeans (pl.)

Jew   der Jude, [-n], -n /die Jüdin, -nen

Jewish   jüdisch

job   der Job, -s; die Stelle, -n; **to have a part-time** ~   jobben (hat gejobbt)

join   bei·treten (ist beigetreten) + dat.; **to** ~ **in**   mit·machen (hat mitgemacht)

joke   der Witz, -e

journalist   der Journalist, [-en], -en/die Journalistin, -nen

joy   die Freude, -n

juice   der Saft, ⸚e

July   der Juli

jump   springen (ist gesprungen)
June   der Juni
just   eben; erst; gerade; halt

K

key   der Schlüssel, -
kick   treten (hat getreten); **to ~ (the ball)**   schießen (hat geschossen)
kilogram   das Kilo(gramm)
kilometer   der Kilometer, -
kind   die Art, -en; **what ~ of . . .?**   was für ein ... ?; *(adj.)* gut; nett
kindergarten   der Kindergarten
king   der König, -e
kingdom   das Königtum, ¨er
kiss   der Kuss, *pl.* Küsse; **to ~**   küssen (hat geküsst)
kitchen   die Küche, -n
knee   das Knie, -
knife   das Messer, -
knock over   um·werfen (hat umgeworfen)
know: to ~ (a fact)   wissen (hat gewusst); **to ~ (be acquainted)**   kennen (hat gekannt); **to ~ something about**   etwas verstehen (hat verstanden) von + *dat.;* **to get to ~**   kennenlernen (hat kennengelernt)
knowledge   die Kenntnis, -se

L

lack   fehlen (hat gefehlt)
lacrosse   das Lacrosse
lake   der See, -n
lame   lahm
lamp   die Lampe, -n
land   das Land, ¨er
landscape   die Landschaft, -en
language   die Sprache, -n; **foreign ~**   die Fremdsprache, -n; **~ institute**   das Sprachinstitut, -e; **~ lab**   das Sprachlabor, -s
laptop computer   der Laptop, -s
large   groß (ö)
last   letzt; **~ night**   gestern Abend; **to ~**   dauern (hat gedauert)
lastly   zuletzt
late   spät
later   später; **until ~**   bis später, tschüss, bis dann, bis bald
latest: at the ~   spätestens
laugh   lachen (hat gelacht); **to ~ about**   lachen über + *acc.*
laundry room   die Waschküche, -n

law   das Gesetz, -e; ~ **(field of study)**   Jura *(no article);* **Basic ~ (German Constitution)**   das Grundgesetz
lawyer   der Rechtsanwalt, ¨e/die Rechtsanwältin, -nen
lay (something down)   legen (hat gelegt)
lazy   faul
lead   führen (hat geführt); leiten (hat geleitet)
leader   der Führer, -(Hitler); der Leiter, -
league   die Liga *(pl.* Ligen)
learn   lernen (hat gelernt)
least: at ~   wenigstens; mindestens
leave   lassen (hat gelassen); verlassen (hat verlassen); weg·fahren (ist weggefahren); ab·fahren (ist abgefahren)
lecture   die Vorlesung, -en; ~ **hall**   der Hörsaal, *pl.* Hörsäle; ~ **notes**   das Skript, -en
left: on/to the ~   links
leg   das Bein, -e
leisure activity   die Freizeitaktivität, -en
lend   leihen (hat geliehen)
lesson   der Unterricht; die Stunde, -n
let   lassen (hat gelassen)
letter   der Brief, -e
lettuce   der Salat, -e
librarian   der Bibliothekar, -e/die Bibliothekarin, -nen
library   die Bibliothek, -en
lie   liegen (hat gelegen); **to ~ down**   (sich) hin·legen (hat sich hingelegt); **to tell a ~**   lügen (hat gelogen)
life   das Leben, -; **life-threatening**   lebensgefährlich
light   das Licht, -er; **traffic ~**   die Ampel, -n; *(adj.)* leicht; ~ *(color)* hell; ~ **blue**   hellblau
lightning: to flash ~   blitzen (es blitzt, es hat geblitzt)
likability   die Sympathie
likable   sympathisch
like   gern haben (hat gern gehabt); mögen (hat gemocht); gefallen (hat gefallen) + *dat.;* **I ~ to swim.**   Ich schwimme gern.; **I (don't) ~ that.**   Das gefällt mir (nicht).; **I'd ~**   ich möchte
limited   begrenzt
line: waiting ~   die Schlange, -n; **to stand in ~**   [in der] Schlange stehen (hat gestanden)
lip   die Lippe, -n
lipstick   der Lippenstift, -e
list   die Liste, -n

listen   zu·hören (hat zugehört) + *dat.;* **to ~ to music**   Musik hören (hat gehört)
liter   der Liter, -
literature   die Literatur, -en
little   klein; wenig; **a ~**   ein bisschen, ein wenig; **Little Red Riding Hood**   Rotkäppchen
live   leben (hat gelebt); wohnen (hat gewohnt); **to ~ together**   zusammen·leben (hat zusammengelebt); **And they ~d happily ever after.**   Und wenn sie nicht gestorben sind, dann leben sie noch heute.
lively   lebendig; schwungvoll
living room   das Wohnzimmer, -
located: to be ~   liegen (hat gelegen)
lock   das Schloss, *pl.* Schlösser; **to un~**   auf·schließen (hat aufgeschlossen)
lodgings: to find ~   unter·kommen (ist untergekommen)
logical   vernünftig
long   lang (ä); lange; **for a ~ time**   lange
longer: no ~   nicht mehr
look   schauen (hat geschaut); **to ~ at**   sich an·schauen (hat angeschaut); **to ~ like**   aus·sehen (hat ausgesehen) wie; **to ~ down**   herab·blicken (hat herabgeblickt); **to ~ for**   suchen (hat gesucht); **to ~ forward to**   sich freuen (hat sich gefreut) auf + *acc.;* **to ~ funny at someone**   (jemanden) schief an·schauen (hat angeschaut); **to ~ through**   durch·gucken (hat durchgeguckt); ~ **!**   Guck mal!
lose   verlieren (hat verloren)
lot: a ~   viel
loud   laut
lousy   mies
love   die Liebe, -n; ~ **poem**   das Liebesgedicht, -e; **to ~**   lieben; **to be in ~ with**   verliebt sein in + *dat.;* **to fall in ~ with**   sich verlieben in + *acc.*
lovesickness   der Liebeskummer
low   gering; niedrig
loyal   treu
loyalty   die Treue
luck   das Glück; **to have bad ~**   Pech haben; **Lots of ~!**   Toi, toi, toi!
lucky: to be ~   Glück haben (hat gehabt); Schwein haben *(colloq.)*
lunch   das Mittagessen; **for ~**   zum Mittagessen; **to have ~**   zu Mittag essen

M

machine die Maschine, -n
magazine die Zeitschrift, -en
magician der Zauberer, -
major subject das Hauptfach, ⸚er
mail die Post; ~**box** das Postfach,
⸚er; ~ **carrier** der Briefträger, -/
die Briefträgerin, -nen; der Postbote,
[-n], -n/die Postbotin, -nen
main Haupt-; ~ **course** das
Hauptgericht, -e; ~ **street** die
Hauptstraße, -n; ~ **street (of
Berlin)** der Kurfürstendamm
(Ku'damm); ~ **train station** der
Hauptbahnhof, ⸚e
major: college ~ das Hauptfach, ⸚er;
What's your ~? Was haben Sie als
Hauptfach?
make machen (hat gemacht); **to** ~ **up
with** sich versöhnen (hat sich
versöhnt) mit + *dat.*
mall das Einkaufszentrum, *pl.* -zentren
man der Mann, ⸚er; **Man!** Mensch!
Mann!
manage schaffen (hat geschafft);
bewerkstelligen (hat bewerkstelligt)
manner die Art
many viele; **how** ~ wie viele; **too** ~
zu viele
map die Landkarte, -n; der Stadtplan, ⸚e
March der März
market der Markt, ⸚e; **indoor** ~ die
Markthalle, -n
marketplace der Marktplatz, ⸚e
marmalade die Marmelade, -n
marriage die Ehe, -n; die Heirat, -en
married verheiratet
marry: to ~, **get married** heiraten (hat
geheiratet)
mass die Masse, -n
match das Spiel, -e
materialistic konsumorientiert
math die Mathematik; die Mathe
matter: What's the ~? Was ist los?
May der Mai
may dürfen (hat gedurft); **that** ~ **well
be** das mag wohl sein
maybe vielleicht
maximal maximal
me mich *(acc.);* mir *(dat.);* ~ **too!** ich
auch!
meadow die Wiese, -n
meal das Essen, -; **Have a good** ~ *(at
lunch).* Mahlzeit.
mean böse; **to** ~ meinen; bedeuten;
What does that ~? Was bedeutet
das?

meaning die Bedeutung, -en
meanwhile inzwischen
meat das Fleisch
mechanic (auto) der Automechaniker,
-/ die Automechanikerin, -nen
medicine die Medizin; das
Medikament, -e
meet treffen (hat getroffen);
kennenlernen (hat kennengelernt)
member das Mitglied, -er
memorial das Mahnmal, -e *(selten:
-mäler);* das Denkmal, ⸚er; die
Gedenkstätte, -n
merchant der Kaufmann, ⸚er/die
Kauffrau, -en; *(pl.)* die Kaufleute
merry lustig
message die Nachricht, -en
meter der Meter, -
Mexican mexikanisch; ~ **(person)** der
Mexikaner, -/die Mexikanerin, -nen
microwave oven der Mikrowellenherd, -e
middle die Mitte, -n
midnight die Mitternacht
milk die Milch
million die Million, -en
mineral water das Mineralwasser
minor subject das Nebenfach, ⸚er
minute die Minute, -n; **(five)** ~**s after
(one)** (fünf) Minuten nach (eins);
(five) ~**s to (two)** (fünf) Minuten
vor (zwei); **Just a** ~ **please!** Einen
Moment, bitte!
miracle das Wunder, -
mirror der Spiegel, -
Miss das Fräulein, - *(for young girls only)*
missing: to be ~ fehlen (hat gefehlt)
mix mischen (hat gemischt)
modern modern
mom die Mutti, -s
moment der Moment, -e; **at the** ~
momentan; im Moment; zur Zeit
monarchy die Monarchie, -n
Monday der Montag
money das Geld
month der Monat, -e
monument das Denkmal, ⸚er
mood die Stimmung, -en; **magical** ~
die Zauberstimmung
more mehr; **no** ~ kein ... mehr; ~
and ~ immer mehr; ~ **or
less** mehr oder weniger
morning der Morgen;
Good ~. Guten Morgen.; Morgen.
this ~ heute Morgen
mornings morgens
mosque die Moschee, -n
most meist-, am meisten; am liebsten;
at the ~ höchstens; ~ **of the
time** meistens

mother die Mutter, ⸚
motivated motiviert
motive das Motiv, -e
motorcycle das Motorrad, ⸚er
mountain der Berg, -e; ~
climbing das Bergsteigen; ~
peak der Gipfel, -
mouth der Mund, ⸚er
move ziehen (ist gezogen);
um·ziehen (ist umgezogen); **to** ~
away weg·ziehen (ist
weggezogen)
movie der Film, -e; ~ **star** der
Filmstar, -s; ~ **theater** das Kino, -s;
to make a ~ einen Film drehen
(hat gedreht)
movies: to go to the ~ ins Kino gehen
Mr. (der) Herr
Mrs. (die) Frau
Ms. (die) Frau
much viel; **how** ~ wie viel; **too** ~ zu
viel
multicultural multikulturell
multiculturalism der
Multikulturalismus
museum das Museum, *pl.* Museen
music die Musik; ~ **conservatory** die
Musikhochschule, -n; ~ **store** das
Musikgeschäft, -e
musical musikalisch *(adj.);* das
Musical, -s; ~ **instrument** das
Musikinstrument, -e
musician der Musiker, -/die Musikerin,
-nen; der Musikant, [-en], -en
must müssen (hat gemusst); **I** ~
not ich darf nicht
my mein
mystery story der Krimi, -s

N

nail polish der Nagellack
name der Name, [-n], -n; **by the** ~
of namens; **first** ~ der Vorname,
[-n], -n; **last** ~ der Nachname, [-n],
-n; **What is your** ~? Wie heißen
Sie?; **to** ~ nennen (hat genannt)
namely nämlich
narrow eng
nationality die Nationalität, -en
naturally klar; natürlich;
selbstverständlich
nature die Natur, -en
Nazi der Nazi, -s; der Nationalsozialist,
[-en], -en; **neo-**~ der Neo-Nazi, -s
near bei + *dat.*
nearer näher
nearby in der Nähe, nah(e)

necessary notwendig

neck der Hals, ¨-e

need brauchen (hat gebraucht); **I don't ~ to** ich muss nicht

neighborhood das Viertel, -

nephew der Neffe, [-n], -n

nervous nervös

never nie, niemals

nevertheless trotzdem

new neu; **What's ~?** Was gibt's Neues?; **~ building** der Neubau, -ten; **~ Year's Day** das Neujahr; **~ Year's Eve** das Silvester

news die Nachricht, -en

newspaper die Zeitung, -en

next nächst; **~ Saturday** nächsten Samstag; **~ to** neben + *dat.*

nice nett; schön

niece die Nichte, -n

night die Nacht, ¨-e; **Good ~** Gute Nacht.; **last ~** gestern Abend; **~mare** der Albtraum, ¨-e

nighttime nächtlich *(adj.)*

no nein; kein; nicht; **~ longer** nicht mehr; **~ more . . .** kein ... mehr

Nobel Prize winner der Nobelpreisträger, -/die Nobelpreisträgerin, -nen

nod nicken (hat genickt)

none kein; **~ at all** überhaupt kein

nonsense der Unsinn

noon der Mittag

no one niemand

north der Norden

North Sea die Nordsee

nose die Nase, -n

not nicht; **isn't that so?** nicht?; nicht wahr?; **~ at all** gar nicht; **~ any** kein; **~ only . . . but also . . .** nicht nur ... sondern auch ...; **~ necessarily** nicht unbedingt

note die Notiz, -en

notebook das Heft, -e

notes: lecture ~ das Skript, -en

nothing nichts; **~ special** nichts Besonderes

notice bemerken (hat bemerkt), merken (hat gemerkt), auf·fallen (ist aufgefallen) + *dat.*

novel der Roman, -e; **crime ~** der Kriminalroman, -e (der Krimi, -s)

November der November

now jetzt; nun; **~ and then** ab und zu; hin und wieder

nowhere nirgendwo

number die Zahl, -en

nurse der Krankenpfleger, -/die Krankenschwester, -n

nursery school der Kindergarten, ¨-

O

object der Gegenstand, ¨-e

obtain bekommen (hat bekommen); kriegen (hat gekriegt); erhalten (hat erhalten); besorgen (hat besorgt)

occupation der Beruf, -e; **~ zone** die Besatzungszone, -n

occupied: to be ~ beschäftigt sein

occupy besetzen (hat besetzt)

occur statt·finden (hat stattgefunden); **to ~ to someone** auf·fallen (ist aufgefallen) + *dat.*

ocean der Ozean, -e; die See, -n

o'clock: at (six) ~ um (sechs) Uhr; **It's (five) ~.** Es ist (fünf) Uhr.

October der Oktober

of von + *dat.;* **~ course** klar

offer an·bieten (hat angeboten); bieten (hat geboten)

office das Büro, -s; (military) die Schreibstube, -n; **~ hours** die Sprechstunde, -n; **doctor's ~** die Praxis, *pl.* Praxen

often oft (ö)

oh ach, ah; aha; **~ I see** ach so; **~ my** o je; **~ well** na ja

okay O.K.; alles klar; okay; ganz gut; **It's (not) ~.** Es geht (nicht).

old alt (ä) **~ town** die Altstadt, ¨-e

Olympic: ~ Games die Olympiade, -n; **~ Stadium** das Olympiastadion

on an; auf + *acc./dat.;* **~ account of** wegen + *gen.;* **~ foot** zu Fuß; **~ one hand** einerseits; **~ (this) Sunday** am Sonntag; **~ Sundays** sonntags [K. 2]

once einmal, mal; **~ more** noch einmal; **~ upon a time, there was . . .** Es war einmal ...

one *(pronoun)* man; **~ another** einander

oneself selbst, selber

only nur; erst; einzig

open offen, geöffnet; **to ~** auf·machen (hat aufgemacht); eröffnen (hat eröffnet); auf·schließen (hat aufgeschlossen); öffnen (hat geöffnet)

opening die Öffnung, -en; **~ time** die Öffnungszeit, -en

opera die Oper, -n

opinion die Meinung, -en; **to have an ~** meinen (hat gemeint); **What's your ~?** Was hältst du davon?; **in my ~** meiner Meinung nach

opportunity die Gelegenheit, -en

or oder

orally mündlich

orange die Apfelsine, -n; die Orange, -n; **~ juice** der Orangensaft; **~ (color)** orange

orchestra das Orchester; **~ conductor** der Dirigent, [-en], -en/die Dirigentin, -nen

order die Ordnung; die Reihenfolge, -n; **in ~** in Ordnung; **in ~ to** um ... zu; **to ~** bestellen (hat bestellt); **to put in ~** ordnen (hat geordnet)

orderly der Krankenpfleger, -; ordentlich

organization die Organisation, -en

organize organisieren (hat organisiert)

origin die Herkunft

original ursprünglich; **~ text** der Originaltext, -e

originate entstehen (ist entstanden)

other ander- (-er, -es, -e); **the ~ way around** umgekehrt

otherwise sonst

our unser

out of aus + *dat.*

outdoors im Freien

outgoing gesellig, kontaktfreudig

outside draußen

over *(time)* vorbei; **~ (position)** über + *acc./dat.;* **~-filled** überfüllt; **~worked** überarbeitet

overcast bedeckt

overhead: ~ projector der Overheadprojektor, -en; **~ transparency** die Folie, -n

oversee übersehen (hat übersehen)

own *(adj.)* eigen; **to ~** besitzen (hat besessen)

P

pack packen (hat gepackt); ein·packen (hat eingepackt)

package das Paket, -e

page die Seite, -n; das Blatt, ¨-er

pain der Schmerz, -en

painkiller die Schmerztablette, -n

palace das Schloss, *pl.* Schlösser

pale blass

pants die Hose, -n

pantyhose die Strumpfhose, -n

paper das Papier; **~ (theme, essay)** die Arbeit, -en; das Referat, -e

paperback das Taschenbuch, ¨-er

parade der Umzug, ¨-e

paradise das Paradies, -e

pardon! Entschuldigung!; **I beg your ~?** Wie bitte?

parents die Eltern *(pl.)*

park der Park, -s; **to ~** parken (hat geparkt)

parka der Anorak, -s

parking: ~ fee die Parkgebühr, -en; **~ garage** das Parkhaus, ¨er; **~ space, lot** der Parkplatz, ¨e; **~ stub** der Parkschein, -e

parliament das Parlament; **German Federal ~** der Bundestag; **German ~ building** der Reichstag

part der Teil, -e; **in ~** zum Teil

participate (in) mit·machen (hat mitgemacht) bei + *dat.*; teil·nehmen (hat teilgenommen) an + *dat.*

particular besonder-

particularly besonders

part-time worker die Aushilfe

party die Party, -s; das Fest, -e; die Fete, -n; **political ~** die Partei, -en; **to give a ~** ein Fest geben; **to go to a ~** auf eine Party (Fete) gehen (ist gegangen)

pass: mountain ~ der Pass, ¨e

passenger der Passagier, -e; **~ vehicle** der Personenkraftwagen, -; der PKW, -s

passionate leidenschaftlich

passive passiv

passport der Pass, ¨e

past *(in clock time)* nach; die Vergangenheit

pastry das Gebäck; **~ shop** die Konditorei, -en

path der Weg, -e

patience die Geduld

pay zahlen (hat gezahlt); **to ~ for** bezahlen (hat bezahlt); **to ~ attention** achten (hat geachtet), auf·passen (hat aufgepasst)

pea die Erbse, -n

peak der Gipfel, -

pearl die Perle, -n

pedestrian der Fußgänger, -/die Fußgängerin, -nen; **~ zone** die Fußgängerzone, -n; der Fußgängerbereich, -e

pen der Kugelschreiber, -; der Kuli, -s; der Stift, -e

pencil der Bleistift, -e

pension die Rente, -n

pensioner der Rentner, -/die Rentnerin, -nen

people die Leute *(pl.)*; die Menschen *(pl.)*; man

pepper der Pfeffer

per pro

percent das Prozent, -e

performance die Vorstellung, -en; die Aufführung, -en

perhaps vielleicht

period der Punkt, -e

permit erlauben (hat erlaubt); lassen (hat gelassen)

permitted erlaubt; **to be ~** dürfen (hat gedurft)

person der Mensch, [-en], -en; die Person, -en

personality die Persönlichkeit, -en

personnel: ~ department die Personalabteilung, -en; **head of ~** der Personalchef, -s/die Personalchefin, -nen

pharmaceutics die Pharmazie

pharmacist der Apotheker, -/die Apothekerin, -nen

pharmacy die Apotheke, -n

Philharmonic Orchestra (of Berlin) die Philharmonie

philosophy die Philosophie

photograph das Bild, das Foto; **to ~** fotografieren (hat fotografiert)

photographer der Fotograf/ die Fotografin

physics die Physik

piano das Klavier, -e; **~ lesson** die Klavierstunde, -n

pick: to ~ out aus·suchen (hat ausgesucht); aus·wählen (hat ausgewählt); **to ~ up** ab·holen (hat abgeholt); **to ~ up (mess)** auf·räumen (hat aufgeräumt)

picture das Bild, -er

piece das Stück, -e

pink rosa

pity: what a ~ schade

place der Platz, ¨e; die Stelle, -n; der Ort, -e; **to my ~** zu mir; **at my ~** bei mir

plan der Plan, ¨e; die Planung, -en; **to ~** vor·haben (hat vorgehabt); planen (hat geplant); **What have you got planned?** Was hast du vor?

planetarium das Planetarium, *pl.* Planeterien

plant die Pflanze, -n; **to ~** pflanzen (hat gepflanzt)

plastic das Plastik

plate der Teller, -

play das Theaterstück, -e; das Drama, *pl.* Dramen; **to ~** spielen (hat gespielt)

playground der Spielplatz, ¨e

plaza der Platz, ¨e

please bitte; **to ~** gefallen (gefällt, hat gefallen) + *dat.*

pleased: to be ~ (about) sich freuen (hat sich gefreut) über + *acc.*

pleasure die Freude, -n; die Lust; das Vergnügen

plot (of a story) die Handlung, -en

plump mollig

pocket die Tasche, -n

poem das Gedicht, -e

poet der Dichter, -/die Dichterin, -nen; der Poet, [-en], -en/die Poetin, -nen

point der Punkt, -e; der Zweck, -e; **to ~ to** zeigen (hat gezeigt) auf + *acc.*; **There's no ~.** Das hat keinen Zweck.

pointless: It's ~. Das hat keinen Zweck.

poison das Gift, -e

poisonous giftig

police die Polizei

political politisch; **~ party** die Partei, -en; **~ science** die Politikwissenschaft, -en

politician der Politiker, -/die Politikerin, -nen

politics die Politik, -en

poor arm (ä)

popular populär; beliebt; **~ music** die Popmusik

pork das Schweinefleisch

portion der Teil, -e; die Portion, -en

portray schildern (hat geschildert)

position die Stelle, -n; **in your ~** an deiner Stelle

position (job) die Stellung, -en; der Job, -s

positive positiv

possible möglich; **It's (not) ~.** Es geht (nicht).

possibility die Möglichkeit, -en

postage stamp die Briefmarke, -n

postal code die Postleitzahl, -en

postcard die Postkarte, -n

poster das Poster, -

post office die Post; **~ box** das Postfach, ¨er; **to go to the ~** auf die Post gehen

pot der Topf, ¨e

potato die Kartoffel, -n

poultry das Geflügel

pound das Pfund, -e; **to ~** pochen (hat gepocht)

power die Macht, ¨e

practical praktisch

practice üben (hat geübt); **to ~ a profession** einen Beruf aus·üben (hat ausgeübt); praktizieren (hat praktiziert)

pray beten (hat gebetet)

prefer: I ~ to work. Ich arbeite lieber.

preparation die Vorbereitung, -en

prepare (for) (sich) vor·bereiten (hat sich vorbereitet) auf + *acc.*

preschool der Kindergarten, ⸚

present (gift) das Geschenk, -e; **(time)** die Gegenwart; **to ~ oneself** sich vor·stellen (hat sich vorgestellt)

presentation das Referat, -e; **to make a ~** ein Referat halten (hat gehalten)

president der Präsident, [-en], -en/ die Präsidentin; -nen; **German Federal ~** der Bundespräsident,[-en], -en/die Bundespräsidentin, -nen

pressure der Druck

prestige das Prestige

pretty schön; (*for women*) hübsch; **~ pale** ganz schön blass

price der Preis, -e

prince der Prinz, [-en], -en; der Königssohn, ⸚e

princess die Prinzessin, -nen; die Königstochter, ⸚

printer der Drucker, -

private privat; **~ bath** das Privatbad, ⸚er; **~ lesson** die Privatstunde, -n

probably wahrscheinlich; wohl

problem das Problem, -e; **without a ~** problemlos

proclaim proklamieren (hat proklamiert); aus·rufen (hat ausgerufen)

produce her·stellen (hat hergestellt); produzieren (hat produziert)

product das Produkt, -e

profession der Beruf, -e

professional der Profi, -s

professor der Professor, -en/die Professorin, -nen; **assistant ~** der Dozent, [-en] -en /die Dozentin, -nen

program das Programm, -e; **TV or radio ~** die Sendung, -en

programmer der Programmierer, -/die Programmiererin, -nen

project das Projekt, -e; das Unternehmen, -

projection screen die Leinwand, ⸚e

promise die Versprechung, -en; **to ~** versprechen (hat versprochen)

protect schützen (hat geschützt)

proud stolz

Prussia (das) Preußen

psychiatry die Psychiatrie

psychology die Psychologie

pub die Kneipe, -n; die Gaststätte, -n; die Bar, -s; das Lokal, -e; **student ~** die Studentenkneipe, -n

public öffentlich

publish veröffentlichen (hat veröffentlicht)

pudding der Pudding, -s

pull ziehen (hat gezogen)

pullover der Pulli, -s; der Pullover, -

punctual pünktlich

pupil der Schüler, -/die Schülerin, -nen

pure rein

purple lila

purpose der Zweck, -e

purse die Handtasche, -n

Puss-in-Boots der gestiefelte Kater

put (*horizontal*) legen (hat gelegt); (*vertical*) stellen (hat gestellt); (*seated*) setzen (hat gesetzt); (*hanging*) hängen (hat gehängt); (*inserted*) stecken (hat gesteckt); (*general*) tun (hat getan);**to ~ up overnight** unter·bringen (hat untergebracht); **to ~ together** zusammen·stellen (hat zusammengestellt); **to ~ on (clothing)** an·ziehen (hat angezogen); **to ~ on makeup** sich schminken (hat sich geschminkt)

Q

qualified qualifiziert

quality die Qualität, -en; **personal ~** die Eigenschaft, -en

quarrel der Krach; der Streit; **to ~ with** sich streiten (hat sich gestritten) mit + *dat.*; Krach haben (hat gehabt)

quarter das Viertel, -; **~ after (five o'clock)** Viertel nach (fünf); **~ to (five o'clock)** Viertel vor (fünf)

queen die Königin, -nen

question die Frage, -n; **~ word** das Fragewort, ⸚er; **to ~** fragen (hat gefragt); **to ask a ~** eine Frage stellen (hat gestellt)

questionable fraglich

quick schnell

quiet die Ruhe; die Stille; ruhig; still

quite ziemlich

R

race rennen (ist gerannt)

racism der Rassismus

radio das Radio, -s

railroad die Bahn, -en

rain der Regen; **to ~** regnen (hat geregnet); **~ shower** der Schauer, -

raincoat der Regenmantel, ⸚

raise: to ~ heben (hat gehoben); **to ~ children** erziehen (hat erzogen)

Ramadan der Ramadan

range (kitchen) der Herd, -e

rank der Rang, ⸚e; die Stellung, -en

rare selten, rar

rather ziemlich; **(in opposition)** sondern; **~ than** lieber als

rave: to ~ about schwärmen (hat geschwärmt) von + *dat.*

raw material der Rohstoff, -e

razor: electric ~ der Rasierapparat, -e

reach erreichen (hat erreicht)

react reagieren (hat reagiert)

reaction die Reaktion, -en

read lesen (hat gelesen)

ready bereit; fertig; **to get ~** sich vor·bereiten (hat sich vorbereitet)

real echt; richtig; wahr; **~ estate agent** der Makler, -/die Maklerin, -nen

reality die Wirklichkeit, -en

really wirklich; richtig; ganz; echt (*slang*); **~ neat** echt toll; ganz toll; **~ bad** ganz schlimm

rear der Hintern

reason der Grund, ⸚e; **for that ~** deshalb; deswegen; aus diesem Grund

reasonable vernünftig; **~ (price)** günstig

reasonably priced preiswert

receipt die Quittung, -en

receive bekommen (hat bekommen)

recently vor kurzem; neulich

reckon with rechnen (hat gerechnet) mit + *dat.*

recognize erkennen (hat erkannt)

recommend empfehlen (hat empfohlen)

recommendation die Empfehlung, -en

reconcile sich versöhnen (hat sich versöhnt)

record die Platte, -n; **~ store** das Musikgeschäft, -e

record player der Plattenspieler, -

recover (from) sich erholen (hat sich erholt) (von + *dat.*)

recuperate (from) sich erholen (hat sich erholt) (von + *dat.*)

recycling das Recycling

red rot (ö)

refrigerator der Kühlschrank, ⸚e

region die Region, -en; der Bereich, -e

register sich ein·schreiben (hat sich eingeschrieben)

regulate regeln (hat geregelt)

rehearsal die Probe, -n

related verwandt

relative der/die Verwandte (*noun decl. like adj.*)

relatives die Verwandtschaft

relax sich aus·ruhen (hat sich ausgeruht)

relaxation die Entspannung, -en

relaxed locker

reliable zuverlässig

religious fromm (ö); religiös

remain bleiben (ist geblieben)

remaining übrig

remember sich erinnern (hat sich erinnert) an + *acc.*

renovate renovieren (hat renoviert)

rent die Miete, -n; **to ~** mieten (hat gemietet); **to ~ out** vermieten (hat vermietet)

repair reparieren (hat repariert); **~ person** der Mechaniker, -/die Mechanikerin, -nen

repeat wiederholen (hat wiederholt)

report der Bericht, -e; das Referat, -e; **to ~** berichten (hat berichtet); sich melden (hat sich gemeldet)

reporter der Reporter, -/die Reporterin, -nen

representative der/die Abgeordnete, -n (*noun decl. like adj.*)

republic die Republik, -en

request bitten (hat gebeten) um + *acc.*; erfordern (hat erfordert)

resistance der Widerstand

resort der Ferienort, -e

resource die Ressource, -n

respect der Respekt

respectable anständig

respectfully (*at end of a letter*) Hochachtungsvoll

responsibility die Verantwortung, -en

responsible verantwortlich; zuständig

rest der Rest, -e; **to ~** sich aus·ruhen (hat sich ausgeruht)

restaurant das Restaurant, -s; die Gaststätte, -n; **town hall ~** der Ratskeller, -

result das Resultat, -e; das Ergebnis, -se

resume (CV) der Lebenslauf, -̈e

return die Rückkehr; **to ~** zurück·fahren (ist zurückgefahren); zurück·gehen (ist zurückgegangen); zurück·kommen (ist zurückgekommen); wieder·kommen (ist wiedergekommen); zurück·kehren (ist zurückgekehrt); **to ~ something** (etwas) zurück·geben (hat zurückgegeben); zurück·nehmen (hat zurückgenommen)

reunification die Wiedervereinigung; die Union

reveal auf·decken (hat aufgedeckt)

rice der Reis

rich reich

ride die Fahrt, -en; **to ~ a bike** Rad fahren (ist Rad gefahren); **to ~ horseback** reiten (ist geritten)

right das Recht, -e; **Is it all ~ with you?** Ist es dir recht?; **to be ~** recht haben; **that's ~** genau; richtig; **on/to the ~** rechts; **~ around the corner** gleich um die Ecke; **~ ?** nicht wahr?

ring der Ring, -e; **to ~** klingeln (hat geklingelt)

rinse spülen (hat gespült)

risk riskieren (hat riskiert)

risky riskant

river der Fluss, *pl.* Flüsse

rock: ~ music die Rockmusik; **~ musician** der Rockmusiker, -/die Rockmusikerin, -nen

role die Rolle, -n

roll das Brötchen, -; die Semmel, -n

rollerblades die Rollerblades (*pl.*)

roll-top shutter der Rollladen, -̈

Roman römisch

romance novel der Liebesroman, -e

romantic romantisch

room das Zimmer, -; der Raum, -̈e; **(space)** der Platz, -̈e; **bathroom** das Badezimmer, -; **bedroom** das Schlafzimmer, -; **classroom** das Klassenzimmer, -; **living ~** das Wohnzimmer, -; **~ mate** der Mitbewohner, -/die Mitbewohnerin, -nen **~ number** die Zimmernummer, -n

round rund; die Runde, -n

routine die Routine, -n; der Alltag

rubble der Schutt

rug der Teppich, -e

rule die Regel, -n

Rumpelstiltskin Rumpelstilzchen

run laufen (ist gelaufen); rennen (ist gerannt)

running das Joggen; das Jogging; das Laufen

Russia (das) Russland

Russian russisch; **~ (language)** (das) Russisch; **~ (person)** der Russe, [-n], -n/die Russin, -nen

S

sack die Tüte, -n

sad traurig

safe sicher

safety die Sicherheit, -en; **~ helmet** der Sicherheitshelm, -e

sail segeln (ist gesegelt)

salad der Salat, -e

salary das Gehalt, -̈er; **~ expectation** die Gehaltsvorstellung, -en

salesperson der Verkäufer, -/die Verkäuferin, -nen

salt das Salz

same (der/das/die) selbe, gleich; **It's all the ~ to me.** Das ist mir egal.; **at the ~ time** gleichzeitig

sandal die Sandale, -n

sandwich das Brot, -e; das Butterbrot, -e; das belegte Brot

satisfied zufrieden

Saturday der Samstag; der Sonnabend

Saturdays samstags; sonnabends

sausage die Wurst, -̈e

save sparen (hat gespart)

savings: ~ account das Sparkonto, *pl.* -konten; **~ bank** die Sparkasse, -n

say sagen (hat gesagt); erzählen (hat erzählt)

scarf der Schal, -s

scene die Szene, -n

scenery die Landschaft, -en

schedule der Stundenplan, -̈e

school die Schule, -n; **elementary ~** die Grundschule, -n; **high ~ (non-college)** die Realschule, -n; **college prep. high ~** das Gymnasium, *pl.* Gymnasien; **technical-vocational ~** die Hauptschule, -n; **~ days** die Schulzeit, -en

science die Wissenschaft, -en; die Naturwissenschaft, -en

scientific wissenschaftlich

scientist der Wissenschaftler, -/die Wissenschaftlerin, -nen

score (in a game) treffen (hat getroffen)

screen die Leinwand, -̈e

sea die See, -n

search die Suche, -n; **to ~ for** suchen (hat gesucht) nach + *dat.*

season die Jahreszeit, -en; **(sports) ~** die Saison, -s

seat der Platz, -̈e; **Is this ~ taken?** Ist hier frei?; **to ~ oneself** sich setzen (hat sich gesetzt)

secretary der Sekretär, -e/ die Sekretärin, -nen

see sehen (hat gesehen)

seem scheinen (hat geschienen)

seldom selten

select wählen (hat gewählt)

selection die Wahl; die Auswahl

self (oneself, myself, itself, etc.) selbst, selber; sich; **~-reliant** selbstständig; **~-assured** selbstsicher

sell verkaufen (hat verkauft)

semester das Semester, -; **break** die Semesterferien *(pl.)*; **bus pass** die Semesterkarte, -n; das Semesterticket, -s

seminar das Seminar, -e; **room** der Seminarraum, ⸚e; **report** die Seminararbeit, -en

send schicken (hat geschickt); senden (hat gesendet)

sense spüren (hat gespürt)

sentence der Satz, ⸚e

separate trennen (hat getrennt); spalten (hat gespaltet)

September der September

sequence die Reihenfolge, -n

serious ernst; **Are you ~?** Ist das dein Ernst?

serve dienen (hat gedient)

set setzen (hat gesetzt); **to ~ the table** den Tisch decken (hat gedeckt); **to ~ off (on a trip)** los·fahren (ist losgefahren)

several einige; mehrere, manche

sexuality die Sexualität

shake rütteln (hat gerüttelt); schütteln (hat geschüttelt); **to ~ hands** die Hand schütteln; die Hand geben (hat gegeben)

shampoo das Shampoo, -s; das Haarwaschmittel, -; **to ~** (sich) die Haare waschen (hat sich gewaschen)

share sich teilen (hat sich geteilt)

shared gemeinsam; **~ bathroom** das Gemeinschaftsbad, ⸚er; **~ kitchen** die Gemeinschaftsküche, -n

shave (sich) rasieren (hat sich rasiert)

shaver (electric) der Rasierapparat, -e

she sie

shelf das Regal, -e

shine scheinen (hat geschienen)

ship das Boot, -e; das Schiff, -e

shirt das Hemd, -en

shock der Schock, -s

shoe der Schuh, -e; **athletic ~** der Turnschuh, -e

shoot schießen (hat geschossen)

shop das Geschäft, -e; der Laden, ⸚; **to ~** ein·kaufen (hat eingekauft)

shopping: to go ~ ein·kaufen gehen (ist einkaufen gegangen); **~ bag** die Einkaufstasche, -n; die Einkaufstüte, -n; die Tragetasche, -n; **~ basket** der Einkaufskorb, ⸚e; **~ center** das Einkaufszentrum, *pl.* -zentren; **~ trip** der Einkaufsbummel

short kurz (ü); **~ (people)** klein; **~ story** die Kurzgeschichte, -n

shorts die Shorts *(pl.)*

should sollen (hat gesollt)

shoulder die Schulter, -n

show zeigen (hat gezeigt)

shower die Dusche, -n; **~ room** der Duschraum, ⸚e; **to ~** (sich) duschen (hat sich geduscht); unter die Dusche gehen (ist gegangen); **rain ~** der Schauer, -

shy schüchtern

siblings die Geschwister *(pl.)*

sick krank

side die Seite, -n

sightseeing attraction die Sehenswürdigkeit, -en

sign das Schild, -er; das Zeichen, -

silence die Stille

silver das Silber

similar ähnlich; gleich

simple einfach; schlicht

simply einfach; bloß

simultaneous gleichzeitig

since seit *(prep.)*; seitdem, da *(conj.)*; **~ when** seit wann

sing singen (hat gesungen)

singer der Sänger, -/die Sängerin, -nen

single ledig; einzeln; **~-family home** das Einfamilienhaus, ⸚er; **~ room** das Einzelzimmer, -

sink das Waschbecken, -; **to ~** sinken (ist gesunken)

sister die Schwester, -n

sit sitzen (hat gesessen); **to ~ down** sich setzen (hat sich gesetzt)

situated: to be ~ liegen (hat gelegen)

situation die Lage, -n; die Situation, -en

size die Größe, -n

skate: roller ~ der Rollschuh, -e; **ice ~** der Schlittschuh, -e; **in-line ~** der Rollerblade, -s: **to ice ~** Schlittschuh laufen (ist gelaufen); **to roller ~** Rollschuh laufen (ist gelaufen)

ski der Ski, -er; **to ~** Ski laufen (ist Ski gelaufen); Ski fahren (ist Ski gefahren); **~ boot** der Skistiefel, -; **~ chalet** die Skihütte, -n; **~ parka** der Skianorak, -s; **~ run, track** die Piste, -n; **cross-country ~ track** die Langlaufloipe, -n

skin die Haut; **~ color** die Hautfarbe, -n

skirt der Rock, ⸚e

slam shut zu·knallen (hat zugeknallt)

sled der Schlitten, -

sleep schlafen (hat geschlafen); **to go to ~** schlafen gehen (ist schlafen gegangen)

sleigh der Schlitten, -; **~ ride** die Schlittelfahrt, -en

slender schlank

slice die Scheibe, -n

slow langsam

small klein

smart intelligent; klug (ü)

smell riechen (hat gerochen); stinken (hat gestunken)

smile lächeln (hat gelächelt)

smoke der Rauch; **to ~** rauchen (hat geraucht)

smooth glatt

snow der Schnee; **powder ~** der Pulverschnee; **to ~** schneien (hat geschneit); **~-covered** verschneit; **Snow White** das Schneewittchen

so so; also; **Isn't that ~?** Nicht?; **~ that** damit; **~ long.** Tschüss.; **I believe ~.** Ich glaube schon/ja.

so-so so lala

soap die Seife, -n; **~ opera** die Seifenoper, -n

soccer der Fußball; **~ field** der Fußballplatz, ⸚e

sociable gesellig; kontaktfreudig

society die Gesellschaft, -en

sociology die Soziologie

sock die Socke, -n

socket: electric ~ die Steckdose, -n

sofa das Sofa, -s

soft drink die Limonade, -n

software die Software

soldier der Soldat, [-en], -en/die Soldatin, -nen

solution die Lösung, -en

solve lösen (hat gelöst)

some etwas; einige; manch (-er, -es, -e); **at ~ point** irgendwann

someone jemand; irgendjemand

something etwas, was; irgendetwas; **~ like that** so was

sometime irgendwann

sometimes manchmal

somewhat etwas; ziemlich

son der Sohn, ⸚e

song das Lied, -er

soon bald; **as ~ as** sobald; wenn

sorcerer der Zauberer, -

sore: ~ muscle der Muskelkater, -

sort die Art, -en; die Sorte, -n; **to ~** sortieren (hat sortiert)

sorry: to be ~ leidtun + *dat.* (hat leidgetan); **I'm ~** es tut mir leid; **~ I'm late.** Entschuldige die Verspätung.

sound klingen (hat geklungen); **That ~s good.** Das klingt gut.; Das hört sich gut an.

soup die Suppe, -n

south der Süden; südlich; **South American** südamerikanisch

southwestern südwestlich

souvenir das Andenken, -

space der Platz, ⸚e

spaghetti die Spaghetti *(pl.)*

Spain (das) Spanien

Spanish spanisch; ~ **(language)** (das) Spanisch

Spaniard der Spanier, -/die Spanierin, -nen

speak reden (hat geredet); sprechen (hat gesprochen)

spectator der Zuschauer, -/die Zuschauerin, -nen

speechless sprachlos

spell buchstabieren (hat buchstabiert); **How do you ~ that?** Wie schreibt man das?

spend (money) aus·geben (hat ausgegeben); **to ~ (time)** verbringen (hat verbracht)

spite: in ~ of trotz + *gen.*

splendid großartig

spontaneity die Spontaneität

spontaneous spontan

spoon der Löffel, -

sport der Sport; **to engage in sports** Sport treiben (hat getrieben); ~ **coat** der/das Sakko, -s; die Jacke, -n

spring der Frühling, -e

stadium das Stadion, *pl.* Stadien

stage (theater) die Bühne, -n

stair die Treppe, -n

stairwell das Treppenhaus, ⸚er

stamp: postage ~ die Briefmarke, -n

stand der Kiosk, -s; der Stand, ⸚e; **to ~** stehen (hat gestanden); **to ~ up** auf·stehen (ist aufgestanden); **to ~/put upright** stellen (hat gestellt)

standing der Rang, ⸚e

standard German (das) Hochdeutsch

stanza die Strophe, -n

stare an·starren (hat angestarrt)

start an·fangen (hat angefangen); beginnen (hat begonnen); **to ~ a conversation** an·sprechen (hat angesprochen)

state (in Germany) das Land, ⸚er; das Bundesland, ⸚er; ~ **(in the U.S.A.)** der Staat, -en; ~ **exam** das Staatsexamen, -

state-owned staatlich

stay der Aufenthalt, -e; **to ~** bleiben (ist geblieben)

step die Treppe, -; **to ~** treten (ist getreten)

stepbrother der Stiefbruder, ⸚

stepdaughter die Stieftochter, ⸚

stepfather der Stiefvater, ⸚

stepmother die Stiefmutter, ⸚

stepsister die Stiefschwester, -n

steps die Treppe, -n

stereo system die Stereoanlage, -n

stick stecken (hat gesteckt)

stiff steif

still still; die Stille; noch; immer noch; noch immer

stomach der Bauch, ⸚e

stomachache die Bauchschmerzen *(pl.)*

stop an·halten (hat angehalten); auf·hören (hat aufgehört); halten (hat gehalten); stehen·bleiben (ist stehengeblieben); **(bus) stop** die Haltestelle, -n

storage room der Abstellraum, ⸚e

store das Geschäft, -e; der Laden, ⸚

storm der Sturm, ⸚e

story die Geschichte, -n; die Erzählung, -en

stove der Herd, -e

straight gerade; ~ **ahead** geradeaus; ~ **hair** glatte Haare

straighten up auf·räumen (hat aufgeräumt)

strange seltsam

street die Straße, -n

streetcar die Straßenbahn, -en

stress der Stress; **to ~ (feel stressed)** stressen (hat gestresst); **stressed** gestresst; **stressful** stressig

strict streng

stroll der Spaziergang, ⸚e; der Bummel, -; **to ~** spazieren gehen (ist spazieren gegangen); bummeln (ist gebummelt)

structure die Struktur, -en

strong stark (ä)

student der Student, [en], -en/die Studentin, -nen; ~ **(university-level)** der/die Studierende, -n *(noun decl. like adj.)*; **fellow ~** der Kommilitone, [-n], -n/die Kommilitonin, -nen; ~ **ID** der Studentenausweis, -e; ~ **room** das Studentenzimmer, -; die Studentenbude, -n

student life das Studentenleben

studies das Studium, *pl.* Studien

study studieren (hat studiert); lernen (hat gelernt); ~ **group** die Arbeitsgruppe, -n; **minor area of ~** das Nebenfach, ⸚er

stuff das Zeug

stupid dumm (ü), doof

subject (academic) das Fach, ⸚er; das Studienfach, ⸚er; **major ~** das Hauptfach, ⸚er; **minor ~** das Nebenfach, ⸚er

subway die U-Bahn, -en

successful erfolgreich

such solch (-er, -es, -e); ~ **a** so ein

suddenly plötzlich

suggest vor·schlagen (hat vorgeschlagen)

suggestion der Vorschlag, ⸚e; der Tipp, -s

suit (man's) der Anzug, ⸚e; **(woman's)** ~ das Kostüm, -e; **to ~** passen (hat gepasst) + *dat.*; stehen (hat gestanden) + *dat.*

suitcase der Koffer, -

summer der Sommer, -; ~ **cottage** das Sommerhäuschen, -

sun die Sonne, -n

Sunday der Sonntag, -e

Sundays sonntags

sunglasses die Sonnenbrille, -n

sunny sonnig

supermarket der Supermarkt, ⸚e

supper das Abendessen; das Abendbrot; **for ~** zum Abendessen; **to have ~** zu Abend essen

supposed: to be ~ to sollen (hat gesollt)

sure sicher; bestimmt; **(agreement)** ~! Natürlich!; Klar!

surf surfen (hat gesurft)

surprise überraschen (hat überrascht)

surprising(ly) überraschend

suspect: to ~ ahnen (hat geahnt)

suspense: to be in ~ gespannt sein

sweater der Pulli, -s; der Pullover, -

swim schwimmen (ist geschwommen); baden (hat gebadet)

swimming pool: indoor ~ das Hallenbad, ⸚er; **outdoor ~** das Frei(schwimm)bad, ⸚er

swimming trunks die Badehose, -n

swim suit der Badeanzug, ⸚e

Swiss *(adj.)* schweizer; ~ **(person)** der Schweizer, -/die Schweizerin, -nen

switch (to change) wechseln (hat gewechselt)

Switzerland die Schweiz

symbol das Wahrzeichen, -; das Symbol, -e

synagogue die Synagoge, -n

T

table der Tisch, -e

take nehmen (hat genommen); **to ~ along** mit·nehmen (hat mitgenommen); **to ~ care of** erledigen (hat erledigt); bewerkstelligen (hat bewerkstelligt); **to ~ off** aus·ziehen (hat ausgezogen); **to ~ place, occur** statt·finden (hat stattgefunden)

talented begabt; talentiert

talk sprechen (hat gesprochen); reden (hat geredet); diskutieren (hat diskutiert); *(dialect)* schwätzen (hat geschwätzt); **to ~ about** reden/sprechen/diskutieren über + *acc.;* **to ~ to** sprechen (etc.) mit + *dat.;* **to ~ over** besprechen (hat besprochen)

tall groß (ö); hoch (höher)

tardiness die Verspätung, -en

target das Ziel, -e

task die Aufgabe, -n

taste der Geschmack; **to ~** schmecken (hat geschmeckt)

tasty lecker

tavern die Wirtschaft, -en

taxi das Taxi, -s

tea der Tee, -s

teach unterrichten (hat unterrichtet); lehren (hat gelehrt)

teacher der Lehrer, -/die Lehrerin, -nen; **~'s degree** das Staatsexamen, -

team die Mannschaft, -en; das Team, -s

telephone das Telefon, -e; **to ~** telefonieren (hat telefoniert); an·rufen (hat angerufen); **~ booth** die Telefonzelle, -n; **by ~** telefonisch; **~ number** die Telefonnummer, -n

televise übertragen (hat übertragen)

television das Fernsehen; **~ set** der Fernseher, -; **color ~** der Farbfernseher; **~ program** die Fernsehsendung, -en; **to watch ~** fern·sehen (hat ferngesehen)

tell sagen (hat gesagt); **to ~ (a story)** erzählen (hat erzählt); **to ~ about** erzählen von + *dat.*

temperature die Temperatur, -en; **the ~ is (ten) degrees** die Temperatur liegt um (zehn) Grad

tennis das Tennis; **~ ball** der Tennisball, ¨e; **~ racket** der Tennisschläger, -; **~ shoe** der Tennisschuh, -e

tent das Zelt, -e

terrace die Terrasse, -n

terrible schlimm; furchtbar; schrecklich

test die Prüfung, -en; **to ~** prüfen (hat geprüft); überprüfen (hat überprüft); **to take a ~** eine Prüfung schreiben (hat geschrieben)

than als

thank danken (hat gedankt) + *dat.* (+ für + *acc.*)

thanks danke; **~ a lot!** danke schön; vielen Dank

that dass; jen- (-er, -es, -e); **~'s why** deshalb; deswegen; **~ is to say** das heißt (d.h.)

the der; das; die; die *(pl.)*

theater das Theater, -; das Schauspielhaus, ¨er; **to go to the ~** ins Theater gehen; **~ play** das Theaterstück, -e

their ihr

them sie *(acc.);* ihnen *(dat.)*

theme das Thema, *pl.* Themen

then dann; da; damals; *(particle)* denn

theory die Theorie, -n

there da; dort; hin; dahin; **over ~** dort drüben; **~ is/are** es gibt (hat gegeben)

therefore also; deshalb; daher; darum; deswegen

these diese

they sie

thick dick

thin dünn, schlank

thing das Ding, -e; die Sache, -n

think denken (hat gedacht); meinen (hat gemeint); glauben (hat geglaubt); **to ~ about** denken an + *acc.;* **to ~ of** halten (hat gehalten) von + *dat.*/für + *acc.;* **to ~ over** sich überlegen (hat sich überlegt); **to ~ something over** nach·denken (hat nachgedacht); **to ~ that** finden (hat gefunden); **What do you ~?** Was meinst du?

third das Drittel, -; dritt-

thirsty durstig; **to be ~** Durst haben

this dies (-er, -es, -e); **~ morning** heute Morgen; **~ afternoon** heute Nachmittag; **~ evening** heute Abend

thorough gründlich

throat der Hals, ¨e; **to have a sore ~** Halsschmerzen haben (hat gehabt)

through durch

throw werfen (hat geworfen); **to ~ away** weg·werfen (hat weggeworfen)

thunder donnern (es donnert, es hat gedonnert)

Thursday der Donnerstag

thus also

ticket die Karte, -n; **airline ~** der Flugschein, -e; das Flugticket, -s

tie (necktie) die Krawatte, -n

time die Zeit, -en; das Mal, -e; **(clocktime)** die Uhr; **at that ~** damals; **at the same ~** zur gleichen Zeit; **for a long ~** lange; **for the first ~** zum ersten Mal; **What ~ is it?** Wie viel Uhr ist es?/Wie spät ist es?; **At what ~?** Um wie viel Uhr?; **~ line** die Zeittafel, -n; **to have ~** frei haben (hat gehabt)

timely hochaktuell

times mal; **[three] ~** [drei]mal

tip das Trinkgeld, -er

tired müde; **dead-~** todmüde

to an; auf, in; nach; zu

today heute; **What day is it ~?** Welcher Tag ist heute?

toe der Zeh, -en

together zusammen; gemeinsam

toilet die Toilette, -n; das WC, -s; das Klo, -s *(colloq.);* **to go to the ~** auf die Toilette/aufs Klo gehen (ist gegangen)

toiletry der Toilettenartikel, -

tolerable erträglich

tolerant tolerant

tolerate ertragen (hat ertragen)

tomato die Tomate, -n

tomorrow morgen; **~ morning** morgen früh; **~ afternoon** morgen Nachmittag; **~ evening** morgen Abend; **day after ~** übermorgen

tonight heute Abend

tongue die Zunge, -n

too zu; **me ~** ich auch; **~ bad** schade; **~ little** zu wenig; **~ many** zu viele; **~ much** zu viel

tooth der Zahn, ¨e

toothache die Zahnschmerzen *(pl.)*

toothbrush die Zahnbürste, -n

toothpaste die Zahnpasta, *pl.* -pasten

topic das Thema, *pl.* Themen

tour die Tour, -en; **~ guide** der Reiseleiter, -/die Reiseleiterin, -nen; der Fremdenführer, -/die Fremdenführerin, -nen

tourism der Tourismus; der Fremdenverkehr

tourist der Tourist, [-en], -en/die Touristin, -nen; **~ office** das Fremdenverkehrsbüro, -s; der Verkehrsverein, -e

towel (bath) das Badetuch, ¨er

tower der Turm, ¨e

town hall das Rathaus, ¨er; **~ restaurant** der Ratskeller, -

track (for skiing) die Piste, -n; **to track** nach·spüren (hat nachgespürt)

traffic der Verkehr; **~ light** die Ampel, -n; **~ regulation** die Verkehrsregel, -n; **~ sign** das Verkehrsschild, -er; das Verkehrszeichen, -

train der Zug, ¨e; die Bahn -en; **~ station** der Bahnhof, ¨e; **main station** der Hauptbahnhof, ¨e; **~ track** die Schiene, -n; das Gleis, -e

trait die Eigenschaft, -en

transfer überweisen (hat überwiesen)

transformation der Wandel

translate übersetzen (hat übersetzt)

translator der Übersetzer, -/die Übersetzerin, -nen

transportation der Verkehr; **means of ~** das Verkehrsmittel, -

travel fahren (ist gefahren); reisen (ist gereist); **~ by train** (mit der) Bahn fahren (ist gefahren); **~ agency** das Reisebüro, -s; das Reiseunternehmen, -; **~ group leader** der Reiseleiter, -/die Reiseleiterin, -nen

treasure der Schatz, ¨e

tree der Baum, ¨e

treaty das Abkommen, -

trifle die Kleinigkeit, -en

trip die Reise, -n; die Fahrt, -en; die Tour, -en; **bike ~** die Radtour, -en; **to take a ~** verreisen (ist verreist)

truck der Lastwagen, -; der LKW, -s

trunk der Kofferraum, ¨e

true wahr; **that's (not) ~** das stimmt (nicht)

trust das Vertrauen; **to ~** vertrauen (hat vertraut)

truth die Wahrheit

try versuchen (hat versucht); probieren (hat probiert); **to ~ on** an·probieren (hat anprobiert)

T-shirt das T-Shirt, -s

Tuesday der Dienstag

tunnel der Tunnel, -s

Turk der Türke, [-n], -n/die Türkin, -nen

Turkish türkisch

Turkey die Türkei

turkey die Pute, -n

turn ab·biegen (ist abgebogen); wenden (hat gewendet); **to ~ around** (sich) um·drehen (hat sich umgedreht); **to ~ in (a paper)** ab·geben (hat abgegeben); **to ~ on** an·drehen (hat angedreht); **to ~ off** aus·machen (hat ausgemacht)

turn, turning die Wende

TV das Fernsehen; **~ set** der Fernseher, -; **~ program** die Fernsehsendung, -en

twice zweimal

type die Art, -en; **to ~** tippen (hat getippt)

U

ugly hässlich

umbrella der Regenschirm, -e; der Schirm, -e

umpteen times zigmal, x-mal

unathletic unsportlich

unattractive unattraktiv

unbelievable unglaublich

uncle der Onkel, -

uncreative einfallslos

under unter; **to keep ~ lock and key** unter Verschluss halten (hat gehalten)

underpaid unterbezahlt

understand verstehen (hat verstanden)

understanding das Verständnis; **international ~** die Völkerverständigung

understood: to make oneself ~ sich verständlich machen (hat sich verständlich gemacht)

undertaking das Unternehmen, -

underway unterwegs

underwear die Unterwäsche

undoubtedly bestimmt

undress (sich) aus·ziehen (hat ausgezogen)

unemployed arbeitslos

unfortunately leider

unfriendly unfreundlich

unhappy unglücklich

unification die Vereinigung

unified vereinigt; vereint

unique einmalig

unity die Einheit

university die Universität, -en; die Uni, -s; die Hochschule, -n; **to attend a ~** an/auf die Universität gehen; studieren (hat studiert); **at the ~** an/auf der Universität

unlikable unsympathisch

unlock auf·schließen (hat aufgeschlossen)

unmusical unmusikalisch

unpaid unbezahlt

unsure unsicher

until bis; **~ now** bisher; **~ later** bis später; tschüss; bis dann; bis bald

up: ~ to bis zu; **~ front** da vorne; **What's ~?** Was gibt's?

uprising der Aufstand, ¨e

urgent dringend; dringlich

U.S.A. die USA (pl.); die Vereinigten Staaten von Amerika; **from the ~** aus den USA

us uns (acc. & dat.)

use benutzen (hat benutzt); gebrauchen (hat gebraucht); verwenden (hat verwendet); **to ~ up** verbrauchen (hat verbraucht)

usual üblich

usually meistens; gewöhnlich

utensil das Gerät, -e

V

vacation der Urlaub; die Ferien (pl.); **~ trip** die Ferienreise, -n; **on/during ~** in Urlaub/in den Ferien; **to go on ~** in Urlaub/in die Ferien fahren (ist gefahren); Urlaub nehmen (hat genommen); **~ home** die Ferienwohnung, -en; **ready for a ~** ferienreif

vacuum der Staubsauger, -; **to ~** staub·saugen (hat gestaubsaugt)

valley das Tal, ¨er

value der Stellenwert, -e

vegetable das Gemüse, -

vending machine der Automat, [-en], -en

very sehr; ganz

veterinarian der Tierarzt, ¨e/die Tierärztin, -nen

vice versa umgekehrt

vicinity die Nähe; **in the ~** in der Nähe

victor die Siegermacht, ¨e

video das Video, -s; **~ camera** die Videokamera, -s; **~ game** das Videospiel, -e; **~ recorder** der Videorecorder, -; **~ store** der Videoverleih, -e

view die Aussicht, -en

village das Dorf, ¨er

violence die Gewalt

visible sichtbar

visit der Besuch, -e; **to ~** besuchen (hat besucht); **to ~ (a museum, etc.)** besichtigen (hat besichtigt)

volleyball der Volleyball

vomit sich übergeben (hat sich übergeben); kotzen (hat gekotzt) (colloq.)

vote die Wahl, -en; **to ~** wählen (hat gewählt)

voter der Wähler, -/die Wählerin, -nen

W

wage rate der Tarif, -e

wait die Wartezeit, -en; **to ~** warten (hat gewartet); **to ~ for** warten (hat gewartet) auf + acc.

waiting period die Wartezeit, -en

waiter/waitress der Kellner, -/die Kellnerin, -nen; **Oh, ~!** Herr Ober! Fräulein! Frau Ober!

wake up auf·wachen (ist aufgewacht)

walk der Spaziergang, ¨e; **to ~** laufen (ist gelaufen); **to take a ~** einen Spaziergang machen; **to go for a ~**

spazieren gehen (ist spazieren gegangen)

wall die Wand, ⸚e; ~ **(exterior)** die Mauer, -n

wallet das Portemonnaie, -s

want (to) wollen (hat gewollt); Lust haben (hat gehabt)

war der Krieg, -e; **(First, Second) World** ~ der (Erste, Zweite) Weltkrieg, -e; **cold** ~ der Kalte Krieg

wardrobe der Kleiderschrank, ⸚e

warm warm (ä)

warn warnen (hat gewarnt)

wash die Wäsche; **to** ~ (sich) waschen (hat gewaschen); **to ~ dishes** ab·waschen (hat abgewaschen); Geschirr spülen (hat gespült)

washing machine die Waschmaschine, -n

wastepaper basket der Papierkorb, ⸚e

watch die Armbanduhr, -en; **to** ~ an·sehen (hat angesehen); schauen (hat geschaut); **to ~ TV** fern·sehen (hat ferngesehen); **to ~ out** auf·passen (hat aufgepasst)

water das Wasser; ~ **sports** der Wassersport; ~ **tower** der Wasserturm, ⸚e; **mineral** ~ das Mineralwasser; **to ~ ski** Wasserski fahren (ist gefahren)

wavy wellig

way der Weg, -e; die Art; **on the** ~ auf dem Weg; **this** ~ so; auf diese Weise

weak schwach (ä)

wear tragen (hat getragen)

weather das Wetter; ~ **map** die Wetterkarte, -n; ~ **report** der Wetterbericht, -e

Website die Website, -s

wedding die Hochzeit, -en

Wednesday der Mittwoch

week die Woche, -n; **a ~ from today** heute in acht Tagen

weekday der Wochentag, -e

weekend das Wochenende; **on the** ~ am Wochenende

weightlifting das Gewichtheben

welcome das Willkommen; **you're** ~ bitte (sehr)

well gut; wohl; ~? na?; **I'm not** ~. Ich fühle mich nicht wohl.; **to get** ~ sich erholen (hat sich erholt); **Get** ~! Gute Besserung!; ~ *(interjection)* Na!; Nun!; ~ **now** na; **oh** ~ na ja

well-known bekannt

west der Westen

we wir

wet nass (a/ä)

what was; ~ **kind (of)**, ~ **a** was für (ein); **What?** Wie bitte?

when wann; wenn; als

whenever immer wenn; sooft

where wo; ~ **(to)** wohin; ~ **do you come from?** Woher kommst du?

whether ob

which welch (-er, -es, -e)

while die Weile, -n; **in a** ~ in einer Weile; während

white weiß

who? wer?; ~ **is that?** Wer ist das?

whole ganz

whom wen *(acc.)*; wem *(dat.)*

whose dessen; ~? wessen?

why warum, wieso, weshalb; **that's** ~ daher; deswegen; deshalb

wife die Frau, -en

win siegen (hat gesiegt); gewinnen (hat gewonnen)

wind der Wind, -e

window das Fenster, -

windy windig

wine der Wein, -e

winter der Winter, -; ~ **sports** der Wintersport

wish der Wunsch, ⸚e; **to** ~ wünschen (hat gewünscht); **I** ~ **I had . . .** Ich wünschte/wollte, ich hätte . . .

witch die Hexe, -n

with mit; ~ **it** damit; **to live** ~ **a family** bei einer Familie wohnen

withdraw (money) ab·heben (hat abgehoben)

without ohne

wizard der Zauberer, -

woman die Frau, -en

wonder das Wunder, -; **I** ~ **if . . .** Ich frage mich, ob . . .

wonderful wunderbar

woods der Wald, ⸚er

word das Wort, ⸚er

work die Arbeit, -en; **to** ~ arbeiten (hat gearbeitet); **to ~ part time** jobben (hat gejobbt); **It doesn't** ~. Es geht nicht., Es funktioniert nicht.; **to ~ out all right** klappen (hat geklappt); ~ **experience** die Arbeitserfahrung, -en; ~ **environment** das Arbeitsklima; ~ **place** der Arbeitsplatz, ⸚e; ~ **quota** die Arbeitsnorm, -en

workbook das Arbeitsbuch, ⸚er

worker der Arbeiter, -/die Arbeiterin, -nen; der Arbeitnehmer, -/die Arbeitnehmerin, -nen

workroom das Arbeitszimmer, -

world die Welt, -en; ~-**famous** weltberühmt; ~ **war** der Weltkrieg, -e

worry die Sorge, -n; **to ~ about** sich Sorgen machen (hat gemacht) um + *acc.;* **Don't** ~. Mach dir keine Sorgen.

worth der Wert; wert; **to be ~ it** sich lohnen (hat sich gelohnt)

worthwhile wert

would würde; ~ **like** möchte; **I** ~ **be** ich wäre; **I** ~ **have** ich hätte; **That ~ be . . .** Das wäre . . .

wound verwunden (hat verwundet)

wow Mensch!

write schreiben (hat geschrieben); **to ~ to** schreiben (hat geschrieben) an + *acc.;* **to ~ down** auf·schreiben (hat aufgeschrieben)

writer der Schriftsteller, -/die Schriftstellerin, -nen; der Autor, -en/die Autorin, -nen

written *(adj.)* schriftlich

wrong falsch; **What's** ~? Was ist los?; **What is ~ with you?** Was hast du?

X

xenophobia die Ausländerfeindlichkeit

Y

yard der Garten, ä-

year das Jahr, -e; **for ~s** seit Jahren

yearly jährlich

yellow gelb

yes ja; *(for emphasis)* doch

yesterday gestern

yet noch; schon; **not** ~ noch nicht

Yiddish das Jiddisch

yogurt der/das Joghurt

you *(informal sing.)* du *(nom.);* dich *(acc.);* dir *(dat.); (formal sing. & pl.)* Sie *(nom. & acc.);* Ihnen *(dat.);* ~ **guys** *(informal pl.)* ihr *(nom.);* euch *(acc. & dat.);* **You're absolutely right.** Du hast vollkommen recht.

young jung; ~ **girl** das Fräulein

your *(informal sing.)* dein; *(informal pl.)* euer; *(formal sing. & pl.)* Ihr

youth die Jugend; der/die Jugendliche *(noun decl. like adj.);* ~ **hostel** die Jugendherberge, -n; **budget** ~ **hotel** das Jugendhotel, -s; ~ **literature** die Jugendliteratur

Z

zero die Null, -en; null

Zip code die Postleitzahl, -en

Index

This index includes grammar topics, topics from the **Wissenswerte Vokabeln, Sprache im Alltag, Brennpunkt Kultur, Deutsch im Beruf,** and common communicative functions. References to student annotations are indicated as [SA]

a/an, 29
abbreviated forms, 30, 48, 58 [SA], 90, 427. *See also* contractions
abbreviations, 21 [SA], 48
aber, 92
ability, expressing, 135
Abitur, 306, 314, 327
academic subjects, 51, 306
accusative case, 56–57. *See also* direct object
    as answer to **wen?/was?**, 56
    of definite articles, 56, 214
    of **der**-words, 233
    of destination, 263
    of indefinite articles, 56, 112, 214
    masculine **N**-nouns in, 57
    of possessive adjectives, 112
    preceded adjectives in, 361
    prepositions taking, 155, 262, 323
    pronouns in, 64
    reflexive pronouns, 324–325
    relative pronouns, 343
    time expressions in, 233 [SA], 274, 318
    and two-case prepositions, 215, 258 [SA]
actions
    describing, 53–54
    purpose of, 280
    repeated, 67
active voice, 450
activities
    describing, 72, 86–90
    proposing, 347–348
    speculating about, 430–437
address, titles of, 16, 60
adjectives, 358
    with accusative case, 361
    comparative, 367–368
    with dative case, 214, 230, 361
    der-words +, 362
    descriptive, 23, 153
    ein-words +, 358, 361
    with genitive case, 410
    with nominative case, 358
    possessive, 90–91, 112, 214 [SA], 358 (*See also* **ein**-words)
    preceded, 358, 410
    superlative, 369–370
    unpreceded, 364
adverbs
    comparative, 367–368
    future-time, 318
    weekday names as, 67

age, asking about, 22
agent, 450
ago, 274
agreeing, 427
alphabet, German, 21
als, 93, 407, 454
am
    + superlative, 369–370
    in time expressions, 274, 318
America. *See* North America
American culture
    German and Austrian influences on, 479
    influences on German-speaking Europe, 475
amounts, specifying, 97–98
an
    names of cities with 255
    da +, 324
    ~ **deiner (Ihrer) Stelle,** 435
    as prefix, 176
    + time expressions, 318
    as two-case preposition, 250, 253, 323
animals, expressions with 205
antecedent, 340
apprenticeships, 317, 346
articles. *See* definite article(s); indefinite article(s)
artists, 353, 458
assumptions, 81, 126
asylum-seekers, 216 [SA], 217
attention-getters, 19 [SA]
auf, 176, 250, 253, 322, 323
Auf Wiedersehen!, 11
aus, 226
außer, 226
Austria, 365–366. *See also* Vienna (Wien)
    culture and customs in, 97, 123, 241, 479
    immigrants from, 47
    language in, 32, 68 [SA]
    map of, 366
    studying in, 123, 327
    authors, 123, 159, 225, 241–242, 353, 381, 472, 477, 479, 485-486
auxiliaries
    English, 53
    German, 170 (*See also* **haben; sein; werden; würde**-construction)
Azubi (Auszubildende), 327, 346, 349

Baden-Württemberg, 260
BAföG, 317

bank accounts, 248 [SA]
bathroom objects, 299
Bavaria (Bayern), 284
beer, 97, 208 [SA]
bei, 226
Belgium, 32
Berlin
    history of, 444, 446–447
    sights in, 422–423, 424 [SA], 430 [SA]
Bern, 403
bicycling, 145
birthdays, 63
bitte, 9, 98, 134
Bitte schön, 98
bleiben, 34 [SA], 171
body, parts of, 232, 303. *See also* physical characteristics
Brücke (art movement), 458
Bundesländer, 111

capitalization, 2 [SA], 3 [SA], 27, 67
cardinal numbers, 22
careers, 119–120, 346 *See also* jobs; professions
cars, 157
characteristics
    of job applicants, 360
    personal, 153, 360
    physical, 23
city names, 215, 227, 255
classroom objects, 27, 29 [SA]
classroom requests, 9
clauses
    infinitive, 195
    main (independent), 192, 194 [SA], 196, 297, 340
    relative, 340
    subordinate (*See* subordinate clause(s))
clock time, 68–69
clothing, articles of, 128–129
cognates, 81, 468
college. *See* university(-ies)
colloquial German. *See* informal German
Cologne (Köln), 278, 390
colors, 29
commands
    formal, 8–9
    imperative mood for, 347
    informal, 131–132, 133
    particles with, 134
    subjunctive vs., 432
    wir, 134
comparative, 367–368

complex sentences, 408
compliments, 230
composers, classical, 177, 353, 354-355.
    365, 485, 472, 479
composers, popular music, 472,
    475, 479
compound nouns, 66
concurrent events, 407
conditional sentences, 437–438
confirming statements, 427
conjunctions
    coordinating, 66, 92, 194 [SA]
        question words as, 196
    subordinating, 192, 193, 194, 195,
        276 [SA], 280, 408
contractions, 109 [SA], 215, 227, 251
contrary-to-fact situations, 437
conversational German. *See* informal
    German
conversational past, 170–176, 178–179,
    406, 407, 452
coordinating conjunctions, 92
countries, 31, 215, 226, 253 [SA]

da-compounds, 324
daily routines, 71, 298
damit, 280
danach, 166 [SA]
Danke schön, 98
dann, 408 [SA]
das, 27, 28, 34
dass, 192, 454
dates, 62, 274
dative case, 212–215
    adjectives in, 214, 230, 361
    of articles, 214
    of **der**-words, 233
    idiomatic expressions with, 228, 231
    indicating location with, 215
    of location, 215, 263
    of personal pronouns, 212
    of possessive adjectives, 214
    prepositions taking, 215, 226–227,
        320, 411
    reflexive pronouns, 300–301
    relative pronouns, 344
    time expressions in, 274, 318
    and two-case prepositions, 215, 250-
        253, 256-257
    verbs taking, 230, 454
days of the week, 66, 274
definite article(s), 27, 113. *See also*
    der-words
    accusative of, 56, 214
    + adjectives, 362, 410
    with countries and nationalities, 31
        [SA], 215
    dative case, 214
    with first names, 165

gender of, 27
genitive of, 410
in nominative case, 34
nominative of, 28, 214
with parts of the body, 300
plural forms, 27
denn, 92 [SA]
dependent clauses. *See* subordinate
    clause(s)
der, 27, 28, 34
der-words, 28, 233, 362, 410. *See also*
    definite article(s)
describing yourself and others, 18, 153
desire, expressing, 137–138, 148
destination, expressing, 250, 262
dictionary forms, 113 [SA]
die, 27, 28, 34
dieser, 233. *See also* **der**-words
diminutives, 402
directions, giving, 261
direct object, 56–57, 170 [SA], 212.
    See also accusative case
divorce, 46 [SA]
doch, 53, 134
doof, 154 [SA]
double-infinitive, 436–437
Dresden, 458
Driver's education, 157
du, 19, 53 [SA], 131–132
du-imperative, 131–132
durch, 155, 450
dürfen, 135, 146, 393, 394 [SA]

EC-Karte, 258 [SA]
education
    German (*See* school system;
        university(-ies))
    international, 123
ein, eine, abbreviated forms of, 30
ein(s) (number), 22, 227
ein-words, 29–30, 90–91. *See also*
    possessive adjectives
    accusative of, 112
    possessive adjectives as, 91
-**el** nouns, 113 [SA]
e-mail, 60
emphasis, 274
emphasis, word order for, 65
English vs. German usage
    choice of present tense verb form in,
        53–54
    cognates, 81, 468
    cultural, 300 [SA]
    indicating possession, 300 [SA],
        409 [SA]
    mixed verb forms, 394 [SA]
    of prepositions, 274, 322
    with reflexive verbs, 296, 300 [SA]
    of relative clauses, 340 [SA], 344 [SA]

in separable-prefix verbs, 71 [SA]
in time expressions, 274
and word meanings, 113 [SA], 147, 170
and word order, 53, 71 [SA], 212
word order in, 54
Entschuldigung, 7
er, 18, 35
es, 35
    ~ **gibt,** 90
    in passive construction, 454
    referring to cities, 112 [SA]
    ~ **war einmal,** 380
etwas, 466
euer, 112 [SA]
European Union, 32, 314
exams, university, 297 [SA]

fairy tales, 380–381
family relationships, 40, 46
farewells, 11
Fasching, Fastnacht, Karneval 390
Ferien, Urlaub vs., 396
film, 177, 447 [SA], 479
fondness, expressing, 137–138
food and drink, 96, 98, 208 [SA], 230.
    See also meals
forms of address, 16
Frankfurt am Main, 159, 255
Frau, 16
Fräulein, 16
friendships, 189
für, 155, 323
future tense, 318–319
future-time expressions, 274, 318–319

ganz, 181
gefallen, 230
gegen, 69, 155
gehen
    conversational past of, 171
    past participle of, 171
    present tense of, 53
    subjunctive of, 440
gender
    of compound nouns, 66
    and definite articles, 27
    and indefinite articles, 29
Geneva (Genf), 403
genitive case, 409–412
geography
    articles used with, 215
    of Austria, 366
    of Germany, 111
    nouns and adjectives for, 31
    pronouns with, 112 [SA]
    of Switzerland, 404
German-Americans, 47
German Democratic Republic, 444,
    446–447, 455

German language. *See also* English vs.
    German usage; informal
  alphabet, 21
  employment opportunities, 119
  English language influences on, 468
  formal, written, 18 [SA], 19, 20, 60
    [SA], 231 [SA], 438
  other language influences on,
    113 [SA]
  study opportunities, 123
  where spoken, 7, 32
Germany
  citizenship in, 44 [SA], 434
  geography of, 111
  history of, 434, 444, 446–447, 455
  immigrants and foreigners in, 123
  influence on America, 47
  map of, 111
gern, 54–55, 137 [SA]
  comparative of, 368
  + haben, 52
  nicht +, 54–55, 71
  nicht ~, 52, 54–55
  position of, 55, 71
  present tense of verbs with, 54
  superlative of, 370
  word order with, 52, 55, 73
Goethe, Johann Wolfgang von, 123, 159,
    472, 477
Goethe-Institut, 123
greetings, 11, 60
Grimm, Jacob and Wilhelm (Brüder
    Grimm), 381
groceries. *See* food; food and drink
Gute Nacht!, 11
Guten Morgen!, 11
Guten Tag!, 11

haben, 48
  as auxiliary, 170–171, 393, 406
  conversational past formed with,
    170
  du-imperative form of, 131
  expressions with, 50
  gern +, 52
  imperative of, 131
  lieb +, 191
  narrative past tense of, 170, 393
  past participle of, 179
  present tense of, 48
  simple past tense of, 170
  subjunctive of, 348 (*See also* **hätte**)
halb, 69
Hamburg, 47 [SA], 177
handeln von, 323 [SA]
hängen, 263
Hanseatic League, 177
hätte, 348, 436, 437
Heidelberg, 100, 102, 106

Heine, Heinrich, 241-242
heißen, 20, 34, 53 [SA]
helping verbs. *See* auxiliaries
Herr(n), 16, 57
hesitation, 427
Hesse, Hermann, 137 [SA], 225, 472
Hessen, 111, 159
hin and **her,** 262
hinter, 251
Hölderlin, Friedrich, 225
holidays, 390, 405. *See also* vacations
house, rooms of a, 216
Humboldt University, 76, 423, 424
hypothetical statements, 348, 349,
    435–438

ich, 18, 48
idea, expressing an, 195
identifying
  family relationships, 46
  people and objects, 27–34, 232
idioms, German, 231
-ieren verbs, past participle of, 172, 178
ihr (her), 90–91, 214 [SA]
Ihr (your, formal), 90–91
ihr (their), 90–91
ihr (you), 18
ihr-imperative, 133
illness, 303, 304 [SA]
immer wenn, 408
immigration, German to North
    America, 47
imperative
  formal, 8–9
  inclusive (wir), 133
  informal (du), 131-132
  informal (ihr), 133
  particles with, 134
imperative mood, 347. *See also*
    commands
impersonal passive, 453–454
in, 215
  + accusative, 322
  + geographic nouns, 215, 227
  and time expressions, 274, 318
  as two-case preposition, 215, 251,
    253, 262
indefinite article(s), 29–30, 34. *See also*
    ein-words
  abbreviated form of, 30
  accusative of, 56, 214
  dative case, 214
  dative of, 214
  gender of, 29
  genitive of, 409–412
  + nationality, profession, or religion,
    31 [SA], 34
  negation of, 30
indefinite time expressions, 409

independent clause. *See* main clause
indicative mood, 347
indirect object, 212. *See also* dative case
indirect questions, 408
infinitive clauses, 195
infinitive(s), 2 [SA], 18 [SA], 53 [SA]
  in brief notes, 67 [SA]
  in formation of formal commands, 8
  modals +, 436–437
  omitted, 94, 109, 135
  of separable-prefix verbs, 71
  zu +, 195
informal German
  abbreviated **ich-**forms, 48
  abbreviated or contracted forms in,
    30, 48, 90, 299 [SA], 324 [SA],
    348 [SA]
  amounts, 98
  animals, expressions with, 205
  article with first names, 165
  assumptions expressed in, 81
  du-imperative, 131–132
  du in, 19, 53 [SA], 131–132
  expressing one's opinion, 228
  ihr-imperative, 133
  interjections, rejoinders, and
    particles, 291
  past tenses in, 170 [SA], 406 (*See also*
    conversational past tense)
  possession in, 227, 411
  replacing genitive in, 411
  wir-imperative, 133
  würde in, 438
informal imperative, 131–134
information questions, 25–26
inseparable prefixes, 71 [SA]
inseparable-prefix verbs, past participle
    of, 178
instruments, musical, 108, 109 [SA]
interjections, 291
internship programs, 123
interrogatives. *See* questions
intransitive verbs, 170–171, 454
inversion, 196. *See also* word order
inversion, subject-verb, 196
invitations, 138
irregular verbs. *See* strong (irregular) verbs
Italy, 32

ja/nein, 66. *See also* yes/no questions
Jena, 309-310
jener, 233 [SA]
jobs. *See also* professions
  applicants, 360
  training, 317

Karneval, 390
kein, keine, 30, 34, 48, 56, 73
  accusative of, 56, 214

kein, keine (*continued*)
dative of, 214
dürfen +, 146
and imperatives, 132, 133
überhaupt +, 57 [SA]
kennen, 112, 174, 394
kennen, wissen vs., 112
kitchen items, 235
können, 109, 135, 393, 431

languages, 51, 109
legen/liegen, 263
Leipzig, 458
leisure time activities, 108
lernen, studieren vs., 306
letter writing, 59, 60, 60 [SA],
62 [SA]
lieber, 93
lieb haben, 191
lieb/lieben/lieber, 62 [SA], 93, 138,
368, 370
Liechtenstein, 32
likes and dislikes, 52, 54–55,
93–94, 230. *See also* **gern;**
mögen; preferences
literature, 137 [SA]
location
asking about, 250
asking for, 250–252
change of, 250, 262
dative of, 215, 226, 263
location, indicating, 215
luck, wishing someone good, 338
Luxembourg, 32

main (independent) clause, 192, 194
[SA], 196, 297, 340, 406, 438
mal, 134, 275
man, 146, 454
Mannheim, 100, 103, 106
Märchen, 380–381
masculine **N**-nouns, 57, 214, 410
meals, 95, 222. *See also* food and drink
metric system, 97, 180 [SA]
minority language, German as, 32
mit, 226
with means of transporation, 276
as prefix, 176
mixed verbs
conversational past of, 174
kennen and **wissen** as, 174
narrative past of, 394–395
past participle of, 174
subjunctive forms of, 440
möchte-forms, 94, 109, 135, 137–138,
192, 393
modal verbs (modals), 94, 109, 135–139,
146–148. *See also* specific modal
verbs, e.g.: **mögen**

and double-infinitive construction,
436–437
expressing desire with, 148
expressing necessity with, 147
expressing permission with, 146
+ infinitive, 109
narrative past forms of, 393
subjunctive forms of, 431, 436–437
summary chart, 148
word order with, 135, 437
mögen, 135, 137, 191, 393
money, 248 [SA]
months, 62
mood, 347–348. *See also* subjunctive mood
Mozart, Wolfgang Amadeus 353
Munich (München), 284
musical instruments, 109 [SA]
müssen, 135, 147, 393, 394 [SA]

nach, 69, 226–227, 323
nachdem, 406
nachher, 166 [SA]
name(s)
abbreviated forms of, 58 [SA]
articles with first, 165
asking for someone's, 20
last, 20, 20 [SA]
showing possession with, 411
narrative (simple) past tense, 388–395,
406, 406 [SA], 407, 451
nationalities, 31, 31 [SA]
neben, 250
necessity, expressing, 147
negation, of indefinite article, 30
newspapers, 174 [SA]
nicht. *See also* **kein**
so/sehr, 52
with commands, 132, 133
+ **dürfen,** 146, 394 [SA]
+ **gern,** 54–55, 71, 73
+ **müssen** +, 147, 394 [SA]
position of, 73
+ **sollen,** 394 [SA]
+ **sondern,** 92
~ **so/sehr,** 52
+ **viel,** 73
nichts, 466
N-nouns, masculine. *See* masculine **N**-nouns
nominative case, 28, 34
adjectives in, 358
definite articles, 34
of definite articles, 214
of **der**-words, 28, 233
of **ein**-words, 30
of indefinite articles, 29–30, 34
of possessive adjectives, 90–91
predicate nominative, 34
of relative pronouns, 340
subject of sentence in, 34

North America, 32, 47
electric current in, 300 [SA]
German immigration to, 47
German influence on, 47
German study in, 123
noun(s)
capitalization of, 2 [SA], 3 [SA], 27
diminutive forms of, 402
gender of, 27, 51 [SA], 66 [SA], 113
of nationality, 31, 31 [SA], 34
N-nouns, 57, 214, 410
plural of, 27, 113, 214, 227 [SA], 231
[SA], 410
predicate, 34
numbers
cardinal, 22
ordinal, 62–63

ob, 192, 408
objects
bathroom, 299
identifying, 113
kitchen items, 235
obligation, expressing, 138
occupations. *See* jobs; professions
oder, 92
ohne, 155
Oktoberfest, 284
opinion, expressing an, 195, 228
ordinal numbers, 62–63
Ostalgie, 447
ownership
and the genitive, 409–412
possessive adjectives and, 90–91, 112,
214 [SA], 358
and possessive **s,** 40 [SA], 227
and proper names, 411
with reflexive pronouns, 300 [SA]
verbs expressing, 48, 230
with **von,** 227

Pardon, 7
particles, 134, 137 [SA], 291
passive voice, 450–454
impersonal, 453–454
past, 452
present, 450
past participles, 172–176, 178–179
-**ieren** verbs, 178
of -**ieren** verbs, 172
of inseparable-prefix verbs, 178
of irregular (strong) and mixed
verbs, 174
in passive, 452
in past-time subjunctive, 436
prefixes and, 176
of regular (weak) verbs, 172
of **sein** and **haben,** 179
of separable-prefix verbs, 176

past perfect tense, 406–407, 452
past tense forms. *See* conversational past
  tense; narrative (simple) past tense
past-time subjunctive, 436
permission, expressing, 146
personal characteristics, 153, 360
personal hygiene, 298, 300
personal items, 128–129
personal pronouns. *See* subject pronouns
personal qualities, 153
personal relationships, 189. 190
phone, answering the, 21 [SA]
physical characteristics, 23. *See also* body,
  parts of
physical characteristics, describing, 23
physical conditions, describing, 50
plural forms, 113
  dative case, 214
  of definite article, 27
Poland, 32
politeness, forms of, 138 [SA], 347–348,
  430, 432
popular culture, 475
possession. *See* ownership; possessive
  adjectives
possessive adjectives, 90–91, 112, 214
  [SA], 358. *See also* **ein**-words
  accusative of, 112
  nominative of, 90–91
possessive **s,** 40 [SA], 227
possibilities, expressing, 109, 347–348, 431
preceded adjectives, 358, 361–362, 410
predicate nominative, 34, 65
preferences, 92, 137–138. *See also* likes
  and dislikes
prefixes
  inseparable, 71 [SA], 178
  separable, 71, 132, 134, 176, 195,
    197, 262, 388, 391
prepositional objects, using verbs
  with, 322
prepositional phrases, 73
preposition(s)
  + accusative, 155, 323
  with accusative, 155
  contractions with, 227, 251 [SA]
  da- and **wo**-compounds with,
    324–325
  + dative, 215, 226–227, 262, 323
  + genitive, 411
  two-case, 215, 250–253, 262–263
present perfect tense. *See* conversational
  past
present tense, 53–54
  to express future time, 318
  passive voice of, 450
  of regular (weak) verbs, 53–54
  separable-prefix verbs, 71, 197
  of stem-vowel changing verbs, 86

present-time subjunctive, 347–348
probability, expressing, 321, 347–348
process, agent vs., 450
professional sports, 265
professions, 34, 113 [SA], 342, 343 [SA],
  346. *See also* jobs
prohibitions, expressing, 146, 147
pronouns, 35
  accusative, 64
  formal, 18 [SA]
  personal (*See* subject pronouns)
  reflexive, 297, 298 [SA], 300–301,
    319 [SA]
  relative, 340–344
  subject, 18, 34
pronunciation
  informal, 348 [SA]
  and verb prefixes, 176

quantifiers, 52, 73 [SA]
quantities, 97
questions
  about time, 408
  indirect, 408
  information, 25–26
  and reflexive pronouns, 297
  yes/no, 26, 54, 73, 192, 408
question words, 25,196

reading strategies, 34 [SA], 307–309
reasons, giving, 194
reflexive pronouns, 297, 298 [SA],
  300–301, 319 [SA]
reflexive verbs, 296, 298 [SA], 319 [SA]
regional German. *See also* Austria,
  language in; Switzerland, Swiss-
  German speech variations in
  northern, 170 [SA], 388 [SA]
  southern, 68 [SA], 170 [SA]
regular verbs. *See* weak (regular) verbs
relationships, 189
relative clauses, 340, 343, 344
relative pronouns, 340–344
religion, nouns of, 34
re-marriage, relationships created by,
  46 [SA]
repeated activities, expressing, 67
requests, 430, 432
Rilke, Rainer Maria, 486
rivers, in city names, 255
rooms of a house, 216

ß (letter), 20 [SA], 53 [SA], 88, 399 [SA]
-**s,** plural formation with, 113 [SA]
same-sex relationships, 190 [SA]
Saxony (Sachsen), 458
school system, 245, 314, 327, 346
seasons, 182, 275
sehen, 86

sehr, 52
sein, 18, 34
  as auxiliary, 170–171, 406
  conversational past formed with, 170–171
  describing yourself with, 18
  du-imperative form of, 131
  and formation of conversational
    past, 170
  imperative of, 131
  narrative past of, 393
  past participle of, 179
  as possessive adjective, 90–91
  present tense of, 18
  Sie-imperative form of, 8
  simple past tense of, 170
  subjunctive of, 348
seit, 227
sentence, subject of, 34
separable-prefix verbs, 71
  conversational past of, 176
  du-imperative form of, 132
  hin/her and, 262
  imperative of, 132, 134
  in narrative past, 388, 391
  past participle of, 176
  in present tense, 71, 197
  in subordinate clauses, 197
  and **zu,** 195
setzen/sitzen, 263
shopping, 253
Sie, 18 [SA], 19, 133 [SA]
sie (she), 18, 35
sie (they), 18, 35
simple past tense. *See* narrative past tense
so, 408 [SA]
  nicht +, 52
soccer, 265
sollen, 135, 138, 393, 394 [SA]
sondern, 92
spatial movement, expressing, 155
spatial relationships, expressing, 226–227
sports, 108, 109 [SA]
Stelle: an deiner (Ihrer), 435
stellen/stehen, 263
stem-changing verbs, 87, 109, 131
stereotypes, 81
Storm, Theodor, 485
strong (irregular) verbs, 86–90
  conversational past of, 174
  narrative past of, 391, 393
  past participle of, 174
  present tense of, 86
  subjunctive of, 439–440
student housing, 211
student(s). *See also* university(-ies)
  employment, 317
  housing, 222
  rooms, 222
  types of, 245 [SA]

studieren, lernen vs., 306
studies, fields of, 51, 306
Stunde/Uhr, 68 [SA]
Stuttgart, 259–260
subject, grammatical, 34, 65
subjects, academic, 51
subjectless passive, 454
subject (personal) pronouns, 18, 34, 212.
    See also specific pronouns
subjunctive mood, 347–348, 430–437
    hätte or wäre, 347–348
    of modal verbs, 431, 436–437
    past-time, 436
    and polite requests, 430, 432
    with strong verbs, 439–440
    subjunctive I vs. subjunctive II,
        437–440
    and unreal situations, 437–440
    with würde, 347, 438, 440
subordinate clause(s), 192, 194, 196.
    See also wenn-clauses
    and double infinitives, 437
    passive voice in, 454
    with question words, 196
    relative clauses as, 340
    verb forms at end of, 196–197
    with weil, 194
    with wenn, 193
    wissen and, 89
    with zu, 195
    and word order, 89, 191, 193–195,
        297, 406, 437
subordinating conjunctions, 192, 194,
    196. *See also specific conjunctions*
suggestions, making, 134, 347–348,
    430, 432
superlative, 103 [SA]
superlatives, 369–370
Swabia, 260
Switzerland, 31 [SA], 403–404
    culture and traditions of, 123
    language in, 32, 68 [SA]
    map of, 404
    North American immigrants from, 47
    preposition in with, 253 [SA]
    school system in, 327, 403
    Swiss-German speech variations in, 20
        [SA], 68 [SA], 402

temperature, 180 [SA], 304 [SA]
tense. *See specific tense, e.g.:* future tense
the, 28
time
    approximate, 155
    in dative and accusative case, 226–227
    duration of, 227
    nach for relationships of, 227
    official, 69 [SA]
    periods of, 68 [SA], 69

questions about, 408
    telling, 68–69
time, (reason), manner, place, 276 [SA],
    278–279, 318 [SA]
time, telling, 68–69
time expressions, 67, 69, 318–319
    in dative and accusative case, 233 [SA],
        274, 318
    of emphasis, 274
    future, 318–319
    genitive, 409
    regularity, expressing, 275
    for repeated activities, 67
titles of address, 16, 60
tourist industry, 119–120
traffic signs, 140, 146
train travel, 150, 234 [SA]
transitive verbs, 170 [SA]
transportation, means of, 145, 150,
    157, 277
Tschüss!, 11
Tübingen, 218, 225
Turnvereine, 265, 266 [SA]
24-hour clock, 69 [SA]
two-case prepositions, 215, 250–253,
    258 [SA], 262–263
two-verb constructions, 71, 436-437

über, 250, 322, 323
überhaupt, 57 [SA]
überhaupt kein, 57 [SA]
Uhr/Stunde, 68 [SA]
um, 69, 155, 261, 274 [SA], 323
und, 92
university(-ies). *See also* student(s)
    academic subjects in, 51
    choice of, 306
    courses of study at, 295, 297 [SA], 306
    exams, 297
    financing, 317
    German system of, 314
    grading at, 311 [SA]
    history of, 225
    and housing for students, 222
    semesters in, 43 [SA]
    in specific cities, 225
    student housing at, 211
    types of, 76
unpreceded adjectives, 364
unreal conditions, expressing,
    437–440
unser, 112 [SA]
unter, 252
Urlaub, Ferien vs., 396

vacations, 396
Verzeihung, 7
viel, 73, 73 [SA]
Vienna (Wien), 353–355

vocational training, 346
voice, 450–454
von, 227
    + agent, 450
    + dative, 323, 411, 450
    showing possession, 227
    and time expressions, 69
vor, 69, 252, 274, 323

wahrscheinlich, 81, 126
wann, 25, 274, 408
wäre
    + past participle, 436
    wie/das + ~, 348
warum, 25
was, 34, 56
    ~ gibt es?, 90
    as question word, 25, 34
weak (regular) verbs, 53–54, 71
    conversational past of, 388
    ending in -ieren, 172, 178
    narrative past of, 388
    past participles of, 172–173
    present tense of, 53–54
    subjunctive of, 438
weather, 180, 183 [SA]
week, days of the, 66
weight, units of. *See* metric system
weil, 194, 280, 454
    with main clause word order, 194 [SA]
    subordinate clauses with, 194
weit, in expressions of distance, 97
wem, 212, 325
wen, 56, 325
Wende, 442 [SA]
wenig, 73 [SA]
wenn, 193, 276 [SA], 408, 437–438
wenn-clauses, 437–440
wer, 25, 34, 56
werden, 319, 321. *See also*
    würde-construction
    as auxiliary, 319, 321, 450
    conversational past of, 452
    in future tense, 319
    narrative past of, 395
    and passive construction, 450, 452
    predicate nominative with, 34 [SA]
    subjunctive of, 347
wessen, 410
wie, 25
    ~ bitte, 26
wine, 97, 208 [SA]
wir, 18
wir-imperative, 133
wissen, 88–89, 112, 174, 192, 395, 440
wo, 25, 247, 250, 252
wo-compounds, 325
woher, 25, 262
wohin, 25, 247, 250, 252, 262

wohl, 81, 126, 321
wollen, 135, 148, 393
womit, 276
worden, 452
word order, 196–197
    coordinating conjunctions and, 66,
      194 [SA]
    creating emphasis with, 65
    direct objects and, 73, 212
    for emphasis, 65
    and the genitive, 410
    with **gern,** 52, 55, 73
    with **gern** and **nicht gern,** 55

    initial subordinate clause and, 406
    with **nicht,** 73
    in the passive, 450
    in questions, 54, 297
    with reflexive pronouns, 297
    in sentence fragments, 67
    with separable prefixes and
      two-part verbs, 71, 197, 318, 388
    subject-verb, 34, 54, 65, 196, 406
    in subordinate clauses, 89, 194–197,
      297, 406, 408, 437
    and time expressions, 276 [SA],
      278–279, 318

würde-construction, 347, 438, 439
    [SA], 440

yes/no questions, 26, 54, 73, 192, 408
you, equivalents of, 19

zu, 195, 227, 261, 323
    infinitive clauses with, 195
    as prefix, 176
Zukunft, 319 [SA]
Zum Beispiel (z. B.), 41 [SA]
zwischen, 252